California Contractors License Law & Reference Book with CD-ROM

2012 Edition

With Rules and Regulations

Contractors State License Board
STATE OF CALIFORNIA
Edmund G. Brown, Jr., *Governor*

This book is an official publication of the State of California. It may not be reproduced in whole or in part without the express permission of the California Contractors State License Board.

The *California Contractors License Law and Reference Book with CD-ROM (2012 Edition)* is available from Matthew Bender & Company, Inc. Copies may be purchased by calling 1-800-533-1637 or faxing 518-462-3788; or by writing to Matthew Bender & Company, Attn. Customer Service, 1275 Broadway, Albany, NY 12204-2694; or at http://www.lexisnexis.com. The price is $23.00, plus $9.49 Shipping & Handling, and is available as follows:

> Mail order:
> Send a check or money order, payable to Matthew Bender & Company, Inc., and include a street address and the recipient's name. *All orders are shipped by carrier and cannot be delivered to a post office box.*

The *California Contractors License Law and Reference Book* is not sold at any office of the Contractors State License Board. Copies may be available from specialty bookstores—check your local telephone directory.

ISBN: 978-1-4224-9820-0

© 2012 California Contractors State License Board

© 2012 Matthew Bender & Company, Inc., a member of the LexisNexis Group.

All rights reserved.

LexisNexis, the knowledge burst logo, and Michie are trademarks of Reed Elsevier Properties Inc., used under license. Matthew Bender is a registered trademark of Matthew Bender Properties Inc.

The California regulations appearing in this publication have been extracted from Barclays Official California Code of Regulations, copyright © 2011, State of California.

This material may not be commercially reproduced or sold in printed or electronic form without written permission of Thomson/West, and is subject to the following disclaimer:

THOMSON/WEST MAKES NO WARRANTY OR REPRESENTATION WHATSO-EVER, EXPRESS OR IMPLIED, WITH RESPECT TO THE MERCHANTABILITY OR FITNESS FOR ANY PARTICULAR PURPOSE WITH RESPECT TO THE INFORMA-TION CONTAINED IN THIS PUBLICATION; AND

THOMSON/WEST ASSUMES NO LIABILITY WHATSOEVER WITH RESPECT TO ANY USE OF THIS PUBLICATION OR ANY PORTION THEREOF OR WITH RE-SPECT TO ANY DAMAGES WHICH MAY RESULT FROM SUCH USE.

Matthew Bender & Company, Inc.
Editorial Offices
701 E. Water Street
Charlottesville, VA 22902
800-446-3410
www.lexisnexis.com

Product Number 2970018

(Pub. 29700)

ABOUT THIS BOOK

The *California Contractors License Law & Reference Book* begins with several narrative chapters that describe many of the legal requirements affecting contractors. These narrative chapters contain references to the laws, rules, and regulations included in the later chapters. The laws and regulations contained in this book are those in effect on January 1, 2012, unless otherwise noted.

———

DEDICATION

The Contractors State License Board dedicates this edition to the 300,000 licensed contractors who abide by California contracting laws and guidelines set forth in this publication, and whose hard work and professionalism help fuel our state's economy.

SUMMARY OF MAJOR CHANGES TO CONTRACTOR LAW

EFFECTIVE JANUARY 1, 2012
unless indicated otherwise

AB 397 (Monning)

Adds Business & Professions Code § 7125.5

Existing law requires private employers to secure the payment of compensation by obtaining and maintaining workers' compensation insurance or to self-insure as an individual employer or as one employer in a group of employers. Contractor License Law requires every licensed contractor to have on file at all times with CSLB a current and valid Certificate of Workers' Compensation Insurance or Certification of Self-Insurance, or a statement certifying that he or she has no employees and is not required to obtain or maintain workers' compensation insurance coverage. **This bill requires, at the time of renewal, an active contractor licensee with an exemption for workers' compensation insurance on file with the board to either recertify the licensee's exemption or to provide a current and valid Certificate of Workers' Compensation Insurance or Certificate of Self-Insurance. The bill also provides for retroactive license renewal, as specified, for otherwise acceptable license renewal applications when the applicant provides the required documentation within 30 days after notification by the board of the renewal rejection.**

(Added Stats 2011 ch 546 § 1, effective January 1, 2012.)

AB 456 (Wagner)

Amends Civil Code §§ 3084 and 8416

The California Constitution gives workers the right to a mechanic's lien for the value of labor and materials provided for the improvement of real property, and authorizes the Legislature to provide for the speedy and efficient enforcement of these liens. Existing law requires a claim of mechanics lien to be served on the owner or reputed owner of the property in order to be valid, and requires a proof of service affidavit to show the name of the person upon whom the mechanics lien was served. **This bill clarifies that the affidavit is required to show the name of the owner or reputed owner of the property, and the title or capacity in which the person or entity was served.**

(Amended Stats 2011 ch 673 §§ 1 and 2, effective January 1, 2012.)

AB 551 (Campos)
Amends Labor Code §§ 1775, 1776, and 1777.1

Existing law generally requires that not less than the general prevailing rate of per diem wages, as specified, be paid to workers employed on a public work, as defined. Existing law requires a contractor or subcontractor to submit, to the state or political subdivision on whose behalf a public work is being performed, a penalty of not more than $50 per calendar day, and not less than $10 per calendar day except in certain cases of a good faith mistake, as provided and determined by the Labor Commissioner, for violations of these prevailing wage provisions. **This bill increases that maximum penalty to $200 for each calendar day and increases the minimum penalty, except in certain cases of a good faith mistake, to no less than $40 for each calendar day. The bill also increases the penalty assessed to contractors and subcontractors with prior violations from $20 to $80, and from $30 to $120 for willful violations.** Existing law requires each contractor and subcontractor performing work on a public work to keep accurate payroll records regarding his or her employees. Existing law requires that these records contain the information specified by the Division of Labor Standards Enforcement (DLSE), and provides that a contractor or subcontractor has 10 days in which to comply after receipt of a written notice requesting the records, or is subject to forfeiting a penalty of $25 for each calendar day for each worker until strict compliance is effectuated. **This bill increases the amount of that penalty to $100 for each calendar day for each worker.** Under existing law, whenever a contractor or subcontractor performing a public works project is found by the Labor Commissioner to be in violation of certain provisions of law relating to payment of prevailing wages, with intent to defraud, or in willful violation of those provisions of law, the contractor or subcontractor or a firm, corporation, partnership, or association in which the contractor or subcontractor has a substantial interest is ineligible to bid on or to receive a public works contract for specified periods of time. **This bill revises that provision to instead make a contractor or subcontractor on a public works project that is found to have committed 2 or more separate willful violations within a 3-year period ineligible for a period of up to 3 years to either bid on or be awarded a contract or perform work as a subcontractor of a public works project. The bill also requires, whenever a contractor or subcontractor performing work on a public works project has failed to provide a timely response to a request by the Division of Labor Standards Enforcement (DLSE), the Division of Apprenticeship Standards (DAS), or the awarding body to produce certified payroll records, the Labor Commissioner to notify the contractor or subcontractor that he or she will be subject to debarment if the certified payroll records are not produced within 30 days after receipt of the written notice, and makes the contractor or subcontractor ineligible to bid on or be awarded a contract or perform work as a subcontractor on a public works project for a period of not less than one year and no more than three years, except as specified.** Existing law also requires the Labor Commissioner, not less than semiannually, to publish and distribute to awarding bodies a list of contractors who are ineligible to bid on or be awarded a public works contract, or to perform work as a subcontractor on a public works project. **This bill instead requires the Labor Commissioner to publish the list described above on the commissioner's website, to notify the Contractors State License Board when the list is updated, and to at least annually notify awarding bodies of the availability of the list of debarred contractors, as specified. This bill incorporates additional AB 766 changes in Labor Code section 1776.**

(Amended Stats 2011 ch 677 §§ 1 through 4, effective January 1, 2012.)

AB 766 (Monning)

Amends Labor Code § 1776

Existing law requires each contractor and subcontractor on a public works project to keep payroll records regarding his or her employees, and requires that these records contain information specified by the Division of Labor Standards Enforcement (DLSE). Existing law requires certain personal identification information, as specified, to be removed when certified payroll records are made available for inspection to the public or to a public agency. **This bill requires non-redacted copies of certified payroll records to be provided, upon request, to any agency included in, and for the purposes of, the Joint Enforcement Strike Force on the Underground Economy, or to any law enforcement agency, but requires any copies of records or certified payroll made available for inspection and furnished upon request to the public by these agencies to be marked or redacted to prevent disclosure of an individual's name, address, and social security number. The bill also provides that an employer is not liable in a civil action for any reasonable act or omission taken in good faith in compliance with these requirements.**

(Amended Stats 2011 ch 481 §§ 1, 1.5, and 2, effective January 1, 2012.)

AB 878 (Berryhill)

Amends Business & Professions Code § 7125
Existing law, the Contractors' State License Law, provides for the licensing and regulation of contractors by the Contractors State License Board. Existing law authorizes the Board to appoint a Registrar of Contractors and requires a workers' compensation insurer to report to the Registrar specified information regarding a licensee's workers' compensation policy. **This bill, additionally, requires a workers' compensation insurer to report to the Registrar a licensee whose workers' compensation insurance policy is canceled by the insurer if the insurer has completed a premium audit or investigation, a material misrepresentation has been made by the insured that results in financial harm to the insurer, and no reimbursement has been paid by the insured to the insurer. The bill provides that that information is not subject to the California Public Records Act. The bill also provides that a willful or deliberate disregard and violation of workers' compensation insurance laws constitute a cause for disciplinary action by the Registrar against the licensee.**

(Amended Stats 2011 ch 686 §§ 1 through 3, effective January 1, 2012.)

AB 1091 (Morrell)

Amends Business & Professions Code § 7068.2

Existing law, the Contractors' State License Law, provides for the licensure and regulation of contractors by the Contractors State License Board. Existing law requires the Board to appoint a Registrar to carry out administrative duties delegated by the Board. Existing law authorizes an applicant for a license to qualify his or her knowledge and experience with a responsible managing officer, employee, member or manager who has certain qualifications. Under existing law, if the responsible managing officer, employee, member, or manager disassociates from the licensed entity, the licensee or the qualifier, as defined, is required to notify the Registrar, as specified. Existing law authorizes the Registrar to accept petitions from licensees disputing matters related to the disassociation. **This bill revises and recasts those provisions by specifying that the notification be provided within 90 days after the date of disassociation. The bill authorizes the Registrar to accept a petition for one 90-day extension to replace the qualifier under limited circumstances and imposes specified requirements related to that submittal. The bill makes other conforming changes.**

(Amended Stats 2011 ch 168 § 1, effective January 1, 2012.)

AB 1307 (Skinner)

Amends Business and Professions Code § 7145.5 and Unemployment Insurance Code § 1088.5 and adds § 6070.5 of the Revenue & Taxation Code

Existing law provides that the Registrar of the Contractors State License Board may refuse to issue, reinstate, reactivate, or renew a license or may suspend the license of a contractor for the failure of the licensee to resolve all outstanding final liabilities, which include taxes, additions to tax, penalties, interest, and any fees that may be assessed by the board, the Department of Industrial Relations, the Employment Development Department, or the Franchise Tax Board. **This bill authorizes the Contractors State License Board, except in certain cases, to take the actions specified above for a licensee's failure to resolve outstanding final liabilities assessed by the State Board of Equalization in addition.**

(Amended Stats 2011 ch 734 §§ 1 and 2, effective January 1, 2012.)

AB 1346 (Atkins)

Amends Labor Code §§ 3099 and 3099.2.

Existing law requires that persons performing work as electricians for specified contractors be certified pursuant to certification standards established by the division.

This bill requires individuals desiring to be certified to submit an application for certification and examination that includes an employment history report from the Social Security Administration. This bill incorporates additional changes to Section 3099.2 of the Labor Code proposed by SB 944.

(Amended Stats 2011 ch 693 §§ 3099 and 3099.2, effective January 1, 2012.)

AB 1424 (Perea)

Amends Business and Professions Code §§ 31 and 476 and adds Business and Professions Code § 494.5 and Public Contract Code § 10295.4

Existing law requires every board, as defined, and the Department of Insurance, upon request of the Franchise Tax Board, to furnish to the Franchise Tax Board certain information with respect to every licensee. **This bill requires the State Board of Equalization, quarterly, and the Franchise Tax Board, at least twice each calendar year, to make available a list of the 500 largest tax delinquencies described above. This bill requires a person whose delinquency appeared on either list and whose name has been removed, as provided, to comply with the terms of the arranged resolution, and authorizes the State Board of Equalization and the Franchise Tax Board, if the person fails to comply with the terms of the arranged resolution, to add the person's name to the list without providing prior written notice, as provided. This bill requires a state governmental licensing entity, other than the Department of Motor Vehicles, State Bar of California, and Alcoholic Beverage Control Board, as provided, that issues professional or occupational licenses, certificates, registrations, or permits, to suspend, revoke, and refuse to issue a license if the licensee's name is** included on either list of the 500 largest tax delinquencies described above. This bill does *not* include the Contractors State License Board in the definition of "state governmental licensing entity." This bill also requires those licensing entities to collect the social security number or federal taxpayer identification number of each individual applicant of that entity for the purpose of matching those applicants to the names on the lists of the 500 largest tax delinquencies, and requires each application for a new license or renewal of a license to indicate on the application that the law allows the State Board of Equalization and the Franchise Tax Board to share taxpayer information with a board and requires the licensee to pay his or her state tax obligation and that his or her license may be suspended if the state tax obligation is not paid. This bill also authorizes the State Board of Equalization and the Franchise Tax Board to disclose to state governmental licensing entities identifying information, as defined, of persons on the list of the 500 largest tax delinquencies, as specified.

(Amended and added stats 2011 ch 455 §§ 1, 2, 3, and 5, effective January 1, 2012.)

SB 190 (Lowenthal)

Amends §§ 7159, 7159.5, 7159.14, and 8513 of the Business and Professions Code, § 8422 of the Civil Code, and § 66499.7 of the Government Code

The California Constitution provides that laborers of every class who have worked upon or have furnished material for a property have a lien upon that property for the value of the labor done and material furnished. The California Constitution requires the Legislature to provide, by law, for the speedy and efficient enforcement of those liens. Existing law, operative July 1, 2012, recodified and revised the law for enforcing mechanic's liens. Existing law provides that certain erroneous information contained in a claim of lien does not invalidate the claim of lien, except as specified. **This bill, operative July 1, 2012, makes various technical, conforming changes related to the recodification of the law for enforcing mechanic's liens. The bill also requires that a person forfeit his or her lien if the** person willfully includes labor or materials in a lien claim that were not furnished to the property in the claim.

(Amended Stats 2011 ch 44 §§ 1 through 7, effective July 1, 2012.)

SB 341 (Lowenthal)

Amends Vehicle Code § 27000

Existing law requires a refuse or garbage truck to be equipped with an automatic backup audible alarm that sounds on backing and is capable of emitting an audible sound meeting specified requirements. A violation of this requirement is a crime. **This bill additionally requires a construction vehicle, as defined, with a gross vehicle weight rating (GVWR) in excess of 14,000 pounds that operates at, or transports any construction or industrial material to and from, a mine or construction site, or both, to be equipped with an automatic backup audible alarm that sounds on backing and is capable of emitting sound audible under normal conditions from a distance of not less than 200 feet.**

(Amends Stats 2011 ch 235 § 27000, effective January 1, 2012.)

SB 454(Pavley)

Amends Public Resources Code § 25900 and Public Utilities Code § 399.4 and adds Public Resources Code § 25402.11

Existing law establishes the State Energy Resources Conservation and Development Commission (CEC, California Energy Commission) and vests with the commission jurisdiction over specified matters related to energy. Existing law requires the Attorney General, upon the request of the commission, to petition a court of competent jurisdiction to enjoin violations of law that is within the subject matter of the commission. Existing law requires the commission to prescribe, by regulation, appliance efficiency standards. **This bill authorizes the commission to establish an administrative enforcement process to enforce the above standards. The bill provides for the assessment of civil penalties by the courts or administrative civil penalties by the commission for a violation of the above standards. The bill requires the penalties collected to be deposited in the Appliance Efficiency Enforcement Subaccount, which this bill would establish in** the Energy Resources Program Account, and authorizes the commission to expend the moneys in the subaccount, upon appropriation by the Legislature, as specified. The bill requires the court, upon granting of relief for a violation of the above standards, to award the commission the reasonable costs incurred by the commission in investigating and prosecuting the action. The bill prohibits the commission from initiating an administrative enforcement process pursuant to those regulations under specified circumstances and until certain events have taken place. Existing law provides that it is the policy of this state and the intent of the Legislature that the commission administer cost-effective energy efficiency programs authorized pursuant to existing statutory authority. Existing law provides for the regulation of public utilities under the Public Utilities Act. A violation of the Public Utilities Act is a crime. This bill prohibits a public utility from issuing rebates or incentives for energy efficiency improvements unless the recipient of the rebate or incentive certifies that the improvement or installation has complied with applicable permitting and licensing requirements, if applicable.

(Amended and added stats 2011 ch 591, §§ 2 through 5, effective January 1, 2012.)

SB 459 (Corbett)

Amends Labor Code §§ 226.8 and 2753

Existing law prescribes comprehensive requirements relating to minimum wages, overtime compensation, and standards for working conditions for the protection of employees applicable to an employment relationship. This bill prohibits willful misclassification, as defined, of individuals as independent contractors. The bill also prohibits charging individuals who have been mischaracterized as independent contractors a fee or making deductions from compensation, as specified, where those acts would have violated the law if the individuals had not been mischaracterized. The bill authorizes the Labor and Workforce Development Agency to assess specified civil penalties from, and would require the agency to take other specified disciplinary actions against, persons or employers violating these prohibitions. It also requires the agency to notify the Contractors State License Board of a violator that is a licensed contractor, and requires the board to initiate an action against the licensee. The bill authorizes an individual to file a complaint, as specified, to request the Labor Commissioner to issue a determination that a person or employer has violated these prohibitions with regard to the individual filing the complaint. The bill authorizes the Labor Commissioner to assess civil and liquidated damages against a person or employer based on a determination that the person or employer has violated these prohibitions. This bill provides that a person who, for money or other valuable consideration, knowingly advises an employer to treat an individual as an independent contractor to avoid employee status for the individual shall be jointly and severally liable with the employer if the individual is not found to be an independent contractor. This bill exempts from the provisions regarding joint and several liability a person who provides advice to his or her employer or an attorney who provides legal advice in the course of practicing law.

(Amended and added stats 2011 ch 706, §§ 1 and 2, effective January 1, 2013.)

SB 541 (Price)

Adds Business and Professions Code § 40

Existing law provides for the licensure and regulation of various professions and vocations by boards within the Department of Consumer Affairs. Existing law establishes standards relating to personal service contracts in state employment. **This bill authorizes boards and bureaus under the Department of Consumer Affairs to enter into an agreement with an expert consultant for specified services.**

(Added Stats 2011 ch 339, § 40, effective immediately, chaptered September 26, 2011.)

SB 543 (Steinberg)

Amends Business and Professions Code §§ 144, 205, 210, 7000.5, 7011

Existing law provides for the licensure and regulation of various businesses and professions by boards within the Department of Consumer Affairs, including the Contractors State License Board. Existing law requires or authorizes these boards to appoint an executive officer, or Registrar of Contractors in CSLB's case. Existing law repeals these provisions on January 1, 2012. Under existing law, boards scheduled for repeal are required to be evaluated by the Joint Sunset Review Committee. **This bill extends the operation of these provisions until January 1, 2016 for CSLB, and instead specifies that the board be subject to review by the appropriate policy committee of the Legislature.**

(Amended Stats 2011 ch 448 §§ 1, 2, 2.5, 3, 21, 22, and 32, effective January 1, 2012.)

SB 944 (Senate Business, Professions and Economic Development Committee)

Amends Business and Professions Code §§ 7027, 7029.5, 7030, 7058.6, 7058.8, 7066.5, Labor Code § 3099.2, and Public Contract Code § 7106

Existing law, the Contractors' State License Law, provides for the licensure and regulation of contractors by the Contractors State License Board. Existing law requires licensed contractors to be classified and authorizes them to be classified as, among other things, a plumbing contractor, an electrical contractor, a sign contractor, and a well-drilling contractor. Existing law requires all plumbing contractors, sign contractors, and well-drilling contractors to display on their business motor vehicle certain identifying information pertaining to their contractors license. **This bill makes that requirement applicable, instead, to C-36 plumbing contractors, C-45 sign contractors, and C-57 well-drilling contractors.** Existing law authorizes persons to obtain blank license application, renewal, or reinstatement forms from the Department of Consumer Affairs. **This bill instead authorizes persons to obtain blank license applications from CSLB.**

(Amended Stats 2011 ch 432 §§ 8, 9, 10, 11, 12, 13, 36, and 37, effective January 1, 2012.)

REMINDER: AB 392, a 2010 law, becomes effective for limited liability companies on January 1, 2012.

SB 392 (Florez)

Amends Business and Professions Code Sections 7025, 7028.5, 7029, 7065, 7065.1, 7065.5, 7068, 7068.1, 7068.2, 7069, 7071, 7071.7, 7071.8, 7071.9, 7071.11, 7071.17, 7072.5, 7075.1, 7076, 7076.2, 7085.6, 7090, 7090.1, 7096, 7121, 7121.1, 7121.5, 7121.6, 7122, 7122.1, 7122.2, 7122.5, 7137, 7138, 7152, 7159, and 7159.10, and adds Sections 7071.6.5 and 7071.19 to the Business and Professions Code.

Contractors' State License Law authorizes the issuance of contractor licenses to individual owners, partnerships, and corporations but does not allow for the issuance of a license to a limited liability company (LLC). This bill requires the Contractors State License Board to, not later than January 1, 2012, begin processing applications for licensure that are submitted by an LLC. The bill requires, as a condition precedent to the issuance, reissuance, reinstatement, reactivation, renewal, or continued valid use of an LLC contractor license, that the licensee have on file a surety bond in the sum of $100,000 for damages arising out of specified claims of employees. The bill also requires, as a condition of licensure, that the LLC licensee maintain a policy or policies of insurance against liability imposed on or against it for damages arising out of claims, and would require the licensed LLC to provide a notice concerning that insurance or security in certain contracts. The liability policy shall be issued for not less than $1 million, and not more than $5 million. The bill provides for the personal liability of persons within the LLC if the license is suspended due to a failure of the LLC to maintain proper registration with the Secretary of State.

The bill also makes other technical, non-substantive changes, and specifies that **the board shall begin processing applications for licensure that are submitted by limited liability companies no later than January 1, 2012.**

(Amended Stats 2010 ch 698 §§ 6-35, effective January 1, 2012.)

SECTIONS AFFECTED BY 2011 LEGISLATION

Business & Professions Code

Business & Professions Code

Business & Professions Code

Section Affected		Type of Change	Chapter Number	Page
7159.14	Further requirements; Statement of agreed amount; Payment due; Punishment for violations; Restitution (Second of two; Operative July 1, 2012)	Amended	44	439
8513	Mechanics' lien; Notice to owner; Release (Second of two; Operative July 1, 2012)	Amended	44	584

Civil Code

Section Affected		Type of Change	Chapter Number	Page
1770	Unlawful practices	Amended	79	623
2782	Construction contracts; Agreements indemnifying promisee or relieving public agency from liability as void; Subcontractor's defense or indemnity obligation; Builder's or general contractor's rights to damages; Equitable indemnity	Amended	707	629
3084	"Claim of lien" or "mechanics lien"; Recordation; Service of mechanics lien (Repealed July 1, 2012)	Amended	673	639
8416	Claim of mechanics lien; Form; Contents; Service; Failure to serve (Operative July 1, 2012)	Added	673	678
8422	Effect of erroneous information (Operative July 1, 2012)	Amended	44	680

Code of Civil Procedure

Section Affected		Type of Change	Chapter Number	Page
116.221	Additional jurisdiction	Amended	64	684

Government Code

Section Affected		Type of Change	Chapter Number	Page
12944	Discrimination by "licensing board"	Amended	261, 719	728
66499.7	Release of security; Notice of completion (Operative July 1, 2012; Repealed January 1, 2016)	Amended	44, 174	731

Labor Code

Section Affected		Type of Change	Chapter Number	Page
226.8	Unlawful activities; Penalties; Disciplinary action; Information to be posted on Internet Web site; Enforcement	Added	706	768

Labor Code

Labor Code

Section Affected		Type of Change	Chapter Number	Page
2753	Liability of person who advises employer to treat individual as independent contractor to avoid employee status	Added	706	794
3099	Responsibilities of Division of Apprenticeship Standards	Amended	693	794
3099.2	Certification of electricians	Amended	432, 693	796

Penal Code

Section Affected		Type of Change	Chapter Number	Page
484b	Diversion of money received for construction of improvements	Amended	15	807

Public Contract Code

Section Affected		Type of Change	Chapter Number	Page
7106	Form of required declaration	Amended	432	823
10262	Payment to subcontractors	Amended	700	825
10295.4	State agency contracts with contractors appearing on tax delinquency list prohibited; Application	Added	455	826

Public Resources Code

Section Affected		Type of Change	Chapter Number	Page
25402.11	Establishment of administrative enforcement process for violation of a regulation and assessment of administrative civil penalty; Considerations; Orders; Cost; Exceptions	Added	591	828
25900	Injunctive relief	Amended	591	830

Public Utilities Code

Section Affected		Type of Change	Chapter Number	Page
399.4	Policy and intent to administer cost-effective energy efficiency programs; Rebates or incentives for an energy efficiency improvement or installation; Evaluation of investments	Amended	591	831

Revenue and Taxation Code

Section Affected		Type of Change	Chapter Number	Page
6070.5	Failure to resolve outstanding liabilities or to comply with terms of installment payment agreement as grounds for refusal to issue or revoke a seller's permit; Notice; Reconsideration	Added	734	833

Unemployment Insurance Code

Section Affected		Type of Change	Chapter Number	Page
1088.5	Information to be reported relating to new employees	Amended	296, 734	837

Vehicle Code

Section Affected		Type of Change	Chapter Number	Page
27000	Horns; Backup device or alarm and video camera on garbage trucks	Amended	235	846

CSLB HISTORY & BACKGROUND

The Contractors State License Board (CSLB) was established in 1929 as the Contractors License Bureau under the Department of Professional and Vocational Standards. Today, CSLB is part of the Department of Consumer Affairs.

A fifteen-member Board appoints CSLB's executive officer, or Registrar of Contractors, and directs administrative policy for the board's operations. CLSB's Board includes nine public members (eight non-contractors and one local building official), five contractors, and one labor representative. The Governor makes eleven appointments and four are made by the Legislature. The Board holds regularly scheduled public meetings throughout the state. These meetings provide the public with an opportunity to testify on agenda items and other issues.

CSLB licenses and regulates contractors in 43 license classifications that constitute the construction industry. Currently, there are about 300,000 contractor licenses in the state. The Registrar oversees approximately 400 employees who work at the headquarters office in Sacramento and field offices throughout the state.

Headquarters staff receives and processes applications for new contractor licenses, additional classifications, changes of license records, and license renewals. Staff also reviews and maintains records of disciplinary actions initiated by the field offices, provides verified certificates of licensure used in court or other legal actions, and provides the status of licensure and other support services.

Headquarters directs the activities of field offices, and initiates all disciplinary actions resulting from investigations. Field office staff investigates consumer complaints against contractors. The Statewide Investigative Fraud Team (SWIFT) addresses unlicensed activity.

CSLB's website, www.cslb.ca.gov or www.CheckTheLicenseFirst.com, provides the ability to look up a contractor by license number, name, or business name, and obtain the licensee's contact information, license status, CSLB legal actions (if any), classifications held, business type, and bond and workers' compensation insurance information.

Identical information is available through CSLB's automated public information line, 1-800-321-CSLB (2752), which operates 24 hours per day. Callers can determine whether a contractor's license is valid by entering the contractor license number. The information provided includes the licensee's business name, license status, classifications held, business type, and CSLB disciplinary actions (if any). Also available is recorded information on licensing and examination procedures, complaint procedures and how to obtain information on a complaint that has been referred for legal action, the location and hours of CSLB offices, and current topics, such as recently passed laws or regulations. Callers can also order forms, applications, and other publications.

CSLB offers a variety of publications and guides to help consumers make informed choices when contracting for home repairs and improvements. Speakers can be provided for groups interested in learning more about CSLB. Check the website for details or write to CSLB Public Affairs, P.O. Box 26000, Sacramento, CA 95826.

CSLB MISSION

The Contractors State License Board protects consumers by regulating the construction industry through policies that promote the health, safety, and general welfare of the public in matters relating to construction.

The Contractors State License Board accomplishes this by:

- *Ensuring that construction is performed in a safe, competent, and professional manner;*

- *Licensing contractors and enforcing licensing laws;*

- *Requiring licensure for any person practicing or offering to practice construction contracting;*

- *Enforcing the laws, regulations, and standards governing construction contracting in a fair and uniform manner;*

- *Providing resolution to disputes that arise from construction activities; and*

- *Educating consumers so they can make informed choices.*

CONTRACTORS STATE LICENSE BOARD OFFICES

Headquarters

Street Address	9821 Business Park Drive Sacramento, CA 95827
Mailing Address	P.O. Box 26000, Sacramento CA 95826
Automated Information	(800) 321-CSLB (2752)
Internet	www.cslb.ca.gov or www.CheckTheLicenseFirst.com

Northern Region

9821 Business Park Drive
Sacramento, CA 95827
Legal Action Disclosure (916) 255-4041
Case Management (916) 255-4027
SWIFT (Unlicensed Activity) (916) 255-2924

Sacramento Intake & Mediation Center
P.O. Box 269116
Sacramento, CA 95826-9116
(800) 321-CSLB (2752)
Fax (916) 255-4449

Fresno Investigative Center
1277 East Alluvial, Ste. 106
Fresno, CA 93720
(800) 321-CSLB (2752)

Oakland Investigative Center *
1515 Clay Street, Suite 1105
Oakland, CA 94612
(800) 321-CSLB (2752)

Sacramento Investigative Center
P.O. Box 269115
Sacramento, CA 95826-9115
(800) 321-CSLB (2752)

San Francisco Investigative Center*
301 Junipero Serra Boulevard, Suite 206
San Francisco, CA 94127-2666
(800) 321-CSLB (2752)

Bakersfield Branch Office*
1601 New Stine Road, Suite 182
Bakersfield, CA 93309
(800) 321-CSLB (2752)

Southern Region

12501 East Imperial Hwy, Suite 600
Norwalk, CA 90650
Legal Action Disclosure (562) 345-7656
Case Management (562) 345-7656
SWIFT (Unlicensed Activity) (562) 345-7600

Norwalk Intake & Mediation Center
12501 East Imperial Hwy, Suite 620
Norwalk, CA 90650
(800) 321-CSLB (2752)
Fax (562) 466-6064

Norwalk Investigative Center
12501 East Imperial Hwy, Suite 630
Norwalk, CA 90650
(800) 321-CSLB (2752)

San Bernardino Investigative Center
1845 Business Center Drive, Suite 206
San Bernardino, CA 92408-3467
(800) 321-CSLB (2752)

San Diego Investigative Center
9246 Lightwave Ave., Ste. 130
San Diego, CA 92123
(800) 321-CSLB (2752)

West Covina Investigative Center
100 N. Barranca St., Suite 300
West Covina, CA 91791
(800) 321-CSLB (2752)

Valencia Investigative Center
28480 Avenue Stanford
Valencia, CA 91355
(800) 321-CSLB (2752)

Santa Rosa Branch Office *
50 D Street, Room 400
Santa Rosa, CA 95404
(800) 321-CSLB (2752)

* Limited office hours

TABLE OF CONTENTS

Section I. The California Contractor License

Section IV. Construction Standards and Safety Regulations

Page

Section V. The Department of Consumer Affairs

Page

Section VI. The Contractors State License Board; License Law, Rules and Regulations, and Related Laws

Page

SECTION I.
THE CALIFORNIA CONTRACTOR LICENSE

Chapter 1.

Becoming a California Licensed Contractor

GENERAL REQUIREMENTS

1. Who can become a licensed contractor?

To qualify for a California contractor license, an individual must be 18 years of age or older, have a valid Social Security number (SSN) issued by the federal Social Security Administration, and have the experience and skills necessary to manage the daily activities of a construction business, including field supervision, or must be represented by someone else with the necessary experience and skills who serves as the qualifying individual.

The person who will act as the qualifying individual must have had, within the ten (10) years immediately before the filing of the application, at least four (4) full years of experience as a journeyman, foreman, supervising employee, or as a foreman, supervisor, or contractor in the classification for which he or she is applying. The experience claimed on the application must be verifiable, and individuals who have knowledge of the experience must certify the accuracy of the experience information as stated on the *Certification of Work Experience* form.

2. Who must be licensed as a contractor?

All businesses or individuals who construct or alter, or offer to construct or alter, any building, highway, road, parking facility, railroad, excavation, or other structure in California must be licensed by the California Contractors State License Board (CSLB) if the total cost (labor and materials) of one or more contracts on the project is $500 or more. Contractors, including subcontractors, specialty contractors, and persons engaged in the business of home

1

improvement (with the exception of joint ventures and projects involving federal funding) must be licensed before submitting bids. Licenses may be issued to individuals, partnerships, corporations, joint ventures or limited liability companies (LLC).

3. Is anyone exempt from the requirement to be licensed?

Yes. Here are some of the exemptions:

- Work on a project for which the combined value of labor, materials, and all other costs on one or more contracts is *less* than $500 falls within the minor work exemption. Work which is part of a larger or major project, whether undertaken by the same or different contractors, may not be divided into amounts less than $500 in an attempt to meet the $500 exemption;

- An employee who is paid wages, who does not usually work in an independently established business, and who does not have direction or control over the performance of work or who does not determine the final results of the work or project;

- Public personnel working on public projects;

- Officers of a court acting within the scope of their office;

- Public utilities working under specified conditions;

- Oil and gas operations performed by an owner or lessee;

- Owner-builders who build or improve structures on their own property if they either do the work themselves or use their own employees (paid in wages) to do the work. This exemption is only valid if the structure is not intended to be offered for sale within one year of completion;

- Owner-builders who build or improve structures on their own property if they contract for the construction with a licensed contractor. This exemption is applicable to the construction of single-family residential structures only if no more than four of such structures are offered for sale in any one calendar year;

- Owner-builders who improve their main place of residence, who have actually resided there for one year prior to completion of the work, and who complete the work prior to sale. This exemption is limited to two structures within a three-year period;

- Sale or installation of finished products that do not become a fixed part of the structure;

- A seller of installed carpets who holds a retail furniture dealer's license but who contracts for installation of the carpet with a licensed carpet installer;

- Security alarm company operators (licensed by the Bureau of Security and Investigative Services) who install, maintain, monitor, sell, alter, or service alarm systems (fire alarm company operators must be licensed by CSLB); and,

- Persons whose activities consist only of installing satellite antenna systems on residential structures or property. These persons must be registered with the Bureau of Electronic and Appliance Repair.

4. Do I have to reside in California to get and keep a CSLB-issued contractor license?

No.

5. Does California recognize contractor licenses issued by other states or countries?

No. However, California does have reciprocal agreements with some states that have comparable license and experience qualifications for certain trades. It is only after the Registrar of Contractors has entered into a reciprocal agreement with the other state and under certain conditions that the Registrar may waive the written trade examination for a contractor licensed in another state. Applicants must still qualify by taking and passing the Law and Business Examination. If you have trade experience or a contractor license issued by another state or country and you want to contract for work in California, this experience may be acceptable. In any case, you must apply for and be issued a license by CSLB. As of this printing, CSLB has reciprocity agreements with Arizona, Nevada, and Utah. Check the CSLB website, www.cslb.ca.gov, for details.

6. What happens if I contract without a license?

A contractor license is not necessary as long as you don't advertise yourself as a licensed contractor and never contract for jobs costing $500 or more in combined labor and materials.

CSLB has established statewide investigative teams that focus on unlicensed contractors and the underground economy. These units conduct stings and sweeps to curtail illegal contracting activities. Stings and sweeps are routinely publicized to ensure maximum consumer education.

Contracting without a license is usually a misdemeanor. Unlicensed contractors face a first offense sentence of up to six months in jail and/or a $5,000 fine, and potential administrative fines of $200 to $15,000. Subsequent violations increase criminal penalties and fines.

However, felony charges may be filed against those who contract without a license for any project that is covered by a state of emergency or disaster proclaimed by the Governor or the President of the United States. Felony convictions may result in a state prison term as specified by the court.

EXPERIENCE REQUIREMENTS

7. What kind of experience is required for a contractor license?

At least four (4) years of journey-level experience in the past 10 years immediately preceding the application is required to qualify for a state contractor license. Credit for experience is given only for experience as a journeyman, foreman, supervising employee, contractor, or owner-builder. These are defined, as follows:

- A journeyman is a person who has completed an apprenticeship program or is an experienced worker, not a trainee, and is fully qualified and able to perform the trade without supervision.

- A foreman or supervising employee is a person who has the knowledge and skill of a journeyman and directly supervises physical construction.

- A contractor is a person who manages the daily activities of a construction business, including field supervision.

- An owner-builder is a person with a minimum of knowledge, skills and abilities of a journeyman, who performs work on his or her own property, and who has the skills necessary to manage the daily activities of a construction business, including field supervision.

All experience claims must be verified by a qualified and responsible person, such as a homeowner, an employer, fellow employee, other journeyman, contractor, union representative, building inspector, architect, engineer, business associate, or a client if the applicant is/was self-employed. The person verifying your experience must have firsthand knowledge of your experience during the time period covered—that is, he or she must have observed the work that you have done and must complete and sign under penalty of perjury the "Certification of Work Experience" form, which is included with the application. Even if you provide a "Certification of Work Experience" form, be prepared to furnish documentation of any experience you claim on the form whenever the documentation is requested. Failure to provide this documentation will result in rejection of your application or denial of the license.

8. Are there education requirements for a license?

No. You do not have to meet any education requirements in order to qualify for a contractor license. However, many community colleges and private schools offer instruction in vocational education. For more information, contact the:

Chancellor's Office, California Community Colleges
1102 Q Street
Sacramento, CA 95811
916.445.8752
www.cccco.edu

(NOTE: CSLB does not make referrals or recommendations regarding license preparation schools.)

9. May I substitute any education, technical training, or apprenticeship training for the required experience?

You may receive credit for technical training, apprenticeship training, or education instead of a portion of the required four years of practical experience; at least one year must be practical experience. You must provide written documentation of any training or education claimed in place of experience. Acceptable documentation includes copies of apprenticeship certificates and college transcripts.

10. How much credit can I expect to receive for technical training, the completion of an approved apprenticeship program, or related college or university education?

CSLB may credit training, apprenticeship, or education, as follows:

A maximum of one-and-one-half (1-1/2) years upon submission of transcripts of the following:

- An Associate of Arts (A.A.) degree from an accredited school or college in building or construction management;

A maximum of two (2) years upon submission of transcripts from any of the following:

- A four-year degree from an accredited college or university in the fields of accounting, business, economics, mathematics, physics, or areas related to the specific trade or craft for which application is being made;
- A professional degree in law; or

- Substantial college or university course work in accounting, architecture, business, construction technology, drafting, economics, engineering, mathematics, or physics.

A maximum of three (3) years upon submission of any of the following:

- A Certificate of Completion of Apprenticeship from an accredited apprenticeship program or a certified statement of completion of apprenticeship training from a union in the classification for which application is being made;

- Transcripts for a four-year degree from an accredited college or university in architecture, construction technology, or any field of engineering that is directly related to the classification for which application is being made; or

- Transcripts for a four-year degree from an accredited college or university in the field of horticulture or landscape horticulture for the C-27 Landscaping classification.

LICENSE CLASSIFICATIONS

11. What are the contractor license classifications?

CSLB issues licenses to contract in particular trades or fields of the construction profession. Each separate trade is recognized as a "classification." Upon qualification (including certification of four years of journey-level experience), there is no limit to the number of classifications that may be added to your license.

CSLB issues licenses for the following classifications:

- **Class "A" — General Engineering Contractor**

  The principal business is in connection with fixed works requiring specialized engineering knowledge and skill.

- **Class "B" — General Building Contractor**

  The principal business is in connection with any structure built, being built, or to be built, requiring in its construction the use of at least two unrelated building trades or crafts; however, framing or carpentry projects may be performed without limitation. A "B" General Building contractor may take a contract for projects involving one trade only if the contractor holds the appropriate specialty license or subcontracts with an appropriately licensed specialty contractor to perform the work.

- **Class "C" — Specialty Contractor**

There are 41 separate "C" license classifications for contractors whose construction work requires specialized skill and whose principal contracting business involves the use of specialized building trades or crafts. Manufacturers are considered to be contractors if engaged in on-site construction, alteration, or repair.

12. In what trades may I obtain a Class "C" Specialty contractor license?

You may obtain a license in any of the classifications listed below. For a detailed description of these classifications, consult the CSLB Rules and Regulations in Chapter 13.

Classification	Code	Section
Boiler, Hot-Water Heating and Steam Fitting	C-4	832.04
Building Moving/Demolition	C-21	832.21
Cabinet, Millwork and Finish Carpentry	C-6	832.06
Ceramic and Mosaic Tile	C-54	832.54
Concrete	C-8	832.08
Construction Zone Traffic Control	C-31	832.31
Drywall	C-9	832.09
Earthwork and Paving	C-12	832.12
Electrical	C-10	832.10
Sign	C-45	832.45
Elevator	C-11	832.11
Fencing	C-13	832.13
Fire Protection	C-16	832.16
Flooring and Floor Covering	C-15	832.15
Framing and Rough Carpentry	C-5	832.05
General Manufactured Housing	C-47	832.47
Glazing	C-17	832.17
Insulation and Acoustical	C-2	832.02
Landscaping	C-27	832.27
Lathing and Plastering	C-35	832.35

Classification	Code	Section
Limited Specialty	C-61	832.61
Lock and Security Equipment	C-28	832.28
Low Voltage Systems	C-7	832.07
Masonry	C-29	832.29
Ornamental Metal	C-23	832.23
Painting and Decorating	C-33	832.33
Parking and Highway Improvement	C-32	832.32
Pipeline	C-34	832.34
Plumbing	C-36	832.36
Refrigeration	C-38	832.38
Roofing	C-39	832.39
Sanitation System	C-42	832.42
Sheet Metal	C-43	832.43
Solar	C-46	832.46
Reinforcing Steel	C-50	832.50
Structural Steel	C-51	832.51
Swimming Pool	C-53	832.53
Warm-Air Heating, Ventilating and Air-Conditioning	C-20	832.20
Water Conditioning	C-55	832.55
Welding	C-60	832.60
Well Drilling	C-57	832.57

Authority cited: B&P Sections 7008 and 7059, Reference: Sections 7058 and 7059

CSLB lists the C-61 Limited Specialty classification in "D" subcategories for administrative tracking. Definitions for the "D" subcategories were developed by staff and approved by the Board as policy. Following are the C-61 Limited Specialty "D" subcategory classifications that CSLB currently issues:

D-03 - Awnings
D-04 - Central Vacuum Systems
D-06 – Concrete-Related Services
D-09 - Drilling, Blasting and Oil Field Work
D-10 - Elevated Floors
D-12 - Synthetic Products
D-16 - Hardware, Locks and Safes
D-21 - Machinery and Pumps
D-24 - Metal Products
D-28 - Doors, Gates and Activating Devices
D-29 - Paperhanging
D-30 - Pile Driving and Pressure Foundation Jacking
D-31 - Pole Installation and Maintenance
D-34 - Prefabricated Equipment
D-35 - Pool and Spa Maintenance
D-38 - Sand and Water Blasting
D-39 - Scaffolding
D-40 - Service Station Equipment and Maintenance
D-41 - Siding and Decking
D-42 - Non-Electrical Sign Installation
D-49 - Tree Service
D-50 - Suspended Ceilings
D-52 - Window Coverings
D-53 - Wood Tanks
D-56 – Trenching
D-59 - Hydroseed Spraying
D-62 - Air and Water Balancing
D-63 - Construction Cleanup
D-64 - Non-specialized
D-65 - Weatherization and Energy Conservation

CSLB's website (**www.cslb.ca.gov** or
www.CheckTheLicenseFirst.com) contains a complete listing of
"D" license classifications and descriptions, plus classifications that
are no longer issued (cross-referenced to current classifications).

13. Are there any special requirements for contractors who work with asbestos or other hazardous substances?

Yes. Contractors who work with asbestos or other hazardous
substances are regulated by the United States Department of Labor,
Federal Occupational Safety and Health Administration, and the
California Department of Industrial Relations, Division of
Occupational Safety and Health (DOSH), as well as by CSLB. These
contractors are subject to a number of certification, registration,
reporting, and safety requirements.

Only the current qualifier on an existing license can apply for the asbestos certification or the hazardous substance certification.

Following are some of CSLB's requirements for asbestos abatement and other hazardous substance removal work:

- Asbestos abatement contractors must be certified by CSLB. To become certified, a contractor must take and pass an EPA-accredited asbestos abatement course, complete the "Application for Asbestos Certification," pass a comprehensive CSLB asbestos abatement exam, and register with the Asbestos Contractor Registration Unit of DOSH.

- Contractors who perform hazardous substance removal work must be certified by CSLB. They must complete an "Application for Hazardous Substance Removal and Remedial Actions," and they must pass a CSLB certification exam.

  Any contractor who has an "A" General Engineering, "B" General Building, "C-36" Plumbing, "C-12" Earthwork and Paving, "C-57" Well Drilling (Water) or, in some cases, "C-61 (D-40)" Service Station Equipment and Maintenance license is eligible to be certified.

In addition, contractors who install or remove underground storage tanks must hold the Hazardous Substance Removal Certification. CSLB Board policy currently limits certified contractors doing underground storage tank work as follows:

- "A" General Engineering contractors may install and/or remove underground storage tanks for any purpose at any location.

- "B" General Building contractors may, in the course of work performed under a contract that meets the requirements for the "B" classification (*see Question 11*), install and/or remove an underground storage tank if they have been properly certified for Hazardous Substance Removal and Remedial Actions.

- C-36 Plumbing contractors may install and/or remove any underground storage tank that provides service to a building, including storage tanks for service stations.

14. Are there any other requirements I need to complete?

FINGERPRINTING – All applicants for licensure are required to submit a full set of fingerprints for the purpose of conducting a criminal background check. Fingerprints will be compared to the records of the California Department of Justice and the Federal

Bureau of Investigation to determine whether a criminal history exists. After submission of an application to CSLB, each individual listed on the application will be sent instructions on the process for obtaining and submitting fingerprints. For more information, visit CSLB's website: http://www.cslb.ca.gov/applicants/FingerprintQA.asp.

ASBESTOS OPEN-BOOK EXAMINATION – Before a license will be issued, every licensee must have completed, signed, and returned the open-book examination contained in the booklet *Asbestos: A Contractor's Guide and Open-Book Examination*. The booklet contains general information about asbestos abatement standards.

APPLYING FOR A LICENSE

15. How do I apply for a contractor license?

You must complete the following steps:

- Obtain an "Application for Original Contractor's License" form from any office of the Contractors State License Board, by telephone from CSLB's 24-hour automated public information line, (800) 321-CSLB (2752), or via the CSLB website, www.cslb.ca.gov or www.CheckTheLicenseFirst.com.

- Take the time to carefully read and follow the general information and instructions included with the application. **Note:** Certifications in support of work experience must be submitted **with the application. No experience certifications will be accepted after the application has been reviewed and accepted.**

- Complete the application and all accompanying forms in black or dark blue ink or with a typewriter. Forms completed in pencil will be returned. Make sure to sign and date the application.

*NOTE: **Applicants with a disability** requiring special testing accommodations must complete Form 13E-77, Special Accommodation Request for Examination. (See page 16 for more information.)*

- Proofread your application for any omissions. If the Board has to return the application to you for any missing information, your license may be delayed.

If you are required to take the exam, you may apply for only one classification at a time, and must pass the examination. After your license is issued, you may apply for any additional classifications for which you qualify.

If you are required to take the exam, you may submit an application for more than one classification at a time only if you have already qualified for each of the classifications for which you are applying.

If you are required to take the examination, take the following steps:

- Submit the application, the application processing fee of $300, and all required application documents to:

  Contractors State License Board
  P.O. Box 26000
  Sacramento, CA 95826

  NOTE: Do not submit any bonds or the initial license fee with your application.

- Be certain to include your return address on the envelope.

- Upon successful completion of your examination, you will be notified to submit the initial license fee of $180 and the documents required for issuance of your license (bonds, proof of workers' compensation insurance, etc.). **You must submit ALL required documents together to avoid delays. Your license will not be issued until all issuance requirements have been met.**

If you are not required to take an examination for any classification for which you are applying, you must:

- Submit an application and $480 ($300 application processing fee and $180 initial license fee, in addition to the $75 for each additional classification);

The following items are required for issuance of a license. They may be submitted with your applications or you may wait until your application is reviewed and a letter requesting the information is received:

- A contractor bond or equivalent in the business name of the applicant, and a bond of qualifying individual or exemption statement for each responsible managing officer or responsible managing employee, as appropriate. The bond of qualifying individual must be in the names of the qualifying individuals and the business.

- Proof of workers' compensation insurance or exemption. If you have no employees, an exemption certificate (Form 13L-50) must be submitted. Please note: if the license is qualified by a responsible managing employee, the qualifier is an employee. This means that workers' compensation insurance is required to cover this employee and an exemption certificate should not be submitted.

Note: All C-39 Roofing contractors must carry workers' compensation insurance regardless of whether they have employees.

If you are applying for an inactive license, you must:

- Submit an application, the appropriate application processing fee, and the initial license fee. The same fees are required for inactive licenses as for active licenses.

NOTE: If your license is to be issued as "inactive," bonds and workers' compensation insurance are NOT required.

16. Will CSLB acknowledge receipt of my application?

CSLB will send you a letter of acknowledgment. This letter will contain two important numbers: a nine-digit Application Fee Number and a four-digit Personal Identification Number (PIN), together with instructions on how to use these numbers to check on the progress of your application.

Your Application Fee Number, also known as your "receipt number," will also appear on the front of your canceled check, on the "Notice to Appear for Examination," and on a request for you to submit the appropriate documents and the initial license fee. Please retain a record of this number and use it in all inquiries regarding your pending application.

17. How long does it take to complete the license application process?

Because there are many factors that affect the time it takes to process an application (type of application, workload, vacancies, etc.), processing times continually change. By using your PIN and your Application Fee Number to do an application status check, you can obtain information on what date the Board is currently working on in regard to your specific type of application. This information is updated weekly and will give you a good idea of when your application will be pulled for processing.

If no exam is required and all license requirements are met, a license can be issued shortly after being pulled for processing. If an exam is required, you will be given an exam date after the date the application is processed and considered acceptable, which means no corrections or additional information is required. Additional time is required to complete application processing after you pass the exam. Your license will not be issued until all issuance requirements have been met.

18. How will I know if my application is approved?

After your application is reviewed and accepted, you will receive either a "Notice to Appear for Examination," or, if the examination is waived, a request for documents and the initial license fee. Some applications are sent for investigation and, even though you may take and pass the exam, the license will not be issued until the application has been approved and all licensing requirements have been met. Applications which require no examination can be submitted with the contractor bond, bond of qualifying individual (if required), proof of workers' compensation insurance, and applicable fees.

19. How can I check on the status of my application?

CSLB will send you an acknowledgment that your application was received. The acknowledgment letter will contain:

- Instructions on how to make inquiries;

- Your Application Fee Number; and

- Your PIN, which will give you private access to your application status. To check on the status of your application, call CSLB's toll-free automated information line, (800) 321-CSLB (2752), or visit the website at www.cslb.ca.gov.

20. What happens if my application is not approved?

Your application may be returned to you if it is insufficient or incomplete. This is known as a "rejection" of the application. You must provide any missing information, make corrections, and return your application to CSLB within 90 days from the date it was rejected. If it is not returned to CSLB within 90 days, your application becomes void. You cannot reinstate it, and you must submit a new application and appropriate processing fee if you wish to pursue a license.

21. If my application is not approved, can you refund my application fee?

No. The $300 fee is for processing the application, whether or not the application is approved. Since each application is filed for processing as soon as it arrives at CSLB, the fee cannot be refunded.

22. How do I apply for a Joint Venture license?

The Joint Venture contractor license is one that is issued to two or more licensees together (sole owners, partnerships, corporations, or other joint ventures) whose licenses are current and active. A Joint Venture license may be issued in any or all of the classifications in which the members of the joint venture are licensed. To apply for a Joint Venture contractor license, you must submit an "Application for Joint Venture Contractor License" form along with the appropriate application fee--$300 application processing fee and $180 initial license fee, in addition to $75 for each additional classification. The following requirements must be met:

- Each of the licensees participating in the joint venture must show the exact business name and license number as it appears in CSLB records;

- One of the official personnel listed on CSLB's records for each participating licensee (the owner, a partner, or an officer of the corporation, but not a responsible managing employee) must sign the application;

- The qualifier for the entity holding the classification applied for must sign the application;

- Provide proof of a contractor bond or submit a $12,500 cash deposit. The bond or cash deposit must bear the same business name as the pending joint venture; and

- Proof of workers' compensation insurance coverage or exemption.

No examination or fingerprinting is required for a Joint Venture license.

23. When does a Joint Venture License Expire?

The Joint Venture license will expire two years from the last day of the month in which the license was issued. Each license included in the joint venture must be current and active before the Joint Venture license can be renewed in active status.

24. What is Cause for Suspension of a Joint Venture License?

If any of the member licenses ceases to be current and active or is suspended for any reason, the Joint Venture license will be suspended.

LICENSING EXAMINATIONS

Special Accommodation Request for Examination

In compliance with the Americans with Disabilities Act (ADA), Public Law 101-336, CSLB provides "reasonable accommodation" for applicants with disabilities that may affect their ability to take required examinations. It is the applicant's responsibility to notify CSLB of any necessary alternative arrangements. CSLB is not required by the ADA to provide special accommodations if they are unaware of specific needs. To request special accommodation, submit Form 13E-77, "Special Accommodation Request for Examination" form. This form is available in any CSLB office and on CSLB's website, www.cslb.ca.gov.

25. Is there an examination requirement for a contractor license?

The qualifying individual for a contractor license is required to pass the written Law and Business Examination and a specific trade examination unless he or she is approved for a waiver.

26. Under what circumstances is a waiver of an examination granted?

The Registrar MAY waive the examination requirement if the qualifying individual meets one of the following conditions:

- The person is currently the qualifying individual for a license in good standing in the same classification for which he or she is applying; or

- The person has been a qualifying individual within the past five (5) years for a license in good standing in the same classification for which he or she is applying; or

- Within the last five (5) years, the person has passed both the Law and Business Examination and the trade examination in the same classification for which he or she is applying.

27. Are there any additional circumstances under which a waiver of an examination may be requested?

Yes, at the Registrar's discretion, an exam waiver may be granted if the qualifying individual meets the following criteria:

The qualifying individual is a member of the immediate family of a licensee whose individual license was active and in good standing for five of the seven years immediately preceding the application. The qualifying individual must have been actively engaged in the licensee's business for five (5) of the previous seven (7) years and be applying in the same classification, and the license must be required in order to continue the operations of an existing family business in the event of the absence or death of the licensee.

28. If I think I am eligible for a waiver, must I complete the experience section of the application?

Even if you think that you are eligible for an examination waiver, you must complete the experience section of the application to document a minimum of five (5) years out of the previous seven (7) years of journey-level experience. All experience claims must be verified by a qualified and responsible person, such as an employer, fellow employee, other journeyman, contractor, union representative, building inspector, architect, or engineer.

The person verifying your claim must have firsthand knowledge of your experience during the time period being verified; that is, he or she must have observed the work that you have done.

EXCEPTIONS

You are not required to document your experience if any of the following conditions exist:

- You are currently a qualifier on a license in good standing in the same classification(s) for which you are applying; or

- You have been a qualifier within the past five (5) years on a license in good standing in the same classification(s) for which you are applying.

29. How will I find out if I have to take the examination?

If you have to take the examination, you will be sent a "Notice to Appear for Examination."

If you qualify for a waiver, you will be sent a notice requesting that the required documents and fees be submitted for your license.

30. How soon after filing my application will I receive my Notice to Appear for Examination?

Scheduling the exam occurs after your application is processed and found acceptable *(see Question 17)*. There are many factors that affect the time it may take to process an application.

You will be scheduled for the exam after the application is accepted. You should receive your examination notice at least three (3) weeks prior to the examination date. *Note: Some applications are sent for formal investigation. Each application must be accepted AND approved in order for the license to be issued, even if the qualifier has passed the exam.*

Please refer to your acknowledgment letter for instructions on how to check the status of your application.

31. Where are the examinations given?

To make the examination procedure more convenient for applicants, CSLB Testing Centers are located throughout the state. The examination sites are located in Fresno, Norwalk, Oakland, Oxnard, Sacramento, San Bernardino, San Diego, and San Jose. CSLB testing staff uses zip codes to assign applicants to the Testing Center nearest to their business address.

The "Notice to Appear for Examination" mailed to the applicant identifies the exam location, what identification is required, and travel directions to the examination site.

32. What are the major components of the examination?

There are two parts to the examination process. All qualifying individuals must pass the standard Law and Business Examination. In addition, all qualifying individuals must pass a second test covering the specific trade or certification area for which they are applying. However, no trade examination is required for the C-61 Limited Specialty classification.

33. What does the Law and Business Examination cover?

The Law and Business Examination consists of multiple choice questions related to business management and construction law. Applicants can find information on the breakdown of the topics covered in the examination in the *Study Guide for the Law and Business Examination* that is sent to applicants along with the "Notice to Appear for Examination."

34. How can I prepare for the Law and Business Examination?

The current edition of the *California Contractors License Law and Reference Book* is the basic study reference. Copies may be purchased by calling 1-800-533-1637, faxing a request to 518-462-3788, through the Internet website at www.lexisnexis.com/bookstore, or by writing to: Matthew Bender & Company, Attn. Customer Service, 1275 Broadway, Albany, NY 12204-2694. When ordering by mail, include a street address and the recipient's name. All orders are shipped by carrier and cannot be delivered to a post office box.

The *California Contractors License Law and Reference Book* is not sold at any CSLB office; however, access to the book is provided on the CSLB website at www.cslb.ca.gov. Copies may be available from some specialty book stores. Please check your local telephone directory.

Other suggested study materials are listed in the resource list included in the *Study Guide for the Law and Business Examination*. The study guide is available by calling CSLB, toll-free, at 1-800-321-CSLB (2752); or via the website at www.cslb.ca.gov.

35. How can I prepare for my trade or certification examination?

A study guide for each examination is available on CSLB's website. Also, CSLB will send it to you with your "Notice to Appear for Examination." The study guide lists the topic areas covered by the examination, shows how each area is weighted, and, in most cases, recommends resource materials to study.

36. What are the trade examinations like?

All trade examinations consist of multiple-choice questions. You will be informed at the test site about the percentage of correct answers needed to pass each examination.

The examinations are developed with the assistance of licensed contractors. Most examinations include questions that refer to accompanying blueprints and/or booklets containing drawings.

37. What should I bring to the examination site?

In order to be admitted to the Testing Center, bring the "Notice to Appear for Examination." You must also bring a government-issued picture identification (a current valid driver license, Department of Motor Vehicles identification card, or military identification card). Pencils, scratch paper, calculators, and scale rulers will be provided. No personal calculators, cell phones, pagers or other electronic devices are permitted in the testing area. All personal items must be placed in a common storage area at your own risk. You are advised to leave articles of value locked in your vehicle since the Testing Center staff does not watch the storage area.

38. How long does the examination take?

You will be given 2-1/2 hours to complete each examination.

39. What is involved with the computer-based testing system?

You will be taking your examination on the easy-to-use State Contractors Official Regulatory Exam (SCORE) system. The SCORE system guides all examinees through a tutorial to help them feel at ease with the computer prior to the exam.

40. What kind of feedback will I receive?

Examinees receive their exam results before they leave the exam site.

Successful examinees are told only that they have passed the examination. They will not be given detailed information about the score.

Unsuccessful examinees are given a statement showing how well they performed in each section of the exam. These sections are described in greater detail in the study guide for that examination so the examinee will know what areas to emphasize in preparing to retake the examination.

41. If I fail to appear for an examination or fail to pass the Law and Business Examination and/or a trade examination, may I retake the examination(s)?

Yes. If you fail to appear for an examination, you must pay a $60 rescheduling fee. If you fail to appear a second time, your application will be considered void, and you will have to submit a new application with new fees. Your examination may be rescheduled one time without a fee if you provide documented evidence that the failure to appear was due to a medical emergency or other circumstance beyond your control.

If you fail the Law and Business Examination and/or your trade examination, you must also pay a $60 fee each time you are rescheduled. You are given 18 months in which to pass the examinations. If you do not pass within 18 months after your application is accepted by the board, your application is considered void, and you will have to submit a new application with new fees. The void date on an application may be extended up to 90 days if you provide documented evidence that the failure to complete the application process was due to a medical emergency or other circumstance beyond your control.

To file for rescheduling, complete the information requested on the bottom of the notice informing you that you failed to pass the examination and submit it with the $60 fee to CSLB. (Please identify any address change on this form.) You will be sent a notice informing you where and when to appear for your next examination.

Examination results are good for five (5) years. If you pass either the trade exam or the Law and Business Examination but fail the other, you need only take the examination you failed as long as you retake and pass the examination within five years.

42. May I review the test questions after the examinations?

No. Test questions and answer keys are not available for review. However, you may file a written protest or critique of any examination question(s) after you have completed your examination and before you turn in your examination materials to the proctor.

43. Are there any penalties for disclosing the contents of a state examination?

Yes. Penalties for conduct that violates the security of the examination include prosecution on misdemeanor charges resulting in a fine of $500, payment of damages of up to $10,000 plus the costs of litigation, and a sentence in county jail. You would also be subject to automatic exam failure; any fee(s) paid to the State of California would not be refunded; and you would not be allowed to apply for any license classification for a period of one (1) year from your examination date.

Conduct which violates the security of the examination includes providing information about test questions to any school, person, or business other than CSLB examination staff; removing examination materials from the examination site (includes writing down examination questions for future use); communicating with other examinees during an examination; copying or permitting your answers to be copied; having in your possession any written material other than test materials provided by CSLB; or taking the examination on behalf of another applicant.

44. What will I receive to show that I'm licensed?

You will receive a wall certificate showing the name of the person or company to which the certificate has been issued, the license number, and the date of issue; and a plastic pocket card showing the license number, business name, classification(s), certifications (if applicable), and the license expiration date. The law requires that you display your wall certificate in your main office or chief place of business. You should also carry your pocket card with you, especially in situations where you think you might be soliciting business or talking to potential customers. CSLB's publication, *What You Should Know Before You Hire a Licensed Contractor*, suggests that customers should ask to see a copy of the pocket card.

45. How long before I receive those documents?

You should receive your wall certificate and pocket card within approximately one week from the time your license is issued.

LICENSE ISSUANCE

46. To whom is a license issued?

A license may be issued to an individual, a partnership, a corporation, a joint venture or a limited liability company. The license belongs to the owner of an individual license, to the partnership, to the corporation as it is registered with the California Secretary of State, or to the combination of licensees who are party to the joint venture or LLC.

47. If the ownership of a business changes, is the contractor license considered to be part of the purchase?

No. With the possible exception of a corporation, the license is not considered part of the business. If the corporation's registration number assigned by the California Secretary of State remains the same, the same license can be used if the license is current and active. The officers and the qualifying individual do not necessarily have to remain the same, although a qualifying individual must be in place in order for the license to be valid.

48. What is the difference between an active and an inactive license?

The holder of an active license is entitled to contract for work in the classifications which appear on the license. While the license is active, the licensee must maintain a current contractor license bond, a bond of qualifying individual (if required), and workers' compensation insurance coverage if employees are hired or if the licensee holds the C-39 Roofing classification.

If a license is inactive, that is, currently renewed but on inactive status, the holder may not bid or contract for work. Neither the contractor bond nor the bond of qualifying individual is required for an inactive license. Also, a licensee does not need to have either the proof of exemption from workers' compensation insurance coverage on file with CSLB while the license is inactive (see Question 59).

49. To whom does the term "qualifying individual" refer?

A qualifying individual, or simply "qualifier," is the person listed in the CSLB records who meets the experience and examination requirements for the license. A qualifying individual is required for every classification on each license issued by CSLB.

50. What is the qualifying individual required to do?

The qualifying individual for a license is responsible for exercising the direct supervision and control of the employer's (or principal's) construction operations.

51. Can the same person serve as the qualifier for more than one license?

A person may act as a qualifying individual for more than one active license only if one of the following conditions exists:

- There is a common ownership of at least 20 percent of the equity of each firm for which the person acts as a qualifier;

- The additional firm is a subsidiary of or a joint venture with the first; or

- The majority of the partners or officers are the same.

Even if he or she meets the above conditions, A PERSON MAY SERVE AS THE QUALIFYING INDIVIDUAL FOR NO MORE THAN THREE (3) FIRMS IN ANY ONE-YEAR PERIOD. If a qualifier disassociates from the third firm, he or she must wait one year before associating with a new third firm.

In most cases, a responsible managing employee (RME) can only act as a qualifying individual for one active license at a time.

52. Who can be a qualifying individual?

If you have an individual license, your qualifier may be either an RME or you.

If you have a partnership license, your qualifier may either be one of the general partners (who shall be designated as the qualifying partner) or an RME.

If you have a corporate license, your qualifier may be either one of the officers listed on CSLB's records for your license (who shall be designated as the responsible managing officer, or RMO) or an RME.

If you have a limited liability company license, your qualifier may be a responsible managing member, responsible managing manager, RMO or RME.

If your qualifying individual is an RME, he or she must be a *bona fide* employee of the firm and may not be the qualifier on any other active license. This means that the RME must be regularly employed by the firm and actively involved in the operation of the business at least 32 hours per week or 80 percent of the total business operating hours per week, whichever is less.

53. Will a conviction for a criminal offense prevent a person from being licensed as a contractor or from serving as a qualifying individual?

CSLB's applications and other forms include questions regarding criminal convictions. CSLB may deny a license if the crime is substantially related to the duties, functions, and qualifications of a contractor. Failure to disclose the requested information may, in and of itself, be grounds for denial of a license.

Even if a crime is found to be substantially related to the duties, functions, and qualifications of a contractor, an individual may be licensed if he or she has demonstrated sufficient rehabilitation. *(See Section 869 in Chapter 13.)*

In 2002, the Legislature mandated that all applicants for licenses and home improvement salesperson registrations be required to submit fingerprints with each application beginning in January 2005. For more information, check CSLB's website at: http://www.cslb.ca.gov/applicants/fingerprintQA.asp.

FINANCIAL REQUIREMENTS

54. Are there any financial requirements to meet in order to qualify for a contractor license?

Yes. All applicants for a new contractor license, other than those applying for a joint venture license, must have more than $2,500 worth of operating capital. Operating capital is defined as your current assets minus your current liabilities.

55. Are there any bond requirements for a contractor license?

Yes. It is your responsibility to file a contractor license bond or cash deposit with the Registrar in the amount of $12,500. In addition, you must submit a separate bond of qualifying individual or cash deposit in the amount of $12,500 for the RME or the RMO. However, a bond of qualifying individual is not required if the RMO certifies that he or she owns 10 percent or more of the voting stock or equity of the corporation for which he or she is to serve as the qualifying individual.

If you have a limited liability company (LLC) license, a separate $100,000 surety bond is required (in addition to the $12,500 contractor bond) for the benefit of any employee or worker damaged by the LLC's failure to pay wages, interest on wages, or fringe benefits, as well as other contributions. *(See Chapter 2 for information about contractor bonds.)*

56. Where do I obtain bonds?

You may purchase bonds from your insurance agent or from one of the private holding companies licensed by the California Department of Insurance. CSLB does not issue bonds. Copies of the approved bond form and information regarding cash alternatives to bonds are available from CSLB upon request.

57. How long is a bond valid?

A bond may be issued for whatever length of time you and your insurance agent or bond company representative arrange. Most bonds are issued for a period of one to three years. At the end of that time, the bond may be canceled, or the bond company may request another premium to extend the life of the bond.

58. What is the total amount of the fees I must pay to obtain a contractor license?

Fees are subject to change. Current fees are printed on the application forms and notices distributed to you. You may check the CSLB website or call the CSLB automated phone system (1-800-321-2752) to verify the current fees. Currently, it costs a total of $480 in fees to obtain a contractor license for one classification. This amount includes both the nonrefundable application processing fee of $300 and the two-year initial license fee of $180.

59. Do I need to be concerned about workers' compensation insurance?

All contractors are required to present proof of workers' compensation insurance coverage as a condition of licensure, or to maintain an active license or to activate an inactive license, unless they are exempt from this requirement. Contractors who do not have employees working for them (except C-39 Roofing licensees) are exempt from the requirement for workers' compensation insurance, but they are required to file a certification of this exemption with the Registrar. If the license is qualified by an RME, an exemption certificate cannot be submitted because the RME is an employee. Neither the proof of coverage nor the exemption is required for an inactive license *(see Question 48)*.

NOTE: All contractors with a C-39 Roofing classification are required by B&P Section 7125 to have a Certificate of Workers' Compensation Insurance or a Certification of Self-Insurance on file with CSLB and are <u>not</u> eligible for exemption.

60. How long is a license valid?

A contractor license is initially issued for a two-year period. It will expire two (2) years from the last day of the month in which it was issued. Licenses are renewed for two years if renewed on active status, or for four (4) years if renewed on inactive status.

Chapter 2.

Your Existing License: Maintaining and Changing It

BONDS

Contractors are required to maintain a surety bond for the benefit of consumers who may be damaged as a result of defective construction or other license law violations, and for the benefit of employees who have not been paid wages that are due to them.

Contractor Bond and Bond of Qualifying Individual

A surety bond is usually a three-party agreement between a surety, the contractor, and a project owner. *(See Chapter 6 for a description of these bonds.)* The contractor license bond is different from most other surety bonds. The contractor bond is executed by a surety in favor of the State of California for the benefit of specific categories of people damaged by a contractor violation of the Contractors State License Law. The list of beneficiaries can be found in Business and Professions (B&P) Code section 7071.5.

Before an active contractor license can be issued or renewed, or an inactive license made active, the licensee must have a current contractor bond, or an approved alternative to the bond (see below), on file with CSLB. The contractor bond shall be in the amount of $12,500 for all classifications.

In addition, a qualifying individual must carry a $12,500 bond, or an approved alternative to the bond, on file for each responsible managing employee (RME). A $12,500 Bond of Qualifying Individual must be on file with CSLB for each responsible managing officer (RMO) unless the RMO owns 10 percent or more of the voting stock of the corporation, and for each responsible managing member or officer, unless he or she owns 10 percent or more of the membership interest in the limited liability company.

If the license is inactive, neither the contractor bond nor the Bond of Qualifying Individual is needed.

Limited Liability Surety Bond

A $100,000 surety bond (in addition to the $12,500 contractor bond) is required for the issuance, reissuance, reinstatement, reactivation, and renewal of a limited liability company license for the benefit of any employee or worker damaged by the LLC's failure to pay wages, interest on wages, or fringe benefits, as well as other contributions (not required for inactive LLC licenses). *(See B&P Code §7071.6.5.)*

Disciplinary Bonds

After a firm's license has been revoked for a violation of Contractors State License Law, the firm must file a disciplinary bond with the Registrar if the license is to be reinstated or reissued, or if the firm seeks to have a new license issued. *(See B&P Code §7071.8.)*

Disciplinary bonds are subject to the following requirements:

- The disciplinary bond must be filed in addition to, and cannot take the place of or be combined with, any other bonds required to maintain an active contractor license;

- The Registrar determines the bond amount, which is based on the seriousness of the violations. The amount may not be less than $15,000 nor greater than ten times the amount of the contractor bond *(See B&P Code §7071.8.)*;

- The disciplinary bond must remain current and on file with the Registrar for at least two (2) years. In some cases, the Registrar may require a longer filing period; and

- The firm's license must remain active and current while the disciplinary bond is on file.

Approved Alternatives to Contractor Bonds

Instead of filing a surety bond with CSLB, a contractor may prefer to use one of the following approved alternatives for filing a security deposit *(See Code of Civil Procedures §995.710.)*.

NOTE: All alternatives to bonds are retained by CSLB for three (3) years after the end of the license period that they cover. If the board is notified of a complaint relative to a claim against the deposit, the deposit shall not be released until the complaint has been adjudicated.

NOTE: It is the contractor's responsibility to make sure the alternative in lieu of a required bond is timely and meets CSLB requirements. Failure to have a required bond or an alternative on file may result in license suspension and a gap in licensure.

Certificate of Deposit

For CSLB to accept certificates of deposit in lieu of a contractor bond, the certificate must meet the board's requirements. As noted above, it is the contractor's responsibility to make sure the financial institution issuing the certificate provides a timely certificate that meets the following requirements:

- It must be issued by a bank or savings and loan association doing business in California;

- It must show the business name of the applicant or the licensee;

- It must be payable to the Contractors State License Board;

- It must be issued for a period of at least one (1) year and be automatically renewable at each maturity date;

- It must state that the interest earned will be paid to the depositor; and

- It must not designate the payee as a "trustee."

Bank Savings Account, Savings and Loan Investment Certificate or Share Account, Credit Union Certificate for Funds or Share Account

It is the contractor's responsibility to make sure the assignment of these accounts or certificates meets the following requirements:

- The account/certificate information must be properly filled out on forms approved by the Registrar and available from CSLB;

- The passbook or certificate must be delivered to the Registrar with the assignment form;

- The passbook or the certificate must show the business name of the applicant or licensee; and

- The passbook or the certificate must be assigned to CSLB.

Cash

A licensee may choose to make a cash deposit with CSLB instead of filing a bond. The cash deposit must be in the form of a cashier's check or a bank-certified check made payable to: Contractors State License Board. A cashier's check must show the name of the purchaser and must be deposited with CSLB.

Bearer Bonds

Bearer bonds must:

- Be issued by the U.S. Government or by the State of California;

- Be delivered to a bank in Sacramento, California, and have a market value equal to or greater than the amounts prescribed in B&P Code sections 7071.6 and 7071.9 or as fixed by the

Registrar, as provided for in B&P Code §7071.8 *(Also see California Code of Regulations (CCR) §856.)*; and

- The bank, as agent for the applicant or licensee, will, on order of the Registrar, deliver the bonds to the Treasurer of the State of California. Under no circumstances are bearer bonds to be delivered to CSLB or the Registrar.

General Requirements for Bonds and Bond Alternatives

The following requirements must be met before your bond (or a bond alternative) can be accepted:

- Bonds are not transferable—do not attempt to transfer a bond from one license to another or from one qualifying individual to another;
- The business name and the license number on the bond must correspond exactly to the information in the records of CSLB;
- The license number on the bond of a qualifying individual must match that of the firm for whom the individual is to serve as the qualifying individual;
- Contractor bonds must be in the correct amount of $12,500;
- A Bond of Qualifying Individual must be in the correct amount of $12,500;
- The bond must have the signature of the attorney-in-fact; and
- Bonds must be filed with CSLB within 90 days of the effective date of the bond.

If you are submitting a bond alternative and the bond alternative is returned for correction, take it and the letter of correction to the issuing entity for correction as soon as possible. Return the corrected document to CSLB as soon as possible.

The Registrar may reinstate your license following a suspension for failing to have a required bond (or bond alternative). However, the suspension may result in a gap in licensure.

Maintaining Bonds

The following guidelines will help you avoid problems with the bonds filed for your license:

- Keep your required bonds, cash deposits, or bond exemptions current at all times;
- Renew your bonds promptly. To avoid a period of suspension, make sure that the effective date of the new bond is the same

as the cancellation date of the old bond. To allow for processing time, arrange for a new bond four (4) weeks before your old one expires;

- Only one bond is in effect at a time. A second bond filed for the same period cancels out the first bond;

- CSLB does not return any bond that has been accepted or processed for an active license; and

- Keep accurate records on your agent, surety company, bond numbers, effective dates, and terms of the bonds.

Suspensions

Your license will be suspended if any of the following bond-related conditions occur:

- Your surety company cancels one or more of your required bonds;

- The voting stock of the responsible managing officer for a corporate license or the membership interest in a limited liability license is no longer at least 10 percent of the total voting stock of the corporation. *(See B&P Code §7071.9.)* Suspension is effective from the date ownership or membership interest terminated unless a bond of qualifying individual, backdated to the date his or her percentage of the stock or membership interest fell below 10 percent, is filed;

- A judgment or payment of claim reduces the amount of any required bond *(See B&P Code §7071.11.)*; and

- You fail to maintain a disciplinary bond or cash deposit in full force and effect for the required amount of time. A suspended license can be reinstated if the surety company sends a "Rescission of Cancellation Notice" to CSLB or if you obtain a new bond and submit it to CSLB within 90 days of the date that the new bond becomes effective or within 90 days of the date the old bond is canceled.

JUDGMENTS AND OUTSTANDING LIABILITIES

Civil Court Judgments

A contractor is required to report a construction-related civil court judgment to CSLB within 90 days of the judgment date. When a copy of the judgment is received by CSLB, the information is entered on the contractor license record and a notice is sent to the contractor. The notice gives the contractor 90 days from the date of the notice to resolve the judgment. After 90 days, if the judgment is not resolved, the contractor license is automatically suspended and remains suspended until the judgment is resolved.

If the contractor fails to report the judgment within 90 days, then when the judgment is reported, his or her contractor license is suspended immediately. The license remains suspended until the judgment is resolved.

NOTE: Anyone can report a construction-related judgment against a contractor by sending a copy of the judgment to the CSLB Judgment Unit at the Sacramento headquarters office. In fact, most of the judgments received by CSLB are sent by the person to whom the contractor owes money.

Once a judgment is entered on a contractor's license record, the unsatisfied judgment can affect any other license that a person is on or any license for which he or she may apply. For example, suppose a contractor has a sole ownership license and a corporation license. If the judgment is against the corporation, then the suspension for failure to resolve the judgment will also suspend the sole ownership license.

These requirements are in B&P Code §7071.17 *(See Chapter 12.).* According to that section, a private arbitration decision is considered the same as a judgment.

Frequently Asked Questions About Judgments

The following questions are those most commonly asked by contractors when a judgment is reported to CSLB:

I was never served or notified of this suit or judgment—what can I do? The judgment wasn't fair, the judge wouldn't listen to me—what can I do?

Whether the suit or judgment was properly served or whether it was fair is for the court to decide. CSLB cannot override a decision made by the court in a civil judgment. If you believe you were not properly served or you think you were treated unfairly, consult an attorney. With a small claims judgment, you can speak with staff from the small claims court in which the judgment was filed.

Can I appeal the court decision?

There are many factors which determine when and why an appeal can be filed, so you should consult an attorney. In the case of a small claims judgment, you can speak with staff from the small claims court in which the judgment was filed.

Why are you suspending my license? I filed an appeal.

Before appeal information can be entered on your license, you must submit a copy of the court-endorsed appeal with proof of a Stay of Enforcement document.

What type of proof do you need to show that I paid the judgment?

Any of the following are satisfactory proof of payment:

- An acknowledgment of Satisfaction of Judgment;

- A notarized, signed statement from the judgment creditor which confirms the judgment has been paid in full; or

- A copy of the front and back of a canceled payment check. CSLB will contact the judgment creditor to verify payment, so please include his or her telephone number. If you cannot contact the person who holds the judgment, consult an attorney. In the case of a small claims judgment, you can speak with staff from the small claims court in which the judgment was filed.

I can't pay the full amount of the judgment. Can I make payments?

You can make payments only if you work out an agreement with the judgment creditor. The judgment creditor is not required to accept payments. If you reach an agreement, it should state the amount owed, the monthly payment amount, the date the payment is due each month, and when a payment will be considered late. All parties must sign the agreement. Once you have a written agreement, submit a copy to CSLB's Judgment Unit. When received at CSLB, the suspension will be lifted. If, however, CSLB is notified by the judgment creditor that you failed to make payments, your license will be suspended immediately.

I filed for bankruptcy. What happens now?

You must provide proof of the bankruptcy filing and confirm that you named the judgment creditor in the bankruptcy. To comply with this requirement, submit a copy of the bankruptcy filing, which must include the page from the creditors list on which the judgment creditor appears.

This judgment isn't construction-related. What can I do?

The applicable section of law (B&P Code §7071.17) actually states that the judgment must be "substantially related . . . to the qualifications, functions, or duties of the license." CSLB broadly interprets this section of law to mean that if the judgment relates to your construction business in any way, it is considered construction-related. It does not mean that you had to necessarily contract with the judgment creditor to build something. If you did not pay your office rent, your office utility bills, your material supplier, subcontractor, employee, or any other bill incurred by your business, CSLB will consider it construction-related. Very few judgments received by CSLB are not construction-related. If you feel confident that your judgment is not construction-related, please provide CSLB with documentation that will support your statement.

Outstanding Liabilities

The state Board of Equalization, Employment Development Department, Department of Industrial Relations, or the Franchise Tax Board can notify CSLB of outstanding final liabilities owed by a contractor to those departments. When CSLB receives such a notification, a letter is sent stating that the contractor has 60 days in which to resolve the outstanding liability or the license will be suspended. When CSLB receives such a notification, a letter is sent to the contractor notifying him or her that the contractor has 60 days in which to resolve the outstanding liability or the license will be suspended. At the end of the 60-day period, if CSLB has not received any information about a resolution, the license will be suspended until the outstanding liability is resolved. The same procedure will be followed if a check submitted to CSLB by a licensee is dishonored.

These requirements are in B&P Code §7145.5. *(See Chapter 12.)*

NOTE: Please do not wait until the last few days before the suspension occurs to try to resolve the judgment. It is often difficult to gather all necessary paperwork at the last minute. Preventing your license from being suspended is a top priority with CSLB; however, sometimes problems arise that cannot be immediately resolved. To avoid delay, promptly submit all necessary documents to the attention of the CSLB Judgment Unit. Once acceptable documentation has been received and the matter has been cleared, a confirmation notice will be sent to you.

WORKERS' COMPENSATION INSURANCE COVERAGE

General Requirements

All contractors are required to submit proof of workers' compensation insurance coverage as a condition of licensure, to maintain a license, to activate an inactive license, or to renew a license, unless they are exempt from this requirement. *(See B&P Code §7125.1.)*

Exemptions

Contractors who do not have employees working for them (except C-39 Roofing licensees) are exempt from the requirement for workers' compensation insurance, but they will be required to file a certification of this exemption with the Registrar. Neither insurance coverage nor the exemption is required for an inactive license.

NOTE: All contractors with a C-39 Roofing classification are required by B&P section 7125 to have a Certificate of Workers' Compensation Insurance or a Certificate of Self-Insurance on file with CSLB and are not eligible for exemption.

LIABILITY INSURANCE COVERAGE FOR LIMITED LIABILITY COMPANIES

Liability insurance with the aggregate limit of $1 million for licensees with five or fewer persons listed as members of the personnel of record is required; plus, an additional $100,000 is required for each additional member of the personnel of record, not to exceed $5 million total. (*See B&P Code §7071.19.*)

ADDING A CLASSIFICATION TO AN EXISTING LICENSE

Under what conditions may I add a classification to my license?

You may add a classification to your existing license only if the license is renewed and current.

How many classifications may I apply for at a time?

In most cases, you must file a separate "Application for Additional Classification" form for each classification you are requesting. However, all of the C-61 (Limited Specialty) classifications you request may be applied for on one application.

What are the requirements for adding a classification to my license?

To add a classification to your license, you must do the following:

- Select a qualifying individual (who may be the licensee) for the new classification you are applying for;

- Have the qualifying individual describe, in detail, four (4) years of experience within the last ten (10) years as a journeyman, foreman, supervisor, or contractor in the classification in which he or she is to serve as the qualifying individual;

- Provide verification for the claimed experience;

- Submit the required application processing fee with the application;
- Unless the qualifying individual for the new classification qualifies for a waiver (see below), he or she must pass the trade examination for that classification. Each qualifying individual must also pass the Law and Business Examination if he or she has not done so previously;
- File any required bonds; and
- If the qualifying individual is an RME, he or she must inactivate his or her individual license.

Under what conditions can I qualify for a waiver of an examination?

- *See Questions 26, 27, and 28 in Chapter 1.*

NOTE: Requesting an exam waiver does not mean you will be automatically granted the waiver. The Registrar has complete discretion regarding the waiver of an exam.

CHANGES IN PERSONNEL

What should I do if any of the official personnel listed on the records for my license leave the firm?

Sole Owner

A sole ownership license is not transferable. If a contracting business is purchased from the holder of a sole ownership license, the contractor license is not part of the purchase. The new owner must apply for and obtain his or her own license before he or she can contract legally.

Partner

If a general or qualifying partner leaves the business, the existing license is canceled. The remaining partners may request a one-year continuance of the license in order to complete projects in progress. The request for a continuance must be submitted to CSLB within 90 days of the date the partner left. Except for those cases where the partner died, the remaining partners cannot contract for any new projects under that license.

The remaining partners must apply for a new license if they choose to remain in business beyond the one (1) year limit of the continuance.

NOTE: Please do not wait until the one year continuance is going to expire before you apply for a new license. Timely processing of your new license is important. In order to avoid a lapse in licensure, please submit the necessary applications promptly.

A limited partner may be added or deleted from a license by submitting a "Change in Limited Partnership" form.

Corporate Officers

If any of the officers listed in CSLB records for a corporate license leaves your business, you must report the change to CSLB within 90 days by submitting a "Disassociation Request." To add personnel, you must complete and submit an "Application to Report New Officers of a Corporation." The status of your license is not affected by adding officers or having any of them leave unless the person who leaves has been serving as a qualifying individual. (See *Qualifying Individual below*.)

Limited Liability Company (LLC) Personnel

If any of the members, managers, or officers listed in CSLB records for an LLC license leaves your business, you must report this change to CSLB within 90 days by submitting a "Disassociation Request." To add personnel, you must complete and submit an "Application to Report New Officers of a Limited Liability Company." If you are adding personnel, the amount of your LLC liability insurance must be sufficient for the total number of personnel of record as required by law. The status of your license is not affected by adding members, managers, or officers or having any of them leave unless the person who leaves has been serving as a qualifying individual. (See *Qualifying Individual below*.)

Qualifying Individual (Responsible Managing Officer, Employee, Member, or Manager)

If an RMO, RME, responsible managing member, or responsible managing manager leaves a business (disassociates), CSLB must be notified in writing within 90 days of the date of disassociation. Use a "Disassociation Notice" form. You must specify:

- ☐ Name of the qualifying individual who left
- ☐ Date of disassociation
- ☐ Name of the business
- ☐ Contractor license number

One of the remaining official personnel listed in CSLB records for that license, or the qualifying individual who is disassociating, must sign the notification of disassociation or your letter.

If you intend to continue to conduct business in the classification for which the qualifying individual was responsible, **you must replace him or her within 90 days of the date of disassociation.** Failure to do so will result in suspension of your license or removal of the classification from your license.

To replace a qualifying individual, you must file an "Application for Replacing the Qualifying Individual" **or** "Application for Limited Liability Company (LLC) Replacing the Qualifying Individual" form and submit the required application fee. This application can also serve as the notice of disassociation. You should act quickly because, within those 90 days, CSLB must process your application and, if necessary, the new qualifying individual must pass the Law and Business Examination and/or trade examination(s).

The requirements for a qualifying individual and the criteria for a waiver of the examinations are described in Chapter 1.

Right to Petition

You may petition the Registrar for reconsideration if you dispute the date of disassociation on which the suspension was based. You may also petition if you can show good cause for your failure to notify the Registrar within 90 days of the date of disassociation. CSLB must receive your petition within 90 days from the date of the board's notice that the license will be suspended if the qualifying individual is not replaced. *(See B&P Code §§7068.2 and 7076.)*

Changes in the Bond Exemption Status of a Responsible Managing Officer of a Corporation, or Officer, Member or Manager of an LLC

If the RMO's share of the voting stock of the corporation, or the RMO, responsible managing member's, or responsible managing manager's membership interest of a limited liability company, falls below 10 percent, he or she will no longer be eligible for exemption from the bond requirements. You must report the change in exemption status and file a "Bond of Qualifying Individual" form within 90 days of the change.

Exemption that Allows an Individual to Serve as the Qualifying Individual for More than One License

A person is allowed to serve as the qualifying individual for more than one license (BUT FOR NO MORE THAN THREE FIRMS IN ANY ONE-YEAR PERIOD) if any of the following conditions exist:

- There is common ownership of at least 20 percent of the equity of each firm involved;

- The other licenses are subsidiaries of, or participants in a joint venture with the first; or

- The majority of partners, officers, or managers are the same.

If this common ownership no longer exists, the qualifying individual must disassociate from each license for which the exemption status no longer applies. *(See B&P Code §7068.1.)*

CHANGES IN BUSINESS NAME OR ADDRESS

Report changes in business name or address as soon as possible, but no later than 90 days after the change.

Business Name

Report a change of the name of your business by completing an "Application to Change Business Name and/or Address" form. Note the following conditions:

- The form must be signed by an owner, partner, officer, member, or manager of the firm.

- If you hold a corporate license or limited liability company license, you must first register the name change with the California Secretary of State. Include a certified copy of the Amendment of Articles of Incorporation (for a corporation) or Statement of Information (for an LLC) form, as appropriate, with your notice.

- The new business name must not conflict with the type of business entity or the classification held.

Business Address

Report a change of the official address of your business by completing the "Application to Change Business Name and/or Address" form. The letter must be signed by the owner, a partner, officer, member, or manager of the firm.

CHANGES IN BUSINESS TYPE

New License Necessary if Business Type Changes

CSLB issues licenses to five types of business entities: sole ownership, partnership, corporation, joint venture, and limited liability company. Licenses are associated with the business and not necessarily the qualifier. Therefore, licenses are not transferable from one business entity to another, even if the qualifying person is the same for both. A new license is required whenever the business entity type is changed. For example, if a contractor with a sole ownership business decides to incorporate, or a partnership splits into multiple sole ownership businesses, a new license is required in each case.

Whenever a business type changes and a new license is not issued, that business faces all the legal risks of an unlicensed contractor. Answers to frequently asked questions about new license requirements are below.

How do I get a license for my new business?

To obtain a license for your new business, you must submit an "Application for Original License" form. Use the "Application for Original License-Examination Waiver (7065)" form if you took the exam for the previous license and are applying for the classification previously held. No exam will be required.

Use the limited liability company version of the forms if you are seeking licensure as an LLC.

Applications can be printed from the CSLB website: www.cslb.ca.gov. You must also pay all the required fees, post new bonds, provide proof of workers' compensation insurance or file a workers' compensation exemption statement, and provide proof of liability insurance coverage, if applicable, for the new business.

Can I keep my old license number?

Only in some cases will the same license number be reissued. If the original license is for a sole ownership business that is being incorporated, or changed to a limited liability company, and the qualifier on the sole ownership business owns 51 percent or more of the voting stock or equity of the new corporation, or of the membership interests of the LLC, will the original license number be reissued. In this situation, a written request asking that your sole ownership license be reissued to the corporation or LLC must accompany your application. The written request must include the contractor's percent of ownership in the corporation or LLC. You can also contact CSLB and the appropriate form will be sent to you.

Often, corporate restructuring will require a new license. Under limited circumstances, a corporation or limited liability company may be allowed to keep the original license number. Under any other circumstance, such as when a business changes from a sole ownership to a partnership or a corporation or LLC to a sole ownership, a new license number will be issued.

Can the license number be changed back to a sole ownership license after it has been used as a corporate or LLC license?

No. Once your license number is reissued to a corporation, it cannot be changed back to a sole ownership license. You will be issued a new license number if you apply for a sole ownership license.

Information about new license requirements can be found on the CSLB website, www.cslb.ca.gov. You can also call CSLB, toll-free: (800) 321-CSLB (2752).

INACTIVATING AND REACTIVATING A LICENSE

What is an inactive license?

An inactive license is "on hold." While your license is inactive, you are not entitled to practice as a contractor or submit a bid for work. You do not need to maintain a bond or workers' compensation or liability insurance coverage, nor do you need to have a qualifying individual on your license. As long as you continue to renew your inactive license you will receive informational bulletins and a renewal application every four (4) years at the address listed in CSLB records for your license.

It is not necessary to inactivate your license because of bond suspension or temporary work stoppages. However, you may be required to inactivate your license if you are applying to serve as the qualifying individual for another license and you do not meet one of the conditions of B&P Code section 7068.1 *(See "Exemption that Allows an Individual to Serve as the Qualifying Individual for More than One License" above.).*

How do I inactivate my license?

The following steps are required to inactivate your license:

- Request the "Application to Inactivate State Contractor's License" form by telephone, in writing from any CSLB office, or online at www.cslb.ca.gov. There is no application fee. (There is, however, a fee for reactivating a license.) If the period of inactivity will be short, read the following section describing how to reactivate a license before you decide to inactivate your license;

- Have the owner; a partner; an officer of your corporation; a member, manager, or officer of your limited liability company; or a member of the Joint Venture license who is listed in CSLB records for your license sign the application; and

- Return your current pocket license with the application. If you have lost your pocket license, check the box on the application and enclose the replacement fee indicated. You will be sent a pocket license stamped "Inactive."

Is an inactive license subject to renewal requirements?

Yes. Every four (4) years, a renewal application will be sent to the business address listed in CSLB records. Please advise CSLB in writing of any change of address. There is no limit on the number of times your contractor license can be renewed on inactive status.

What should I do if I want to resume contracting?

If you want to resume contracting and your license is inactive, you must reactivate your license before you begin contracting. *(See B&P Code §7076.5 and CCR §867.)*

How do I reactivate my license?

To reactivate an inactive license, request a reactivation application by telephone or in writing from CSLB's Sacramento headquarters office, complete the application, and meet the following conditions:

- Verify that your operating capital exceeds $2,500;

- Meet all bond requirements including any disciplinary bond, contractor bond, LLC surety bond, or bond of qualifying individual. Attach all required bonds to the application. Do not send bonds separately;

- Submit proof of workers' compensation insurance or exemption;

- For limited liability company licenses only, submit proof of liability insurance in the amount that is required for the number of personnel on the license;

- The application must be signed by **all** qualifying partners, responsible managing employees, responsible managing members, responsible managing managers, and responsible managing officers. If applying to reactivate a sole ownership license, the **owner** must sign; if a partnership license, all **partners** must sign; if a corporation, **one corporate officer** must sign; if a limited liability company, **one member, manager, or officer** must sign; and if a joint venture license, the **qualifying individuals of each entity** must sign;

- Comply with any special requirements for the qualifying individual, such as the need to disassociate from any other license for which he or she is currently serving as the qualifying individual and inactivation of his or her individual license, unless he or she can provide verification of common ownership of at least 20 percent of the equity of every business for which he or she is serving as the qualifying individual; and

- Submit the required fee.

What other conditions must I consider when reactivating any license?

If there has been a change in the form of your business (for example, you have formed a partnership, corporation, or limited liability company) or if a partner has been added to or left your business, you will need a new license.

If you hold a corporate license, and you wish to make any additions to the list of officers, you must complete and submit an "Application to Report New Officers of a Corporation" form. To delete officers, complete and submit a "Disassociation Request." To change the qualifier, request the "Application to Replace the Qualifying Individual" form. For changes to the personnel or LLCs, you must complete and submit the comparable LLC forms.

Contractors are required to submit proof of workers' compensation insurance coverage, and liability insurance coverage if applicable, before a license can be activated, unless they are exempt from the workers' compensation insurance requirement. Contractors who do not have employees working for them are exempt from the requirement for workers' compensation insurance, but they will be required to file a certification of this exemption with the Registrar *(See B&P Code §7125.1.)*. Download the exemption form from the CSLB website www.cslb.ca.gov, or request the form by telephone at 1-800-321-CSLB (2752).

What is the effective date of reactivation?

Your reactivated license will be effective the date on which the required fee, an acceptable application, and other required documents are received and processed by CSLB. After your reactivation application has been processed, your license will be active for a full two (2) years from the end of the month in which it was reactivated. *(See B&P Code §7076.5 and CCR §867.)*

How do I order a new wall or pocket license?

Official personnel for the license may send the appropriate form to CSLB to order a new or an additional wall or pocket license. Specify the license number and whether you are requesting the wall or pocket license. The form must be signed by current personnel listed on the license (owner, partners, officers, managers, members, or RMEs). A fee is required for each copy and is subject to change. (Call CSLB or check the website for the current fee.) **Make the check payable to: Registrar of Contractors; do not send cash.**

RENEWING YOUR LICENSE

Active licenses expire every two (2) years. Inactive licenses expire every four (4) years. Check your current pocket license for the expiration date on your license.

How do I renew my license?

Approximately 60 days before your license is due to expire, CSLB will send you a renewal application. It is important to notify CSLB if your address has changed since your license was issued or renewed. **It is your responsibility to make sure your license is renewed even if you don't receive the form.** You may not contract for work with an expired license. When you receive the renewal application, complete it and promptly send it to CSLB. Keep the following things in mind as you complete your application:

- The application and requirements must be acceptable;

- You must submit the required fee;

- The renewal application must be completed and signed; and

- Your renewed license may be either active or inactive. If you renew the license as inactive, you do not need to maintain any bonds or designate a qualifying individual. If you wish to change the license from inactive to active at the time of renewal, see the question above *"How do I reactivate my license?"*

What happens if I don't renew my license by the expiration date?

You may not contract for work with an expired license.

An acceptable license renewal form must be received by CSLB prior to the expiration date of the license. If you renew your license after the expiration date, or if you send a form that is not considered acceptable, your renewal will be considered delinquent, and the license record will show a break in license status. During any such period, the contractor will be considered unlicensed. In addition, if the license is expired, a delinquent fee of 50 percent of the renewal fee will be required.

You may renew an expired license any time within five (5) years after its expiration. After five years, it becomes void, and if you wish to contract, you must apply for a new license and fulfill the examination or waiver requirements again.

You may petition the Registrar of Contractor to renew your license retroactive to the renewal date. Your petition will only be considered under the following conditions:

- The Registrar must receive the petition within 90 days of the expiration date;

- You must be able to show that the delay was due to circumstances beyond your control; and

- You must pay the delinquent renewal fee.

May I renew my license if it is suspended?

A suspended license may be renewed as active or inactive. However, you may not contract for work with an inactive or suspended license and you will not be issued a wall or pocket license. If you wish to contract for work, you must clear the suspension before your license can be renewed as active. *(See B&P Code §§7140-7145 and CCR §853.)*

CANCELLATION OF A LICENSE

Under what circumstances is a license canceled?

A license is canceled when any of the following conditions arise:

- Individual license: death of the owner;

- Partnership license: death or disassociation of a general or qualifying partner;

- Corporate and limited liability company license: notification by the licensee of merger, dissolution, or surrender of the right to do business in California; and/or

- Joint Venture license: cancellation, revocation, or withdrawal of any of the businesses that formed the joint venture.

A corporation or limited liability company license shall also be canceled 60 days after CSLB discovers that the corporation or LLC has merged, dissolved, or surrendered the right to do business.

A licensee may also voluntarily request cancellation of a license at any time. **Remember that it is illegal to contract with a canceled license.**

How do I cancel my license?

You must notify CSLB in writing within 90 days of the event that causes you to request the cancellation. There is no fee for cancellation. Return your wall certificate and your current pocket license with your written request for cancellation.

Depending on the type of license you hold, your request for cancellation must fulfill the following requirements:

- The owner of an Individual license must sign the request for voluntary cancellation. In the case of the owner's death, a family member or administrator of the estate of the deceased must sign the request, state the date of death, and provide a copy of the death certificate;

- If a Partnership license must be canceled due to the disassociation of a partner, a general partner must sign the request and state the date of disassociation; in the case of a partner's death, a remaining partner must sign the request, state the date of death, and provide a copy of the death certificate;

- To cancel a Corporate license, two officers listed on the license, or the remaining officer if only one officer remains, must sign the request and state the date of the event causing cancellation or enclose a copy of the corporate minutes documenting the dissolution or merger or enclose a copy of the dissolution papers issued by the California Secretary of State;

- To cancel a Limited Liability Company license, two members, managers, or officers listed on the license, or the remaining officer if only one remains, must sign the request and state the date of the event causing cancellation or enclose a copy of the dissolution papers issued by the California Secretary of State; and

- To cancel a Joint Venture license, one of the official personnel (other than an RME) listed in CSLB's records for the license of any of the businesses forming the joint venture must sign the request and state the date of the event causing the cancellation.

What is the effective date of my license cancellation?

The effective date of cancellation of a license is usually either the date the request for cancellation is received by CSLB or the date of the event causing the cancellation.

NOTE: A cancellation is not effective until it has been accepted by CSLB. The board may decide not to cancel a license if disciplinary action is pending.

If an event occurs which makes a license subject to cancellation, is there a means by which a business can temporarily continue to operate?

Yes. Under certain circumstances, the Registrar may grant a continuance for up to one (1) year. There are restrictions on who may apply for the continuance or on one's right to enter into new contracts. If a continuance is granted, this is a temporary period for the business to use to reorganize. If a business wants to continue beyond the temporary period, it must submit an application as soon as possible.

Who may apply for a continuance?

The rules as to who may apply for a continuance vary depending on the type of license:

- Sole Ownership
  If the licensee dies, a member of his or her immediate family may apply to continue the family business;

- Partnership
  The remaining partners, as listed in the Board's records, may apply; or

- Joint Venture
  The remaining businesses listed in the records of CSLB as those who formed the joint venture may apply.

NOTE: Since corporate and limited liability company licenses are granted to the corporation or LLC as a whole, the status of the license is not affected if one of the officers, members, or managers leaves. Therefore, continuances are not granted for corporate or LLC licenses.

How do I apply for a continuance?

To apply for a continuance, submit a written request to CSLB as soon as possible but no later than 90 days from the date of the death or disassociation, stating why a continuance is necessary.

What does a continuance allow me to do?

Under a continuance of an Individual or of a Partnership license (when one of the partners has died), you may continue normal business operations and enter into new contracts during the period for which the continuance is granted.

Under a continuance of a Joint Venture license or of a Partnership license (when one of the partners has disassociated), you may conduct business only on those contracts entered into before the event necessitating cancellation occurred. You may not enter into any new contracts.

Can a continuance be extended?

Yes. The Registrar may approve an extension to the one-year provision if additional time is necessary to complete projects contracted for or commenced before the disassociation or death. A license extended under these circumstances is subject to all provisions including those relating to renewal and bond requirements.

Chapter 3.

Access to Information About Licensees

DOCUMENTS AVAILABLE, COMPLAINT RECORDS, FEES

You may obtain license information by calling the CSLB automated toll-free line: (800) 321-CSLB (2752), 24/7, or on CSLB's website www.cslb.ca.gov. Information on CSLB's website is available Monday at 6:00 a.m. through Sunday at 8:30 p.m. (PST). The website is not available from 8:30 p.m. Sunday to 6:30 a.m. Monday.

Callers can enter the contractor license number to determine whether a contractor's license is valid and whether the contractor has disclosable complaints.

Visit CSLB's website for general information regarding licensing, consumer assistance services (such as selecting a contractor during a state of emergency), consumer complaint services, online publications, and license status information. To obtain written information or copies of documents in CSLB's possession, send a written request to CSLB, P.O. Box 26000, Sacramento, CA 95826. Provide the full name, business name, or contractor license number, and specify exactly what kind of information you are seeking. CSLB provides copies of records with personal and confidential information deleted.

INFORMATION REGARDING INDIVIDUAL LICENSE RECORDS

CSLB will provide the following information after receiving a written request and the appropriate fees. *(See chart on following pages.)*

- Report of current bond information

- Report of current license status

- Records search and certified report of license history (past 10 years only unless a specific time period is requested)

- Records search and certified report of no license history (past 10 years only unless supporting documents are submitted to support the need for more than 10 years)

- Records search and certified report of home improvement salesperson registration

- Copies of documents (personal and confidential information deleted)
- Disclosure of complaints resulting in legal action and a history of legal actions taken by the Board against current license holders
- Disclosure of open complaints that meet the criteria of B&P Code section 7124.6 in that they: "have been referred for investigation after a determination by board enforcement staff that a probable violation has occurred, and have been reviewed by a supervisor, and [the complaints] regard allegations that if proven would present a risk of harm to the public and would be appropriate for suspension or revocation of the contractor's license or criminal prosecution."

INFORMATION ABOUT LARGE NUMBERS OF CONTRACTORS

Public Sales Custom Order Form

With this form you may order license information within specified parameters, including license status, license classification(s), geographical locations, etc. The information provided is in Text File Format, and includes: contractor license number, business name, address and telephone number, license classification(s), business county, bond company, and workers' compensation information. **NO E-MAIL ADDRESSES ARE PROVIDED**. Record layout may be viewed at www.cslb.ca.gov. Click on "Forms and Applications," then on "Public Sales – Lists." There is a **$245 non-refundable fee** for this service.

Full File/Update File Order Form - CD/DVD & Cartridge Tapes

CSLB license information is available in Text File Format on CD/DVD. Available files include:

License Master Full File*, License Master Update File, Business Principal Full File, Business Principal Update File, Action Code Full File, Action Code Update File, Workers' Compensation Full File, Workers' Compensation Update File, Complaint Disclosure/Legal Action Full File, and Complaint Disclosure/Legal Action Update File.

* Full Files may require the use of software to read large files, e.g., LTF (large text files) viewer 5.2u.

Record layouts may be viewed at www.cslb.ca.gov, click on "Forms and Applications," then on "Public Sales – CSLB Files."

TELEPHONE NUMBERS ARE PROVIDED ON THE LICENSE MASTER FILE ONLY. There is a **$235 non-refundable fee** for each file.

To obtain an order form, call 1-800-321-2752, or download the form at www.cslb.ca.gov, click on "Forms and Applications," then on "Public Sales – CSLB Files" or "Public Sales – Lists." Submit the completed form to:

> Contractors State License Board
> Attn: Data Services Unit
> P O Box 26000
> Sacramento, CA 95826

Fees must be paid in advance by check or money order. DO NOT SEND CASH. If you have questions about ordering, call the CSLB Help Desk at (916) 255-3975.

INFORMATION REGARDING PENDING APPLICATION RECORDS

CSLB provides a Web page that allows users to download the **Pending Application Master Postlist** and **Pending Application Personnel File** on a daily basis.

The **Pending Application Master Postlist** includes application number, business type, business name and address, license classification(s), and examinee name (if an exam is required). **NO TELEPHONE NUMBERS ARE PROVIDED.**

The **Pending Application Personnel File** includes application number, personnel name, position, and license classification(s). **NO TELEPHONE NUMBERS ARE PROVIDED.**

To access this information on the Internet, visit: www.cslb.ca.gov/consumers/data.asp.

If you have questions about accessing this data, call the CSLB Help Desk at (916) 255-3975.

INFORMATION REGARDING LEGAL ACTION AGAINST CONTRACTORS

CSLB can provide public information on complaints that have been investigated and referred for legal action, or concluded in legal action administered by the Board against a license. The fact that a complaint against a contractor has been referred for legal action does not mean the contractor has necessarily committed a violation of

Contractors State License Law; no conclusions or judgments as to the validity of the charges are assumed.

You may obtain a "Request for Disclosure of Contractor's License Information" form from the CSLB website.

The above-mentioned website and toll-free information line can also provide the following information:

- General license information, including business name, license number, license classification(s), address of record, and official personnel listed for a license;

- Bond information, including bond amount, bond identification number, and name of bonding company; and

- Workers' compensation information, including workers' compensation insurance carrier, policy number, effective date, and expiration date.

DOCUMENTS AVAILABLE FROM CSLB

PLEASE NOTE: All fees are current as of January 1, 2012. For verification of current fees, check CSLB's website, www.cslb.ca.gov, or contact CSLB, toll-free, at (800) 321-CSLB (2752).

TYPE OF INFORMATION	PROVIDES	DISTRIBUTION/ AVAILABLE	FEE
BOND STATUS LETTER Submit a "Request for Current Bond Information" form	Current bond(s) information; names/addresses of surety companies that provide bonds; issuance, renewal, and expiration/ cancellation dates; entity status; business name of contractor, address, and classification(s) held.	Public; Available at: www.cslb.ca.gov (800) 321-CSLB	$8 each

TYPE OF INFORMATION	PROVIDES	DISTRIBUTION/ AVAILABLE	FEE
CERTIFIED COPY OF THE WALL OR POCKET LICENSE of a currently renewed license Submit a "Wall and/or Pocket Certificate" form (also used to change a business name and/or address).	Replacement copy	Members of the licensed entity; Available at: www.cslb.ca.gov	$11 each
CERTIFIED COPY OF HOME IMPROVEMENT SALESPERSON REGISTRATION Pocket Card of a currently renewed registration Submit a "Changing HIS Address or Request for Pocket Registration Card" form	Replacement copy	Registered salesperson; Available at: www.cslb.ca.gov	$11 each
PHOTOCOPIES OF DOCUMENTS Submit a "Request for Copies" form	Copy with all personal or confidential information deleted	Public; Available at: www.cslb.ca.gov (800) 321-CSLB	10¢ per page
CERTIFIED COPIES OF PHOTOCOPIED DOCUMENTS Submit a "Request for Copies" form	Board certification of authenticity, currency, and accuracy	Public; Available at: www.cslb.ca.gov (800) 321-CSLB	$2 certification fee per license PLUS 10¢ per page copied
GENERAL STATUS LETTER Submit a "Request for General Status Letter" form	Current license information excluding bond status: NOT certified	Public; Available at: www.cslb.ca.gov (800) 321-CSLB	$8 each

TYPE OF INFORMATION	PROVIDES	DISTRIBUTION/ AVAILABLE	FEE
CERTIFIED LICENSE HISTORY Admissible as *prima facie* evidence of the facts stated. (Used primarily for court actions.) Submit a "Request for Certified License History" form, three (3) months IN ADVANCE of need.	Certified history of license ("record") or absence of license ("No-record" / "Certificate of Non-licensee") for a given time period. Includes: classification(s) held; license personnel, any disciplinary actions on bond but NO OTHER bond information UNLESS specially requested, and the standing of the license at all times during the period covered by the certificate.	Public; Available at: www.cslb.ca.gov (800) 321-CSLB	$67 each
CERTIFIED LICENSE HISTORY Home Improvement Salesperson Submit a "Request for Home Improvement Salesperson Registration Information" form two to three weeks IN ADVANCE of need	Certified history of Home Improvement Salesperson Registration. A "record" certificate includes the registration number, effective date, business name, and the license number of the contractor with whom the salesperson is registered. If the person is not registered, a "no-record" certificate is issued.	Public; Available at: www.cslb.ca.gov	$67 each

TYPE OF INFORMATION	PROVIDES	DISTRIBUTION/ AVAILABLE	FEE
ELECTRONIC MEDIA Submit a "Full File/ Update File Order" form Information is available in Text File Format on CD/DVD. Full Files are produced twice a year. Update Files, showing the past month's activity, are produced monthly.	Four different file formats are available: • License file • Business principal file (all personnel of record for each license) • Workers' compensation file • Action codes or complaint disclosure/legal action file	Public; available at: www.cslb.ca.gov	$235.00 each file, non-refundable
SPECIAL INFORMATION REQUEST Submit a "Public Sales Custom Order" form	Specially compiled list of contractors, according to a variety of criteria that you select. With this service, you can specify geographical area, license classification, license status, etc. The information provided is in Text File Format, and includes the business name, business address and telephone number, license number, and license classification(s).	Public; available at: www.cslb.ca.gov	$245 nonrefund-able fee

TYPE OF INFORMATION	PROVIDES	DISTRIBUTION/ AVAILABLE	FEE
INTERNET ACCESS TO PENDING APPLICATION RECORDS	The FTP process allows downloads of the Pending Application MASTER and PERSONNEL Posting List on a daily basis. Available information includes the name, address, personnel, and classification(s) for all applications that are posted by CSLB.	Public; Access this information on the Internet at: www.cslb.ca.gov/ consumers/dada. asp For help, call the CSLB Help Desk at (916) 255-3975.	No fee

Chapter 4.

Enforcement Procedures: Complaints and Citations

Section I

Complaints against contractors may be filed with CSLB by homeowners, other contractors, subcontractors, material suppliers, or employees. Public agencies may also file complaints.

Most complaints made against contractors involve poor workmanship; abandonment of a project; failure to pay subcontractors, suppliers, or employees; building code violations; lack of reasonable diligence in executing a construction project; use of false, misleading, or deceptive advertising; and violations of the law governing home improvement contracts.

COMPLAINTS AGAINST LICENSED CONTRACTORS

When a complaint is made against a licensed contractor, the CSLB Intake and Mediation Center nearest the location of the alleged violation receives and processes the complaint. Each written complaint is reviewed to determine if it falls within CSLB's jurisdiction. CSLB sends a confirmation to the complainant that the complaint has been received. CSLB also sends a notice to the licensed contractor to determine if the complaint can be resolved without further board involvement.

If, after notification to the contractor, the complaint has not been resolved, a consumer services representative (CSR) may contact the complainant and respondent (the licensee) to request additional information and, if necessary, documentation. If appropriate, the CSR will attempt mediation. If mediation is unsuccessful, the CSR may recommend settlement through CSLB's arbitration program, or may recommend that the complainant contact the surety company that issued the contractor's bond, file a claim in small claims court, or file a civil suit in superior court.

If CSLB believes that a complaint fits the criteria for assignment to an enforcement representative (ER), an investigation may be conducted to determine if there are violations of the Contractors State License Law. Such an investigation may include interviewing the complainant, the contractor, and any other parties who can furnish relevant information.

What happens if a violation is established?

If a violation is established but it is an isolated or minor one, CSLB may send the licensee a warning letter. The warning letter informs the licensee that CSLB is aware of the violation and that a future occurrence of the same violation may result in more stringent board actions.

If, on the other hand, a more serious violation is established, the Registrar of Contractors may issue a citation, which can include an order to correct a project, make restitution to an injured party, and pay a civil penalty of up to $5,000 for violations by licensees and $15,000 for unlicensed contractors. (*See B&P §7099.2(b) regarding $15,000 citations for B&P §7114 and B&P §7118 violations.*)

If the licensee complies with the citation orders, CSLB takes no further action. If the licensee contests all or any part of the citation, a mandatory settlement conference may be held to resolve the citation. If the matter is not settled, a hearing can be set before an administrative law judge of the State of California. At the hearing, the licensee can argue against the citation orders. If the licensee prevails at this hearing, CSLB takes no further action. If, however, the licensee does not prevail and does not comply with a final citation order, the license may be suspended and then revoked.

For flagrant violations of law, the Registrar will take administrative action by filing an accusation with the state Attorney General stating the board's intent to suspend or revoke the license. The licensee may be provided the opportunity to resolve the matter at a Mandatory Settlement Conference. If the matter is not settled, the licensee is given an opportunity to defend himself or herself at a hearing before a state administrative law judge. The following procedures may be used to decide a case:

- The licensee may choose to have a hearing before a state administrative law judge. The recommendation of this judge is used by the Registrar in determining the appropriate action to take;

- The licensee and the Registrar may negotiate a settlement of the case. This settlement is known as a "stipulation;" or

- If the licensee fails to respond to the accusation, the case will be considered to be in default. The Registrar will decide on the appropriate action to take against the licensee.

The decision of the Registrar may include various remedies:

- **Revocation of the License**

  The licensee's right to engage in contracting is taken away. The license shall not be reinstated or reissued for one (1) to five (5) years from the effective date of the decision.

None of the official personnel who are listed in the CSLB records for a revoked license and who have been found to have had knowledge of, or participated in, the acts or omissions constituting grounds for the revocation may apply for a license until the penalty period is over. The licensee must also show that he or she has complied with all provisions of the decision and settled any loss caused by the act or omission that resulted in the revocation of the license and must file a disciplinary bond in the amount set by the Registrar.

- **Suspension of the License**

  The licensee is not entitled to operate during the period of suspension. A disciplinary bond must be filed before the license will be reinstated or reissued.

- **Stay of Suspension or Revocation (probation)**

  The licensee must abide by certain terms and conditions to keep the suspension or revocation from going into effect. He or she must also file a disciplinary bond in order to remain in business during this period. Suspension or revocation of the license will result if any of the terms of the agreement are violated.

- **Recovery of Investigation and Enforcement Costs**

  The licensee, in order to maintain good and clear standing or as a condition for renewal and reinstatement of his or her license, must pay the costs as ordered or as stipulated.

- **Dismissal with No Penalties**

  Matters that have been dismissed are not disclosed to the public.

- **Injunction Against Unlawful Activity**

  Upon establishing that a blatant violation of the law has occurred, CSLB may go to court to request an injunction, which would immediately stop the unlawful activity.

- **Criminal Charges**

  Upon establishing that a blatant violation of the law has occurred, CSLB may refer the complaint to the local office of the district attorney for a possible criminal filing.

Complaint Disclosure

Once CSLB has determined that a probable violation of law has occurred, which, if proven, would present a risk of harm to the public, and for which suspension or revocation of the contractor's license would be appropriate, the date, nature, and status of the complaint will be disclosed to the public. A disclaimer stating that the complaint is, at this time, only an allegation will accompany this disclosure.

Citations will be disclosed to the public from date of issuance and for five (5) years from the date of compliance.

Accusations that result in suspension or stayed revocation of the contractor license shall be disclosed from the date the accusation is filed and for seven (7) years after the accusation has been settled, including the terms and conditions of probation. All revocations that are not stayed shall be disclosed indefinitely from the effective date of the revocation.

ADDRESSING COMPLAINTS AGAINST UNLICENSED CONTRACTORS

In California, it is a misdemeanor to engage in the business or act in the capacity of a contractor without a contractor license unless the contractor meets the criteria for exemption specified in Business and Professions Code sections 7040 through 7054.5.

When a complaint is filed against an unlicensed contractor, CSLB will verify that the accused individual or firm contracted without a contractor license and will, with sufficient evidence, determine the amount of financial injury involved.

How does CSLB process complaints against unlicensed contractors?

When the Board receives a complaint against an unlicensed contractor, it may issue an administrative citation or file a criminal action with the local district attorney's office. In some cases, it may initiate injunction proceedings against the non-licensee through the Office of the Attorney General or the district attorney.

- **Citation**

  The Registrar may issue a citation to an unlicensed contractor when there is probable cause to believe that the person is acting in the capacity of a contractor or engaging in the business of contracting without a license that is in good standing with CSLB. The citation includes an **order of abatement** to cease and desist and a **civil penalty** of up to $15,000. Unless the board receives a written appeal within fifteen (15) working days after the citation is served, the citation becomes a final order of the Registrar. The civil penalty is paid to CSLB.

If the citation is appealed, a mandatory settlement conference may be held to resolve the citation. If the matter is not settled, the appeal will be heard before an administrative law judge. The administrative law judge submits a decision to uphold, modify, or dismiss the citation. The decision is sent to the Registrar for adoption.

If the cited unlicensed contractor continues to contract without a license, the Registrar may refer the case to the local district attorney for criminal action.

- **Criminal Action**

  CSLB may refer investigations to the local prosecutor to file criminal charges. If criminal charges are filed, the unlicensed contractor appears in local court, which renders a final decision on the case. The court may order a fine, probation, restitution, a jail sentence, or all of these.

- **Injunction**

  The Registrar may apply for an injunction with the superior court of either the county in which an alleged practice or transaction took place or the county in which the unlicensed person maintains a business or residence. An injunction restrains an unlicensed person from acting in the capacity or engaging in the business of contracting without a license that is in good standing with CSLB.

How does CSLB process complaints against unregistered salespersons?

The same citation process used for complaints against unlicensed contractors is used for complaints against unregistered home improvement salespersons. Disciplinary action can also be taken against the licensed contractor who employs the unregistered salesperson.

Statewide Investigative Fraud Team

In addition to the complaint process, CSLB established the Enforcement division Statewide Investigative Fraud Team (SWIFT) that focuses on the underground economy and the unlicensed contractor who prospers at the expense of consumers and legitimate businesses. The SWIFT unit has the authority to visit any job site without cause or complaint, ask contractors to produce proof of licensure in good standing, and cite those who are not properly licensed. *(See B&P Code §§ 7011.4 and 7099.)*

SECTION II.
HOME IMPROVEMENT

Chapter 5.

Home Improvement

Home improvement is the repairing, remodeling, altering, converting, or modernizing of, or adding to, residential property and includes, but is not limited to, the construction, erection, replacement, or improvement of driveways, swimming pools (including spas and hot tubs), terraces, patios, awnings, storm windows, landscaping, fences, porches, garages, fallout shelters, basements, and other improvements of the structures or land that is adjacent to a dwelling. Home improvement is also the installation of home improvement goods or the furnishing of home improvement services.

HOME IMPROVEMENT CONTRACTOR

A home improvement contractor, including a swimming pool contractor, is a contractor licensed by the Contractors State License Board (CSLB) who is engaged in the business of home improvement either full-time or part-time.

HOME IMPROVEMENT CONTRACTS

The home improvement business in California constitutes a large portion of the state's construction industry. Because of the very nature of the home improvement field, there is a potential for problems or abuses. Abuses are usually caused by unlicensed operators or unethical or incompetent contractors. Problems can occur because of a general misunderstanding of basic requirements and of the agreement entered into by the owner and the contractor. Special requirements concerning the home improvement contract were placed into the law as an attempt to eliminate as many of these problems as possible. It is important for contractors stay current on all requirements.

The most recent changes to home improvement contract law resulted from the passage of Senate Bill (SB) 30 in 2004, and SB 1113 and Assembly Bill (AB) 316 in 2005. The Legislature made significant additions to the information the contractor must provide to the buyer of home improvements. The idea behind the legislation is to use the contract itself to inform homeowners of the most important contract requirements. With this information in hand, consumers are better able to understand the process. CSLB expects the availability of this simple consumer protection information to reduce the number of disputes between contractors and homeowners and, therefore, the number of complaints homeowners make to the board.

SB 30 maintained many of the existing home improvement contract provisions and added some new requirements, as well. Among the requirements: any changes made to contracts must be in writing, be legible, be easy to understand, and inform a consumer of his or her right to cancel or rescind the contract, and a home improvement contract must contain various information, notices, and disclosures for the protection of the consumer. SB 30 also created a "service and repair contract" to be used by licensed contractors for jobs of $750 or less, provided that the contract meets all four of the new requirements. The bill enacted various disclosure requirements applicable to the service and repair contract. SB 30 provided that any violation of the provisions subjects the contractor to discipline. The bill made conforming changes, and revised and recast certain existing provisions regarding home improvement contracts and related matters. SB 30 was to become operative on July 1, 2005. (Read SB 1113.)

SB 1113 postponed implementation of the SB 30 provisions until January 1, 2006. The bill also revised and recast some of the provisions and made other related changes in other provisions of law. SB 1113 took effect immediately as an emergency statute.

AB 316 revised and recast the service and repair contract requirements and set forth information, notices, and disclosures required to be included as part of the contract. In addition, a service and repair contract that does not meet specified requirements is subject to the requirements applicable to a home improvement contract regardless of the aggregate contract price.

In developing contracts, contractors should pay strict attention to the requirements for print typeface and point size of the notices and disclosures. For example, unless a larger print typeface is specified, text in any printed form shall be in at least 10-point type and the headings shall be in at least 10-point boldface type.

For more detailed information on the home improvement contract requirements, visit CSLB's website at www.cslb.ca.gov. CSLB has developed two comprehensive guides regarding home improvement contract requirements

for both contractors and consumers. Please visit CSLB's website to view or place a publication order.

HOME WARRANTIES

Home warranties generally are not transferrable, except as provided for home roof warranties in Chapter 5. Home Roof Warranties of the California Civil Code:

> For any contract subject to this chapter that is entered into on or after January 1, 1994, the warranty obligations shall inure to the benefit of, and shall be directly enforceable by, all subsequent purchasers and transferees of the residential structure, without limitation, unless the contract contains a clear and conspicuous provision limiting transferability of the warranty (*See Civil Code §1797.62.*).

HOME IMPROVEMENT SALESPERSON (HIS) REGISTRATION

Anyone who solicits, sells, negotiates, or executes home improvement contracts for a licensed contractor outside of the contractor's normal place of business, regardless of the dollar amount of those contracts, must be registered with CSLB as a Home Improvement Salesperson (HIS).

Who is exempt from the HIS registration requirement?

Salespersons who only sell goods or negotiate contracts at a fixed business establishment where the goods or services are exhibited or offered for sale are not considered home improvement salespersons.

The official personnel listed in CSLB's records for the contractor license are also exempt from registration requirements. This includes individual contractors, qualifying individuals, partners, officers of the corporation, and responsible managing officers, members, managers or employees.

Other exemptions from the registration requirements include people who contact prospective buyers for the exclusive purpose of scheduling appointments for a registered home improvement salesperson, and *bona fide* service or repair people who are in the employ of a licensed contractor and whose repair or service calls are limited to the service or repair initially requested by the buyer.

May a home improvement salesperson work for more than one contractor?

Yes. A home improvement salesperson may work for any number of contractors and sell a variety of goods and services, but **a**

salesperson employed by more than one contractor must register separately for each contractor. Each registration will require a separate application and registration fee. Each time a home improvement salesperson changes employment from one contractor to another, or is employed by an additional contractor, he or she must become registered as a home improvement salesperson for the new contractor. Each contractor's license must be current and active.

What are the qualifications for a home improvement salesperson?

A home improvement salesperson must be at least 18 years of age. There are no educational, residency, or experience requirements.

How do I apply for registration?

Obtain an "Application for Registration as a Home Improvement Salesperson" form from any CSLB office by calling CSLB, toll-free: (800) 321-CSLB (2752) or downloading the application from www.cslb.ca.gov. Then, do the following:

- Carefully read and follow all instructions on the application;

- Complete the form in blue or black ink or use a typewriter. Both you and your employer must sign the application; and

- Submit the required nonrefundable, nontransferable application fee, and your application to the CSLB headquarters office.

May I begin working as an HIS as soon as I have submitted my registration application and fee to CSLB?

No. Your application must be reviewed and a registration number must be issued to you before you may legally work as a home improvement salesperson.

How long will it take to become registered?

CSLB's processing times vary depending on its workload, staff vacancies, etc. CSLB's website includes a processing time chart that indicates the date of documents that are currently being processed, including home improvement salesperson applications and renewals. The chart is updated weekly and helps to keep customers informed on current processing times.

When does my HIS registration expire?

The HIS registration expires two (2) years from the last day of the month in which it was issued. CSLB will mail a renewal application to your address of record several weeks before your registration expires. Upon verification of the renewal, a new registration certificate will be mailed showing the new expiration date.

If your address has changed since your registration was issued or last renewed, it is your responsibility to notify CSLB in writing within 90 days of the change.

If you have not received an advance notification of renewal, notify CSLB. This should be done no later than three (3) weeks before your registration expires.

Is a contract sold or negotiated by an unregistered salesperson enforceable?

The law does not specifically state that the contract would be unenforceable, but since other factors involved could have a bearing on its enforceability, questions about specific contracts should be referred to an attorney. According to Business and Professions (B&P) Code section 7154, a contractor who employs an unregistered person to negotiate home improvement contracts is subject to disciplinary action by the Registrar. Furthermore, B&P Code section 7153 states that it is a misdemeanor for a person to act as a home improvement salesperson without being registered. In addition to possible criminal action, the same section provides that an administrative citation may be issued to any unregistered person who engages in the HIS occupation.

For additional information, refer to B&P Code sections 7150 through 7173 in Chapter 12 of this book.

REGISTRAR-APPROVED JOINT CONTROL AGREEMENTS

B&P Code provides for the use of a joint control agreement approved by the Registrar of Contractors "covering full performance and completion of the contract" as an alternative to certain contract requirements. When a joint control is used, no schedule of payments is required in the contract.

A joint control is a builder's construction control service, which acts as an escrow holder of a consumer's money. A joint control company manages the disbursement of funds to prevent the contractor from being paid more than the value of the work already completed. A joint control also safeguards the consumer's property from mechanic's liens by requiring the contractor to supply lien releases as progress payments are made.

A joint control normally includes an analysis of the contract and building plans or specifications, breakdown of costs, and the preparation of an account from which the funds will be disbursed on regularly scheduled progress payments. An addendum *(See page 69)* must be incorporated into joint control agreements for any joint control company to be considered approved by the Registrar.

CSLB does not license joint control companies, nor does CSLB have any legal jurisdiction over joint control company activities. The criteria for "Registrar approval" was developed through mutual agreement of CSLB and joint control company representatives. The resulting addendum (which follows), if included in the control agreement and followed, should prove to be beneficial to both contractors and consumers.

CSLB does not maintain lists of approved joint control companies nor monitor their activities. Registrar approval is implicit if the addendum is used. Responsibility for incorporating the addendum in agreements will rest solely with the joint control companies. Contractors and consumers should compare any joint control agreement with the following addendum to ensure that the Control supplies the services required for approval.

NOTE: The last paragraph in the joint control addendum pertains to home improvement contracts other than swimming pool contracts. **Effective January 1, 2006, the same down payment provisions applied to swimming pools as to other home improvement projects: $1,000 or 10 percent of the total contract price, whichever is less.**

MECHANIC'S LIEN WARNING

Effective January 1, 2006, the "Mechanic's Lien Warning" *(See page 71)* will replace the previously-used "Notice to Owner." This notice describes, in non-technical language, pertinent provisions of the state's mechanic's lien laws that specify the rights and responsibilities of both the property owner and the contractor.

The Mechanic's Lien Warning must be a part of any home improvement contract, including swimming pool contracts. This notice is not required for a contract that meets the service and repair contract requirements.

JOINT CONTROL ADDENDUM

Addendum to Control Agreement/Escrow Instructions

This addendum is hereby incorporated into and becomes a part of the Control Agreement attached hereto, dated _____.

1. Should any of the terms or provisions of the contract between Owner and Contractor or of the contract into which this Addendum is incorporated conflict with any of the terms or provisions of this Addendum, then the terms of this Addendum shall prevail.

2. Control agrees to control and disburse funds in the following manner:

   a) Supplier or subcontractor submits to contractor duplicate copies of invoices requesting payment;

   b) If payment is justified, based on work completed, control accepts disbursement order or voucher in favor of payee for net amount;

   c) After signing by the contractor and the payee concerned, order for payment (together with copies of invoices, unconditional lien releases and/or other substantiating data) is delivered or mailed to the Control for payment.

3. Prior to issuing payment, Control agrees to verify:

   a) That all vouchers have authorized signatures;

   b) That adequate unconditional lien releases have been submitted in writing; and

   c) That sufficient funds are on hand to pay the specific invoice(s) submitted.

4. Prior to issuing final payment, Control agrees to verify that project has passed final inspection by local building authorities, unless the scope of the contracted project does not require a final inspection.

5. After verification of the above, checks shall be made payable to the supplier or subcontractor, or to the prime contractor and supplier or subcontractor, jointly.

6. Control agrees that in no event shall it disburse payments in excess of 100 percent of the value of the work

performed on the project at any time, excluding finance charges.

7. The funds from this account shall be used only for the project described in the contract. Control warrants that work and material paid for by Control has been provided.

8. If this agreement is terminated for any reason prior to disbursement of all monies payable under the contract between Owner and Contractor, all subsequent disbursements to Contractor shall conform to the requirements of Business and Professions Code section 7159.

NOTE: B&P Code section 7159 requires that all change orders be in writing and signed by all parties.

SO AGREED this _____ day of _____, 20_____.

_____   _____
CONTROL   **OWNER**

_____   _____
CONTRACTOR   **OWNER**

Contractors who furnish a joint control as part of the terms of a home improvement contract should be aware that the law prohibits them from having any financial or other interest in the joint control company. Also, it is the contractor's responsibility to determine whether the above addendum is included in the control agreement.

If an approved joint control or bond covering the complete contract is not furnished with a home improvement contract, the contractor may not require a down payment in excess of $1,000 or 10 percent of the total contract price, whichever is less. The contract must also contain a schedule of payments stated in dollars and cents, specifically referenced to the work or services to be performed or the materials and equipment to be supplied. Also, no payments other than the down payment can be in excess of the value of the work (excluding finance charges) performed at any time on the project.

MECHANIC'S LIEN WARNING

Anyone who helps improve property, but who is not paid for performed work or supplied materials, may record what is called a mechanic's lien against that property. A mechanic's lien is a claim, like a mortgage or home equity loan, made against the property and recorded with the county recorder.

Even if the contractor is paid in full, unpaid subcontractors, suppliers, and laborers who helped to improve the property may record mechanic's liens and sue the property owner in court to foreclose a lien. If a court finds the lien is valid, the property owner could be forced to pay additional monies or have a court officer sell the home to pay the lien. Liens can also affect personal credit records.

20-DAY PRELIMINARY NOTICE

To preserve their right to record a lien, each subcontractor and material supplier **must provide the property owner with a document called a "20-Day Preliminary Notice."** This notice is not a lien. The purpose of the notice is to let the property owner know that the person who is sending the notice has the *right* to record a lien on the property if he or she is not paid.

The Preliminary Notice can be sent up to 20 days after the subcontractor starts work or the supplier provides material. The prime contractor and laborers do not send 20-Day Preliminary Notices; contractor law assumes the property owner already knows they are improving the property.

A list of all contractors, subcontractors, and material suppliers that work on project can be provided to the property owner to help avoid confusion.

PAYING WITH JOINT CHECKS

Joint checks are a protective method to make sure the subcontractor or material supplier is paid. When the contractor tells the property owner that it is time to pay for the work of a subcontractor or supplier who has sent the property owner a Preliminary Notice, a joint check payable to both the contractor and the subcontractor or material supplier is written to confirm payment.

For other ways to prevent liens, visit CSLB's website at www.cslb.ca.gov or call CSLB at 800-321-CSLB (2752).

Effective January 1, 2011, the definitions of "claim of lien" and "mechanic's lien" are the same. It also requires that a Notice of Mechanic's Lien be served on the owner or person believed to be the owner of the property or on the

construction lender or original contractor, <u>and</u> that a "proof of service affidavit" to the above mentioned party or parties be completed and signed by the person serving the Notice of Mechanic's Lien. <u>Failure to serve the mechanic's lien and confirm a proof of service affidavit will cause the mechanic's lien to be unenforceable.</u>

SECTION III.
BUSINESS MANAGEMENT

Chapter
6.   Managing a Business

Chapter 6.

Managing a Business

The construction industry, while one of the largest segments of the economy, includes many small businesses that employ fewer than eight people. The industry is somewhat easy to enter because relatively little money is needed to get started; however, the number of bankruptcies and closures is also quite high. This chapter will focus on business and management principles that may reduce the chance of business failure.

While it may be simple to establish your contracting business, the knowledge and concepts outlined in the following pages should be mastered to enable you to become an effective manager. The terms and ideas used here should become as familiar to you as the technical construction language you use every day.

This chapter will show you how good management and accounting techniques can be applied to the construction industry. The numbers used in the examples were chosen to illustrate the average successful small contracting business. The numbers and ratios provide only a starting point for your job of managing.

THE CONTRACTOR MANAGER

The average contractor has knowledge and skills in many of the phases of construction learned from firsthand experience. However, upon starting a business, the contractor must become a business manager, often without experience or training.

Statistics show that 90 percent of bankruptcies and business closures result from poor management. The specific reasons include an inability to plan, manage, and control business affairs (managerial competence); insufficient on-the-job supervisory experience or the inability to manage employees (people competence); and the lack of knowledge of business practices (technical competence). Hard work is not enough. You learned your building trade skills through on-the-job training, and these skills must now be balanced by learning management skills, as well.

The main duties of the contractor who is a manager are to plan and direct the major activities of the business; coordinate employee work and materials; and train, direct, and advise employees in supervisory and non-supervisory positions. The key to successful management is the ability to review available information and arrive at informed decisions. Information must be current and accurate. Setting up a record-keeping and reporting system is the first step in being able to use and apply the information. The manager is responsible for making sure that this information is complete and accurate.

PRINCIPLES OF MANAGEMENT

The most difficult part of changing roles from employee to manager may be in developing the clear understanding of what is important for successful management. Management theory has been divided into two different areas: functional and behavioral.

The Functional Areas of Management Include:

- **Planning**

  Good planning is one of the most important, but most neglected, management duties. The large amount of information from within the business must be put together with information from outside the business to schedule business activities. Planning is essential to make sure that resources, money, people, and equipment are available to the business in the right amounts and at the right time.

- **Decision-Making/Delegation**

  It is important for the manager to avoid spending too much time involved in the details of everyday work. Employees should be trained and encouraged to assume responsibility for routine decision-making. The manager's responsibility is to make sure that these decisions fit together with the plans for the project and the business as a whole.

- **Standardization**

  For the greatest efficiency, it is important to standardize methods for routine, ongoing operations. When the best method has been determined, it should be adopted as the pattern for similar operations in the future. Standardization also makes it easier for decisions to be made at lower levels.

- **Controls**

  Controls are established to inform the manager when the actual business outcome is different from what was expected. Controls should be designed to warn the manager before the differences become too great. The manager can both check on the progress of the business and evaluate overall performance by comparing results with plans. Effective controls must be established and rigidly enforced. The manager can then adapt to change rather than resist change.

  The functional areas of management relate mostly to the technical side of business. The people or behavioral side of business is equally important and must not be ignored.

The Behavioral Aspects of Management Include:

- **Human Relations**

  Management should always remember to consider each problem from the other person's point of view. The success or failure of a business depends largely upon the proper handling and treatment of the personnel.

- **Cooperation**

  Cooperation between individuals in any group must be encouraged by management. This ensures that their combined efforts, working toward a common goal, will produce far greater results than the combined total produced by each working as an individual. The spirit of cooperation is usually inspired by the conduct of the manager. Cooperation cannot be imposed; it can only be achieved by leadership.

- **Responsibility**

  Each individual in an organization should be responsible for one or more phases of operation. These responsibilities should be clearly understood, and the individual should be given the authority to carry them out and be held accountable for their completion. One of the most consistent failings of management is in neglecting to instruct personnel about their responsibilities and delegating adequate authority to exercise those responsibilities.

- **Communication**

  Effective communication is an important part of any sound organization. All personnel are entitled to be advised about any subjects that concern them individually. Good communication improves morale and productivity.

- **Executive Ability**

  As the size of the contracting business increases, the contractor must spend more time and energy in the role of a manager. Executive ability can be realized to the fullest extent only when the manager is relieved of all unnecessary detail or routine work. When standards of performance are established, definite plans and policies formulated, and adequate controls installed, the manager may focus attention on those matters that are the exception to the normal operation. Time spent on the job should be limited to cases where it is necessary.

Guidelines

Do not make the common mistake of thinking these principles do not apply to you. Many managers feel that because these principles make common sense and represent facts they know, that they are applying them, when actually the reverse is true. Managers can test their observance of the principles of management by reviewing the following questions:

- Are all jobs planned carefully in advance?

- Is each worker in the right place?

- Is each worker sufficiently trained for the job assigned?

- Are the best possible practices established as standards for all routine operations?

- Is the business capable of rapid adjustment to changing conditions?

- Does each worker have the required materials, supplies, and equipment to complete the job effectively?

- Is each worker directed by one supervisor only?

- Have all overlapping authority and responsibility been eliminated?

- Does every worker clearly understand the assigned task and the start and completion schedule for the task?

- Has all duplication of effort been eliminated?

Management should be able to answer "yes" to all of these questions. Any hesitancy or "no" answer puts the immediate obligation on the manager to review the situation and, if necessary, take corrective action.

ESTABLISHING YOUR BUSINESS

Forms of Business

The legal form of the business will determine the available sources of financing, the extent of personal liability, the extent of control, and the tax liabilities. The legal form may change as the business grows and should be reviewed as financing requirements change. The sole owner often lacks the personal capital sources necessary to sustain growth. The partnership is usually created to expand the source of funds. Continued growth and the resulting larger financing needs may lead to incorporation, which, in turn, provides access to external funds.

- **Sole Ownership**

  Sole ownership (often called personal ownership or sole proprietorship) is the simplest form of business organization and relies primarily on the financial resources available to an individual. The owner has sole responsibility and complete control. He/she must obtain all the financing and is personally liable for any claims against the business.

  The sole ownership is easy to set up and is subject to minimum regulations. For tax purposes, business income is reported as personal income. Sole ownership appeals to individuals who value smallness, simplicity, and personal control. *(See Chapter 2 for information about maintaining a sole ownership license.)*

- **General Partnership**

  The general partnership uses the financial and personal resources of two or more individuals who share in the ownership and operation of the business. The general partnership requires registration of the name of the business. A lawyer should be consulted to formalize the rights and responsibilities of the partners regarding management and profit-sharing.

  Under most circumstances, a partnership agreement terminates with the death or withdrawal of a partner or the addition of a new partner. Some partnership agreements avoid termination by entering into a prior written agreement allowing the partnership to continue. However, when a contractor license is issued to a general partnership and a general partner leaves for any reason or the partnership wants to add another general partner, the license is cancelled. *(See Chapter 2 for a discussion of partnership and ways to continue as a partnership for a short period of time after cancellation.)*

Section III

The partnership is not an entity separate from the partners. Each partner may be personally liable to the extent of his or her personal assets and may be legally responsible for the negligent acts of the other partner(s). For tax purposes, an individual's share of the partnership income is taxed as personal income.

- **Limited Partnership**

  The limited partnership allows investors to join in a partnership without taking full responsibility for the business. The limited partner risks only his or her original investment. In this case, there must be at least one general partner who runs the business and who remains fully responsible for the liabilities of the business. (*See Chapter 2 for a discussion of what to do if a limited partner leaves the partnership.*)

- **Corporation**

  A corporation is a separate legal entity created by the government. It can make contracts, be held legally liable, and is taxed. The corporation may raise capital by selling stock to private investors or to the public. Stockholders are usually not liable for claims against the corporation beyond their original investment. Creditors may claim only the corporate assets, although corporate officers may be personally liable.

  Incorporation begins by filing articles of incorporation with the Secretary of State. The corporation has no fixed life. The death of a stockholder or sale of one's personal investment will not disrupt the business.

- **"S" Chapter Corporation**

  Another type of corporation is an "S Chapter" corporation. "S" corporations must meet certain restrictions and can report the business income as individual income. This benefit is designed to remove the tax considerations from the decision regarding the form of business organization for the small business. The business can operate in corporate form to reduce the owner's liability, but is taxed like a partnership. Since the corporation is not taxed separately, only an information return similar to the partnership tax return need be filed. For the small business, this avoids the double taxation of corporate income that results when the corporation is taxed on earnings and the owners are taxed on dividends distributed by the corporation.

- **Limited Liability Company**

  A California LLC generally offers liability protection similar to that of a corporation but is taxed differently. Domestic LLCs may be managed by one or more managers or one or more members. In addition to filing the applicable documents with the Secretary of State, an operating agreement among the members as to the affairs of the LLC and the conduct of its business is required. The LLC does not file the operating agreement with the Secretary of State but maintains it at the office where the LLC's records are kept.

To form an LLC in California, **Articles of Organization** (Form LLC–1) must be filed with the California Secretary of State's office.

Inventory of Resources

You should consider many details before establishing a contracting business, beginning with the understanding that the company should be managed by individuals who have acquired technical expertise through experience. The contractor/manager is motivated by the desire to achieve personal independence, demonstrate greater efficiency, and make more profit. Your careful consideration of the following questions will help you to identify common obstacles to the successful operation of a business.

- What financial resources do I have and what financial resources will be required? Funds must be available to purchase equipment, rent office space, and meet payroll and personal living expenses until income is received.

- Am I willing to take risks—risks that include the cost and availability of materials and services, weather, delays brought about by government regulation and required inspections, and reliance on the expertise of architects?

- What resources do I have to attract sufficient business? Is the level of building activity in the area high enough to support a new business?

- What type of contracting business do I specialize in? Will it be custom building, speculative building, remodeling and home improvement, or general contracting?

- Who will handle the bookkeeping and record keeping that is essential for planning, coordination, and control?

- Do I have the resources to handle personnel, financial, and legal reporting requirements?

It is important for you to obtain the necessary resources before attempting to establish your business.

Section III

Taxes and Permits

The owner(s) of the business is required to pay taxes and fees at the federal, state, and local levels. If the business is a sole ownership or partnership, estimated federal and state income taxes must be prepaid or paid quarterly.

An Employer Identification Number (EIN) must be requested from the Internal Revenue Service, and the federal income and Social Security taxes withheld from employee wages must be paid quarterly, monthly, or semimonthly, as required.

The contractor must register with the Employment Development Department, obtain a state EIN, and pay state payroll and unemployment insurance taxes for employees who earn over $100 in a calendar quarter.

California requires a Seller's Permit for businesses that sell tangible personal property. The State Board of Equalization can require a deposit of the estimated sales tax for the first six months. The contractor must collect the required sales tax from the customer unless the tax on materials was already paid at the time of purchase.

Contractors must also obtain the required city or county permits before starting the job. Business licenses and construction permits are a cost of doing business, a fact that must be recognized at the outset. In addition, the contractor must be familiar with zoning laws and building codes.

Bonds

A requirement for bonding is generally mandatory for large jobs financed by institutional lenders, such as savings and loans, insurance companies, or commercial banks. In addition, many owners and lenders, as well as other contractors, impose bonding requirements. Bonds can be obtained from bonding companies for a percentage of the contract price, usually in the 1 to 2 percent range. This requirement is a cost of doing business that should be recognized when the bid is submitted. Bonds may be classified as follows:

- **Performance bonds** guarantee the project's completion according to the building plans and specifications. If the job is abandoned or the work unacceptable, the bonding company has the option of hiring another contractor to complete the work or settling for damages.

- **Payment bonds** assure the owner that no liens for labor and materials will be filed against the property.

- **Contract bonds** guarantee both job completion and payment of all labor and materials.

In general, unless the bonding company has taken on responsibility for completing the project, the bonding company will not have to pay more than the face amount of the bond.

The new contractor should be aware that bonding requirements may exclude the new business from bidding on desired jobs. Bonding companies will not take risks without verifying the technical and resource capabilities of the bonded contractor. It is essential to practice sound business management techniques if you hope to be able to qualify for bonding in the future.

Contractor License Bonds

Contractor license bonds are different from performance, payment, and contract bonds. Each licensed contractor is required to carry a contractor bond. Unlike payment, performance, and contract bonds, which are usually written to cover specific projects, a contractor license bond is written to cover any project the contractor agrees to perform. The penal sum of the contractor license bond is $12,500. The bond for qualifiers is $12,500.

Limited Liability Company Surety Bond

A $100,000 surety bond (in addition to the $12,500 contractor bond) is required for the issuance, reissuance, reinstatement, reactivation, and renewal of an LLC license for the benefit of any employee or worker damaged by the LLC's failure to pay wages, interest on wages, or fringe benefits, as well as other contributions. (*See B&P Code §7071.6.5.*)

Commercial General Liability Insurance

Just as an accident can happen to anyone, everyone makes mistakes. Many California contractors address accidents and mistakes through commercial general liability (CGL) insurance. As the International Risk Management Institute explains in its *Guide to Construction Insurance*, CGL insurance protects "the insured contractor from liability to members of the public (other than employees) for bodily injury, property damage, or personal injury caused by virtually any activity." Thus, CGL insurance can shift the risk of liability for accidents and mistakes from the contractor to the insurance company.

Contractors who carry CGL insurance generally find this insurance to be well worth the cost. The insurance company:

- Provides a claim-handling process;
- Defends the contractor against insurance claims;
- Pays claims for covered damages; and

- Pays for immediately necessary medical treatment, even when the contractor is not ultimately found to be liable.

Contractors State License Law does not require contractors to carry CGL insurance unless their business entity is a limited liability company (See below.). Even though it is not universally required by licensing law, commercial property owners routinely require the contractors they hire to carry CGL insurance. These property owners understand that numerous, expensive mishaps can, and do, occur in construction projects.

On the other hand, when a homeowner hires a contractor to perform home improvement work, the homeowner rarely requires the contractor to carry CGL insurance. The primary reason given by homeowners for not requiring the contractor to carry CGL insurance is that it doesn't occur to a homeowner that a contractor would work on the house without being insured. According to the California Code of Regulations (CCR) section 872(a), in order to alert homeowners to the value of CGL insurance, beginning in February 2002, home improvement contractors were required to:

- Disclose in writing whether they carry commercial general liability insurance.
- If they do carry CGL insurance, the contractors are required to provide the homeowner with the name and telephone number of the insurance company, in writing, so the homeowner can verify coverage.

This requirement changed under the new home improvement contract requirements. *(See Chapter 5.)* On January 1, 2006, SB 30 became effective, requiring the contractor to provide CGL insurance information to homeowners as part of the contract.

$1 Million Liability Insurance Minimum

Liability insurance with the aggregate limit of $1 million for licensees with five or fewer persons listed as members of the personnel of record is required for a limited liability company; plus, an additional $100,000 is required for each additional member of the personnel of record, not to exceed $5 million total. *(See B&P Code §7071.19.)*

For more information about the risks covered by insurance, see "Risk Management" on page 107.

Workers' Compensation Insurance

The California workers' compensation insurance laws are administered by the State Department of Industrial Relations through the Division of Workers' Compensation. The following paragraphs highlight some important provisions of workers' compensation law found in the California Labor Code.

Workers' Compensation Defined

California workers' compensation law establishes a no-fault insurance plan purchased by the employer-contractor and administered by the state to:

- Limit the employer-contractor's liability and avoid costly lawsuits; and

- Guarantee that an injured worker receives prompt and complete medical treatment and specific benefits for job-related injury or illness. Under some circumstances, an employer-contractor can be sued for damages. For example, the harmed parties may sue if an employee is injured when the employer is illegally uninsured, or if the employer conceals the existence of an employee's injury and its connection with employment. Please check with the Department of Industrial Relations for more information.

Employer Liability

An employer-contractor is REQUIRED to provide weekly benefit payments (indemnity) and necessary medical and hospital treatment to all of his or her employees for work-incurred injuries and illness. This liability of the employer extends to employed relatives on the same basis as any other employee.

If the employer has one or more employees, even part-time, he or she is required to insure for workers' compensation claims. An "owner-operator" or "independent contractor" should consult an attorney to determine insurance liability and should pay particular attention to Labor Code §2750.5.

Workers' Compensation Insurance Coverage

The employer-contractor may provide insurance protection in one of three ways:

- By a standard approved policy of workers' compensation insurance available through any licensed carrier;

- By securing a permit from the Director of the State Department of Industrial Relations to become a self-insurer *(Labor Code §3700)*; or

- By participating in a collectively bargained alternative dispute resolution program recognized by the Division of Workers' Compensation *(Labor Code §3201.5)*.

Section III

In general, if a contractor carries compensation insurance, the compensation insurance company assumes the obligation of the contractor under the workers' compensation laws. Some exceptions include penalties based on:

- The contractor's serious and willful misconduct *(Labor Code §4553)*;

- Injury to an illegally employed person under 16 years of age *(Labor Code §4557)*; and

- Instances where the employer discriminates against an employee because an industrial injury claim was filed *(Labor Code §132a)*.

Reporting Name of Insurer

Every licensed contractor must report, in writing, the name and address of the insurer carrying workers' compensation on his or her employees to the Registrar of Contractors within 90 days after any policy of insurance is issued to him or her. He or she must send a copy of this report to the insurer. Failure to make such a report is a misdemeanor *(Business and Professions Code §§7125-7126)*.

Reporting Occupational Injury or Illness

- An employer-contractor MUST file a complete report of every employee occupational injury or occupational illness that results in lost time beyond the date of injury or illness, or which requires medical treatment beyond first aid, with the Department of Industrial Relations through its Division of Labor Statistics and Research or, if an insured employer, with the insurer *(Labor Code §6409.1)*.

The report filed shall be the original of the form prescribed for that purpose by the Division of Labor Statistics and Research. A report shall be filed concerning each injury and illness that has, or is alleged to have, arisen out of and in the course of employment, within five (5) days after the employer obtains knowledge of the injury or illness. Each report of occupational injury or occupational illness must indicate the Social Security number of the injured employee *(Labor Code §6409.1)*.

The insured employer must file with his or her insurer a complete report of every injury or illness to each employee. If a report is not filed with the insurance carrier, the Workers' Compensation Appeals Board may issue an order directing the insured employer to report the injury or illness within five (5) days. Failure of the employer to comply with this order may be punished as contempt *(Labor Code §3760)*.

- In every case involving a serious injury or illness, or death, IN ADDITION TO the report described above, the employer must report immediately by telephone to the Division of Occupational Safety and Health *(Labor Code 6409.1)*.

Employee Notification and Posting Requirements

Every employer-contractor subject to the provisions of the workers' compensation laws MUST:

- Give every new employee, either at the time the employee is hired or by the end of his or her first pay period, written notice of the employee's right to receive workers' compensation benefits should he or she be injured on the job at any time while working for the employer. The content of the notice must be approved by the Administrative Director of the Division of Workers' Compensation and must contain the information listed in Section 9880 of CCR Title 8. *The notice shall be available in both English and Spanish when there are Spanish-speaking employees (Labor Code §3551).*

- Post conspicuously, in a location frequented by employees, a Notice to Employees poster. *The Notice to Employees must be posted in English (and Spanish where there are Spanish-speaking employees).* The Notice to Employees poster must contain the information listed in Section 9881 of CCR Title 8 or the employer may post the Administrative Director's approved Notice to Employees poster provided in Section 9881.1 of CCR Title 8 [DWC 7 (8/1/04)]. Failure to keep such a notice conspicuously posted is punishable as a misdemeanor. *(Labor Code §3550)*

- Post information regarding protections and obligations of employees under occupational safety and health laws, and related citations *(Labor Code §6408). (See Chapter 7 in this book for details.)*

- Give any employee who is a victim of workplace crime written notification that the employee is eligible for workers' compensation *(Labor Code §3553)*.

- The contractor or his or her insurance company should notify his or her employee, in case of an injury, of a physician who will provide professional care. ("Physician" as used here, includes physicians and surgeons, psychologists, acupuncturists, optometrists, dentists, podiatrists, and osteopathic and chiropractic practitioners, each in his or her respective field.)

Section III

Benefits to Which Workers May Be Entitled

- **Medical Treatment**

  Since April 19, 2004, employers have been required to authorize medical treatment consistent with the American College of Occupational and Environmental Medicine's (ACOEM) Occupational Medicine Practice Guidelines, Second Edition, or the treatment utilization schedule adopted by the Administrative Director to cure or relieve the injured worker from the effects of his or her injury. Within one working day of receiving the employee's claim form, the employer must authorize treatment for the alleged industrial injury and must continue to provide the treatment until the date that liability for the claim is either accepted or rejected by the employer. Until the date the claim is accepted or rejected, liability for medical treatment is limited to $10,000 *(Labor Code §§4600, 4604.5, 4610, 5307.27, and 5402)*.

- **Supplemental Job Displacement Benefit**

  After January 1, 2004, the worker may be entitled to a supplemental job displacement benefit if he or she cannot return to work for the employer within 60 days following the end of the temporary disability period. The amount of the benefit is based on the employee's permanent disability level and must be used for retraining, skill enhancement, or job placement assistance *(Labor Code §4658.5)*.

- **Temporary Disability**

  The worker is also entitled to temporary disability payments while recovering from the injury. These weekly payments begin after the third day of disability and are based upon two-thirds of the weekly earnings, *up to a legal maximum*. The amount of these payments is determined by state law. The compensation insurance company should be able to provide information on current rates. Where temporary disability extends beyond 14 days or requires overnight hospitalization, the three-day waiting period is eliminated *(Labor Code §§4453, 4650, 4652, and 4653)*.

- **Permanent Disability**

  If a permanent disability arises out of an industrial injury, the worker is entitled to compensation based on the rated degree of disability. Benefits are based on the earning of the disabled worker, and the range of benefit amounts are set by state law. For permanent disability ratings between 70 percent and 99 3/4 percent, a life pension is granted *(Labor Code §4453)*.

- **Death Benefits**

  If the injury causes death, a benefit is payable to those dependent on the deceased for support at the time of injury. In addition, burial expenses are allowed up to a prescribed amount *(Labor Code §§4701 and 4702)*.

- **Compensation for Serious and Willful Employer Misconduct**

  The amount of compensation otherwise recoverable can be increased one-half, together with costs and expenses not to exceed $250, where the employee is injured by reason of the serious or willful misconduct of the employer or his or her managing representative, partner, executive, managing officer, or general superintendent. The insurance company is not liable for the increase and is not permitted to cover it under the insurance policy *(Labor Code §§4550 and 4553; Insurance Code §11661)*.

Penalties for Noncompliance

- Failure to secure payment of compensation as required by law is a misdemeanor *(Labor Code §3700.5)*.

- A contractor's license may be suspended or revoked by the Registrar of Contractors if the contractor fails to secure the payment of compensation *(Business and Professions Code §7110)*.

- The Department of Industrial Relations, Division of Labor Standards Enforcement may also take action against a contractor who has failed to secure the payment of compensation. This may include:

  - Issuing a "stop order," prohibiting the use of employee labor until insurance is provided *(Labor Code §3710.1)*;

  - Obtaining a restraining order in superior court against the contractor *(Labor Code §3712)*;

  - Issuing a penalty assessment order (Penalties for an uninsured contractor may be either the greater of twice the amount the contractor would have paid in premiums during the period he or she was uninsured or $1,000 per employee employed during that same period. If the contractor's uninsured status is discovered following the filing of a claim for compensation, the penalty shall be either $2,000 for each employee employed on the date of injury in non-compensable cases, and $10,000 for each employee in compensable cases *(Labor Code §3722)*; or

- o Recording a lien against the real property and personal property of the contractor as a security interest *(Labor Code §3727)*.

- If a contractor willfully fails to provide compensation insurance for an employee and an injury occurs, the contractor must pay the disability compensation plus a penalty of 10 percent and attorney fees. He or she must also supply all necessary medical treatment. In addition, he or she is liable for damages in a civil action, with a legal presumption that the injury was caused by the employer's negligence. Contributory negligence of the employee is no defense *(Labor Code §§3706, 3708, 4554, and 4555)*.

- Every employer, and every employee having direction, management control, or custody of employment of any other employee, who willfully violates any occupational safety or health standard that causes the death of any employee or the prolonged impairment of the body of any employee shall, upon conviction, be punished by a fine and or imprisonment *(Labor Code §6425)*.

Additional Information

For additional information, consult the white pages of your local telephone book under:

"State Government/Industrial Relations, Workers' Compensation"

- Contact the Division's headquarters office at:

  Department of Industrial Relations
  Division of Workers' Compensation
  1515 Clay Street, 17th Floor
  Oakland, California 94612
  (510) 286-7100

- Visit the Division's website: www.dir.ca.gov/dwc.

- Call 1-800-736-7401 for recorded messages.

- The Division of Workers' Compensation publishes an *Employer's Guide* that can be requested by calling one of the numbers listed above.

FINANCIAL RESPONSIBILITY AND CONTROL

Finance has frequently been called the "language of business." This is because financial statements are a method of communicating business information. Financial statements contain the information necessary for planning, coordination, and control. The success of your business will depend on your ability to react to change. Financial statements provide the basic tools for this analysis. The foremost objective of the accounting process is to arrive at an estimate of the periodic income and expenses of a business. With this information, the owner can make the decisions that will increase the potential for profit. In this section, an attempt is made to keep the definitions and examples as simple as possible, yet realistic enough to provide understanding.

Records

Every business must keep records. Good records are essential for effective management. They are required when seeking outside financing and, in some cases, are mandated by law. State and federal agencies frequently specify certain records that must be maintained and made available for government audits and to substantiate tax reporting. For a description of the records specifically required under Contractors State License Law, see Business and Professions Code section 7111.

Accurate accounting records must be kept to provide the base to construct financial statements. The information summarized in these statements highlights the total operational costs, individual job costs, and other costs that affect your ability to make a profit. Accurate records also provide information on cash receipts and a basis for control of disbursements. The contractor can, by reviewing these records, determine the cash flow requirements of other jobs that he or she has completed to help in estimating the costs of future jobs.

Accounting Methods

Is it necessary for contractors to understand detailed accounting methods? In general, it is not. The manager's role is not to compile the statements, but rather to use these statements as tools of management. It is not necessary for the contractor to be an expert in accounting but, as a manager, he or she must understand and be able to take action based on the statement numbers.

Understand the Fundamental Terms of Accounting

- **Cash Basis of Accounting**

    Under the cash basis of accounting, revenue is recognized when cash is actually or constructively received, and expenses are deductible in the year paid (unless they should be taken in a different period in order to clearly reflect income).

    A cash basis of accounting may be appropriate where no prepaid expenses (e.g., insurance, rent), depreciable assets, or inventories exist, and where revenue is received during the accounting period.

Information regarding cash flow, as provided by the cash basis of accounting method, can be valuable in judging the ability of the business to pay its debts, to finance replacements of productive assets, and to expand the scope of business operations. However, a strict cash method neither records receivables nor payables since these items have not been received or disbursed. This failure to match income and expenses for a given accounting period restricts the information available to the manager using a cash basis of accounting.

Additionally, where depreciation and inventories are utilized, the accrual method is necessary to accurately reflect expenses and income. For federal income tax purposes, the accrual method is required when inventories are utilized.

The net increase or decrease in cash during a given period is not very useful in evaluating a company's operating performance because, although progress payments come in during the course of a job, final profit cannot be determined until after the job is completed. For these reasons, the cash basis of accounting is not recommended for contractors.

- **Accrual Basis of Accounting**

  The accrual basis of accounting is a method that recognizes revenues when earned and expenses when incurred, regardless of when payment is received or made. Thus, this method allows the matching of revenues and associated expenses for individual periods of time.

  In a contracting business that has qualifying long-term projects, the accrual basis of accounting is often further modified using two methods: 1) the **percentage of completion** and 2) the **completed contract** methods.

  1) The percentage of completion method will report profits and losses regularly on the basis of actual work accomplished on each job. For example, if the work performed in a given year is estimated to represent 50 percent of total performance under contract, then 50 percent of the total estimated revenue and profit is considered earned.

  2) The completed contract method allows for the gross income and related costs for each contract to be reported in the year in which such a contract is completed.

- **Financial Statements**

  The balance sheet and income statement summarize the firm's internal data. These statements, in turn, provide the information for ratio analysis that highlights the strengths and exposes the weaknesses of the company.

- **Balance Sheet**

  The balance sheet is a statement of financial condition of an individual business at a certain point in time. The balance sheet is often referred to as a "snap shot." The accountant will usually provide two balance sheets, one for the current year just ending and another for the prior year. An example of a balance sheet for a corporation is shown on page 88. This balance sheet lets the reader compare where the company stood at the end of each of the past two years.

  The balance sheet is a statement of the company's resources, financial obligations, and ownership investment. The balance sheet is divided into two sides: on the left are shown the assets; on the right are shown the company's liabilities and stockholders' equity (the owners' investment). Both sides are always equal or in balance. The company's assets include its cash, physical goods, and its financial claims on others. Liabilities represent the claims others have on the company. The stockholder's equity section includes the original investment of the owners. Since this example is a corporation, the equity section includes undistributed profits earned by the corporation to date (additional investment of earnings held by the corporation).

This section briefly describes some of the important features of the balance sheet:

Typical Construction Company, Inc.
Balance Sheet
December 31, 2011

Assets	Current Year	Prior Year	Liabilities and Stockholders' Equity	Current Year	Prior Year
Current Assets			**Liabilities**		
Cash	$10,000	$15,000	Current Liabilities		
Retention	$40,000	$35,000	Accounts payable	$80,000	$60,000
Accounts Receivable	$70,000	$50,000	Notes payable	$25,000	$30,000
Total current assets	**$120,000**	**$100,000**	Accrued expenses payable	$20,000	$20,000
			Accrued payroll	$20,000	$18,000
Inventories			Misc taxes payable	$5,000	$10,000
Construction in progress	$200,000	$160,000	Federal income taxes payable	$30,000	$12,000
Less: partial billings or contracts	-$120,000	-$100,000	**Total, current liabilities**	**$180,000**	**$150,000**
Costs or contracts in excess of billings	**$80,000**	**$60,000**	Long-term liabilities		
Raw Materials	$30,000	$30,000	Bank loan, truck and equipment; 14% due	$100,000	$90,000
Total Inventories	**$110,000**	**$90,000**	**Total, Liabilities**	**$280,000**	**$240,000**
Prepaid Expenses (permits and licenses, etc)	$20,000	$25,000			
Total, Current Assets	**$250,000**	**$215,000**	**Stockholders' Equity**		
			Common stock, $5 par value, authorized, issued and outstanding 10,000 shares	$50,000	$50,000
Property, plant and equipment					
Leasehold improvements	$4,000	$4,000	Retained earnings	$70,000	$60,000
Office furniture and fixtures	$2,000	$2,000			
Small tools	$10,000	$10,000	**Total, Stockholders' Equity**	**$120,000**	**$110,000**
Construction equipment	$154,000	$130,000	**Total, Liabilities and Stockholders' Equity**	**$400,000**	**$350,000**
Less: accumulated depreciation	-$20,000	-$15,000			
Net property, plant and equipment	**$150,000**	**$131,000**			
Other Assets		$4,000			
Total Assets	**$400,000**	**$350,000**			

ASSETS (left columns)

Assets are categorized as either current or fixed. Assets are listed in order of declining liquidity. (Liquidity refers to the speed with which an item can be converted into cash or, put another way, the ability of the organization to pay its current debt). Current assets are the first items listed on the left side of the balance sheet. These are the assets that are either cash or capable of being converted into cash in the normal course of business, generally within one year from the date of the balance sheet. In addition to cash (money on hand and deposits in the bank), the other items that will be turned into cash include retentions, accounts receivable, inventories, and prepaid expenses. After current assets, the balance sheet lists fixed assets.

Each of these is briefly described below:

- **Cash**: Immediately available or liquid funds.

- **Retention**: A specified amount, usually 10%, withheld from progress payments to the contractor pending satisfactory completion and final acceptance of the project. This amount you have already earned even though you have not yet been paid.

- **Accounts Receivable**: The amounts due from customers (other than retentions) in payment for construction projects.

- **Inventory**: Includes all materials, labor, and direct and indirect overhead on jobs currently in progress. (For an example of direct and indirect costs, refer to the Internal Revenue Code Sections 263A (capitalization and inclusion in inventory costs of certain expenses) and 451 (general rule for taxable year of inclusion).

- **Prepaid Expenses**: Goods or services the company buys and pays for before use. Examples are insurance premiums and office supplies.

- **Property, Plant, and Equipment**: The next major category on the balance sheet is property, plant, and equipment, sometimes called fixed assets or plant and equipment. This group of assets includes physical resources a contractor owns or acquires for use in operations and has no intention to resell. Regardless of their current market value, fixed assets are valued at their original cost less accumulated depreciation. Sometimes property, plant, and equipment may be leased rather than owned. The value of the leased property is often included with the fixed assets and the lease payments are included with the liabilities.

- **Other Assets**: Resources not included under current assets, or under "Property, Plant, and Equipment" are placed here. Examples include scrap materials or equipment held for resale and long-term receivables.

LIABILITIES (right columns)

Liabilities, like assets, are broken down into two major categories: current liabilities and long-term liabilities. Liabilities represent obligations to pay money or other assets or to render future services to others. The relationship of current and fixed assets and current and long-term liabilities will become apparent when you learn how to analyze the information presented in the financial statements.

Current Liabilities: This item includes debts of the company that become due within one year of the balance sheet date. Current assets are the source from which these payments are usually made. Management must be aware of this relationship and maintain sufficient current assets or control the amount of current liabilities to avoid becoming delinquent in its bills. In our example, "Typical Construction Company, Inc." has $180,000 of current liabilities composed of the following items:

- **Accounts Payable**: Money owed to suppliers and subcontractors.

- **Notes Payable**: Balance of the principal owed on a written promissory note.

- **Accrued Expenses Payable**: Monies owed for interest, services, insurance premiums, and other fees that are not included under accounts payable. Thus, expenses that have been incurred but are not due for payment on the date of the balance sheet are grouped under accrued expenses payable.

- **Accrued Payroll**: Salaries and wages the contractor currently owes to employees.

- **Miscellaneous Taxes Payable**: Amounts estimated by the accountant to have been incurred during the accounting period and are owed to local and state governmental agencies.

- **Federal Income Taxes Payable**: Amount of liability for taxes owed to the federal government. *(Note: Different organizational forms will have different tax obligations.)*

LONG-TERM LIABILITIES

Long-term liabilities are notes or mortgages due one year beyond the balance sheet date. In our sample balance sheet, Typical Construction Company, Inc. owed $100,000 on a bank loan due more than a year in the future. This loan was secured by using certain equipment as collateral.

Stockholders' Equity (right column): The stockholders' equity section of the balance sheet, also called net worth or equity, represents the claim of the owners on the assets of the business. Different organizational forms use different names for this section of the balance sheet, but basically this is the original investment of the owners. Our example is a corporation, and the stockholders' equity section has two accounts.

Capital Stock: The total amount invested in the business by the contractor in exchange for shares of common stock at par value. Par value is arbitrarily established and need not be the same as the current market price of that share of stock.

Retained Earnings: Total corporation earnings from its beginning, minus the total dividends declared (distributions to owners) since the corporation was founded. This account represents additional investment by the owners who were willing to forego a larger distribution of the company's earnings.

INCOME STATEMENT

The income statement summarizes the operations of the company over a period of time. For the Typical Construction Company, Inc. (see next page) the period of time is one year. The balance sheets presented for Typical were year-end balance sheets with the income statement summarizing the operations during the intervening time period. Income statements are often prepared to cover shorter operational periods (e.g., quarter or month). Basically, the income statement shows business revenue, expenses, and the resulting profit or loss for a given accounting period. Since the revenues are matched against the related costs and expenses, the difference between the two is how much the corporation makes or loses. This profit or loss is often called the "bottom line" because it is an important indicator of performance, and it is also the last line of the income statement. Note, however, that this is only one performance indicator that financial statements report. The relationships of the various expense categories to total revenue presented in this statement must be understood if the company is to be effectively managed.

Section III

The components of this income statement are illustrated as follows:

Typical Construction Company, Inc.
Income Statement
for the year ending December 31, 2011

	Current Year	Prior Year
Sales of Residences	$1,250,000	$1,000,000
Cost of Operations		
Cost of Sales	1,030,000	850,000
General and administrative expenses	91,000	75,000
Operating expenses	23,900	22,000
Total operating expenses	1,145,000	947,000
Income Before Provision for Federal Income Tax	105,000	53,000
Provision for Federal Income Tax	30,000	12,000
Net Profit for year	$75,000	$41,000

Income: The revenue amount reflects all the billings made to customers for completed projects, as well as work in progress. This is an example of the accrual basis previously discussed. In our example for Typical Construction Company, Inc., the sales of residences for the current year were $1,250,000, which represents amounts billed for completed projects and work in progress.

Cost of Operations: Cost of operations in the contracting business is comprised of all costs and expenses associated with running the business, with the exception that federal income taxes are shown on another line. By totaling all the costs of operations and subtracting these from the revenue, the operating profit of the company can be found. In our example, Typical Construction Company, Inc., the total cost of operations for the current year is $1,145,000, which, when subtracted from the net sales, leaves an operating profit of $105,000. This represents the amount of profit earned by the contractor without taking into consideration federal income taxes.

Within the Cost of Operations section of the Income Statement are several important amounts we will now briefly describe.

Direct Labor: The actual cost for labor payroll for all jobs worked on during the period covered by the income statement. The amount of direct labor and the percentage of direct labor to the total cost of any particular project should be closely monitored by management. Direct labor expense is an important variable in determining the ultimate profit of the company. The labor percentage is also a direct measurement of the efficiency of the workers and the performance of supervision.

Direct Labor Burden: This includes all payroll taxes, insurance, and employee benefits associated with the labor payroll. If the workers belong to a union, the direct labor burden will include union benefit assessments and, in some cases, association fees.

Materials Used: This includes the cost of all materials used on the job, and is usually the largest single expense item on the income statement. Since materials comprise such a large part of the total cost of contracting, this account should be carefully controlled and every effort made to ensure that purchasing is done efficiently.

Other Direct Costs: These costs include all items, other than those listed above, that are directly chargeable to individual jobs. For example, permits, bonds, insurance, and equipment rentals would be included here.

General and Administrative Expenses: This figure on the income statement is comprised of all items of expense of a general nature that cannot be specifically attributed to individual construction projects. In the example of Typical Construction Company, Inc., these expenses are summarized for the year on a separate schedule, which supplements the income statement.

Note that the items covered in our example will differ somewhat between companies, depending upon the type of contracting. The extent to which individual expenses will be listed separately or combined with others will also vary among accountants and contractors.

Pretax Income: To get this figure, the total operating expenses were subtracted from the sales of residences. This figure is called Income Before Provision for Federal Income Tax for those corporations that are subject to federal taxation. Certain corporations, as well as sole ownerships and partnerships, do not pay taxes on income; the income is reported on the owner's personal tax returns. This is another example of how the organizational form the contractor initially chooses will influence the content of the financial statements.

Net Profit for Year: This figure is often called net income and represents the sum of all revenues minus all expenses including taxes if applicable. Net profit or income is commonly referred to as the "bottom line."

Statement of Changes in Financial Position

The Statement of Changes in Financial Position, also called the
Statement of Sources and Applications of Funds, is a third major
financial statement. It shows how funds were obtained and where
funds were used. We do not show an example of this statement
because in many small operations it is not used. However, if a
contracting company is going to be audited by certified public
accountants for the purpose of presenting financial statements to
creditors or others, a Statement of Changes in Financial Position may
be necessary.

Financial Analysis and Ratios

While the figures listed in the financial statements are meaningful
and important taken alone, they become even more valuable when
compared to other information. For example, comparing any balance
sheet item for the current year with the prior year immediately gives
us added information. Did the figure increase? Decrease? If so, by
how much in absolute dollars? How much in percentage terms?

The comparison of financial relationships is often done in three ways.
The first method is the comparison of current financial data with
prior years. Very often, businesses will compare three to five years of
key items such as revenue and net income. This type of comparison
gives the reader an idea as to the trends over time.

The second method is to compare the current financial data with that
of other businesses within the same industry. Sources for industry
data are provided by organizations, such as Robert Morris Associates,
Dun and Bradstreet, Inc., and Standard and Poor's. This information
is often available at large local libraries and at local California State
University libraries.

The third method used in interpreting financial statements is ratio
analysis. The relationship between any two figures within the current
financial data is called a ratio. For example, if current assets are
$100,000 and current liabilities are $50,000, the relationship of
current assets to current liabilities ($100,000/50,000) may be shown
as 2 to 1, or 2:1 (ratio). The bank loan officer who is to recommend the
establishment of a line of credit (short-term loan) would be interested
in the current ratio and quick ratio, as the bank would expect the
contractor to repay the loan in the near term.

Current Ratio

One very important kind of information that can be readily
determined from the balance sheet is the ability of the company to
pay debts when due (sometimes referred to as liquidity). The
difference between the total current assets and the total current

liabilities is called **working capital**. One way of looking at working capital is that it represents the amount that is free and clear if all current debts are paid off. A comfortable amount of working capital gives a company the ability to meet its obligations and take advantage of opportunities.

What is a comfortable amount of working capital? To help answer this question, the current ratio provides additional helpful information. To calculate the current ratio, divide total current assets by total current liabilities. In the example of Typical Construction Company, Inc., the figures are:

$$\frac{\text{Current Assets}}{\text{Current Liabilities}} \quad \frac{\$250,000}{\$180,000} = 1.39$$

Therefore, for each $1 of current liabilities there is $1.39 in current assets to back it up.

Quick Ratio

The quick ratio is another, more conservative way of testing the adequacy of the current liquidity of the company. Instead of using current assets, quick assets are substituted because these are quickly converted into cash. One simple method of determining the quick assets is total current assets minus inventories. In our example:

Current Assets	$250,000
−Inventories	−110,000
Quick Assets	$140,000

Quick Ratio:

$$\frac{\text{Quick Assets}}{\text{CURRENT LIABILITIES}} \quad \frac{140,000}{180,000} = .78$$

For the above analysis, we can see that we have $.78 of assets that may readily be converted into cash for each $1 of current liabilities that will require cash payments shortly.

The long-term creditors (banks or insurance companies) would be interested in the ratio of total liabilities to net worth. This measure indicates the relative proportions of the contractor's assets supplied by creditors and owners. In the event that the company defaulted on its debts, this ratio indicates the degree of safety for the creditors.

Net sales to net working capital, net sales to total assets, and net income to net worth are all measures of the efficiency of the company's use of its resources. These measures are important indicators to management. Net sales to net working capital (low ratio) might be attributed either to an excess of working capital or to inadequate sales. Management should examine each ratio keeping in mind that if the ratios reflect a weakness, the manager then must analyze the problem area and develop possible solutions, e.g., more vigorous collection effort to reduce the size of receivables. Keep in mind that the ratios also are interdependent. When the receivables are reduced, the cash generated by the collection effort may be used to reduce long-term liabilities and improve the debt ratio. Management must not focus its attention narrowly. The broad perspective created by knowledge of business principles is essential for success.

FINANCIAL MANAGEMENT

The section about accounting control focused on the technical documents and interpretations that make up the information flow the contractor must learn to use. The financial management section focuses first, on the need for financial resources; second, on the sources; and finally, on how to best determine whether those financial resources are being fully utilized.

Capitalization

Capitalization refers to the total of financial resources made available to the owner. These financial resources are used to acquire the physical assets necessary to conduct the business. As you assess your financial requirements, the more obvious needs to finance the tools, vehicles, and other equipment (physical resources) used daily in the business are recognized first. The need for additional financing of office expenses, licenses, payroll expenses, bonding, rentals, etc., because of the differences between when you must pay and when you get paid, is critical for the business. A lack of enough working capital and insufficient cash liquidity generally result in business failure.

The amount of working capital required depends on the type of contracting business. The progress payments required under contracts for custom building and remodeling may be used to meet payroll expenses and material costs. The typical contract provides for three or more payments, 90 percent during the construction phase and the final 10 percent upon completion and expiration of the lien period. This final 10 percent is the "retention." The contractor cannot collect more than the percentage already completed. The contractor must be aware that differences in the timing of expenditures and receipts may limit his or her capacity to finance the business, particularly if the company commits itself to new jobs before final payments on completed jobs have been received.

The significance of "retention" must not be underestimated. Retention usually exceeds profits and therefore represents a claim on working

Section III

capital. Retention payments to the individual contractor may be held up through no fault of the contractor. The total project must be accepted before retentions are released. The problem is even greater for the subcontractor who completes his or her phase early in the project and must contend with a long waiting period. Since these funds are not available for use elsewhere in the business, the contractor must often finance the costs through borrowing. Speculative builders require larger amounts of capital than custom builders. This would imply that the speculative builder must provide substantial financial resources to qualify for loan commitments. Growth that is too rapid can overextend the company to the extent that its solvency may be jeopardized. Financial planning will help avoid cash shortages.

Sources of Financing

The new business owner typically lacks the required financial resources. Two types of external financing are available – **equity funds** and **debt**. Equity funds are supplied by investors who acquire some control of the business and a share of future profits. These funds remain in the business. Debt represents borrowed dollars that require both the repayment of the original amount and periodic interest payments. The owner does not normally give up control of the business.

Equity

The typical sources of these funds are acquaintances of the new owner-contractor. Equity funds are sometimes available from private venture capital companies, small business investment corporations that are funded by the federal Small Business Administration, and minority enterprise small business investment companies. These sources are usually restricted to businesses with a proven track record in a growing industry.

DEBT

Long-Term

Banks may offer long-term financing to contractors with good credit ratings, technical knowledge, and capacity for repayment as evidenced by financial planning in the form of projected balance sheets, income statements, and cash budgets.

The Small Business Administration (SBA) can make direct loans, but prefers to provide funds by guaranteeing up to 90 percent of a bank loan. SBA will not review a direct loan application unless the firm has been refused by at least one bank, and if the city's population exceeds

200,000. SBA prefers an equal dollar share to be put up by the owner for loans under either the guarantee program or direct loan program.

Short-Term

The operating business may want to establish a line of credit with a bank to meet some of its short-term needs for working capital. Through the line of credit, commercial banks can provide the working capital necessary to complete the awarded contract, with the loan requiring repayment when the contractor is paid.

The bank loan officer will normally require balance sheets and income statements on the business for the current period, as well as over several prior years. The contractor is advised to have these reports prepared by a Certified Public Accountant (CPA) so that they meet professional accounting standards. The lender will expect to be provided with information on the contract up for bid, as well as all uncompleted contracts. The loan officer will evaluate:

Character: Includes experience with similar jobs and locations; business reputation with lenders, suppliers, and subcontractors; and reasonableness of bid.

Capacity: Requires an evaluation of current workload, availability of equipment, and financial resources available to withstand any reasonable loss. The financial strengths of the awarding agency and subcontractors and suppliers are also important considerations.

Certainty: What are the chances that repayment will be affected by unexpected losses on existing business? Are completion dates realistic? Is there a chance that penalties will be assessed for delays?

Bank loans to speculative builders may include funds necessary to provide offsite improvements, as well as the construction of buildings. Funding may also be arranged to acquire land for future development.

OPERATIONS MANAGEMENT

Job Selection

Job selection is the key to making a profit. The planning involved in job selection requires a knowledge of the general level of business activity in the local area, the need for new construction, costs of materials and labor, the contractor's current financial resources, and any new architectural or structural advances. (The goal is to select individual projects for which the contractor has technical expertise.)

Bidding and Estimation (Planning)

Accurate bidding requires that the contractor plan the entire construction process on paper. The time spent on this detailed work ensures the accuracy of cost estimates necessary for the contractor to make a profit. Careful review of the job requires on-site inspection (walk the job), review of plans and specifications, identification of equipment required and the financing method (purchase, lease, rental), and the need for subcontractors.

Materials required are determined from takeoffs (quantity and measurements taken from plans) that are converted to costs on the estimation form. Prices should be obtained from published price lists and quotes from suppliers and subcontractors. It is important to include sales tax and freight costs. Cash discounts should not be included unless the contractor is certain that sufficient financial resources will be available so that accounts payable may be repaid during the discount period.

Labor costs are calculated according to work classification. These costs include not only the hourly wage rate, but also payroll taxes, health and welfare benefits, vacation pay, and required insurance. The contractor should also be aware that wage settlements could affect these rates and that job actions could affect the availability of these workers.

Other direct costs that must be examined include permits and other fees; interest, loan commitment fees, points, and other charges on borrowed funds; equipment owned or rented; and any additional insurance that may be required.

Fuel and lubricant expenses, general maintenance, and small tools represent indirect costs that may be charged to the project and should not be overlooked.

The contractor must also identify the overhead expenses. Overhead normally includes such expenses as office rental, supplies and wages, advertising, bad debts, storage charges, and any other general administrative costs. The appropriate portion should be allocated to the job.

When all the costs have been totaled, the contractor must add profit. Profit is essential to the continuation of the business and represents the return for bearing risk. The contractor will seriously jeopardize the business by omitting the allowance for profit, especially if the bid is low margin and there is any chance of underestimation. Insufficient profits threaten both capitalization (losses reduce retained earnings) and cash flow (payments to vendors may exceed

Section III

receipts) to the extent that bankruptcy and/or dissolution may be the result.

Common pitfalls that can be avoided include: bidding on projects for which the plans and specifications are not completely understood; insufficient planning so that hurried analysis becomes necessary; overextension of the managerial and/or financial resources of the company; and bidding against the competition and not on the job. It is easier to avoid financial difficulty by not bidding on a job for which you lack the capability than to try to salvage the job after a poor bid has been accepted.

The Construction Process (Coordination and Control)

The estimate that is the basis for the bid becomes a budget for the project. Without extensive planning and scheduling, lack of coordination can result in added costs which quickly reduce the profits.

If the estimation has been done properly, the job was broken down into a job schedule to arrive at the number of labor hours required. Actual construction, however, requires that materials and labor be brought together at the proper time. Two methods of production scheduling may be used to accomplish this coordination.

The **bar chart** (Figure 6.A) is a fundamental scheduling technique that shows graphically the starting and finishing times for the individual tasks that make up the job. This scheduling approach is simple but overlooks some interrelated tasks.

The **critical path** method (Figure 6.B) is a more complex tool that inter-relates the tasks better. This technique derives its name from the key path through the network that takes into account all the tasks to be completed.

Any delay in one of these tasks will result in overall delay of the project. This procedure, therefore, identifies the tasks upon which the manager must focus attention to ensure completion of the project on time. Since the contractor's time is a scarce resource, this approach can save on this important factor.

FIGURE 6.A
Building a New Home: Construction Schedule

FIGURE 6.B
Building a New Home: Critical Path Analysis

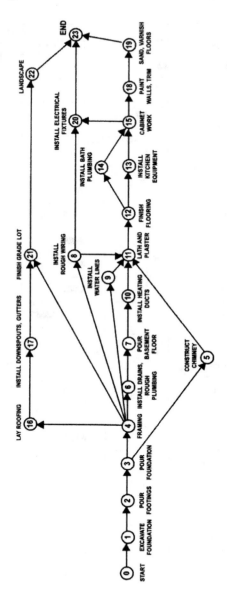

Controlling Costs

Contractors typically have a small permanent payroll that consists of a foreperson and skilled journeypersons. This force can be expanded by union hiring halls, which means that the contractor must be knowledgeable about the union's master labor contract. The work of the various subcontractors must be scheduled and coordinated with the overall job. The small contractor must expect to spend most of the day at the site, coordinating these activities and resolving conflicts. Subcontractors should be chosen on the basis of their ability to perform, as well as cost, since untimely delays quickly eliminate the potential savings of the lowest bid.

Purchasing is an essential part of the job because of the high cost of carrying materials inventory. As with subcontractors, reliability is equally important as price. The contractor will typically develop trade relations with a limited number of suppliers. Costs are best controlled by checking with other suppliers if prices increase significantly, by verifying order quantities, by taking cash discounts when offered, and by not overstocking.

Risk Management

Businesses operate under conditions of uncertainty. Profits are the price charged to bear risk. Unexpected property and casualty losses can severely damage the business' prospects. Insurance is a means of reducing the company's exposure to risk. The contractor should consult an insurance agent or broker to design a comprehensive insurance package to meet the company's specific needs. This package could include:

- fire insurance,
- liability insurance,
- automobile insurance,
- workers' compensation insurance,
- fidelity bonds,
- business interruption insurance,
- employee health and life insurance, and
- "key person" insurance.

Insurance costs can be minimized by obtaining a number of quotes for new or renewal policies or by enrolling in special plans offered by trade associations.

Section III

If the contractor lacks sufficient funds for total coverage, a planned approach to risk management becomes necessary. The principles that should be followed include:

- The largest loss exposure should be covered first. Property and liability insurance should be reviewed yearly to reflect changes in valuation and to reflect current court judgments.

- The use of deductibles will significantly reduce costs.

- Coverage should be reviewed yearly to reflect changes in the business.

- Take time to understand the implications of any changes in the insurer's contracts.

Marketing Management

Personal contacts represent the major source of business for the new contractor. Small and medium-sized contracting businesses rely on referrals. The extent of the marketing effort is limited by the sources available to the contractor.

The development of a formal marketing program is helpful to the contractor to ensure that continued effort and attention is placed in this vital area. Inattention to the marketing program could weaken the entire effort of the company, regardless of how strong the other areas may be.

LEGAL CONSIDERATIONS AND REMEDIES

A continuing relationship with an attorney familiar with the construction business is helpful. Printed standard forms of agreements used in the industry are available from the contractor's particular trade association, The American Institute of Architects, or the Associated General Contractors of America. It is a good idea to have the attorney double-check the contract for compliance with all regulatory agency requirements.

Lawyers are often located through friends, other contractors, suppliers, trade associations, or through listings in telephone directories. Local bar associations can arrange a meeting between a contractor and a practicing attorney in the area. In addition to helping with the interpretation of contracts, the attorney can help in choosing the form of business organization; making sure all necessary documents are filed with city, county, and state governments; and helping resolve any differences that might occur between the contractor and other business parties.

There are typically four types of contractual agreements between the builder and owner with which the contractor should be familiar. These are the lump-sum, the cost-plus, the unit-price, and the guaranteed-maximum cost contract. Each of these contract types specifies different terms and obligations with which the contractor must be familiar.

In addition, the contractor has to be aware of the proper filing methods, the number of days for filing, and other documents such as lien release notices, lien claims, and notices of completion. It is essential for the contractor to be familiar with the California Mechanic's Lien Law.

Disputes

A good manager will minimize the likelihood of a dispute; and, if involved in one, a good manager will have enhanced his or her chances of success.

At the outset, you should be aware that there is no good lawsuit. Everyone is a loser. You will never be fully compensated for your out-of-pocket expenses, much less for the physical, emotional, and business disruption that a lawsuit can create. Therefore, you should do everything within reason to settle your differences. This can be done in a number of ways:

Get It in Writing

Besides the statutory requirement that certain contracts be in writing, it is extremely important that a contract of any significance at all be in writing. First, a written document will not be forgotten like a verbal agreement and is more likely to keep the parties aware of their rights and responsibilities.

Second, if there is a dispute and an arbitrator or judge is asked to interpret the agreement, he or she is more likely to find in accordance with your true intent if that intent is in writing.

Extras

"Changes" or "extras" added to a contract tend to contribute to disputes. To determine if something is an extra or outside the scope of the original agreement, you must be able to accurately determine what the original agreement states. If the original agreement is well defined and in writing, it will be much easier to determine if something is an extra.

Once you determine that a request is different than what has been agreed upon (whether more or less), document that fact in writing. You should also immediately negotiate the effect of the change such as cost and time. Tell your customer what is going on and allow the customer to determine if the change is worth it. If you and your customer agreed to the change, make sure both parties sign the written change order.

Communication

Whenever possible you should communicate with your customer and encourage your customer to communicate with you. Frequent "punch lists" are a good idea. A walk-through near the end of the job to determine the items that are left to be completed is recommended. Correct any deficiencies quickly.

It is a good idea to document the progress of the project and keep your customer up-to-date.

Closely allied with the communication of progress is frequent billing. By invoicing regularly you will minimize your business's cash demands while keeping your customer informed. Let your customer know what is going on; and, if there is a problem, face it head on before it becomes insurmountable.

Even if you have done everything you could, you may still find yourself involved in a dispute. You have various options:

Settlement

Lawsuits are costly, time-consuming, and disruptive. If at all possible, you should attempt to settle your differences. Fighting for principles may be less rewarding than you would anticipate.

Small Claims

If you are owed money and cannot settle your dispute, you might consider filing suit in small claims court rather than courts of greater jurisdiction. Although you cannot foreclose on a mechanic's lien in small claims court, you may get a monetary judgment of up to $7,500. Aside from the fact that if a defendant loses, he or she has an automatic right of appeal, small claims judgments are as valid and binding as courts of greater jurisdiction.

Small claims courts are fast and economical. Your claim can usually be heard within one month and the entire cost should be minimal. You and your customer must represent yourselves. Neither you nor your customer may be represented by an attorney. For information about small claims court topics, such as filing a complaint and collecting a judgment, see the California Court website: http://www.courtinfo.ca.gov/selfhelp/smallclaims. If the defendant loses in small claims court, there is an automatic right of appeal. But even that appeal is usually within a month or two. You will not have to wait for long.

Arbitration

Another option for settling disputes is arbitration. CSLB has its own arbitration program, but many contractors choose to bring their disputes to private arbitrators.

The advantage of arbitration lies in its relative speed and its low cost in comparison to court proceedings.

Arbitration is different from court proceedings in a number of ways. Usually both parties must agree to arbitration and can often have a say in choosing the arbitrator. Both parties often choose an arbitrator who has some familiarity with construction. This is one of the reasons arbitration can be cost-effective.

Either side may present its own case or use an attorney.

Because of its more informal nature, some of the protections afforded in court, such as the rules of evidence, are not always followed. Arbitrators tend to allow much more evidence than would be allowed in court. Most arbitration decisions are binding (the arbitrator's decision is final). Finally, there are very few grounds for appeal of an arbitration decision.

If you want potential disputes to be solved via *private* arbitration, the arbitration notice in Business and Professions Code section 7191 must be used. However, if the parties to the contract agree to such a notice, they will not be allowed access to CSLB's arbitration program (unless both parties later sign a waiver of the contractual arbitration clause).

CSLB Arbitration Program

To help resolve complaints filed with the board, CSLB offers two free arbitration programs—a mandatory program for disputes involving alleged damages of less than $12,500 and a voluntary program for disputes involving alleged damages of between $12,500 and $50,000. When the alleged damages are less than $12,500, CSLB has the power to order the contractor to CSLB arbitration.

Section III

In order to qualify for CSLB arbitration, disputes must comply with certain criteria:

- the contractor's license must be in good standing at the time of the alleged violation;

- the contractor cannot have a record of prior violations; and

- the parties cannot have previously agreed to private arbitration in the contract or elsewhere.

Mechanic's Liens

Mechanic's liens and "stop notices" are briefly touched upon in this portion of the book; these two avenues are discussed at great detail in the next portion. However, you should note that, as a contractor (one who enhances the value of property), you are entitled to a lien on the property and may be entitled to a lien on any construction funds. The manner in which these liens are perfected is very technical and the time limits are short. You should be thoroughly familiar with the manner and means of perfecting your lien rights, such as giving the preliminary notice, recording the mechanic's lien, filing a stop notice, and filing suit to foreclose. These remedies are rather speedy and can be utilized by anyone who improves the property.

Filing Suit

Regardless of your mechanic's lien rights, as any other businessperson, you are entitled to file suit for breach of the construction contract if someone does not fulfill his or her obligation. Certainly, if the customer does not pay you money when it is due, you are entitled to file suit. In the event that you have been unsuccessful in resolving the dispute and have not availed yourself of the mechanic's lien rights due to your failure to comply with the strict statutory requirements, you can still file suit as any other businessperson. The seller of any product or service is entitled to his or her compensation. You, as a contractor, are also entitled to your money.

If you are a corporation, you cannot represent yourself in court and must obtain the services of an attorney. In the event that you are a partnership or a sole proprietor, you can represent yourself in court and are not required to have an attorney represent you. It is, however, a good idea to have an attorney represent you in court due to the technical requirements of the court procedure.

Summary

You are normally much better off staying out of disputes. You can greatly minimize the likelihood of a dispute by documenting your agreements, meeting problems head-on, seeking solutions, negotiating and documenting changes as they occur, communicating with your customer, and invoicing regularly.

If you find yourself in a dispute, make reasonable efforts to settle it. If you can't, you may choose between small claims court, arbitration, or civil litigation.

CALIFORNIA MECHANIC'S LIENS AND STOP NOTICES

Mechanic's Liens

In the State of California, mechanic's liens are provided for in the California Constitution. Article 14, Section 3 of the California Constitution provides:

> "Mechanics, persons furnishing materials, artisans, and laborers of every class, shall have a lien upon the property upon which they have bestowed labor or furnished materials for the value of such labor done and materials furnished; and the Legislature shall provide, by law, for the speedy and efficient enforcement of such liens."

The manner in which mechanic's lien rights are perfected is based on statutes. The California Supreme Court has held that mechanic's lien rights are constitutional.

The list of people who may claim liens as provided by the Constitution, as well as the California Civil Code, is as follows: mechanics; persons furnishing materials; contractors; subcontractors; lessors of equipment; artisans; architects; registered engineers; licensed land surveyors; machinists; builders; teamsters; draymen; and all persons and laborers performing labor on or bestowing skill or other necessary services to, furnishing material or leasing equipment to be used or consumed in, or furnishing appliances, teams, or power contributing to a work of improvement. This does not mean that these people must have a contract directly with the owner. However, they must have a contract with the agent of the owner and every contractor, subcontractor, architect, builder, or other person having charge of a work of improvement is held to be the agent of the owner.

A material supplier is not the agent of the owner; and, therefore, a material supplier's supplier is not entitled to a statutory lien. Further, in order to be able to perfect your lien, the work and/or materials, etc. must be incorporated into the structure. That is to say that it has to be installed.

Section III

Stop Notices

A mechanic's lien is a lien on property. A stop notice is a lien on funds. You may use one or the other, or both. However, it should be noted that in public works, you cannot file a mechanic's lien; and, therefore, your only remedy may be a stop notice. Since the stop notice is a lien on funds, it may be preferable to a mechanic's lien in some instances.

Other Remedies

Even though you may be one of the people protected by the mechanic's lien laws of the State of California, you are not precluded from other remedies. You can still sue on a contract theory or on any other legal theory available. So, even if you have not availed yourself of the mechanic's lien rights, you still have alternative legal remedies.

Procedure

The mechanic's lien laws and stop notice requirements are relatively complicated and must be adhered to very strictly. Listed below is a procedural checklist that you may use to formulate an office procedure to help you complete each step necessary in a timely manner. It is best to become thoroughly familiar with the process and discuss it with your attorney before establishing your office procedure and training staff on these steps.

Mechanic's Lien and Stop Notice Checklist

I. Prior to Serving the Notices

Before serving the notices, it is important to do all of the following:

    A. Obtain the legal description of the property;

    B. Determine the name of the owner and the extent of the owner's interest in the property;

    C. Determine whether the owner is the one who is requesting the improvement. (If not, what is the interest of the person requesting it and are there any others who claim an interest in the property, such as lenders, etc.);

    D. Determine whether you are a prime contractor, subcontractor, laborer, or material supplier;

    E. Determine the name of the construction lender (if any); and

    F. Consider the effect of a bond or joint control.

II. Subcontractors and Material Suppliers

A. Within twenty days (20) from first furnishing labor or materials, serve a "Preliminary 20-day Notice" on the owner, the original contractor, and construction lender. No matter how many deliveries you make, or the time span over which you furnish labor or materials, only one Preliminary Notice is required.

Changes to the text of the Preliminary Notice became effective on January 1, 2004. Under the new notice, you must use specific wording to inform a property owner of a new responsibility to notify anyone who served a Preliminary Notice. (*See Civil Code §3097 Title 15, Works of Improvement,* in the Appendix.)

NOTE: You may also file the Preliminary 20-day Notice with the County Recorder in the county in which the property is located. The County Recorder will then notify you when a Notice of Completion or Notice of Cessation is recorded on the property.

The most common method for serving a notice is to use first class certified or registered mail, return receipt requested, postage prepaid, addressed to the residence or place of business of the person being served, or at the address shown by the building permit, or at an address contained on a recorded mortgage or trust deed. Be sure to keep post office receipts for later use if you need to file a claim and prove it in court. A Preliminary Notice also may be served by personal delivery or by leaving it with a "person in charge" at the residence or place of business of the person you wish to serve (must be an adult).

B. After the work is completed or ceases, the following apply:

1. If the owner records a Notice of Completion after completion of work of improvement (this requires signature of owner or owner's agent), you should not do additional work under the contract. (While this Notice provision is designed to primarily protect the owner, it might serve to increase the funds accessible to satisfy your claim and indicate that you have performed your contractual obligations.)

2. Labor must have ceased for at least 30 days before the owner is entitled to record a Notice of Cessation. If the owner files a Notice of Cessation of labor or a Notice of Completion, then:

Section III

(a) Within 30 days of the owner recording either a Notice of Cessation or Completion, the subcontractor must record a Claim of Lien with County Recorder. Also at this time, serve stop notices (see below).

Note: A new law, effective January 1, 2004, requires an owner who files a Notice of Cessation or a Notice of Completion to notify any potential lien claimants within 10 days of recording the notices. This notification is designed to let you, the potential lien claimant, know that the time for filing a Claim of Lien has been reduced. This provision does not apply to a residential property of four or fewer units.

(b) File Lien Foreclosure Action within 90 days of recording a Claim of Lien, and record a *Lis Pendens* at the same time. You must also file an action on the stop notice at this time, if applicable. If you want more than 90 days in which to foreclose, then after recording the lien, but before 90 days elapses, give credit to the owner and record a notice of the fact and terms of credit. Within 90 days after your offer expires, you must foreclose. You can keep granting extensions by the above procedure, but you must foreclose within one (1) year after work is completed. The action should be brought to trial within two (2) years after commencement.

3. If no Notice of Completion or Notice of Cessation is recorded and either:

(a) Labor ceases and the owner or agent uses work of improvement, or

(b) The owner or agent accepts improvement, then:

(1) Within 90 days of any of the above acts, record a Claim of Lien. Also at this time, serve stop notices. (See below.)

(2) Within 90 days of recording the lien, file a Lien Foreclosure Action and record a *Lis Pendens* at the same time. If you want to extend the time in which to file a foreclosure action, after you record the Claim of Lien, but before 90 days elapse, give credit to the owner and record a notice of the fact and terms of credit. The extension will be for 90 days after the credit expires, but even with extensions you must foreclose within one (1) year after the

work is completed. The action should be brought to trial within two (2) years after commencement.

4. Stop Notices:

   (a) Serve stop notices on the owner, bonded stop notice on the construction lender, or anyone holding funds.

   (b) If no mechanic's lien has been recorded, and a surety payment bond has been recorded, then the notice must be served on the surety.

   (c) File suit on the notice at the same time that you file a Lien Foreclosure Action.

III. Prime Contractors

A. Within 10 days after completion, you may record a Notice of Completion. (While this notice provision is designed to primarily protect the owner, it might serve to increase the funds accessible to satisfy your claim and indicate that you have performed your contractual obligations.) Do not do additional work under the contract. This notice requires the signature of the owner or the owner's agent.

B. Within 60 days of recording the above, record the Claim of Lien.

C. Within 90 days of recording the lien, file a Lien Foreclosure Action and record a *Lis Pendens* at the same time. If you want to extend the time in which to file a foreclosure action, after you record the Claim of Lien, but before 90 days elapse, give credit to the owner and record a notice of the fact and terms of credit. The extension will be for 90 days after the credit expires, but even with extensions you must foreclose within one (1) year after the work is completed. The action should be brought to trial within two (2) years after commencement.

D. If the owner records a Notice of Cessation of Labor or a Notice of Completion, do the following:

NOTE: Labor must have ceased for at least 30 days before the owner is entitled to record the Notice of Cessation.

   1. Within 60 days of recording of a Notice of Cessation or a Notice of Completion, the contractor must record a Claim of Lien.

   2. Within 90 days of recording the Claim of Lien, file a Lien Foreclosure Action, and record a *Lis Pendens*. If you want

more than 90 days in which to foreclose, then after recording the lien, but before the first 90 days elapse, give credit to the owner and record a notice of fact and terms of credit. Within 90 days after your "offer" expires, you must foreclose. You can keep granting extensions by the above procedure, but you must foreclose within one (1) year after work is completed. The action should be brought to trial two (2) years after commencement.

E. If no Notice of Completion or Cessation is recorded, and either;

    1. Labor ceases and owner or agent uses the work of improvement or

    2. Owner or agent accepts improvement, then:

        (a) Within 90 days of any of the above acts, record a Claim of Lien.

        (b) File Lien Foreclosure Action within 90 days of recording Claim of Lien and record a *Lis Pendens* at the same time. If you want more than 90 days in which to foreclose, then after recording the lien, but before the first 90 days elapse, give credit to the owner and record a notice of the fact and terms of credit. Within 90 days after your offer expires, you must foreclose. You can keep granting extensions by the above procedure, but you must foreclose within one (1) year after work is completed. The action should be brought to trial within two (2) years after commencement.

NOTE: Per AB 457, passed in 2009, effective January 1, 2011, the definitions of "claim of lien" and "mechanic's lien" are the same. This law also requires that a Notice of Mechanic's Lien be served on the owner or person believed to be the owner of the property or on the construction lender or original contractor, <u>and</u> that a "proof of service affidavit" to the above mentioned party or parties be completed and signed by the person serving the Notice of Mechanic's Lien. Failure to serve the mechanic's lien and confirm a proof of service affidavit will cause the mechanic's lien to be unenforceable. These requirements are detailed at the following link: <u>http://www.leginfo.ca.gov/pub/09-10/bill/asm/ab_0451-0500/ab_457_bill_20090806_chaptered.html</u>

FIGURE 6.C

Mechanic's Lien and Stop Notice Process

(See also the Mechanic's Lien and Stop Notice Checklist, page 114)

(See also the Mechanic's Lien and Stop Notice Checklist, page 114)

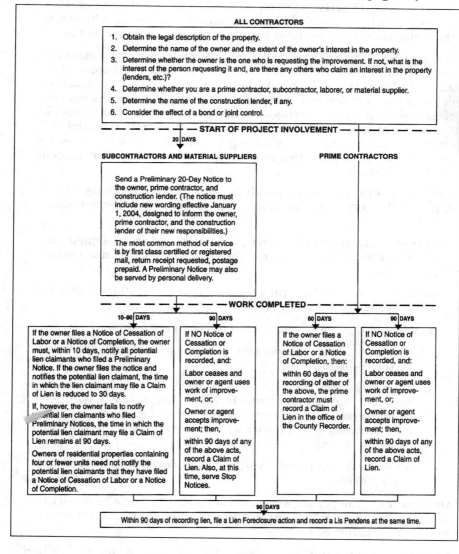

ALL CONTRACTORS

1. Obtain the legal description of the property.
2. Determine the name of the owner and the extent of the owner's interest in the property.
3. Determine whether the owner is the one who is requesting the improvement. If not, what is the interest of the person requesting it and, are there any others who claim an interest in the property (lenders, etc.)?
4. Determine whether you are a prime contractor, subcontractor, laborer, or material supplier.
5. Determine the name of the construction lender, if any.
6. Consider the effect of a bond or joint control.

— — — — — — — **START OF PROJECT INVOLVEMENT** — — — — — — —

20 DAYS

SUBCONTRACTORS AND MATERIAL SUPPLIERS   **PRIME CONTRACTORS**

Send a Preliminary 20-Day Notice to the owner, prime contractor, and construction lender. (The notice must include new wording effective January 1, 2004, designed to inform the owner, prime contractor, and the construction lender of their new responsibilities.)

The most common method of service is by first class certified or registered mail, return receipt requested, postage prepaid. A Preliminary Notice may also be served by personal delivery.

— — — — — — **WORK COMPLETED** — — — — — —

10–90 DAYS   **90 DAYS**   **60 DAYS**   **90 DAYS**

| If the owner files a Notice of Cessation of Labor or a Notice of Completion, the owner must, within 10 days, notify all potential lien claimants who filed a Preliminary Notice. If the owner files the notice and notifies the potential lien claimant, the time in which the lien claimant may file a Claim of Lien is reduced to 30 days.

 If, however, the owner fails to notify potential lien claimants who filed Preliminary Notices, the time in which the potential lien claimant may file a Claim of Lien remains at 90 days.

 Owners of residential properties containing four or fewer units need not notify the potential lien claimants that they have filed a Notice of Cessation of Labor or a Notice of Completion. | If NO Notice of Cessation or Completion is recorded, and:

 Labor ceases and owner or agent uses work of improvement, or;

 Owner or agent accepts improvement; then,

 within 90 days of any of the above acts, record a Claim of Lien. Also, at this time, serve Stop Notices. | If the owner files a Notice of Cessation of Labor or a Notice of Completion, then:

 within 60 days of the recording of either of the above, the prime contractor must record a Claim of Lien in the office of the County Recorder. | If NO Notice of Cessation or Completion is recorded, and:

 Labor ceases and owner or agent uses work of improvement, or;

 Owner or agent accepts improvement; then,

 within 90 days of any of the above acts, record a Claim of Lien. |

90 DAYS

Within 90 days of recording lien, file a Lien Foreclosure action and record a Lis Pendens at the same time.

Section III

GLOSSARY OF TERMS
ASSOCIATED WITH MECHANIC'S LIENS

Awarding Authority is the owner or the agent of the owner who awards an original building or construction contract, also known as the prime contract. This term is usually used with public works.

Bonded Stop Notice is a bond that accompanies a stop notice to a construction lender and must be in a sum equal to 1-1/4 times the amount of the claim. The bond, along with the stop notice, must be delivered by certified or registered mail or in person, to the persons responsible for administering or holding construction funds. Should the claimant lose his/her action (lawsuit on the bond), then the claimant must pay all costs that may be awarded against the owner or contractor or construction lenders. This is the reason for the bond on the stop notice.

Claimant is the person who is claiming or asserting the right or demand (the person who is claiming mechanic's lien or stop notice rights).

Claim of Lien (mechanic's lien) is a written statement signed and verified by the claimant or by the claimant's agent that must state the following:

(a) the amount of claimant's demand (after deducting credits and offsets);

(b) the name of the owner or reputed owner, if known;

(c) the kind of labor, services, equipment, or materials furnished by the claimant;

(d) the name of the person by whom the claimant was employed or to whom the claimant furnished the labor, services, equipment, or materials (the contractor who hired you if you are a subcontractor or the owner who hired you if you are the prime contractor); and,

(e) a description of the site sufficient for identification (*See Civil Code §3084*).

Defendant is the person who defends him/herself or who denies a claim. A defendant is the person against whom relief or recovery is sought in an action or suit.

Lien Foreclosure Action is a lawsuit to foreclose the mechanic's lien.

Lis Pendens is a notice that a lawsuit is pending and that the lawsuit affects real property. It warns everyone who might acquire the property that he or she may be bound by an adverse judgment (*See Civil Code §3146*).

Notice of Cessation is a written notice, signed and verified by the owner or his/her agent, stating:

(a) the approximate date when labor on the job stopped;

(b) that no further labor has been performed since the recording of this notice;

(c) the name and address of the owner;

(d) the nature of the interest or estate of the owner;

(e) the street address of the site, if any, or a description of the site sufficient for identification; and

(f) the name of the original contractor, if any, for the work of improvement.

The Notice of Cessation must be recorded in the Office of the County Recorder of the county in which the site is located and will be effective only if labor has ceased continuously for at least 30 days prior to the recording (*See Civil Code §3092*).

Notice of Completion is a written notice, signed and verified by the owner or his/her agent, stating:

(a) the date that the job is finished;

(b) the name and address of the owner;

(c) the nature of the interest or estate of the owner;

(d) the street address of the site, if any, or a description of the site sufficient for identification; and

(e) the name of the original contractor, if any, for the contract covering the portion of the work of improvement completed.

The Notice of Completion must be recorded in the Office of the County Recorder of the county in which the site is located within ten days after completion of the project (*See Civil Code §3093*). If the Notice of Completion is recorded, then the time within which you have to record your mechanic's lien is 60 days if you are a prime contractor and 30 days if you are a subcontractor. If this notice is not filed in a timely manner, you have a 90-day period within which to record the claim.

Notice of Non-Responsibility is a written notice, as described below, which is signed and verified by a person or that person's agent who owns or claims to have an interest in the property that is being

Section III

improved and who has not caused the work of improvement. For example, the owner completes this notice when his/her tenant is requiring the work of improvement without the owner's direction. This notice must contain:

(a) a description of the site sufficient for identification,

(b) the name and nature of the title or interest of the person giving the notice,

(c) the name of the purchaser or person holding the lease (lessee), if known, and

(d) a statement by the person giving the notice that he/ she will NOT be responsible for any claims arising from the work of improvement.

Within 10 days of discovering the work of improvement, the person asserting non-responsibility must POST this notice in a conspicuous place on the site AND must RECORD the notice in the Office of the County Recorder of the county in which the site is located (*See Civil Code §3094*).

Original Contractor, also known as prime contractor, is usually a general contractor.

Owner includes any person(s) having some title or interest in a parcel of real property.

Payment Bond is a bond that is usually procured by the owner or contractor that is in an amount sufficient to pay all claims of claimants. The bond gives the claimant the right to recover in any suit brought on the bond. Usually the bond is used to protect against mechanic's liens and substitutes the bond as security instead of the real property.

Prime Contractor See "Original Contractor" above.

Stop Notice is a written notice, signed and verified by the claimant or the claimant's agent, that puts a lender or anyone else holding construction funds on notice that there is money due and owing to the claimant. It must state the following:

(a) the kind of labor, services, equipment, or materials furnished or agreed to be furnished by the claimant;

(b) the name of the person to or for whom the labor, services, etc. were furnished; and

(c) the amount, based on value as near as possible, of the work or equipment already completed or furnished and the amount of the whole work agreed to be done or furnished.

If involving a private work of improvement, the notice must be delivered to the owner personally or left at his/her residence or place of business with a person in charge or delivered to his/her architect, if any; and, if the notice is served upon a construction lender holding construction funds and maintaining branch offices, it must be delivered to the manager or other responsible person at the office or branch administering or holding the construction funds.

If involving any public work for the state, the notice must be filed with the director of the department that let the contract.

If involving any other public work, the notice must be filed in the office of the controller, auditor, or other public disbursing officer whose duty it is to make payments under the provisions of the contract or with the commissioners, managers, trustees, officers, board of supervisors, board of trustees, common council, or other body by whom the contract was awarded.

Any stop notice may be served by registered or certified mail with the same effect as personal service (*See Civil Code §3103*).

The stop notice obligates the person holding construction funds to withhold sufficient funds to satisfy the amount in the stop notice. If the person holding the funds does not withhold sufficient funds to satisfy the stop notice, then the lender or whoever else is holding the funds may be responsible to the claimant directly.

In order to bind a construction lender, the stop notice must be bonded. The bond that accompanies a stop notice to any construction lender must be in the sum equal to one and one-quarter (1-1/4) times the amount of the claim. The bond must be delivered along with the stop notice in person or by certified or registered mail to the persons responsible for administering or holding the construction funds.

Should the claimant lose in his/her action (lawsuit on the bond), then the claimant must pay all costs that may be awarded against the owner or contractor or construction lender. That is the reason for the bond on the stop notice (*See Civil Code §3083*).

Subcontractor is any person who does not have a contract directly with an owner. The subcontractor has a contract with and from the prime contractor or another subcontractor. A subcontractor is usually a specialty contractor, but can also be a general contractor.

EXPERT ADVISORS

The new contractor must be prepared to seek out and utilize the expertise of specialists in business affairs, just as the contractor has come to rely upon skilled specialists in the building trades. If the business is to be organized as a partnership or corporation, an attorney, preferably one who specializes in drawing up partnership agreements or incorporation papers, should be consulted. The local bar association should be able to provide recommendations.

The accounting records should be prepared by a certified public accountant (CPA) whose practice specializes in building trade industry clients, if at all possible. The CPA or tax lawyer should be consulted for specialized tax problems.

The U.S. Small Business Administration (SBA) along with its resource partners, Service Corps of Retired Executives (SCORE), Small Business Development Centers (SBDC), and Small Business Information Centers (BIC), offer a wide variety of services to individuals wanting to start or grow their business. Services include one-on-one counseling, workshops, training, business seminars, and SBA's guaranteed loan programs designed to help with your business financing needs. Contact them at:

U.S. Small Business Administration
(800) U ASK SBA (827-5722)
www.sba.gov
Email: answerdesk@sba.gov

BIDDING ON GOVERNMENT CONTRACTS

Contractors bidding in California should know that there are a variety of federal, state, and local governmental agencies, as well as public utilities and private corporations, which may require a bidder to take specific steps to achieve established minority, women, and disabled veteran business enterprise (DVBE) goals. For information on fulfilling these goals on bids for certain government contracts, check with the following agencies:

California Department of General Services,
Procurement Division
Office of Small Business and DVBE Certification (OSDC)
707 Third Street, 1st Floor, Room 400
West Sacramento, CA 95605

Phone: (916) 375-4940
Fax: (916) 375-4950
www.pd.dgs.ca.gov/smbus/default.htm

The U.S. Department of Commerce Minority Business Development Agency provides direct business development services to minority businesses through a network of Minority Business Development Centers (MBDCs) located in most major cities throughout the country. Services may include identification of contracting opportunities, preparation of bid proposals, identification of lending sources, preparation of loan applications, etc.

As per Presidential Executive Order 11625, the following ethnic groups are among those eligible for assistance from MBDA funded organizations: African Americans, Puerto Ricans, Spanish-speaking Americans, Native Americans, Eskimos, Aleuts, Hasidic Jews, Asian-Pacific Islanders, and Asian Indians.

U.S. Department of Commerce
Minority Business Development Agency
221 Main Street, Suite 1280
San Francisco, CA 94105

Phone: (415) 744-3001
Fax: (415) 744-3061
www.mbda.gov

Section III

SECTION IV.

CONSTRUCTION STANDARDS AND SAFETY REGULATIONS

Chapter 7.

Safety and Health in Construction

According to the California Division of Labor Statistics and Research, the construction industry has one of the highest occupational injury rates of any major industry in the state. A substantial portion of these injuries could be prevented if employers complied with occupational safety and health standards.

The following is a description of many of the general safety and health requirements and practices that affect contractors in California. In addition, there are many safety and health requirements that apply to specific construction trades and activities.

It is your responsibility to be informed about the local, state, and federal laws and regulations which affect your business, as well as which regulatory agencies have or share jurisdiction in your area.

RESPONSIBLE AGENCIES

Regulatory and advisory roles pertaining to construction safety and health in California are performed by several state agencies. The following agencies are those with whom contractors and their employees are most likely to be involved.

California Department of Industrial Relations, Division of Occupational Safety and Health (DOSH)

DOSH, within the Department of Industrial Relations, is given the authority to implement and enforce the Cal/OSHA program according to the provisions of California Labor Law. The Cal/OSHA program is approved, monitored, and partially funded by Federal OSHA in accordance with the Federal Occupational Safety and Health Act

Section IV

(OSHA) of 1970. To ensure that working conditions are safe and healthful and that employers meet their obligations to provide such conditions, the DOSH Enforcement Unit enforces the occupational safety and health regulations, responds to employees' complaints, makes routine inspections of workplaces, and investigates serious and fatal job-related injuries and illnesses.

DOSH works to ensure safe and healthful working conditions for California employees through standards enforcement, consultation service to employers, occupational safety and health research, and by providing information and publications.

Cal/OSHA Consultation Service

The Cal/OSHA Consultation Service provides free on-site consultation. Its goal is to help employers develop solutions to their occupational safety and health problems so that they can voluntarily comply with safety and health standards. The Consultation Service staff identifies workplace hazards and helps employers develop and improve the company's Injury and Illness Prevention Program (IIPP), as per Title 8 California Code of Regulations (*T8 CCR §3203*).

When the Consultation Service staff visits a jobsite and reviews the contractor's IIPP, they not only identify occupational hazards, but also point out areas where the safety orders require specific actions and recommend ways to achieve compliance.

In contrast to DOSH Enforcement, the Consultation Service staff does not issue citations or penalties. Instead, they give the contractor a report that outlines the conditions found and describe the need for corrective action.

Occupational Safety and Health Standards Board

The Occupational Safety and Health Standards Board adopts, amends, or repeals California safety and health standards. (State standards must be at least as strict as the federal OSHA standards.) The Standards Board also has the authority to grant petitions to adopt or amend regulations, and to grant variances to employers. Anyone may participate in standards development by participating at the Standards Board's public hearings or as members of advisory committees.

To keep current on any proposed or new construction safety orders, such as washing facilities at construction job sites (*T8 CCR §1527*) and fall protection for residential type framing activities (*T8 CCR §1716.2*), visit the website at http://www.dir.ca.gov/OSHSB.

Occupational Safety and Health Appeals Board

The Occupational Safety and Health Appeals Board hears and makes decisions on appeals concerning citations, orders, civil penalties, and abatement dates issued by DOSH Enforcement. Employers, employees, and employee representatives may participate in proceedings of the Appeals Board.

Other Agencies Share Responsibility

The following agencies share additional responsibilities in the area of hazardous substances: California Department of Public Health; Department of Toxic Substances Control; California Environmental Protection Agency; State Allocation Board, Office of Public School Construction; California Department of Resources Recycling and Recovery; Department of Fish and Game; California Highway Patrol; California Department of Forestry and Fire Protection; U.S. Environmental Protection Agency; and regional air emissions control boards.

NOTE: The Contractors State License Board may also take action against a contractor who has violated regulations under the jurisdiction of other agencies.

CONSTRUCTION SAFETY LEGAL REQUIREMENTS

Every employer and employee must comply with all applicable occupational safety and health standards, rules, regulations, and orders. The bulk of the legal requirements governing employer responsibilities and employee rights can be found in the California Labor Code and Title 8 of the California Code of Regulations (CCR). Title 8 regulations that pertain to most construction contractors can be found in the Construction Safety Orders (beginning with Section 1500) and the General Industry Safety Orders (beginning with Section 3200). Title 8 regulations also include many other safety orders that encompass regulations that govern more limited trades and activities, such as the Electrical Safety Orders and Compressed Air Safety Orders. Title 8 includes requirements for permits, safe work practices, operations, and equipment. In some cases, detailed specifications, which apply to construction work, are included.

Many of the employer responsibilities and employee rights are detailed in the Cal/OSHA poster, *Safety and Health Protection on the Job*. **Each construction contractor is required to post at least one copy of this poster and the Code of Safe Practices** at each location where employees report to work each day, or, if the employees do not usually work at or report to a single establishment, the notice shall be posted at the location(s) from which the employees operate to carry out their activities (*Labor Code §6408(a); T8 CCR §340*). The notice must be posted in a conspicuous place where notices to employees are customarily posted.

MULTIPLE EMPLOYER WORK SITES

Construction and non-construction work sites may have multiple employers (*T8 CCR §§336.10-336.11*). When multiple employers are involved, DOSH has developed the following enforcement criteria to categorize employers into four types:

- *Exposing Employer*: the employer whose employees were exposed to the hazard.

- *Creating Employer*: the employer who actually created the hazard.

- *Controlling Employer*: the employer who was responsible, by contract or who has the authority for ensuring that the hazardous condition is corrected.

- *Correcting Employer*: the employer who had the responsibility for actually correcting the hazard.

NOTE: DOSH may cite the Creating, Controlling, or Correcting Employers regardless of whether their own employees were exposed to the hazard.

DOSH may determine whether the available information indicates that the Exposing Employer meets each of the following five (5) criteria for an affirmative defense:

1) The employer did not create the hazard;

2) The employer did not have the responsibility or the authority to have the hazard corrected;

3) The employer did not have the ability to correct or remove the hazard;

4) The employer can demonstrate that the Creating, the Controlling, and/or the Correcting employers, as appropriate, were specifically notified or were aware of the hazards to which the employees were exposed; and

5) The employer took appropriate feasible steps to protect the employees from the hazard; instructed them to recognize the hazard; and, where necessary, informed them of how to avoid dangers associated with it, including removing the employees from the job if the hazard was extreme and there was no other way to protect them from the hazard.

INJURY AND ILLNESS PREVENTION PROGRAM (IIPP)

Accidents are costly. These costs may include:

- Productive time lost by the injured employee;

- Productive time lost by employees and supervisors attending to the accident victim;

- Clean-up and start-up of operations interrupted by the accident;

- Time to hire or to retrain other individuals to replace the injured employee until his or her return;

- Time and costs for repair or replacement of any damaged equipment or materials;

- Costs of continuing all or part of the employee's wages, in addition to compensation;

- Reduced morale among employees, and perhaps lower efficiency;

- Increased workers' compensation insurance rates;

- Costs of completing paperwork generated by the incident; and

- Costs of legal representation in civil and criminal cases.

In California, every employer is required to provide a safe and healthful workplace for his or her employees by doing everything reasonably necessary to protect their lives, safety, and health (*Labor Code §§6400, 6401, 6401.7, 6402, and 6403*). The key to accomplishing this goal of maintaining a safe and healthful workplace is the requirement that every employer have and maintain an effective IIPP. Senate Bill 198 placed strict guidelines for such a program into law in 1989. The regulations required by that law, and other related laws, can be found in *T8 CCR §§1509, 1510, 1511, 1512, 1514, and 3203*. Professional consultants from the Cal/OSHA Consultation Service are available to provide free assistance to employers and employees on how to set up an effective IIPP at your job site. These consultants can also provide safety and health training to your employees at your job site.

Required IIPP Elements

Your IIPP must be a WRITTEN PLAN that includes procedures and is PUT INTO PRACTICE and DOCUMENTED. Some of the requirements are:

- **Management commitment to safety and health**

    This commitment should be evident from strong organizational policies, procedures, incentives, and disciplinary actions necessary to ensure employee compliance with safe and healthful work practices. Management commitment is also demonstrated by the allocation of company resources—financial, material, and personnel —for identifying and controlling hazards, purchasing protective equipment, and training employees in safety and health.

- **Identify the person(s) with program implementation authority and responsibility**

- **System for communicating with employees**

  Communicate with employees in a form that is readily understandable by all affected employees—on matters relating to occupational safety and health. Employees should be encouraged to report unsafe conditions—with the assurance that management will take action to correct the problem and that the employee need not fear reprisal for reporting the problem.

  o As part of this communication system, every construction contractor must adopt a written Code of Safe Practices. The contents must include language equivalent to the applicable general statements included in Plate A-3 of the appendix to the Construction Safety Orders in Title 8. In addition, each employer should include other safety guidelines that fit the operations more exactly. The Code of Safe Practices must be posted at a conspicuous location at each job site office or be provided to each supervisory employee, who shall have it readily available.

- **System for identifying, evaluating and controlling existing or potential workplace hazards**

  o No employee shall be required or knowingly permitted to work in an unsafe place, unless for the purpose of making it safe, and then, only after proper precautions have been taken to protect the employee while doing such work.

  o Prior to starting work, the employer must survey the job site to determine what hazards may be involved and what safeguards will be necessary to ensure that the work is performed safely.

  o Periodic, scheduled inspections must be conducted to identify unsafe conditions and work practices. The frequency of inspections should be determined by the type and magnitude of the hazards, the proficiency of the employees, how recently any changes in equipment or procedures were introduced, and the history of workplace injuries and illnesses.

o Occupational illnesses and accidents must be investigated. The investigatory procedures must include a written report of each event.

o The employer shall permit only qualified persons to operate equipment and machinery.

o Every employer must provide and require employees to use safety devices. Employers must adopt and require the use of methods and procedures that are reasonably adequate to make the work and workplace safe.

- **Develop, maintain, and document training programs for both supervisors and employees**

Every employer program should provide information about general safe work practices, plus specific instruction with regard to hazards that are unique to a job assignment.

o When employees are first hired, they must be given instructions regarding job hazards, safety precautions, and the employer's Code of Safe Practices.

o Employees given new job assignments must be given training for this work.

o Supervisors must conduct "toolbox" or "tailgate" safety meetings with their crews at least every ten (10) working days.

o Where employees may be subjected to known or new job site hazards, such as flammable liquids, gases, poisons, caustics, harmful plants and animals, toxic materials, confined spaces, etc., they must be instructed in the recognition of the hazard, in the procedures for protecting themselves from injury, and in the first aid procedure in the event of injury. (_NOTE_: _Specific requirements pertaining to exposure to hazardous substances are discussed below._)

o Employees need instruction whenever new protective equipment or different work practices are to be used on existing hazards.

- **Ensure the availability of emergency medical services for employees**

  Every employer must have a suitable number of appropriately trained and available staff to render first aid. A first aid kit must be present at each workplace.

  Keep in mind that safety regulations and codes establish minimum standards. It is up to each contractor to implement a comprehensive safety program that goes above and beyond these safety standards.

EMPLOYEE COMPLAINT RIGHTS AND PROTECTIONS

Employees or their representatives who believe that unsafe or unhealthful conditions exist in their workplace have the right to file a complaint with any DOSH Enforcement Unit office. DOSH Enforcement must investigate good faith complaints of serious violations within three (3) working days of receiving the complaint. Complaints of non-serious violations must be investigated within 14 calendar days (*Labor Code §6309*).

The name of the person making the complaint will be kept confidential by DOSH (*Labor Code §6309*). Employees may not be fired or otherwise punished for filing a good faith complaint with DOSH or for cooperating in any investigation of unsafe working conditions or work practices (*Labor Code §6310*). Employees have a right to refuse to perform work that would violate any Labor Code provision or occupational safety or health regulation, where the violation would create a real and apparent hazard to the employee or other employees. No employee may be laid off or discharged for refusing to perform such work (*Labor Code §6311*).

INJURY AND ILLNESS REPORTING AND RECORDKEEPING REQUIREMENTS

In addition to the documentation of safety inspections and employee training described above, employers must file reports and maintain records of occupational injuries or illnesses. There are specific requirements for the form and content of this information.

Reporting Requirements

- Employers must report immediately by telephone or other immediate contact method to the nearest DOSH district office any work-related fatality or serious injury or illness suffered by an employee. "Immediately" means as soon as practically possible, but not longer than eight (8) hours after the employer knows of, or, with diligent inquiry would have known of, the incident (*T8 CCR §342*). "Serious injury or illness," in general, means any employment-related injury or illness which requires inpatient hospitalization for a period in excess of 24 hours for other than medical observation, or in which an employee suffers a loss of any member of the body or suffers any serious degree of permanent disfigurement (*T8 CCR §330*).

- Employers must file a complete report of every occupational injury or illness that results in absence from work for a full day or shift beyond the date of the injury or illness, or which requires medical treatment beyond first aid (*Labor Code §5401(a); Labor Code § 6409.1; T8 CCR §14001*).

    The report must be made within five (5) days of the incident, using Form 5020, "Employer's Report of Occupational Injury or Illness," which is published by the Department of Industrial Relations, Division of Labor Statistics and Research. In the event an employer has filed a report of injury or illness, and the employee subsequently dies as a result of the reported injury or illness, the employer must file an amended report, which indicates the death. This amended report must be filed within five (5) days after the employer is notified or learns of the death. Self-insured employers shall report directly to the Division. Employers who are insured by a workers' compensation insurance carrier shall file the report with the carrier.

    NOTE: Insured employers are required to file a report with their carriers of EVERY work-related illness or injury (*Labor Code §3760*).

Recordkeeping Requirements

Records of accidents, work-related injuries, illnesses, and property losses serve a valuable purpose. As stated above, occupational illnesses, accidents, and near misses must be investigated. Your standard investigatory procedures must include a written report of each incident. You are also required to maintain records of your scheduled periodic hazard identification inspections and the safety training that your employees and supervisors have received. When you review all of these records together, causes of the injuries and accidents can be identified. You may determine that you need different or additional inspection and/or training practices that will be more likely to prevent similar illnesses or accidents from recurring.

Employers must keep records when injuries or illnesses occur on the Cal/OSHA Form 300, "Log of Work-Related Injuries and Illnesses."

The only exception applies to employers who had no more than ten (10) employees for all shifts combined during any 24-hour period during the previous calendar year. The Cal/OSHA Form 300, "Log of Work-Related Injuries and Illnesses," is the basic document on which work-related employee injuries and illnesses are recorded. Employees, former employees, and their representatives shall have access to the Form 300 log.

For more details on this regulation see Title 8 CCR Sections 14300–14300.48.

PERMITS

Permits must be obtained from the DOSH Enforcement Unit before an employer undertakes the following kinds of work (*T8 CCR §341*):

- Construction of trenches or excavations which are five (5) feet or more deep, into which a person is required to descend;

- Construction of any building, structure, falsework, or scaffolding more than three (3) stories high (A story is 12 feet in height. A tower crane erected on a construction project is considered, for the purposes of these requirements, to be a structure.);

- Demolition of any building, structure, or the dismantling of falsework, or scaffolding more than three (3) stories high or the equivalent height (36 feet); and

- The underground use of diesel engines for work in mines and tunnels.

The contractor should contact the local DOSH Enforcement Unit office to obtain information regarding who must obtain the permit, when the permit must be obtained, the fees charged to obtain the permit, and any additional requirements the employer must comply with before the permit can be granted.

Annual permits may be obtained for the erection and dismantling of scaffolds, falsework, vertical shoring systems, and construction of excavations or trenches (*T8 CCR §341.1*).

The DOSH Enforcement Unit may conduct an investigation or require a safety conference prior to issuance of the permit. Employees or their representatives are to be included in any required pre-job safety conference (*T8 CCR §341.1*).

Permits must be posted at or near each place of employment requiring a permit (*T8 CCR §341.4*).

An employer who is denied a permit by the DOSH Enforcement Unit may appeal that denial to the Director of the Department of Industrial Relations (*T8 CCR §341.2*).

The DOSH Enforcement Unit may at any time, upon a showing of good cause and after notice and an opportunity to be heard, revoke or suspend a permit (*T8 CCR §341.5*). The employer may appeal the revocation or suspension to the Director.

VARIANCES

Permanent Variance

An employer may apply to the Standards Board for a permanent variance from a California occupational safety and health standard, order, or special order, if the employer demonstrates that an equivalent method, device, or process can be used that will provide equal or better safety for employees. Applications are considered at variance hearings conducted by the Standards Board. Rules of procedure are contained in Chapter 3.5 of Title 8 of the California Code of Regulations.

Temporary Variance

DOSH may grant a temporary variance to employers if the employer files a proper application and establishes that (*Labor Code §§6450– 6457*):

- The employer is unable to comply with a standard by its effective date because of unavailability of professional or technical personnel or of materials and equipment needed to come into compliance with the standard or because necessary construction or alteration of facilities cannot be completed by the effective date;

- The employer is taking all available steps to safeguard his or her employees against the hazards covered by the standard; and

- The employer has an effective program for coming into compliance with the standard as quickly as practicable.

A temporary variance of up to one (1) year may be granted only after notice is given to employees and a hearing is held by DOSH. The temporary order may be renewed up to two times, for a maximum of 180 days each time. Anyone adversely affected by the granting or denial of a temporary variance may appeal that action to the Standards Board.

Section IV

INVESTIGATIONS OF UNSAFE CONDITIONS

Employers may be subject to an inspection (without advance notice) in response to one or more of the DOSH criteria: imminent danger, fatality or serious accident, investigations of serious injuries or illness, employee complaint, public complaint, high hazards list, permits, etc. Also, firms in industries with higher-than-average potential risk are scheduled for inspections. During the inspection, employees may be interviewed and photographs may be taken. An employee representative must have an opportunity to accompany the DOSH investigator on worksite inspections (*Labor Code §6314*).

The employer is protected from having to reveal trade secrets as a result of an inspection or subsequent proceedings (*Labor Code §§6322 and 6396*).

When, in the opinion of the DOSH Enforcement officer, a place of employment or piece of equipment is in a dangerous condition, is not properly guarded, or is dangerously placed so as to constitute an imminent hazard to employees, DOSH may prohibit entry into the area or use of the equipment (other than, with DOSH approval, to eliminate the dangerous condition). The DOSH Enforcement officer will attach a conspicuous notice stating the limitations. The notice must remain in place until removed by a DOSH Enforcement officer after the area or equipment is made safe and the required safeguards or safety devices are provided (*Labor Code §6325*).

As a result of the investigation, the employer may receive a citation, notice, special order, information memorandum, or an order to take special action for any alleged violation of standards, rules, orders, or regulations. Violations will be classified as serious, general, or regulatory, and may be designated as repeat or willful. Citations issued will have financial penalty assessments.

Any citation (or copy of a citation) issued for safety and health violations must be posted at or near the place of violation where it is readily observable by affected employees for a period of three (3) working days or until the condition is corrected, whichever is longer (*Labor Code §6318; T8 CCR §332.4*).

The employer may contest any citations, penalties, and abatement (correction) requirements through both formal and informal proceedings (*Labor Code §6319*).

Penalties will be determined, based on the gravity and severity of the violation (*Labor Code §§6319, 6423-6435*).

Penalties may be adjusted, based on:

- The size of the business;

- The good faith of the employer, including timely abatement; and

- The employer's history of previous violations.

Employers who do not have an Injury and Illness Prevention Program shall receive no adjustment for either good faith or a positive history (*Labor Code §6428*).

The law contains other misdemeanor provisions relating to such matters as revealing trade secrets and unauthorized advance notice of an inspection.

If, after inspection or investigation, the DOSH Enforcement Unit issues a citation for a serious violation, it may conduct a reinspection at the end of the period fixed for abatement of the violation (*Labor Code §6320*).

HAZARDOUS SUBSTANCES

Information and Training

All employers who use hazardous substances and whose employees might be exposed under either normal work conditions or reasonably foreseeable emergency conditions resulting from workplace operations (e.g., equipment failure, rupture of containers, failure of control equipment, etc.) must provide their employees with information and training about these substances, the hazards of these substances, and how to handle these substances under normal and emergency conditions.

Manufacturers of these substances must prepare Material Safety Data Sheets (MSDS), and the manufacturers or sellers of these substances must provide the MSDS to anyone who purchases them.

Employers and employees can find out what hazards are associated with particular substances or chemicals in the workplace, the recommended exposure levels, and the precautions to take in using these substances or chemicals by writing to:

HESIS-TRS (Hazard Evaluation System and
Information Service)
850 Marina Bay Parkway
Bldg. P, 3rd Floor
Richmond, CA 94804

www.cdph.ca.gov/programs/hesis/Pages/default.aspx

In your letter or phone contact with HESIS, please include the following information:

- Your name;
- Job title;
- Mailing address;
- Phone number (include area code);
- Chemical name (not just the product name);
- How the chemical is used;
- How any exposure to the chemical occurred; and
- When the exposure occurred.

California residents may also call the following numbers:

HESIS WORKPLACE HAZARD HELPLINE
System (English) ....(866) 282-5516

Free publications on workplace hazards ....(866) 627-1586

Fax ....(510) 620-5743

Employers must notify any employee who has been or is being exposed to toxic substances or harmful physical agents in concentrations at levels exceeding those prescribed by applicable standards, orders, or special orders, and inform any employee so exposed of corrective action being taken (*Labor Code §6408(e)*).

Employers must allow employees to observe monitoring or measuring of exposure to hazards (*Labor Code §6408(c)*).

Employees must have access to their medical records and exposure records to potentially toxic materials or harmful physical agents (*Labor Code §6408(d); T8 CCR §3204*).

Hazardous Substance Removal Work and Remedial Actions

NOTE: The removal of hazardous substances and related remedial actions do not include asbestos-related work, as defined in Labor Code §6501.8, or work related to a hazardous substance spill on a highway (*B&P Code §7058.7*).

As of May 1, 1988, a contractor must have passed an approved hazardous substance removal certification examination before removing hazardous substances or taking related remedial actions (as defined in Chapter 6.8 of Division 20 of the Health and Safety Code) in cases that involve digging into the surface of the earth and removing the material from:

- A site listed pursuant to Section 25356 of the Health and Safety Code;

- A site listed as a hazardous waste site by the Department of Toxic Substances Control; or

- A site listed on the National Priorities List compiled pursuant to the Comprehensive Environmental Response, Compensation, and Liability Act of 1980 (42 U.S.C. Section 9601 et seq.).

The Contractors State License Board may require currently certified licensees to pass additional updated, approved hazardous substance removal certification examinations based on new public or occupational health and safety information. (*B&P Code §7058.7; Labor Code §142.7*).

Contractors must also comply with the "Hazardous Waste Operations and Emergency Response Standards" (*Labor Code §142.7; T8 CCR §5192*). These require:

- Specific work practices;

- The certification of employees and supervisors involved in hazardous substance removal work;

- The designation of a qualified person who shall be responsible for scheduling any air sampling, laboratory calibration of sampling equipment, evaluation of soil or other contaminated materials sampling results, and for conducting any equipment testing and evaluating the results of the tests; and

- Holding a safety and health conference for all hazardous substance removal jobs before the start of actual work. The conference shall include representatives of the owner or contracting agency, the contractor, the employer, employees, and employee representatives. It shall include a discussion of the employer's safety and health program and the means that the employer intends to use in order to provide a safe and healthy place of employment.

Any contractor who engages in hazardous substance work, or any contractor or employer who either knowingly or negligently enters into a contract with another person to do hazardous substance work, when that person is required to be but is not certified pursuant to B&P Code §7058.7, is subject to penalty (*B&P Code §7028.1 and 7118.6*).

Lead in Construction Work

This section applies to all construction work where an employee may be occupationally exposed to lead. Construction work, in general, is defined as work for construction, alteration, and/or repair, including

Section IV

painting and decoration (*T8 CCR §1532.1*). Lead is defined as metallic lead, all inorganic lead compounds, and organic lead soaps.

Employers shall provide a written lead-work pre-job notification to the nearest DOSH District office as per T8 CCR §1532.1 (p)(1) to (p)(4) when work is planned that includes any of the tasks listed in subsection (d)(2). Also the employers are responsible for being knowledgeable about the permissible exposure limit (PEL); exposure assessment; methods of compliance; respiratory protection; protective work clothing and equipment; housekeeping procedures; and hygiene facilities, practices, and establishing regulated areas. The employer must also know the medical surveillance program and medical removal protection practices. Lastly, the employer is to display appropriate signs and allow employees to observe monitoring procedures.

The employer is required to provide employee information, training, and certification as per T8 CCR §1532.1(l). As required by T8 CCR §1532.1(l)(3), the employer shall ensure that all employees and supervisors that perform any lead-related construction work are trained by an accredited training provider and they are then certified by the California Department of Health Services.

CARCINOGEN CONTROL

LAW: Employers in California must meet strict standards for the occupational health and safety of employees who handle carcinogenic (cancer-causing) substances on their jobs—for example, asbestos. These standards are part of the "Construction Safety Orders and General Industry Safety Orders" in Title 8 of the California Code of Regulations. Due to the extent and complexity of the many code requirements, contractors are urged to read the regulations themselves. Regulated carcinogen means a recognized cancer-causing substance, compound, mixture, or product regulated by Sections 1529, 1532, 1535, 8358, or Article 110 Sections 5200-5220.

Registration Required for Carcinogen Use

Businesses involved in the use of carcinogens must inform DOSH as per T8 CCR §5203. Report of Use must be mailed to:

> Occupational Carcinogen Control Unit
> Division of Occupational Safety and Health
> 1515 Clay Street, Suite 1901
> Oakland, CA 94612

Requirements for Asbestos-Related Work

Asbestos is the most common carcinogen in construction and demolition work. Persons engaged in insulation, plasterboard, siding, and ceiling plasterwork risk higher than usual exposure to asbestos. Failure to adopt safe work practices for handling asbestos has caused many employees to develop asbestos-related disabilities and fatal diseases. It is your responsibility to familiarize yourself with the laws pertaining to asbestos.

The owner of a commercial or industrial building or structure, an employer, or a contractor who engages in, or contracts for, asbestos-related work must make a good faith effort to determine if asbestos is present before the work is begun. The contractor or employer must first ask the owner of a building or structure built prior to 1978 if asbestos is present. Failure to do so may result in penalty (*Labor Code §§6501.9 and 6505.5*). Similar requirements exist in T8 CCR § 1529(k)(1) and (2), "Communication of Hazards and Duties of Building and Facility Owners."

If DOSH has reasonable cause to believe that any workplace contains asbestos, and if there appears to be inadequate protection for employees at that workplace from the hazards of airborne asbestos fibers, DOSH may issue an order prohibiting use (*Labor Code §6325.5*).

"Asbestos-related work" means any activity which by disturbing asbestos-containing construction materials may release asbestos fibers into the air and which is not related to its manufacture, the mining or excavation of asbestos-bearing ore or materials, or the installation or repair of automotive materials containing asbestos (*Labor Code §6501.8*).

"Asbestos-containing construction material" means any manufactured construction material which contains more than one-tenth of one percent (0.1%) asbestos by weight (*T8 CCR §341.6*).

Asbestos Removal Certification

A contractor may not engage in asbestos-related work which involves 100 square feet or more of surface area of asbestos-containing materials unless the qualifier for the license has passed an asbestos certification examination that is developed and administered by the Contractors State License Board (CSLB). Exceptions include contractors involved with the installation, maintenance, and repair of asbestos cement pipe or sheets, vinyl asbestos floor materials, or asbestos bituminous or resinous materials (*B&P Code §§7058.5 and 7065.01*).

Section IV

Any contractor who engages in asbestos-related work, or any contractor or employer who either knowingly or negligently enters into a contract with another person to do asbestos-related work, when that person is required to be but is not certified pursuant to B&P Code §7058.5, is subject to penalty (*B&P Code §§7028.1 and 7118.5*). A contractor who *is not* certified for asbestos-related work may bid on a project involving this work if a contractor who is properly certified by CSLB and registered by DOSH performs the asbestos-related work.

Asbestos Removal Registration

All contractors who engage in asbestos-related work that involves 100 square feet or more of surface area of asbestos-containing material that will be handled during the course of work being performed at a single worksite must register with DOSH. A "single work site" includes all buildings, structures, premises, fixtures, machinery, or other areas where asbestos-containing construction material will be handled during the course of the work for which the employer has contracted, whether pursuant to single or multiple contracts with the same hirer (*Labor Code §6501.5; T8 CCR §341.6*).

THERE ARE NO EXEMPTIONS FROM REGISTRATION. Those contractors who are exempt from CSLB certification (see above) must still register with DOSH if they are performing asbestos-related work. In addition, the State of California, a city, city and county, county, district, or public utility subject to the jurisdiction of the Public Utilities Commission shall be required to apply for a registration through the designated chief executive officer of that body. No registration fees shall be required, however, of any public agencies (*Labor Code §6508.5*).

Applications, applications for renewal, and information can be obtained from Asbestos Contractors Registration Unit (ACRU) at:

ACRU-DOSH
1515 Clay Street, Suite 1901
Oakland, CA 94612
(510) 286-7362

Notification and Posting of Asbestos-Related Work

When an employer will be conducting separate jobs or phases of work that require asbestos removal registration, or where the work process may differ or is performed at noncontiguous locations, written notice must be provided to the nearest DOSH Enforcement district office prior to commencement of any work (*Labor Code §6501.5; T8 CCR §341.7*). Furthermore, the employer must post a sign readable at 20 feet at the location where any asbestos-related work is to be conducted that states "Danger–Asbestos. Cancer and Lung Hazard. Keep Out."

Asbestos-Related Work in Schools

When asbestos-related work is done in elementary or secondary schools, either public or private, additional standards must be met as per Title 40, Code of Federal Regulations (CFR) Part 763, Asbestos Hazard Emergency Response Act (AHERA).

Local education agencies are required to use only AHERA-accredited persons to perform the following tasks:

- Inspecting for asbestos-containing materials in school buildings;

- Preparing management plans concerning the presence of asbestos-containing materials in schools;

- Designing and drafting specifications for asbestos abatement projects; and

- Supervising and conducting the abatement work.

Persons seeking to be accredited must complete a training course that has been approved by DOSH and pass an examination for that course. There are separate course requirements for inspectors, management planners, project designers, asbestos abatement contractors and supervisors, and for asbestos abatement workers.

NOTE: For schools to receive funding for asbestos abatement programs, they must comply with the rules and regulations of the State Allocation Board, Office of Public School Construction (OPSC). Since prompt payment to the contractor may be closely related to the school's receipt of OPSC funding, it is important that the contractor be aware of and encourage compliance with the OPSC requirements.

Renovation and Demolition Work

Renovation and demolition jobs are subject to the National Emission Standards for Hazardous Air Pollutants (NESHAP), which are enforced by the Federal Environmental Protection Agency and local air quality and air pollution districts. Before a renovation or demolition job begins on a site that may include asbestos-containing materials, one of these agencies must be notified. There are strict penalties for violations of the NESHAP requirements.

Disposal of Asbestos

The California Department of Toxic Substances Control, Hazardous Waste Management Branch, enforces the requirements governing the disposal of waste that contains asbestos. These requirements include the following (*Health and Safety Code §25143.7*):

- If a landfill is used, it must meet waste disposal requirements issued by the regional water quality control board that allows the disposal of such waste; and

- The wastes must be handled and disposed of in accordance with the Toxic Substances Control Act (*Public Law §94-469*) and all other applicable laws and regulations.

CONFINED SPACES

Safety and health practices for confined spaces are outlined in Title 8 of the California Code of Regulations Sections 5156, 5157, and 5158 (*Labor Code §142.3*). A permit-required confined space (*T8 CCR §5157*) is defined as a space large enough and so configured that an employee can bodily enter and perform assigned work; has limited or restricted means for entry or exit; and is not designed for continuous employee occupancy. In other confined space operations (*T8 CCR §5158*), confined space is defined by the concurrent existence of conditions where the existing ventilation is insufficient to remove dangerous air contamination, oxygen enrichment and/or oxygen deficiency which may exist or develop; and where ready access or egress for the removal of a suddenly disabled employee is difficult due to the location or size of the openings.

EXCAVATIONS AND TRENCHES

For regulations relating to permits for excavations and trenches, refer to the California Code of Regulations Title 8, Chapter 3.2, Article 2, Section 341 of the California Occupational Safety and Health Regulations (Cal/OSHA).

For definitions, general requirements, and information pertaining to excavations and trenching safety orders, see Title 8 of the California Code of Regulations, §1504, 1539–1547 and Labor Code §142.3.

HOW TO OBTAIN ADDITIONAL INFORMATION

WHAT YOU NEED	WHERE TO GET IT
Browse and order free DOSH publications	*http://www.dir.ca.gov/dosh/puborder.asp*
California Occupational Safety and Health Standards— *Title 8 California Code of Regulations, Industrial Relations.* The entire Title 8 and the Safety Orders for each industry are available for purchase.	Barclays Official Code of Regulations P.O. Box 2006 San Francisco, CA 94126 (800) 888-3600 or: *www.dir.ca.gov*
Information concerning California Occupational Safety and Health requirements Free on-site consultation to discuss particular problems and obtain assistance and advice DOSH workplace posters	Cal/OSHA Consultation Services Offices (see list on the next page) or order posters on-line at: *http://www.dir.ca.gov/wp.asp*
Recordkeeping and Reporting Requirements *Log and Summary of Occupational Injuries and Illnesses (OSHA Form 300)* *California Work Injuries and Illnesses— Annual Report* *Work Injuries and Illnesses—Quarterly Report*	Department of Industrial Relations Division of Labor Statistics and Research P.O. Box 420603 San Francisco, CA 94142 (415) 703-3020

Section IV

Cal/OSHA Enforcement Unit District Offices

Concord	1450 Enea Circle, Ste. 525, Bldg. C, Concord, CA 94520	(925) 602-6517 Fax (925) 676-0227
Foster City	1065 East Hillsdale Blvd., Suite 110, Foster City, CA 94404	(650) 573-3812 Fax (650) 573-3817
Fremont	39141 Civic Center Dr., Suite 310, Fremont, CA 94538-5818	(510) 794-2521 Fax (510) 794-3889
Fresno	2550 Mariposa Street, Suite 4000, Fresno, CA 93721	(559) 445-5302 Fax (559) 445-5786
Los Angeles	320 West 4th Street, Suite 850, Los Angeles, CA 90013	(213) 576-7451 Fax (213) 576-7461
Modesto	1209 Woodrow, Suite C-4, Modesto, CA 95350	(209) 576-6260 Fax (209) 576-6191
Monrovia	750 Royal Oaks Drive, Suite 104, Monrovia, CA 91016	(626) 256-7913 Fax (626) 359-4291
Oakland	1515 Clay Street, Suite 1301, Oakland, CA 94612	(510) 622-2916 Fax (510) 622-2908
Redding	381 Hemsted Drive, Redding, CA 96002	(530) 224-4743 Fax (530) 224-4747
Sacramento	2424 Arden Way, Suite 165, Sacramento, CA 95825	(916) 263-2800 Fax (916) 263-2798
San Bernardino	464 W. 4th Street, Suite 332, San Bernardino, CA 92401	(909) 383-4321 Fax (909) 383-6789
San Diego	7575 Metropolitan Drive, Suite 207, San Diego, CA 92108	(619) 767-2280 Fax (619) 767-2299
San Francisco	121 Spear Street, Suite 430, San Francisco, CA 94105	(415) 972-8670 Fax (415) 972-8686
Santa Ana	2000 E. McFadden Ave., Ste. 122, Santa Ana, CA 92705	(714) 558-4451 Fax (714) 558-2035
Santa Rosa	1221 Farmers Lane, Suite 300, Santa Rosa, CA 95405	(707) 576-2388 Fax (707) 576-2598
Torrance	680 Knox Street, Suite 100, Torrance, CA 90502	(310) 516-3734 Fax (310) 516-4253
Van Nuys	6150 Van Nuys Boulevard, Suite 405, Van Nuys, CA 91401	(818) 901-5403 Fax (818) 901-5578
Ventura	1000 Hill Road, Suite 110, Ventura, CA 93003	(805) 654-4581 Fax (805) 654-4852
West Covina	1906 West Garvey Ave. South, Ste 200, West Covina, CA 91790	(626) 472-0046 Fax (626) 472-7708

High Hazard Compliance Unit

Oakland	1515 Clay Street, Suite 1303, Oakland, CA 94612	(510) 622-3009

		Fax (510) 622-3025
Santa Ana	2000 E. McFadden Ave., Suite 111 Santa Ana, CA 92705	(714) 567-7100 Fax (714) 567-6074

Cal/OSHA Consultation Service Area Offices—Consultation Toll-Free Number (800) 963-9424

Northern California	2424 Arden Way, Suite 410, Sacramento, CA 95825	(916) 263-0704
San Francisco Bay Area	1515 Clay Street, Suite 1103, Oakland, CA 94612	(510) 622-2891
Central Valley	1901 North Gateway Blvd., Suite 102, Fresno, CA 93727	(559) 454-1295
San Fernando Valley	6150 Van Nuys Blvd., Suite 307, Van Nuys, CA 91401	(818) 901-5754
Los Angeles	10350 Heritage Park Dr., Suite 201, Santa Fe Springs, CA 90670	(562) 944-9366
San Bernardino, Orange	464 W. 4th Street, Suite 339, San Bernardino, CA 92401	(909) 383-4567
San Diego	7575 Metropolitan Drive, Suite 204, San Diego, CA 92108	(619) 767-2060

Process Safety Management Unit

Torrance	680 Knox Street, Suite 100, Torrance, CA 90502	(310) 217-6902 Fax (310) 217-6969
Concord	1450 Enea Circle, Ste. 550, Concord, CA 94520	(925) 602-2665 Fax (925) 602-2668

Mining and Tunneling Unit

Sacramento	2211 Park Towne Circle, Suite 2, Sacramento, CA 95825	(916) 574-2540 Fax (916) 574-2542
Van Nuys	6150 Van Nuys Boulevard, Suite 310, Van Nuys, CA 91401	(818) 901-5420 Fax (818) 901-5579
San Bernardino	464 West 4th Street, Suite 354, San Bernardino, CA 92401	(909) 383-6782 Fax (909) 388-7132

Other Resources

Occupational Safety & Health Standards Board
2520 Venture Oaks Way, Ste. 350, Sacramento, CA 95833   (916) 274-5721

Occupational Safety & Health Appeals Board
2520 Venture Oaks Way, Ste. 300, Sacramento, CA 95833   (916) 274-5751

DOSH Asbestos Contractors Registration Unit
1515 Clay St., Ste. 1901, Oakland, CA 94612   (510) 286-7362

Department of Toxic Substances Control
1001 I Street, P.O. Box 806, Sacramento, CA 95812   (800) 728-6942

Section IV

State Allocation Board/Public School Construction
1130 K Street, Suite 400, Sacramento, CA 95814-2928   (916) 445-3160

Chapter 8.

Regional Notification Centers: Underground Service Alert

What is a Regional Notification Center?

A regional notification center is an association of owners and operators of subsurface installations (water, gas, electric, telephone, sewer, oil lines, etc.). Damage to underground structures may result in the disruption of essential public services and pose a threat to workers, the public, and environmental safety. The purpose of the center is to provide a single telephone number that excavators can use to give the center's members advance notification of their intent to excavate. The operators of the underground installations are then responsible for providing information about the locations of the facility, or marking or staking the approximate location of their facility, or advising the excavator of clearance. The operators are only responsible for facilities they own; the operators are not responsible for facilities they do not own.

Contacting a Regional Notification Center is a Requirement—Not an Option.

California Government Code §§4216-4216.9 require anyone planning to excavate to contact the appropriate regional notification center at least two (2) working days (but not more than 14 calendar days) before beginning to excavate. The center will issue an inquiry identification number to the excavator as confirmation of the call.

NOTE: An excavation permit is not valid without this identification number.

Who Must Comply:

- Any person or entity who plans to disturb the surface of the ground, whether by digging, drilling, boring, etc.

Exempt Persons:

- An owner of private property who contracts with a contractor or subcontractor (contractor/subcontractor must be licensed) for an excavation project that does not require an excavation permit;

- An owner of private property (who is not a licensed contractor or subcontractor) who, as a part of improving his or her

151

principal residence, does work which does not require an excavation permit.

- Regardless of whether an equipment operator is provided for that piece of equipment, any person or private entity that leases or rents power-operated or power-driven excavating or boring equipment to a contractor or subcontractor licensed pursuant to the Contractors State License Law if the signed rental agreement between the person or private entity and the contractor or subcontractor contains the following provision: "It is the sole responsibility of the lessee or renter to follow the requirements of the regional notification center law pursuant to Article 2 (commencing with Section 4216) of Chapter 3.1 of Division 5 of Title 1 of the Government Code. By signing this contract, the lessee or renter accepts all liabilities and responsibilities contained in the regional notification center law."

Steps Required for Compliance:

- Every general contractor, contractor, or subcontractor excavating at a job site must have his or her own Underground Service Alert (USA) identification (ticket) number for the excavation work he or she is performing.

- Excluding emergency situations, parties planning excavation activities must contact the appropriate regional notification center not less than two (2) working days, nor more than 14 calendar days, prior to the start of work.

NOTE: THE REGIONAL NOTIFICATION CENTER CALL IS FREE: 811 / 800-227-2600.

- Upon notification, the center will issue an identification (ticket) number. The ticket number will be valid for 28 calendar days. If work is to continue past 28 calendar days, the ticket number must be revalidated by again notifying the center before the ticket number expires.

- At the site, excavators must clearly mark the boundaries of the work area, usually with white paint.

- Within these boundary markings, operators of underground installations must then provide information about their facilities, mark or stake the location of their lines clearly using the appropriate color to show what type of installation is present, or advise of clearance.

- If, during the course of the job, the operator's markings become no longer visible, the excavator must contact the regional center and request the operator to re-mark the lines within two (2) working days.

- Using the operator's markings, an excavator must determine the exact location of underground facilities with hand tools before any power equipment may be used.

Helpful Hints

- Be prepared to provide the beginning date and time of your excavation.

- Provide your name, company's name, company's mailing address, telephone number where you can be contacted, nature of work (grading, drilling, etc.), who the work is being done for, the name of the foreman, permit name and number, whether you have outlined your excavation in white paint, and a description of your excavation site.

- When giving the description of your excavation site, be sure to give the address or description of where you will be digging (including side of street, which corner of the intersection, footage, and total distances or other tie-in measurements), nearest intersecting street, city, and county.

Penalties

- Any operator or excavator who NEGLIGENTLY violates any portion of Government Code sections 4216–4216.9 is subject to a fine not to exceed $10,000.

- Any operator or excavator who KNOWINGLY AND WILLFULLY violates any portion of Government Code sections 4216–4216.9 is subject to a fine not to exceed $50,000.

- An excavator may also be subject to third party claims for damages arising from the excavation work.

- Violation of Government Code sections 4216–4216.9 could result in disciplinary action and possible revocation of your contractor license by the Contractors State License Board.

REGIONAL NOTIFICATION CENTERS

Underground Service Alert of Northern California and Nevada: 811 / (800) 227-2600, www.usasnorth.org

Serves the following counties in Northern California:

Alameda, Alpine, Amador, Butte, Calaveras, Colusa, Contra Costa, Del Norte, El Dorado, Fresno, Glenn, Humboldt, Kern, Kings, Lake, Lassen, Madera, Marin, Mariposa, Mendocino, Merced, Modoc, Mono, Monterey, Napa, Nevada, Placer, Plumas, Sacramento, San Benito,

Section IV

San Francisco, San Joaquin, San Luis Obispo, San Mateo, Santa Clara, Santa Cruz, Shasta, Sierra, Siskiyou, Solano, Sonoma, Stanislaus, Sutter, Tehama, Trinity, Tulare, Tuolumne, Yolo, and Yuba.

Serves the entire state of Nevada.

Service: Monday–Friday, 6 a.m.–7 p.m., excluding holidays

Underground Service Alert of Southern California—

811 / (800) 227-2600, www.digalert.org

Serves the following counties in Southern California:

Imperial, Inyo, Los Angeles, Orange, Riverside, San Bernardino, San Diego, Santa Barbara, and Ventura

Service: Monday–Friday, 6 a.m.–7 p.m., excluding holidays

Five Steps to a Safe Excavation:

1) Survey and mark.

2) Call before you dig.

3) Wait the required time.

4) Respect the marks.

5) Dig with care.

Whatever you do, do it safe, but CALL AT LEAST TWO (2) WORKING DAYS TO FOURTEEN (14) CALENDAR DAYS BEFORE YOU DIG.

Chapter 9.

Preservation of Native American Remains

California has one of the largest Native American populations in the United States. With approximately 115 federally recognized tribes and many more applying for recognition, California Native American lands include reservations and rancherias in over half of California's counties. Historically, Native American land holdings encompassed the entire State of California.

There has been an increasing rate of vandalism and inadvertent destruction of Native American burial grounds, human remains, and associated grave goods. Several laws provide for the protection and sensitive treatment of these human remains and associated burial goods (Health and Safety Code section 7050.5; Public Resources Code sections 5097.9-5097.991). The intent of the law is to provide protection to Native American burials and associated grave goods from vandalism and inadvertent destruction.

REPORTING REQUIREMENT

In the event of discovery or recognition of any human remains in any location other than a dedicated cemetery, there shall be no further excavation or disturbance of the site or nearby area. Upon the discovery of human remains or burial artifacts at any site other than a dedicated cemetery, the following actions MUST BE TAKEN IMMEDIATELY:

- Stop work immediately at that site and any nearby area reasonably suspected to have remains, and contact the county coroner.

- The coroner has two (2) working days to examine the remains after being notified by the person responsible for the excavation. If the remains are Native American, the coroner has 24 hours to notify the Native American Heritage Commission.

- The Native American Heritage Commission will immediately notify the person it believes to be the most likely descendant of the deceased Native American.

- The most likely descendant has 24 hours to make recommendations to the owner, or representative, for the treatment and disposition, with proper dignity, of the remains and grave goods.

- If the owner doesn't accept the descendant's recommendations, the owner or the descendant may request mediation by the Native American Heritage Commission.

- If mediation fails to provide measures acceptable to the landowner, the landowner or his or her authorized representative shall reinter the human remains and items associated with Native American burials, with appropriate dignity, and in a location on the property that is not subject to further subsurface disturbance.

PENALTIES

It is a felony to obtain or possess Native American remains or associated grave goods. (See Public Resource Code sections 5097.94, 5097.98, and 5097.99.) Any person who knowingly or willfully removes, obtains, or possesses any Native American remains or associated burial artifacts, without authority of law, is guilty of a felony, punishable by imprisonment in the state prison.

ADDITIONAL INFORMATION

To learn more about the protection and preservation of Native American burial grounds, human remains, and associated grave goods, contact the Native American Heritage Commission at:

> Native American Heritage Commission
> 915 Capitol Mall, Room 364
> Sacramento, CA 95814
> (916) 653-4082
> www.nahc.ca.gov

Chapter 10.

Construction of Wells

LICENSE REQUIRED FOR WATER WELLS

Section 13750.5 of the California Water Code states:

> "No person shall undertake to dig, bore, or drill a water well, cathodic protection well, groundwater monitoring well, or geothermal heat exchange well, to deepen or re-perforate such a well, or to abandon or destroy such a well, unless the person responsible for that construction, alteration, destruction, or abandonment possesses a C-57 Water Well contractor's license."

REPORTING REQUIREMENTS

Water Wells, Cathodic Protection Wells, and Monitoring Wells

California Water Code sections 13751 through 13754, requires persons who construct, alter, (including, but not limited to, drilling, deepening, re-perforation, or abandonment), or destroy a water well, cathodic protection well, monitoring well, or geothermal heat exchange well, to file a report of completion, called the "Well Completion Report, DWR 188," with the California Department of Water Resources (DWR) within 60 days after completion of the work. Earlier versions of the form were called "Water Well Driller's Report." All of these reports are also called "well logs" or "driller's logs."

This requirement also applies to persons who convert—for use as a water well, cathodic protection well, or monitoring well—any oil or gas well originally constructed under the jurisdiction of the California Department of Conservation.

The State of California and other agencies use the information provided by these reports to evaluate ground water resources, to protect ground water quality, and to conserve water supplies. In addition, the Water Code was amended in 2002 to require that certain specifics be included in groundwater management plans adopted by local water management agencies. Knowledge of the construction details of wells and the local geology will be useful in developing such plans.

NOTE: Failure to file the Well Completion Report is a misdemeanor (*Water Code §13754*) and constitutes cause for

disciplinary action against your contractor license (*Business and Professions Code section 7110*).

How and Where to File

The Department of Water Resources will provide the proper forms for your report and pertinent sections of the California Water Code. You may obtain hard copies from any of the DWR district offices listed below or, if your computer has Adobe Acrobat, you can download a blank copy of the "Well Completion Report" from DWR's website at the URL following this paragraph. If you download the form from the website, be sure to obtain the unique sequential number at the top of the form before downloading. DWR staff uses this number to enter the information into the database.

http://www.water.ca.gov/groundwater/well_info_and_other/well_comp letion_reports.cfm

A number of county health departments also have paper copies available.

The ***How to Fill Out a Well Completion Report*** - *Instruction Pamphlet* can also be downloaded from the website at the URL shown above, as well as several other publications relating to groundwater. Software that allows you to fill in the Well Completion Report on your computer and store it in digital format can be purchased from several firms.

Submit your completed reports to the DWR district office that has jurisdiction over the county in which the well is located. For the appropriate office address, find the county and its corresponding district office in the table below.

CALIFORNIA DEPARTMENT OF WATER RESOURCES
DISTRICT OFFICES

Butte, Colusa, Del Norte, Glenn, Humboldt, Lake, Lassen, Modoc, Plumas, Shasta, Siskiyou, Tehama and Trinity	Northern District 2440 Main Street Red Bluff, CA 96080-2398 (530) 529-7300
Alameda, Alpine, Amador, Calaveras, Contra Costa, El Dorado, Marin, Mendocino, Mono (North), Napa, Nevada, Placer, Sacramento, San Francisco, San Joaquin, San Mateo, Santa Clara, Sierra, Solano, Sonoma, Sutter, Tuolumne, Yolo and Yuba	Central District 3500 Industrial Blvd. West Sacramento, CA 95691 (916) 376-9600
Fresno, Kern (Valley), Kings, Madera, Mariposa, Merced, Monterey, San Benito, Santa Cruz, Stanislaus and Tulare	San Joaquin District 3374 E. Shields Avenue Fresno, CA 93726-6913 (559) 230-3300
Imperial, Inyo, Kern (Desert), Los Angeles, Mono (South), Orange, Riverside, San Bernardino, San Diego, San Luis Obispo, Santa Barbara and Ventura	Southern District 770 Fairmont Avenue, Suite 102 Glendale, CA 91203-1035 (818) 500-1645

Section IV

WELL STANDARDS

Standards for construction, modification, rehabilitation, and destruction of water wells, monitoring wells, and cathodic protection wells are published by DWR in Bulletin 74-90, supplement to Bulletin 74-81, entitled *California Well Standards: Water Wells, Monitoring Wells, Cathodic Protection Wells.* Copies can be obtained from:

Publications/Department of Water Resources
P.O. Box 942836
Sacramento, CA 94236-0001
(916) 653-1097

California Well Standards, and standards for the construction, rehabilitation, and destruction of geothermal heat exchange wells (also called ground source heat pumps) in *California Laws for Wells (March 2003)* can be viewed on DWR's website: *http://www.groundwater.water.ca.gov/technical_assistance/gw_wells /gww_standards/index.cfm*.

Counties and other local government jurisdictions that have been designated local enforcing agencies may have adopted standards in addition to the statewide standards contained in Bulletin 74-90. These local agencies should be contacted whenever work on a well is being planned to ensure compliance with local ordinances. Many of these local agencies require permits for any work on a well, and charge a fee for that permit. For information, contact the local agency, which is usually the county Department of Environmental Health.

Questions about well standards should be directed to the local enforcing agency, to the DWR district offices listed above, or to DWR's Division of Planning and Local Assistance Headquarters at (916) 651-9649.

SECTION V.

THE DEPARTMENT OF CONSUMER AFFAIRS

Chapter 11.

Laws Governing the Department of Consumer Affairs

The Department of Consumer Affairs includes 40 regulatory entities—among them the Contractors State License Board—which regulate various services and industries in the state. Some of the other boards and bureaus under the department's purview include the Medical Board of California, the Structural Pest Control Board, and the Bureau of Automotive Repair. The department's mission, through its regulatory boards, is "to promote and protect the interests of California consumers by serving as guardian and advocate for their health, safety, privacy, and economic well being; enhancing public participation in regulatory decision-making; promoting legal and ethical standards of professional conduct; identifying marketplace trends so that the Department's programs and policies are contemporary, relevant, and responsive; partnering with business and consumer groups in California and the nation; and working with law enforcement to combat fraud and enforce consumer protection laws vigorously and fairly." The laws governing the department and the CSLB are part of California's Business and Professions Code. What follows are selected sections from the codes that relate, in general or in specifics, to the purpose and function of the department.

BUSINESS & PROFESSIONS CODE

GENERAL PROVISIONS

§ 7.5.   "Conviction"; When action by board following establishment of conviction may be taken; Prohibition against denial of licensure; Application of section

§ 7.5.   "Conviction"; When action by board following establishment of conviction may be taken; Prohibition against denial of licensure; Application of section

A conviction within the meaning of this code means a plea or verdict of guilty or a conviction following a plea of nolo contendere. Any
action which a board is permitted to take following the establishment
of a conviction may be taken when the time for appeal has elapsed, or
the judgment of conviction has been affirmed on appeal or when an
order granting probation is made suspending the imposition of sentence, irrespective of a subsequent order under the provisions of Section 1203.4 of the Penal Code. However, a board may not deny a license to an applicant who is otherwise qualified pursuant to subdivision (b) of Section 480.

Nothing in this section shall apply to the licensure of persons pursuant to Chapter 4 (commencing with Section 6000) of Division 3.

Added Stats 1979 ch 876 § 1.

§ 8.   Governing provisions

Unless the context otherwise requires, the general provisions he-
reinafter set forth shall govern the construction of this code.

Enacted Stats 1937.

§ 9. Effect of headings

Division, part, chapter, article and section headings contained herein shall not be deemed to govern, limit, modify, or in any manner affect the scope, meaning, or intent of the provisions of this code.

Enacted Stats 1937.

§ 10. Authority of deputies

Whenever, by the provisions of this code, a power is granted to a public officer or a duty imposed upon such an officer, the power may be exercised or duty performed by a deputy of the officer or by a person authorized pursuant to law by the officer, unless it is expressly otherwise provided.

Enacted Stats 1937.

§ 12.5. Violation of regulation adopted pursuant to code provision; Issuance of citation

Whenever in any provision of this code authority is granted to issue a citation for a violation of any provision of this code, that authority also includes the authority to issue a citation for the violation of any regulation adopted pursuant to any provision of this code.

Added Stats 1986 ch 1379 § 1.

§ 14.1. Legislative intent

The Legislature hereby declares its intent that the terms "man" or "men" where appropriate shall be deemed "person" or "persons" and any references to the terms "man" or "men" in sections of this code be changed to "person" or "persons" when such code sections are being amended for any purpose. This act is declaratory and not amendatory of existing law.

Added Stats 1976 ch 1171 § 1.

§ 22. "Board"

"Board," as used in any provision of this code, refers to the board in which the administration of the provision is vested, and unless otherwise expressly provided, shall include "bureau," "commission," "committee," "department," "division," "examining committee," "program," and "agency."

Enacted Stats 1937. Amended Stats 1947 ch 1350 § 1; Stats 1980 ch 676 § 1; Stats 1991 ch 654 § 1 (AB 1893); Stats 1999 ch 656 § 1 (SB 1306); Stats 2004 ch 33 § 1 (AB 1467), effective April 13, 2004; Stats 2010 ch 670 § 1 (AB 2130), effective January 1, 2011.

Section V

§ 23.5. "Director"

"Director," unless otherwise defined, refers to the Director of Consumer Affairs.

Wherever the laws of this state refer to the Director of Professional and Vocational Standards, the reference shall be construed to be to the Director of Consumer Affairs.

Added Stats 1939 ch 30 § 2. Amended Stats 1971 ch 716 § 2.

§ 23.6. "Appointing power"

"Appointing power," unless otherwise defined, refers to the Director of Consumer Affairs.

Added Stats 1945 ch 1276 § 1. Amended Stats 1971 ch 716 § 3.

§ 23.7. "License"

Unless otherwise expressly provided, "license" means license, certificate, registration, or other means to engage in a business or profession regulated by this code or referred to in Section 1000 or 3600.

Added Stats 1994 ch 26 § 1 (AB 1807), effective March 30, 1994.

§ 23.8. "Licentiate"

"Licentiate" means any person authorized by a license, certificate, registration, or other means to engage in a business or profession regulated by this code or referred to in Sections 1000 and 3600.

Added Stats 1961 ch 2232 § 1.

§ 23.9. Licensing eligibility of prison releasees

Notwithstanding any other provision of this code, any individual who, while imprisoned in a state prison or other correctional institution, is trained, in the course of a rehabilitation program approved by the particular licensing agency concerned and provided by the prison or other correctional institution, in a particular skill, occupation, or profession for which a state license, certificate, or other evidence of proficiency is required by this code shall not, when released from the prison or institution, be denied the right to take the next regularly scheduled state examination or any examination thereafter required to obtain the license, certificate, or other evidence of proficiency and shall not be denied such license, certificate, or other evidence of proficiency, because of his imprisonment or the conviction from which the imprisonment resulted, or because he obtained his training in prison or in the correctional institution, if the licensing agency, upon recommendation of the Adult Authority or the Department of the Youth Authority, as the case may be, finds that he is a fit person to be licensed.

Added Stats 1967 ch 1690 § 1, as B & P C § 23.8. Amended and Renumbered by Stats 1971 ch 582 § 1.

§ 26. Rules and regulations regarding building standards

Wherever, pursuant to this code, any state department, officer, board, agency, committee, or commission is authorized to adopt rules and regulations, such rules and regulations which are building standards, as defined in Section 18909 of the Health and Safety Code, shall be adopted pursuant to the provisions of Part 2.5 (commencing with Section 18901) of Division 13 of the Health and Safety Code unless the provisions of Sections 18930, 18933, 18938, 18940, 18943, 18944, and 18945 of the Health and Safety Code are expressly excepted in the provision of this code under which the authority to adopt the specific building standard is delegated. Any building standard adopted in violation of this section shall have no force or effect. Any building standard adopted prior to January 1, 1980, pursuant to this code and not expressly excepted by statute from such provisions of the State Building Standards Law shall remain in effect only until January 1, 1985, or until adopted, amended, or superseded by provisions published in the State Building Standards Code, whichever occurs sooner.

Added Stats 1979 ch 1152 § 1.

§ 27. Information to be provided on Internet; Entities in Department of Consumer Affairs required to comply

(a) Each entity specified in subdivisions (c), (d), and (e) shall provide on the Internet information regarding the status of every license issued by that entity in accordance with the California Public Records Act (Chapter 3.5 (commencing with Section 6250) of Division 7 of Title 1 of the Government Code) and the Information Practices Act of 1977 (Chapter 1 (commencing with Section 1798) of Title 1.8 of Part 4 of Division 3 of the Civil Code). The public information to be provided on the Internet shall include information on suspensions and revocations of licenses issued by the entity and other related enforcement action, including accusations filed pursuant to the Administrative Procedure Act (Chapter 3.5 (commencing with Section 11340) of Part 1 of Division 3 of Title 2 of the Government Code) taken by the entity relative to persons, businesses, or facilities subject to licensure or regulation by the entity. The information may not include personal information, including home telephone number, date of birth, or social security number. Each entity shall disclose a licensee's address of record. However, each entity shall allow a licensee to provide a post office box number or other alternate address, instead of his or her home address, as the address of record. This section shall not prec-

Section V

lude an entity from also requiring a licensee, who has provided a post office box number or other alternative mailing address as his or her address of record, to provide a physical business address or residence address only for the entity's internal administrative use and not for disclosure as the licensee's address of record or disclosure on the Internet.

(b) In providing information on the Internet, each entity specified in subdivisions (c) and (d) shall comply with the Department of Consumer Affairs Guidelines for Access to Public Records.

(c) Each of the following entities within the Department of Consumer Affairs shall comply with the requirements of this section:

(1) The Board for Professional Engineers , Land Surveyors, and Geologists shall disclose information on its registrants and licensees.

(2) The Bureau of Automotive Repair shall disclose information on its licensees, including auto repair dealers, smog stations, lamp and brake stations, smog check technicians, and smog inspection certification stations.

(3) The Bureau of Electronic and Appliance Repair, Home Furnishings, and Thermal Insulation shall disclose information on its licensees and registrants, including major appliance repair dealers, combination dealers (electronic and appliance), electronic repair dealers, service contract sellers, and service contract administrators.

(4) The Cemetery and Funeral Bureau shall disclose information on its licensees, including cemetery brokers, cemetery salespersons, cemetery managers, crematory managers, cemetery authorities, crematories, cremated remains disposers, embalmers, funeral establishments, and funeral directors.

(5) The Professional Fiduciaries Bureau shall disclose information on its licensees.

(6) The Contractors' State License Board shall disclose information on its licensees and registrants in accordance with Chapter 9 (commencing with Section 7000) of Division 3. In addition to information related to licenses as specified in subdivision (a), the board shall also disclose information provided to the board by the Labor Commissioner pursuant to Section 98.9 of the Labor Code.

(7) The Bureau for Private Postsecondary Education shall disclose information on private postsecondary institutions under its jurisdiction, including disclosure of notices to comply issued pursuant to Section 94935 of the Education Code.

(8) The California Board of Accountancy shall disclose information on its licensees and registrants.

(9) The California Architects Board shall disclose information on its licensees, including architects and landscape architects.

(10) The State Athletic Commission shall disclose information on its licensees and registrants.

(11) The State Board of Barbering and Cosmetology shall disclose information on its licensees.

(12) The State Board of Guide Dogs for the Blind shall disclose information on its licensees and registrants.

(13) The Acupuncture Board shall disclose information on its licensees.

(14) The Board of Behavioral Sciences shall disclose information on its licensees, including marriage and family therapists, licensed clinical social workers, licensed educational psychologists, and licensed professional clinical counselors.

(15) The Dental Board of California shall disclose information on its licensees.

(16) The State Board of Optometry shall disclose information regarding certificates of registration to practice optometry, statements of licensure, optometric corporation registrations, branch office licenses, and fictitious name permits of its licensees.

(17) The Board of Psychology shall disclose information on its licensees, including psychologists, psychological assistants, and registered psychologists.

(d) The State Board of Chiropractic Examiners shall disclose information on its licensees.

(e) The Structural Pest Control Board shall disclose information on its licensees, including applicators, field representatives, and operators in the areas of fumigation, general pest and wood destroying pests and organisms, and wood roof cleaning and treatment.

(f) "Internet" for the purposes of this section has the meaning set forth in paragraph (6) of subdivision (f) of Section 17538.

Added Stats 1997 ch 661 § 1 (SB 492). Amended Stats 1998 ch 59 § 1 (AB 969); Stats 1999 ch 655 § 1 (SB 1308); Stats 2000 ch 927 § 1 (SB 1889); Stats 2001 ch 159 § 1 (SB 662); Stats 2003 ch 849 § 1 (AB 1418); Stats 2009 ch 308 § 1 (SB 819), effective January 1, 2010, ch 310 § 1.5 (AB 48), effective January 1, 2010; Stats 2011 ch 381 § 2 (SB 146), effective January 1, 2012, ch 712 § 1 (SB 706), effective January 1, 2012.

§ 29.5.   Additional qualifications for licensure

In addition to other qualifications for licensure prescribed by the various acts of boards under the department, applicants for licensure and licensees renewing their licenses shall also comply with Section 17520 of the Family Code.

Added Stats 1991 ch 542 § 1 (SB 1161). Amended Stats 2003 ch 607 § 1 (SB 1077).

—*See Family Code Section 17520, Compliance with Support Orders by Applicants for Professional Licenses, in Appendix.*

Section V

§ 30. Provision of federal employer identification number or social security number by licensee

(a) Notwithstanding any other provision of law, any board, as defined in Section 22, and the State Bar and the Department of Real Estate shall at the time of issuance of the license require that the licensee provide its federal employer identification number, if the licensee is a partnership, or his or her social security number for all others.

(b) Any licensee failing to provide the federal identification number or social security number shall be reported by the licensing board to the Franchise Tax Board and, if failing to provide after notification pursuant to paragraph (1) of subdivision (b) of Section 19528 of the Revenue and Taxation Code, shall be subject to the penalty provided in paragraph (2) of subdivision (b) of Section 19528 of the Revenue and Taxation Code.

(c) In addition to the penalty specified in subdivision (b), a licensing board may not process any application for an original license unless the applicant or licensee provides its federal employer identification number or social security number where requested on the application.

(d) A licensing board shall, upon request of the Franchise Tax Board, furnish to the Franchise Tax Board the following information with respect to every licensee:

(1) Name.

(2) Address or addresses of record.

(3) Federal employer identification number if the entity is a partnership or social security number for all others.

(4) Type of license.

(5) Effective date of license or a renewal.

(6) Expiration date of license.

(7) Whether license is active or inactive, if known.

(8) Whether license is new or a renewal.

(e) For the purposes of this section:

(1) "Licensee" means any entity, other than a corporation, authorized by a license, certificate, registration, or other means to engage in a business or profession regulated by this code or referred to in Section 1000 or 3600.

(2) "License" includes a certificate, registration, or any other authorization needed to engage in a business or profession regulated by this code or referred to in Section 1000 or 3600.

(3) "Licensing board" means any board, as defined in Section 22, the State Bar, and the Department of Real Estate.

(f) The reports required under this section shall be filed on magnetic media or in other machine-readable form, according to standards furnished by the Franchise Tax Board.

(g) Licensing boards shall provide to the Franchise Tax Board the information required by this section at a time that the Franchise Tax Board may require.

(h) Notwithstanding Chapter 3.5 (commencing with Section 6250) of Division 7 of Title 1 of the Government Code, the social security number and federal employer identification number furnished pursuant to this section shall not be deemed to be a public record and shall not be open to the public for inspection.

(i) Any deputy, agent, clerk, officer, or employee of any licensing board described in subdivision (a), or any former officer or employee or other individual who in the course of his or her employment or duty has or has had access to the information required to be furnished under this section, may not disclose or make known in any manner that information, except as provided in this section to the Franchise Tax Board or as provided in subdivision (k).

(j) It is the intent of the Legislature in enacting this section to utilize the social security account number or federal employer identification number for the purpose of establishing the identification of persons affected by state tax laws and for purposes of compliance with Section 17520 of the Family Code and, to that end, the information furnished pursuant to this section shall be used exclusively for those purposes.

(k) If the board utilizes a national examination to issue a license, and if a reciprocity agreement or comity exists between the State of California and the state requesting release of the social security number, any deputy, agent, clerk, officer, or employee of any licensing board described in subdivision (a) may release a social security number to an examination or licensing entity, only for the purpose of verification of licensure or examination status.

(*l*) For the purposes of enforcement of Section 17520 of the Family Code, and notwithstanding any other provision of law, any board, as defined in Section 22, and the State Bar and the Department of Real Estate shall at the time of issuance of the license require that each licensee provide the social security number of each individual listed on the license and any person who qualifies the license. For the purposes of this subdivision, "licensee" means any entity that is issued a license by any board, as defined in Section 22, the State Bar, the Department of Real Estate, and the Department of Motor Vehicles.

Added Stats 1986 ch 1361 § 1. Amended Stats 1988 ch 1333 § 1, effective September 24, 1988; Stats 1991 ch 542 § 2 (SB 1161), ch 654 § 1.5 (AB 1893); Stats 1994 ch 1135 § 1 (AB 3302); Stats 1997 ch 17 § 1 (SB 947) (ch 604 prevails), ch 604 § 1 (SB 1106), effective October 3, 1997, ch 605 § 1 (AB 1040); Stats 1999 ch 652 § 1.5 (SB 240); Stats 2006 ch 658 § 1 (SB 1476), effective January 1, 2007.

Section V

§ 31. Compliance with judgment or order for support upon issuance or renewal of license

(a) As used in this section, "board" means any entity listed in Section 101, the entities referred to in Sections 1000 and 3600, the State Bar, the Department of Real Estate, and any other state agency that issues a license, certificate, or registration authorizing a person to engage in a business or profession.

(b) Each applicant for the issuance or renewal of a license, certificate, registration, or other means to engage in a business or profession regulated by a board who is not in compliance with a judgment or order for support shall be subject to Section 17520 of the Family Code.

(c) "Compliance with a judgment or order for support" has the meaning given in paragraph (4) of subdivision (a) of Section 17520 of the Family Code.

(d) Each licensee or applicant whose name appears on a list of the 500 largest tax delinquencies pursuant to Section 7063 or 19195 of the Revenue and Taxation Code shall be subject to Section 494.5.

(e) Each application for a new license or renewal of a license shall indicate on the application that the law allows the State Board of Equalization and the Franchise Tax Board to share taxpayer information with a board and requires the licensee to pay his or her state tax obligation and that his or her license may be suspended if the state tax obligation is not paid.

(f) For purposes of this section, "tax obligation" means the tax imposed under, or in accordance with, Part 1 (commencing with Section 6001), Part 1.5 (commencing with Section 7200), Part 1.6 (commencing with Section 7251), Part 1.7 (commencing with Section 7280), Part 10 (commencing with Section 17001), or Part 11 (commencing with Section 23001) of Division 2 of the Revenue and Taxation Code.

Added Stats 1991 ch 110 § 4 (SB 101). Amended Stats 1991 ch 542 § 3 (SB 1161); Stats 2010 ch 328 § 1 (SB 1330), effective January 1, 2011; Stats 2011 ch 455 § 1 (AB 1424), effective January 1, 2012.

§ 35. Provision in rules and regulations for evaluation experience obtained in armed services

It is the policy of this state that, consistent with the provision of high-quality services, persons with skills, knowledge, and experience obtained in the armed services of the United States should be permitted to apply this learning and contribute to the employment needs of the state at the maximum level of responsibility and skill for which they are qualified. To this end, rules and regulations of boards provided for in this code shall provide for methods of evaluating education, training, and experience obtained in the armed services, if applicable to the requirements of the business, occupation, or profession regulated. These rules and regulations shall also specify how this education, training, and experience may be used to meet the licensure requirements for the particular business, occupation, or profession regulated. Each board shall consult with the Department of Veterans Affairs and the Military Department before adopting these rules and regulations. Each board shall perform the duties required by this section within existing budgetary resources of the agency within which the board operates.

Added Stats 1994 ch 987 § 1 (SB 1646), effective September 28, 1994. Amended Stats 1995 ch 91 § 1 (SB 975); Stats 2010 ch 214 § 1 (AB 2783), effective January 1, 2011.

§ 40. State Board of Chiropractic Examiners or Osteopathic Medical Board of California expert consultant agreements

(a) Subject to the standards described in Section 19130 of the Government Code, any board, as defined in Section 22, the State Board of Chiropractic Examiners, or the Osteopathic Medical Board of California may enter into an agreement with an expert consultant to do any of the following:

(1) Provide an expert opinion on enforcement-related matters, including providing testimony at an administrative hearing.

(2) Assist the board as a subject matter expert in examination development, examination validation, or occupational analyses.

(3) Evaluate the mental or physical health of a licensee or an applicant for a license as may be necessary to protect the public health and safety.

(b) An executed contract between a board and an expert consultant shall be exempt from the provisions of Part 2 (commencing with Section 10100) of Division 2 of the Public Contract Code.

(c) Each board shall establish policies and procedures for the selection and use of expert consultants.

(d) Nothing in this section shall be construed to expand the scope of practice of an expert consultant providing services pursuant to this section.

Added Stats 2011 ch 339 § 1 (SB 541), effective September 26, 2011.

DIVISION 1

DEPARTMENT OF CONSUMER AFFAIRS

Chapter 1

The Department

Chapter 2

The Director of Consumer Affairs

Chapter 3

Funds of the Department

Chapter 4

Consumer Affairs

Article 1

General Provisions and Definitions

Article 2

Director and Employees

Article 3

Powers and Duties

Article 3.6

Uniform Standards Regarding Substance-Abusing Healing Arts Licensees

Article 4

Representation of Consumers

Article 5

Consumer Complaints

Article 7

Personal Information and Privacy Protection

Section V

Article 7

Rules and Regulations

Chapter 1

The Department

§ 100. Establishment

There is in the state government, in the State and Consumer Services Agency, a Department of Consumer Affairs.

Enacted Stats 1937. Amended Stats 1969 ch 138 § 5; Stats 1971 ch 716 § 4; Stats 1984 ch 144 § 1.

§ 101. Composition of department

The department is comprised of:
(a) The Dental Board of California.
(b) The Medical Board of California.
(c) The State Board of Optometry.
(d) The California State Board of Pharmacy.
(e) The Veterinary Medical Board.
(f) The California Board of Accountancy.
(g) The California Architects Board.
(h) The Bureau of Barbering and Cosmetology.
(i) The Board for Professional Engineers and Land Surveyors.
(j) The Contractors' State License Board.
(k) The Bureau for Private Postsecondary Education.
(*l*) The Bureau of Electronic and Appliance Repair, Home Furnishings, and Thermal Insulation.
(m) The Board of Registered Nursing.
(n) The Board of Behavioral Sciences.
(o) The State Athletic Commission.
(p) The Cemetery and Funeral Bureau.
(q) The State Board of Guide Dogs for the Blind.
(r) The Bureau of Security and Investigative Services.
(s) The Court Reporters Board of California.
(t) The Board of Vocational Nursing and Psychiatric Technicians.
(u) The Landscape Architects Technical Committee.
(v) The Division of Investigation.
(w) The Bureau of Automotive Repair.

(x) The Respiratory Care Board of California.

(y) The Acupuncture Board.

(z) The Board of Psychology.

(aa) The California Board of Podiatric Medicine.

(ab) The Physical Therapy Board of California.

(ac) The Arbitration Review Program.

(ad) The Physician Assistant Committee.

(ae) The Speech-Language Pathology and Audiology Board.

(af) The California Board of Occupational Therapy.

(ag) The Osteopathic Medical Board of California.

(ah) The Naturopathic Medicine Committee.

(ai) The Dental Hygiene Committee of California.

(aj) The Professional Fiduciaries Bureau.

(ak) Any other boards, offices, or officers subject to its jurisdiction by law.

Enacted Stats 1937. Amended Stats 1939 ch 651 § 1; Stats 1947 ch 1350 § 2; Stats 1953 ch 966 § 1; Stats 1955 ch 965 § 1; Stats 1961 ch 1095 § 1; Stats 1968 ch 444 § 1, ch 1323 § 1; Stats 1969 ch 1249 § 5; Stats 1971 ch 716 § 5, ch 1578 § 1, ch 1593 § 23.1, operative July 1, 1973; Stats 1972 ch 749 § 1, ch 1396 § 2; Stats 1973 ch 122 § 2.2, effective June 29, 1973, ch 863 § 1; Stats 1974 ch 546 § 1; Stats 1977 ch 141 § 1, effective June 29, 1977; Stats 1983 ch 150 § 1; Stats 1985 ch 1230 § 1; Stats 1987 ch 925 § 1, effective September 22, 1987; Stats 1989 ch 886 § 1; Stats 1990 ch 1256 § 1 (AB 2649); Stats 1991 ch 359 § 1 (AB 1332), ch 654 § 2 (AB 1893); Stats 1993 ch 1263 § 1 (AB 936); Stats 1994 ch 26 § 3 (AB 1807), effective March 30, 1994, ch 1274 § 1 (SB 2039), ch 1275 § 1 (SB 2101); Stats 1995 ch 60 § 1 (SB 42), effective July 6, 1995; Stats 1997 ch 758 § 1 (SB 1346), ch 759 § 1.5 (SB 827); Stats 1998 ch 59 § 2 (AB 969); Stats 1999 ch 655 § 1.1 (SB 1308); Stats 2000 ch 697 § 1 (SB 1046); Stats 2001 ch 615 § 1 (SB 26), effective October 9, 2001, ch 687 § 1.5 (AB 1409); Stats 2003 ch 485 § 1 (SB 907); Stats. 2009, Ch. 308, 309, 310 (SB 819).

§ 101.1.   [Section repealed 2011.]

Added Stats 1994 ch 908 § 2 (SB 2036). Amended Stats 1999 ch 983 § 1 (SB 1307). Repealed Stats 2010 ch 670 § 2 (AB 2130), effective January 1, 2011. The repealed section related to legislative intent regarding existing and proposed consumer-related boards.

§ 101.6.   Purpose

The boards, bureaus, and commissions in the department are established for the purpose of ensuring that those private businesses and professions deemed to engage in activities which have potential impact upon the public health, safety, and welfare are adequately regulated in order to protect the people of California.

To this end, they establish minimum qualifications and levels of competency and license persons desiring to engage in the occupations they regulate upon determining that such persons possess the requisite skills and qualifications necessary to provide safe and effective services to the public, or register or otherwise certify persons in order to identify practitioners and ensure performance according to set and accepted professional standards. They provide a means for redress of grievances by investigating allegations of unprofessional conduct, incompetence, fraudulent action, or unlawful activity brought to their attention by members of the public and institute disciplinary action against persons licensed or registered under the provisions of this code when such action is warranted. In addition, they conduct periodic checks of licensees, registrants, or otherwise certified persons in order to ensure compliance with the relevant sections of this code.

Added Stats 1980 ch 375 § 1.

§ 101.7. Meetings of boards; Regular and special

(a) Notwithstanding any other provision of law, boards shall meet at least three times each calendar year. Boards shall meet at least once each calendar year in northern California and once each calendar year in southern California in order to facilitate participation by the public and its licensees.

(b) The director at his or her discretion may exempt any board from the requirement in subdivision (a) upon a showing of good cause that the board is not able to meet at least three times in a calendar year.

(c) The director may call for a special meeting of the board when a board is not fulfilling its duties.

Added Stats 2007 ch 354 § 1 (SB 1047), effective January 1, 2008.

§ 102. Assumption of duties of board created by initiative

Upon the request of any board regulating, licensing, or controlling any professional or vocational occupation created by an initiative act, the Director of Consumer Affairs may take over the duties of the board under the same conditions and in the same manner as provided in this code for other boards of like character. Such boards shall pay a proportionate cost of the administration of the department on the same basis as is charged other boards included within the department. Upon request from any such board which has adopted the provisions of Chapter 5 (commencing with Section 11500) of Part 1 of Division 3 of Title 2 of the Government Code as rules of procedure in proceedings before it, the director shall assign hearing officers for such proceedings in accordance with Section 110.5.

Enacted Stats 1937. Amended Stats 1945 ch 869 § 1; Stats 1971 ch 716 § 6.

§ 102.3. Interagency agreement to delegate duties of certain repealed boards; Technical committees for regulation of professions under delegated authority; Renewal of agreement

(a) The director may enter into an interagency agreement with an appropriate entity within the Department of Consumer Affairs as provided for in Section 101 to delegate the duties, powers, purposes, responsibilities, and jurisdiction that have been succeeded and vested with the department, of a board, as defined in Section 477, which became inoperative and was repealed in accordance with Chapter 908 of the Statutes of 1994.

(b)(1) Where, pursuant to subdivision (a), an interagency agreement is entered into between the director and that entity, the entity receiving the delegation of authority may establish a technical committee to regulate, as directed by the entity, the profession subject to the authority that has been delegated. The entity may delegate to the technical committee only those powers that it received pursuant to the interagency agreement with the director. The technical committee shall have only those powers that have been delegated to it by the entity.

(2) Where the entity delegates its authority to adopt, amend, or repeal regulations to the technical committee, all regulations adopted, amended, or repealed by the technical committee shall be subject to the review and approval of the entity.

(3) The entity shall not delegate to a technical committee its authority to discipline a licentiate who has violated the provisions of the applicable chapter of the Business and Professions Code that is subject to the director's delegation of authority to the entity.

(c) An interagency agreement entered into, pursuant to subdivision (a), shall continue until such time as the licensing program administered by the technical committee has undergone a review by the Joint Committee on Boards, Commissions, and Consumer Protection to evaluate and determine whether the licensing program has demonstrated a public need for its continued existence. Thereafter, at the director's discretion, the interagency agreement may be renewed.

Added Stats 1997 ch 475 § 1 (AB 1546). Amended Stats 2004 ch 33 § 2 (AB 1467), effective April 13, 2004.

§ 103. Compensation and reimbursement for expenses

Each member of a board, commission, or committee created in the various chapters of Division 2 (commencing with Section 500) and Division 3 (commencing with Section 5000), and in Chapter 2 (commencing with Section 18600) and Chapter 3 (commencing with Section 19000) of Division 8, shall receive the moneys specified in this section when authorized by the respective provisions.

Section V

Each such member shall receive a per diem of one hundred dollars ($100) for each day actually spent in the discharge of official duties, and shall be reimbursed for traveling and other expenses necessarily incurred in the performance of official duties.

The payments in each instance shall be made only from the fund from which the expenses of the agency are paid and shall be subject to the availability of money.

Notwithstanding any other provision of law, no public officer or employee shall receive per diem salary compensation for serving on those boards, commissions, committees, or the Consumer Advisory Council on any day when the officer or employee also received compensation for his or her regular public employment.

Added Stats 1959 ch 1645 § 1. Amended Stats 1978 ch 1141 § 1; Stats 1985 ch 502 § 1; Stats 1987 ch 850 § 1; Stats 1993 ch 1264 § 1 (SB 574).

§ 105.5. Tenure of members of boards, etc., within department

Notwithstanding any other provision of this code, each member of a board, commission, examining committee, or other similarly constituted agency within the department shall hold office until the appointment and qualification of his successor or until one year shall have elapsed since the expiration of the term for which he was appointed, whichever first occurs.

Added Stats 1967 ch 524 § 1.

§ 106. Removal of board members

The Governor has power to remove from office at any time, any member of any board appointed by him for continued neglect of duties required by law, or for incompetence, or unprofessional or dishonorable conduct. Nothing in this section shall be construed as a limitation or restriction on the power of the Governor, conferred on him by any other provision of law, to remove any member of any board.

Enacted Stats 1937. Amended Stats 1945 ch 1276 § 3.

§ 106.5. Removal of member of licensing board for disclosure of examination information

Notwithstanding any other provision of law, the Governor may remove from office a member of a board or other licensing entity in the department if it is shown that such member has knowledge of the specific questions to be asked on the licensing entity's next examination and directly or indirectly discloses any such question or questions in advance of or during the examination to any applicant for that examination.

The proceedings for removal shall be conducted in accordance with the provisions of Chapter 5 of Part 1 of Division 3 of Title 2 of the Government Code, and the Governor shall have all the powers granted therein.

Added Stats 1977 ch 482 § 1.

§ 107. Executive officers (First of two; Operative until July 1, 2012)

Pursuant to subdivision (e) of Section 4 of Article VII of the California Constitution, each board may appoint a person exempt from civil service and may fix his or her salary, with the approval of the Department of Personnel Administration pursuant to Section 19825 of the Government Code, who shall be designated as an executive officer unless the licensing act of the particular board designates the person as a registrar.

Enacted Stats 1937. Amended Stats 1984 ch 47 § 2, effective March 21, 1984; Stats 1987 ch 850 § 2.

§ 107. Executive officers (Second of two; Operative July 1, 2012)

Pursuant to subdivision (e) of Section 4 of Article VII of the California Constitution, each board may appoint a person exempt from civil service and may fix his or her salary, with the approval of the Department of Human Resources pursuant to Section 19825 of the Government Code, who shall be designated as an executive officer unless the licensing act of the particular board designates the person as a registrar.

Enacted Stats 1937. Amended Stats 1984 ch 47 § 2, effective March 21, 1984; Stats 1987 ch 850 § 2. Amended by 2011 Governor's Reorganization Plan No. 1 § 1, effective September 9, 2011, operative July 1, 2012.

§ 107.5. Official seals

If any board in the department uses an official seal pursuant to any provision of this code, the seal shall contain the words "State of California" and "Department of Consumer Affairs" in addition to the title of the board, and shall be in a form approved by the director.

Added Stats 1967 ch 1272 § 1. Amended Stats 1971 ch 716 § 7.

§ 108. Status and powers of boards

Each of the boards comprising the department exists as a separate unit, and has the functions of setting standards, holding meetings, and setting dates thereof, preparing and conducting examinations,

Section V

passing upon applicants, conducting investigations of violations of laws under its jurisdiction, issuing citations and holding hearings for the revocation of licenses, and the imposing of penalties following those hearings, insofar as these powers are given by statute to each respective board.

Enacted Stats 1937. Amended Stats 2008 ch 179 § 1 (SB 1498), effective January 1, 2009.

§ 108.5. Witness fees and expenses

In any investigation, proceeding or hearing which any board, commission or officer in the department is empowered to institute, conduct, or hold, any witness appearing at such investigation, proceeding or hearing whether upon a subpoena or voluntarily, may be paid the sum of twelve dollars ($12) per day for every day in actual attendance at such investigation, proceeding or hearing and for his actual, necessary and reasonable expenses and such sums shall be a legal charge against the funds of the respective board, commission or officer; provided further, that no witness appearing other than at the instance of the board, commission or officer may be compensated out of such fund.

The board, commission or officer will determine the sums due any such witness and enter the amount on its minutes.

Added Stats 1943 ch 1035 § 1. Amended Stats 1957 ch 1908 § 6; Stats 1970 ch 1061 § 1.

§ 109. Review of decisions; Investigations

(a) The decisions of any of the boards comprising the department with respect to setting standards, conducting examinations, passing candidates, and revoking licenses, are not subject to review by the director, but are final within the limits provided by this code which are applicable to the particular board, except as provided in this section.

(b) The director may initiate an investigation of any allegations of misconduct in the preparation, administration, or scoring of an examination which is administered by a board, or in the review of qualifications which are a part of the licensing process of any board. A request for investigation shall be made by the director to the Division of Investigation through the chief of the division or to any law enforcement agency in the jurisdiction where the alleged misconduct occurred.

(c) The director may intervene in any matter of any board where an investigation by the Division of Investigation discloses probable cause to believe that the conduct or activity of a board, or its members or employees constitutes a violation of criminal law.

The term "intervene," as used in paragraph (c) of this section may include, but is not limited to, an application for a restraining order or injunctive relief as specified in Section 123.5, or a referral or request for criminal prosecution. For purposes of this section, the director shall be deemed to have standing under Section 123.5 and shall seek representation of the Attorney General, or other appropriate counsel in the event of a conflict in pursuing that action.

Enacted Stats 1937. Amended Stats 1991 ch 1013 § 1 (SB 961).

§ 110. Records and property

The department shall have possession and control of all records, books, papers, offices, equipment, supplies, funds, appropriations, land and other property—real or personal—now or hereafter held for the benefit or use of all of the bodies, offices or officers comprising the department. The title to all property held by any of these bodies, offices or officers for the use and benefit of the state, is vested in the State of California to be held in the possession of the department. Except as authorized by a board, the department shall not have the possession and control of examination questions prior to submission to applicants at scheduled examinations.

Enacted Stats 1937. Amended Stats 1996 ch 829 § 1 (AB 3473).

§ 111. Commissioners on examination

Unless otherwise expressly provided, any board may, with the approval of the appointing power, appoint qualified persons, who shall be designated as commissioners on examination, to give the whole or any portion of any examination. A commissioner on examination need not be a member of the board but he shall have the same qualifications as one and shall be subject to the same rules.

Added Stats 1937 ch 474. Amended Stats 1947 ch 1350 § 3; Stats 1978 ch 1161 § 1.

§ 112. Publication and sale of directories of authorized persons

Notwithstanding any other provision of this code, no agency in the department, with the exception of the Board for Professional Engineers and Land Surveyors, shall be required to compile, publish, sell, or otherwise distribute a directory. When an agency deems it necessary to compile and publish a directory, the agency shall cooperate with the director in determining its form and content, the time and frequency of its publication, the persons to whom it is to be sold or otherwise distributed, and its price if it is sold. Any agency that requires the approval of the director for the compilation, publication, or distribution of a directory, under the law in effect at the time the amendment made to this section at the 1970 Regular Session of the Legislature becomes effective, shall continue to require that approval. As used in this section, "directory" means a directory, roster, register, or similar compila-

Section V

tion of the names of persons who hold a license, certificate, permit, registration, or similar indicia of authority from the agency.

Added Stats 1937 ch 474. Amended Stats 1968 ch 1345 § 1; Stats 1970 ch 475 § 1; Stats 1998 ch 59 § 3 (AB 969).

§ 113. Conferences; Traveling expenses

Upon recommendation of the director, officers, and employees of the department, and the officers, members, and employees of the boards, committees, and commissions comprising it or subject to its jurisdiction may confer, in this state or elsewhere, with officers or employees of this state, its political subdivisions, other states, or the United States, or with other persons, associations, or organizations as may be of assistance to the department, board, committee, or commission in the conduct of its work. The officers, members, and employees shall be entitled to their actual traveling expenses incurred in pursuance hereof, but when these expenses are incurred with respect to travel outside of the state, they shall be subject to the approval of the Governor and the Director of Finance.

Added Stats 1937 ch 474. Amended Stats 1941 ch 885 § 1; Stats 2000 ch 277 § 1 (AB 2697); Stats 2001 ch 159 § 2 (SB 662).

§ 114. Reinstatement of expired license of licensee serving in military

(a) Notwithstanding any other provision of this code, any licensee or registrant of any board, commission, or bureau within the department whose license expired while the licensee or registrant was on active duty as a member of the California National Guard or the United States Armed Forces, may, upon application, reinstate his or her license or registration without examination or penalty, provided that all of the following requirements are satisfied:

(1) His or her license or registration was valid at the time he or she entered the California National Guard or the United States Armed Forces.

(2) The application for reinstatement is made while serving in the California National Guard or the United States Armed Forces, or not later than one year from the date of discharge from active service or return to inactive military status.

(3) The application for reinstatement is accompanied by an affidavit showing the date of entrance into the service, whether still in the service, or date of discharge, and the renewal fee for the current renewal period in which the application is filed is paid.

(b) If application for reinstatement is filed more than one year after discharge or return to inactive status, the applicant, in the discretion of the licensing agency, may be required to pass an examination.

(c) If application for reinstatement is filed and the licensing agency determines that the applicant has not actively engaged in the practice of his or her profession while on active duty, then the licensing agency may require the applicant to pass an examination.

(d) Unless otherwise specifically provided in this code, any licensee or registrant who, either part time or full time, practices in this state the profession or vocation for which he or she is licensed or registered shall be required to maintain his or her license in good standing even though he or she is in military service.

For the purposes in this section, time spent by a licensee in receiving treatment or hospitalization in any veterans' facility during which he or she is prevented from practicing his or her profession or vocation shall be excluded from said period of one year.

Added Stats 1951 ch 185 § 2. Amended Stats 1953 ch 423 § 1; Stats 1961 ch 1253 § 1; Stats 2010 ch 389 § 1 (AB 2500), effective January 1, 2011; Stats 2011 ch 296 § 1 (AB 1023), effective January 1, 2012.

§ 114.5.   [Section repealed 2011.]

Added Stats 1953 ch 423 § 2. Repealed Stats 2010 ch 389 § 2 (AB 2500), effective January 1, 2011. The repealed section related to the meaning of "War".

§ 115.   Applicability of Section 114

The provisions of Section 114 of this code are also applicable to a licensee or registrant whose license or registration was obtained while in the armed services.

Added Stats 1951 ch 1577 § 1.

§ 118.   Effect of withdrawal of application; Effect of suspension, forfeiture, etc., of license

(a) The withdrawal of an application for a license after it has been filed with a board in the department shall not, unless the board has consented in writing to such withdrawal, deprive the board of its authority to institute or continue a proceeding against the applicant for the denial of the license upon any ground provided by law or to enter an order denying the license upon any such ground.

(b) The suspension, expiration, or forfeiture by operation of law of a license issued by a board in the department, or its suspension, forfeiture, or cancellation by order of the board or by order of a court of law, or its surrender without the written consent of the board, shall not, during any period in which it may be renewed, restored, reissued, or reinstated, deprive the board of its authority to institute or continue a disciplinary proceeding against the licensee upon any ground provided by law or to enter an order suspending or revoking the li-

Section V

cense or otherwise taking disciplinary action against the licensee on any such ground.

(c) As used in this section, "board" includes an individual who is authorized by any provision of this code to issue, suspend, or revoke a license, and "license" includes "certificate," "registration," and "permit."

Added Stats 1961 ch 1079 § 1.

§ 119. Misdemeanors pertaining to use of licenses

Any person who does any of the following is guilty of a misdemeanor:

(a) Displays or causes or permits to be displayed or has in his or her possession either of the following:

(1) A canceled, revoked, suspended, or fraudulently altered license.

(2) A fictitious license or any document simulating a license or purporting to be or have been issued as a license.

(b) Lends his or her license to any other person or knowingly permits the use thereof by another.

(c) Displays or represents any license not issued to him or her as being his or her license.

(d) Fails or refuses to surrender to the issuing authority upon its lawful written demand any license, registration, permit, or certificate which has been suspended, revoked, or canceled.

(e) Knowingly permits any unlawful use of a license issued to him or her.

(f) Photographs, photostats, duplicates, manufactures, or in any way reproduces any license or facsimile thereof in a manner that it could be mistaken for a valid license, or displays or has in his or her possession any such photograph, photostat, duplicate, reproduction, or facsimile unless authorized by this code.

(g) Buys or receives a fraudulent, forged, or counterfeited license knowing that it is fraudulent, forged, or counterfeited. For purposes of this subdivision, "fraudulent" means containing any misrepresentation of fact.

As used in this section, "license" includes "certificate," "permit," "authority," and "registration" or any other indicia giving authorization to engage in a business or profession regulated by this code or referred to in Section 1000 or 3600.

Added Stats 1965 ch 1083 § 1. Amended Stats 1990 ch 350 § 1 (SB 2084) (ch 1207 prevails), ch 1207 § 1 (AB 3242); Stats 1994 ch 1206 § 1 (SB 1775); Stats 2000 ch 568 § 1 (AB 2888).

§ 121. Practice during period between renewal and receipt of evidence of renewal

No licensee who has complied with the provisions of this code relating to the renewal of his or her license prior to expiration of such license shall be deemed to be engaged illegally in the practice of his or her business or profession during any period between such renewal and receipt of evidence of such renewal which may occur due to delay not the fault of the applicant.

As used in this section, "license" includes "certificate," "permit," "authorization," and "registration," or any other indicia giving authorization, by any agency, board, bureau, commission, committee, or entity within the Department of Consumer Affairs, to engage in a business or profession regulated by this code or by the board referred to in the Chiropractic Act or the Osteopathic Act.

Added Stats 1979 ch 77 § 1.

§ 121.5. Application of fees to licenses or registrations lawfully inactivated

Except as otherwise provided in this code, the application of delinquency fees or accrued and unpaid renewal fees for the renewal of expired licenses or registrations shall not apply to licenses or registrations that have lawfully been designated as inactive or retired.

Added Stats 2001 ch 435 § 1 (SB 349).

§ 122. Fee for issuance of duplicate certificate

Except as otherwise provided by law, the department and each of the boards, bureaus, committees, and commissions within the department may charge a fee for the processing and issuance of a duplicate copy of any certificate of licensure or other form evidencing licensure or renewal of licensure. The fee shall be in an amount sufficient to cover all costs incident to the issuance of the duplicate certificate or other form but shall not exceed twenty-five dollars ($25).

Added Stats 1986 ch 951 § 1.

§ 123. Conduct constituting subversion of licensing examination; Penalties and damages

It is a misdemeanor for any person to engage in any conduct which subverts or attempts to subvert any licensing examination or the administration of an examination, including, but not limited to:

(a) Conduct which violates the security of the examination materials; removing from the examination room any examination materials without authorization; the unauthorized reproduction by any means of any portion of the actual licensing examination; aiding by any means the unauthorized reproduction of any portion of the actual licensing examination; paying or using professional or paid examination-takers for the purpose of reconstructing any portion of the licensing examination; obtaining examination questions or other examination material, except by specific authorization either before, during, or after an examination; or using or purporting to use any examination questions or materials which were improperly removed or taken from any examination for the purpose of instructing or preparing any applicant for examination; or selling, distributing, buying, receiving, or having unauthorized possession of any portion of a future, current, or previously administered licensing examination.

(b) Communicating with any other examinee during the administration of a licensing examination; copying answers from another examinee or permitting one's answers to be copied by another examinee; having in one's possession during the administration of the licensing examination any books, equipment, notes, written or printed materials, or data of any kind, other than the examination materials distributed, or otherwise authorized to be in one's possession during the examination; or impersonating any examinee or having an impersonator take the licensing examination on one's behalf.

Nothing in this section shall preclude prosecution under the authority provided for in any other provision of law.

In addition to any other penalties, a person found guilty of violating this section, shall be liable for the actual damages sustained by the agency administering the examination not to exceed ten thousand dollars ($10,000) and the costs of litigation.

(c) If any provision of this section or the application thereof to any person or circumstances is held invalid, that invalidity shall not affect other provisions or applications of the section that can be given effect without the invalid provision or application, and to this end the provisions of this section are severable.

Added Stats 1989 ch 1022 § 1. Amended Stats 1991 ch 647 § 1 (SB 879).

§ 123.5. Enjoining violations

Whenever any person has engaged, or is about to engage, in any acts or practices which constitute, or will constitute, a violation of Section 123, the superior court in and for the county wherein the acts or practices take place, or are about to take place, may issue an injunction, or other appropriate order, restraining such conduct on application of a board, the Attorney General or the district attorney of the county.

The proceedings under this section shall be governed by Chapter 3 (commencing with Section 525) of Title 7 of Part 2 of the Code of Civil Procedure.

The remedy provided for by this section shall be in addition to, and not a limitation on, the authority provided for in any other provision of law.

Added Stats 1983 ch 95 § 2, as B & P C § 497. Amended and Renumbered by Stats 1989 ch 1022 § 4.

§ 124. Manner of notice

Notwithstanding subdivision (c) of Section 11505 of the Government Code, whenever written notice, including a notice, order, or document served pursuant to Chapter 3.5 (commencing with Section 11340), Chapter 4 (commencing with Section 11370), or Chapter 5 (commencing with Section 11500), of Part 1 of Division 3 of Title 2 of the Government Code, is required to be given by any board in the department, the notice may be given by regular mail addressed to the last known address of the licentiate or by personal service, at the option of the board.

Added Stats 1961 ch 1253 § 2. Amended Stats 1994 ch 26 § 4 (AB 1807), effective March 30, 1994; Stats 1995 ch 938 § 1 (SB 523), operative July 1, 1997.

§ 125. Misdemeanor offenses by licensees

Any person, licensed under Division 1 (commencing with Section 100), Division 2(commencing with Section 500), or Division 3(commencing with Section 5000) is guilty of a misdemeanor and subject to the disciplinary provisions of this code applicable to him or her, who conspires with a person not so licensed to violate any provision of this code, or who, with intent to aid or assist that person in violating those provisions does either of the following:
(a) Allows his or her license to be used by that person.
(b) Acts as his or her agent or partner.

Added Stats 1949 ch 308 § 1. Amended Stats 1994 ch 1206 § 2 (SB 1775).

§ 125.3. Direction to licentiate violating licensing act to pay costs of investigation and enforcement

(a) Except as otherwise provided by law, in any order issued in resolution of a disciplinary proceeding before any board within the department or before the Osteopathic Medical Board, upon request of the entity bringing the proceeding, the administrative law judge may direct a licentiate found to have committed a violation or violations of the licensing act to pay a sum not to exceed the reasonable costs of the investigation and enforcement of the case.
(b) In the case of a disciplined licentiate that is a corporation or a partnership, the order may be made against the licensed corporate entity or licensed partnership.

(c) A certified copy of the actual costs, or a good faith estimate of costs where actual costs are not available, signed by the entity bringing the proceeding or its designated representative shall be prima facie evidence of reasonable costs of investigation and prosecution of the case. The costs shall include the amount of investigative and enforcement costs up to the date of the hearing, including, but not limited to, charges imposed by the Attorney General.

(d) The administrative law judge shall make a proposed finding of the amount of reasonable costs of investigation and prosecution of the case when requested pursuant to subdivision (a). The finding of the administrative law judge with regard to costs shall not be reviewable by the board to increase the cost award. The board may reduce or eliminate the cost award, or remand to the administrative law judge if the proposed decision fails to make a finding on costs requested pursuant to subdivision (a).

(e) If an order for recovery of costs is made and timely payment is not made as directed in the board's decision, the board may enforce the order for repayment in any appropriate court. This right of enforcement shall be in addition to any other rights the board may have as to any licentiate to pay costs.

(f) In any action for recovery of costs, proof of the board's decision shall be conclusive proof of the validity of the order of payment and the terms for payment.

(g)(1) Except as provided in paragraph (2), the board shall not renew or reinstate the license of any licentiate who has failed to pay all of the costs ordered under this section.

(2) Notwithstanding paragraph (1), the board may, in its discretion, conditionally renew or reinstate for a maximum of one year the license of any licentiate who demonstrates financial hardship and who enters into a formal agreement with the board to reimburse the board within that one-year period for the unpaid costs.

(h) All costs recovered under this section shall be considered a reimbursement for costs incurred and shall be deposited in the fund of the board recovering the costs to be available upon appropriation by the Legislature.

(i) Nothing in this section shall preclude a board from including the recovery of the costs of investigation and enforcement of a case in any stipulated settlement.

(j) This section does not apply to any board if a specific statutory provision in that board's licensing act provides for recovery of costs in an administrative disciplinary proceeding.

(k) Notwithstanding the provisions of this section, the Medical Board of California shall not request nor obtain from a physician and surgeon, investigation and prosecution costs for a disciplinary proceeding against the licentiate. The board shall ensure that this subdivision is revenue neutral with regard to it and that any loss of revenue or increase in costs resulting from this subdivision is offset by an increase in the amount of the initial license fee and the biennial renewal fee, as provided in subdivision (e) of Section 2435.

Added Stats 1992 ch 1059 § 1 (AB 3745), ch 1289 § 1 (AB 2743). Amended Stats 2001 ch 728 § 1 (SB 724); Stats 2005 ch 674 § 2 (SB 231), effective January 1, 2006; Stats 2006 ch 223 § 2 (SB 1438), effective January 1, 2007.

§ 125.5. Enjoining violations; Restitution orders

(a) The superior court for the county in which any person has engaged or is about to engage in any act which constitutes a violation of a chapter of this code administered or enforced by a board within the department may, upon a petition filed by the board with the approval of the director, issue an injunction or other appropriate order restraining such conduct. The proceedings under this section shall be governed by Chapter 3 (commencing with Section 525) of Title 7 of Part 2 of the Code of Civil Procedure. As used in this section, "board" includes commission, bureau, division, agency and a medical quality review committee.

(b) The superior court for the county in which any person has engaged in any act which constitutes a violation of a chapter of this code administered or enforced by a board within the department may, upon a petition filed by the board with the approval of the director, order such person to make restitution to persons injured as a result of such violation.

(c) The court may order a person subject to an injunction or restraining order, provided for in subdivision (a) of this section, or subject to an order requiring restitution pursuant to subdivision (b), to reimburse the petitioning board for expenses incurred by the board in its investigation related to its petition.

(d) The remedy provided for by this section shall be in addition to, and not a limitation on, the authority provided for in any other section of this code.

Added Stats 1972 ch 1238 § 1. Amended Stats 1973 ch 632 § 1; Stats 2d Ex Sess 1975 ch 1 § 2; Stats 1982 ch 517 § 1.

§ 125.6. Unlawful discrimination by licensees

(a) With regard to an applicant, every person who holds a license under the provisions of this code is subject to disciplinary action under the disciplinary provisions of this code applicable to that person if, because of any characteristic listed or defined in subdivision (b) or (e) of Section 51 of the Civil Code, he or she refuses to perform the licensed activity or aids or incites the refusal to perform that licensed activity by another licensee, or if, because of any characteristic listed or defined in subdivision (b) or (e) of Section 51 of the Civil Code, he or she makes any discrimination, or restriction in the performance of the licensed activity. Nothing in this section shall be interpreted to apply to discrimination by employers with regard to employees or prospective employees, nor shall this section authorize action against any club license issued pursuant to Article 4 (commencing with Section 23425) of Chapter 3 of Division 9 because of discriminatory membership policy. The presence of architectural barriers to an individual with physical disabilities that conform to applicable state or local building codes and regulations shall not constitute discrimination under this section.

(b)(1) Nothing in this section requires a person licensed pursuant to Division 2 (commencing with Section 500) to permit an individual to participate in, or benefit from, the licensed activity of the licensee where that individual poses a direct threat to the health or safety of others. For this purpose, the term "direct threat" means a significant risk to the health or safety of others that cannot be eliminated by a modification of policies, practices, or procedures or by the provision of auxiliary aids and services.

(2) Nothing in this section requires a person licensed pursuant to Division 2 (commencing with Section 500) to perform a licensed activity for which he or she is not qualified to perform.

(c)(1) "Applicant," as used in this section, means a person applying for licensed services provided by a person licensed under this code.

(2) "License," as used in this section, includes "certificate," "permit," "authority," and "registration" or any other indicia giving authorization to engage in a business or profession regulated by this code.

Added Stats 1974 ch 1350 § 1. Amended Stats 1977 ch 293 § 1; Stats 1980 ch 191 § 1; Stats 1992 ch 913 § 2 (AB 1077); Stats 2007 ch 568 § 2 (AB 14), effective January 1, 2008.

§ 125.7. Restraining orders

In addition to the remedy provided for in Section 125.5, the superior court for the county in which any licensee licensed under Division 2 (commencing with Section 500), or any initiative act referred to in that division, has engaged or is about to engage in any act that constitutes a violation of a chapter of this code administered or enforced by a board referred to in Division 2 (commencing with Section 500), may, upon a petition filed by the board and accompanied by an affidavit or affidavits in support thereof and a memorandum of points and authorities, issue a temporary restraining order or other appropriate order restraining the licensee from engaging in the business or profession for which the person is licensed or from any part thereof, in accordance with this section.

(a) If the affidavits in support of the petition show that the licensee has engaged or is about to engage in acts or omissions constituting a violation of a chapter of this code and if the court is satisfied that permitting the licensee to continue to engage in the business or profession for which the license was issued will endanger the public health, safety, or welfare, the court may issue an order temporarily restraining the licensee from engaging in the profession for which he or she is licensed.

(b) The order may not be issued without notice to the licensee unless it appears from facts shown by the affidavits that serious injury would result to the public before the matter can be heard on notice.

(c) Except as otherwise specifically provided by this section, proceedings under this section shall be governed by Chapter 3 (commencing with Section 525) of Title 7 of Part 2 of the Code of Civil Procedure.

(d) When a restraining order is issued pursuant to this section, or within a time to be allowed by the superior court, but in any case not more than 30 days after the restraining order is issued, an accusation shall be filed with the board pursuant to Section 11503 of the Government Code or, in the case of a licensee of the State Department of Health Services, with that department pursuant to Section 100171 of the Health and Safety Code. The accusation shall be served upon the licensee as provided by Section 11505 of the Government Code. The licensee shall have all of the rights and privileges available as specified in Chapter 5 (commencing with Section 11500) of Part 1 of Division 3 of Title 2 of the Government Code. However, if the licensee requests a hearing on the accusation, the board shall provide the licensee with a hearing within 30 days of the request and a decision within 15 days of the date the decision is received from the administrative law judge, or the court may nullify the restraining order previously issued. Any restraining order issued pursuant to this section shall be dissolved by operation of law at the time the board's decision is subject to judicial review pursuant to Section 1094.5 of the Code of Civil Procedure.

(e) The remedy provided for in this section shall be in addition to, and not a limitation upon, the authority provided by any other provision of this code.

Added Stats 1977 ch 292 § 1. Amended Stats 1982 ch 517 § 2; Stats 1994 ch 1206 § 3 (SB 1775); Stats 1997 ch 220 § 1 (SB 68), effective August 4, 1997; Stats 1998 ch 878 § 1.5 (SB 2239).

§ 125.8.   Temporary order restraining licensee engaged or about to engage in violation of law

In addition to the remedy provided for in Section 125.5, the superior court for the county in which any licensee licensed under Division 3 (commencing with Section 5000) or Chapter 2 (commencing with Section 18600) or Chapter 3 (commencing with Section 19000) of Division 8 has engaged or is about to engage in any act which

constitutes a violation of a chapter of this code administered or enforced by a board referred to in Division 3 (commencing with Section
5000) or Chapter 2 (commencing with Section 18600) or Chapter 3
(commencing with Section 19000) of Division 8 may, upon a petition
filed by the board and accompanied by an affidavit or affidavits in
support thereof and a memorandum of points and authorities, issue
a temporary restraining order or other appropriate order restraining the licensee from engaging in the business or profession for
which the person is licensed or from any part thereof, in accordance
with the provisions of this section.

(a) If the affidavits in support of the petition show that the licensee
has engaged or is about to engage in acts or omissions constituting a
violation of a chapter of this code and if the court is satisfied that
permitting the licensee to continue to engage in the business or profession for which the license was issued will endanger the public
health, safety, or welfare, the court may issue an order temporarily
restraining the licensee from engaging in the profession for which he
is licensed.

(b) Such order may not be issued without notice to the licensee unless it appears from facts shown by the affidavits that serious injury
would result to the public before the matter can be heard on notice.

(c) Except as otherwise specifically provided by this section, proceedings under this section shall be governed by Chapter 3 (commencing
with Section 525) of Title 7 of Part 2 of the Code of Civil Procedure.

(d) When a restraining order is issued pursuant to this section, or
within a time to be allowed by the superior court, but in any case not
more than 30 days after the restraining order is issued, an accusation
shall be filed with the board pursuant to Section 11503 of the Government Code. The accusation shall be served upon the licensee as
provided by Section 11505 of the Government Code. The licensee
shall have all of the rights and privileges available as specified in
Chapter 5 (commencing with Section 11500) of Part 1 of Division 3 of
Title 2 of the Government Code; however, if the licensee requests a
hearing on the accusation, the board must provide the licensee with a
hearing within 30 days of the request and a decision within 15 days of
the date of the conclusion of the hearing, or the court may nullify the
restraining order previously issued. Any restraining order issued
pursuant to this section shall be dissolved by operation of law at such
time the board's decision is subject to judicial review pursuant to Section 1094.5 of the Code of Civil Procedure.

Added Stats 1977 ch 443 § 1. Amended Stats 1982 ch 517 § 3.

§ 125.9. System for issuance of citations to licensees; Contents; Fines

(a) Except with respect to persons regulated under Chapter 11 (commencing with Section 7500), and Chapter 11.6 (commencing with Section 7590) of Division 3, any board, bureau, or commission within the department, the board created by the Chiropractic Initiative Act, and the Osteopathic Medical Board of California, may establish, by regulation, a system for the issuance to a licensee of a citation which may contain an order of abatement or an order to pay an administrative fine assessed by the board, bureau, or commission where the licensee is in violation of the applicable licensing act or any regulation adopted pursuant thereto.

(b) The system shall contain the following provisions:

(1) Citations shall be in writing and shall describe with particularity the nature of the violation, including specific reference to the provision of law determined to have been violated.

(2) Whenever appropriate, the citation shall contain an order of abatement fixing a reasonable time for abatement of the violation.

(3) In no event shall the administrative fine assessed by the board, bureau, or commission exceed fivethousand dollars ($5,000) for each inspection or each investigation made with respect to the violation, or five thousand dollars ($5,000) for each violation or count if the violation involves fraudulent billing submitted to an insurance company, the Medi-Cal program, or Medicare. In assessing a fine, the board, bureau, or commission shall give due consideration to the appropriateness of the amount of the fine with respect to factors such as the gravity of the violation, the good faith of the licensee, and the history of previous violations.

(4) A citation or fine assessment issued pursuant to a citation shall inform the licensee that if he or she desires a hearing to contest the finding of a violation, that hearing shall be requested by written notice to the board, bureau, or commission within 30 days of the date of issuance of the citation or assessment. If a hearing is not requested pursuant to this section, payment of any fine shall not constitute an admission of the violation charged. Hearings shall be held pursuant to Chapter 5 (commencing with Section 11500) of Part 1 of Division 3 of Title 2 of the Government Code.

(5) Failure of a licensee to pay a fine within 30 days of the date of assessment, unless the citation is being appealed, may result in disciplinary action being taken by the board, bureau, or commission. Where a citation is not contested and a fine is not paid, the full amount of the assessed fine shall be added to the fee for renewal of the license. A license shall not be renewed without payment of the renewal fee and fine.

(c) The system may contain the following provisions:

(1) A citation may be issued without the assessment of an administrative fine.

(2) Assessment of administrative fines may be limited to only particular violations of the applicable licensing act.

(d) Notwithstanding any other provision of law, if a fine is paid to satisfy an assessment based on the finding of a violation, payment of the fine shall be represented as satisfactory resolution of the matter for purposes of public disclosure.

(e) Administrative fines collected pursuant to this section shall be deposited in the special fund of the particular board, bureau, or commission.

Added Stats 1986 ch 1379 § 2. Amended Stats 1987 ch 1088 § 1; Stats 1991 ch 521 § 1 (SB 650); Stats 1995 ch 381 § 4 (AB 910), effective August 4, 1995, ch 708 § 1 (SB 609); Stats 2000 ch 197 § 1 (SB 1636); Stats 2001 ch 309 § 1 (AB 761), ch 728 § 1.2 (SB 724); Stats 2003 ch 788 § 1 (SB 362).

§ 126. Submission of reports to Governor

Notwithstanding any other provision of this code, any board, commission, examining committee, or other similarly constituted agency within the department required prior to the effective date of this section to submit reports to the Governor under any provision of this code shall not be required to submit such reports.

Added Stats 1967 ch 660 § 1.

§ 127. Submission of reports to director

Notwithstanding any other provision of this code, the director may require such reports from any board, commission, examining committee, or other similarly constituted agency within the department as he deems reasonably necessary on any phase of their operations.

Added Stats 1967 ch 660 § 2.

§ 128. Sale of equipment, supplies, or services for use in violation of licensing requirements

Notwithstanding any other provision of law, it is a misdemeanor to sell equipment, supplies, or services to any person with knowledge that the equipment, supplies, or services are to be used in the performance of a service or contract in violation of the licensing requirements of this code.

The provisions of this section shall not be applicable to cash sales of less than one hundred dollars ($100).

For the purposes of this section, "person" includes, but is not limited to, a company, partnership, limited liability company, firm, or corporation.

For the purposes of this section, "license" includes certificate or registration.

A violation of this section shall be punishable by a fine of not less than one thousand dollars ($1,000) and by imprisonment in the county jail not exceeding six months.

Added Stats 1971 ch 1052 § 1. Amended Stats 1994 ch 1010 § 1 (SB 2053).

§ 128.5. Reduction of license fees in event of surplus funds

(a) Notwithstanding any other provision of law, if at the end of any fiscal year, an agency within the Department of Consumer Affairs, except the agencies referred to in subdivision (b), has unencumbered funds in an amount that equals or is more than the agency's operating budget for the next two fiscal years, the agency shall reduce license or other fees, whether the license or other fees be fixed by statute or may be determined by the agency within limits fixed by statute, during the following fiscal year in an amount that will reduce any surplus funds of the agency to an amount less than the agency's operating budget for the next two fiscal years.

(b) Notwithstanding any other provision of law, if at the end of any fiscal year, the California Architects Board, the Board of Behavioral Sciences, the Veterinary Medical Board, the Court Reporters Board of California, the Medical Board of California, the Board of Vocational Nursing and Psychiatric Technicians, or the Bureau of Security and Investigative Services has unencumbered funds in an amount that equals or is more than the agency's operating budget for the next two fiscal years, the agency shall reduce license or other fees, whether the license or other fees be fixed by statute or may be determined by the agency within limits fixed by statute, during the following fiscal year in an amount that will reduce any surplus funds of the agency to an amount less than the agency's operating budget for the next two fiscal years.

Added Stats 1972 ch 938 § 2, effective August 16, 1972, as B & P C § 128. Amended Stats 1973 ch 863 § 3. Amended and Renumbered by Stats 1978 ch 1161 § 4. Amended Stats 1987 ch 850 § 3; Stats 1989 ch 886 § 2; Stats 1993 ch 1263 § 2 (AB 936); Stats 1994 ch 26 § 5 (AB 1807), effective March 30, 1994; Stats 1995 ch 60 § 2 (SB 42), effective July 6, 1995; Stats 1997 ch 759 § 2 (SB 827); Stats 2000 ch 1054 § 1 (SB 1863); Stats. 2009, Ch. 308 (SB 819).

§ 129. Handling of complaints; Reports to Legislature

(a) As used in this section, "board" means every board, bureau, commission, committee and similarly constituted agency in the department which issues licenses.

(b) Each board shall, upon receipt of any complaint respecting a licentiate thereof, notify the complainant of the initial administrative action taken on his complaint within 10 days of receipt. Each board shall thereafter notify the complainant of the final action taken on his complaint. There shall be a notification made in every case in which the complainant is known. If the complaint is not within the jurisdiction of the board or if the board is unable to dispose satisfactorily of the complaint, the board shall transmit the complaint together with any evidence or information it has concerning the complaint to the agency, public or private, whose authority in the opinion of the board will provide the most effective means to secure the relief sought. The board shall notify the complainant of such action and of any other means which may be available to the complainant to secure relief.

(c) The board shall, when the board deems it appropriate, notify the person against whom the complaint is made of the nature of the complaint, may request appropriate relief for the complainant, and may meet and confer with the complainant and the licentiate in order to mediate the complaint. Nothing in this subdivision shall be construed as authorizing or requiring any board to set or to modify any fee charged by a licentiate.

(d) It shall be the continuing duty of the board to ascertain patterns of complaints and to report on all actions taken with respect to such patterns of complaints to the director and to the Legislature at least once a year. The board shall evaluate those complaints dismissed for lack of jurisdiction or no violation and recommend to the director and to the Legislature at least once a year such statutory changes as it deems necessary to implement the board's functions and responsibilities under this section.

(e) It shall be the continuing duty of the board to take whatever action it deems necessary, with the approval of the director, to inform the public of its functions under this section.

Added Stats 1972 ch 1041 § 1.

§ 130. Terms of office of agency members

(a) Notwithstanding any other provision of law, the term of office of any member of an agency designated in subdivision (b) shall be for a term of four years expiring on June 1.

(b) Subdivision (a) applies to the following boards or committees:

(1) The Medical Board of California.

(2) The California Board of Podiatric Medicine.

(3) The Physical Therapy Board of California.

(4) The Board of Registered Nursing.

(5) The Board of Vocational Nursing and Psychiatric Technicians.

(6) The State Board of Optometry.

(7) The California State Board of Pharmacy.

(8) The Veterinary Medical Board.

(9) The California Architects Board.

(10) The Landscape Architect Technical Committee.

(11) The Board for Professional Engineers and Land Surveyors.
(12) The Contractors' State License Board.
(13) The State Board of Guide Dogs for the Blind.
(14) The Board of Behavioral Sciences.
(15) The Structural Pest Control Board.
(16) The Bureau of Electronic and Appliance Repair.
(17) The Court Reporters Board of California.
(18) The State Board for Geologists and Geophysicists.
(19) The State Athletic Commission.
(20) The Osteopathic Medical Board of California.
(21) The Respiratory Care Board of California.
(22) The Acupuncture Board.
(23) The Board of Psychology.

Added Stats 1969 ch 465 § 1. Amended Stats 1971 ch 716 § 8; Stats 1978 ch 1161 § 5; Stats 1983 ch 150 § 2; Stats 1986 ch 655 § 1; Stats 1987 ch 850 § 4; Stats 1989 ch 886 § 3; Stats 1990 ch 1256 § 2 (AB 2649); Stats 1991 ch 359 § 2 (AB 1332); Stats 1994 ch 26 § 6 (AB 1807), effective March 30, 1994, ch 1274 § 1.3 (SB 2039); Stats 1995 ch 60 § 3 (SB 42), effective July 6, 1995; Stats 1997 ch 759 § 3 (SB 827); Stats 1998 ch 59 § 4 (AB 969), ch 970 § 1 (AB 2802), ch 971 § 1 (AB 2721); Stats 2000 ch 1054 § 2 (SB 1863); Stats 2001 ch 159 § 3 (SB 662).

§ 131. Maximum number of terms

Notwithstanding any other provision of law, no member of an agency designated in subdivision (b) of Section 130 or member of a board, commission, committee, or similarly constituted agency in the department shall serve more than two consecutive full terms.

Added Stats 1970 ch 1394 § 1, operative July 1, 1971. Amended Stats 1987 ch 850 § 5.

§ 134. Proration of license fees

When the term of any license issued by any agency in the department exceeds one year, initial license fees for licenses which are issued during a current license term shall be prorated on a yearly basis.

Added Stats 1974 ch 743 § 1. Amended Stats 1978 ch 1161 § 6.

§ 135. Reexamination of applicants

No agency in the department shall, on the basis of an applicant's failure to successfully complete prior examinations, impose any additional limitations, restrictions, prerequisites, or requirements on any applicant who wishes to participate in subsequent examinations except that any examining agency which allows an applicant conditional credit for successfully completing a divisible part of an examination may require that an applicant be reexamined in those parts successfully completed if such applicant has not successfully completed all parts of the examination within a required period of time established

Section V

by the examining agency. Nothing in this section, however, requires the exemption of such applicant from the regular fees and requirements normally associated with examinations.

Added Stats 1974 ch 743 § 2.

§ 136. Notification of change of address; Punishment for failure to comply

(a) Each person holding a license, certificate, registration, permit, or other authority to engage in a profession or occupation issued by a board within the department shall notify the issuing board at its principal office of any change in his or her mailing address within 30 days after the change, unless the board has specified by regulations a shorter time period.

(b) Except as otherwise provided by law, failure of a licentiate to comply with the requirement in subdivision (a) constitutes grounds for the issuance of a citation and administrative fine, if the board has the authority to issue citations and administrative fines.

Added Stats 1994 ch 26 § 7 (AB 1807), effective March 30, 1994.

§ 137. Regulations requiring inclusion of license numbers in advertising, etc.

Any agency within the department may promulgate regulations requiring licensees to include their license numbers in any advertising, soliciting, or other presentments to the public.

However, nothing in this section shall be construed to authorize regulation of any person not a licensee who engages in advertising, solicitation, or who makes any other presentment to the public on behalf of a licensee. Such a person shall incur no liability pursuant to this section for communicating in any advertising, soliciting, or other presentment to the public a licensee's license number exactly as provided to him by the licensee or for failure to communicate such number if none is provided to him by the licensee.

Added Stats 1974 ch 743 § 3.

§ 138. Notice that practitioner is licensed; Evaluation of licensing examination

Every board in the department, as defined in Section 22, shall initiate the process of adopting regulations on or before June 30, 1999, to require its licentiates, as defined in Section 23.8, to provide notice to their clients or customers that the practitioner is licensed by this state. A board shall be exempt from the requirement to adopt regulations pursuant to this section if the board has in place, in statute or regulation, a requirement that provides for consumer notice of a practitioner's status as a licensee of this state.

Added Stats 1998 ch 879 § 1 (SB 2238). Amended Stats 1999 ch 67 § 1 (AB 1105), effective July 6, 1999.

§ 139. Policy for examination development and validation, and occupational analysis

(a) The Legislature finds and declares that occupational analyses and examination validation studies are fundamental components of licensure programs. It is the intent of the Legislature that the policy developed by the department pursuant to subdivision (b) be used by the fiscal, policy, and sunset review committees of the Legislature in their annual reviews of these boards, programs, and bureaus.

(b) Notwithstanding any other provision of law, the department shall develop, in consultation with the boards, programs, bureaus, and divisions under its jurisdiction, and the Osteopathic Medical Board of California and the State Board of Chiropractic Examiners, a policy regarding examination development and validation, and occupational analysis. The department shall finalize and distribute this policy by September 30, 1999, to each of the boards, programs, bureaus, and divisions under its jurisdiction and to the Osteopathic Medical Board of California and the State Board of Chiropractic Examiners. This policy shall be submitted in draft form at least 30 days prior to that date to the appropriate fiscal, policy, and sunset review committees of the Legislature for review. This policy shall address, but shall not be limited to, the following issues:

(1) An appropriate schedule for examination validation and occupational analyses, and circumstances under which more frequent reviews are appropriate.

(2) Minimum requirements for psychometrically sound examination validation, examination development, and occupational analyses, including standards for sufficient number of test items.

(3) Standards for review of state and national examinations.

(4) Setting of passing standards.

(5) Appropriate funding sources for examination validations and occupational analyses.

(6) Conditions under which boards, programs, and bureaus should use internal and external entities to conduct these reviews.

(7) Standards for determining appropriate costs of reviews of different types of examinations, measured in terms of hours required.

(8) Conditions under which it is appropriate to fund permanent and limited term positions within a board, program, or bureau to manage these reviews.

(c) Every regulatory board and bureau, as defined in Section 22, and every program and bureau administered by the department, the

Section V

Osteopathic Medical Board of California, and the State Board of Chiropractic Examiners, shall submit to the director on or before December 1, 1999, and on or before December 1 of each subsequent year, its method for ensuring that every licensing examination administered by or pursuant to contract with the board is subject to periodic evaluation. The evaluation shall include (1) a description of the occupational analysis serving as the basis for the examination; (2) sufficient item analysis data to permit a psychometric evaluation of the items; (3) an assessment of the appropriateness of prerequisites for admittance to the examination; and (4) an estimate of the costs and personnel required to perform these functions. The evaluation shall be revised and a new evaluation submitted to the director whenever, in the judgment of the board, program, or bureau, there is a substantial change in the examination or the prerequisites for admittance to the examination.

(d) The evaluation may be conducted by the board, program, or bureau, the Office of Professional Examination Services of the department, the Osteopathic Medical Board of California, or the State Board of Chiropractic Examiners or pursuant to a contract with a qualified private testing firm. A board, program, or bureau that provides for development or administration of a licensing examination pursuant to contract with a public or private entity may rely on an occupational analysis or item analysis conducted by that entity. The department shall compile this information, along with a schedule specifying when examination validations and occupational analyses shall be performed, and submit it to the appropriate fiscal, policy, and sunset review committees of the Legislature by September 30 of each year. It is the intent of the Legislature that the method specified in this report be consistent with the policy developed by the department pursuant to subdivision (b).

Added Stats 1999 ch 67 § 2 (AB 1105), effective July 6, 1999. Amended Stats. 2009, Ch. 307 (SB 821)

§ 140. Disciplinary action; Licensee's failure to record cash transactions in payment of employee wages

Any board, as defined in Section 22, which is authorized under this code to take disciplinary action against a person who holds a license may take disciplinary action upon the ground that the licensee has failed to record and preserve for not less than three years, any and all cash transactions involved in the payment of employee wages by a licensee. Failure to make these records available to an authorized representative of the board may be made grounds for disciplinary action. In any action brought and sustained by the board which involves a violation of this section and any regulation adopted thereto, the board may assess the licensee with the actual investigative costs incurred, not to exceed two thousand five hundred dollars ($2,500). Failure to pay those costs may result in revocation of the license. Any moneys collected pursuant to this section shall be deposited in the respective fund of the board.

Added Stats 1984 ch 1490 § 2, effective September 27, 1984.

§ 141. Disciplinary action by foreign jurisdiction; Grounds for disciplinary action by state licensing board

(a) For any licensee holding a license issued by a board under the jurisdiction of the department, a disciplinary action taken by another state, by any agency of the federal government, or by another country for any act substantially related to the practice regulated by the California license, may be a ground for disciplinary action by the respective state licensing board. A certified copy of the record of the disciplinary action taken against the licensee by another state, an agency of the federal government, or another country shall be conclusive evidence of the events related therein.

(b) Nothing in this section shall preclude a board from applying a specific statutory provision in the licensing act administered by that board that provides for discipline based upon a disciplinary action taken against the licensee by another state, an agency of the federal government, or another country.

Added Stats 1994 ch 1275 § 2 (SB 2101).

§ 143. Proof of license as condition of bringing action for collection of compensation

(a) No person engaged in any business or profession for which a license is required under this code governing the department or any board, bureau, commission, committee, or program within the department, may bring or maintain any action, or recover in law or equity in any action, in any court of this state for the collection of compensation for the performance of any act or contract for which a license is required without alleging and proving that he or she was duly licensed at all times during the performance of that act or contract, regardless of the merits of the cause of action brought by the person.

(b) The judicial doctrine of substantial compliance shall not apply to this section.

(c) This section shall not apply to an act or contract that is considered to qualify as lawful practice of a licensed occupation or profession pursuant to Section 121.

Added Stats 1990 ch 1207 § 1.5 (AB 3242).

Section V

§ 144. Requirement of fingerprints for criminal record checks; Applicability

(a) Notwithstanding any other provision of law, an agency designated in subdivision (b) shall require an applicant to furnish to the agency a full set of fingerprints for purposes of conducting criminal history record checks. Any agency designated in subdivision (b) may obtain and receive, at its discretion, criminal history information from the Department of Justice and the United States Federal Bureau of Investigation.

(b) Subdivision (a) applies to the following:

(1) California Board of Accountancy.

(2) State Athletic Commission.

(3) Board of Behavioral Sciences.

(4) Court Reporters Board of California.

(5) State Board of Guide Dogs for the Blind.

(6) California State Board of Pharmacy.

(7) Board of Registered Nursing.

(8) Veterinary Medical Board.

(9) Board of Vocational Nursing and Psychiatric Technicians.

(10) Respiratory Care Board of California.

(11) Physical Therapy Board of California.

(12) Physician Assistant Committee of the Medical Board of California.

(13) Speech-Language Pathology and Audiology and Hearing Aid Dispenser Board.

(14) Medical Board of California.

(15) State Board of Optometry.

(16) Acupuncture Board.

(17) Cemetery and Funeral Bureau.

(18) Bureau of Security and Investigative Services.

(19) Division of Investigation.

(20) Board of Psychology.

(21) California Board of Occupational Therapy.

(22) Structural Pest Control Board.

(23) Contractors' State License Board.

(24) Naturopathic Medicine Committee.

(25) Professional Fiduciaries Bureau.

(26) Board for Professional Engineers, Land Surveyors, and Geologists.

(c) For purposes of paragraph (26) of subdivision (b), the term "applicant" shall be limited to an initial applicant who has never been registered or licensed by the board or to an applicant for a new licensure or registration category.

Added Stats 1997 ch 758 § 2 (SB 1346). Amended Stats 2000 ch 697 § 1.2 (SB 1046), operative January 1, 2001; Stats 2001 ch 159 § 4 (SB 662), ch 687 § 2 (AB 1409) (ch 687 prevails); Stats 2002 ch 744 § 1 (SB 1953), ch 825 § 1 (SB 1952); Stats 2003 ch 485 § 2 (SB 907), ch 789 § 1 (SB 364), ch 874 § 1 (SB 363); Stats 2004 ch 909 § 1.2 (SB 136), effective September 30, 2004; Stats 2009 ch 308 § 4 (SB 819), effective January 1, 2010; Stats 2011 ch 448 § 1 (SB 543), effective January 1, 2012.

Chapter 2
The Director of Consumer Affairs

§ 150. Designation

The department is under the control of a civil executive officer who is known as the Director of Consumer Affairs.

Enacted Stats 1937. Amended Stats 1971 ch 716 § 9.

§ 151. Appointment and tenure; Salary and traveling expenses

The director is appointed by the Governor and holds office at the Governor's pleasure. The director shall receive the annual salary provided for by Chapter 6 (commencing with Section 11550) of Part 1 of Division 3 of Title 2 of the Government Code, and his or her necessary traveling expenses.

Enacted Stats 1937. Amended Stats 1943 ch 1029 § 1; Stats 1945 ch 1185 § 2; Stats 1947 ch 1442 § 1; Stats 1951 ch 1613 § 14; Stats 1984 ch 144 § 2, ch 268 § 0.1, effective June 30, 1984; Stats 1985 ch 106 § 1.

§ 152. Departmental organization

For the purpose of administration, the reregistration and clerical work of the department is organized by the director, subject to the approval of the Governor, in such manner as he deems necessary properly to segregate and conduct the work of the department.

Enacted Stats 1937.

§ 152.5. Extension of renewal dates

For purposes of distributing the reregistration work of the department uniformly throughout the year as nearly as practicable, the boards in the department may, with the approval of the director, extend by not more than six months the date fixed by law for the renewal of any license, certificate or permit issued by them, except that in such event any renewal fee which may be involved shall be prorated in such manner that no person shall be required to pay a greater or lesser fee than would have been required had the change in renewal dates not occurred.

Section V

Added Stats 1959 ch 1707 § 1.

§ 152.6. Establishment of license periods and renewal dates

Notwithstanding any other provision of this code, each board within the department shall, in cooperation with the director, establish such license periods and renewal dates for all licenses in such manner as best to distribute the renewal work of all boards throughout each year and permit the most efficient, and economical use of personnel and equipment. To the extent practicable, provision shall be made for the proration or other adjustment of fees in such manner that no person shall be required to pay a greater or lesser fee than he would have been required to pay if the change in license periods or renewal dates had not occurred.

As used in this section "license" includes "certificate," "permit," "authority," "registration," and similar indicia of authority to engage in a business or profession, and "board" includes "board," "commission," "committee," and an individual who is authorized to renew a license.

Added Stats 1968 ch 1248 § 1.

§ 153. Investigations

The director may investigate the work of the several boards in his department and may obtain a copy of all records and full and complete data in all official matters in possession of the boards, their members, officers, or employees, other than examination questions prior to submission to applicants at scheduled examinations.

Enacted Stats 1937.

§ 154. Matters relating to employees of boards

Any and all matters relating to employment, tenure or discipline of employees of any board, agency or commission, shall be initiated by said board, agency or commission, but all such actions shall, before reference to the State Personnel Board, receive the approval of the appointing power.

To effect the purposes of Division 1 of this code and each agency of the department, employment of all personnel shall be in accord with Article XXIV of the Constitution, the law and rules and regulations of the State Personnel Board. Each board, agency or commission, shall select its employees from a list of eligibles obtained by the appointing power from the State Personnel Board. The person selected by the board, agency or commission to fill any position or vacancy shall thereafter be reported by the board, agency or commission, to the appointing power.

Enacted Stats 1937. Amended Stats 1945 ch 1276 § 4.

§ 154.5. Legal assistance for experts aiding in investigations of licensees

If a person, not a regular employee of a board under this code, including the Board of Chiropractic Examiners and the Osteopathic Medical Board of California, is hired or under contract to provide expertise to the board in the evaluation of an applicant or the conduct of a licensee, and that person is named as a defendant in a civil action arising out of the evaluation or any opinions rendered, statements made, or testimony given to the board or its representatives, the board shall provide for representation required to defend the defendant in that civil action. The board shall not be liable for any judgment rendered against the person. The Attorney General shall be utilized in the action and his or her services shall be a charge against the board.

Added Stats 1986 ch 1205 § 1, as B & P C § 483. Amended and Renumbered by Stats 1987 ch 850 § 8. Amended Stats 1991 ch 359 § 3 (AB 1332).

§ 155. Employment of investigators; Inspectors as employees or under contract

(a) In accordance with Section 159.5, the director may employ such investigators, inspectors, and deputies as are necessary properly to investigate and prosecute all violations of any law, the enforcement of which is charged to the department or to any board, agency, or commission in the department.

(b) It is the intent of the Legislature that inspectors used by boards, bureaus, or commissions in the department shall not be required to be employees of the Division of Investigation, but may either be employees of, or under contract to, the boards, bureaus, or commissions. Contracts for services shall be consistent with Article 4.5 (commencing with Section 19130) of Chapter 6 of Part 2 of Division 5 of Title 2 of the Government Code. All civil service employees currently employed as inspectors whose functions are transferred as a result of this section shall retain their positions, status, and rights in accordance with Section 19994.10 of the Government Code and the State Civil Service Act (Part 2 (commencing with Section 18500) of Division 5 of Title 2 of the Government Code).

(c) Nothing in this section limits the authority of, or prohibits, investigators in the Division of Investigation in the conduct of inspections or investigations of any licensee, or in the conduct of investigations of any officer or employee of a board or the department at the specific request of the director or his or her designee.

Enacted Stats 1937. Amended Stats 1945 ch 1276 § 5; Stats 1971 ch 716 § 10; Stats 1985 ch 1382 § 1.

Section V

§ 156. Contractual authority

(a) The director may, for the department and at the request and with the consent of a board within the department on whose behalf the contract is to be made, enter into contracts pursuant to Chapter 3 (commencing with Section 11250) of Part 1 of Division 3 of Title 2 of the Government Code or Chapter 2 (commencing with Section 10290) of Part 2 of Division 2 of the Public Contract Code for and on behalf of any board within the department.

(b) In accordance with subdivision (a), the director may, in his or her discretion, negotiate and execute contracts for examination purposes which include provisions which hold harmless a contractor where liability resulting from a contract between a board in the department and the contractor is traceable to the state or its officers, agents, or employees.

Added Stats 1953 ch 864 § 1. Amended Stats 1984 ch 144 § 3; Stats 1988 ch 1448 § 1.

§ 156.1. Retention of records by providers of services related to treatment of alcohol or drug impairment

(a) Notwithstanding any other provision of law, individuals or entities contracting with the department or any board within the department for the provision of services relating to the treatment and rehabilitation of licentiates impaired by alcohol or dangerous drugs shall retain all records and documents pertaining to those services until such time as these records and documents have been reviewed for audit by the department. These records and documents shall be retained for three years from the date of the last treatment or service rendered to that licentiate, after which time the records and documents may be purged and destroyed by the contract vendor. This provision shall supersede any other provision of law relating to the purging or destruction of records pertaining to those treatment and rehabilitation programs.

(b) Unless otherwise expressly provided by statute or regulation, all records and documents pertaining to services for the treatment and rehabilitation of licentiates impaired by alcohol or dangerous drugs provided by any contract vendor to the department or to any board within the department shall be kept confidential and are not subject to discovery or subpoena.

(c) With respect to all other contracts for services with the department or any board within the department other than those set forth in subdivision (a), the director or chief deputy director may request an examination and audit by the department's internal auditor of all performance under the contract. For this purpose, all documents and records of the contract vendor in connection with such performance shall be retained by such vendor for a period of three years after final payment under the contract. Nothing in this section shall affect the authority of the State Auditor to conduct any examination or audit under the terms of Section 8546.7 of the Government Code.

Added Stats 1991 ch 654 § 3 (AB 1893). Amended Stats 2003 ch 107 § 1 (AB 569); Stats 2010 ch 517 § 1 (SB 1172), effective January 1, 2011.

§ 156.5. Leases for examination or meeting purposes

The director may negotiate and execute for the department and for its component agencies, rental agreements for short-term hiring of space and furnishings for examination or meeting purposes. The director may, in his or her discretion, negotiate and execute contracts for that space which include provisions which hold harmless the provider of the space where liability resulting from use of the space under the contract is traceable to the state or its officers, agents, or employees. Notwithstanding any other provision of law, the director may, in his or her discretion, advance payments as deposits to reserve and hold examination or meeting space. Any such agreement is subject to the approval of the legal office of the Department of General Services.

Added Stats 1967 ch 1235 § 1. Amended Stats 1988 ch 1448 § 1.5.

§ 157. Expenses in criminal prosecutions and unprofessional conduct proceedings

Expenses incurred by any board or on behalf of any board in any criminal prosecution or unprofessional conduct proceeding constitute proper charges against the funds of the board.

Added Stats 1937 ch 474.

§ 158. Refunds to applicants

With the approval of the Director of Consumer Affairs, the boards and commissions comprising the department or subject to its jurisdiction may make refunds to applicants who are found ineligible to take the examinations or whose credentials are insufficient to entitle them to certificates or licenses.

Notwithstanding any other provision of law any application fees, license fees or penalties imposed and collected illegally, by mistake, inadvertence, or error shall be refunded. Claims authorized by the department shall be filed with the State Controller, and the Controller shall draw his warrant against the fund of the agency in payment of such refund.

Added Stats 1937 ch 474. Amended Stats 1945 ch 1378 § 1; Stats 1971 ch 716 § 11.

Section V

§ 159. Administration of oaths

The members and the executive officer of each board, agency, bureau, division, or commission have power to administer oaths and affirmations in the performance of any business of the board, and to certify to official acts.

Added Stats 1947 ch 1350 § 5.

§ 159.5. Division of Investigation; Appointments

There is in the department the Division of Investigation. The division is in the charge of a person with the title of chief of the division.

Except as provided in Section 160, investigators who have the authority of peace officers, as specified in subdivision (a) of Section 160 and in subdivision (a) of Section 830.3 of the Penal Code, shall be in the division and shall be appointed by the director.

Added Stats 1971 ch 716 § 12. Amended Stats 1985 ch 1382 § 2; Stats 2010 ch 719 § 2 (SB 856), effective October 19, 2010.

§ 161. Sale of copies of public records

The department, or any board in the department, may sell copies of any part of its respective public records, or compilations, extracts, or summaries of information contained in its public records, at a charge sufficient to pay the actual cost thereof. Such charge, and the conditions under which sales may be made, shall be determined by the director with the approval of the Department of General Services.

Added Stats 1949 ch 704 § 1. Amended Stats 1963 ch 590 § 1; Stats 1965 ch 371 § 9.

§ 162. Evidentiary effect of certificate of records officer as to license, etc.

The certificate of the officer in charge of the records of any board in the department that any person was or was not on a specified date, or during a specified period of time, licensed, certified or registered under the provisions of law administered by the board, or that the license, certificate or registration of any person was revoked or under suspension, shall be admitted in any court as prima facie evidence of the facts therein recited.

Added Stats 1949 ch 355 § 1.

§ 163. Fee for certification of records, etc.

Except as otherwise expressly provided by law, the department and each board in the department shall charge a fee of two dollars ($2) for the certification of a copy of any record, document, or paper in its custody or for the certification of any document evidencing the content of any such record, document or paper.

Added Stats 1961 ch 1858 § 1. Amended Stats 1963 ch 590 § 2.

§ 163.5. Delinquency fees; Reinstatement fees

Except as otherwise provided by law, the delinquency, penalty, or late fee for any licensee within the Department of Consumer Affairs shall be 50 percent of the renewal fee for such license in effect on the date of the renewal of the license, but not less than twenty-five dollars ($25) nor more than one hundred fifty dollars ($150).

A delinquency, penalty, or late fee shall not be assessed until 30 days have elapsed from the date that the licensing agency mailed a notice of renewal to the licensee at the licensee's last known address of record. The notice shall specify the date for timely renewal, and that failure to renew in a timely fashion shall result in the assessment of a delinquency, penalty, or late fee.

In the event a reinstatement or like fee is charged for the reinstatement of a license, the reinstatement fee shall be 150 percent of the renewal fee for such license in effect on the date of the reinstatement of the license, but not more than twenty-five dollars ($25) in excess of the renewal fee, except that in the event that such a fee is fixed by statute at less than 150 percent of the renewal fee and less than the renewal fee plus twenty-five dollars ($25), the fee so fixed shall be charged.

Added Stats 1974 ch 743 § 4. Amended Stats 1985 ch 587 § 1.

§ 163.6. [Section repealed 1992.]

Added Stats 1985 ch 587 § 2. Inoperative June 30, 1991. Repealed, operative January 1, 1992, by its own terms. The repealed section related to reduction in license renewal fees to offset increase in revenue.

§ 164. Form and content of license, certificate, permit, or similar indicia of authority

The form and content of any license, certificate, permit, or similar indicia of authority issued by any agency in the department, including any document evidencing renewal of a license, certificate, permit, or similar indicia of authority, shall be determined by the director after consultation with and consideration of the views of the agency concerned.

Added Stats 1971 ch 716 § 15. Amended Stats 1987 ch 850 § 6.

Section V

§ 165. Prohibition against submission of fiscal impact analysis relating to pending legislation without prior submission to director for comment

Notwithstanding any other provision of law, no board, bureau, committee, commission, or program in the Department of Consumer Affairs shall submit to the Legislature any fiscal impact analysis relating to legislation pending before the Legislature until the analysis has been submitted to the Director of Consumer Affairs, or his or her designee, for review and comment. The boards, bureaus, committees, commissions, and programs shall include the comments of the director when submitting any fiscal impact analysis to the Legislature. This section shall not be construed to prohibit boards, bureaus, committees, commissions, and programs from responding to direct requests for fiscal data from Members of the Legislature or their staffs. In those instances it shall be the responsibility of boards, bureaus, committees, commissions, and programs to also transmit that information to the director, or his or her designee, within five working days.

Added Stats 1984 ch 268 § 0.2, effective June 30, 1984.

§ 166. Development of guidelines for mandatory continuing education programs

The director shall, by regulation, develop guidelines to prescribe components for mandatory continuing education programs administered by any board within the department.

(a) The guidelines shall be developed to ensure that mandatory continuing education is used as a means to create a more competent licensing population, thereby enhancing public protection. The guidelines shall require mandatory continuing education programs to address, at least, the following:

(1) Course validity.

(2) Occupational relevancy.

(3) Effective presentation.

(4) Actual attendance.

(5) Material assimilation.

(6) Potential for application.

(b) The director shall consider educational principles, and the guidelines shall prescribe mandatory continuing education program formats to include, but not be limited to, the following:

(1) The specified audience.

(2) Identification of what is to be learned.

(3) Clear goals and objectives.

(4) Relevant learning methods (participatory, hands-on, or clinical setting).

(5) Evaluation, focused on the learner and the assessment of the intended learning outcomes (goals and objectives).

(c) Any board within the department that, after January 1, 1993, proposes a mandatory continuing education program for its licensees shall submit the proposed program to the director for review to assure that the program contains all the elements set forth in this section and complies with the guidelines developed by the director.

(d) Any board administering a mandatory continuing education program that proposes to amend its current program shall do so in a manner consistent with this section.

(e) Any board currently administering a mandatory continuing education program shall review the components and requirements of the program to determine the extent to which they are consistent with the guidelines developed under this section. The board shall submit a report of their findings to the director. The report shall identify the similarities and differences of its mandatory continuing education program. The report shall include any board-specific needs to explain the variation from the director's guidelines.

(f) Any board administering a mandatory continuing education program, when accepting hours for credit which are obtained out of state, shall ensure that the course for which credit is given is administered in accordance with the guidelines addressed in subdivision (a).

(g) Nothing in this section or in the guidelines adopted by the director shall be construed to repeal any requirements for continuing education programs set forth in any other provision of this code.

Added Stats 1992 ch 1135 § 2.2 (SB 2044). Amended Stats 1994 ch 146 § 1 (AB 3601).

Chapter 3

Funds of the Department

§ 200.1.   Fund accruals exempt from transfer

(a) Any accruals that occur on or after September 11, 1993, to any funds or accounts within the Professions and Vocations Fund that realize increased revenues to that fund or account as a result of legislation enacted on or after September 11, 1993, and that have not been transferred pursuant to Sections 13.50, 13.60, and 13.70 of the Budget Act of 1993 on the effective date of the act that enacted this section, shall be exempt from the transfers contained in Sections 13.50, 13.60, and 13.70 of the Budget Act of 1993. These funds shall include, but not be limited to, all of the following:

(1) Athletic Commission Fund.

(2) Bureau of Home Furnishings and Thermal Insulation Fund.

(3) Contractors' License Fund.

(4) Private Investigator Fund.

(5) Respiratory Care Fund.
(6) Vocational Nursing and Psychiatric Technicians Fund.
(b) Subdivision (a) shall not apply to the Contingent Fund of the Medical Board of California.

Added Stats 1994 ch 26 § 10 (AB 1807), effective March 30, 1994. Amended Stats 1997 ch 759 § 4 (SB 827).

§ 201. Levy for administrative expenses

A charge for the estimated administrative expenses of the department, not to exceed the available balance in any appropriation for any one fiscal year, may be levied in advance on a pro rata share basis against any of the funds of any of the boards, bureaus, commissions, divisions, and agencies, at the discretion of the director and with the approval of the Department of Finance.

Enacted Stats 1937. Amended Stats 1947 ch 1350 § 4; Stats 1965 ch 371 § 10; Stats 1974 ch 1221 § 1.

§ 202.5. Itemized statement of services and changes from Department of Justice

Prior to payment to the Department of Justice of any charges for legal services rendered to any board within the department, the Department of Justice shall submit to the board an itemized statement of the services and charges. The itemized statement shall include detailed information regarding the services performed and the amount of time billed for each of those services.

Added Stats 1994 ch 1273 § 1 (SB 2038).

§ 205. Professions and Vocations Fund

(a) There is in the State Treasury the Professions and Vocations Fund. The fund shall consist of the following special funds:
(1) Accountancy Fund.
(2) California Architects Board Fund.
(3) Athletic Commission Fund.
(4) Barbering and Cosmetology Contingent Fund.
(5) Cemetery Fund.
(6) Contractors' License Fund.
(7) State Dentistry Fund.
(8) State Funeral Directors and Embalmers Fund.
(9) Guide Dogs for the Blind Fund.
(10) Home Furnishings and Thermal Insulation Fund.
(11) California Architects Board-Landscape Architects Fund.
(12) Contingent Fund of the Medical Board of California.
(13) Optometry Fund.
(14) Pharmacy Board Contingent Fund.

(15) Physical Therapy Fund.

(16) Private Investigator Fund.

(17) Professional Engineer's and Land Surveyor's Fund.

(18) Consumer Affairs Fund.

(19) Behavioral Sciences Fund.

(20) Licensed Midwifery Fund.

(21) Court Reporters' Fund.

(22) Veterinary Medical Board Contingent Fund.

(23) Vocational Nurses Account of the Vocational Nursing and Psychiatric Technicians Fund.

(24) Electronic and Appliance Repair Fund.

(25) Geology and Geophysics Account of the Professional Engineer's and Land Surveyor's Fund.

(26) Dispensing Opticians Fund.

(27) Acupuncture Fund.

(28) Physician Assistant Fund.

(29) Board of Podiatric Medicine Fund.

(30) Psychology Fund.

(31) Respiratory Care Fund.

(32) Speech-Language Pathology and Audiology and Hearing Aid Dispensers Fund.

(33) Board of Registered Nursing Fund.

(34) Psychiatric Technician Examiners Account of the Vocational Nursing and Psychiatric Technicians Fund.

(35) Animal Health Technician Examining Committee Fund.

(36) State Dental Hygiene Fund.

(37) State Dental Assistant Fund.

(b) For accounting and recordkeeping purposes, the Professions and Vocations Fund shall be deemed to be a single special fund, and each of the several special funds therein shall constitute and be deemed to be a separate account in the Professions and Vocations Fund. Each account or fund shall be available for expenditure only for the purposes as are now or may hereafter be provided by law.

Added Stats 1959 ch 1242 § 1. Amended Stats 1969 ch 1249 § 6; Stats 1971 ch 716 § 17.5; Stats 1972 ch 749 § 3; Stats 1973 ch 863 § 4; Stats 1983 ch 150 § 3; Stats 1985 ch 1230 § 2. Repealed Stats 1987 ch 850 § 7 (1987 ch 925 prevails). Amended Stats 1987 ch 925 § 2, effective September 22, 1987; Stats 1994 ch 26 § 11 (AB 1807), effective March 30, 1994, ch 149 § 1 (AB 2388), effective July 9, 1994, ch 1275 § 3 (SB 2101); Stats 1995 ch 60 § 5 (SB 42), effective July 6, 1995; Stats 1997 ch 759 § 5 (SB 827); Stats 2000 ch 1054 § 4.5 (SB 1863); Stats 2001 ch 687 § 3 (AB 1409); Stats 2008 ch 31 § 2 (SB 853), effective January 1, 2009; Stats 2009–2010 4th Ex Sess ch 18 § 4 (AB 20XXXX), effective October 23, 2009; Stats 2009 ch 309 § 3 (AB 1535), effective January 1, 2010; Stats 2011 ch 448 § 2 (SB 543), effective January 1, 2012, ch 449 § 1.5 (SB 933), effective January 1, 2012.

§ 206. Dishonored check tendered for payment of fine, fee, or penalty

Notwithstanding any other provision of law, any person tendering a check for payment of a fee, fine, or penalty that was subsequently dishonored, shall not be granted a license, or other authority that they were seeking, until the applicant pays the amount outstanding from the dishonored payment together with the applicable fee, including any delinquency fee. The board may require the person whose check was returned unpaid to make payment of all fees by cashier's check or money order.

Added Stats 1994 ch 26 § 12 (AB 1807), effective March 30, 1994.

§ 210. Contract with vendor of BreEZe system after written notification to certain committees of the Legislature; Term; Amount; Submission of report (Subdivision (b) inoperative December 1, 2018; Subdivision (c) operative term contingent)

(a) (1) The department may enter into a contract with a vendor for the BreEZe system, the integrated, enterprisewide enforcement case management and licensing system described in the department's strategic plan, no sooner than 30 days after notification in writing to the chairpersons of the Appropriations Committees of each house of the Legislature and the Chairperson of the Joint Legislative Budget Committee.

(2) The amount of BreEZe system vendor contract funds, authorized pursuant to this section, shall be consistent with the project costs approved by the office of the State Chief Information Officer based on its review and approval of the most recent BreEZe Special Project Report to be submitted by the department prior to contract award at the conclusion of procurement activities.

(3) Paragraph (2) shall apply to all Budget Act items for the department that have an appropriation for the BreEZe system.

(b) (1) If the department enters into a contract with a vendor for the BreEZe system pursuant to subdivision (a), the department shall, by December 31, 2014, submit to the Legislature, the Senate Committee on Business, Professions and Economic Development, the Assembly Committee on Business, Professions and Consumer Protection, and the budget committees of each house, a report analyzing the workload of licensing personnel employed by boards within the department participating in the BreEZe system.

(2) A report to the Legislature pursuant to this subdivision shall be submitted in compliance with Section 9795 of the Government Code.

(3) This subdivision shall become inoperative on December 1, 2018, pursuant to Section 10231.5 of the Government Code.

(c) (1) Notwithstanding any other provision of law, upon the request of the Department of Consumer Affairs, the Department of Finance may augment the budgets of the boards, bureaus, commissions, committees, programs, and divisions that comprise the Department of Consumer Affairs, as defined in Section 101, for expenditure of non-General Fund moneys to pay BreEZe project costs. The augmentation may be made no sooner than 30 days after notification in writing to the chairpersons of the committees in each house of the Legislature that consider appropriations and the Chairperson of the Joint Legislative Budget Committee, or no sooner than whatever lesser time the chairperson of the joint committee may in each instance determine. The amount of funds augmented pursuant to the authority of this subdivision shall be consistent with project cost increases approved by the Secretary of California Technology based on the secretary's review and approval of the most recent BreEZe Special Project Report to be submitted at the conclusion of procurement activities. This subdivision shall apply to all Budget Act items for the boards, bureaus, commissions, committees, programs, and divisions that comprise the Department of Consumer Affairs, as defined in Section 101, that have an appropriation for the BreEZe system in the Budget Act of 2011.

(2) This subdivision shall become inoperative upon enactment of the Budget Act of 2012.

Added Stats 2010 ch 719 § 4 (SB 856), effective October 19, 2010. Amended Stats 2011 ch 448 § 3 (SB 543), effective January 1, 2012.

Chapter 4

Consumer Affairs

Article 1

General Provisions and Definitions

§ 300.   Citation of chapter

This chapter may be cited as the Consumer Affairs Act

Added Stats 1970 ch 1394 § 3, operative July 1, 1971.

§ 301.   Declaration of intent

It is the intent of the Legislature and the purpose of this chapter to promote and protect the interests of the people as consumers. The Legislature finds that vigorous representation and protection of consumer interests are essential to the fair and efficient functioning of a free enterprise market economy. The Legislature declares that government advances the interests of consumers by facilitating the proper functioning of the free enterprise market economy through (a) educating and informing the consumer to insure rational consumer choice in the marketplace; (b) protecting the consumer from the sale of goods and services through the use of deceptive methods, acts, or practices which are inimical to the general welfare of consumers; (c) fostering competition; and (d) promoting effective representation of consumers' interests in all branches and levels of government.

Added Stats 1970 ch 1394 § 3, operative July 1, 1971. Amended Stats 1975 ch 1262 § 1.

§ 302. Definitions

As used in this chapter, the following terms have the following meanings:

(a) "Department" means the Department of Consumer Affairs.

(b) "Director" means the Director of the Department of Consumer Affairs.

(c) "Consumer" means any individual who seeks or acquires, by purchase or lease, any goods, services, money, or credit for personal, family, or household purposes.

(d) "Person" means an individual, partnership, corporation, limited liability company, association, or other group, however organized.

(e) "Individual" does not include a partnership, corporation, association, or other group, however organized.

(f) "Division" means the Division of Consumer Services.

(g) "Interests of consumers" is limited to the cost, quality, purity, safety, durability, performance, effectiveness, dependability, availability, and adequacy of choice of goods and services offered or furnished to consumers and the adequacy and accuracy of information relating to consumer goods, services, money, or credit (including labeling, packaging, and advertising of contents, qualities, and terms of sales).

Added Stats 1970 ch 1394 § 3, operative July 1, 1971. Amended Stats 1972 ch 808 § 1; Stats 1975 ch 1262 § 2; Stats 1994 ch 1010 § 2 (SB 2053).

§ 303. Division of Consumer Services; Chief

There is in the department a Division of Consumer Services under the supervision and control of a chief. The chief shall be appointed by the Governor and shall serve at his pleasure. His compensation shall be fixed by the director in accordance with law.

Added Stats 1972 ch 808 § 2.

Article 2

Director and Employees

§ 305. Administration of chapter

The director shall administer and enforce the provisions of this chapter. Every power granted or duty imposed upon the director under this chapter may be exercised or performed in the name of the director by a deputy or assistant director or the chief of the department's Division of Consumer Services, subject to such conditions and limitations as the director may prescribe.

Added Stats 1970 ch 1394 § 3, operative July 1, 1971. Amended Stats 1971 ch 114 § 1, effective June 2, 1971, operative July 1, 1971.

§ 306. Employment matters

The director, in accordance with the State Civil Service Act, may appoint and fix the compensation of such clerical or other personnel as may be necessary to carry out the provisions of this chapter. All such personnel shall perform their respective duties under the supervision and the direction of the director.

Added Stats 1970 ch 1394 § 3, operative July 1, 1971.

§ 307. Experts and consultants

The director may contract for the services of experts and consultants where necessary to carry out the provisions of this chapter and may provide compensation and reimbursement of expenses for such experts and consultants in accordance with state law.

Added Stats 1975 ch 1262 § 3.

Article 3

Powers and Duties

§ 310. Director's powers and duties

The director shall have the following powers and it shall be his duty to:

(a) Recommend and propose the enactment of such legislation as necessary to protect and promote the interests of consumers.

(b) Represent the consumer's interests before federal and state legislative hearings and executive commissions.

(c) Assist, advise, and cooperate with federal, state, and local agencies and officials to protect and promote the interests of consumers.

(d) Study, investigate, research, and analyze matters affecting the interests of consumers.

Section V

(e) Hold public hearings, subpoena witnesses, take testimony, compel the production of books, papers, documents, and other evidence, and call upon other state agencies for information.

(f) Propose and assist in the creation and development of consumer education programs.

(g) Promote ethical standards of conduct for business and consumers and undertake activities to encourage public responsibility in the production, promotion, sale and lease of consumer goods and services.

(h) Advise the Governor and Legislature on all matters affecting the interests of consumers.

(i) Exercise and perform such other functions, powers and duties as may be deemed appropriate to protect and promote the interests of consumers as directed by the Governor or the Legislature.

(j) Maintain contact and liaison with consumer groups in California and nationally.

Added Stats 1970 ch 1394 § 3, operative July 1, 1971. Amended Stats 1975 ch 1262 § 4.

§ 311. Interdepartmental committee

The director may create an interdepartmental committee to assist and advise him in the implementation of his duties. The members of such committee shall consist of the heads of state departments, or their designees. Members of such committee shall serve without compensation but shall be reimbursed for the expenses actually and necessarily incurred by them in the performance of their duties.

Added Stats 1970 ch 1394 § 3, operative July 1, 1971.

§ 312. Report to Governor and Legislature

The director shall submit to the Governor and the Legislature on or before January 1, 2003, and annually thereafter, a report of programmatic and statistical information regarding the activities of the department and its constituent entities. The report shall include information concerning the director's activities pursuant to Section 326, including the number and general patterns of consumer complaints and the action taken on those complaints.

Added Stats 1970 ch 1394 § 3, operative July 1, 1971. Amended Stats 1975 ch 1262 § 5; Stats 1998 ch 829 § 1 SB 1652); Stats 2002 ch 405 § 3 (AB 2973).

§ 313.2. Adoption of regulations in conformance with Americans with Disabilities Act

The director shall adopt regulations to implement, interpret, and make specific the provisions of the Americans with Disabilities Act (P.L. 101–336), as they relate to the examination process for professional licensing and certification programs under the purview of the department.

Added Stats 1992 ch 1289 § 3 (AB 2743).

§ 313.5. Publication of consumer information bibliography

The director shall periodically publish a bibliography of consumer information available in the department library and elsewhere. Such bibliography shall be sent to subscribers upon payment of a reasonable fee therefor.

Added Stats 1972 ch 1251 § 2. Amended Stats 1975 ch 1262 § 7.

Article 3.6

Uniform Standards Regarding Substance-Abusing Healing Arts Licensees

§ 315.2. Cease practice order

(a) A board, as described in Section 315, shall order a licensee of the board to cease practice if the licensee tests positive for any substance that is prohibited under the terms of the licensee's probation or diversion program.

(b) An order to cease practice under this section shall not be governed by the provisions of Chapter 5 (commencing with Section 11500) of Part 1 of Division 3 of Title 2 of the Government Code.

(c) A cease practice order under this section shall not constitute disciplinary action.

(d) This section shall have no effect on the Board of Registered Nursing pursuant to Article 3.1 (commencing with Section 2770) of Chapter 6 of Division 2.

Added Stats 2010 ch 517 § 2 (SB 1172), effective January 1, 2011.

§ 315.4. Cease practice order for violation of probation or diversion program

(a) A board, as described in Section 315, may adopt regulations authorizing the board to order a licensee on probation or in a diversion program to cease practice for major violations and when the board orders a licensee to undergo a clinical diagnostic evaluation pursuant to the uniform and specific standards adopted and authorized under Section 315.

(b) An order to cease practice under this section shall not be governed by the provisions of Chapter 5 (commencing with Section 11500) of Part 1 of Division 3 of Title 2 of the Government Code.

(c) A cease practice order under this section shall not constitute disciplinary action.

(d) This section shall have no effect on the Board of Registered Nursing pursuant to Article 3.1 (commencing with Section 2770) of Chapter 6 of Division 2.

Added Stats 2010 ch 517 § 3 (SB 1172), effective January 1, 2011.

Article 4

Representation of Consumers

§ 320. Intervention in administrative or judicial proceedings

Whenever there is pending before any state commission, regulatory agency, department, or other state agency, or any state or federal court or agency, any matter or proceeding which the director finds may affect substantially the interests of consumers within California, the director, or the Attorney General, may intervene in such matter or proceeding in any appropriate manner to represent the interests of consumers. The director, or any officer or employee designated by the director for that purpose, or the Attorney General, may thereafter present to such agency, court, or department, in conformity with the rules of practice and procedure thereof, such evidence and argument as he shall determine to be necessary, for the effective protection of the interests of consumers.

Added Stats 1970 ch 1394 § 3, operative July 1, 1971. Amended Stats 1975 ch 1262 § 8.

§ 321. Commencement of legal proceedings

Whenever it appears to the director that the interests of the consumers of this state are being damaged, or may be damaged, by any person who engaged in, or intends to engage in, any acts or practices in violation of any law of this state, or any federal law, the director or any officer or employee designated by the director, or the Attorney General, may commence legal proceedings in the appropriate forum to enjoin such acts or practices and may seek other appropriate relief on behalf of such consumers.

Added Stats 1975 ch 1262 § 9.

Article 5

Consumer Complaints

§ 325. Actionable complaints

It shall be the duty of the director to receive complaints from consumers concerning (a) unfair methods of competition and unfair or deceptive acts or practices undertaken by any person in the conduct of any trade or commerce; (b) the production, distribution, sale, and lease of any goods and services undertaken by any person which may endanger the public health, safety, or welfare; (c) violations of provisions of this code relating to businesses and professions licensed by any agency of the department, and regulations promulgated pursuant thereto; and (d) other matters consistent with the purposes of this chapter, whenever appropriate.

Added Stats 1970 ch 1394 § 3, operative July 1, 1971.

§ 325.3. Consumer complaints on paging services

In addition to the duties prescribed by Section 325, it shall be the duty of the director to receive complaints from consumers concerning services provided by the entities described in paragraph (2) of subdivision (b) of Section 234 of the Public Utilities Code.

Added Stats 1995 ch 357 § 1 (AB 202).

§ 326. Proceedings on receipt of complaint

(a) Upon receipt of any complaint pursuant to Section 325, the director may notify the person against whom the complaint is made of the nature of the complaint and may request appropriate relief for the consumer.

(b) The director shall also transmit any valid complaint to the local, state or federal agency whose authority provides the most effective means to secure the relief.

The director shall, if appropriate, advise the consumer of the action taken on the complaint and of any other means which may be available to the consumer to secure relief.

(c) If the director receives a complaint or receives information from any source indicating a probable violation of any law, rule, or order of any regulatory agency of the state, or if a pattern of complaints from consumers develops, the director shall transmit any complaint he or she considers to be valid to any appropriate law enforcement or regulatory agency and any evidence or information he or she may have concerning the probable violation or pattern of complaints or request the Attorney General to undertake appropriate legal action. It shall be the continuing duty of the director to discern patterns of complaints and to ascertain the nature and extent of action taken with respect to the probable violations or pattern of complaints.

Added Stats 1970 ch 1394 § 3, operative July 1, 1971. Amended Stats 1978 ch 1161 § 8; Stats 1989 ch 1360 § 1.

Section V

Article 7

Personal Information and Privacy Protection

§ 350. [Section repealed 2008.]

Added Stats 2000 ch 984 § 1 (SB 129). Amended Stats 2001 ch 159 § 5 (SB 662). Repealed Stats 2007 ch 183 § 1 (SB 90), effective January 1, 2008. The repealed section related to the office of privacy protection.

§ 352. [Section repealed 2008.]

Added Stats 2000 ch 984 § 1 (SB 129). Amended Stats 2004 ch 227 § 1 (SB 1102), effective August 16, 2004, operation contingent. Repealed Stats 2007 ch 183 § 2 (SB 90), effective January 1, 2008. The repealed section related to commencement of activities under the article and funding for such.

Chapter 6

Public Members

§ 450. Qualifications generally

In addition to the qualifications provided in the respective chapters of this code, a public member or a lay member of any board shall not be, nor shall he have been within the period of five years immediately preceding his appointment, any of the following:

(a) An employer, or an officer, director, or substantially fulltime representative of an employer or group of employers, of any licentiate of such board, except that this shall not preclude the appointment of a person which maintains infrequent employer status with such licentiate, or maintains a client, patient, or customer relationship with any such licentiate which does not constitute more than 2 percent of the practice or business of the licentiate.

(b) A person maintaining a contractual relationship with a licentiate of such board, which would constitute more than 2 percent of the practice or business of any such licentiate, or an officer, director, or substantially full-time representative of such person or group of persons.

(c) An employee of any licentiate of such board, or a representative of such employee, except that this shall not preclude the appointment of a person who maintains an infrequent employee relationship or a person rendering professional or related services to a licentiate if such employment or service does not constitute more than 2 percent of the employment or practice of the member of the board.

Added Stats 1961 ch 2232 § 2.

§ 450.3.   Conflicting pecuniary interests

No public member shall either at the time of his appointment or during his tenure in office have any financial interest in any organization subject to regulation by the board, commission or committee of which he is a member.

Added Stats 1972 ch 1032 § 1.

§ 450.4.   [Section repealed 2003.]

Added Stats 1976 ch 1188 § 1. Repealed Stats 2003 ch 563 § 1 (AB 827). The repealed section related to expertise required by board members.

§ 450.5.   Prior industrial and professional pursuits

A public member, or a lay member, at any time within five years immediately preceding his or her appointment, shall not have been engaged in pursuits which lie within the field of the industry or profession, or have provided representation to the industry or profession, regulated by the board of which he or she is a member, nor shall he or she engage in those pursuits or provide that representation during his or her term of office.

Added Stats 1961 ch 2232 § 2. Amended Stats 2003 ch 563 § 2 (AB 827).

§ 450.6.   Age

Notwithstanding any other section of law, a public member may be appointed without regard to age so long as the public member has reached the age of majority prior to appointment.

Added Stats 1976 ch 1188 § 1.3.

§ 451.   Delegation of duties

If any board shall as a part of its functions delegate any duty or responsibility to be performed by a single member of such board, such delegation shall not be made solely to any public member or any lay member of the board in any of the following instances:

(a) The actual preparation of, the administration of, and the grading of, examinations.

(b) The inspection or investigation of licentiates, the manner or method of practice or doing business, or their place of practice or business.

Nothing in this section shall be construed as precluding a public member or a lay member from participating in the formation of policy relating to the scope of the activities set forth in subdivisions (a) and (b) or in the approval, disapproval or modification of the action of its individual members, nor preclude such member from participating as a member of a subcommittee consisting of more than one member of the board in the performance of any duty.

Added Stats 1961 ch 2232 § 2.

§ 452. "Board"

"Board," as used in this chapter, includes a board, advisory board, commission, examining committee, committee or other similarly constituted body exercising powers under this code.

Added Stats 1961 ch 2232 § 2. Amended Stats 1976 ch 1188 § 1.5.

Chapter 7

Licensee

§ 460. Powers of local governmental entities

(a) No city or county shall prohibit a person or group of persons, authorized by one of the agencies in the Department of Consumer Affairs by a license, certificate, or other such means to engage in a particular business, from engaging in that business,occupation, or profession or any portion thereof.

(b) No city, county, or city and county shall prohibit a healingarts professional licensed with the state under Division 2 (commencing with Section 500) from engaging in any act or performing any procedure that falls within the professionally recognized scopeof practice of that licensee.

(1) This subdivision shall not be construed to prohibit the enforcement of a local ordinance in effect prior to January 1, 2010,related to any act or procedure that falls within the professionally recognized scope of practice of a healing arts professional licensed under Division 2 (commencing with Section 500).

(2) This subdivision shall not be construed to prevent a city,county, or city and county from adopting or enforcing any local ordinance governing zoning, business licensing, or reasonable health and safety requirements for establishments or businesses of a healing arts professional licensed under Division 2 (commencing with Section500).

(c) Nothing in this section shall prohibit any city, county, or city and county from levying a business license tax solely forrevenue purposes, nor any city or county from levying a license taxsolely for the purpose of covering the cost of regulation.

Added Stats 1967 ch 1095 § 1. Amended Stats 1971 ch 716 § 24; Stats. 2009, Ch. 16.

§ 461. Asking applicant to reveal arrest record prohibited

No public agency, state or local, shall, on an initial application form for any license, certificate or registration, ask for or require the applicant to reveal a record of arrest that did not result in a conviction or a plea of nolo contendere. A violation of this section is a misdemeanor.

This section shall apply in the case of any license, certificate or registration provided for by any law of this state or local government, including, but not limited to, this code, the Corporations Code, the Education Code, and the Insurance Code.

Added Stats 1975 ch 883 § 1.

§ 462. Inactive category of licensure

(a) Any of the boards, bureaus, commissions, or programs within the department may establish, by regulation, a system for an inactive category of licensure for persons who are not actively engaged in the practice of their profession or vocation.

(b) The regulation shall contain the following provisions:

(1) The holder of an inactive license issued pursuant to this section shall not engage in any activity for which a license is required.

(2) An inactive license issued pursuant to this section shall be renewed during the same time period in which an active license is renewed. The holder of an inactive license need not comply with any continuing education requirement for renewal of an active license.

(3) The renewal fee for a license in an active status shall apply also for a renewal of a license in an inactive status, unless a lesser renewal fee is specified by the board.

(4) In order for the holder of an inactive license issued pursuant to this section to restore his or her license to an active status, the holder of an inactive license shall comply with all the following:

(A) Pay the renewal fee.

(B) If the board requires completion of continuing education for renewal of an active license, complete continuing education equivalent to that required for renewal of an active license, unless a different requirement is specified by the board.

(c) This section shall not apply to any healing arts board as specified in Section 701.

Added Stats 1994 ch 26 § 14 (AB 1807), effective March 30, 1994.

Section V

Chapter 8

Dispute Resolution Programs

Article 1

Legislative Purpose

§ 465.5. Legislative intent

It is the intent of the Legislature to permit counties to accomplish all of the following:

(a) Encouragement and support of the development and use of alternative dispute resolution techniques.

(b) Encouragement and support of community participation in the development, administration, and oversight of local programs designed to facilitate the informal resolution of disputes among members of the community.

(c) Development of structures for dispute resolution that may serve as models for resolution programs in other communities.

(d) Education of communities with regard to the availability and benefits of alternative dispute resolution techniques.

(e) Encouragement of courts, prosecuting authorities, public defenders, law enforcement agencies, and administrative agencies to work in cooperation with, and to make referrals to, dispute resolution programs.

At the time that the state assumes the responsibility for the funding of California trial courts, consideration shall be given to the Dispute Resolution Advisory Council's evaluation of the effectiveness of alternative dispute resolution programs and the feasibility of the operation of a statewide program of grants, with the intention of funding alternative dispute resolution programs on a statewide basis.

Added Stats 1986 ch 1313 § 1.

Article 3

Establishment and Administration of Programs

§ 467. Dispute Resolution Advisory Council

(a) There is in the Division of Consumer Services of the Department of Consumer Affairs a Dispute Resolution Advisory Council. The advisory council shall complete the duties required by this chapter no later than January 1, 1989.

(b) The advisory council shall consist of seven persons, five of whom shall be appointed by the Governor. One member shall be appointed by the Senate Rules Committee, and one member shall be appointed by the Speaker of the Assembly. At least four of the persons appointed to the advisory council shall be active members of the State

Bar of California, and at least four persons appointed to the advisory council shall have a minimum of two years of direct experience in utilizing dispute resolution techniques. The members of the advisory council shall reflect the racial, ethnic, sexual, and geographic diversity of the State of California.

(c) The members of the advisory council shall not receive a salary for their services but shall be reimbursed for their actual and necessary travel and other expenses incurred in the performance of their duties.

Added Stats 1986 ch 1313 § 1. Amended Stats 1987 ch 28 § 1, effective May 28, 1987.

§ 467.1. Contract requirements; County programs

(a) A program funded pursuant to this chapter shall be operated pursuant to contract with the county and shall comply with all of the requirements of this chapter and the rules and regulations of the advisory council.

(b) Counties may establish a program of grants to public entities and nonpartisan nonprofit corporations for the establishment and continuance of programs to be operated under the requirements of this chapter and the standards developed by the advisory council. The board of supervisors of a county in which, because of the county's size, the distribution authorized by Section 470.5 is insufficient to establish a county program may enter into an agreement with the board of supervisors of one or more other such counties to establish a program authorized by this chapter on a regional basis.

Added Stats 1986 ch 1313 § 1. Amended Stats 1987 ch 28 § 2, effective May 28, 1987; Stats 2005 ch 75 § 2 (AB 145), effective July 19, 2005, operative January 1, 2006.

§ 467.2. Eligibility for program funding

A program shall not be eligible for funding under this chapter unless it meets all of the following requirements:

(a) Compliance with this chapter and the applicable rules and regulations of the advisory council.

(b) Provision of neutral persons adequately trained in conflict resolution techniques as required by the rules and regulations promulgated by the advisory council pursuant to Section 471.

(c) Provision of dispute resolution, on a sliding scale basis, and without cost to indigents.

(d) Provision that, upon consent of the parties, a written agreement or an award resolving a dispute will be issued setting out a settlement of the issues involved in the dispute and the future responsibilities of each party.

(e) Provision of neutral procedures applicable equally to all participants without any special benefit or consideration given to persons or entities providing funding for the programs.

Section V

(f) Provision that participation in the program is voluntary and that the parties are not coerced to enter dispute resolution.

(g) Provision of alternative dispute resolution is the primary purpose of the program.

(h) Programs operated by counties that receive funding under this chapter shall be operated primarily for the purposes of dispute resolution, consistent with the purposes of this chapter.

Added Stats 1986 ch 1313 § 1.

§ 467.3. Provision of written statement to parties; Contents

Programs funded pursuant to this chapter shall provide persons indicating an intention to utilize the dispute resolution process with a written statement prior to the dispute resolution proceeding, in language easy to read and understand, stating all of the following:

(a) The nature of the dispute.

(b) The nature of the dispute resolution process.

(c) The rights and obligations of the parties, including, but not limited to, all of the following:

(1) The right to call and examine witnesses.

(2) The right of the parties to be accompanied by counsel, who may participate as permitted under the rules and procedures of the program.

(d) The procedures under which the dispute resolution will be conducted.

(e) If the parties enter into arbitration, whether the dispute resolution process will be binding.

Added Stats 1986 ch 1313 § 1.

§ 467.4. Agreements resolving disputes; Enforcement; Admissibility in evidence; Tolling statute of limitations

(a) An agreement resolving a dispute entered into with the assistance of a program shall not be enforceable in a court nor shall it be admissible as evidence in any judicial or administrative proceeding, unless the consent of the parties or the agreement includes a provision that clearly states the intention of the parties that the agreement or any resulting award shall be so enforceable or admissible as evidence.

(b) The parties may agree in writing to toll the applicable statute of limitations during the pendency of the dispute resolution process.

Added Stats 1986 ch 1313 § 1.

§ 467.5. Communications during mediation proceedings

Notwithstanding the express application of Chapter 2 (commencing with Section 1115) of Division 9 of the Evidence Code to mediations, all proceedings conducted by a program funded pursuant to this chapter, including, but not limited to, arbitrations and conciliations, are subject to Chapter 2 (commencing with Section 1115) of Division 9 of the Evidence Code.

Added Stats 1988 ch 188 § 2. Amended Stats 1997 ch 772 § 1 (AB 939).

§ 467.6. Statistical records; Anonymity of parties

Each program shall maintain those statistical records required by Section 471.5, and as may be required by the county. The records shall maintain the confidentiality and anonymity of the parties.

Added Stats 1986 ch 1313 § 1.

§ 467.7. Withdrawal from dispute resolution; Criminal complaints; Waiver of right to counsel

(a) Unless the parties have agreed to a binding award, nothing in this chapter shall be construed to prohibit any person who voluntarily enters the dispute resolution process from revoking his or her consent, withdrawing from dispute resolution, and seeking judicial or administrative redress.

(b) In cases in which a criminal complaint has been filed by a prosecutor, other than for an infraction, the advice of counsel shall be obtained before any dispute resolution process is initiated. Nothing in this subdivision shall be construed to preclude a defendant from knowingly and voluntarily waiving the right to counsel. A defendant who indicates a desire to waive the right to counsel shall be encouraged to consult with the public defender or private counsel before waiving that right.

Added Stats 1986 ch 1313 § 1.

Section V

Article 4

Application Procedures

§ 468.1. Selection of programs

Programs shall be selected for funding by a county from the applications submitted therefor.

Added Stats 1986 ch 1313 § 1.

§ 468.2. Applications; Required information

Applications submitted for funding shall include, but need not be limited to, all of the following information:

(a) Evidence of compliance with Sections 467.2, 467.3, and 467.4.

(b) A description of the proposed community area of service, cost of the principal components of operation, and any other characteristics, as determined by rules of the advisory council.

(c) A description of available dispute resolution services and facilities within the defined geographical area.

(d) A description of the applicant's proposed program, by type and purpose, including evidence of community support, the present availability of resources, and the applicant's administrative capability.

(e) A description of existing or planned cooperation between the applicant and local human service and justice system agencies.

(f) A demonstrated effort on the part of the applicant to show the manner in which funds that may be awarded under this program may be coordinated or consolidated with other local, state, or federal funds available for the activities described in Sections 467.2, 467.3, and 467.4.

(g) An explanation of the methods to be used for selecting and training mediators and other facilitators used in the dispute resolution process.

(h) Such additional information as may be required by the county.

Added Stats 1986 ch 1313 § 1.

§ 468.3. Funding priorities; Criteria

Data supplied by each applicant shall be used to assign relative funding priority on the basis of criteria developed by the advisory council. The criteria may include, but shall not be limited to, all of the following, in addition to the criteria set forth in Section 468.2:

(a) Unit cost, according to the type and scope of the proposed program.

(b) Quality and validity of the program.

(c) Number of participants who may be served.

(d) Administrative capability.

(e) Community support factors.

Added Stats 1986 ch 1313 § 1.

Article 6

Funding

§ 470.1. Acceptance of funds by grant recipients

(a) A grant recipient may accept funds from any public or private source for the purposes of this chapter.

(b) A county and its representatives may inspect, examine, and audit the fiscal affairs of the programs and the projects funded under this chapter.

(c) Programs shall, whenever reasonably possible, make use of public facilities at free or nominal costs.

Added Stats 1986 ch 1313 § 1.

§ 470.2. County's share of funding

A county's share of the funding pursuant to this chapter shall not exceed 50 percent of the approved estimated cost of the program.

Added Stats 1986 ch 1313 § 1.

§ 470.3. [Section repealed 2006.]

Added Stats 1986 ch 1313 § 1. Amended Stats 1987 ch 28 § 3, effective May 28, 1987, ch 1431 § 1; Stats 1992 ch 685 § 2 (SB 1707), effective September 12, 1992; Stats 1998 ch 931 § 1 (SB 2139), effective September 28, 1998. Repealed Stats 2005 ch 75 § 3 (AB 145), effective July 19, 2005, operative January 1, 2006. The repealed section related to fees for support of programs.

§ 470.5. Monthly distributions from filing fees for support of dispute resolution programs

(a) On and after January 1, 2006, as described in Section 68085.1 of the Government Code, the Administrative Office of the Courts shall make monthly distributions from superior court filing fees for the support of dispute resolution programs under this chapter in each county that has acted to establish a program. The amount distributed in each county shall be equal to the following:

(1) From each first paper filing fee collected by the court as provided under Section 70611 or 70612, subdivision (a) of Section 70613, subdivision (a) of Section 70614, or Section 70670 of the Government Code, and each first paper or petition filing fee collected by the court in a probate matter as provided under Section 70650, 70651, 70652, 70653, or 70655 of the Government Code, the same amount as was required to be collected for the support of dispute resolution programs in that county as of December 31, 2005, when a fee was collected for the filing of a first paper in a civil action under Section 26820.4 of the Government Code.

(2) From each first paper filing fee in a limited civil case collected by the court as provided under subdivision (b) of Section 70613 or subdivision (b) of Section 70614 of the Government Code, and each first paper or petition filing fee collected by the court in a probate matter as provided under Section 70654, 70656, or 70658 of the Government Code, the same amount as was required to be collected for the support of dispute resolution programs in that county as of December 31, 2005, when a fee was collected for the filing of a first paper in a civil action under Section 72055 of the Government Code where the amount demanded, excluding attorney's fees and costs, was ten thousand dollars ($10,000) or less.

(b) Distributions under this section shall be used only for the support of dispute resolution programs authorized by this chapter. The county shall deposit the amounts distributed under this section in an account created and maintained for this purpose by the county. Records of these distributions shall be available for inspection by the public upon request.

(c) After January 1, 2006, a county that does not already have a distribution from superior court filing fees under this section and that establishes a dispute resolution program authorized by this chapter may approve a distribution under this section. A county that already has a distribution under this section may change the amount of the distribution. The total amount to be distributed for the support of dispute resolution programs under this section may not exceed eight dollars ($8) per filing fee.

(d) The county may make changes under subdivision (c) to be effective January 1 or July 1 of any year, on and after January 1, 2006. The county shall provide the Administrative Office of the Courts with a copy of the action of the board of supervisors that establishes the change at least 15 days before the date that the change goes into effect.

Added Stats 2005 ch 75 § 4 (AB 145), effective July 19, 2005, operative January 1, 2006.

§ 470.6. Carry over of moneys and fees

A county may carry over moneys received from distributions under Section 470.5 and from the fees for the support of dispute resolution programs authorized by this chapter that were added to fees for filing a first paper in a civil action in superior court under the laws in effect before January 1, 2006.

Added Stats 2005 ch 75 § 5 (AB 145), effective July 19, 2005, operative January 1, 2006.

Article 7

Rules and Regulations

§ 471.3. Statewide uniformity with guidelines contained in rules and regulations

The rules and regulations adopted by the advisory council pursuant to Section 471 shall be formulated to promote statewide uniformity with the guidelines contained in those rules and regulations.

Added Stats 1987 ch 28 § 6, effective May 28, 1987.

§ 471.5. Annual provision of statistical data

Each program funded pursuant to this chapter shall annually provide the county with statistical data regarding its operating budget; the number of referrals, categories, or types of cases referred to the program; the number of persons served by the program; the number of disputes resolved; the nature of the disputes resolved; rates of compliance; the number of persons utilizing the process more than once; the duration of and the estimated costs of the hearings conducted by the programs; and any other information that the county may require. The data shall maintain the confidentiality and anonymity of the persons employing the dispute resolution process.

Added Stats 1986 ch 1313 § 1. Amended Stats 1987 ch 56 § 1.

DIVISION 1.2

JOINT COMMITTEE ON BOARDS, COMMISSIONS, AND CONSUMER PROTECTION

Chapter 1

Review of Boards under the Department of Consumer Affairs

§ 473.   [Section repealed 2011.]
§ 473.1.   [Section repealed 2011.]
§ 473.15.   [Section repealed 2011.]
§ 473.16.   [Section repealed 2011.]
§ 473.17.   [Section repealed 2000.]
§ 473.2.   [Section repealed 2011.]
§ 473.3.   [Section repealed 2011.]
§ 473.4.   [Section repealed 2011.]
§ 473.5.   [Section repealed 2011.]
§ 473.6.   [Section repealed 2011.]

§ 473.   [Section repealed 2011.]

Added Stats 1994 ch 908 § 5 (SB 2036). Amended Stats 1998 ch 991 § 2 (SB 1980); Stats 2003 ch 874 § 2 (SB 363); Stats 2004 ch 33 § 3 (AB 1467), effective April 13, 2004. Repealed Stats 2010 ch 670 § 3 (AB 2130), effective January 1, 2011. The repealed section related to the establishment of the Joint Committee on Boards, Commissions, and Consumer Protection, powers and duties, designation of staff, and termination of Committee.

§ 473.1.   [Section repealed 2011.]

Added Stats 1994 ch 908 § 5 (SB 2036). Amended Stats 1997 ch 78 § 3.5 (AB 71); Stats 2000 ch 393 § 1 (SB 2028); Stats 2002 ch 825 § 2 (SB 1952); Stats 2003 ch 789 § 3 (SB 364); Stats 2009 ch 310 § 5 (AB 48), effective January 1, 2010. Repealed Stats 2010 ch 670 § 3 (AB 2130), effective January 1, 2011. The repealed section related to applicability of chapter "Review of Boards under the Department of Consumer Affairs."

§ 473.15.   [Section repealed 2011.]

Added Stats 1997 ch 759 § 6 (SB 827). Amended Stats 2000 ch 199 § 1 (SB 2034); Stats 2002 ch 681 § 1 (SB 1954), ch 1012 § 1.5 (SB 2025), effective September 27, 2002; Stats

2004 ch 33 § 4 (AB 1467), effective April 13, 2004; Stats 2005 ch 659 § 0.5 (SB 248), effective January 1, 2006; Stats 2006 ch 658 § 4 (SB 1476), effective January 1, 2007. Repealed Stats 2010 ch 670 § 3 (AB 2130), effective January 1, 2011. The repealed section related to review of specified boards by committee and legislative intent.

§ 473.16.   [Section repealed 2011.]

Added Stats 2005 ch 674 § 3 (SB 231), effective January 1, 2006. Repealed Stats 2010 ch 670 § 3 (AB 2130), effective January 1, 2011. The repealed section related to examination and report of Medical Board of California's composition, initial and biennial fees, and report of findings.

§ 473.17.   [Section repealed 2000.]

Added Stats ch 736 § 1 (SB 1981). Repealed Stats 2000 ch 393 § 3 (SB 2028). The repealed section related to review of referral of cases by specified boards to Licensing and Health Quality Enforcement Sections of Attorney General's office.

§ 473.2.   [Section repealed 2011.]

Added Stats 1994 ch 908 § 5 (SB 2036). Amended Stats 2000 ch 393 § 4 (SB 2028); Stats 2003 ch 789 § 4 (SB 364); Stats 2004 ch 33 § 5 (AB 1467), effective April 13, 2004. Repealed Stats 2010 ch 670 § 3 (AB 2130), effective January 1, 2011. The repealed section related to submission of analysis and report to committee concerning the board.

§ 473.3.   [Section repealed 2011.]

Added Stats 1994 ch 908 § 5 (SB 2036). Amended Stats 1997 ch 78 § 3.7 (AB 71); Stats 2000 ch 393 § 5 (SB 2028); Stats 2001 ch 399 § 1 (AB 1720); Stats 2003 ch 789 § 5 (SB 364); Stats 2004 ch 33 § 6 (AB 1467), effective April 13, 2004. Repealed Stats 2010 ch 670 § 3 (AB 2130), effective January 1, 2011. The repealed section related to public hearings prior to termination, continuation, or reestablishment of any board, the review of the Bureau for Private Postsecondary and Vocational Education and Bureau of Automotive Repair.

§ 473.4.   [Section repealed 2011.]

Added Stats 1994 ch 908 § 5 (SB 2036). Amended Stats 2004 ch 33 § 7 (AB 1467), effective April 13, 2004. Repealed Stats 2010 ch 670 § 3 (AB 2130), effective January 1, 2011. The repealed section related to the evaluation of boards and regulatory programs and determination of need for continued existence.

§ 473.5.   [Section repealed 2011.]

Added Stats 1994 ch 908 § 5 (SB 2036). Amended Stats 2000 ch 393 § 6 (SB 2028); Stats 2004 ch 33 § 8 (AB 1467), effective April 13, 2004. Repealed Stats 2010 ch 670 § 3 (AB 2130), effective January 1, 2011. The repealed section related to report of findings and preliminary recommendations by Joint Committee on Boards, Commissions, and Consumer Protection.

§ 473.6.   [Section repealed 2011.]

Added Stats 1997 ch 759 § 7 (SB 827). Amended Stats 2002 ch 1012 § 2 (SB 2025), effective September 27, 2002; Stats 2004 ch 33 § 9 (AB 1467), effective April 13, 2004, ch 909 § 1.5 (SB 136), effective September 30, 2004. Repealed Stats 2010 ch 670 § 3 (AB

2130), effective January 1, 2011. The repealed section related to the referral of proposals to create new licensure categories, change requirements, or create new licensing board to Joint Committee.

DIVISION 1.5

DENIAL, SUSPENSION AND REVOCATION OF LICENSES

Chapter 1

General Provisions

Chapter 2

Denial of Licenses

Chapter 3

Suspension and Revocation of Licenses

Chapter 4

Public Reprovals

Chapter 5

Examination Security

Chapter 1

General Provisions

§ 475. Applicability of division

(a) Notwithstanding any other provisions of this code, the provisions of this division shall govern the denial of licenses on the grounds of:

(1) Knowingly making a false statement of material fact, or knowingly omitting to state a material fact, in an application for a license.

(2) Conviction of a crime.

(3) Commission of any act involving dishonesty, fraud or deceit with the intent to substantially benefit himself or another, or substantially injure another.

(4) Commission of any act which, if done by a licentiate of the business or profession in question, would be grounds for suspension or revocation of license.

(b) Notwithstanding any other provisions of this code, the provisions of this division shall govern the suspension and revocation of licenses on grounds specified in paragraphs (1) and (2) of subdivision (a).

(c) A license shall not be denied, suspended, or revoked on the grounds of a lack of good moral character or any similar ground relating to an applicant's character, reputation, personality, or habits.

Added Stats 1972 ch 903 § 1. Amended Stats 1974 ch 1321 § 1; Stats 1992 ch 1289 § 5 (AB 2743).

§ 476. Exemptions

(a) Except as provided in subdivision (b), nothing in this division shall apply to the licensure or registration of persons pursuant to Chapter 4 (commencing with Section 6000) of Division 3, or pursuant to Division 9 (commencing with Section 23000) or pursuant to Chapter 5 (commencing with Section 19800) of Division 8.

(b) Section 494.5 shall apply to the licensure of persons authorized to practice law pursuant to Chapter 4 (commencing with Section 6000) of Division 3, and the licensure or registration of persons pursuant to Chapter 5 (commencing with Section 19800) of Division 8 or pursuant to Division 9 (commencing with Section 23000).

Added Stats 1972 ch 903 § 1. Amended Stats 1983 ch 721 § 1; Stats 2011 ch 455 § 2 (AB 1424), effective January 1, 2012.

§ 477.   "Board"; "License"

As used in this division:

(a) "Board" includes "bureau," "commission," "committee," "department," "division," "examining committee," "program," and "agency."

(b) "License" includes certificate, registration or other means to engage in a business or profession regulated by this code.

Added Stats 1972 ch 903 § 1. Amended Stats 1974 ch 1321 § 2; Stats 1983 ch 95 § 1; Stats 1991 ch 654 § 5 (AB 1893).

§ 478.   "Application"; "Material"

(a) As used in this division, "application" includes the original documents or writings filed and any other supporting documents or writings including supporting documents provided or filed contemporaneously, or later, in support of the application whether provided or filed by the applicant or by any other person in support of the application.

(b) As used in this division, "material" includes a statement or omission substantially related to the qualifications, functions, or duties of the business or profession.

Added Stats 1992 ch 1289 § 6 (AB 2743).

Chapter 2

Denial of Licenses

§ 480.   Grounds for denial; Effect of obtaining certificate of rehabilitation

(a) A board may deny a license regulated by this code on the grounds that the applicant has one of the following:

(1) Been convicted of a crime. A conviction within the meaning of this section means a plea or verdict of guilty or a conviction following a plea of nolo contendere. Any action that a board is permitted to take following the establishment of a conviction may be taken when the time for appeal has elapsed, or the judgment of conviction has been affirmed on appeal, or when an order granting probation is made suspending the imposition of sentence, irrespective of a subsequent order under the provisions of Section 1203.4 of the Penal Code.

(2) Done any act involving dishonesty, fraud, or deceit with the intent to substantially benefit himself or herself or another, or substantially injure another.

(3) (A) Done any act that if done by a licentiate of the business or profession in question, would be grounds for suspension or revocation of license.

(B) The board may deny a license pursuant to this subdivision only if the crime or act is substantially related to the qualifications, functions, or duties of the business or profession for which application is made.

(b) Notwithstanding any other provision of this code, no person shall be denied a license solely on the basis that he or she has been convicted of a felony if he or she has obtained a certificate of rehabilitation under Chapter 3.5 (commencing with Section 4852.01) of Title 6 of Part 3 of the Penal Code or that he or she has been convicted of a misdemeanor if he or she has met all applicable requirements of the criteria of rehabilitation developed by the board to evaluate the rehabilitation of a person when considering the denial of a license under subdivision (a) of Section 482.

(c) A board may deny a license regulated by this code on the ground that the applicant knowingly made a false statement of fact required to be revealed in the application for the license.

Added Stats 1974 ch 1321 § 4. Amended Stats 1976 ch 947 § 1; Stats 1979 ch 876 § 2; Stats 2008 ch 179 § 2 (SB 1498), effective January 1, 2009.

§ 481. Crime and job-fitness criteria

Each board under the provisions of this code shall develop criteria to aid it, when considering the denial, suspension or revocation of a license, to determine whether a crime or act is substantially related to the qualifications, functions, or duties of the business or profession it regulates.

Added Stats 1974 ch 1321 § 6.

§ 482. Rehabilitation criteria

Each board under the provisions of this code shall develop criteria to evaluate the rehabilitation of a person when:

(a) Considering the denial of a license by the board under Section 480; or

(b) Considering suspension or revocation of a license under Section 490.

Each board shall take into account all competent evidence of rehabilitation furnished by the applicant or licensee.

Added Stats 1972 ch 903 § 1. Amended Stats 1974 ch 1321 § 7.

§ 484. Attestation to good moral character of applicant

No person applying for licensure under this code shall be required to submit to any licensing board any attestation by other persons to his good moral character.

Added Stats 1972 ch 903 § 1. Amended Stats 1974 ch 1321 § 9.

§ 485. Procedure upon denial

Upon denial of an application for a license under this chapter or Section 496, the board shall do either of the following:

(a) File and serve a statement of issues in accordance with Chapter 5 (commencing with Section 11500) of Part 1 of Division 3 of Title 2 of the Government Code.

(b) Notify the applicant that the application is denied, stating (1) the reason for the denial, and (2) that the applicant has the right to a hearing under Chapter 5 (commencing with Section 11500) of Part 1 of Division 3 of Title 2 of the Government Code if written request for hearing is made within 60 days after service of the notice of denial. Unless written request for hearing is made within the 60-day period, the applicant's right to a hearing is deemed waived.

Service of the notice of denial may be made in the manner authorized for service of summons in civil actions, or by registered mail addressed to the applicant at the latest address filed by the applicant in writing with the board in his or her application or otherwise. Service by mail is complete on the date of mailing.

Added Stats 1972 ch 903 § 1. Amended Stats 1997 ch 758 § 2.3 (SB 1346).

§ 486. Contents of decision or notice

Where the board has denied an application for a license under this chapter or Section 496, it shall, in its decision, or in its notice under subdivision (b) of Section 485, inform the applicant of the following:

(a) The earliest date on which the applicant may reapply for a license which shall be one year from the effective date of the decision, or service of the notice under subdivision (b) of Section 485, unless the board prescribes an earlier date or a later date is prescribed by another statute.

(b) That all competent evidence of rehabilitation presented will be considered upon a reapplication.

Along with the decision, or the notice under subdivision (b) of Section 485, the board shall serve a copy of the criteria relating to rehabilitation formulated under Section 482.

Added Stats 1972 ch 903 § 1. Amended Stats 1974 ch 1321 § 9.5; Stats 1997 ch 758 § 2.4 (SB 1346).

Section V

§ 487. Hearing; Time

If a hearing is requested by the applicant, the board shall conduct such hearing within 90 days from the date the hearing is requested unless the applicant shall request or agree in writing to a postponement or continuance of the hearing. Notwithstanding the above, the Office of Administrative Hearings may order, or on a showing of good cause, grant a request for, up to 45 additional days within which to conduct a hearing, except in cases involving alleged examination or licensing fraud, in which cases the period may be up to 180 days. In no case shall more than two such orders be made or requests be granted.

Added Stats 1972 ch 903 § 1. Amended Stats 1974 ch 1321 § 10; Stats 1986 ch 220 § 1, effective June 30, 1986.

§ 488. Hearing request

Except as otherwise provided by law, following a hearing requested by an applicant pursuant to subdivision (b) of Section 485, the board may take any of the following actions:

(a) Grant the license effective upon completion of all licensing requirements by the applicant.

(b) Grant the license effective upon completion of all licensing requirements by the applicant, immediately revoke the license, stay the revocation, and impose probationary conditions on the license, which may include suspension.

(c) Deny the license.

(d) Take other action in relation to denying or granting the license as the board in its discretion may deem proper.

Added Stats 2000 ch 568 § 2 (AB 2888).

§ 489. Denial of application without a hearing

Any agency in the department which is authorized by law to deny an application for a license upon the grounds specified in Section 480 or 496, may without a hearing deny an application upon any of those grounds, if within one year previously, and after proceedings conducted in accordance with Chapter 5 (commencing with Section 11500) of Part 1 of Division 3 of Title 2 of the Government Code, that agency has denied an application from the same applicant upon the same ground.

Added Stats 1955 ch 1151 § 1, as B & P C § 116. Amended Stats 1978 ch 1161 § 2. Renumbered by Stats 1989 ch 1104 § 1. Amended Stats 1997 ch 758 § 2.5 (SB 1346).

Chapter 3

Suspension and Revocation of Licenses

§ 490. Grounds for suspension or revocation; Discipline for substantially related crimes; Conviction; Legislative findings

(a) In addition to any other action that a board is permitted to take against a licensee, a board may suspend or revoke a license on the ground that the licensee has been convicted of a crime, if the crime is substantially related to the qualifications, functions, or duties of the business or profession for which the license was issued.

(b) Notwithstanding any other provision of law, a board may exercise any authority to discipline a licensee for conviction of a crime that is independent of the authority granted under subdivision (a) only if the crime is substantially related to the qualifications, functions, or duties of the business or profession for which the licensee's license was issued.

(c) A conviction within the meaning of this section means a plea or verdict of guilty or a conviction following a plea of nolo contendere. An action that a board is permitted to take following the establishment of a conviction may be taken when the time for appeal has elapsed, or the judgment of conviction has been affirmed on appeal, or when an order granting probation is made suspending the imposition of sentence, irrespective of a subsequent order under Section 1203.4 of the Penal Code.

(d) The Legislature hereby finds and declares that the application of this section has been made unclear by the holding in Petropoulos v. Department of Real Estate (2006) 142 Cal.App.4th 554, and that the holding in that case has placed a significant number of statutes and regulations in question, resulting in potential harm to the consumers of California from licensees who have been convicted of crimes. Therefore, the Legislature finds and declares that this section establishes an independent basis for a board to impose discipline upon a licensee, and that the amendments to this section made by Chapter 33 of the Statutes of 2008 do not constitute a change to, but rather are declaratory of, existing law.

Added Stats 1974 ch 1321 § 13. Amended Stats 1979 ch 876 § 3; Stats 1980 ch 548 § 1; Stats 1992 ch 1289 § 7 (AB 2743); Stats 2008 ch 33 § 2 (SB 797) (ch 33 prevails), effective June 23, 2008, ch 179 § 3 (SB 1498), effective January 1, 2009; Stats 2010 ch 328 § 2 (SB 1330), effective January 1, 2011.

Section V

§ 490.5. Suspension of license for failure to comply with child support order

A board may suspend a license pursuant to Section 17520 of the Family Code if a licensee is not in compliance with a child support order or judgment.

Added Stats 1994 ch 906 § 1 (AB 923), operative January 1, 1996. Amended Stats 2010 ch 328 § 3 (SB 1330), effective January 1, 2011.

§ 491. Procedure upon suspension or revocation

Upon suspension or revocation of a license by a board on one or more of the grounds specified in Section 490, the board shall:

(a) Send a copy of the provisions of Section 11522 of the Government Code to the ex-licensee.

(b) Send a copy of the criteria relating to rehabilitation formulated under Section 482 to the ex-licensee.

Added Stats 1972 ch 903 § 1. Amended Stats 1974 ch 1321 § 14; Stats 1975 ch 678 § 1.

§ 493. Evidentiary effect of record of conviction of crime substantially related to licensee's qualifications, functions, and duties

Notwithstanding any other provision of law, in a proceeding conducted by a board within the department pursuant to law to deny an application for a license or to suspend or revoke a license or otherwise take disciplinary action against a person who holds a license, upon the ground that the applicant or the licensee has been convicted of a crime substantially related to the qualifications, functions, and duties of the licensee in question, the record of conviction of the crime shall be conclusive evidence of the fact that the conviction occurred, but only of that fact, and the board may inquire into the circumstances surrounding the commission of the crime in order to fix the degree of discipline or to determine if the conviction is substantially related to the qualifications, functions, and duties of the licensee in question.

As used in this section, "license" includes "certificate," "permit," "authority," and "registration."

Added Stats 1961 ch 934 § 1, as B & P C § 117. Amended Stats 1978 ch 1161 § 3. Renumbered by Stats 1989 ch 1104 § 1.3.

§ 494. Interim suspension or restriction order

(a) A board or an administrative law judge sitting alone, as provided in subdivision (h), may, upon petition, issue an interim order suspending any licentiate or imposing license restrictions, including, but not limited to, mandatory biological fluid testing, supervision, or remedial training. The petition shall include affidavits that demonstrate, to the satisfaction of the board, both of the following:

(1) The licentiate has engaged in acts or omissions constituting a violation of this code or has been convicted of a crime substantially related to the licensed activity.

(2) Permitting the licentiate to continue to engage in the licensed activity, or permitting the licentiate to continue in the licensed activity without restrictions, would endanger the public health, safety, or welfare.

(b) No interim order provided for in this section shall be issued without notice to the licentiate unless it appears from the petition and supporting documents that serious injury would result to the public before the matter could be heard on notice.

(c) Except as provided in subdivision (b), the licentiate shall be given at least 15 days' notice of the hearing on the petition for an interim order. The notice shall include documents submitted to the board in support of the petition. If the order was initially issued without notice as provided in subdivision (b), the licentiate shall be entitled to a hearing on the petition within 20 days of the issuance of the interim order without notice. The licentiate shall be given notice of the hearing within two days after issuance of the initial interim order, and shall receive all documents in support of the petition. The failure of the board to provide a hearing within 20 days following the issuance of the interim order without notice, unless the licentiate waives his or her right to the hearing, shall result in the dissolution of the interim order by operation of law.

(d) At the hearing on the petition for an interim order, the licentiate may:

(1) Be represented by counsel.

(2) Have a record made of the proceedings, copies of which shall be available to the licentiate upon payment of costs computed in accordance with the provisions for transcript costs for judicial review contained in Section 11523 of the Government Code.

(3) Present affidavits and other documentary evidence.

(4) Present oral argument.

(e) The board, or an administrative law judge sitting alone as provided in subdivision (h), shall issue a decision on the petition for interim order within five business days following submission of the matter. The standard of proof required to obtain an interim order pursuant to this section shall be a preponderance of the evidence standard. If the interim order was previously issued without notice, the board shall determine whether the order shall remain in effect, be dissolved, or modified.

(f) The board shall file an accusation within 15 days of the issuance of an interim order. In the case of an interim order issued without notice, the time shall run from the date of the order issued after the noticed hearing. If the licentiate files a Notice of Defense, the hearing shall be held within 30 days of the agency's receipt of the Notice of Defense. A decision shall be rendered on the accusation no later than 30 days after submission of the matter. Failure to comply with any of the requirements in this subdivision shall dissolve the interim order by operation of law.

(g) Interim orders shall be subject to judicial review pursuant to Section 1094.5 of the Code of Civil Procedure and shall be heard only in the superior court in and for the Counties of Sacramento, San Francisco, Los Angeles, or San Diego. The review of an interim order shall be limited to a determination of whether the board abused its discretion in the issuance of the interim order. Abuse of discretion is established if the respondent board has not proceeded in the manner required by law, or if the court determines that the interim order is not supported by substantial evidence in light of the whole record.

(h) The board may, in its sole discretion, delegate the hearing on any petition for an interim order to an administrative law judge in the Office of Administrative Hearings. If the board hears the noticed petition itself, an administrative law judge shall preside at the hearing, rule on the admission and exclusion of evidence, and advise the board on matters of law. The board shall exercise all other powers relating to the conduct of the hearing but may delegate any or all of them to the administrative law judge. When the petition has been delegated to an administrative law judge, he or she shall sit alone and exercise all of the powers of the board relating to the conduct of the hearing. A decision issued by an administrative law judge sitting alone shall be final when it is filed with the board. If the administrative law judge issues an interim order without notice, he or she shall preside at the noticed hearing, unless unavailable, in which case another administrative law judge may hear the matter. The decision of the administrative law judge sitting alone on the petition for an interim order is final, subject only to judicial review in accordance with subdivision (g).

(i) Failure to comply with an interim order issued pursuant to subdivision (a) or (b) shall constitute a separate cause for disciplinary action against any licentiate, and may be heard at, and as a part of, the noticed hearing provided for in subdivision (f). Allegations of noncompliance with the interim order may be filed at any time prior to the rendering of a decision on the accusation. Violation of the interim order is established upon proof that the licentiate was on notice of the interim order and its terms, and that the order was in effect at the time of the violation. The finding of a violation of an interim order made at the hearing on the accusation shall be reviewed as a part of any review of a final decision of the agency.

If the interim order issued by the agency provides for anything less than a complete suspension of the licentiate from his or her business or profession, and the licentiate violates the interim order prior to the hearing on the accusation provided for in subdivision (f), the agency may, upon notice to the licentiate and proof of violation, modify or expand the interim order.

(j) A plea or verdict of guilty or a conviction after a plea of nolo contendere is deemed to be a conviction within the meaning of this section. A certified record of the conviction shall be conclusive evidence of the fact that the conviction occurred. A board may take action under this section notwithstanding the fact that an appeal of the conviction may be taken.

(k) The interim orders provided for by this section shall be in addition to, and not a limitation on, the authority to seek injunctive relief provided in any other provision of law.

(l) In the case of a board, a petition for an interim order may be filed by the executive officer. In the case of a bureau or program, a petition may be filed by the chief or program administrator, as the case may be.

(m) "Board," as used in this section, shall include any agency described in Section 22, and any allied health agency within the jurisdiction of the Medical Board of California. Board shall also include the Osteopathic Medical Board of California and the State Board of Chiropractic Examiners. The provisions of this section shall not be applicable to the Medical Board of California, the Board of Podiatric Medicine, or the State Athletic Commission.

Added Stats 1993 ch 840 § 1 (SB 842). Amended Stats 1994 ch 1275 § 4 (SB 2101).

§ 494.5. Agency actions when licensee is on certified list; Definitions; Collection and distribution of certified list information; Timing; Notices; Challenges by applicants and licensees; Release forms; Interagency agreements; Fees; Remedies; Inquiries and disclosure of information; Severability

(a) (1) Except as provided in paragraphs (2), (3), and (4), a state governmental licensing entity shall refuse to issue, reactivate, reinstate, or renew a license and shall suspend a license if a licensee's name is included on a certified list.

(2) The Department of Motor Vehicles shall suspend a license if a licensee's name is included on a certified list. Any reference in this section to the issuance, reactivation, reinstatement, renewal, or denial of a license shall not apply to the Department of Motor Vehicles.

(3) The State Bar of California may recommend to refuse to issue, reactivate, reinstate, or renew a license and may recommend to suspend a license if a licensee's name is included on a certified list. The word "may" shall be substituted for the word "shall" relating to the

issuance of a temporary license, refusal to issue, reactivate, reinstate, renew, or suspend a license in this section for licenses under the jurisdiction of the California Supreme Court.

(4) The Alcoholic Beverage Control Board may refuse to issue, reactivate, reinstate, or renew a license, and may suspend a license, if a licensee's name is included on a certified list.

(b) For purposes of this section:

(1) "Certified list" means either the list provided by the State Board of Equalization or the list provided by the Franchise Tax Board of persons whose names appear on the lists of the 500 largest tax delinquencies pursuant to Section 7063 or 19195 of the Revenue and Taxation Code, as applicable.

(2) "License" includes a certificate, registration, or any other authorization to engage in a profession or occupation issued by a state governmental licensing entity. "License" includes a driver's license issued pursuant to Chapter 1 (commencing with Section 12500) of Division 6 of the Vehicle Code. "License" excludes a vehicle registration issued pursuant to Division 3 (commencing with Section 4000) of the Vehicle Code.

(3) "Licensee" means an individual authorized by a license to drive a motor vehicle or authorized by a license, certificate, registration, or other authorization to engage in a profession or occupation issued by a state governmental licensing entity.

(4) "State governmental licensing entity" means any entity listed in Section 101, 1000, or 19420, the office of the Attorney General, the Department of Insurance, the Department of Motor Vehicles, the State Bar of California, the Department of Real Estate, and any other state agency, board, or commission that issues a license, certificate, or registration authorizing an individual to engage in a profession or occupation, including any certificate, business or occupational license, or permit or license issued by the Department of Motor Vehicles or the Department of the California Highway Patrol. "State governmental licensing entity" shall not include the Contractors' State License Board.

(c) The State Board of Equalization and the Franchise Tax Board shall each submit its respective certified list to every state governmental licensing entity. The certified lists shall include the name, social security number or taxpayer identification number, and the last known address of the persons identified on the certified lists.

(d) Notwithstanding any other law, each state governmental licensing entity shall collect the social security number or the federal taxpayer identification number from all applicants for the purposes of matching the names of the certified lists provided by the State Board of Equalization and the Franchise Tax Board to applicants and licensees.

(e) (1) Each state governmental licensing entity shall determine whether an applicant or licensee is on the most recent certified list provided by the State Board of Equalization and the Franchise Tax Board.

(2) If an applicant or licensee is on either of the certified lists, the state governmental licensing entity shall immediately provide a preliminary notice to the applicant or licensee of the entity's intent to suspend or withhold issuance or renewal of the license. The preliminary notice shall be delivered personally or by mail to the applicant's or licensee's last known mailing address on file with the state governmental licensing entity within 30 days of receipt of the certified list. Service by mail shall be completed in accordance with Section 1013 of the Code of Civil Procedure.

(A) The state governmental licensing entity shall issue a temporary license valid for a period of 90 days to any applicant whose name is on a certified list if the applicant is otherwise eligible for a license.

(B) The 90-day time period for a temporary license shall not be extended. Only one temporary license shall be issued during a regular license term and the term of the temporary license shall coincide with the first 90 days of the regular license term. A license for the full term or the remainder of the license term may be issued or renewed only upon compliance with this section.

(C) In the event that a license is suspended or an application for a license or the renewal of a license is denied pursuant to this section, any funds paid by the applicant or licensee shall not be refunded by the state governmental licensing entity.

(f) (1) A state governmental licensing entity shall refuse to issue or shall suspend a license pursuant to this section no sooner than 90 days and no later than 120 days of the mailing of the preliminary notice described in paragraph (2) of subdivision (e), unless the state governmental licensing entity has received a release pursuant to subdivision (h). The procedures in the administrative adjudication provisions of the Administrative Procedure Act (Chapter 4.5 (commencing with Section 11400) and Chapter 5 (commencing with Section 11500) of Part 1 of Division 3 of Title 2 of the Government Code) shall not apply to the denial or suspension of, or refusal to renew, a license or the issuance of a temporary license pursuant to this section.

(2) Notwithstanding any other law, if a board, bureau, or commission listed in Section 101, other than the Contractors' State License Board, fails to take action in accordance with this section, the Department of Consumer Affairs shall issue a temporary license or suspend or refuse to issue, reactivate, reinstate, or renew a license, as appropriate.

(g) Notices shall be developed by each state governmental licensing entity. For an applicant or licensee on the State Board of Equalization's certified list, the notice shall include the address and telephone number of the State Board of Equalization, and shall emphasize the necessity of obtaining a release from the State Board of Equalization as a condition for the issuance, renewal, or continued valid status of a license or licenses. For an applicant or licensee on the Franchise Tax Board's certified list, the notice shall include the address and telephone number of the Franchise Tax Board, and shall emphasize the necessity of obtaining a release from the Franchise Tax Board as a condition for the issuance, renewal, or continued valid status of a license or licenses.

(1) The notice shall inform the applicant that the state governmental licensing entity shall issue a temporary license, as provided in subparagraph (A) of paragraph (2) of subdivision (e), for 90 calendar days if the applicant is otherwise eligible and that upon expiration of that time period, the license will be denied unless the state governmental licensing entity has received a release from the State Board of Equalization or the Franchise Tax Board, whichever is applicable.

(2) The notice shall inform the licensee that any license suspended under this section will remain suspended until the state governmental licensing entity receives a release along with applications and fees, if applicable, to reinstate the license.

(3) The notice shall also inform the applicant or licensee that if an application is denied or a license is suspended pursuant to this section, any moneys paid by the applicant or licensee shall not be refunded by the state governmental licensing entity. The state governmental licensing entity shall also develop a form that the applicant or licensee shall use to request a release by the State Board of Equalization or the Franchise Tax Board. A copy of this form shall be included with every notice sent pursuant to this subdivision.

(h) If the applicant or licensee wishes to challenge the submission of his or her name on a certified list, the applicant or licensee shall make a timely written request for release to the State Board of Equalization or the Franchise Tax Board, whichever is applicable. The State Board of Equalization or the Franchise Tax Board shall immediately send a release to the appropriate state governmental licensing entity and the applicant or licensee, if any of the following conditions are met:

(1) The applicant or licensee has complied with the tax obligation, either by payment of the unpaid taxes or entry into an installment payment agreement, as described in Section 6832 or 19008 of the Revenue and Taxation Code, to satisfy the unpaid taxes.

(2) The applicant or licensee has submitted a request for release not later than 45 days after the applicant's or licensee's receipt of a preliminary notice described in paragraph (2) of subdivision (e), but the State Board of Equalization or the Franchise Tax Board, whichever is applicable, will be unable to complete the release review and send notice of its findings to the applicant or licensee and state govern-

mental licensing entity within 45 days after the State Board of Equalization's or the Franchise Tax Board's receipt of the applicant's or licensee's request for release. Whenever a release is granted under this paragraph, and, notwithstanding that release, the applicable license or licenses have been suspended erroneously, the state governmental licensing entity shall reinstate the applicable licenses with retroactive effect back to the date of the erroneous suspension and that suspension shall not be reflected on any license record.

(3) The applicant or licensee is unable to pay the outstanding tax obligation due to a current financial hardship. "Financial hardship" means financial hardship as determined by the State Board of Equalization or the Franchise Tax Board, whichever is applicable, where the applicant or licensee is unable to pay any part of the outstanding liability and the applicant or licensee is unable to qualify for an installment payment arrangement as provided for by Section 6832 or Section 19008 of the Revenue and Taxation Code. In order to establish the existence of a financial hardship, the applicant or licensee shall submit any information, including information related to reasonable business and personal expenses, requested by the State Board of Equalization or the Franchise Tax Board, whichever is applicable, for purposes of making that determination.

(i) An applicant or licensee is required to act with diligence in responding to notices from the state governmental licensing entity and the State Board of Equalization or the Franchise Tax Board with the recognition that the temporary license will lapse or the license suspension will go into effect after 90 days and that the State Board of Equalization or the Franchise Tax Board must have time to act within that period. An applicant's or licensee's delay in acting, without good cause, which directly results in the inability of the State Board of Equalization or the Franchise Tax Board, whichever is applicable, to complete a review of the applicant's or licensee's request for release shall not constitute the diligence required under this section which would justify the issuance of a release. An applicant or licensee shall have the burden of establishing that he or she diligently responded to notices from the state governmental licensing entity or the State Board of Equalization or the Franchise Tax Board and that any delay was not without good cause.

(j) The State Board of Equalization or the Franchise Tax Board shall create release forms for use pursuant to this section. When the applicant or licensee has complied with the tax obligation by payment of the unpaid taxes, or entry into an installment payment agreement, or establishing the existence of a current financial hardship as defined in paragraph (3) of subdivision (h), the State Board of Equalization or the Franchise Tax Board, whichever is applicable, shall mail a release form to the applicant or licensee and provide a release to the appropriate state governmental licensing entity. Any state govern-

Section V

mental licensing entity that has received a release from the State Board of Equalization and the Franchise Tax Board pursuant to this subdivision shall process the release within five business days of its receipt. If the State Board of Equalization or the Franchise Tax Board determines subsequent to the issuance of a release that the licensee has not complied with their installment payment agreement, the State Board of Equalization or the Franchise Tax Board, whichever is applicable, shall notify the state governmental licensing entity and the licensee in a format prescribed by the State Board of Equalization or the Franchise Tax Board, whichever is applicable, that the licensee is not in compliance and the release shall be rescinded. The State Board of Equalization and the Franchise Tax Board may, when it is economically feasible for the state governmental licensing entity to develop an automated process for complying with this subdivision, notify the state governmental licensing entity in a manner prescribed by the State Board of Equalization or the Franchise Tax Board, whichever is applicable, that the licensee has not complied with the installment payment agreement. Upon receipt of this notice, the state governmental licensing entity shall immediately notify the licensee on a form prescribed by the state governmental licensing entity that the licensee's license will be suspended on a specific date, and this date shall be no longer than 30 days from the date the form is mailed. The licensee shall be further notified that the license will remain suspended until a new release is issued in accordance with this subdivision.

(k) The State Board of Equalization and the Franchise Tax Board may enter into interagency agreements with the state governmental licensing entities necessary to implement this section.

(l) Notwithstanding any other law, a state governmental licensing entity, with the approval of the appropriate department director or governing body, may impose a fee on a licensee whose license has been suspended pursuant to this section. The fee shall not exceed the amount necessary for the state governmental licensing entity to cover its costs in carrying out the provisions of this section. Fees imposed pursuant to this section shall be deposited in the fund in which other fees imposed by the state governmental licensing entity are deposited and shall be available to that entity upon appropriation in the annual Budget Act.

(m) The process described in subdivision (h) shall constitute the sole administrative remedy for contesting the issuance of a temporary license or the denial or suspension of a license under this section.

(n) Any state governmental licensing entity receiving an inquiry as to the licensed status of an applicant or licensee who has had a license denied or suspended under this section or who has been granted a temporary license under this section shall respond that the license was denied or suspended or the temporary license was issued only because the licensee appeared on a list of the 500 largest tax delinquencies pursuant to Section 7063 or 19195 of the Revenue and Taxation Code. Information collected pursuant to this section by any state agency, board, or department shall be subject to the Information Practices Act of 1977 (Chapter 1 (commencing with Section 1798) of Title 1.8 of Part 4 of Division 3 of the Civil Code). Any state governmental licensing entity that discloses on its Internet Web site or other publication that the licensee has had a license denied or suspended under this section or has been granted a temporary license under this section shall prominently disclose, in bold and adjacent to the information regarding the status of the license, that the only reason the license was denied, suspended, or temporarily issued is because the licensee failed to pay taxes.

(o) Any rules and regulations issued pursuant to this section by any state agency, board, or department may be adopted as emergency regulations in accordance with the rulemaking provisions of the Administrative Procedure Act (Chapter 3.5 (commencing with Section 11340) of Part 1 of Division 3 of Title 2 of the Government Code). The adoption of these regulations shall be deemed an emergency and necessary for the immediate preservation of the public peace, health, and safety, or general welfare. The regulations shall become effective immediately upon filing with the Secretary of State.

(p) The State Board of Equalization, the Franchise Tax Board, and state governmental licensing entities, as appropriate, shall adopt regulations as necessary to implement this section.

(q) (1) Neither the state governmental licensing entity, nor any officer, employee, or agent, or former officer, employee, or agent of a state governmental licensing entity, may disclose or use any information obtained from the State Board of Equalization or the Franchise Tax Board, pursuant to this section, except to inform the public of the denial, refusal to renew, or suspension of a license or the issuance of a temporary license pursuant to this section. The release or other use of information received by a state governmental licensing entity pursuant to this section, except as authorized by this section, is punishable as a misdemeanor. This subdivision may not be interpreted to prevent the State Bar of California from filing a request with the Supreme Court of California to suspend a member of the bar pursuant to this section.

(2) A suspension of, or refusal to renew, a license or issuance of a temporary license pursuant to this section does not constitute denial or discipline of a licensee for purposes of any reporting requirements to the National Practitioner Data Bank and shall not be reported to the National Practitioner Data Bank or the Healthcare Integrity and Protection Data Bank.

(3) Upon release from the certified list, the suspension or revocation of the applicant's or licensee's license shall be purged from the state

governmental licensing entity's Internet Web site or other publication within three business days. This paragraph shall not apply to the State Bar of California.

(r) If any provision of this section or the application thereof to any person or circumstance is held invalid, that invalidity shall not affect other provisions or applications of this section that can be given effect without the invalid provision or application, and to this end the provisions of this section are severable.

(s) All rights to review afforded by this section to an applicant shall also be afforded to a licensee.

(t) Unless otherwise provided in this section, the policies, practices, and procedures of a state governmental licensing entity with respect to license suspensions under this section shall be the same as those applicable with respect to suspensions pursuant to Section 17520 of the Family Code.

(u) No provision of this section shall be interpreted to allow a court to review and prevent the collection of taxes prior to the payment of those taxes in violation of the California Constitution.

(v) This section shall apply to any licensee whose name appears on a list of the 500 largest tax delinquencies pursuant to Section 7063 or 19195 of the Revenue and Taxation Code on or after July 1, 2012.

Added Stats 2011 ch 455 § 3 (AB 1424), effective January 1, 2012.

Chapter 4

Public Reprovals

§ 495. Public reproval of licentiate or certificate holder for act constituting grounds for suspension or revocation of license or certificate; Proceedings

Notwithstanding any other provision of law, any entity authorized to issue a license or certificate pursuant to this code may publicly reprove a licentiate or certificate holder thereof, for any act that would constitute grounds to suspend or revoke a license or certificate. Any proceedings for public reproval, public reproval and suspension, or public reproval and revocation shall be conducted in accordance with Chapter 5 (commencing with Section 11500) of Part 1 of Division 3 of Title 2 of the Government Code, or, in the case of a licensee or certificate holder under the jurisdiction of the State Department of Health Services, in accordance with Section 100171 of the Health and Safety Code.

Added Stats 1977 ch 886 § 1. Amended Stats 1997 ch 220 § 2 (SB 68), effective August 4, 1997.

Chapter 5

Examination Security

§ 496.   Grounds for denial, suspension, or revocation of license

A board may deny, suspend, revoke, or otherwise restrict a license on the ground that an applicant or licensee has violated Section 123 pertaining to subversion of licensing examinations.

Added Stats 1989 ch 1022 § 3.

§ 498.   Fraud, deceit or misrepresentation as grounds for action against license

A board may revoke, suspend, or otherwise restrict a license on the ground that the licensee secured the license by fraud, deceit, or knowing misrepresentation of a material fact or by knowingly omitting to state a material fact.

Added Stats 1992 ch 1289 § 8 (AB 2743).

§ 499.   Action against license based on licentiate's actions regarding application of another

A board may revoke, suspend, or otherwise restrict a license on the ground that the licensee, in support of another person's application for license, knowingly made a false statement of a material fact or knowingly omitted to state a material fact to the board regarding the application.

Added Stats 1992 ch 1289 § 9 (AB 2743).

Section V

SECTION VI.

THE CONTRACTORS STATE LICENSE BOARD; LICENSE LAW, RULES AND REGULATIONS, AND RELATED LAWS

Chapter 12.
Contractors' State License Law

BUSINESS & PROFESSIONS CODE

DIVISION 3
PROFESSIONS AND VOCATIONS GENERALLY

Chapter 9

Contractors

Article 1

Administration

Article 2

Application of Chapter

Article 3

Exemptions

Section VI

Section VI

Article 7

Disciplinary Proceedings

Article 7.5

Workers' Compensation Insurance Reports

Section VI

Article 8

Revenue

Article 8.5

The Construction Management Education Sponsorship Act of 1991

Article 9

Renewal of Licenses

Article 10

Home Improvement Business

Article 11

Asbestos Consultants

Article 12

Prohibitions

Chapter 9.3

Home Inspectors

Chapter 9.4

Home Energy Rating System (HERS) Home Inspections

Chapter 9

Contractors

Article 1

Administration

§ 7000. Citation of chapter

This chapter constitutes, and may be cited as, the Contractors' State License Law.

Added Stats 1961 ch 1822 § 2. Amended Stats 1984 ch 193 § 1.

§ 7000.2. Requiring contractors to show proof of compliance with local business tax requirements prior to permit issuance; Limit on business taxes

Nothing in this code shall be interpreted to prohibit cities, counties, and cities and counties from requiring contractors to show proof that they are in compliance with local business tax requirements of the entity prior to issuing any city, county, or city and county permit. Nothing in this code shall be interpreted to prohibit cities, counties, and cities and counties from denying the issuance of a permit to a licensed contractor who is not in compliance with local business tax requirements.

Any business tax required or collected as part of this process shall not exceed the amount of the license tax or license fee authorized by Section 37101 of the Government Code or Section 16000 of the Business and Professions Code.

Added Stats 1992 ch 325 § 1 (AB 2710).

§ 7000.5. Contractors' State License Board; Members; Effect of repeal (Repealed January 1, 2016)

(a) There is in the Department of Consumer Affairs a Contractors' State License Board, which consists of 15 members.

(b) Notwithstanding any other provision of law, the repeal of this section renders the board subject to review by the appropriate policy committees of the Legislature.

(c) This section shall remain in effect only until January 1, 2016, and as of that date is repealed, unless a later enacted statute, that is enacted before January 1, 2016, deletes or extends that date.

Added Stats 1939 ch 37 § 1, as B & P C § 7000. Amended Stats 1961 ch 1821 § 61. Amended and renumbered by Stats 1961 ch 1822 § 3. Amended Stats 1963 ch 1098 § 1; Stats 1971 ch 716 § 98; Stats 1972 ch 1314 § 1; Stats 1975 ch 1153 § 1; Stats 1982 ch 676 § 40; Stats 1994 ch 908 § 48 (SB 2036); Stats 1997 ch 812 § 1 (SB 857), ch 813 § 1 (SB 825); Stats 1999 ch 656 § 5 (SB 1306); Stats 2000 ch 1005 § 1 (SB 2029); Stats 2002 ch 744 § 2 (SB 1953); Stats 2004 ch 33 § 24 (AB 1467), effective April 13, 2004; Stats 2005 ch 675 § 10 (SB 232), effective January 1, 2006; Stats 2006 ch 658 § 105 (SB 1476), effective January 1, 2007; Stats 2008 ch 385 § 7 (SB 963), effective January 1, 2009; Stats 2010 ch 695 § 37 (SB 294), effective January 1, 2011, repealed January 1, 2012; Stats 2011 ch 448 § 21 (SB 543), effective January 1, 2012, repealed January 1, 2016.

§ 7000.6.   Priority of board; Protection of the public

Protection of the public shall be the highest priority for the Contractors' State License Board in exercising its licensing, regulatory, and disciplinary functions. Whenever the protection of the public is inconsistent with other interests sought to be promoted, the protection of the public shall be paramount.

Added Stats 2002 ch 744 § 3 (SB 1953).

§ 7001.   Members of board; Qualifications; Public member

All members of the board, except the public members, shall be contractors actively engaged in the contracting business, have been so engaged for a period of not less than five years preceding the date of their appointment and shall so continue in the contracting business during the term of their office. No one, except a public member, shall be eligible for appointment who does not at the time hold an unexpired license to operate as a contractor.

The public members shall not be licentiates of the board.

Added Stats 1939 ch 37 § 1. Amended Stats 1961 ch 1821 § 62; Stats 1971 ch 716 § 99; Stats 2000 ch 1005 § 2 (SB 2029).

§ 7002.   Board members; Kinds of contractors and qualifications; Definitions

(a) One member of the board shall be a general engineering contractor, two members shall be general building contractors, two members shall be specialty contractors, one member shall be a member of a labor organization representing the building trades, one member shall be an active local building official, and eight members shall be public members, one of whom shall be from a statewide senior citizen organization.

(b) No public member shall be a current or former licensee of the board or a close family member of a licensee or be currently or formerly connected with the construction industry or have any financial interest in the business of a licensee of the board. Each public member shall meet all of the requirements for public membership on a board as set forth in Chapter 6 (commencing with Section 450) of Division 1. Notwithstanding the provisions of this subdivision and those of Section 450, a representative of a labor organization shall be eligible for appointment to serve as a public member of the board.

(c) Each contractor member of the board shall be of recognized standing in his or her branch of the contracting business and hold an unexpired license to operate as a contractor. In addition, each contractor member shall, as of the date of his or her appointment, be actively engaged in the contracting business and have been so engaged for a period of not less than five years. Each contractor member shall remain actively engaged in the contracting business during the entire term of his or her membership on the board.

(d) Each member of the board shall be at least 30 years of age and of good character. In addition, each member shall have been a citizen and resident of the State of California for at least five years next preceding his or her appointment.

(e) For the purposes of construing this article, the terms "general engineering contractor," "general building contractor," and "specialty contractor" shall have the meanings given in Article 4 (commencing with Section 7055) of this chapter.

Added Stats 1939 ch 37 § 1. Amended 1941 ch 971 § 1; Stats 1961 ch 1821 § 63; Stats 1963 ch 1098 § 2; Stats 1971 ch 716 § 100; Stats 1972 ch 1314 § 2; Stats 1973 ch 319 § 32; Stats 1975 ch 1153 § 2; Stats 1976 ch 1188 § 39; Stats 1991 ch 1160 § 1 (AB 2190); Stats 1994 ch 279 § 1 (AB 203); Stats 2000 ch 1005 § 3 (SB 2029).

§ 7003. Terms, vacancies, and appointment of successors

Except as otherwise provided, an appointment to fill a vacancy caused by the expiration of the term of office shall be for a term of four years and shall be filled, except for a vacancy in the term of a public member, by a member from the same branch of the contracting business as was the branch of the member whose term has expired. A vacancy in the term of a public member shall be filled by another public member. Each member shall hold office until the appointment and qualification of his or her successor or until the office is deemed to be vacant pursuant to Section 1774 of the Government Code, whichever first occurs.

Vacancies occurring in the membership of the board for any cause shall be filled by appointment for the balance of the unexpired term.

No person shall serve as a member of the board for more than two consecutive terms.

The Governor shall appoint four of the public members, including the public member who is from a statewide senior citizen organization, the local building official, the member of a labor organization representing the building trades, and the five contractor members qualified as provided in Section 7002. The Senate Rules Committee and the Speaker of the Assembly shall each appoint two public members.

Added Stats 1939 ch 37 § 1. Amended Stats 1955 ch 1532 § 1; Stats 1961 ch 1821 § 64; Stats 1963 ch 1098 § 3; Stats 1971 ch 716 § 101; Stats 1972 ch 1314 § 3; Stats 1973 ch

319 § 33; Stats 1975 ch 1153 § 3; Stats 1976 ch 1188 § 40; Stats 1982 ch 676 § 41; Stats 1991 ch 1160 § 2 (AB 2190); Stats 1994 ch 279 § 2 (AB 203); Stats 1999 ch 983 § 5 (SB 1307); Stats 2000 ch 1005 § 4 (SB 2029).

—See Government Code 1774, Vacancies; Appointments and Reappointments by the Governor and Senate, in Appendix.

§ 7005. Removal of members; Grounds

The Governor may remove any member of the board for misconduct, incompetency or neglect of duty.

Added Stats 1939 ch 37 § 1.

§ 7006. Meetings of board; Regular and special

The board shall meet at least once each calendar quarter for the purpose of transacting business as may properly come before it.

Special meetings of the board may be held at times as the board may provide in its bylaws. Four members of the board may call a special meeting at any time.

Added Stats 1939 ch 37 § 1. Amended Stats 2001 ch 728 § 52 (SB 724).

§ 7007. Quorum; Notice of meetings

Eight members constitute a quorum at a board meeting.

Due notice of each meeting and the time and place thereof shall be given each member in the manner provided by the bylaws.

Added Stats 1939 ch 37 § 1. Amended Stats 1961 ch 1821 § 65; Stats 1972 ch 1314 § 4; Stats 1975 ch 1153 § 4; Stats 2000 ch 1005 § 5 (SB 2029).

§ 7008. Appointment of committees; Making of rules and regulations

The board may appoint such committees and make such rules and regulations as are reasonably necessary to carry out the provisions of this chapter. Such rules and regulations shall be adopted in accordance with the provisions of the Administrative Procedure Act.

Added Stats 1939 ch 37 § 1. Amended Stats 1957 ch 2084 § 20; Stats 1983 ch 891 § 1.

§ 7009. Administration of oaths and taking of proofs

Any member or committee of the board may administer oaths and may take testimony and proofs concerning all matters within the jurisdiction of the board.

Added Stats 1939 ch 37 § 1.

§ 7010.   Functions and duties of board

The board is vested with all functions and duties relating to the administration of this chapter, except those functions and duties vested in the director under the provisions of Division I of this code.

Added Stats 1939 ch 37 § 1.

§ 7011.   Registrar of contractors (Repealed January 1, 2016)

(a) The board, by and with the approval of the director, shall appoint a registrar of contractors and fix his or her compensation.

(b) The registrar shall be the executive officer and secretary of the board and shall carry out all of the administrative duties as provided in this chapter and as delegated to him or her by the board.

(c) For the purpose of administration of this chapter, there may be appointed a deputy registrar, a chief reviewing and hearing officer, and, subject to Section 159.5, other assistants and subordinates as may be necessary.

(d) Appointments shall be made in accordance with the provisions of civil service laws.

(e) This section shall remain in effect only until January 1, 2016, and as of that date is repealed, unless a later enacted statute, that is enacted before January 1, 2016, deletes or extends that date.

Added Stats 1939 ch 37 § 1. Amended Stats 1947 ch 1406 § 1; Stats 1951 ch 1613 § 16; Stats 1963 ch 1587 § 1; Stats 1971 ch 716 § 102; Stats 1994 ch 908 § 49 (SB 2036); Stats 1997 ch 812 § 2 (SB 857), ch 813 § 2 (SB 825); Stats 1999 ch 656 § 6 (SB 1306); Stats 2001 ch 615 § 9 (SB 26), effective October 9, 2001; Stats 2002 ch 744 § 4 (SB 1953); Stats 2005 ch 675 § 11 (SB 232), effective January 1, 2006; Stats 2006 ch 658 § 106 (SB 1476), effective January 1, 2007; Stats 2008 ch 385 § 8 (SB 963), effective January 1, 2009; Stats 2010 ch 695 § 38 (SB 294), effective January 1, 2011, repealed January 1, 2012; Stats 2011 ch 448 § 22 (SB 543), effective January 1, 2012, repealed January 1, 2016.

§ 7011.3.   Prohibition against double penalty for same offense

The registrar shall not assess a civil penalty against a licensed contractor who has been assessed a specified civil penalty by the Labor Commissioner under Section 1020 or 1022 of the Labor Code for the same offense.

Added Stats 1982 ch 327 § 5, effective June 30, 1982.

§ 7011.4.   Enforcement of licensing provisions

(a) Notwithstanding Section 7011, there is in the Contractors' State License Board, a separate enforcement unit which shall rigorously enforce this chapter prohibiting all forms of unlicensed activity.

(b) Persons employed as enforcement representatives in this unit and designated by the Director of Consumer Affairs are not peace officers and are not entitled to safety member retirement benefits. They do not have the power of arrest. However, they may issue a written notice to appear in court pursuant to Chapter 5c (commencing with Section 853.5) of Title 3 of Part 2 of the Penal Code.

Added Stats 1989 ch 1363 § 1. Amended Stats 1994 ch 413 § 1 (SB 1694); Stats 2004 ch 865 § 4 (SB 1914).

—*See Government Code Section 11181, Powers in Connection with Investigations and Actions, in Appendix.*

§ 7011.5.　Investigators as peace officers

Persons employed as investigators of the Special Investigations Unit of the Contractors' State License Board and designated by the Director of Consumer Affairs have the authority of peace officers while engaged in exercising the powers granted or performing the duties imposed upon them in investigating the laws administered by the Contractors' State License Board or commencing directly or indirectly any criminal prosecution arising from any investigation conducted under these laws. All persons herein referred to shall be deemed to be acting within the scope of employment with respect to all acts and matters in this section set forth.

Added Stats 1982 ch 1277 § 1.

§ 7011.7.　Reviewing and investigating complaints

(a) The registrar shall review and investigate complaints filed in a manner consistent with this chapter and the Budget Act. It is the intent of the Legislature that complaints be reviewed and investigated as promptly as resources allow.

(b) The board shall set as a goal the improvement of its disciplinary system so that an average of no more than six months elapses from the receipt of a complaint to the completion of an investigation.

(c) Notwithstanding subdivision (a), the goal for completing the review and investigation of complaints that, in the opinion of the board, involve complex fraud issues or complex contractual arrangements, should be no more than one year.

Added Stats 1983 ch 1301 § 1, operative January 1, 1984. Amended Stats 1989 ch 1132 § 1, effective September 29, 1989; Stats 2000 ch 1005 § 6 (SB 2029).

§ 7011.8.　False complaints against contractors; Penalties

(a) Any person who reports to, or causes a complaint to be filed with, the Contractors' State License Board that a person licensed by that entity has engaged in professional misconduct, knowing the report or complaint to be false, is guilty of an infraction punishable by a fine not to exceed one thousand dollars ($1,000).

(b) The board may notify the appropriate district attorney or city attorney that a person has made or filed what the entity believes to be a false report or complaint against a licensee.

Added Stats 1992 ch 437 § 1 (AB 2966). Amended Stats 2001 ch 745 § 5 (SB 1191), effective October 12, 2001.

§ 7012. Cooperation in enforcement of legislation relating to construction industry; Assistants

The registrar, with the approval of the board and the director, may, when funds are available, cooperate in the enforcement of governmental legislation relating to the construction industry, and, except as provided by Section 159.5, shall appoint such assistants as may be necessary therefor.

Added Stats 1939 ch 37 § 1. Amended Stats 1971 ch 716 § 103.

§ 7013. Review of registrar's acts or decisions by board; Application of section

The board may in its discretion review and sustain or reverse by a majority vote any action or decision of the registrar.

This section shall apply to any action, decision, order, or proceeding of the registrar conducted in accordance with the provisions of Chapter 5 (commencing with Section 11500) of Part 1 of Division 3 of Title 2 of the Government Code.

Added Stats 1939 ch 37 § 1. Amended Stats 1961 ch 941 § 1; Stats 1979 ch 410 § 1.

§ 7013.5. Transcript of witness as evidence

In all application, citation, or disciplinary proceedings pursuant to this chapter and conducted in accordance with the provisions of Chapter 5 (commencing with Section 11500) of Part 1 of Division 3 of Title 2 of the Government Code, the testimony of a witness given in any contested civil or criminal action or special proceeding, in any state or before any governmental body or agency, to which the licensee or person complained against is a party, or in whose behalf the action or proceeding is prosecuted or defended, may be received in evidence, so far as relevant and material to the issues in the proceedings, by means of a duly authenticated transcript of that testimony and without proof of the unavailability of the witness; provided that the registrar may order the production of and testimony by that witness, in lieu of or in addition to receiving a transcript of his or her testimony and may decline to receive in evidence the transcript of testimony, in whole or in part, when it appears that the testimony was given under circumstances that did not require or allow an opportunity for full cross-examination.

Added Stats 2003 ch 607 § 30 (SB 1077).

§ 7014.   Equipment and records; Procurement

The board may procure equipment and records necessary to carry out the provisions of this chapter.

Added Stats 1939 ch 37 § 1.

§ 7015.   Seal of board

The board shall adopt a seal for its own use. The seal shall have the words "Contractors' State License Board, State of California, Department of Consumer Affairs," and the care and custody thereof shall be in the hands of the registrar.

Added Stats 1939 ch 37 § 1. Amended Stats 1972 ch 1138 § 1.

§ 7016.   Per diem and expenses of members of board

Each member of the board shall receive a per diem and expenses as provided in Section 103.

Added Stats 1959 ch 1645 § 27.

§ 7017.3.   Report on complaints and case aging statistics

The Contractors' State License Board shall report annually to the Legislature, not later than October 1 of each year, the following statistical information for the prior fiscal year. The following data shall be reported on complaints filed with the board against licensed contractors, registered home improvement salespersons, and unlicensed persons acting as licensees or registrants:

(a) The number of complaints received by the board categorized by source, such as public, trade, profession, government agency, or board-initiated, and by type of complaint, such as licensee or nonlicensee.

(b) The number of complaints closed prior to referral for field investigation, categorized by the reason for the closure, such as settled, referred for mandatory arbitration, or referred for voluntary arbitration.

(c) The number of complaints referred for field investigation categorized by the type of complaint, such as licensee or nonlicensee.

(d) The number of complaints closed after referral for field investigation categorized by the reason for the closure, such as settled, referred for mandatory arbitration, or referred for voluntary arbitration.

(e) For the board's Intake/Mediation Center and the board's Investigation Center closures, respectively, the total number of complaints closed prior to a field investigation per consumer services representative, and the total number of complaints closed after referral for a field investigation per enforcement representative. Additionally, the board shall report the total number of complaints closed by other board staff during the year.

(f) The number of complaints pending at the end of the fiscal year grouped in 90-day increments, and the percentage of total complaints pending, represented by the number of complaints in each grouping.

(g) The number of citations issued to licensees categorized by the type of citation such as order of correction only or order of correction and fine, and the number of citations issued to licensees that were vacated or withdrawn.

(h) The number of citations issued to nonlicensees and the number of these citations that were vacated or withdrawn.

(i) The number of complaints referred to a local prosecutor for criminal investigation or prosecution, the number of complaints referred to the Attorney General for the filing of an accusation, and the number of complaints referred to both a local prosecutor and the Attorney General, categorized by type of complaint, such as licensee and nonlicensee.

(j) Actions taken by the board, including, but not limited to, the following:

(1) The number of disciplinary actions categorized by type, such as revocations or suspensions, categorized by whether the disciplinary action resulted from an accusation, failure to comply with a citation, or failure to comply with an arbitration award.

(2) The number of accusations dismissed or withdrawn.

(k) For subdivisions (g) and (j), the number of cases containing violations of Sections 7121 and 7121.5, and paragraph (5) of subdivision (a) of Section 7159.5, categorized by section.

(l) The number of interim suspension orders sought, the number of interim suspension orders granted, the number of temporary restraining orders sought, and the number of temporary restraining orders granted.

(m) The amount of cost recovery ordered and the amount collected.

(n) Case aging data, including data for each major stage of the enforcement process, including the following:

(1) The average number of days from the filing of a complaint to its closure by the board's Intake/Mediation Center prior to the referral for an investigation categorized by the type of complaint, such as licensee or nonlicensee.

(2) The average number of days from the referral of a complaint for an investigation to its closure by the Investigation Center categorized by the type of complaint, such as licensee or nonlicensee.

(3) The average number of days from the filing of a complaint to the referral of the completed investigation to the Attorney General.

(4) The average number of days from the referral of a completed investigation to the Attorney General to the filing of an accusation by the Attorney General.

(5) The average number of days from the filing of an accusation to the first hearing date or date of a stipulated settlement.

(6) The average number of days from the receipt of the Administrative Law Judge's proposed decision to the registrar's final decision.

Added Stats 2002 ch 744 § 5 (SB 1953). Amended Stats 2006 ch 106 § 1 (AB 2457), effective January 1, 2007; Stats 2007 ch 130 § 28 (AB 299), effective January 1, 2008.

—*See Civil Code Section 3097, Preliminary 20-Day Notice (Private Work), in Appendix.*

§ 7019. Contract with licensed professionals for site investigation of consumer complaints

(a) If funding is made available for that purpose, the board may contract with licensed professionals, as appropriate, for the site investigation of consumer complaints.

(b) The board may contract with other professionals, including, but not limited to, interpreters and manufacturer's representatives, whose skills or expertise are required to aid in the investigation or prosecution of a licensee, registrant, applicant for a license or registration, or those subject to licensure or registration by the board.

(c) The registrar shall determine the rate of reimbursement for those individuals providing assistance to the board pursuant to this section. All reports shall be completed on a form prescribed by the registrar.

(d) As used in this section, "licensed professionals" means, but is not limited to, engineers, architects, landscape architects, geologists, and accountants licensed, certificated, or registered pursuant to this division.

Added Stats 1987 ch 1264 § 2, effective September 28, 1987. Amended Stats 1991 ch 1160 § 4 (AB 2190); Stats 2002 ch 1013 § 59 (SB 2026).

§ 7019.1. [Section repealed 2001.]

Added Stats 1997 ch 812 § 2 (SB 857), operative until July 1, 2000. Repealed, operative January 1, 2001, by its own terms. The repealed section related to copy of opinion.

—*See Unemployment Insurance Code Section 329, Joint Enforcement Strike Force on the Underground Economy, in Appendix.*

—*See also Labor Code Section 106, Authority of the Labor Commissioner, in the Appendix.*

§ 7020. Computerized enforcement tracking system for consumer complaints

The board shall maintain a computerized enforcement tracking system for consumer complaints.

Added Stats 1987 ch 1264 § 3, effective September 28, 1987. Amended Stats 1991 ch 1160 § 5 (AB 2190).

Article 2
Application of Chapter

§ 7025. "Members of the personnel of record"; "Person"; "Qualifying person"; "Qualifying individual"; "Qualifier"

(a) "Members of the personnel of record" as used in this chapter means every person listed in the records of the registrar as then associated with a licensee.

(b) "Person" as used in this chapter includes an individual, a firm, partnership, corporation, limited liability company, association or other organization, or any combination thereof.

(c) "Qualifying person," "qualifying individual," or "qualifier," as used in this chapter, means a person who qualifies for a license pursuant to Section 7068.

Added Stats 1939 ch 37 § 1. Amended Stats 2010 ch 698 § 2 (SB 392), effective January 1, 2011.

§ 7026. "Contractor"; "Roadway"

"Contractor," for the purposes of this chapter, is synonymous with "builder" and, within the meaning of this chapter, a contractor is any person who undertakes to or offers to undertake to, or purports to have the capacity to undertake to, or submits a bid to, or does himself or herself or by or through others, construct, alter, repair, add to, subtract from, improve, move, wreck or demolish any building, highway, road, parking facility, railroad, excavation or other structure, project, development or improvement, or to do any part thereof, including the erection of scaffolding or other structures or works in connection therewith, or the cleaning of grounds or structures in connection therewith, or the preparation and removal of roadway construction zones, lane closures, flagging, or traffic diversions, or the installation, repair, maintenance, or calibration of monitoring equipment for underground storage tanks, and whether or not the performance of work herein described involves the addition to, or fabrication into, any structure, project, development or improvement herein described of any material or article of merchandise. "Contractor" includes subcontractor and specialty contractor. "Roadway" includes, but is not limited to, public or city streets, highways, or any public conveyance.

Added Stats 1939 ch 37 § 1. Amended Stats 1939 ch 1091 § 1; Stats 1941 ch 971 § 2; Stats 1949 ch 90 § 1; Stats 1963 ch 972 § 1; Stats 1969 ch 761 § 1; Stats 1970 ch 340 § 1; Stats 1973 ch 892 § 1; Stats 1977 ch 429 § 1; Stats 1999 ch 708 § 1 (AB 1206); Stats 2001 ch 728 § 53 (SB 724).

§ 7026.1. "Contractor"

The term "contractor" includes all of the following:

(a) Any person not exempt under Section 7053 who maintains or services air-conditioning, heating, or refrigeration equipment that is a fixed part of the structure to which it is attached.

(b) Any person, consultant to an owner-builder, firm, association, organization, partnership, business trust, corporation, or company, who or which undertakes, offers to undertake, purports to have the capacity to undertake, or submits a bid, to construct any building or home improvement project, or part thereof.

(c) A temporary labor service agency that, as the employer, provides employees for the performance of work covered by this chapter. The provisions of this subdivision shall not apply if there is a properly licensed contractor who exercises supervision in accordance with Section 7068.1 and who is directly responsible for the final results of the work. Nothing in this subdivision shall require a qualifying individual, as provided in Section 7068, to be present during the supervision of work covered by this chapter. A contractor requesting the services of a temporary labor service agency shall provide his or her license number to that temporary labor service agency.

(d) Any person not otherwise exempt by this chapter, who performs tree removal, tree pruning, stump removal, or engages in tree or limb cabling or guying. The term contractor does not include a person performing the activities of a nurseryperson who in the normal course of routine work performs incidental pruning of trees, or guying of planted trees and their limbs. The term contractor does not include a gardener who in the normal course of routine work performs incidental pruning of trees measuring less than 15 feet in height after planting.

(e) Any person engaged in the business of drilling, digging, boring, or otherwise constructing, deepening, repairing, reperforating, or abandoning any water well, cathodic protection well, or monitoring well.

Added Stats 1971 ch 1365 § 1. Amended Stats 1991 ch 1160 § 6 (AB 2190); Stats 2003 ch 759 § 1 (AB 544); Stats 2004 ch 183 § 10 (AB 3082).

§ 7026.2. Definitions

(a) For the purposes of this chapter, "contractor" includes any person engaged in the business of the construction, installation, alteration, repair, or preparation for moving of a mobilehome or mobilehome accessory buildings and structures upon a site for the purpose of occupancy as a dwelling.

(b) "Contractor" does not include the manufacturer of the mobile-home or mobilehome accessory building or structure if it is constructed at a place other than the site upon which it is installed for the purpose of occupancy as a dwelling, and does not include the manufacturer when the manufacturer is solely performing work in compliance with the manufacturer's warranty. "Contractor" includes the manufacturer if the manufacturer is engaged in onsite construction, alteration, or repair of a mobilehome or mobilehome accessory buildings and structures pursuant to specialized plans, specifications, or models, or any work other than in compliance with the manufacturer's warranty.

(c) "Contractor" does not include a seller of a manufactured home or mobilehome who holds a retail manufactured home or mobilehome dealer's license under Chapter 7 (commencing with Section 18045) of Part 2 of Division 13 of the Health and Safety Code, if the installation of the manufactured home or mobilehome is to be performed by a licensed contractor and the seller certifies that fact in writing to the buyer prior to the performance of the installation. The certification shall include the name, business address, and contractor's license number of the licensed contractor by whom the installation will be performed.

(d) For the purposes of this chapter, the following terms have the following meanings:

(1) "Mobilehome" means a vehicle defined in Section 18008 of the Health and Safety Code.

(2) "Mobilehome accessory building or structure" means a building or structure defined in Section 18008.5 of the Health and Safety Code.

(3) "Manufactured home" means a structure defined in Section 18007 of the Health and Safety Code.

Added Stats 1969 ch 761 § 2 as § 7027. Amended Stats 1970 ch 340 § 2; Stats 1973 ch 892 § 2; Stats 1983 ch 891 § 1.5; Stats 1986 ch 851 § 1. Renumbered by Stats 1991 ch 1160 § 17 (AB 2190).

—See *California Water Code Section 13750.5, License Required for Water Wells, in the Appendix.*

§ 7026.3. Persons who install or contract for the installation of carpet

For the purpose of this chapter, "contractor" includes any person who installs or contracts for the installation of carpet wherein the carpet is attached to the structure by any conventional method as determined by custom and usage in the trade; except that a seller of installed carpet who holds a retail furniture dealer's license under

Chapter 3 (commencing with Section 19000) of Division 8 shall not be required to have a contractor's license if the installation of the carpet is performed by a licensed contractor and the seller so certifies in writing to the buyer prior to the performance of the installation, which certification shall include the name, business address, and contractor's license number of the licensed contractor by whom the installation will be performed.

Added Stats 1991 ch 1160 § 9 (AB 2190).

§ 7026.11. Permissible scope of work for the General Manufactured Housing Contractor (C-47) license classification

Notwithstanding any other provision of law, the permissible scope of work for the General Manufactured Housing Contractor (C-47) license classification set forth in Section 832.47 of Division 8 of Title 16 of the California Code of Regulations shall include manufactured homes, as defined in Section 18007 of the Health and Safety Code, mobilehomes, as defined in Section 18008 of the Health and Safety Code, and multifamily manufactured homes, as defined in Section 18008.7 of the Health and Safety Code.

Added Stats 2007 ch 540 § 1 (SB 538), effective January 1, 2008.

§ 7026.12. Installations of fire protection systems

The installation of a fire protection system, excluding an electrical alarm system, shall be performed only by a contractor holding a fire protection contractor classification as defined in the regulations of the board or by an owner-builder of an owner-occupied, single-family dwelling, if not more than two single-family dwellings on the same parcel are constructed within one year, plans are submitted to and approved by the city, county, or city and county authority, and the city, county, or city and county authority inspects and approves the installation.

Added Stats 1988 ch 1035 § 1. Amended Stats 1994 ch 185 § 1 (AB 2646).

§ 7027. Advertising as contractor

Any person who advertises or puts out any sign or card or other device that would indicate to the public that he or she is a contractor, or who causes his or her name or business name to be included in a classified advertisement or directory under a classification for construction or work of improvement covered by this chapter is subject to the provisions of this chapter regardless of whether his or her operations as a builder are otherwise exempted.

Added Stats 1957 ch 948 § 1, as B & P C § 7026.6. Amended Stats 1978 ch 771 § 1. Amended and renumbered by Stats 1991 ch 1160 § 12 (AB 2190); Stats 2011 ch 432 § 8 (SB 944), effective January 1, 2012.

§ 7027.1. Advertising by unlicensed person; Penalties

(a) It is a misdemeanor for any person to advertise for construction or work of improvement covered by this chapter unless that person holds a valid license under this chapter in the classification so advertised, except that a licensed building or engineering contractor may advertise as a general contractor.

(b) "Advertise," as used in this section, includes, but not by way of limitation, the issuance of any card, sign, or device to any person, the causing, permitting, or allowing of any sign or marking on or in any building or structure, or in any newspaper, magazine, or by airwave or any electronic transmission, or in any directory under a listing for construction or work of improvement covered by this chapter, with or without any limiting qualifications.

(c) A violation of this section is punishable by a fine of not less than seven hundred dollars ($700) and not more than one thousand dollars ($1,000), which fine shall be in addition to any other punishment imposed for a violation of this section.

(d) If upon investigation, the registrar has probable cause to believe that an unlicensed individual is in violation of this section, the registrar may issue a citation pursuant to Section 7028.7 or 7099.10.

Added Stats 1957 ch 948 § 2, as B & P C § 7026.7. Amended Stats 1978 ch 771 § 2; Stats 1986 ch 518 § 1. Amended and renumbered by Stats 1991 ch 1160 § 13 (AB 2190). Amended Stats 1994 ch 413 § 2 (SB 1694); Stats 1998 ch 599 § 2 (SB 597).

§ 7027.2. Advertising by person not licensed

Notwithstanding any other provision of this chapter, any person not licensed pursuant to this chapter may advertise for construction work or work of improvement covered by this chapter, provided that he or she shall state in the advertisement that he or she is not licensed under this chapter.

Added Stats 1978 ch 771 § 3, as B & P C § 7026.8. Amended and renumbered by Stats 1991 ch 1160 § 14 (AB 2190).

§ 7027.3. Penalties for fraudulent use of incorrect license number

Any person, licensed or unlicensed, who willfully and intentionally uses, with intent to defraud, a contractor's license number that does not correspond to the number on a currently valid contractor's license held by that person, is punishable by a fine not exceeding ten thousand dollars ($10,000), or by imprisonment in state prison, or in county jail for not more than one year, or by both that fine and imprisonment. The penalty provided by this section is cumulative to the penalties available under all other laws of this state. If, upon investigation, the registrar has probable cause to believe that an unlicensed individual is in violation of this section, the registrar may issue a citation pursuant to Section 7028.7.

Added Stats 1984 ch 815 § 1, as B & P C § 7026.10. Amended Stats 1987 ch 930 § 1, effective September 22, 1987. Amended and renumbered by Stats 1991 ch 1160 § 15 (AB 2190). Amended Stats 2001 ch 728 § 54 (SB 724).

§ 7027.4. Advertising as insured or bonded; Requirements; Cause for discipline

(a) It is a cause for discipline for any contractor to advertise that he or she is "insured" or has insurance without identifying in the advertisement the type of insurance, including, for example, "commercial general liability insurance" or "workers' compensation insurance" that is carried by the contractor. The contractor may abbreviate the title of the type of insurance.

(b) It is cause for discipline for a contractor to advertise that he or she is "bonded" if the reference is to a contractor's license bond required pursuant to Section 7071.6 or to a disciplinary bond required pursuant to Section 7071.8.

(c) "Advertise," as used in this section, includes, but is not limited to, the issuance of any card, sign, or device to any person, the causing, permitting, or allowing of any sign or marking on or in any building or structure or business vehicle or in any newspaper, magazine, or by airwave or any electronic transmission, or in any directory under a listing for construction or work of improvement covered by this chapter, for the direct or indirect purpose of performing or offering to perform services that require a contractor's license.

Added Stats 2003 ch 607 § 31 (SB 1077).

§ 7027.5. Authority for landscape contractor to design systems or facilities; Prime contract for pool, spa, hot tub, outdoor cooking center or fireplace; Subcontracting work outside of the field and scope of activities

(a) A landscape contractor working within the classification for which the license is issued may design systems or facilities for work to be performed and supervised by that contractor.

(b) Notwithstanding any other provision of this chapter, a landscape contractor working within the classification for which the license is issued may enter into a prime contract for the construction of any of the following:

(1) A swimming pool, spa, or hot tub, provided that the improvements are included within the landscape project that the landscape contractor is supervising and the construction of any swimming pool,

spa, or hot tub is subcontracted to a single licensed contractor holding a Swimming Pool (C-53) classification, as set forth in Section 832.53 of Title 16 of the California Code of Regulations, or performed by the landscape contractor if the landscape contractor also holds a Swimming Pool (C-53) classification. The contractor constructing the swimming pool, spa, or hot tub may subcontract with other appropriately licensed contractors for the completion of individual components of the construction.

(2) An outdoor cooking center, provided that the improvements are included within a residential landscape project that the contractor is supervising. For purposes of this subdivision, "outdoor cooking center" means an unenclosed area within a landscape that is used for the cooking or preparation of food or beverages.

(3) An outdoor fireplace, provided that it is included within a residential landscape project that the contractor is supervising and is not attached to a dwelling.

(c) Work performed in connection with a residential landscape project specified in paragraph (2) or (3) of subdivision (b) that is outside of the field and scope of activities authorized to be performed under the Landscape Contractor classification (C-27), as set forth in Section 832.27 of Title 16 of the California Code of Regulations, may only be performed by a landscape contractor if the landscape contractor also either holds an appropriate specialty license classification to perform the work or is licensed as a general building contractor. If the landscape contractor neither holds an appropriate specialty license classification to perform the work nor is licensed as a general building contractor, the work shall be performed by a specialty contractor holding the appropriate license classification or by a general building contractor performing work in accordance with the requirements of subdivision (b) of Section 7057.

(d) A violation of this section shall be cause for disciplinary action.

Added Stats 1983 ch 699 § 12. Amended Stats 2003 ch 34 § 1 (AB 341); Stats 2007 ch 107 § 1 (AB 711), effective January 1, 2008; Stats 2008 ch 179 § 17 (SB 1498), effective January 1, 2009.

§ 7028. Engaging in business without license; Fine and punishment; Statute of limitations

(a) It is a misdemeanor for a person to engage in the business or act in the capacity of a contractor within this state without having a license therefor, unless the person is particularly exempted from the provisions of this chapter.

(b) A first conviction for the offense described in this section is punishable by a fine not exceeding five thousand dollars ($5,000) or by imprisonment in a county jail not exceeding six months, or by both that fine and imprisonment.

(c) If a person has been previously convicted of the offense described in this section, unless the provisions of subdivision (d) are applicable, the court shall impose a fine of 20 percent of the contract price, or 20 percent of the aggregate payments made to, or at the direction of, the unlicensed contractor, or five thousand dollars ($5,000)whichever is greater, and, unless the sentence prescribed in subdivision (d) is imposed, the person shall be confined in a county jail for not less than 90 days, except in an unusual case where the interests of justice would be served by imposition of a lesser sentence or a fine. If the court imposes only a fine or a jail sentence of less than 90 days for second or subsequent convictions under this section, the court shall state the reasons for its sentencing choice on the record.

(d) A third or subsequent conviction for the offense described in this section is punishable by a fine of not less than five thousand dollars ($5,000) nor more than the greater amount of ten thousand dollars ($10,000) or 20 percent of the contract price, or 20 percent of the aggregate payments made to, or at the direction of, the unlicensed contractor, and by imprisonment in a county jail for not more than one year or less than 90 days. The penalty provided by this subdivision is cumulative to the penalties available under all other laws of this state.

(e) A person who violates this section is subject to the penalties prescribed in subdivision (d) if the person was named on a license that was previously revoked and, either in fact or under law, was held responsible for any act or omission resulting in the revocation.

(f) If the person engaging in the business of or acting in the capacity of an unlicensed contractor has agreed to furnish materials and labor on an hourly basis, "the contract price" for the purposes of this section means the aggregate sum of the cost of materials and labor furnishedand the cost of completing the work to be performed.

(g) Notwithstanding any other provision of law, an indictment for any violation of this section by the unlicensed contractor shall be found or an information or complaint filed within four years from the date of the contract proposal, contract, completion, or abandonment of the work, whichever occurs last.

(h) For any conviction under this section, a person who utilized the services of the unlicensed contractor is a victim of crime and is eligible, pursuant to subdivision (f) of Section 1202.4 of the Penal Code, for restitution for economic losses, regardless of whether that person had knowledge that the contractor was unlicensed.

Added Stats 1939 ch 37 § 1. Amended Stats 1963 ch 1883 § 1; Stats 1969 ch 1583 § 4; Stats 1972 ch 125 § 1; Stats 1982 ch 607 § 1; Stats 1989 ch 366 § 1; Stats 1995 ch 467 § 1 (SB 1061); Stats 1996 ch 145 § 1 (AB 2958); Stats 2003 ch 706 § 1 (SB 443); Stats 2004 ch 183 § 11 (AB 3082); Stats 2005 ch 205 § 1 (SB 488), effective January 1, 2006; Stats 2008 ch 33 § 13 (SB 797), effective June 23, 2008; Stats 2009 ch 319 § 1 (AB 370), effective January 1, 2010; Stats 2010 ch 328 § 15 (SB 1330), effective January 1, 2011.

§ 7028.1. Penalties against uncertified contractors performing asbestos-related work

It is a misdemeanor for any contractor, whether licensed or unlicensed, to perform or engage in asbestos-related work, as defined in Section 6501.8 of the Labor Code, without certification pursuant to Section 7058.5 of this code, or to perform or engage in a removal or remedial action, as defined in subdivision (d) of Section 7058.7, or, unless otherwise exempted by this chapter, to bid for the installation or removal of, or to install or remove, an underground storage tank, without certification pursuant to Section 7058.7. A contractor in violation of this section is subject to one of the following penalties:

(a) Conviction of a first offense is punishable by a fine of not less than one thousand dollars ($1,000) or more than three thousand dollars ($3,000), and by possible revocation or suspension of any contractor's license.

(b) Conviction of a subsequent offense requires a fine of not less than three thousand dollars ($3,000) or more than five thousand dollars ($5,000), or imprisonment in the county jail not exceeding one year, or both the fine and imprisonment, and a mandatory action to suspend or revoke any contractor's license.

Added Stats 1985 ch 1587 § 1, effective October 2, 1985. Amended Stats 1986 ch 1443 § 1, effective September 30, 1986, ch 1451 § 1.4, effective September 30, 1986; Stats 1990 ch 1366 § 1 (SB 2004), effective September 26, 1990; Stats 1991 ch 1160 § 18 (AB 2190); Stats 1993 ch 589 § 10 (AB 2211); Stats 1996 ch 712 § 1 (SB 1557); Stats 2004 ch 865 § 7 (SB 1914).

§ 7028.2. Complaints; Disposition of penalties

A criminal complaint pursuant to this chapter may be brought by the Attorney General or by the district attorney or prosecuting attorney of any city, in any county in the state with jurisdiction over the contractor or employer, by reason of the contractor's or employer's act, or failure to act, within that jurisdiction. Any penalty assessed by the court shall be paid to the office of the prosecutor bringing the complaint.

Added Stats 1985 ch 1587 § 2, effective October 2, 1985. Amended Stats 1986 ch 1451 § 1.5, effective September 30, 1986; Stats 1989 ch 366 § 2; Stats 1998 ch 931 § 8 (SB 2139), effective September 28, 1998.

§ 7028.3. Injunction against violations

In addition to all other remedies, when it appears to the registrar, either upon complaint or otherwise, that a licensee has engaged in, or is engaging in, any act, practice, or transaction which constitutes a violation of this chapter whereby another person may be substantially injured, or that any person, who does not hold a state contractor's license in any classification, has engaged in, or is engaging in, any

Section VI

act, practice, or transaction which constitutes a violation of this chapter, whether or not there is substantial injury, the registrar may, either through the Attorney General or through the district attorney of the county in which the act, practice, or transaction is alleged to have been committed, apply to the superior court of that county or any other county in which such person maintains a place of business or resides, for an injunction restraining such person from acting in the capacity of a contractor without a license in violation of this chapter, or from acting in violation of this chapter when another person may be substantially injured, and, upon a proper showing, a temporary restraining order, a preliminary injunction, or a permanent injunction shall be granted.

Added Stats 1965 ch 942 § 1. Amended Stats 1969 ch 698 § 1, ch 1583 § 7; Stats 1982 ch 517 § 17.

§ 7028.4.   Injunction against continuing violation by person not holding state contractor's license

In addition to the remedies set forth in Section 7028.3, on proper showing by (1) a licensed contractor, or an association of contractors, (2) a consumer affected by the violation, (3) a district attorney, or (4) the Attorney General, of a continuing violation of this chapter by a person who does not hold a state contractor's license in any classification, an injunction shall issue by a court specified in Section 7028.3 at the request of any such party, prohibiting such violation. The plaintiff in any such action shall not be required to prove irreparable injury.

Added Stats 1969 ch 1583 § 8. Amended Stats 1971 ch 442 § 1.

§ 7028.5.   Specified individuals acting as contractor without license

It is unlawful for a person who is or has been a partner, officer, director, manager, responsible managing employee, responsible managing member, responsible managing manager, or responsible managing officer of, or an individual who is listed in the personnel of record of, a licensed partnership, corporation, limited liability company, firm, association or other organization to individually engage in the business or individually act in the capacity of a contractor within this state without having a license in good standing to so engage or act.

Added Stats 1941 ch 971 § 3. Amended Stats 2010 ch 698 § 3 (SB 392), effective January 1, 2011.

§ 7028.6.   Authority to issue citations

The Registrar of Contractors is hereby empowered to issue citations containing orders of abatement and civil penalties against persons acting in the capacity of or engaging in the business of a contractor within this state without having a license in good standing to so act or engage.

Added Stats 1981 ch 1124 § 1. Amended Stats 1998 ch 633 § 1 (SB 2217); Stats 2010 ch 415 § 17 (SB 1491), effective January 1, 2011.

§ 7028.7.   Issuance of citation

(a) If upon inspection or investigation, either upon complaint or otherwise, the registrar has probable cause to believe that a person is acting in the capacity of or engaging in the business of a contractor or salesperson within this state without having a license or registration in good standing to so act or engage, and the person is not otherwise exempted from this chapter, the registrar shall issue a citation to that person.

(b) Within 72 hours of receiving notice that a public entity is intending to award, or has awarded, a contract to an unlicensed contractor, the registrar shall give written notice to the public entity that a citation may be issued if a contract is awarded to an unlicensed contractor. If after receiving the written notice from the registrar that the public entity has awarded or awards the contract to an unlicensed contractor, the registrar may issue a citation to the responsible officer or employee of the public entity as specified in Section 7028.15.

(c) Each citation shall be in writing and shall describe with particularity the basis of the citation. Notwithstanding Sections 125.9 and 148, each citation shall contain an order of abatement and an assessment of a civil penalty in an amount not less than two hundred dollars ($200) nor more than fifteen thousand dollars ($15,000).

(d) With the approval of the Contractors' State License Board, the registrar shall prescribe procedures for the issuance of a citation under this section. The board shall adopt regulations covering the assessment of a civil penalty that shall give due consideration to the gravity of the violation, and any history of previous violations.

(e) The sanctions authorized under this section shall be separate from, and in addition to, all other remedies either civil or criminal.

Added Stats 1986 ch 995 § 3, operative January 1, 1988. Amended Stats 1990 ch 774 § 1 (SB 1079), effective September 11, 1990; Stats 1991 ch 785 § 1 (AB 800); Stats 1992 ch 606 § 1 (AB 3240); Stats 2001 ch 728 § 55 (SB 724); Stats 2009 ch 307 § 69 (SB 821), effective January 1, 2010; Stats 2010 ch 415 § 18 (SB 1491), effective January 1, 2011.

§ 7028.8.   Service of citation

Service of a citation issued under Section 7028.7 may be made by certified mail at the last known business address or residence address of the person cited.

Added Stats 1981 ch 1124 § 3.

Section VI

§ 7028.9.   Limitations period

A citation under Section 7028.7 shall be issued by the registrar within four years after the act or omission that is the basis for the citation or within 18 months after the date of the filing of the complaint with the registrar, whichever is later.

Added Stats 1981 ch 1124 § 4. Amended Stats 1996 ch 145 § 2 (AB 2958); Stats 2010 ch 415 § 19 (SB 1491), effective January 1, 2011.

§ 7028.10.   Appeal to registrar

Any person served with a citation under Section 7028.7 may appeal to the registrar within 15 working days after service of the citation with respect to violations alleged, scope of the order of abatement, or amount of civil penalty assessed.

Added Stats 1981 ch 1124 § 5. Amended Stats 1985 ch 1281 § 1.

§ 7028.11.   Citation as final order

If within 15 working days after service of the citation, the person cited fails to notify the registrar that he or she intends to appeal the citation, the citation shall be deemed a final order of the registrar and not subject to review by any court or agency. The 15-day period may be extended by the registrar for good cause.

Added Stats 1981 ch 1124 § 6. Amended Stats 1985 ch 1281 § 2.

§ 7028.12.   Hearing; Decision

If the person cited under Section 7028.7 timely notifies the registrar that he or she intends to contest the citation, the registrar shall afford an opportunity for a hearing. The registrar shall thereafter issue a decision, based on findings of fact, affirming, modifying, or vacating the citation or directing other appropriate relief. The proceedings under this section shall be conducted in accordance with the provisions of Chapter 5 (commencing with Section 11500) of Part 1 of Division 3 of Title 2 of the Government Code, and the registrar shall have all the powers granted therein.

Added Stats 1981 ch 1124 § 7.

§ 7028.13.   Application for court order; Collection of civil penalty; Assignment of rights to civil penalty; Time limit for collection of penalty

(a) After the exhaustion of the review procedures provided for in Sections 7028.10 to 7028.12, inclusive, the registrar may apply to the appropriate superior court for a judgment in the amount of the civil penalty and an order compelling the cited person to comply with the order of abatement. The application, which shall include a certified copy of the final order of the registrar, shall constitute a sufficient showing to warrant the issuance of the judgment and order. If the cited person did not appeal the citation, a certified copy of the citation and proof of service, and a certification that the person cited is not or was not a licensed contractor or applicant for a license at the time of issuance of the citation, shall constitute a sufficient showing to warrant the issuance of the judgment and order.

(b) Notwithstanding any other provision of law, the registrar may delegate the collection of the civil penalty for any citation issued to any person or entity legally authorized to engage in collections. Costs of collection shall be borne by the person cited. The registrar shall not delegate the authority to enforce the order of abatement.

(c) Notwithstanding any other provision of law, the registrar shall have the authority to assign the rights to the civil penalty, or a portion thereof, for adequate consideration. The assignee and the registrar shall have all the rights afforded under the ordinary laws of assignment of rights and delegation of duties. The registrar shall not assign the order of abatement. The assignee may apply to the appropriate superior court for a judgment based upon the assigned rights upon the same evidentiary showing as set forth in subdivision (a).

(d) Notwithstanding any other provision of law, including subdivisions (a) and (b) of Section 340 of the Code of Civil Procedure, the registrar or his or her designee or assignee shall have four years from the date of the final order to collect civil penalties except that the registrar or his or her designee or assignee shall have 10 years from the date of the judgment to enforce civil penalties on citations that have been converted to judgments through the process described in subdivisions (a) and (c).

Added Stats 1981 ch 1124 § 8. Amended Stats 2001 ch 728 § 56 (SB 724); Stats 2005 ch 280 § 2 (SB 1112), effective January 1, 2006.

§ 7028.14. Waiver of part of civil penalty on issuance of license

Notwithstanding any other provision of the law, the registrar may waive part of the civil penalty if the person against whom the civil penalty is assessed satisfactorily completes all the requirements for, and is issued, a contractor's license. Any outstanding injury to the public shall be satisfactorily settled prior to issuance of the license.

Added Stats 1989 ch 1174 § 1.

§ 7028.15. License required to submit bid to public agency; Exceptions

(a) It is a misdemeanor for any person to submit a bid to a public agency in order to engage in the business or act in the capacity of a contractor within this state without having a license therefor, except in any of the following cases:

(1) The person is particularly exempted from this chapter.

(2) The bid is submitted on a state project governed by Section 10164 of the Public Contract Code or on any local agency project governed by Section 20103.5 of the Public Contract Code.

(b) If a person has been previously convicted of the offense described in this section, the court shall impose a fine of 20 percent of the price of the contract under which the unlicensed person performed contracting work, or four thousand five hundred dollars ($4,500), whichever is greater, or imprisonment in the county jail for not less than 10 days nor more than six months, or both.

In the event the person performing the contracting work has agreed to furnish materials and labor on an hourly basis, "the price of the contract" for the purposes of this subdivision means the aggregate sum of the cost of materials and labor furnished and the cost of completing the work to be performed.

(c) This section shall not apply to a joint venture license, as required by Section 7029.1. However, at the time of making a bid as a joint venture, each person submitting the bid shall be subject to this section with respect to his or her individual licensure.

(d) This section shall not affect the right or ability of a licensed architect, land surveyor, or registered professional engineer to form joint ventures with licensed contractors to render services within the scope of their respective practices.

(e) Unless one of the foregoing exceptions applies, a bid submitted to a public agency by a contractor who is not licensed in accordance with this chapter shall be considered nonresponsive and shall be rejected by the public agency. Unless one of the foregoing exceptions applies, a local public agency shall, before awarding a contract or issuing a purchase order, verify that the contractor was properly licensed when the contractor submitted the bid. Notwithstanding any other provision of law, unless one of the foregoing exceptions applies, the registrar may issue a citation to any public officer or employee of a public entity who knowingly awards a contract or issues a purchase order to a contractor who is not licensed pursuant to this chapter. The amount of civil penalties, appeal, and finality of such citations shall be subject to Sections 7028.7 to 7028.13, inclusive. Any contract awarded to, or any purchase order issued to, a contractor who is not licensed pursuant to this chapter is void.

(f) Any compliance or noncompliance with subdivision (e) of this section, as added by Chapter 863 of the Statutes of 1989, shall not invalidate any contract or bid awarded by a public agency during which time that subdivision was in effect.

(g) A public employee or officer shall not be subject to a citation pursuant to this section if the public employee, officer, or employing agency made an inquiry to the board for the purposes of verifying the license status of any person or contractor and the board failed to respond to the inquiry within three business days. For purposes of this section, a telephone response by the board shall be deemed sufficient.

Added Stats 1989 ch 863 § 1. Amended Stats 1990 ch 321 § 1 (SB 929), effective July 16, 1990; Stats 1991 ch 785 § 2 (AB 800); Stats 1992 ch 294 § 1 (AB 2347).

—See *Public Contract Code Section 10164, License Required for Award of Contract on State Project; 10262 Payment to Subcontractors, and 20103.5, Public Works Contracts: Bidder or Contract Not Licensed; Penalties, in Appendix.*

§ 7028.16. Punishment for engaging in business without license with respect to structures damaged by natural disaster for which state of emergency has been declared

A person who engages in the business or acts in the capacity of a contractor, without having a license therefor, in connection with the offer or performance of repairs to a residential or nonresidential structure for damage caused by a natural disaster for which a state of emergency is proclaimed by the Governor pursuant to Section 8625 of the Government Code, or for which an emergency or major disaster is declared by the President of the United States, shall be punished by a fine up to ten thousand dollars ($10,000), or by imprisonment pursuant to subdivision (h) of Section 1170 of the Penal Code for 16 months, or for two or three years, or by both that fine and imprisonment, or by a fine up to one thousand dollars ($1,000), or by imprisonment in a county jail not exceeding one year, or by both that fine and imprisonment. In addition, a person who utilized the services of the unlicensed contractor is a victim of crime regardless of whether that person had knowledge that the contractor was unlicensed.

Added Stats 1st Ex Sess 1989-1990 ch 36 § 3, effective September 22, 1990. Amended Stats 2009 ch 319 § 2 (AB 370), effective January 1, 2010; Stats 2011 ch 15 § 18 (AB 109), effective April 4, 2011, operative October 1, 2011.

—See *Penal Code Sections 670, State of Emergency; Fraud of Owners or Lessees of Residential Structures; Penalties; 667.16, Enhanced Sentence for Fraud in Repairing Natural Disaster Damage; 551, Insurance Fraud, in Appendix.*

§ 7028.17. Failure of unlicensed person to comply with citation; Distribution of fines

(a) The failure of an unlicensed individual to comply with a citation after it is final is a misdemeanor.

(b) Notwithstanding Section 1462.5 or 1463 of the Penal Code or any other provision of law, any fine collected upon conviction in a criminal action brought under this section shall be distributed as follows:

(1) If the action is brought by a district attorney, any fine collected shall be paid to the treasurer of the county in which the judgment was entered to be designated for use by the district attorney.

(2) If the action is brought by a city attorney or city prosecutor, any fine collected shall be paid to the treasurer of the city in which the judgment was entered, to be designated for use by the city attorney.

Added Stats 1988 ch 725 § 1, as B & P C § 7099.85. Amended Stats 1989 ch 366 § 3. Amended and renumbered by Stats 1991 ch 1160 § 30 (AB 2190).

§ 7029. Issuance and suspension of joint venture license

A joint venture license is a license issued to any combination of individuals, corporations, limited liability companies, partnerships, or other joint ventures, each of which holds a current, active license in good standing. A joint venture license may be issued in any classification in which at least one of the entities is licensed. An active joint venture license shall be automatically suspended by operation of law during any period in which any member of the entity does not hold a current, active license in good standing.

Added Stats 1983 ch 891 § 3. Amended Stats 1984 ch 1174 § 1; Stats 2010 ch 698 § 4 (SB 392), effective January 1, 2011.

§ 7029.1. Unlawfully acting in joint venture without license

(a) Except as provided in this section, it is unlawful for any two or more licensees, each of whom has been issued a license to act separately in the capacity of a contractor within this state, to be awarded a contract jointly or otherwise act as a contractor without first having secured a joint venture license in accordance with the provisions of this chapter.

(b) Prior to obtaining a joint venture license, contractors licensed in accordance with this chapter may jointly bid for the performance of work covered by this section. If a combination of licensees submit a bid for the performance of work for which a joint venture license is required, a failure to obtain that license shall not prevent the imposition of any penalty specified by law for the failure of a contractor who submits a bid to enter into a contract pursuant to the bid.

(c) A violation of this section constitutes a cause for disciplinary action.

Added Stats 1983 ch 891 § 4. Amended Stats 1987 ch 930 § 3, effective September 22, 1987; Stats 2003 ch 607 § 32 (SB 1077).

§ 7029.5. Display of name, business address and business license number on commercial vehicles

Every C-36 plumbing contractor, C-45 sign contractor, and C-57 well-drilling contractor licensed under this chapter shall have displayed on each side of each motor vehicle used in his or her business, for which a commercial vehicle registration fee has been paid pursuant to Article 3 (commencing with Section 9400) of Chapter 6 of Division 3 of the Vehicle Code, his or her name, permanent business address, and contractor's license number, all in letters and numerals not less than 1½ inches high.

The identification requirements of this section shall also apply to any drill rig used for the drilling of water wells.

Failure to comply with this section constitutes a cause for disciplinary action.

Added Stats 1972 ch 681 § 1, operative July 1, 1973, as B & P C § 7029.6. Amended and renumbered by Stats 1991 ch 1160 § 20 (AB 2190); Stats 2011 ch 432 § 9 (SB 944), effective January 1, 2012.

§ 7029.6. Display of business name and contractors' license number

Except for contractors identified in Section 7029.5, every contractor licensed under this chapter shall have displayed, in or on each motor vehicle used in his or her construction business, for which a commercial vehicle registration fee has been paid pursuant to Article 3 (commencing with Section 9400) of Chapter 6 of Division 3 of the Vehicle Code, his or her business name and contractors' license number in a clearly visible location in print type of at least 72-point font or three-quarters of an inch in height and width.

Added Stats 2003 ch 118 § 1 (AB 1538).

§ 7030. Licensee's statement on contracts; Notice requirements; Exceptions

(a) Except for contractors writing home improvement contracts pursuant to Section 7151.2 and contractors writing service and repair contracts pursuant to Section 7159.10, every person licensed pursuant to this chapter shall include the following statement in at least 10-point type on all written contracts with respect to which the person is a prime contractor:

"Contractors are required by law to be licensed and regulated by the Contractors' State License Board which has jurisdiction to investigate complaints against contractors if a complaint regarding a patent act or omission is filed within four years of the date of the alleged violation. A complaint regarding a latent act or omission pertaining to structural defects must be filed within 10 years of the date of the alleged violation. Any questions concerning a contractor may be referred to the Registrar, Contractors' State License Board, P.O. Box 26000, Sacramento, CA 95826."

(b) Every person licensed pursuant to this chapter shall include the following statement in at least 12-point type in all home improvement contracts written pursuant to Section 7151.2 and service and repair contracts written pursuant to Section 7159.10:

"Information about the Contractors' State License Board (CSLB):

CSLB is the state consumer protection agency that licenses and regulates construction contractors.

Contact CSLB for information about the licensed contractor you are considering, including information about disclosable complaints, disciplinary actions and civil judgments that are reported to CSLB.

Use only licensed contractors. If you file a complaint against a licensed contractor within the legal deadline (usually four years), CSLB has authority to investigate the complaint. If you use an unlicensed contractor, CSLB may not be able to help you resolve your complaint. Your only remedy may be in civil court, and you may be liable for damages arising out of any injuries to the unlicensed contractor or the unlicensed contractor's employees.

For more information:

Visit CSLB's Internet Web site at www.cslb.ca.gov

Call CSLB at 800-321-CSLB (2752)

Write CSLB at P.O. Box 26000, Sacramento, CA 95826."

(c) Failure to comply with the notice requirements set forth in subdivision (a) or (b) of this section is cause for disciplinary action.

Added Stats 2005 ch 48 § 5 (SB 1113), effective July 18, 2005, operative January 1, 2006. Amended Stats 2011 ch 432 § 10 (SB 944), effective January 1, 2012.

§ 7030.1. Disclosure

(a) A contractor, who has his or her license suspended or revoked two or more times within an eight-year period, shall disclose either in capital letters in 10-point roman boldface type or in contrasting red print in at least 8-point roman boldface type, in a document provided prior to entering into a contract to perform work on residential property with four or fewer units, any disciplinary license suspension, or license revocation during the last eight years resulting from any violation of this chapter by the contractor, whether or not the suspension or revocation was stayed.

(b) The disclosure notice required by this section may be provided in a bid, estimate, or other document prior to entering into a contract.

(c) A violation of this section is subject to the following penalties:

(1) A penalty of one thousand dollars ($1,000) shall be assessed for the first violation.

(2) A penalty of two thousand five hundred dollars ($2,500) shall be assessed for the second violation.

(3) A penalty of five thousand dollars ($5,000) shall be assessed for a third violation in addition to a one-year suspension of license by operation of law.

(4) A fourth violation shall result in the revocation of license in accordance with this chapter.

Added Stats 1996 ch 282 § 3 (AB 2494).

§ 7030.5. Inclusion of license number in contracts, bids, and advertising

Every person licensed pursuant to this chapter shall include his license number in: (a) all construction contracts; (b) subcontracts and calls for bid; and (c) all forms of advertising, as prescribed by the registrar of contractors, used by such a person.

Added Stats 1972 ch 124 § 1, operative July 1, 1973. Amended Stats 1973 ch 153 § 1, effective July 6, 1973, operative July 1, 1973.

§ 7031. Allegation and proof of license in action on contract; Recovery of compensation paid to unlicensed contractor; Substantial compliance; Exceptions

(a) Except as provided in subdivision (e), no person engaged in the business or acting in the capacity of a contractor, may bring or maintain any action, or recover in law or equity in any action, in any court of this state for the collection of compensation for the performance of any act or contract where a license is required by this chapter without alleging that he or she was a duly licensed contractor at all times during the performance of that act or contract, regardless of the merits of the cause of action brought by the person, except that this prohibition shall not apply to contractors who are each individually licensed under this chapter but who fail to comply with Section 7029.

(b) Except as provided in subdivision (e), a person who utilizes the services of an unlicensed contractor may bring an action in any court of competent jurisdiction in this state to recover all compensation paid to the unlicensed contractor for performance of any act or contract.

(c) A security interest taken to secure any payment for the performance of any act or contract for which a license is required by this chapter is unenforceable if the person performing the act or contract

was not a duly licensed contractor at all times during the performance of the act or contract.

(d) If licensure or proper licensure is controverted, then proof of licensure pursuant to this section shall be made by production of a verified certificate of licensure from the Contractors' State License
Board which establishes that the individual or entity bringing the
action was duly licensed in the proper classification of contractors at
all times during the performance of any act or contract covered by the
action. Nothing in this subdivision shall require any person or entity
controverting licensure or proper licensure to produce a verified certificate. When licensure or proper licensure is controverted, the burden of proof to establish licensure or proper licensure shall be on the
licensee.

(e) The judicial doctrine of substantial compliance shall not apply
under this section where the person who engaged in the business or
acted in the capacity of a contractor has never been a duly licensed
contractor in this state. However, notwithstanding subdivision (b) of
Section 143, the court may determine that there has been substantial
compliance with licensure requirements under this section if it is
shown at an evidentiary hearing that the person who engaged in the
business or acted in the capacity of a contractor (1) had been duly licensed as a contractor in this state prior to the performance of the act
or contract, (2) acted reasonably and in good faith to maintain proper
licensure, (3) did not know or reasonably should not have known that
he or she was not duly licensed when performance of the act or contract commenced, and (4) acted promptly and in good faith to reinstate his or her license upon learning it was invalid.

(f) The exceptions to the prohibition against the application of the
judicial doctrine of substantial compliance found in subdivision (e)
shall apply to all contracts entered into on or after January 1, 1992,
and to all actions or arbitrations arising therefrom, except that the
amendments to subdivisions (e) and (f) enacted during the 1994 portion of the 1993–94 Regular Session of the Legislature shall not apply
to either of the following:

(1) Any legal action or arbitration commenced prior to January 1,
1995, regardless of the date on which the parties entered into the contract.

(2) Any legal action or arbitration commenced on or after January
1, 1995, if the legal action or arbitration was commenced prior to
January 1, 1995, and was subsequently dismissed.

Added Stats 1939 ch 37 § 1. Amended Stats 1957 ch 845 § 1; Stats 1961 ch 1325 § 1;
Stats 1965 ch 681 § 1; Stats 1989 ch 368 § 1; Stats 1991 ch 632 § 1 (AB 1382); Stats
1992 ch 229 § 1 (AB 2413); Stats 1993 ch 797 § 1 (AB 628); Stats 1994 ch 550 § 1 (SB
1844); Stats 2001 ch 226 § 1 (AB 678); Stats 2003 ch 289 § 1 (AB 1386).

§ 7031.5.   Applicant's statement as to license required by city or county permit regulations; Penalty for violation

Each county or city which requires the issuance of a permit as a condition precedent to the construction, alteration, improvement, demolition or repair of any building or structure shall also require that each applicant for such a permit file as a condition precedent to the issuance of a permit a statement which he has prepared and signed stating that the applicant is licensed under the provisions of this chapter, giving the number of the license and stating that it is in full force and effect, or, if the applicant is exempt from the provisions of this chapter, the basis for the alleged exemption.

Any violation of this section by any applicant for a permit shall be subject to a civil penalty of not more than five hundred dollars ($500).

Added Stats 1963 ch 1140 § 1. Amended Stats 1977 ch 1052 § 1.

§ 7032.   Construction of chapter; Complaints to registrar against licensees

Nothing in this chapter shall limit the power of a city or county to regulate the quality and character of installations made by contractors through a system of permits and inspections which are designed to secure compliance with and aid in the enforcement of applicable state and local building laws, or to enforce other local laws necessary for the protection of the public health and safety. Nothing in this chapter shall limit the power of a city or county to adopt any system of permits requiring submission to and approval by the city or county of plans and specifications for an installation prior to the commencement of construction of the installation.

Cities or counties may direct complaints to the registrar against licensees based upon determinations by city or county enforcement officers of violations by such licensees of codes the enforcement of which is the responsibility of the complaining city or county. Such complaints shall to the extent determined to be necessary by the registrar be given priority in processing over other complaints.

Nothing contained in this section shall be construed as authorizing a city or county to enact regulations relating to the qualifications necessary to engage in the business of contracting.

Added Stats 1959 ch 1403 § 1, effective July 1, 1959. Amended Stats 1961 ch 198 § 1.

§ 7033.   Requirement of filing by licensee or applicant statement as to license, or exemption and proof thereof

Every city or city and county which requires the issuance of a business license as a condition precedent to engaging, within the city or city and county, in a business which is subject to regulation under this chapter, shall require that each licensee and each applicant for issuance or renewal of such license shall file, or have on file, with such city or city and county, a signed statement that such licensee or applicant is licensed under the provisions of this chapter and stating that the license is in full force and effect, or, if such licensee or applicant is exempt from the provisions of this chapter, he shall furnish proof of the facts which entitle him to such exemption.

Added Stats 1965 ch 1082 § 1.

—*See Government Code Section 37101.7, Licensing for Revenue by Cities, in Appendix.*

§ 7034. Insertion of void or unenforceable provisions in contract prohibited (First of two; Operative until July 1, 2012)

(a) No contractor who is required to be licensed under this chapter shall insert in any contract, or be a party, with a subcontractor who is licensed under this chapter to any contract which contains, a provision, clause, covenant, or agreement which is void or unenforceable under Section 2782 of the Civil Code.

(b) No contractor who is required to be licensed under this chapter shall require a waiver of lien rights from any subcontractor, employee, or supplier in violation of Section 3262 of the Civil Code.

Added Stats 1976 ch 411 § 1. Amended Stats 1979 ch 1013 § 3.

—*See Civil Code Sections 2782 Construction Contracts; Invalidity of Provisions to Indemnify Promissee Against Liability; Exceptions and 2782.6 Exception for Professional Engineer or Geologist; "Hazardous Materials" Defined, in Appendix.*

§ 7034. Insertion of void or unenforceable provisions in contract prohibited (Second of two; Operative July 1, 2012)

(a) No contractor that is required to be licensed under this chapter shall insert in any contract, or be a party, with a subcontractor that is licensed under this chapter to any contract which contains, a provision, clause, covenant, or agreement which is void or unenforceable under Section 2782 of the Civil Code.

(b) No contractor that is required to be licensed under this chapter shall require a waiver of lien rights from any subcontractor, employee, or supplier in violation of Section 8122 of the Civil Code.

Added Stats 1976 ch 411 § 1. Amended Stats 1979 ch 1013 § 3; Stats 2010 ch 697 § 1 (SB 189), effective January 1, 2011, operative July 1, 2012.

—*See Civil Code Sections 2782 Construction Contracts; Invalidity of Provisions to Indemnify Promissee Against Liability; Exceptions and 2782.6 Exception for Professional Engineer or Geologist; "Hazardous Materials" Defined, in Appendix.*

Article 3
Exemptions

§ 7040. United States, State, and subdivisions

(a) This chapter does not apply to an authorized representative of the United States government, the State of California, or any incorporated town, city, county, irrigation district, reclamation district or other municipal or political corporation or subdivision of this state when the entity or its representative is acting within the scope of the entity's or representative's official capacity.

(b) Nothing in this section authorizes the entity or it's authorized representative thereof either to enter into or authorize a contract with an unlicensed contractor for work which is required by this chapter to be performed by a licensed contractor.

Added Stats 1939 ch 37 § 1. Amended Stats 1986 ch 1230 § 1; Stats 1995 ch 467 § 2 (SB 1061).

—*See Public Contract Code Section 6100 License Required for Award of Contract, in Appendix.*

§ 7041. Court officers

This chapter does not apply to officers of a court when they are acting within the scope of their office.

Added Stats 1939 ch 37 § 1.

§ 7042. Public utilities in their own business operations

This chapter does not apply to public utilities operating under the regulation of the State Railroad Commission on construction, maintenance and development work incidental to their own business.

Added Stats 1939 ch 37 § 1.

§ 7042.1. Adoption fees; Deferral, waiver, or reduction

(a) Notwithstanding any other provisions of this chapter, gas heat, or electrical corporations and their subsidiaries that are regulated as public utilities by the Public Utilities Commission shall not conduct work for which a contractor's license is required, except under any one or more of the following conditions:

(1) The work is performed upon the gas, heat, or electrical corporation's properties.

(2) The work is performed through a contract with a contractor or contractors licensed pursuant to this chapter or the work is performed for low-income citizens pursuant to a program authorized by order of the Public Utilities Commission.

(3) The work is undertaken by the gas, heat, or electrical corporation in furtherance of the generation, transmission, or distribution of electricity, gas, or steam, whether within or without the service area of the corporation, if any work performed within a structure and beyond a customer's utility meter is necessary to protect the public safety or to avoid interruption of service.

(4) The work is otherwise exempt from the provisions of this chapter.

(5) The work is performed to comply with programs or procedures ordered or authorized by the Public Utilities Commission not inconsistent with the objectives expressed in Chapter 984 of the Statutes of 1983.

(b) For the purposes of this section, the following terms have the following meanings:

(1) "Gas, heat, or electrical corporation properties" means properties which a gas, heat, or electrical corporation owns or leases, or over which it has been granted an easement for utility purposes, or facilities which a gas, heat, or electrical corporation owns or operates for utility purposes.

(2) "Subsidiaries" means subsidiaries of a gas, heat, or electrical corporation regulated as public utilities by the Public Utilities Commission which carry out activities solely for utility purposes.

(c) It is the intention of the Legislature in enacting this section that public utility regulations be clearly based on the principle that the energy conservation industry should be allowed to develop in a competitive manner, as declared in Chapter 984 of the Statutes of 1983.

Added Stats 1984 ch 1136 § 1. Amended Stats 1989 ch 29 § 1.

—*See Labor Code Section 3099 Electrician Competency and Training Standards, in Appendix.*

§ 7042.5. Application of chapter; Underground trenching operations; Cable television corporation defined

This chapter does not apply to public utilities operating under the regulation of the Public Utilities Commission on construction, maintenance, and development work incidental to their own business, or to those activities of a cable television corporation subject to regulation pursuant to Section 768.5 of the Public Utilities Code, except underground trenching by a cable television corporation within the public streets, other than that necessary solely for the connection of its distribution system to, or within the properties of, subscribers or potential subscribers.

As used in this section, a cable television corporation is a corporation or person that transmits television programs by cable to subscribers for a fee.

Added Stats 1983 ch 1230 § 1. Amended Stats 1984 ch 945 § 1.

§ 7043. Oil or gas drilling and operation

This chapter does not apply to any construction, repair or operation incidental to the discovering or producing of petroleum or gas, or the drilling, testing, abandoning or other operation of any petroleum or gas well, when performed by an owner or lessee.

Added Stats 1939 ch 37 § 1.

§ 7044. Property owner making own improvements

(a) This chapter does not apply to any of the following:

(1) An owner who builds or improves a structure on his or her property, provided that both of the following conditions are met:

(A) None of the improvements are intended or offered for sale.

(B) The property owner personally performs all of the work or any work not performed by the owner is performed by the owner's employees with wages as their sole compensation.

(2) An owner who builds or improves a structure on his or her property, provided that both of the following conditions are met:

(A) The owner directly contracts with licensees who are duly licensed to contract for the work of the respective trades involved in completing the project.

(B) For projects involving single-family residential structures, no more than four of these structures are intended or offered for sale in a calendar year. This subparagraph shall not apply if the owner contracts with a general contractor for the construction.

(3) A homeowner improving his or her principal place of residence or appurtenances thereto, provided that all of the following conditions exist:

(A) The work is performed prior to sale.

(B) The homeowner has actually resided in the residence for the 12 months prior to completion of the work.

(C) The homeowner has not availed himself or herself of the exemption in this paragraph on more than two structures more than once during any three-year period.

(b) In all actions brought under this chapter, both of the following shall apply:

(1) Except as provided in paragraph (2), proof of the sale or offering for sale of a structure by or for the owner-builder within one year after completion of the structure constitutes a rebuttable presumption affecting the burden of proof that the structure was undertaken for purposes of sale.

(2) Proof of the sale or offering for sale of five or more structures by the owner-builder within one year after completion constitutes a conclusive presumption that the structures were undertaken for purposes of sale.

Added Stats 1981 ch 1124 § 10. Amended Stats 1988 ch 1035 § 1.3; Stats. 2009, Ch. 307 (SB 821).

§ 7044.01.   Remedies; Violations; Fees and costs

In addition to all other remedies, any licensed contractor or association of contractors, labor organization, consumer affected by the violation, district attorney, or the Attorney General shall be entitled to seek injunctive relief prohibiting any violation of this chapter by an owner-builder who is neither licensed nor exempted from licensure under this chapter. The plaintiff in that action shall not be required to prove irreparable injury and shall be entitled to attorney's fees and all costs incurred in the prosecution of the action, provided the plaintiff is the prevailing party. The defendant in that action shall be entitled to attorney's fees and all costs incurred in the defense against the action, provided the defendant is the prevailing party.

Enacted by Stats. 2009, Ch. 307.

§ 7044.1.   Real estate licensee acting within scope of license

This chapter does not apply to a real estate licensee acting within the course and scope of his or her license pursuant to the Real Estate Law (Part 1 (commencing with Section 10000) of Division 4). However, nothing in this section shall authorize a real estate licensee or a property manager to act in the capacity of a contractor unless licensed by the board.

Added Stats 1994 ch 361 § 1 (AB 2636).

§ 7044.2.   Inapplicability of chapter

This chapter does not apply to an admitted surety insurer whenever that surety insurer engages a contractor to undertake the completion of a contract on which a performance or completion bond was issued by the surety insurer, provided all actual construction work is performed by duly licensed contractors.

Added Stats 1996 ch 287 § 1 (SB 2002). Amended Stats 1997 ch 17 § 7 (SB 947).

§ 7045.   Sale or installation of products not part of structure

This chapter does not apply to the sale or installation of any finished products, materials, or articles of merchandise that do not become a fixed part of the structure, nor shall it apply to a material supplier or manufacturer furnishing finished products, materials, or articles of merchandise who does not install or contract for the installation of those items. The term "finished products" shall not include installed carpets or mobilehomes or mobilehome accessory structures, as defined in Section 7026.2.

This chapter shall apply to the installation of home improvement goods, as defined in Section 7151.

Added Stats 1939 ch 37 § 1. Amended Stats 1961 ch 1585 § 1; Stats 1967 ch 687 § 1; Stats 1969 ch 761 § 3; Stats 1970 ch 340 § 3; Stats 1973 ch 892 § 3; Stats 1979 ch 1012 § 1; Stats 1981 ch 916 § 1; Stats 1991 ch 1160 § 23 (AB 2190); Stats 1993 ch 589 § 11 (AB 2211).

§ 7046. Personal property work; Mobilehome accessory buildings or structures

This chapter does not apply to any construction, alteration, improvement, or repair of personal property. The term "personal property" shall not include mobilehomes or mobilehome accessory structures as defined in Section 7026.2.

Added Stats 1939 ch 37 § 1. Amended Stats 1969 ch 761 § 4; Stats 1970 ch 340 § 4; Stats 1973 ch 892 § 4; Stats 1991 ch 1160 § 24 (AB 2190).

§ 7048. Contracts aggregating less than specified amount; When exemption not applicable

This chapter does not apply to any work or operation on one undertaking or project by one or more contracts, the aggregate contract price which for labor, materials, and all other items, is less than five hundred dollars ($500), that work or operations being considered of casual, minor, or inconsequential nature.

This exemption does not apply in any case wherein the work of construction is only a part of a larger or major operation, whether undertaken by the same or a different contractor, or in which a division of the operation is made in contracts of amounts less than five hundred dollars ($500) for the purpose of evasion of this chapter or otherwise.

This exemption does not apply to a person who advertises or puts out any sign or card or other device which might indicate to the public that he or she is a contractor or that he or she is qualified to engage in the business of a contractor.

Added Stats 1939 ch 37 § 1. Amended Stats 1945 ch 1361 § 1; Stats 1977 ch 416 § 1; Stats 1986 ch 293 § 1; Stats 1998 ch 633 § 3 (SB 2217); Stats 2004 ch 865 § 8 (SB 1914).

§ 7049. Ditch work and agricultural or fire prevention work

This chapter does not apply to any construction or operation incidental to the construction and repair of irrigation and drainage ditches of regularly constituted irrigation districts, reclamation districts, or to farming, dairying, agriculture, viticulture, horticulture, or stock or poultry raising, or clearing or other work upon the land in rural districts for fire prevention purposes, except when performed by a licensee under this chapter.

The provisions of this chapter do apply to the business of drilling, digging, boring, or otherwise constructing, deepening, repairing, reperforating, or abandoning water wells.

Added Stats 1939 ch 37 § 1. Amended 1959 ch 1691 § 2.

§ 7051. Application of chapter to certain licensees or registrants

This chapter does not apply to a licensed architect or a registered civil or professional engineer acting solely in his or her professional capacity or to a licensed structural pest control operator acting within the scope of his or her license or a licensee operating within the scope of the Geologist and Geophysicist Act.

Added Stats 1949 ch 90 § 4. Amended Stats 1955 ch 1532 § 4; Stats 1994 ch 26 § 206 (AB 1807), effective March 30, 1994.

§ 7052. People furnishing material or supplies

This chapter does not apply to any person who only furnishes materials or supplies without fabricating them into, or consuming them in the performance of, the work of the contractor.

Added Stats 1949 ch 90 § 5.

§ 7053. Employees

Except as provided in Article 10 (commencing with Section 7150), this chapter does not apply to any person who engages in the activities herein regulated as an employee who receives wages as his or her sole compensation, does not customarily engage in an independently established business, and does not have the right to control or discretion as to the manner of performance so as to determine the final results of the work performed.

Added Stats 1949 ch 90 § 6. Amended Stats 1970 ch 227 § 1; Stats 1974 ch 434 § 1; Stats 1982 ch 1427 § 2.

§ 7054. Inapplicability of chapter to licensed alarm company operators

This chapter does not apply to any person who performs work in the installation, maintenance, monitoring, selling, alteration, or servicing of alarm systems, as defined in subdivision (n) of Section 7590.1, and who holds an alarm company operator's license issued pursuant to Chapter 11.6 (commencing with Section 7590).

Added Stats 1982 ch 1210 § 1. Amended Stats 1991 ch 1160 § 25 (AB 2190).

§ 7054.5. Application of licensing provisions to installation of satellite antenna systems on residential structures

The licensing provisions of this chapter do not apply to any person registered under Chapter 20 (commencing with Section 9800) if that person's activities consist only of installing satellite antenna systems on residential structures or property.

Added Stats 1987 ch 422 § 1.

—*See Business & Professions Code Sections 7590.1, Definitions; 5537 Licensed Contractor Exemptions from the Architect Act 5537.2 Exemptions and 6737.5, Exemptions for the Provisions of the Engineers Act, in Appendix.*

Article 4
Classifications

§ 7055. Branches of contracting business

For the purpose of classification, the contracting business includes any or all of the following branches:
(a) General engineering contracting.
(b) General building contracting.
(c) Specialty contracting.

Added Stats 1945 ch 1159 § 1.

§ 7056. General engineering contractor

A general engineering contractor is a contractor whose principal contracting business is in connection with fixed works requiring specialized engineering knowledge and skill, including the following divisions or subjects: irrigation, drainage, water power, water supply, flood control, inland waterways, harbors, docks and wharves, shipyards and ports, dams and hydroelectric projects, levees, river control and reclamation works, railroads, highways, streets and roads, tunnels, airports and airways, sewers and sewage disposal plants and systems, waste reduction plants, bridges, overpasses, underpasses and other similar works, pipelines and other systems for the transmission of petroleum and other liquid or gaseous substances, parks, playgrounds and other recreational works, refineries, chemical plants and similar industrial plants requiring specialized engineering knowledge and skill, powerhouses, powerplants and other utility plants and installations, mines and metallurgical plants, land leveling and earthmoving projects, excavating, grading, trenching, paving and surfacing work and cement and concrete works in connection with the above-mentioned fixed works.

Added Stats 1945 ch 1159 § 2. Amended Stats 1951 ch 1606 § 1; Stats 2011 ch 296 § 12 (AB 1023), effective January 1, 2012.

Section VI

§ 7057. General building contractor

(a) Except as provided in this section, a general building contractor is a contractor whose principal contracting business is in connection with any structure built, being built, or to be built, for the support, shelter, and enclosure of persons, animals, chattels, or movable property of any kind, requiring in its construction the use of at least two unrelated building trades or crafts, or to do or superintend the whole or any part thereof.

This does not include anyone who merely furnishes materials or supplies under Section 7045 without fabricating them into, or consuming them in the performance of the work of the general building contractor.

(b) A general building contractor may take a prime contract or a subcontract for a framing or carpentry project. However, a general building contractor shall not take a prime contract for any project involving trades other than framing or carpentry unless the prime contract requires at least two unrelated building trades or crafts other than framing or carpentry, or unless the general building contractor holds the appropriate license classification or subcontracts with an appropriately licensed contractor to perform the work. A general building contractor shall not take a subcontract involving trades other than framing or carpentry, unless the subcontract requires at least two unrelated trades or crafts other than framing or carpentry, or unless the general building contractor holds the appropriate license classification. The general building contractor may not count framing or carpentry in calculating the two unrelated trades necessary in order for the general building contractor to be able to take a prime contract or subcontract for a project involving other trades.

(c) No general building contractor shall contract for any project that includes the "C–16" Fire Protection classification as provided for in Section 7026.12 or the "C–57" Well Drilling classification as provided for in Section 13750.5 of the Water Code, unless the general building contractor holds the appropriate license classification, or subcontracts with the appropriately licensed contractor.

Added Stats 1945 ch 1159 § 3. Amended Stats 1997 ch 812 § 2 (SB 857); Stats 2002 ch 1013 § 60 (SB 2026).

§ 7058. "Specialty contractor"

(a) A specialty contractor is a contractor whose operations involve the performance of construction work requiring special skill and whose principal contracting business involves the use of specialized building trades or crafts.

(b) A specialty contractor includes a contractor whose operations include the business of servicing or testing fire extinguishing systems.

(c) A specialty contractor includes a contractor whose operations are concerned with the installation and laying of carpets, linoleum, and resilient floor covering.

(d) A specialty contractor includes a contractor whose operations are concerned with preparing or removing roadway construction zones, lane closures, flagging, or traffic diversions on roadways, including, but not limited to, public streets, highways, or any public conveyance.

Added Stats 1945 ch 1159 § 4. Amended Stats 1959 ch 2175 § 1; Stats 1963 ch 1320 § 1; Stats 1967 ch 687 § 2; Stats 1985 ch 253 § 1; Stats 1991 ch 1160 § 26 (AB 2190); Stats 1999 ch 708 § 2 (AB 1206); Stats 2007 ch 354 § 15 (SB 1047), effective January 1, 2008.

§ 7058.1. [Section repealed 2002.]

Added Stats 1999 ch 708 § 3 (AB 1206). Repealed Stats 2002 ch 1013 § 61 (SB 2026). The repealed section related to requirements for exemption from testing.

§ 7058.5. Certification of contractors performing asbestos-related work

(a) No contractor shall engage in asbestos-related work, as defined in Section 6501.8 of the Labor Code, that involves 100 square feet or more of surface area of asbestos containing materials, unless the qualifier for the license passes an asbestos certification examination. Additional updated asbestos certification examinations may be required based on new health and safety information. The decision on whether to require an updated certification examination shall be made by the Contractors State License Board, in consultation with the Division of Occupational Safety and Health in the Department of Industrial Relations and the Division of Environmental and Occupational Disease Control in the State Department of Public Health.

No asbestos certification examination shall be required for contractors involved with the installation, maintenance, and repair of asbestos cement pipe or sheets, vinyl asbestos floor materials, or asbestos bituminous or resinous materials.

"Asbestos," as used in this section, has the same meaning as defined in Section 6501.7 of the Labor Code.

(b) The Contractors State License Board shall make available to all applicants, either on the board's Internet Web site or, if requested, in hard copy, a booklet containing information relative to handling and disposal of asbestos, together with an open book examination concerning asbestos-related work. All applicants for an initial contractor license shall complete the open book examination and, prior to the issuance of a contractor's license, submit it to the board electronically or by mail if the applicant elects to use the hard-copy format.

Added Stats 1985 ch 1587 § 3, effective October 2, 1985. Amended Stats 1986 ch 1451 § 2, effective September 30, 1986; Stats 1987 ch 930 § 4, effective September 22, 1987; Stats 1991 ch 1160 § 27 (AB 2190); Stats 2010 ch 415 § 20 (SB 1491), effective January 1, 2011.

§ 7058.6.   Registration with Division of Occupational Safety and Health as condition of asbestos certification; Certification examination; Proof of current registration

(a) The board shall not issue an asbestos certification, as required by Section 7058.5, unless the contractor is registered with the Division of Occupational Safety and Health of the Department of Industrial Relations pursuant to Section 6501.5 of the Labor Code. The board may issue an asbestos certification to a contractor who is not registered, provided the contractor in a written statement acknowledges that he or she does not perform asbestos-related work. The board shall notify both the division and the contractor, in writing, of the contractor's passage of the certification examination, for the purpose of allowing the contractor to satisfy the requirement of paragraph (1) of subdivision (a) of Section 6501.5 of the Labor Code. The contractor shall register with the division within 90 days from the date the contractor is notified of the passage of the certification examination. The board may require a reexamination if the contractor fails to register within 90 days following issuance of the notification. Applicable test fees shall be paid for any reexamination required under this section.

(b) Any contractor who is certified to engage in asbestos-related work shall present proof of current registration with the division pursuant to Section 6501.5 of the Labor Code upon application for renewal of his or her license, if the contractor engages in asbestos-related work, as defined in Section 6501.8 of the Labor Code.

(c) A contractor who is not certified pursuant to this section may bid on and contract to perform a project involving asbestos-related work as long as the asbestos-related work is performed by a contractor who is certified and registered pursuant to this section and Section 6501.5 of the Labor Code.

(d) The board shall obtain and periodically update the list of contractors certified to engage in asbestos-related work who are registered pursuant to Section 6501.5 of the Labor Code.

Added Stats 1988 ch 1003 § 1.5, operative July 1, 1989. Amended Stats 1995 ch 467 § 3 (SB 1061); Stats 2011 ch 432 § 11 (SB 944), effective January 1, 2012.

§ 7058.7.   Hazardous substance certification examination

(a) No contractor may engage in a removal or remedial action, as defined in subdivision (d), unless the qualifier for the license has passed an approved hazardous substance certification examination.

(b)(1) The Contractors' State License Board, the Division of Occupational Safety and Health of the Department of Industrial Relations, and the Department of Toxic Substances Control shall jointly select an advisory committee, which shall be composed of two representatives of hazardous substance removal workers in California, two general engineering contractors in California, and two representatives of insurance companies in California who shall be selected by the Insurance Commissioner.

(2) The Contractors' State License Board shall develop a written test for the certification of contractors engaged in hazardous substance removal or remedial action, in consultation with the Division of Occupational Safety and Health, the State Water Resources Control Board, the Department of Toxic Substances Control, and the advisory committee.

(c) The Contractors' State License Board may require additional updated approved hazardous substance certification examinations of licensees currently certified based on new public or occupational health and safety information. The Contractors' State License Board, in consultation with the Department of Toxic Substances Control and the State Water Resources Control Board, shall approve other initial and updated hazardous substance certification examinations and determine whether to require an updated certification examination of all current certificate holders.

(d) For purposes of this section "removal or remedial action" has the same meaning as found in Chapter 6.8 (commencing with Section 25300) of Division 20 of the Health and Safety Code, if the action requires the contractor to dig into the surface of the earth and remove the dug material and the action is at a site listed pursuant to Section 25356 of the Health and Safety Code or any other site listed as a hazardous substance release site by the Department of Toxic Substances Control or a site listed on the National Priorities List compiled pursuant to the Comprehensive Environmental Response, Compensation, and Liability Act of 1980 (42 U.S.C. Sec. 9601 et seq.). "Removal or remedial action" does not include asbestos-related work, as defined in Section 6501.8 of the Labor Code, or work related to a hazardous substance spill on a highway.

(e)(1) A contractor may not install or remove an underground storage tank, unless the contractor has passed the hazardous substance certification examination developed pursuant to this section.

(2) A contractor who is not certified may bid on or contract for the installation or removal of an underground tank, if the work is performed by a contractor who is certified pursuant to this section.

(3) For purposes of this subdivision, "underground storage tank" has the same meaning as defined in subdivision (y) of Section 25281 of the Health and Safety Code.

Added Stats 1986 ch 1443 § 2, effective September 30, 1986. Amended Stats 1990 ch 1366 § 2 (SB 2004), effective September 26, 1990; Stats 1992 ch 1289 § 42.5 (AB 2743), ch 1290 § 1 (AB 3188), effective September 30, 1992; Stats 1993 ch 168 § 1 (AB 427); Stats 2002 ch 999 § 1 (AB 2481).

—See Health and Safety Code Section 25281 Definitions in Appendix.

—See Labor Code Sections 6501.5 Asbestos Certification, 6501.7 Asbestos: Definitions and 6501.8 Asbestos-Related Work Containing Construction Material, in Appendix.

—See also Health and Safety Code Sections 25914 Asbestos and Hazardous Removal Contracts Intent, 25914.1 Definitions, 25914.2 Need for Separate Contract; Emergency Conditions and 25914.3 Certification Requirements: Bids, in Appendix

§ 7058.8.   Information to public regarding removal or encapsulation of asbestos-containing materials

The board shall make available to the public upon request information about contracting for the removal or encapsulation of asbestos-containing materials in a building including all of the following:

(a) Steps to take when contracting with a company to remove asbestos.

(b) Existing laws and regulations pertaining to asbestos-related work in California.

(c) Basic health information as contained in the United States Environmental Protection Agency publication, "Guidance for Controlling Asbestos-Containing Materials in Buildings."

(d) A current list of contractors who are certified pursuant to Section 7058.5 to engage in asbestos-related work and who are registered pursuant to Section 6501.5 of the Labor Code.

Added Stats 1988 ch 1003 § 2, operative July 1, 1989. Amended Stats 2011 ch 432 § 12 (SB 944), effective January 1, 2012.

§ 7059.   Rules and regulations affecting classification of contractors; Contracts involving two or more crafts; Public works contracts

(a) The board may adopt reasonably necessary rules and regulations to effect the classification of contractors in a manner consistent with established usage and procedure as found in the construction business, and may limit the field and scope of the operations of a licensed contractor to those in which he or she is classified and qualified to engage, as defined by Sections 7055, 7056, 7057, and 7058. A licensee may make application for classification and be classified in more than one classification if the licensee meets the qualifications prescribed by the board for such additional classification or classifications. The application shall be in a form as prescribed by the registrar and shall be accompanied by the application fee fixed by this chapter.

No license fee shall be charged for an additional classification or classifications.

Nothing contained in this section shall prohibit a specialty contractor from taking and executing a contract involving the use of two or more crafts or trades, if the performance of the work in the crafts or trades, other than in which he or she is licensed, is incidental and supplemental to the performance of the work in the craft for which the specialty contractor is licensed.

(b) In public works contracts, as defined in Section 1101 of the Public Contract Code, the awarding authority shall determine the license classification necessary to bid and perform the project. In no case shall the awarding authority award a prime contract to a specialty contractor whose classification constitutes less than a majority of the project. When a specialty contractor is authorized to bid a project, all work to be performed outside of his or her license specialty, except work authorized by subdivision (a), shall be performed by a licensed subcontractor in compliance with the Subletting and Subcontracting Fair Practices Act (Chapter 4 (commencing with Section 4100) of Part 1 of Division 2 of the Public Contract Code).

Added Stats 1939 ch 37 § 1. Amended Stats 1941 ch 971 § 9; Stats 1945 ch 1159 § 5; Stats 1957 ch 2084 § 21; Stats 1966 ch 4 § 1; Stats 1983 ch 891 § 5; Stats 1987 ch 485 § 1.

§ 7059.1. Misleading or incompatible use of name styles

(a) A licensee shall not use any business name that indicates the licensee is qualified to perform work in classifications other than those issued for that license, or any business name that is incompatible with the type of business entity licensed.

(b) A licensee shall not conduct business under more than one name for each license. Nothing in this section shall prevent a licensee from obtaining a business name change as otherwise provided by this chapter.

Added Stats 1983 ch 891 § 6. Amended Stats 2001 ch 728 § 57 (SB 724).

Article 5
Licensing

§ 7065. Investigation, classification, and examinations

(a) Under rules and regulations adopted by the board and approved by the director, the registrar shall investigate, classify, and qualify applicants for contractors' licenses by written examination. This examination shall include questions designed to show that the applicant has the necessary degree of knowledge required by Section 7068 and shall include pertinent questions relating to the laws of this state and the contracting business and trade.

Section VI

(b) Contractors' licenses are to be issued to individual owners, partnerships, corporations, and limited liability companies in accordance with this chapter.

(1) Every person who is an officer, member, responsible manager, or director of a corporation or limited liability company seeking licensure under this chapter shall be listed on the application as a member of the personnel of record.

(2) Every person who is a member of a partnership seeking licensure under this chapter shall be listed on the application as a member of the personnel record.

(c) An applicant shall qualify for licensure in accordance with this subdivision as follows:

(1) An individual owner may qualify by examination for a contractor's license upon the appearance of the owner or a qualifying individual appearing as a responsible managing employee on behalf of the owner.

(2) A partnership may qualify by examination for a contractor's license upon the appearance of a partner or a qualifying individual appearing as a responsible managing employee on behalf of the partnership.

(3) A corporation may qualify by examination for a contractor's license upon the appearance of a qualifying individual appearing either as a responsible managing officer or a responsible managing employee on behalf of the corporation.

(4) A limited liability company may qualify by examination for a contractor's license upon the appearance of a qualifying individual appearing as a responsible managing officer, a responsible managing manager, a responsible managing member, or a responsible managing employee on behalf of the company.

(d) No examination shall be required of a qualifying individual if, within the five-year period immediately preceding the application for licensure, the qualifying individual has either personally passed the written examination for the same classification being applied for, or has served as the qualifying individual for a licensee whose license was in good standing at any time during the five-year period immediately preceding the application for licensure and in the same classification being applied for.

Added Stats 1939 ch 37 § 1. Amended Stats 1979 ch 1013 § 4; Stats 1980 ch 138 § 1, effective May 30, 1980; Stats 1981 ch 1122 § 1; Stats 1982 ch 378 § 1, ch 1347 § 2; Stats 1989 ch 350 § 1; Stats 2010 ch 698 § 5 (SB 392), effective January 1, 2011; Stats 2011 ch 296 § 13 (AB 1023), effective January 1, 2012.

—*See Government Code Section 12944, Discrimination by "Licensing Board," in Appendix.*

§ 7065.01. Examination not required for limited specialty license classification

Notwithstanding Section 7065, no trade examination shall be required of an applicant for the limited specialty license classification.

Added Stats 2002 ch 311 § 2 (AB 264).

§ 7065.05. Review and revision of examination contents

The board shall periodically review and, if needed, revise the contents of qualifying examinations to insure that the examination questions are timely and relevant to the business of contracting. The board shall, in addition, construct and conduct examinations in such a manner as to preclude the possibility of any applicant having prior knowledge of any specific examination question.

Added Stats 1979 ch 1013 § 5. Amended Stats 2000 ch 1005 § 8 (SB 2029); Stats 2005 ch 280 § 3 (SB 1112), effective January 1, 2006.

§ 7065.1. Waiver of examination

Notwithstanding Section 7065, the registrar may waive the examination for a contractor's license under any of the following circumstances:

(a) The qualifying individual has, for five of the seven years immediately preceding the application for licensure, been listed on the official records of the board as a member of the personnel of any licensee who held a license, which was active and in good standing, in the same classification being applied for, and who during the period listed on the license has been actively engaged in a licensee's construction activities in the same classification within which the applicant applies for a license.

(b) The qualifying individual is an immediate member of the family of a licensee whose individual license was active and in good standing for five of the seven years immediately preceding the application for licensure, and the qualifying individual is able to show all of the following:

(1) The qualifying individual has been actively engaged in the licensee's business for five of the seven years immediately preceding the application for licensure.

(2) The license is required to continue the existing family business in the event of the absence or death of the licensee.

(3) An application is made for a new license in the same classifications in which the licensee is or was licensed.

(c) The qualifying individual is an employee of a corporation or a limited liability company seeking to replace its former qualifying individual and has been employed by that corporation or limited liability company under the following conditions:

(1) For five of the seven years immediately preceding the application for licensure, the qualifying individual has been continually employed by the corporation or limited liability company in a supervisory capacity in the same classifications being applied for.

(2) For five of the seven years immediately preceding the application for licensure, the corporation or limited liability company has held an active license in good standing in the same classifications being applied for.

(3) The corporation or limited liability company has not requested a waiver under this subdivision within the past five years.

For purposes of this section, employees of a corporation or limited liability company shall include, but not be limited to, the officers of a corporation and the officers and managers of a limited liability company.

Added Stats 1981 ch 1122 § 3. Amended Stats 1982 ch 378 § 2; Stats 1986 ch 27 § 1; Stats 1990 ch 1456 § 1 (SB 2476); Stats 1992 ch 746 § 1 (AB 2424); Stats 2010 ch 698 § 6 (SB 392), effective January 1, 2011.

§ 7065.2. Waiver of examination

Notwithstanding Section 7065, the registrar may waive the examination for a contractor's license if the applicant has previously held a valid contractor's license in this state and has been acting in the capacity of a contractor for the United States government in a position exempt from licensure under this chapter.

Added Stats 1987 ch 630 § 1.

§ 7065.3. Additional classification without examination under specified conditions

Notwithstanding Section 7065, upon a conclusive showing by a licensee that he or she possesses experience satisfactory to the registrar in the classification applied for, an additional classification may be added, without further examination, under all of the following conditions:

(a) For five of the seven years immediately preceding the application, the qualifying individual of the licensee has been listed as a member of the personnel of any licensee whose license was active and in good standing, and who during the period listed on a license was actively engaged in the licensee's construction activities.

(b) The qualifying individual for the applicant has had within the last 10 years immediately preceding the filing of the application, not less than four years experience as a journeyman, foreman, supervising employee or contractor in the classification within which the licensee intends to engage in the additional classification as a contractor.

(c) The application is, as determined by the registrar, for a classification which is closely related to the classification or classifications in which the licensee is licensed, or the qualifying individual is associated with a licensed general engineering contractor or licensed general building contractor and is applying for a classification which is a significant component of the licensed contractor's construction business as determined by the registrar. This section shall not apply to an applicant who is licensed solely within the limited-specialty classifications.

Pursuant to Section 7065, the registrar shall conduct a comprehensive field investigation of no less than 3 percent of applications filed under this section to ensure that the applicants met the experience requirements of this section and shall make public, at quarterly meetings of the Contractors' State License Board, a listing of all applications approved under this section during the previous 12 months, including, but not limited to, the name of the applicant, license number, classification applied for, and existing classifications.

Added Stats 1990 ch 1456 § 3 (SB 2476).

§ 7065.4. Reciprocity

The registrar may accept the qualifications of an applicant who is licensed as a contractor in a similar classification in another state if that state accepts the qualifications of a contractor licensed in this state for purposes of licensure in that other state, and if the board ascertains, on a case-by-case basis, that the professional qualifications and conditions of good standing for licensure and continued licensure are at least the same or greater in that state as in California. The registrar may waive the trade examination for that applicant if the applicant provides written certification from that other state in which he or she is licensed, that the applicant's license has been in good standing for the previous five years.

Added Stats 1990 ch 1326 § 2 (AB 3480), effective September 25, 1990.

§ 7065.5. Minor not to be licensed unless guardian appointed

No license shall be issued to a minor, nor to any partnership a partner of which is a minor, nor to any corporation any officer, director or responsible managing employee of which is a minor, nor to any limited liability company any officer, manager, or responsible managing employee of which is a minor, nor to any other kind of business organization in which a minor holds a responsible official position, unless the minor shall first have had a guardian appointed by a court of competent jurisdiction.

Added Stats 1941 ch 971 § 10. Amended Stats 2010 ch 698 § 7 (SB 392), effective January 1, 2011.

§ 7066. Application; Form and contents; Fee

To obtain an original license, an applicant shall submit to the registrar an application in writing containing the statement that the applicant desires the issuance of a license under the terms of this chapter.

The application shall be made on a form prescribed by the registrar in accordance with the rules and regulations adopted by the board and shall be accompanied by the fee fixed by this chapter.

Added Stats 1939 ch 37 § 1.

§ 7066.5. Blank forms

Any person may obtain blank license application forms from the board or may cause to be printed forms used by or approved by the Registrar of Contractors.

Added Stats 1984 ch 1252 § 1. Amended Stats 2011 ch 432 § 13 (SB 944), effective January 1, 2012.

§ 7067.5. Financial solvency; Requirements as to license applicant; Financial statements of licensees

Every applicant for an original license, or for the reactivation of an inactive license, or for the reissuance or reinstatement of a revoked license shall possess and every such applicant, other than one applying under Section 7029 unless required by the registrar, shall evidence financial solvency. The registrar shall deny the application of any applicant who fails to comply with this section. For purposes of this section financial solvency shall mean that the applicant's operating capital shall exceed two thousand five hundred dollars ($2500).

The applicant shall provide answers to questions contained in a standard form of questionnaire as required by the registrar relative to his financial ability and condition and signed by the applicant under penalty of perjury.

In any case in which further financial information would assist the registrar in an investigation, the registrar may obtain such information or may require any licensee or applicant under investigation pursuant to this chapter to provide such additional financial information as the registrar may deem necessary.

The financial information required by the registrar shall be confidential and not a public record, but, where relevant, shall be admissible as evidence in any administrative hearing or judicial action or proceeding.

The registrar may destroy any financial information which has been on file for a period of at least three years.

Added Stats 1965 ch 636 § 1. Amended Stats 1969 ch 735 § 1; Stats 1974 ch 435 § 1; Stats 1979 ch 1013 § 6.

§ 7067.6. Application form; Signatures required

Every application form for an original license, for renewal thereof, for reinstatement or for reissuance, including both active and inactive licenses, shall be signed by both the applicant and by the person qualifying on behalf of an individual or firm as referred to in Section 7068.1.

Added Stats 1963 ch 1016 § 1.

§ 7068. Qualifications

(a) The board shall require an applicant to show the degree of knowledge and experience in the classification applied for, and the general knowledge of the building, safety, health, and lien laws of the state and of the administrative principles of the contracting business that the board deems necessary for the safety and protection of the public.

(b) An applicant shall qualify in regard to his or her experience and knowledge in one of the following ways:

(1) If an individual, he or she shall qualify by personal appearance or by the appearance of his or her responsible managing employee who is qualified for the same license classification as the classification being applied for.

(2) If a partnership or a limited partnership, it shall qualify by the appearance of a general partner or by the appearance of a responsible managing employee who is qualified for the same license classification as the classification being applied for.

(3) If a corporation, or any other combination or organization, it shall qualify by the appearance of a responsible managing officer or responsible managing employee who is qualified for the same license classification as the classification being applied for.

(4) If a limited liability company, it shall qualify by the appearance of a responsible managing officer, a responsible managing manager, responsible managing member, or a responsible managing employee who is qualified for the same license classification as the classification being applied for.

(c) A responsible managing employee for the purpose of this chapter shall mean an individual who is a bona fide employee of the applicant and is actively engaged in the classification of work for which that responsible managing employee is the qualifying person on behalf of the applicant.

(d) The board shall, in addition, require an applicant who qualifies by means of a responsible managing employee under either paragraph (1) or (2) of subdivision (b) to show his or her general know-

Section VI

ledge of the building, safety, health, and lien laws of the state and of the administrative principles of the contracting business as the board deems necessary for the safety and protection of the public.

(e) Except in accordance with Section 7068.1, no person qualifying on behalf of an individual or firm under paragraph (1), (2), (3), or (4) of subdivision (b) shall hold any other active contractor's license while acting in the capacity of a qualifying individual pursuant to this section.

(f) At the time of application for renewal of a license, the current qualifying individual shall file a statement with the registrar, on a form prescribed by the registrar, verifying his or her capacity as a qualifying individual to the licensee.

(g) Statements made by or on behalf of an applicant as to the applicant's experience in the classification applied for shall be verified by a qualified and responsible person. In addition, the registrar shall, as specified by board regulation, randomly review a percentage of such statements for their veracity.

(h) The registrar shall review experience gained by applicants from other states to determine whether all of that experience was gained in a lawful manner in that state.

Added Stats 1939 ch 37 § 1. Amended Stats 1941 ch 971 § 11; Stats 1957 ch 720 § 1; Stats 1959 ch 407 § 1; Stats 1963 ch 1017 § 1; Stats 1967 ch 1368 § 1; Stats 1979 ch 1013 § 7; Stats 1980 ch 138 § 2, effective May 30, 1980; Stats 1986 ch 995 § 4; Stats 1989 ch 1174 § 2; Stats 1991 ch 1160 § 28 (AB 2190); Stats 2004 ch 865 § 9 (SB 1914); Stats 2010 ch 698 § 8 (SB 392), effective January 1, 2011.

—See Unemployment Code Section 1095, Permissible Uses for EDD Data, in Appendix.

§ 7068.1. Duty of individual qualifying on behalf of another; Acting as qualifying individual for additional person or firm

The person qualifying on behalf of an individual or firm under paragraph (1), (2), (3), or (4) of subdivision (b) of Section 7068 shall be responsible for exercising that direct supervision and control of his or her employer's or principal's construction operations as is necessary to secure full compliance with this chapter and the rules and regulations of the board relating to the construction operations. This person shall not act in the capacity of the qualifying person for an additional individual or firm unless one of the following conditions exists:

(a) There is a common ownership of at least 20 percent of the equity of each individual or firm for which the person acts in a qualifying capacity.

(b) The additional firm is a subsidiary of or a joint venture with the first. "Subsidiary," as used in this subdivision, means any firm at least 20 percent of the equity of which is owned by the other firm.

(c) With respect to a firm under paragraph (2), (3), or (4) of subdivision (b) of Section 7068, the majority of the partners, officers, or managers are the same.

(d) Notwithstanding subdivisions (a), (b), and (c), a qualifying individual may act as the qualifier for no more than three firms in any one-year period.

"Firm," as used in this section, means a partnership, a limited partnership, a corporation, a limited liability company, or any other combination or organization described in Section 7068.

"Person," as used in this section, is limited to natural persons, notwithstanding the definition of "person" in Section 7025.

The board shall require every applicant or licensee qualifying by the appearance of a qualifying individual to submit detailed information on the qualifying individual's duties and responsibilities for supervision and control of the applicant's construction operations.

Added Stats 1959 ch 407 § 2. Amended Stats 1961 ch 1777 § 1; Stats 1963 ch 1016 § 2; Stats 1967 ch 1368 § 2; Stats 1979 ch 1013 § 8; Stats 1991 ch 145 § 1 (AB 425); Stats 2006 ch 106 § 2 (AB 2457), effective January 1, 2007; Stats 2010 ch 698 § 9 (SB 392), effective January 1, 2011; Stats 2011 ch 296 § 14 (AB 1023), effective January 1, 2012.

§ 7068.2. Disassociation of responsible managing officer; Notice; Replacement; Petition of licensee; Failure to notify registrar

(a) If the responsible managing officer, responsible managing employee, responsible managing member, or responsible managing manager, disassociates from the licensed entity, the licensee, or the qualifier shall notify the registrar in writing within 90 days after the date of disassociation. The licensee shall have 90 days after the date of disassociation in which to replace the qualifier. Upon failure to replace the qualifier within 90 days after the date of disassociation, the license shall be automatically suspended or the classification removed at the end of the 90 days.

(b) To replace a responsible managing officer, responsible managing employee, responsible managing member, or responsible managing manager, the licensee shall file an application as prescribed by the registrar, accompanied by the fee fixed by this chapter, designating an individual to qualify as required by this chapter.

(c) Upon failure of the licensee or the qualifier to notify the registrar of the disassociation of the qualifier within 90 days after the date of disassociation, the license shall be automatically suspended or the classification removed and the qualifier removed from the license effective the date the written notification is received at the board's headquarters office.

(d) The person qualifying on behalf of a licensee under Section 7068 shall be responsible for the licensee's construction operations until

Section VI

the date of disassociation or the date the board receives the written notification of disassociation, whichever is later.

(e) (1) Upon a showing of good cause by the licensee, the registrar may review and accept a petition for one 90-day extension to replace the qualifier immediately following the initial 90-day period described in subdivision (a) only under one or more of the following circumstances:

(A) If the licensee is disputing the date of disassociation.

(B) If the responsible managing officer, employee, member, or manager has died.

(C) If there has been delay in processing the application to replace the qualifier that is out of the applicant's control and it is the responsibility of the board or another state or federal agency that is relied upon in the application process.

(2) This petition shall be received within 90 days after the date of disassociation or death or delay. The petition shall only be considered if an application to replace the qualifier as prescribed by the registrar is on file with the board. Under the circumstances described in subparagraphs (A) and (B) of paragraph (1), the licensee shall have no more than a total of 180 days after the date of disassociation or death in which to replace the qualifier.

(f) Failure of the licensee or the qualifier to notify the registrar of the qualifier's disassociation within 90 days after the date of disassociation shall constitute grounds for disciplinary action.

Added Stats 1983 ch 891 § 9. Amended Stats 1984 ch 1174 § 3; Stats 1987 ch 930 § 5, effective September 22, 1987; Stats 2010 ch 698 § 10 (SB 392), effective January 1, 2011; Stats 2011 ch 168 § 1 (AB 1091), effective January 1, 2012.

§ 7068.5.   Taking qualifying examination on behalf of applicant for contractor's license; Misdemeanor

It is a misdemeanor for any person other than the examinee named in the application to take the qualifying examination on behalf of an applicant for a contractor's license.

Added Stats 1961 ch 491 § 1.

§ 7068.7.   Obtaining examination for another; Misdemeanor

Any person who obtains and provides for another the qualifying examination, or any part thereof, when not authorized to do so, is guilty of a misdemeanor.

Added Stats 1979 ch 1013 § 9.

§ 7069. Grounds for denial of license; Fingerprints of applicants; Criminal history and subsequent arrest information

(a) An applicant, and each officer, director, partner, manager, associate, and responsible managing employee thereof, shall not have committed acts or crimes that are grounds for denial of licensure under Section 480.

(b) As part of an application for a contractor's license, the board shall require an applicant to furnish a full set of fingerprints for purposes of conducting a criminal history record check. Fingerprints furnished pursuant to this subdivision shall be submitted in an electronic format if readily available. Requests for alternative methods of furnishing fingerprints are subject to the approval of the registrar. The board shall use the fingerprints furnished by an applicant to obtain criminal history information on the applicant from the Department of Justice and the United States Federal Bureau of Investigation, and the board may obtain any subsequent arrest information that is available.

Added Stats 1939 ch 37 § 1. Amended Stats 1941 ch 971 § 12; Stats 1955 ch 1547 § 1; Stats 1978 ch 1161 § 362; Stats 2002 ch 744 § 6 (SB 1953); Stats 2003 ch 874 § 20 (SB 363); Stats 2004 ch 909 § 27.3 (SB 136), effective September 30, 2004; Stats 2007 ch 240 § 1 (AB 936), effective January 1, 2008; Stats 2010 ch 698 § 11 (SB 392), effective January 1, 2011.

§ 7069.1. Arrest of licensee or home improvement salesperson

(a) Upon notification of an arrest of a member of the personnel of a licensee or a home improvement salesperson, the registrar, by first-class mail to the last official address of record, may require the arrestee to provide proof of the disposition of the matter.

(b) The proof required by this section shall be satisfactory for carrying out the purposes of this chapter, and at the registrar's discretion may include, but is not limited to, certified court documents, certified court orders, or sentencing documents. Any proof required by this section shall be received by the registrar within 90 days of the date of the disposition, or within 90 days of the registrar's demand for information if that date is later.

(c) Failure to comply with the provisions of this section constitutes cause for disciplinary action.

Added Stats 2004 ch 586 § 1 (AB 2216).

§ 7070. Showing that no license was refused or revoked

An applicant shall show that he or she has never been denied a license or had a license revoked for reasons that would preclude the granting of the license applied for. Where the board has denied an application for license under this chapter or Chapter 2 (commencing

Section VI

with Section 480) of Division 1.5, it shall, in its decision, or in its notice under subdivision (b) of Section 485, inform the applicant of the earliest date that the applicant may reapply for a license, which shall be one year from the effective date of the decision or service of notice under subdivision (b) of Section 485, unless the board prescribes an earlier date.

Added Stats 1939 ch 37 § 1. Amended Stats 1997 ch 334 § 1 (SB 299).

§ 7071. Refusal to corporation, partnership, or limited liability company for member's lack of qualifications

No license shall be issued to a corporation, partnership, limited liability company, or other combination or organization if a responsible officer or director of the corporation, or other combination or organization, or a partner of the partnership, or a manager or officer of the limited liability company, or any member of an organization seeking licensure under this chapter does not meet the qualifications required of an applicant other than those qualifications relating to knowledge and experience.

Added Stats 1939 ch 37 § 1. Amended Stats 1955 ch 1267 § 1; Stats 2010 ch 698 § 12 (SB 392), effective January 1, 2011; Stats 2011 ch 296 § 15 (AB 1023), effective January 1, 2012.

§ 7071.3. Entry into armed forces by licensee; Designation of manager to act for such entrant; Renewal fee and duration of license

Notwithstanding any other provision of this code, the holder of a current valid license under this chapter who has entered or enters the armed forces of the United States may designate a responsible managing person or persons to act for him while in the armed forces and until one year after his discharge therefrom, after which time the authority to so act for the licensee shall terminate. The renewal fee shall be paid for any such licensee so designating others to act for him.

Any license shall remain in full force and effect for 30 days after the entrance of the licensee into the armed forces, but he shall prior to the expiration of such 30-day period provide the registrar with the name or names of the persons so designated to conduct his business. The registrar may qualify such persons in any manner he may adopt. Persons so designated shall not have committed acts or crimes constituting grounds for denial of licensure under Section 480.

Persons so designated committing any of the acts or crimes constituting grounds for denial of licensure under Section 480 shall be removed from the business of such licensee after a hearing as provided in this chapter.

Added Stats 1945 ch 452 § 1, effective May 24, 1945. Amended Stats 1961 ch 1636 § 1, operative October 1, 1962; Stats 1978 ch 1161 § 363.

§ 7071.5. Contractor's bond (First of two; Operative until July 1, 2012)

The contractor's bond required by this article shall be executed by an admitted surety in favor of the State of California, in a form acceptable to the registrar and filed with the registrar by the licensee or applicant. The contractor's bond shall be for the benefit of the following:

(a) A homeowner contracting for home improvement upon the homeowner's personal family residence damaged as a result of a violation of this chapter by the licensee.

(b) A property owner contracting for the construction of a single-family dwelling who is damaged as a result of a violation of this chapter by the licensee. That property owner shall only recover under this subdivision if the single-family dwelling is not intended for sale or offered for sale at the time the damages were incurred.

(c) A person damaged as a result of a willful and deliberate violation of this chapter by the licensee, or by the fraud of the licensee in the execution or performance of a construction contract.

(d) An employee of the licensee damaged by the licensee's failure to pay wages.

(e) A person or entity, including an express trust fund described in Section 3111 of the Civil Code, to whom a portion of the compensation of an employee of a licensee is paid by agreement with that employee or the collective bargaining agent of that employee, damaged as the result of the licensee's failure to pay fringe benefits for its employees, including, but not limited to, employer payments described in Section 1773.1 of the Labor Code and regulations thereunder (without regard to whether the work was performed on a private or public work). Damage to an express trust fund is limited to actual employer payments required to be made on behalf of employees of the licensee, as part of the overall compensation of those employees, which the licensee fails to pay.

Added Stats 1967 ch 1604 § 6, operative July 1, 1969. Amended Stats 1979 ch 1013 § 10, ch 1138 § 1.5; Stats 1980 ch 27 § 1.5, effective March 5, 1980; Stats 1982 ch 517 § 18; Stats 1999 ch 795 § 1 (SB 914); Stats 2008 ch 157 § 1 (SB 1432), effective January 1, 2009.

—*See Code of Civil Procedure, Bond and Undertaking Law Sections 995.010 to 996.560 in Appendix.*

Section VI

§ 7071.5.   Contractor's bond (Second of two; Operative July 1, 2012)

The contractor's bond required by this article shall be executed by an admitted surety in favor of the State of California, in a form acceptable to the registrar and filed with the registrar by the licensee or applicant. The contractor's bond shall be for the benefit of the following:

(a) A homeowner contracting for home improvement upon the homeowner's personal family residence damaged as a result of a violation of this chapter by the licensee.

(b) A property owner contracting for the construction of a single-family dwelling who is damaged as a result of a violation of this chapter by the licensee. That property owner shall only recover under this subdivision if the single-family dwelling is not intended for sale or offered for sale at the time the damages were incurred.

(c) A person damaged as a result of a willful and deliberate violation of this chapter by the licensee, or by the fraud of the licensee in the execution or performance of a construction contract.

(d) An employee of the licensee damaged by the licensee's failure to pay wages.

(e) A person or entity, including a laborer described in subdivision (b) of Section 8024 of the Civil Code, to which a portion of the compensation of an employee of a licensee is paid by agreement with that employee or the collective bargaining agent of that employee, damaged as the result of the licensee's failure to pay fringe benefits for its employees, including, but not limited to, employer payments described in Section 1773.1 of the Labor Code and regulations thereunder (without regard to whether the work was performed on a private or public work). Damage to a person or entity under this subdivision is limited to actual employer payments required to be made on behalf of employees of the licensee, as part of the overall compensation of those employees, which the licensee fails to pay.

Added Stats 1967 ch 1604 § 6, operative July 1, 1969. Amended Stats 1979 ch 1013 § 10, ch 1138 § 1.5; Stats 1980 ch 27 § 1.5, effective March 5, 1980; Stats 1982 ch 517 § 18; Stats 1999 ch 795 § 1 (SB 914); Stats 2008 ch 157 § 1 (SB 1432), effective January 1, 2009; Stats 2010 ch 697 § 2 (SB 189), effective January 1, 2011, operative July 1, 2012.

—See Code of Civil Procedure, Bond and Undertaking Law Sections 995.010 to 996.560 in Appendix.

§ 7071.6.   Bond as condition precedent to license

(a) The board shall require as a condition precedent to the issuance, reinstatement, reactivation, renewal, or continued maintenance of a license, that the applicant or licensee file or have on file a contractor's bond in the sum of twelve thousand five hundred dollars ($12,500).

(b) Excluding the claims brought by the beneficiaries specified in subdivision (a) of Section 7071.5, the aggregate liability of a surety on claims brought against a bond required by this section shall not exceed the sum of seven thousand five hundred dollars ($7,500). The bond proceeds in excess of seven thousand five hundred dollars ($7,500) shall be reserved exclusively for the claims of the beneficiaries specified in subdivision (a) of Section 7071.5. However, nothing in this section shall be construed so as to prevent any beneficiary specified in subdivision (a) of Section 7071.5 from claiming or recovering the full measure of the bond required by this section.

(c) No bond shall be required of a holder of a license that has been inactivated on the official records of the board during the period the license is inactive.

(d) Notwithstanding any other provision of law, as a condition precedent to licensure, the board may require an applicant to post a contractor's bond in twice the amount required pursuant to subdivision (a) until the time that the license is renewed, under the following conditions:

(1) The applicant has either been convicted of a violation of Section 7028 or has been cited pursuant to Section 7028.7.

(2) If the applicant has been cited pursuant to Section 7028.7, the citation has been reduced to a final order of the registrar.

(3) The violation of Section 7028, or the basis for the citation issued pursuant to Section 7028.7, constituted a substantial injury to the public.

Added Stats 2002 ch 1123 § 2 (SB 1919), operative January 1, 2004. Amended Stats 2005 ch 280 § 4 (SB 1112), effective January 1, 2006; Stats 2007 ch 354 § 16 (SB 1047), effective January 1, 2008.

§ 7071.6.5.   Surety bond as condition precedent to license

(a) The board shall require, as a condition precedent to the issuance, reissuance, reinstatement, reactivation, renewal, or continued valid use of a limited liability company license, that the applicant or licensee file or have on file a surety bond in the sum of one hundred thousand dollars ($100,000).

(b) The bond required by this section shall be executed by an admitted surety in favor of the State of California, in a form acceptable to the registrar and filed with the registrar, electronically or otherwise, by the applicant or licensee.

(c) The bond required by this section shall be for the benefit of any employee damaged by his or her employer's failure to pay wages, interest on wages, or fringe benefits and is intended to serve as an additional safeguard for workers employed by or contracted to work for a limited liability company.

Section VI

(d) If an applicant or licensee subject to subdivision (a) is also a party to a collective bargaining agreement, the bond required by this section shall also cover, in addition to the coverage described in subdivision (c), welfare fund contributions, pension fund contributions, and apprentice program contributions.

(e) The bond required by this section shall not be applicable to a licensee whose license has been inactivated on the official records of the board during the period the license is inactive.

Added Stats 2010 ch 698 § 13 (SB 392), effective January 1, 2011.

§ 7071.7.   Acceptance of bond as of effective date; Retroactive reinstatement of license

(a) Except as provided in subdivision (b), the registrar shall accept a bond required by Section 7071.6, 7071.6.5, 7071.8, or 7071.9 as of the effective date shown on the bond, if the bond is received by the registrar within 90 days after that date, and shall reinstate the license to which the bond pertains, if otherwise eligible, retroactive to the effective date of the bond.

(b) Notwithstanding subdivision (a), the registrar shall accept a bond as of the effective date shown on the bond, even if the bond is not received by the registrar within 90 days after that date, upon a showing by the licensee, on a form acceptable to the registrar, that the failure to have a bond on file was due to circumstances beyond the control of the licensee. The registrar shall reinstate the license to which the bond pertains, if otherwise eligible, retroactive to the effective date of the bond.

Added Stats 1986 ch 27 § 2. Amended Stats 2010 ch 698 § 14 (SB 392), effective January 1, 2011.

§ 7071.8.   Bond required for restoration of suspended or revoked license

(a) This section applies to an application for a license, for renewal or restoration of a license, an application to change officers or members of a corporation or a limited liability company, or for continued valid use of a license which has been disciplined, whether or not the disciplinary action has been stayed, made by any of the following persons or firms:

(1) A person whose license has been suspended or revoked as a result of disciplinary action, or a person who was a qualifying individual for a licensee at any time during which cause for disciplinary action occurred resulting in suspension or revocation of the licensee's license, whether or not the qualifying individual had knowledge or participated in the prohibited act or omission.

(2) A person who was an officer, director, manager, partner, or member of the personnel of record of a licensee at any time during which cause for disciplinary action occurred resulting in suspension or revocation of the licensee's license and who had knowledge of or participated in the act or omission which was the cause for the disciplinary action.

(3) A partnership, corporation, limited liability company, firm, or association of which an existing or new officer, director, manager, partner, qualifying person, or member of the personnel of record has had a license suspended or revoked as a result of disciplinary action.

(4) A partnership, corporation, limited liability company, firm, or association of which a member of the personnel of record, including, but not limited to, an officer, director, manager, partner, or qualifying person was, likewise, a manager, officer, director, or partner of a licensee at any time during which cause for disciplinary action occurred resulting in suspension or revocation of the license, and who had knowledge of or participated in the act or omission which was the cause for the disciplinary action.

(b) The board shall require as a condition precedent to the issuance, reissuance, renewal, or restoration of a license to the applicant, or to the approval of an application to change officers of a corporationor a limited liability company, or removal of suspension, or to the continued valid use of a license which has been suspended or revoked, but which suspension or revocation has been stayed, that the applicant or licensee file or have on file a contractor's bond in a sum to be fixed by the registrar based upon the seriousness of the violation, but which sum shall not be less than fifteen thousand dollars ($15,000) nor more than 10 times that amount required by Section 7071.6.

(c) The bond is in addition to, may not be combined with, and does not replace any other type of bond required by this chapter. The bond shall remain on file with the registrar for a period of at least two years and for any additional time that the registrar determines. The bond period shall run only while the license is current, active, and in good standing, and shall be extended until the license has been current, active, and in good standing for the required period. Each applicant or licensee shall be required to file only one disciplinary contractor's bond of the type described in this section for each application or license subject to this bond requirement.

Added 1941 ch 882 § 1, as B & P C § 7071.5. Amended Stats 1961 ch 1125 § 1; Stats 1963 ch 1972 § 1; Stats 1965 ch 1022 § 1, ch 1025 § 1. Amended and renumbered Stats 1967 ch 1604 § 1, operative July 1, 1969. Amended Stats 1968 ch 482 § 2, operative July 1, 1969; Stats 1974 ch 434 § 2; Stats 1982 ch 517 § 20; Stats 1986 ch 79 § 1; Stats 1992 ch 294 § 2 (AB 2347); Stats 1994 ch 192 § 1 (AB 3475); Stats 2010 ch 698 § 15 (SB 392), effective January 1, 2011.

Section VI

§ 7071.9. Requirement of qualifying individual's bond as condition precedent to license

(a) If the qualifying individual, as referred to in Sections 7068 and 7068.1, is neither the proprietor, a general partner, nor a joint licensee, he or she shall file or have on file a qualifying individual's bond as provided in Section 7071.10 in the sum of twelve thousand five hundred dollars ($12,500). This bond is in addition to, and may not be combined with, any contractor's bond required by Sections 7071.5 to 7071.8, inclusive, and is required for the issuance, reinstatement, reactivation, or continued valid use of a license.

(b) Excluding the claims brought by the beneficiaries specified in paragraph (1) of subdivision (a) of Section 7071.10, the aggregate liability of a surety on claims brought against the bond required by this section shall not exceed the sum of seven thousand five hundred dollars ($7,500). The bond proceeds in excess of seven thousand five hundred dollars ($7,500) shall be reserved exclusively for the claims of the beneficiaries specified in paragraph (1) of subdivision (a) of Section 7071.10. However, nothing in this section shall be construed to prevent any beneficiary specified in paragraph (1) of subdivision (a) of Section 7071.10 from claiming or recovering the full measure of the bond required by this section. This bond is in addition to, and may not be combined with, any contractor's bond required by Sections 7071.5 to 7071.8, inclusive, and is required for the issuance, reinstatement, reactivation, or continued valid use of a license.

(c) The responsible managing officer of a corporation shall not be required to file or have on file a qualifying individual's bond, if he or she owns 10 percent or more of the voting stock of the corporation and certifies to that fact on a form prescribed by the registrar.

(d) The qualifying individual for a limited liability company shall not be required to file or have on file a qualifying individual' s bond if he or she owns at least a 10-percent membership interest in the limited liability company and certifies to that fact on a form prescribed by the registrar.

Added Stats 1967 ch 1604 § 7, operative July 1, 1970. Amended Stats 1968 ch 482 § 3, operative July 1, 1970; Stats 1971 ch 669 § 2; Stats 1972 ch 7 § 2, effective February 29, 1972, operative March 4, 1972; Stats 1973 ch 319 § 36, Stats 1979 ch 1013 § 12; Stats 1980 ch 27 § 3, effective March 5, 1980; Stats 1982 ch 517 § 21; Stats 1986 ch 27 § 3; Stats 1993 ch 1264 § 6.4 (SB 574); Stats 2004 ch 865 § 10 (SB 1914); Stats 2007 ch 354 § 17 (SB 1047), effective January 1, 2008; Stats 2010 ch 698 § 16 (SB 392), effective January 1, 2011.

§ 7071.10. Qualifying individual's bond (First of two; Operative until July 1, 2012)

The qualifying individual's bond required by this article shall be executed by an admitted surety insurer in favor of the State of California, in a form acceptable to the registrar and filed with the registrar by the qualifying individual. The qualifying individual's bond shall not be required in addition to the contractor's bond when, as set forth under paragraph (1) of subdivision (b) of Section 7068, the individual proprietor has qualified for the license by his or her personal appearance, or the qualifier is a general partner as set forth under paragraph (2) of subdivision (b) of Section 7068. The qualifying individual's bond shall be for the benefit of the following persons:

(a) A homeowner contracting for home improvement upon the homeowner's personal family residence damaged as a result of a violation of this chapter by the licensee.

(b) A property owner contracting for the construction of a single-family dwelling who is damaged as a result of a violation of this chapter by the licensee. That property owner shall only recover under this subdivision if the single-family dwelling is not intended for sale or offered for sale at the time the damages were incurred.

(c) A person damaged as a result of a willful and deliberate violation of this chapter by the licensee, or by the fraud of the licensee in the execution or performance of a construction contract.

(d) An employee of the licensee damaged by the licensee's failure to pay wages.

(e) A person or entity, including an express trust fund described in Section 3111 of the Civil Code, to whom a portion of the compensation of an employee of a licensee is paid by agreement with that employee or the collective bargaining agent of that employee, that is damaged as the result of the licensee's failure to pay fringe benefits for its employees including, but not limited to, employer payments described in Section 1773.1 of the Labor Code and regulations adopted thereunder (without regard to whether the work was performed on a public or private work). Damage to an express trust fund is limited to employer payments required to be made on behalf of employees of the licensee, as part of the overall compensation of those employees, which the licensee fails to pay.

Added Stats 1967 ch 1604 § 8, operative July 1, 1969. Amended Stats 1968 ch 482 § 4, operative July 1, 1969; Stats 1979 ch 1013 § 13, ch 1138 § 2.5; Stats 1982 ch 517 § 22; Stats 1999 ch 795 § 2 (SB 914); Stats 2008 ch 157 § 2 (SB 1432), effective January 1, 2009.

§ 7071.10. Qualifying individual's bond (Second of two; Operative July 1, 2012)

The qualifying individual's bond required by this article shall be executed by an admitted surety insurer in favor of the State of California, in a form acceptable to the registrar and filed with the registrar by the qualifying individual. The qualifying individual's bond shall not be required in addition to the contractor's bond when, as set forth under paragraph (1) of subdivision (b) of Section 7068, the individual proprietor has qualified for the license by his or her personal appearance, or the qualifier is a general partner as set forth under paragraph (2) of subdivision (b) of Section 7068. The qualifying individual's bond shall be for the benefit of the following persons:

(a) A homeowner contracting for home improvement upon the homeowner's personal family residence damaged as a result of a violation of this chapter by the licensee.

(b) A property owner contracting for the construction of a single-family dwelling who is damaged as a result of a violation of this chapter by the licensee. That property owner shall only recover under this subdivision if the single-family dwelling is not intended for sale or offered for sale at the time the damages were incurred.

(c) A person damaged as a result of a willful and deliberate violation of this chapter by the licensee, or by the fraud of the licensee in the execution or performance of a construction contract.

(d) An employee of the licensee damaged by the licensee's failure to pay wages.

(e) A person or entity, including a laborer described in subdivision (b) of Section 8024 of the Civil Code, to which a portion of the compensation of an employee of a licensee is paid by agreement with that employee or the collective bargaining agent of that employee, that is damaged as the result of the licensee's failure to pay fringe benefits for its employees including, but not limited to, employer payments described in Section 1773.1 of the Labor Code and regulations adopted thereunder (without regard to whether the work was performed on a public or private work). Damage to a person or entity under this subdivision is limited to employer payments required to be made on behalf of employees of the licensee, as part of the overall compensation of those employees, which the licensee fails to pay.

Added Stats 1967 ch 1604 § 8, operative July 1, 1969. Amended Stats 1968 ch 482 § 4, operative July 1, 1969; Stats 1979 ch 1013 § 13, ch 1138 § 2.5; Stats 1982 ch 517 § 22; Stats 1999 ch 795 § 2 (SB 914); Stats 2008 ch 157 § 2 (SB 1432), effective January 1, 2009; Stats 2010 ch 697 § 3 (SB 189), effective January 1, 2011, operative July 1, 2012.

§ 7071.11. Aggregate liability of surety on claim for wages and benefits; Renewal of license contingent on satisfaction of claims and debts; Limitations periods; Notice of payment; Protest of settlement; Accord; Legal fees not to be charged

(a) The aggregate liability of a surety on a claim for wages and fringe benefits brought against a bond required by this article, other than a bond required by Section 7071.8, shall not exceed the sum of four thousand dollars ($4,000). If a bond required by this article is insufficient to pay all claims in full, the sum of the bond shall be distributed to all claimants in proportion to the amount of their respective claims.

(b) No license may be renewed, reissued, or reinstated while a judgment or admitted claim in excess of the amount of the bond remains unsatisfied.

(c) Except for claims covered by subdivision (d), any action against a bond required under this article, excluding the judgment bond specified under Section 7071.17, shall be brought in accordance with the following:

(1) Within two years after the expiration of the license period during which the act or omission occurred. The provisions of this paragraph shall be applicable only if the license has not been inactivated, canceled, or revoked during the license period for which the bond was posted and accepted by the registrar as specified under Section 7071.7.

(2) If the license has been inactivated, canceled, or revoked, an action shall be brought within two years of the date the license of the active licensee would have expired had the license not been inactivated, canceled, or revoked. For the provisions of this paragraph to be applicable, the act or omission for which the action is filed must have occurred prior to the date the license was inactivated, canceled, or revoked.

(3) An action against a disciplinary bond filed by an active licensee pursuant to Section 7071.8 shall be brought in accordance with the provisions of paragraph (1) or (2), as applicable, or within two years after the last date for which a disciplinary bond filed pursuant to Section 7071.8 was required, whichever date is first.

(d) A claim to recover wages or fringe benefits shall be brought within six months from the date that the wage or fringe benefit delinquencies were discovered, but in no event shall a civil action thereon be brought later than two years from the date the wage or fringe benefit contributions were due.

(e) Whenever the surety makes payment on a claim against a bond required by this article, whether or not payment is made through a court action or otherwise, the surety shall, within 30 days of the payment, provide notice to the registrar. The notice required by this subdivision shall provide the following information by declaration on a form prescribed by the registrar:

(1) The name and license number of the contractor.

(2) The surety bond number.

(3) The amount of payment.

(4) The statutory basis upon which the claim is made.

(5) The names of the person or persons to whom payments have been made.

(6) Whether or not the payments were the result of a good faith action by the surety.

The notice shall also clearly indicate whether or not the licensee filed a protest in accordance with this section.

(f) Prior to the settlement of a claim through a good faith payment by the surety, a licensee shall have not less than 15 days in which to provide a written protest. This protest shall instruct the surety not to make payment from the bond on the licensee's account upon the specific grounds that the claim is opposed by the licensee, and provide the surety a specific and reasonable basis for the licensee's opposition to payment.

(1) Whenever a licensee files a protest in accordance with this subdivision, the board shall investigate the matter and file disciplinary action as set forth under this chapter if there is evidence that the surety has sustained a loss as the result of a good faith payment made for the purpose of mitigating any damages incurred by any person or entity covered under Section 7071.5.

(2) A licensee that fails to file a protest as specified in this subdivision shall have 90 days from the date of notification by the board to submit proof of payment of the actual amount owed to the surety and, if applicable, proof of payment of any judgment or admitted claim in excess of the amount of the bond or, by operation of law, the license shall be suspended at the end of the 90 days. A license suspension pursuant to this subdivision shall be disclosed indefinitely as a failure to settle outstanding final liabilities in violation of this chapter. The disclosure specified by this subdivision shall also be applicable to all licenses covered by the provisions of subdivision (g).

(g) During any period in which a surety remains unreimbursed for a loss or expense sustained on a bond issued pursuant to this article, the license for which the bond was issued, and any other license on which any member of the licensee's personnel of record has also been listed, may not be renewed, reissued, or reinstated while the licensee was subject to suspension or disciplinary action under this section.

(h) The licensee may provide the board with a notarized copy of an accord, reached with the surety to satisfy the debt in lieu of full payment. By operation of law, failure to abide by the accord shall result in the automatic suspension of a license to which this section applies. A license that is suspended for failure to abide by the accord may only be renewed or reinstated when proof of satisfaction of all debts is made.

(i) Legal fees may not be charged against the bond by the board.

Added Stats 1963 ch 1972 § 2, as B & P C § 7071.6. Amended Stats 1965 ch 1022 § 2. Amended and renumbered by Stats 1967 ch 1604 § 2, operative July 1, 1969. Amended Stats 1968 ch 482 § 5, operative July 1, 1969; Stats 1972 ch 7 § 3, effective February 29, 1972, operative March 4, 1972; Stats 1974 ch 201 § 1; Stats 1977 ch 280 § 1, effective July 7, 1977; Stats 1979 ch 1013 § 14, ch 1138 § 3.5; Stats 1980 ch 27 § 3.5, effective March 5, 1980; Stats 1982 ch 517 § 23; Stats 1986 ch 1353 § 1, operative July 1, 1987; Stats 1990 ch 1326 § 3 (AB 3480), effective September 25, 1990; Stats 1993 ch

1264 § 7 (SB 574); Stats 1999 ch 795 § 3 (SB 914); Stats 2001 ch 728 § 58 (SB 724); Stats 2002 ch 311 § 3 (AB 264); Stats 2004 ch 865 § 11 (SB 1914); Stats 2005 ch 280 § 5 (SB 1112), effective January 1, 2006; Stats 2008 ch 157 § 3 (SB 1432), effective January 1, 2009; Stats 2010 ch 698 § 17 (SB 392), effective January 1, 2011.

—*See Code of Civil Procedure, Bond and Undertaking Law Sections 995.010 to 996.560 in Appendix.*

§ 7071.12.   Deposit in lieu of bond; When released; Limitations periods; Filing of claims for nonpayment of wages or benefits

(a) Instead of the bond provided by this article a deposit may be given pursuant to Article 7 (commencing with Section 995.710) of Chapter 2 of Title 14 of Part 2 of the Code of Civil Procedure.

(b) If the board is notified, in writing, of a civil action against the deposit authorized under this section, the deposit or any portion thereof shall not be released for any purpose, except as determined by the court.

(c) If any deposit authorized under this section is insufficient to pay, in full, all claims that have been adjudicated under any action filed in accordance with this section, the sum of the deposit shall be distributed to all claimants in proportion to the amount of their respective claims.

(d) The following limitations periods apply to deposits in lieu of the bond required by this article:

(1) Any action, other than an action to recover wages or fringe benefits, against a deposit given in lieu of a contractor's bond or bond of a qualifying individual filed by an active licensee shall be brought within three years after the expiration of the license period during which the act or omission occurred, or within three years of the date the license of the active licensee was inactivated, canceled, or revoked by the board, whichever occurs first.

(2) Any action, other than an action to recover wages or fringe benefits, against a deposit given in lieu of a disciplinary bond filed by an active licensee pursuant to Section 7071.8 shall be brought within three years after the expiration of the license period during which the act or omission occurred, or within three years of the date the license of the active licensee was inactivated, canceled, or revoked by the board, or within three years after the last date for which a deposit given in lieu of a disciplinary bond filed pursuant to Section 7071.8 was required, whichever date is first.

(3) A claim to recover wages or fringe benefits shall be brought within six months from the date that the wage or fringe benefit delinquencies were discovered, but in no event shall a civil action thereon be brought later than two years from the date the wage or fringe benefit contributions were due.

(e) In any case in which a claim is filed against a deposit given in lieu of a bond by any employee or by an employee organization on behalf of an employee, concerning wages or fringe benefits based upon the employee's employment, claims for the nonpayment shall be filed with the Labor Commissioner. The Labor Commissioner shall, pursuant to the authority vested by Section 96.5 of the Labor Code, conduct hearings to determine whether or not the wages or fringe benefits should be paid to the complainant. Upon a finding by the commissioner that the wages or fringe benefits should be paid to the complainant, the commissioner shall notify the register of the findings. The registrar shall not make payment from the deposit on the basis of findings by the commissioner for a period of 10 days following determination of the findings. If, within the period, the complainant or the contractor files written notice with the registrar and the commissioner of an intention to seek judicial review of the findings pursuant to Section 11523 of the Government Code, the registrar shall not make payment if an action is actually filed, except as determined by the court. If, thereafter, no action is filed within 60 days following determination of findings by the commissioner, the registrar shall make payment from the deposit to the complainant.

(f) Legal fees may not be charged by the board against any deposit posted pursuant to this section.

Added Stats 1982 ch 517 § 24.5. Amended Stats 2005 ch 280 § 6 (SB 1112), effective January 1, 2006.

§ 7071.13. Reference to bond in advertising, soliciting, or other presentments as ground for suspension of license

Any reference by a contractor in his advertising, soliciting, or other presentments to the public to any bond required to be filed pursuant to this chapter is a ground for the suspension of the license of such contractor.

Added Stats 1963 ch 1972 § 4, as B & P C § 7071.8. Renumbered Stats 1967 ch 1604 § 4, operative July 1, 1969.

§ 7071.14. Prohibited discrimination in denying license bond; Liability for damages

No licensee or applicant for a license under this chapter shall be denied a contractor's license bond solely because of his race, religious creed, color, national origin, ancestry, or sex. Whoever denies a contractor's license bond solely on the grounds specified herein is liable for each and every such offense for the actual damages, and two hundred fifty dollars ($250) in addition thereto, suffered by the licensee or applicant for a license.

Added Stats 1971 ch 669 § 4.

§ 7071.15. Revocation or suspension of license for failure to maintain bond

If a licensee fails to maintain a sufficient bond required by this article, the license is subject to suspension or revocation pursuant to Section 996.020 of the Code of Civil Procedure.

Added Stats 1983 ch 18 § 1.5, effective April 21, 1983.

§ 7071.17. Bond required where applicant or licensee has unsatisfied final judgment for failure to pay contractor, subcontractor, consumer, materials supplier, or employee; Notice of unsatisfied final judgments; Suspension for noncompliance; Reinstatement; Disqualification from serving as personnel of record for other licensee; Disciplinary action

(a) Notwithstanding any other provision of law, the board shall require, as a condition precedent to accepting an application for licensure, renewal, reinstatement, or to change officers or other personnel of record, that an applicant, previously found to have failed or refused to pay a contractor, subcontractor, consumer, materials supplier, or employee based on an unsatisfied final judgment, file or have on file with the board a bond sufficient to guarantee payment of an amount equal to the unsatisfied final judgment or judgments. The applicant shall have 90 days from the date of notification by the board to file the bond or the application shall become void and the applicant shall reapply for issuance, reinstatement, or reactivation of a license. The board may not issue, reinstate, or reactivate a license until the bond is filed with the board. The bond required by this section is in addition to the contractor's bond. The bond shall be on file for a minimum of one year, after which the bond may be removed by submitting proof of satisfaction of all debts. The applicant may provide the board with a notarized copy of any accord, reached with any individual holding an unsatisfied final judgment, to satisfy a debt in lieu of filing the bond. The board shall include on the license application for issuance, reinstatement, or reactivation, a statement, to be made under penalty of perjury, as to whether there are any unsatisfied judgments against the applicant on behalf of contractors, subcontractors, consumers, materials suppliers, or the applicant's employees. Notwithstanding any other provision of law, if it is found that the applicant falsified the statement then the license will be retroactively suspended to the date of issuance and the license will stay suspended until the bond, satisfaction of judgment, or notarized copy of any accord applicable under this section is filed.

(b) Notwithstanding any other provision of law, all licensees shall notify the registrar in writing of any unsatisfied final judgment imposed on the licensee. If the licensee fails to notify the registrar in writing within 90 days, the license shall be automatically suspended on the date that the registrar is informed, or is made aware of the unsatisfied final judgment. The suspension shall not be removed until proof of satisfaction of the judgment, or in lieu thereof, a notarized copy of an accord is submitted to the registrar. If the licensee notifies the registrar in writing within 90 days of the imposition of any unsatisfied final judgment, the licensee shall, as a condition to the continual maintenance of the license, file or have on file with the board a bond sufficient to guarantee payment of an amount equal to all unsatisfied judgments applicable under this section. The licensee has 90 days from date of notification by the board to file the bond or at the end of the 90 days the license shall be automatically suspended. In lieu of filing the bond required by this section, the licensee may provide the board with a notarized copy of any accord reached with any individual holding an unsatisfied final judgment.

(c) By operation of law, failure to maintain the bond or failure to abide by the accord shall result in the automatic suspension of any license to which this section applies.

(d) A license that is suspended for failure to comply with the provisions of this section can only be reinstated when proof of satisfaction of all debts is made, or when a notarized copy of an accord has been filed as set forth under this section.

(e) This section applies only with respect to an unsatisfied final judgment that is substantially related to the construction activities of a licensee licensed under this chapter, or to the qualifications, functions, or duties of the license.

(f) Except as otherwise provided, this section shall not apply to an applicant or licensee when the financial obligation covered by this section has been discharged in a bankruptcy proceeding.

(g) Except as otherwise provided, the bond shall remain in full force in the amount posted until the entire debt is satisfied. If, at the time of renewal, the licensee submits proof of partial satisfaction of the financial obligations covered by this section, the board may authorize the bond to be reduced to the amount of the unsatisfied portion of the outstanding judgment. When the licensee submits proof of satisfaction of all debts, the bond requirement may be removed.

(h) The board shall take the actions required by this section upon notification by any party having knowledge of the outstanding judgment upon a showing of proof of the judgment.

(i) For the purposes of this section, the term "judgment" also includes any final arbitration award where the time to file a petition for a trial de novo or a petition to vacate or correct the arbitration award has expired, and no petition is pending.

(j) The qualifying person and any partner of the licensee or personnel of the licensee named as a judgment debtor in an unsatisfied final judgment shall be automatically prohibited from serving as an officer, director, associate, partner, owner, manager, qualifying individual, or other personnel of record of another licensee. This prohibition shall cause the license of any other existing renewable licensed entity with any of the same personnel of record as the judgment debtor licensee to be suspended until the license of the judgment debtor is reinstated or until those same personnel of record disassociate themselves from the renewable licensed entity.

(k) For purposes of this section, a cash deposit may be submitted in lieu of the bond.

(*l*) Notwithstanding subdivision (f), the failure of a licensee to notify the registrar of an unsatisfied final judgment in accordance with this section is cause for disciplinary action.

Added Stats 1995 ch 467 § 6 (SB 1061). Amended Stats 1997 ch 469 § 1 (AB 772); Stats 2003 ch 363 § 1 (AB 1382); Stats 2010 ch 698 § 18 (SB 392), effective January 1, 2011.

—*See Code of Civil Procedure Section 116.220 Jurisdiction of Small Claims Court, in Appendix.*

—*See Code of Civil Procedure, Bond and Undertaking Law Sections 995.010 to 996.560 in Appendix.*

§ 7071.19. Insurance as condition precedent to license; Aggregate limit of liability; Compliance with financial security requirements; Duties of registrar

(a) As a condition of the issuance, reinstatement, reactivation, or continued valid use of a license under this chapter, in addition to any bond required under this article, a limited liability company shall, in accordance with the provisions of this section, maintain a policy or policies of insurance against liability imposed on or against it by law for damages arising out of claims based upon acts, errors, or omissions arising out of the contracting services it provides.

(b) The total aggregate limit of liability under the policy or policies of insurance required under this section shall be as follows:

(1) For a limited liability company licensee with five or fewer persons listed on the members of the personnel of record, the aggregate limit shall not be less than one million dollars ($1,000,000).

(2) For a limited liability company licensee with more than five persons listed on the members of the personnel of record, an additional one hundred thousand dollars ($100,000) of insurance shall be obtained for each person listed on the personnel of record of the licensee except that the maximum amount of insurance is not required to exceed five million dollars ($5,000,000) in any one designated period, less amounts paid in defending, settling, or discharging claims as set forth under this section.

(c) The policy or policies required by this section may be issued on a claims-made or occurrence basis, and shall cover: (1) in the case of a claims-made policy, claims initially asserted in the designated period, and (2) in the case of an occurrence policy, occurrences during the designated period. For purposes of this section, "designated period" means a policy year or any other period designated in the policy that is not greater than 12 months. Any policy or policies secured to satisfy the provisions of this section shall be written by an insurer or insurers duly licensed by this state, and may be in a form reasonably available in the commercial insurance market and may be subject to those terms, conditions, exclusions, and endorsements that are typically contained in those policies. A policy or policies of insurance maintained pursuant to this section may be subject to a deductible or self-insured retention.

(d) The impairment or exhaustion of the aggregate limit of liability by amounts paid under any policy in connection with the settlement, discharge, or defense of claims applicable to a designated period shall not require the licensee to acquire additional insurance coverage for that designated period. However, the aggregate limit of liability coverage (coverage limit) required by this section shall be reinstated by not later than the commencement date of the next designated period, and the license of any licensee that fails to comply with this provision shall be suspended by operation of law until the date that the licensee complies with the coverage limit requirements of this section. In addition, the amount to which any coverage limit is depleted may be reported on the license record.

(e) Upon the dissolution and winding up of the company, the company shall, with respect to any insurance policy or policies then maintained pursuant to this section, maintain or obtain an extended reporting period endorsement or equivalent provision in the maximum total aggregate limit of liability required to comply with this section for a minimum of three years if reasonably available from the insurer.

(f) Prior to the issuance, reinstatement, or reactivation of a limited liability company license as provided under this chapter, the applicant or licensee shall, in the manner prescribed by the registrar, submit the information and documentation required by this section and requested by the registrar, demonstrating compliance with the financial security requirements specified by this section.

(g) For any insurance policy secured by a licensee in satisfaction of this section, a Certificate of Liability Insurance, signed by an authorized agent or employee of the insurer, shall be submitted electronically or otherwise to the registrar. The insurer issuing the certificate shall report to the registrar the following information for any policy required under this section: name, license number, policy number, dates that coverage is scheduled to commence and lapse, the date and amount of any payment of claims, and cancellation date if applicable.

(h) Upon the issuance, reinstatement, or reactivation of a license under this section, the registrar may post the following information to the licensee's license record on the Internet:

(1) The name of the insurer or insurers providing the liability policy or policies submitted by the licensee for the most recent designated period.

(2) The policy number(s) and the sum of the aggregate limit of liability provided by each.

Added Stats 2010 ch 698 § 19 (SB 392), effective January 1, 2011.

§ 7072. Issuance of license

Following receipt of the application fee and an application furnishing complete information in the manner required by the registrar, and after such examination and investigation as he may require, the registrar, within 15 days after approval of the application, shall notify the applicant that a license may be issued to him on payment of the initial license fee provided in Article 8 (commencing at Section 7135), and, when the initial license fee is paid, shall issue a license to him permitting him to engage in business as a contractor under the terms of this chapter.

Added Stats 1939 ch 37 § 1. Amended Stats 1961 ch 1636 § 3, operative October 1, 1962; Stats 1970 ch 340 § 5.

§ 7072.5. Issuance of pocket card

(a) Upon the issuance of a license, a plasticized pocket card of a size, design, and content as may be determined by the registrar shall be issued at no cost to each licensee, or to the partners, managers, officers, or responsible managing officers of licensees licensed as other than individuals, which card shall be evidence that the licensee is duly licensed pursuant to this chapter. All cards issued shall be surrendered upon the suspension, revocation, or denial of renewal of the license, and shall be mailed or delivered to the board within five days of the suspension, revocation, or denial.

(b) When a person to whom a card is issued terminates his or her position, office, or association with a licensee that is licensed as other than an individual, that person shall surrender his or her card to the licensee and within five days thereafter the card shall be mailed or delivered by the licensee to the board for cancellation.

Added Stats 1988 ch 1495 § 1. Amended Stats 2006 ch 106 § 3 (AB 2457), effective January 1, 2007; Stats 2010 ch 698 § 20 (SB 392), effective January 1, 2011.

§ 7073. Grounds and procedures for denial of application; Rehabilitation and reapplication; Probationary license in lieu of denial

(a) The registrar may deny any application for a license or supplemental classification where the applicant has failed to comply with any rule or regulation adopted pursuant to this chapter or where there are grounds for denial under Section 480. Procedures for denial of an application shall be conducted in accordance with Section 485.

(b) When the board has denied an application for a license on grounds that the applicant has committed a crime substantially related to qualifications, functions, or duties of a contractor, it shall, in its decision or in its notice under subdivision (b) of Section 485, inform the applicant of the earliest date on which the applicant may reapply for a license. The board shall develop criteria, similar to the criteria developed to evaluate rehabilitation, to establish the earliest date on which the applicant may reapply. The date set by the registrar shall not be more than five years from the effective date of the decision or service of notice under subdivision (b) of Section 485.

(c) The board shall inform an applicant that all competent evidence of rehabilitation shall be considered upon reapplication.

(d) Along with the decision or notice under subdivision (b) of Section 485, the board shall serve a copy of the criteria for rehabilitation formulated under Section 482.

(e) In lieu of denying licensure as authorized under this section, the registrar may issue an applicant a probationary license with terms and conditions. During the probationary period, if information is brought to the attention of the registrar regarding any act or omission of the licensee constituting grounds for discipline or denial of licensure for which the registrar determines that revocation of the probationary license would be proper, the registrar shall notify the applicant to show cause within 30 days why the probationary license should not be revoked. The proceedings shall be conducted in accordance with the provisions of Chapter 5 (commencing with Section 11500) of Part 1 of Division 3 of Title 2 of the Government Code, and the registrar shall have all the powers granted therein. A probationary license shall not be renewed during any period in which any proceeding brought pursuant to this section is pending.

Added Stats 1983 ch 891 § 11. Amended Stats 2004 ch 586 § 2 (AB 2216); Stats 2005 ch 280 § 7 (SB 1112), effective January 1, 2006.

§ 7074. When application becomes void; Disposition of application; Fee for reapplication

(a) Except as otherwise provided by this section, an application for an original license, for an additional classification or for a change of qualifier shall become void when:

(1) The applicant or examinee for the applicant has failed to appear for the scheduled qualifying examination and fails to request and pay the fee for rescheduling within 90 days of notification of failure to appear, or, after being rescheduled, has failed to appear for a second examination.

(2) The applicant or the examinee for the applicant has failed to achieve a passing grade in the scheduled qualifying examination, and fails to request and pay the fee for rescheduling within 90 days of notification of failure to pass the examination.

(3) The applicant or the examinee for the applicant has failed to achieve a passing grade in the qualifying examination within 18 months after the application has been deemed acceptable by the board.

(4) The applicant for an original license, after having been notified to do so, fails to pay the initial license fee within 90 days from the date of the notice.

(5) The applicant, after having been notified to do so, fails to file within 90 days from the date of the notice any bond or cash deposit or other documents that may be required for issuance or granting pursuant to this chapter.

(6) After filing, the applicant withdraws the application.

(7) The applicant fails to return the application rejected by the board for insufficiency or incompleteness within 90 days from the date of original notice or rejection.

(8) The application is denied after disciplinary proceedings conducted in accordance with the provisions of this code.

(b) The void date on an application may be extended up to 90 days or one examination may be rescheduled without a fee upon documented evidence by the applicant that the failure to complete the application process or to appear for an examination was due to a medical emergency or other circumstance beyond the control of the applicant.

(c) An application voided pursuant to the provisions of this section shall remain in the possession of the registrar for the period as he or she deems necessary and shall not be returned to the applicant. Any reapplication for a license shall be accompanied by the fee fixed by this chapter.

Added Stats 1983 ch 891 § 13. Amended Stats 2001 ch 728 § 59 (SB 724).

§ 7075. Display of license

The license shall be displayed in the licensee's main office or chief place of business. Satisfactory evidence of the possession of a license and the current renewal thereof shall be provided by the licensee upon demand.

Added Stats 1939 ch 37 § 1. Amended Stats 1961 ch 1636 § 4, operative October 1, 1962; Stats 1963 ch 1016 § 3; Stats 1971 ch 716 § 104; Stats 1990 ch 1326 § 4 (AB 3480), effective September 25, 1990.

Section VI

§ 7075.1. Nontransferability of license

(a) No license, regardless of type or classification, shall be transferable to any other person or entity under any circumstances.

(b) A license number may be reissued after cancellation, revocation, suspension, or expiration beyond the renewal period specified in Section 7141, only under the following circumstances:

(1) To an individual upon application.

(2) To a partnership upon application if there is no change in the partners or partnership structure.

(3) To a corporation upon application if there is no change in the status of the corporation as registered with the Secretary of State.

(4) To a limited liability company upon application if there is no change in the status of the company as registered with the Secretary of State.

(c) A license number may be reissued or reassigned to a different entity only under the following conditions:

(1) To a corporation when the parent corporation has merged or created a subsidiary, the subsidiary has merged into the parent corporation, or the corporation has changed its filing status with the Secretary of State from a domestic corporation to a foreign corporation or from a foreign corporation to a domestic corporation, and the new entity is being formed to continue the business of the formerly licensed corporation.

(2) To a limited liability company when the parent limited liability company has merged or created a subsidiary, the subsidiary has merged into the parent limited liability company, or the limited liability company has changed its filing status with the Secretary of State from a domestic limited liability company to a foreign limited liability company or from a foreign limited liability company to a domestic limited liability company, and the new entity is being formed to continue the business of the formerly licensed limited liability company.

(3) To an individual when the individual is an immediate family member of a licensed individual who is deceased or absent and the license is required to continue an existing family contracting business.

(4) To a corporation or limited liability company when created by immediate members of an individual licensee's family to continue an existing deceased or absent individual licensee's contracting business.

(5) To a corporation or limited liability company when the corporation or limited liability company is formed by an individual licensee and the individual licensee maintains ownership directly or indirectly of shares or membership interests evidencing more than 50 percent of the voting power.

(6) To a corporation or limited liability company that acquires a spouse, brother, sister, son, daughter, stepson, stepdaughter, grand-

son, granddaughter, son-in-law, licensee pursuant to an asset sale provided that the corporation or limited liability company has a qualifier as required by Section 7068.

(7) To a limited liability company that is formed by a corporation to continue the business of the corporation subsequent to the cancellation of the corporate entity's license, provided the personnel listed for each entity are the same.

For purposes of this section, an immediate family member of a deceased or absent licensed individual is either a spouse, father, mother, brother, sister, son, daughter, stepson, stepdaughter, grandson, granddaughter, son-in-law, or daughter-in-law.

Added Stats 1990 ch 1326 § 4.5 (AB 3480), effective September 25, 1990. Amended Stats 1992 ch 746 § 2 (AB 2424); Stats 2010 ch 698 § 21 (SB 392), effective January 1, 2011.

§ 7076. Events resulting in cancellation of license; Continuance of license

(a) An individual license shall be canceled upon the death of a person licensed as an individual. An immediate member of the family of the deceased licensee may request a continuance of the license to complete projects in progress and undertake new work for a reasonable amount of time to be determined by rules of the board. The request for a continuance must be made in writing and received at the board's headquarters office within 90 days after the death. Approval of the continuance of an individual license may be contingent upon meeting the bond requirements of Sections 7071.5 and 7071.6 within 90 days of notification by the board of that requirement. The immediate member of the family must apply for and obtain his or her own license to continue contracting after the continuance expires.

(b) A partnership license shall be canceled upon the death of a general partner. The remaining partner or partners shall notify the registrar in writing within 90 days of the death of a general partner. Failure to notify the registrar within 90 days of the death is grounds for disciplinary action.

The remaining general partner or partners may request a continuance of the license to complete projects in progress and undertake new work for a reasonable amount of time to be determined by rules of the board. The request for a continuance must be made in writing and received at the board's headquarters office within 90 days after the death. The remaining general partner or partners must apply for and obtain a new license to continue contracting after the continuance expires.

(c) A partnership license shall be canceled upon the disassociation of a general partner or upon the dissolution of the partnership. The disassociating partner or the remaining partner or partners shall notify the registrar in writing within 90 days of the disassociation of a general partner or dissolution of the partnership. Failure to notify the registrar of the disassociation or dissolution within 90 days shall cause the license to be canceled effective the date the written notification is received at the board's headquarters office. Failure to notify the registrar within 90 days of the disassociation or dissolution is grounds for disciplinary action. The remaining general partner or partners may request a continuance of the license to complete projects contracted for or in progress prior to the date of disassociation or dissolution for a reasonable length of time to be determined by rules of the board. The request for a continuance must be made in writing and received at the board's headquarters office within 90 days after the disassociation or dissolution. The remaining general partner or partners must apply for and obtain a new license to undertake new work and to continue contracting after the continuance expires.

(d) The general partner or partners shall notify the registrar in writing within 90 days of the death of a limited partner. Failure to notify the registrar within 90 days of the death is grounds for disciplinary action.

The death of a limited partner will not affect the partnership license unless the partnership license has only one limited partner. In this case, the license will be canceled upon the death of the limited partner unless a new limited partner is added to the license within 90 days of the death.

If the license is canceled, the remaining general partner or partners may request a continuance of the license to complete projects in progress and to undertake new work for a reasonable amount of time to be determined by rules of the board. The request for a continuance must be made in writing and received at the board's headquarters office within 90 days after the death. The remaining general partner or partners must apply for and obtain a new license to continue contracting after the continuance expires.

(e) The general partner or partners shall notify the registrar in writing within 90 days of the disassociation of a limited partner. Failure to notify the registrar of the disassociation, within 90 days, shall cause the disassociation to be effective the date the written notification is received at the board's headquarters office. Failure to notify the registrar within 90 days of the disassociation is grounds for disciplinary action.

The disassociation of a limited partner will not affect the partnership license unless the partnership license has only one limited partner. In this case, the license will be canceled upon the disassociation of the limited partner unless a new limited partner is added to the license within 90 days of the disassociation. If the license is canceled, the remaining general partner or partners may request a continuance of the license to complete projects contracted for or in progress prior to the date of disassociation for a reasonable amount of time to be determined by rules of the board. The request for a continuance must be made in writing and received at the board's headquarters office within 90 days after the death. The remaining general partner or partners must apply for and obtain a new license to undertake new work and to continue contracting after the continuance expires.

(f) A joint venture license shall be canceled upon the cancellation, revocation, or disassociation of any of its entity licenses or upon the dissolution of the joint venture. The registrar shall be notified in writing within 90 days of the disassociation of a joint venture entity or dissolution of the joint venture. Failure to notify the registrar of the disassociation or dissolution within 90 days shall cause the license to be canceled effective the date the written notification is received at the board's headquarters office. Failure to notify the registrar within 90 days of the disassociation or dissolution is grounds for disciplinary action.

Any remaining entity or entities may request a continuance of the license to complete projects contracted for or in progress prior to the date of disassociation or dissolution for a reasonable amount of time to be determined by rules of the board. The request for a continuance must be made in writing and received at the board's headquarters office within 90 days of the disassociation or dissolution. The remaining entity or entities must apply for and obtain a new license to undertake new work and to continue contracting after the continuance expires.

(g) Any individual, partnership, or joint venture license continued in accordance with this section is subject to all other provisions of this chapter.

(h) A corporation license shall be canceled upon the corporation's dissolution, merger, or surrender of its right to do business in this state. The corporation shall notify the registrar in writing within 90 days of the dissolution, merger, or surrender. Failure to notify the registrar of the dissolution, merger, or surrender within 90 days shall cause the license to be canceled effective the date written notification is received at the board's headquarters office. If the corporation fails to notify the board of the dissolution, merger, or surrender, the corporation license shall be canceled 60 days after the board's discovery when researching the corporate records of the Secretary of State. Failure to notify the registrar within 90 days of the dissolution, merger, or surrender is grounds for disciplinary action.

(i) A limited liability company license shall be canceled upon the company's dissolution, merger, or surrender of its right to do business in this state. The limited liability company shall notify the registrar in writing within 90 days of the dissolution, merger, or surrender. Failure to notify the registrar of the dissolution, merger, or surrender within 90 days shall cause the license to be canceled effective the date written notification is received at the board's headquarters office. If the limited liability company fails to notify the board of the dissolution, merger, or surrender, the limited liability company license shall be canceled 60 days after the board's discovery when researching the records of the Secretary of State. Failure to notify the registrar within 90 days of the dissolution, merger, or surrender is grounds for disciplinary action.

(j) The registrar shall review and accept the petition of a licensee who disputes the date of cancellation upon a showing of good cause. This petition shall be received within 90 days of the board's official notice of cancellation.

Added Stats 1995 ch 467 § 8 (SB 1061). Amended Stats 2010 ch 698 § 22 (SB 392), effective January 1, 2011.

§ 7076.1. Voluntary surrender of license

Upon the voluntary surrender of a license by a licensee, the registrar shall order the license canceled. Cancellation will be effected upon receipt of the request by the registrar. No refund will be made of any fee which a licensee may have paid prior to the surrender of the license.

To reinstate a canceled license the licensee must pay all of the fees and meet all of the qualifications and requirements set forth in this chapter for obtaining an original license.

Added Stats 1975 ch 329 § 1.

§ 7076.2. Suspension for failure to be registered and in good standing after notice; Personal liability

(a) Notwithstanding any other provision of law, the failure of a contractor licensed to do business as a corporation or limited liability company in this state to be registered and in good standing with the Secretary of State after notice from the registrar shall result in the automatic suspension of the license by operation of law. The registrar shall notify the licensee in writing of its failure to be registered and in good standing with the Secretary of State and that the licensee shall be suspended 30 days from the date of the notice if the licensee does not provide proof satisfactory to the registrar that it is properly registered and in good standing with the Secretary of State. Reinstatement may be made at any time following the suspension by providing proof satisfactory to the registrar that the license is properly registered and in good standing.

(b) Where the license of a limited liability company is suspended pursuant to subdivision (a), each person within the company identified in Section 7028.5 shall be personally liable up to one million dollars ($1,000,000) each for damages resulting to third parties in connection with the company's performance, during the period of suspension, of any act or contract where a license is required by this chapter. This personal liability shall not apply where there has been substantial compliance with the licensure requirements, as described in subdivision (e) of Section 7031.

Added Stats 1995 ch 467 § 9 (SB 1061). Amended Stats 2010 ch 698 § 23 (SB 392), effective January 1, 2011.

§ 7076.5. Inactive license certificate; Reinstatement; Holder not entitled to practice

(a) A contractor may inactivate his or her license by submitting a form prescribed by the registrar accompanied by the current active license certificate. When the current license certificate has been lost, the licensee shall pay the fee prescribed by law to replace the license certificate. Upon receipt of an acceptable application to inactivate, the registrar shall issue an inactive license certificate to the contractor. The holder of an inactive license shall not be entitled to practice as a contractor until his or her license is reactivated.

(b) Any licensed contractor who is not engaged in work or activities which require a contractor's license may apply for an inactive license.

(c) Inactive licenses shall be valid for a period of four years from their due date.

(d) During the period that an existing license is inactive, no bonding requirement pursuant to Section 7071.6, 7071.8 or 7071.9 or qualifier requirement pursuant to Section 7068 shall apply. An applicant for license having met the qualifications for issuance may request that the license be issued inactive unless the applicant is subject to the provisions of Section 7071.8.

(e) The board shall not refund any of the renewal fee which a licensee may have paid prior to the inactivation of his or her license.

(f) An inactive license shall be renewed on each established renewal date by submitting the renewal application and paying the inactive renewal fee.

(g) An inactive license may be reactivated by submitting an application acceptable to the registrar, by paying the full renewal fee for an active license and by fulfilling all other requirements of this chapter. No examination shall be required to reactivate an inactive license.

(h) The inactive status of a license shall not bar any disciplinary action by the board against a licensee for any of the causes stated in this chapter.

Added Stats 1983 ch 891 § 18. Amended Stats 1987 ch 875 § 1.

§ 7077. Original license probationary; Revocation

Every original license, except an additional classification issued pursuant to Section 7059, shall be a probationary license until such time as the license is renewed. If information is brought to the attention of the registrar, during such probationary period, regarding any act or omission of the licensee constituting grounds for denial, revocation, or suspension of an application or license, such that, in the registrar's discretion, it would be proper to revoke the probationary license, the registrar shall forthwith notify the applicant to show cause within not more than 30 days, why the probationary license should not be revoked. The proceedings shall be conducted in accordance with the provisions of Chapter 5 (commencing with Section 11500) of Part 1 of Division 3 of Title 2 of the Government Code, and the registrar shall have all the powers granted therein. A probationary license shall not be renewed during the pendency of any proceedings brought pursuant to this section.

Added Stats 1979 ch 1013 § 15.

Article 6
Records

§ 7080.5. Public posting following acceptance of application

When an application has been accepted by the registrar, the name and address of the applicant, every classification for which the applicant has applied, and the names and titles of all personnel who have signed the application shall be publicly posted by the registrar, on the day following acceptance, in the office of the Contractors' State License Board in Sacramento.

Added Stats 1984 ch 1252 § 2.

§ 7081. List of contractors

Whenever funds are available for the purpose, the registrar shall publish a list of the names and addresses of contractors, registered under this chapter and of the licenses issued, suspended or revoked, and such further information with respect to this chapter and its administration as he deems proper.

He may furnish the lists to such public works and building departments, public officials or public bodies, and other persons interested in or allied with the building and construction industry in this or any other State as he deems advisable and, at such intervals as he deems necessary whenever funds are available.

Copies of the lists may also be furnished by the registrar upon request to any firm or individual upon payment of a reasonable fee fixed by the registrar.

Added Stats 1939 ch 37 § 1.

§ 7082. Publication and distribution of information of industry

Whenever funds are available for the purpose, the registrar may publish and disseminate to licentiates of the board, and public officials or other persons interested in or allied with the building and construction industry, such information with relation to the administration and enforcement of this chapter as he deems necessary to carry out its purposes.

Added Stats 1939 ch 37 § 1.

§ 7083. Notification by licensees of changes in recorded information

All licensees shall notify the registrar, on a form prescribed by the registrar, in writing within 90 days of any change to information recorded under this chapter. This notification requirement shall include, but not be limited to, changes in business address, personnel, business name, qualifying individual bond exemption pursuant to Section 7071.9, or exemption to qualify multiple licenses pursuant to Section 7068.1.

Failure of the licensee to notify the registrar of any change to information within 90 days shall cause the change to be effective the date the written notification is received at the board's headquarters office.

Failure to notify the registrar of the changes within the 90 days is grounds for disciplinary action.

Added Stats 1983 ch 891 § 21. Amended Stats 1984 ch 1174 § 5; Stats 1986 ch 27 § 4; Stats 1990 ch 1326 § 7 (AB 3480), effective September 25, 1990; Stats 2004 ch 865 § 12 (SB 1914).

§ 7083.1. Notification of registrar of change of address of licensee whose license is expired, suspended, or cancelled

A licensee whose license is expired or suspended, and is renewable under Section 7141, or whose license is canceled, shall notify the registrar in writing of a change of address of record within 90 days, and shall maintain a current address of record during the five-year period immediately following the expiration or cancellation of the license.

Added Stats 1987 ch 930 § 6, effective September 22, 1987. Amended Stats 2007 ch 240 § 2 (AB 936), effective January 1, 2008.

§ 7084. Rules and regulations to carry out article

The registrar, with the approval of the director may adopt and promulgate the rules and regulations he deems necessary to carry out the provisions of this article.

Added Stats 1939 ch 37 § 1.

Article 6.2

Arbitration

§ 7085.   Referral to arbitration; Conditions

(a) After investigating any verified complaint alleging a violation of Section 7107, 7109, 7110, 7113, 7119, or 7120, and any complaint arising from a contract involving works of improvement and finding a possible violation, the registrar may, with the concurrence of both the licensee and the complainant, refer the alleged violation, and any dispute between the licensee and the complainant arising thereunder, to arbitration pursuant to this article, provided the registrar finds that:

(1) There is evidence that the complainant has suffered or is likely to suffer material damages as a result of a violation of Section 7107, 7109, 7110, 7113, 7119, or 7120, and any complaint arising from a contract involving works of improvement.

(2) There are reasonable grounds for the registrar to believe that the public interest would be better served by arbitration than by disciplinary action.

(3) The licensee does not have a history of repeated or similar violations.

(4) The licensee was in good standing at the time of the alleged violation.

(5) The licensee does not have any outstanding disciplinary actions filed against him or her.

(6) The parties have not previously agreed to private arbitration of the dispute pursuant to contract or otherwise.

(7) The parties have been advised of the provisions of Section 2855 of the Civil Code.

For the purposes of paragraph (1), "material damages" means damages greater than the amount of the bond required under subdivision (a) of Section 7071.6, but less than fifty thousand dollars ($50,000).

(b) In all cases in which a possible violation of the sections set forth in paragraph (1) of subdivision (a) exists and the contract price, or the demand for damages is equal to or less than the amount of the bond required under Section 7071.6, but, regardless of the contract price, the complaint shall be referred to arbitration, utilizing the criteria set forth in paragraphs (2) to (6), inclusive, of subdivision (a).

Added Stats 1979 ch 1013 § 16. Amended Stats 1987 ch 1311 § 1, effective September 28, 1987; Stats 1989 ch 1132 § 2, effective September 29, 1989; Stats 1992 ch 597 § 1 (AB 497); Stats 1998 ch 492 § 1 (SB 1792); Stats 2002 ch 312 § 1 (AB 728); Stats 2004 ch 865 § 13 (SB 1914); Stats 2005 ch 280 § 8 (SB 1112), effective January 1, 2006.

§ 7085.2. Arbitrator's award deemed award of registrar

An arbitrator may render an award and that award shall be deemed to be an order of the registrar.

Added Stats 1987 ch 1311 § 2, effective September 28, 1987.

§ 7085.3. Notice; Consequences of election; Right to retain counsel; Agreement to arbitrate

Once the registrar determines that arbitration pursuant to subdivision (a) of Section 7085 would be a suitable means of resolving the dispute, the registrar shall notify the complainant and the licensee of this decision. The registrar shall also notify the complainant of the consequences of selecting administrative arbitration over judicial remedies and advise the parties of their rights to retain counsel at their own expense. The registrar shall forward an "agreement to arbitrate" to the complainant and the licensee. This agreement shall be returned to the registrar within 30 calendar days of the date that the agreement is mailed by the registrar. The return of this agreement by the parties shall authorize the registrar to proceed with administrative arbitration.

Added Stats 1979 ch 1013 § 16. Amended Stats 1987 ch 1311 § 3, effective September 28, 1987; Stats 1989 ch 1132 § 3, effective September 29, 1989.

§ 7085.4. Referral of agreement to arbitrate to arbitrator or arbitration association; Notification of complainant and licensee

(a) For cases that the registrar determines to refer to arbitration under subdivision (a) of Section 7085, once the complainant and the licensee authorize the registrar to proceed with administrative arbitration, the registrar shall refer the agreement to arbitrate to an arbitrator or an arbitration association approved by the board.

(b) Once the registrar determines that a complaint must be referred to arbitration pursuant to subdivision (b) of Section 7085, the registrar shall notify the complainant and the licensee of that decision. The registrar shall inform the parties of the consequences of administrative arbitration over judicial remedies and shall advise the parties of their right to retain counsel at their own expense if they so choose. The registrar shall forward a notice to arbitrate to the complainant and the licensee. This notice shall be returned to the registrar within 30 calendar days of the date that the notice is mailed by the registrar. The complainant's failure to return an executed copy of the notice shall result in the closure of the complaint.

Notwithstanding Section 7085.5, a licensee's failure to return an executed copy of the notice shall not prohibit the registrar from refer-

Section VI

ring the dispute to arbitration or bar the registrar from issuing an order enforcing any award resulting therefrom, pursuant to Section 7085.6, whether the award resulted from a contested hearing or a noncontested hearing.

Added Stats 1979 ch 1013 § 16. Amended Stats 1987 ch 1311 § 4, effective September 28, 1987; Stats 1989 ch 1132 § 4, effective September 29, 1989.

§ 7085.5. Rules of conduct for arbitrations; court procedure and exclusion of liability

Arbitrations of disputes arising out of cases filed with or by the board shall be conducted in accordance with the following rules:

(a) All "agreements to arbitrate" shall include the names, addresses, and telephone numbers of the parties to the dispute, the issue in dispute, and the amount in dollars or any other remedy sought. The appropriate fee shall be paid by the board from the Contractors' License Fund.

(b)(1) The board or appointed arbitration association shall appoint an arbitrator in the following manner: immediately after the filing of the agreement to arbitrate, the board or appointed arbitration association shall submit simultaneously to each party to the dispute, an identical list of names of persons chosen from the panel. Each party to the dispute shall have seven days from the mailing date in which to cross off any names to which it objects, number the remaining names to indicate the order of preference, and return the list to the board or appointed arbitration association. If a party does not return the list within the time specified, all persons named in the list are acceptable. From among the persons who have been approved on both lists, and in accordance with the designated order of mutual preference, the board or appointed arbitration association shall appoint an arbitrator to serve. If the parties fail to agree on any of the parties named, if acceptable arbitrators are unable to act, or if, for any other reason, the appointment cannot be made from the submitted lists, the board or appointed arbitration association shall have the power to make the appointment from among other members of the panel without the submission of any additional lists. Each dispute shall be heard and determined by one arbitrator unless the board or appointed arbitration association, in its discretion, directs that a greater number of arbitrators be appointed.

(2) In all cases in which a complaint has been referred to arbitration pursuant to subdivision (b) of Section 7085, the board or the appointed arbitration association shall have the power to appoint an arbitrator to hear the matter.

(3) The board shall adopt regulations setting minimum qualification standards for listed arbitrators based upon relevant training, experience, and performance.

(c) No person shall serve as an arbitrator in any arbitration in which that person has any financial or personal interest in the result of the arbitration. Prior to accepting an appointment, the prospective arbitrator shall disclose any circumstances likely to prevent a prompt hearing or to create a presumption of bias. Upon receipt of that information, the board or appointed arbitration association shall immediately replace the arbitrator or communicate the information to the parties for their comments. Thereafter, the board or appointed arbitration association shall determine whether the arbitrator should be disqualified and shall inform the parties of its decision, which shall be conclusive.

(d) The board or appointed arbitration association may appoint another arbitrator if a vacancy occurs, or if an appointed arbitrator is unable to serve in a timely manner.

(e)(1) The board or appointed arbitration association shall provide the parties with a list of the times and dates, and locations of the hearing to be held. The parties shall notify the arbitrator, within seven calendar days of the mailing of the list, of the times and dates convenient to each party. If the parties fail to respond to the arbitrator within the seven-day period, the arbitrator shall fix the time, place, and location of the hearing. An arbitrator may, at the arbitrator's sole discretion, make an inspection of the construction site which is the subject of the arbitration. The arbitrator shall notify the parties of the time and date set for the inspection. Any party who so desires may be present at the inspection.

(2) The board or appointed arbitration association shall fix the time, place, and location of the hearing for all cases referred to arbitration pursuant to subdivision (b) of Section 7085. An arbitrator may, at the arbitrator's sole discretion, make an inspection of the construction site which is the subject of the arbitration. The arbitrator shall notify the parties of the time and date set for the inspection. Any party who desires may be present at the inspection.

(f) Any person having a direct interest in the arbitration is entitled to attend the hearing. The arbitrator shall otherwise have the power to require the exclusion of any witness, other than a party or other essential person, during the testimony of any other witness. It shall be discretionary with the arbitrator to determine the propriety of the attendance of any other person.

(g) Hearings shall be adjourned by the arbitrator only for good cause.

(h) A record is not required to be taken of the proceedings. However, any party to the proceeding may have a record made at its own expense. The parties may make appropriate notes of the proceedings.

(i) The hearing shall be conducted by the arbitrator in any manner which will permit full and expeditious presentation of the case by both parties. Consistent with the expedited nature of arbitration, the arbitrator shall establish the extent of, and schedule for, the production of relevant documents and other information, the identification of any witnesses to be called, and a schedule for any hearings to elicit facts solely within the knowledge of one party. The complaining party shall present its claims, proofs, and witnesses, who shall submit to questions or other examination. The defending party shall then present its defenses, proofs, and witnesses, who shall submit to questions or other examination. The arbitrator has discretion to vary this procedure but shall afford full and equal opportunity to the parties for the presentation of any material or relevant proofs.

(j) The arbitration may proceed in the absence of any party who, after due notice, fails to be present. The arbitrator shall require the attending party to submit supporting evidence in order to make an award. An award for the attending party shall not be based solely on the fact that the other party has failed to appear at the arbitration hearing.

(k) The arbitrator shall be the sole judge of the relevancy and materiality of the evidence offered and conformity to legal rules of evidence shall not be required.

(l) The arbitrator may receive and consider documentary evidence. Documents to be considered by the arbitrator may be submitted prior to the hearing. However, a copy shall be simultaneously transmitted to all other parties and to the board or appointed arbitration association for transmittal to the arbitrator or board appointed arbitrator.

(m) The arbitrator shall specifically inquire of the parties whether they have any further proofs to offer or witnesses to be heard. Upon receiving negative replies, the arbitrator shall declare the hearing closed and minutes thereof shall be recorded. If briefs are to be filed, the hearing shall be declared closed as of the final date set by the arbitrator for the receipt of briefs. If documents are to be filed as requested by the arbitrator and the date set for their receipt is later than that set for the receipt of briefs, the later date shall be the date of closing the hearings. The time limit within which the arbitrator is required to make the award shall commence to run, in the absence of other agreements by the parties, upon the closing of the hearings.

(n) The hearing may be reopened on the arbitrator's own motion.

(o) Any party who proceeds with the arbitration after knowledge that any provision or requirement of these rules has not been complied with, and who fails to state his or her objections to the arbitrator in writing, within 10 calendar days of close of hearing, shall be deemed to have waived his or her right to object.

(p)(1) Except as provided in paragraph (2), any papers or process necessary or proper for the initiation or continuation of an arbitration under these rules and for any court action in connection therewith, or for the entry of judgment on an award made thereunder, may be served upon any party (A) by regular mail addressed to that party or his or her attorney at the party's last known address, or (B) by personal service.

(2) Notwithstanding paragraph (1), in all cases referred to arbitration pursuant to subdivision (b) of Section 7085 in which the contractor fails or refuses to return an executed copy of the notice to arbitrate within the time specified, any papers or process specified in paragraph (1) to be sent to the contractor, including the notice of hearing, shall be mailed by certified mail to the contractor's address of record.

(q) The award shall be made promptly by the arbitrator, and unless otherwise agreed by the parties, no later than 30 calendar days from the date of closing the hearing, closing a reopened hearing, or if oral hearing has been waived, from the date of transmitting the final statements and proofs to the arbitrator.

The arbitrator may for good cause extend any period of time established by these rules, except the time for making the award. The arbitrator shall notify the parties of any extension and the reason therefor.

(r)(1) The arbitrator may grant any remedy or relief that the arbitrator deems just and equitable and within the scope of the board's referral and the requirements of the board. The arbitrator, in his or her sole discretion, may award costs or expenses.

(2) The amendments made in paragraph (1) during the 2003–04 Regular Session shall not be interpreted to prevent an arbitrator from awarding a complainant all direct costs and expenses for the completion or repair of the project.

(s) The award shall become final 30 calendar days from the date the arbitration award is issued. The arbitrator, upon written application of a party to the arbitration, may correct the award upon the following grounds:

(1) There was an evident miscalculation of figures or an evident mistake in the description of any person, things, or property referred to in the award.

(2) There is any other clerical error in the award, not affecting the merits of the controversy.

An application for correction of the award shall be made within 10 calendar days of the date of service of the award by serving a copy of the application on the arbitrator, and all other parties to the arbitration. Any party to the arbitration may make a written objection to the application for correction by serving a copy of the written objection on the arbitrator, the board, and all other parties to the arbitration, within 10 calendar days of the date of service of the application for correction.

The arbitrator shall either deny the application or correct the award within 30 calendar days of the date of service of the original award by mailing a copy of the denial or correction to all parties to the arbitration. Any appeal from the denial or correction shall be filed with a court of competent jurisdiction and a true copy thereof shall be filed with the arbitrator or appointed arbitration association within 30 calendar days after the award has become final. The award shall be in writing, and shall be signed by the arbitrator or a majority of them. If no appeal is filed within the 30-calendar day period, it shall become a final order of the registrar.

(t) Service of the award by certified mail shall be effective if a certified letter containing the award, or a true copy thereof, is mailed by the arbitrator or arbitration association to each party or to a party's attorney of record at their last known address, address of record, or by personally serving any party. Service may be proved in the manner authorized in civil actions.

(u) The board shall pay the expenses of one expert witness appointed by the board when the services of an expert witness are requested by either party involved in arbitration pursuant to this article and the case involves workmanship issues that are itemized in the complaint and have not been repaired or replaced. Parties who choose to present the findings of another expert witness as evidence shall pay for those services. Payment for expert witnesses appointed by the board shall be limited to the expert witness costs for inspection of the problem at the construction site, preparation of the expert witness' report, and expert witness fees for appearing or testifying at a hearing. All requests for payment to an expert witness shall be submitted on a form that has been approved by the registrar. All requests for payment to an expert witness shall be reviewed and approved by the board prior to payment. The registrar shall advise the parties that names of industry experts may be obtained by requesting this information from the registrar.

(v) The arbitrator shall interpret and apply these rules insofar as they relate to his or her powers and duties.

(w) The following shall apply as to court procedure and exclusion of liability:

(1) The board, the appointed arbitration association, or any arbitrator in a proceeding under these rules is not a necessary party in judicial proceedings relating to the arbitration.

(2) Parties to these rules shall be deemed to have consented that judgment upon the arbitration award may be entered in any federal or state court having jurisdiction thereof.

(3) The board, the appointed arbitration association, or any arbitrator is not liable to any party for any act or omission in connection with any arbitration conducted under these rules.

Added Stats 1987 ch 1311 § 5, effective September 28, 1987. Amended Stats 1988 ch 160 § 3; Stats 1989 ch 1132 § 5, effective September 29, 1989; Stats 1998 ch 492 § 2 (SB 1792); Stats 2003 ch 363 § 2 (AB 1382).

§ 7085.6. Failure to comply with award as grounds for automatic suspension; Appeal; Reinstatement; Delay in revocation for good cause; Dissociation from other licensee

(a)(1) The failure of a licensee to comply with an arbitration award rendered under this article shall result in the automatic suspension of a license by operation of law.

(2) The registrar shall notify the licensee by certified mail of the failure to comply with the arbitrator's award, and that the license shall be automatically suspended 30 calendar days from the date of that notice.

(3) The licensee may appeal the suspension for noncompliance within 15 calendar days after service of the notice by written notice to the registrar.

(4) Reinstatement may be made at any time following the suspension by complying with the arbitrator's award and the final order of the registrar. If no reinstatement of the license is made within 90 days of the date of the automatic suspension, the license and any other contractor's license issued to the licensee shall be automatically revoked by operation of law for a period to be determined by the registrar pursuant to Section 7102.

(5) The registrar may delay, for good cause, the revocation of a contractor's license for failure to comply with the arbitration award. The delay in the revocation of the license shall not exceed one year. When seeking a delay of the revocation of his or her license, a licensee shall apply to the registrar in writing prior to the date of the revocation of the licensee's license by operation of law and state the reasons that establish good cause for the delay. The registrar's power to grant a delay of the revocation shall expire upon the effective date of the revocation of the licensee's license by operation of law.

(b) The licensee shall be automatically prohibited from serving as an officer, director, associate, partner, manager, or qualifying individual of another licensee, for the period determined by the registrar and the employment, election, or association of that person by another licensee shall constitute grounds for disciplinary action. A qualifier disassociated pursuant to this section shall be replaced within 90 days from the date of disassociation. Upon failure to replace the qualifier within 90 days of the disassociation, the license of the other licensee shall be automatically suspended or the qualifier's classification removed at the end of the 90 days.

Added Stats 1979 ch 1013 § 16. Amended Stats 1987 ch 1311 § 6, effective September 28, 1987; Stats 1988 ch 1619 § 2, effective September 30, 1988; Stats 2003 ch 363 § 3 (AB 1382); Stats 2010 ch 698 § 24 (SB 392), effective January 1, 2011.

Section VI

§ 7085.7.   Enforcement of award

A complainant may enforce an arbitrator's award in accordance with Chapter 2 (commencing with Section 1285) of Title 9 of Part 3 of the Code of Civil Procedure.

Added Stats 1987 ch 1311 § 8, effective September 28, 1987.

§ 7085.9.   Disclosure to public of complaint referred to arbitration

Notwithstanding any other provision of law, a complaint referred to arbitration pursuant to Section 7085 is not subject to disclosure to the public until such time as an investigation into an alleged violation of Section 7085.6 has been initiated by the registrar.

Added Stats 1988 ch 1035 § 2.

Article 7
Disciplinary Proceedings

§ 7090.   Investigation, suspension, revocation; Construction without permit as violation; Burden of proof

The registrar may upon his or her own motion and shall upon the verified complaint in writing of any person, investigate the actions of any applicant, contractor, or home improvement salesperson within the state and may deny the licensure or the renewal of licensure of, or cite, temporarily suspend, or permanently revoke any license or registration if the applicant, licensee, or registrant, is guilty of or commits any one or more of the acts or omissions constituting causes for disciplinary action.

The registrar may proceed to take disciplinary action as in this article provided against an applicant or a person licensed or registered under the provisions of this chapter even though the grounds or cause for such disciplinary action arose upon projects or while the applicant, licensee, or registrant was acting in a capacity or under circumstances or facts which, under the provisions of Sections 7044, 7045, 7046, and 7048, would otherwise exempt the person or his or her operations from the provisions of this chapter.

Notwithstanding any provision of this chapter, if the registrar finds that any contractor licensed or registered under the provisions of this chapter has willfully and deliberately violated any state or local law relating to the issuance of building permits, other than failure to obtain a county or city permit for repair, maintenance, and adjustment of equipment where such repair, maintenance, or adjustment is valued at less than five hundred dollars ($500) for labor or materials, or where the repair of a part or component part of mechanical equipment consists of replacing such part or component part of mechanical equipment in need of repair with the identical part or component part, the registrar shall take disciplinary action against the contractor's license in accordance with this chapter.

For the purpose of this section, there shall be a rebuttable presumption affecting the burden of proof that construction performed without a permit is a willful and deliberate violation.

For the purposes of this section, with respect to administrative proceedings or hearings to suspend or revoke a contractor's license, the registrar at all times shall have the burden of proof to establish by clear and convincing evidence that he or she is entitled to the relief sought in the petition.

Added Stats 1939 ch 37 § 1. Amended Stats 1941 ch 971 § 15; Stats 1972 ch 1138 § 3.5; Stats 1974 ch 717 § 1; Stats 1975 ch 772 § 1; Stats 1984 ch 1174 § 6; Stats 1997 ch 334 § 2 (SB 299); Stats 2010 ch 698 § 25 (SB 392), effective January 1, 2011.

§ 7090.1. Automatic suspension of license for failure to pay civil penalty or comply with order of correction; Contest of determination; Reinstatement; Delay in revocation for good cause; Dissociation from other licensee

(a)(1) Notwithstanding any other provisions of law, the failure to pay a civil penalty, or to comply with an order of correction or an order to pay a specified sum to an injured party in lieu of correction once the order has become final, shall result in the automatic suspension of a license by operation of law 30 days after noncompliance with the terms of the order.

(2) The registrar shall notify the licensee in writing of the failure to comply with the final order and that the license shall be suspended 30 days from the date of the notice.

(3) The licensee may contest the determination of noncompliance within 15 days after service of the notice, by written notice to the registrar. Upon receipt of the written notice, the registrar may reconsider the determination and after reconsideration may affirm or set aside the suspension.

(4) Reinstatement may be made at any time following the suspension by complying with the final order of the citation. If no reinstatement of the license is made within 90 days of the date of the automatic suspension, the cited license and any other contractors' license issued to the licensee shall be automatically revoked by operation of law for a period to be determined by the registrar pursuant to Section 7102.

(5) The registrar may delay, for good cause, the revocation of a contractor's license for failure to comply with the final order of the citation. The delay in the revocation of the license shall not exceed one year. When seeking a delay of the revocation of his or her license, a

licensee shall apply to the registrar in writing prior to the date of the revocation of the licensee's license by operation of law and state the reasons that establish good cause for the delay. The registrar's power to grant a delay of the revocation shall expire upon the effective date of the revocation of the licensee's license by operation of law.

(b) The cited licensee shall also be automatically prohibited from serving as an officer, director, associate, partner, manager, or qualifying individual of another licensee, for the period determined by the registrar, and the employment, election, or association of that person by a licensee shall constitute grounds for disciplinary action. A qualifier disassociated pursuant to this section shall be replaced within 90 days of the date of disassociation. Upon failure to replace the qualifier within 90 days of the prohibition, the license of the other licensee shall be automatically suspended or the qualifier's classification removed at the end of the 90 days.

Added Stats 1984 ch 1174 § 7. Amended Stats 1986 ch 27 § 5; Stats 1987 ch 831 § 1; Stats 1988 ch 1619 § 3, effective September 30, 1988; Stats 2003 ch 363 § 4 (AB 1382); Stats 2004 ch 865 § 14 (SB 1914); Stats 2010 ch 698 § 26 (SB 392), effective January 1, 2011.

§ 7090.5. Effect of correction of condition caused by fraudulent act

In the event a licensee commits a fraudulent act which is a ground for disciplinary action under Section 7116 of this article, the correction of any condition resulting from such act shall not in and of itself preclude the registrar from taking disciplinary action under this article.

If the registrar finds a licensee has engaged in repeated acts which would be grounds for disciplinary action under this article, and if by correction of conditions resulting from those acts the licensee avoided disciplinary action as to each individual act, the correction of those conditions shall not in and of itself preclude the registrar from taking disciplinary action under this article.

Added Stats 1953 ch 576 § 1. Amended Stats 1978 ch 985 § 1.

§ 7091. Filing complaints and disciplinary actions

(a)(1) A complaint against a licensee alleging commission of any patent acts or omissions that may be grounds for legal action shall be filed in writing with the registrar within four years after the act or omission alleged as the ground for the disciplinary action.

(2) A disciplinary action against a licensee relevant to this subdivision shall be filed or a referral to the arbitration program outlined in Section 7085 shall be referred within four years after the patent act or omission alleged as the ground for disciplinary action or arbitration or within 18 months from the date of the filing of the complaint with the registrar, whichever is later.

(b)(1) A complaint against a licensee alleging commission of any latent acts or omissions that may be grounds for legal action pursuant to subdivision (a) of Section 7109 regarding structural defects, as defined by regulation, shall be filed in writing with the registrar within 10 years after the act or omission alleged as the ground for the disciplinary action.

(2) A disciplinary action against a licensee relevant to this subdivision shall be filed within 10 years after the latent act or omission alleged as the ground for disciplinary action or within 18 months from the date of the filing of the complaint with the registrar, whichever is later. As used in this subdivision "latent act or omission" means an act or omission that is not apparent by reasonable inspection.

(c) A disciplinary action alleging a violation of Section 7112 shall be filed within two years after the discovery by the registrar or by the board of the alleged facts constituting the fraud or misrepresentation prohibited by the section.

(d) With respect to a licensee who has been convicted of a crime and, as a result of that conviction is subject to discipline under Section 7123, the disciplinary action shall be filed within two years after the discovery of the conviction by the registrar or by the board.

(e) A disciplinary action regarding an alleged breach of an express, written warranty issued by the contractor shall be filed not later than 18 months from the expiration of the warranty.

(f) The proceedings under this article shall be conducted in accordance with the provisions of Chapter 5 (commencing with Section 11500) of Part 1 of Division 3 of Title 2 of the Government Code, and the registrar shall have all the powers granted therein.

(g) Nothing in this section shall be construed to affect the liability of a surety or the period of limitations prescribed by law for the commencement of actions against a surety or cash deposit.

Added Stats 1939 ch 37 § 1. Amended Stats 1945 ch 886 § 2; Stats 1955 ch 1532 § 5; Stats 1963 ch 1258 § 1; Stats 1980 ch 865 § 1, ch 1210 § 2; Stats 1987 ch 1264 § 5, effective September 28, 1987; Stats 1994 ch 1135 § 2 (AB 3302); Stats 2001 ch 728 § 60 (SB 724); Stats 2002 ch 312 § 3 (AB 728); Stats 2007 ch 85 § 1 (AB 243), effective January 1, 2008.

§ 7095. Decision of registrar

The decision may:

(a) Provide for the immediate complete suspension by the licensee of all operations as a contractor during the period fixed by the decision.

(b) Permit the licensee to complete any or all contracts shown by competent evidence taken at the hearing to be then uncompleted.

(c) Impose upon the licensee compliance with such specific conditions as may be just in connection with his operations as a contractor disclosed at the hearing and may further provide that until such conditions are complied with no application for restoration of the suspended or revoked license shall be accepted by the registrar.

Added Stats 1939 ch 37 § 1.

§ 7096. "Licensee"

For the purposes of this chapter, the term "licensee" shall include an individual, partnership, corporation, limited liability company, joint venture, or any combination or organization licensed under this chapter, and shall also include any named responsible managing officer, responsible managing manager, responsible managing member, or personnel of that licentiate whose appearance has qualified the licentiate under the provisions of Section 7068.

Added Stats 1957 ch 1712 § 1. Amended Stats 1995 ch 467 § 10 (SB 1061); Stats 2010 ch 698 § 27 (SB 392), effective January 1, 2011.

§ 7097. Suspension of additional license issued following suspension of any license

Notwithstanding the provisions of Sections 7121 and 7122, when any license has been suspended by a decision of the registrar pursuant to an accusation or pursuant to subdivision (b) of Section 7071.17, Section 7085.6 or 7090.1, any additional license issued under this chapter in the name of the licensee or for which the licensee furnished qualifying experience and appearance under the provisions of Section 7068, may be suspended by the registrar without further notice.

Added Stats 1957 ch 1712 § 2. Amended Stats 1995 ch 467 § 11 (SB 1061).

§ 7098. Revocation of additional license issued following revocation of license

Notwithstanding the provisions of Sections 7121 and 7122, when any license has been revoked under the provisions of this chapter, any additional license issued under this chapter in the name of the licensee or for which the licensee furnished qualifying experience and appearance under the provisions of Section 7068, may be revoked by the registrar without further notice.

Added Stats 1957 ch 1712 § 3. Amended Stats 1995 ch 467 § 12 (SB 1061).

§ 7099. Citation

If, upon investigation, the registrar has probable cause to believe that a licensee, or an applicant for a license under this chapter, has committed any acts or omissions which are grounds for denial, revocation, or suspension of license, he or she may, in lieu of proceeding pursuant to this article, issue a citation to the licensee or applicant.

Each citation shall be in writing and shall describe with particularity the nature of the violation, including a reference to the provisions alleged to have been violated. In addition, each citation may contain an order of correction fixing a reasonable time for correction of the violation or an order, against the licensee only, for payment of a specified sum to an injured party in lieu of correction, and may contain an assessment of a civil penalty.

Added Stats 1979 ch 1013 § 17. Amended Stats 1983 ch 891 § 22; Stats 1984 ch 606 § 1; Stats 1985 ch 1281 § 3; Stats 1986 ch 27 § 6; Stats 1987 ch 930 § 7, effective September 22, 1987.

§ 7099.1. Regulations for order of correction

The board shall promulgate regulations covering the formulation of an order of correction which gives due consideration to the time required to correct and the practical feasibility of correction.

Added Stats 1979 ch 1013 § 18.

§ 7099.2. Regulations for assessment of civil penalties; Factors; Maximum amount

(a) The board shall promulgate regulations covering the assessment of civil penalties under this article that give due consideration to the appropriateness of the penalty with respect to the following factors:
(1) The gravity of the violation.
(2) The good faith of the licensee or applicant for licensure being charged.
(3) The history of previous violations.
(b) Except as otherwise provided by this chapter, no civil penalty shall be assessed in an amount greater than five thousand dollars ($5,000). Notwithstanding Section 125.9, a civil penalty not to exceed fifteen thousand dollars ($15,000) may be assessed for a violation of Section 7114 or 7118.

Added Stats 1979 ch 1013 § 19. Amended Stats 1984 ch 606 § 1.5; Stats 1992 ch 606 § 2 (AB 3240); Stats 1996 ch 282 § 4 (AB 2494); Stats 2003 ch 363 § 5 (AB 1382); Stats 2010 ch 415 § 21 (SB 1491), effective January 1, 2011.

§ 7099.3. Appeal to registrar

Any licensee or applicant for licensure served with a citation pursuant to Section 7099, may appeal to the registrar within 15 working days from service of the citation with respect to violations alleged by the registrar, correction periods, amount of penalties, and the reasonableness of the change required by the registrar to correct the condition.

Added Stats 1979 ch 1013 § 20. Amended Stats 1983 ch 891 § 23; Stats 1984 ch 606 § 2.

§ 7099.4. Time to contest citation

If within 15 working days from service of the citation issued by the registrar, the licensee or applicant for licensure fails to notify the registrar that he or she intends to contest the citation, the citation shall be deemed a final order of the registrar and not be subject to review by any court or agency. The 15-day period may be extended by the registrar for cause.

Added Stats 1979 ch 1013 § 21. Amended Stats 1983 ch 891 § 24; Stats 1984 ch 606 § 3.

§ 7099.5. Hearing

If a licensee or applicant for licensure notifies the registrar that he or she intends to contest a citation issued under Section 7099, the registrar shall afford an opportunity for a hearing. The registrar shall thereafter issue a decision, based on findings of fact, affirming, modifying, or vacating the citation or penalty, or directing other appropriate relief. The proceedings under this section shall be conducted in accordance with the provisions of Chapter 5 (commencing with Section 11500) of Part 1 of Division 3 of Title 2 of the Government Code, and the registrar shall have all the powers granted therein.

Added Stats 1979 ch 1013 § 22. Amended Stats 1984 ch 606 § 4.

§ 7099.6. Failure to comply with citation as ground for denial, suspension, or revocation of license

(a) The failure of a licensee to comply with a citation after it is final is a ground for suspension or revocation of license.

(b) The failure of an applicant for licensure to comply with a citation after it is final is a ground for denial of license.

Added Stats 1979 ch 1013 § 23. Amended Stats 1984 ch 606 § 5; Stats 1986 ch 1205 § 2.

§ 7099.7. Bond exempt from payment of civil penalty

No order for payment of a civil penalty shall be made against any bond required pursuant to Sections 7071.5 to 7071.8.

Added Stats 1979 ch 1013 § 24.

§ 7099.10. Citation; Hearing; Disconnection of telephone service

(a) If, upon investigation, the registrar has probable cause to believe that a licensee, an applicant for a license, or an unlicensed individual acting in the capacity of a contractor who is not otherwise exempted from the provisions of this chapter, has violated Section 7027.1 by advertising for construction or work of improvement covered by this chapter in an alphabetical or classified directory, without being properly licensed, the registrar may issue a citation under Section 7099 containing an order of correction which requires the violator to cease the unlawful advertising and to notify the telephone company furnishing services to the violator to disconnect the telephone service furnished to any telephone number contained in the unlawful advertising, and that subsequent calls to that number shall not be referred by the telephone company to any new telephone number obtained by that person.

(b) If the person to whom a citation is issued under subdivision (a) notifies the registrar that he or she intends to contest the citation, the registrar shall afford an opportunity for a hearing, as specified in Section 7099.5, within 90 days after receiving the notification.

(c) If the person to whom a citation and order of correction is issued under subdivision (a) fails to comply with the order of correction after the order is final, the registrar shall inform the Public Utilities Commission of the violation, and the Public Utilities Commission shall require the telephone corporation furnishing services to that person to disconnect the telephone service furnished to any telephone number contained in the unlawful advertising.

(d) The good faith compliance by a telephone corporation with an order of the Public Utilities Commission to terminate service issued pursuant to this section shall constitute a complete defense to any civil or criminal action brought against the telephone corporation arising from the termination of service.

Added Stats 1986 ch 518 § 2. Amended Stats 1991 ch 1160 § 32 (AB 2190); Stats 1992 ch 294 § 3 (AB 2347).

§ 7099.11. Advertising to promote services for asbestos removal; Notice to comply; Citation

(a) No person shall advertise, as that term is defined in Section 7027.1, to promote his or her services for the removal of asbestos unless he or she is certified to engage in asbestos-related work pursuant to Section 7058.5, and registered for that purpose pursuant to Section 6501.5 of the Labor Code. Each advertisement shall include that person's certification and registration numbers and shall use the same name under which that person is certified and registered.

(b) The registrar shall issue a notice to comply with the order of correction provisions of subdivision (a) of Section 7099.10, to any person who is certified and registered, as described in subdivision (a), and who fails to include in any advertisement his or her certification and registration numbers.

(c) The registrar shall issue a citation pursuant to Section 7099 to any person who fails to comply with the notice required by subdivision (b), or who advertises to promote his or her services for the removal of asbestos but does not possess valid certification and registration numbers as required by subdivision (a), or who fails to use in that advertisement the same name under which he or she is certified and registered.

Citations shall be issued and conducted pursuant to Sections 7099 to 7099.10, inclusive.

Added Stats 1988 ch 1003 § 1, operative July 1, 1989, as § 7030.6. Amended and renumbered by Stats 1991 ch 1160 § 22 (AB 2190). Amended Stats 1992 ch 294 § 4 (AB 2347).

§ 7100.   Continuance of business pending review

In any proceeding for review by a court, the court may in its discretion, upon the filing of a proper bond by the licensee in an amount to be fixed by the court, but not less than one thousand dollars ($1,000) or an amount the court finds is sufficient to protect the public, whichever is greater, guaranteeing the compliance by the licensee with specific conditions imposed upon him by the registrar's decision, if any, permit the licensee to continue to do business as a contractor pending entry of judgment by the court in the case. There shall be no stay of the registrar's decision pending an appeal or review of any such proceeding unless the appellant or applicant for review shall file a bond in all respects conditioned as, and similar to, the bond required to stay the effect of the registrar's decision in the first instance.

Added Stats 1939 ch 37 § 1. Amended Stats 1945 ch 886 § 3; Stats 1949 ch 753 § 1; Stats 1979 ch 1013 § 27.

§ 7102.   Reinstatement or reissuance of license

After suspension of a license upon any of the grounds set forth in this chapter, the registrar may reinstate the license upon proof of compliance by the contractor with all provisions of the decision as to reinstatement or, in the absence of a decision or any provisions of reinstatement, in the sound discretion of the registrar.

After revocation of a license upon any of the grounds set forth in this chapter, the license shall not be reinstated or reissued and a license shall not be issued to any member of the personnel of the revoked licensee found to have had knowledge of or participated in the acts or omissions constituting grounds for revocation, within a minimum period of one year and a maximum period of five years after the final decision of revocation and then only on proper showing that all loss caused by the act or omission for which the license was revoked has been fully satisfied and that all conditions imposed by the decision of revocation have been complied with.

The board shall promulgate regulations covering the criteria to be considered when extending the minimum one-year period. The criteria shall give due consideration to the appropriateness of the extension of time with respect to the following factors:

(a) The gravity of the violation.

(b) The history of previous violations.

(c) Criminal convictions.

When any loss has been reduced to a monetary obligation or debt, however, the satisfaction of the monetary obligation or debt as a prerequisite for the issuance, reissuance, or reinstatement of a license shall not be required to the extent the monetary obligation or debt was discharged in a bankruptcy proceeding. However, any nonmonetary condition not discharged in a bankruptcy proceeding shall be complied with prior to the issuance, the reissuance, or reinstatement of the license.

Added Stats 1939 ch 37 § 1. Amended Stats 1961 ch 1635 § 5, operative October 1, 1962; Stats 1975 ch 818 § 1; Stats 1983 ch 891 § 25; Stats 1987 ch 831 § 2; Stats 1995 ch 467 § 13 (SB 1061); Stats 2006 ch 123 § 1 (AB 2658), effective January 1, 2007.

§ 7103. Effect of disciplinary action by another state

The revocation, suspension, or other disciplinary action of a license to act as a contractor by another state shall constitute grounds for disciplinary action in this state if the individual is a licensee, or applies for a license, in this state. A certified copy of the revocation, suspension, or other disciplinary action by the other state is conclusive evidence of that action.

Added Stats 1994 ch 1135 § 2 (AB 3302).

§ 7104. Notice to complainant of resolution of complaint

When the board resolves a complaint, the board shall notify the complainant in writing of its action and the reasons for taking that action. The board shall provide the same notice in writing to the contractor provided that the contractor is licensed and the notification would not jeopardize an action or investigation that involves the contractor.

Added Stats 1994 ch 1135 § 4 (AB 3302).

§ 7106. Revocation or suspension of license incident to court action

The suspension or revocation of license as in this chapter provided may also be embraced in any action otherwise proper in any court involving the licensee's performance of his legal obligation as a contractor.

Added Stats 1939 ch 37 § 1.

Section VI

§ 7106.5. Effect of expiration or suspension of license on jurisdiction of registrar

The expiration, cancellation, forfeiture, or suspension of a license by operation of law or by order or decision of the registrar or a court of law, or the voluntary surrender of a license by a licensee shall not deprive the registrar of jurisdiction to proceed with any investigation of or action or disciplinary proceeding against the license, or to render a decision suspending or revoking the license.

Added Stats 1941 ch 971 § 16. Amended Stats 1961 ch 1636 § 6, operative October 1, 1962; Stats 2002 ch 1013 § 61.3 (SB 2026).

§ 7107. Abandonment of contract

Abandonment without legal excuse of any construction project or operation engaged in or undertaken by the licensee as a contractor constitutes a cause for disciplinary action.

Added Stats 1939 ch 37 § 1.

§ 7108. Diversion or misapplication of funds or property

Diversion of funds or property received for prosecution or completion of a specific construction project or operation, or for a specified purpose in the prosecution or completion of any construction project or operation, or failure substantially to account for the application or use of such funds or property on the construction project or operation for which such funds or property were received constitutes a cause for disciplinary action.

Added Stats 1939 ch 37 § 1. Amended Stats 1959 ch 97 § 1.

—*See Penal Code Section 484b, Wrongful Diversion of Public Funds, a Public Offense, in Appendix.*

§ 7108.5. Failure to pay subcontractors

(a) A prime contractor or subcontractor shall pay to any subcontractor, not later than seven days after receipt of each progress payment, unless otherwise agreed to in writing, the respective amounts allowed the contractor on account of the work performed by the subcontractors, to the extent of each subcontractor's interest therein. In the event that there is a good faith dispute over all or any portion of the amount due on a progress payment from the prime contractor or subcontractor to a subcontractor, the prime contractor or subcontractor may withhold no more than 150 percent of the disputed amount.

(b) Any violation of this section shall constitute a cause for disciplinary action and shall subject the licensee to a penalty, payable to the subcontractor, of 2 percent of the amount due per month for every month that payment is not made.

(c) In any action for the collection of funds wrongfully withheld, the prevailing party shall be entitled to his or her attorney's fees and costs.

(d) The sanctions authorized under this section shall be separate from, and in addition to, all other remedies, either civil, administrative, or criminal.

(e) This section applies to all private works of improvement and to all public works of improvement, except where Section 10262 of the Public Contract Code applies.

Added Stats 2009 ch 307 § 73 (SB 821), effective January 1, 2010. Amended Stats 2010 ch 328 § 16 (SB 1330), effective January 1, 2011; Stats 2011 ch 700 § 1 (SB 293), effective January 1, 2012.

—*See Public Contract Code Section 10262, in the Appendix.*

§ 7108.6. Failure to pay transportation charges submitted by dump truck carrier

A licensed contractor is required to pay all transportation charges submitted by a duly authorized motor carrier of property in dump truck equipment by the 20th day following the last day of the calendar month in which the transportation was performed, if the charges, including all necessary documentation, are submitted by the fifth day following the last day of the calendar month in which the transportation was performed. The payment shall be made unless otherwise agreed to in writing by the contractor and by the duly authorized motor carrier of property in dump truck equipment. In the event that there is a good faith dispute over a portion of the charges claimed, the contractor may withhold payment of up to 150 percent of the disputed amount or an amount otherwise agreed to by the parties. A violation of this section constitutes a cause for disciplinary action under Section 7120 and shall also subject the contractor licensee to a penalty, payable to the carrier, of 2 percent of the amount due per month for every month that payment is outstanding. In an action for the collection of moneys not paid in accordance with this section, the prevailing party shall be entitled to his or her attorney's fees and costs.

This section applies to all private works of improvement and to all public works of improvement.

Added Stats 1984 ch 1494 § 1. Amended Stats 1995 ch 37 § 1 (AB 311); Stats 1996 ch 712 § 3 (SB 1557).

Section VI

§ 7109. Departure from accepted trade standards; Departure from plans or specifications

(a) A willful departure in any material respect from accepted trade standards for good and workmanlike construction constitutes a cause for disciplinary action, unless the departure was in accordance with plans and specifications prepared by or under the direct supervision of an architect.

(b) A willful departure from or disregard of plans or specifications in any material respect, which is prejudicial to another, without the consent of the owner or his or her duly authorized representative and without the consent of the person entitled to have the particular construction project or operation completed in accordance with such plans or specifications, constitutes a cause for disciplinary action.

Added Stats 1939 ch 37 § 1. Amended Stats 1963 ch 1611 § 1; Stats 1988 ch 1619 § 4, effective September 30, 1988.

—*See Business & Professions Code Section 8556 Removal and Replacement of Pest Damage Areas; Application of Wood Preservatives: Contracting for Performance of Soil Treatment Pest Control Work, in Appendix.*

§ 7109.5. Violation of safety provisions

Violation of any safety provision in, or authorized by, Division 5 (commencing with Section 6300) of the Labor Code resulting in death or serious injury to an employee constitutes a cause for disciplinary action.

Added Stats 1963 ch 1083 § 2.

§ 7110. Disregard or violation of statutes

Willful or deliberate disregard and violation of the building laws of the state, or of any political subdivision thereof, or of Section 8550 or 8556 of this code, or of Sections 1689.5 to 1689.15, inclusive, or Sections 1689.10 to 1689.13, inclusive, of the Civil Code, or of the safety laws or labor laws or compensation insurance laws or Unemployment Insurance Code of the state, or of the Subletting and Subcontracting Fair Practices Act (Chapter 4 (commencing with Section 4100) of Part 1 of Division 2 of the Public Contract Code), or violation by any licensee of any provision of the Health and Safety Code or Water Code, relating to the digging, boring, or drilling of water wells, or Article 2 (commencing with Section 4216) of Chapter 3.1 of Division 5 of Title 1 of the Government Code, constitutes a cause for disciplinary action.

Added Stats 1939 ch 37 § 1. Amended Stats 1949 ch 1433 § 1; Stats 1965 ch 583 § 1; Stats 1968 ch 804 § 1; Stats 1969 ch 820 § 3; Stats 1974 ch 433 § 2; Stats 1979 ch 747 § 1.5, ch 1012 § 1.7; Stats 1994 ch 362 § 1 (AB 2719); Stats 2002 ch 1013 § 61.5 (SB 2026); Stats 2010 ch 415 § 22 (SB 1491), effective January 1, 2011.

—*See Public Contract Code Sections 4107 and 4110.*

§ 7110.1. Requiring or causing execution of release

The requiring of an execution of release of any claim or the causing of the execution of any such release in violation of Section 206.5 of the Labor Code is a cause for disciplinary action.

Added Stats 1959 ch 1066 § 2.

—*See Labor Code Section 206.5, Violation: Release of Claim for Wages, in Appendix.*

§ 7110.5. Initiation of action against contractor after receipt of Labor Commissioner's finding of willful violation of Labor Code

Upon receipt of a certified copy of the Labor Commissioner's finding of a willful or deliberate violation of the Labor Code by a licensee, pursuant to Section 98.9 of the Labor Code, the registrar shall initiate disciplinary action against the licensee within 30 days of notification.

Added Stats 1978 ch 1247 § 1. Amended Stats 2005 ch 280 § 9 (SB 1112), effective January 1, 2006.

§ 7111. Failure to make and keep records for inspection; Disciplinary action

(a) Failure to make and keep records showing all contracts, documents, records, receipts, and disbursements by a licensee of all of his or her transactions as a contractor, and failure to have those records available for inspection by the registrar or his or her duly authorized representative for a period of not less than five years after completion of any construction project or operation to which the records refer, or refusal by a licensee to comply with a written request of the registrar to make the records available for inspection constitutes a cause for disciplinary action.

(b) Failure of a licensee, applicant, or registrant subject to the provisions of this chapter, who without lawful excuse, delays, obstructs, or refuses to comply with a written request of the registrar or designee for information or records, to provide that information or make available those records, when the information or records are required in the attempt to discharge any duty of the registrar, constitutes a cause for disciplinary action.

Added Stats 1939 ch 37 § 1. Amended Stats 1959 ch 98 § 1; Stats 1988 ch 1035 § 3; Stats 1991 ch 1160 § 33 (AB 2190).

§ 7111.1.   Failure to respond to request to cooperate in investigation of complaint

The failure of, or refusal by, a licensee to respond to a written request of the registrar to cooperate in the investigation of a complaint against that licensee constitutes a cause for disciplinary action.

Added Stats 1984 ch 1174 § 8.

§ 7112.   Omission or misrepresentation of material fact by applicant

Omission or misrepresentation of a material fact by an applicant or a licensee in obtaining, or renewing a license, or in adding a classification to an existing license constitutes a cause for disciplinary action.

Added Stats 1939 ch 37 § 1. Amended Stats 2001 ch 728 § 61 (SB 724).

§ 7112.1.   Expungement of classification due to omission or misrepresentation

Any classification that has been added to an existing license record as a result of an applicant or licensee omitting or misrepresenting a material fact shall be expunged from the license record pursuant to a final order of the registrar evidencing a violation of Section 7112.

Added Stats 2001 ch 728 § 62 (SB 724).

§ 7113.   Failure to complete project for contract price

Failure in a material respect on the part of a licensee to complete any construction project or operation for the price stated in the contract for such construction project or operation or in any modification of such contract constitutes a cause for disciplinary action.

Added Stats 1939 ch 37 § 1.

§ 7113.5.   Avoidance or settlement of obligations for less than full amount

The avoidance or settlement by a licensee for less than the full amount of the lawful obligations of the licensee incurred as a contractor, whether by (a) composition, arrangement, or reorganization with creditors under state law, (b) composition, arrangement, or reorganization with creditors under any agreement or understanding, (c) receivership as provided in Chapter 5 (commencing at Section 564) of Title 7 of Part 2 of the Code of Civil Procedure, (d) assignment for the benefit of creditors, (e) trusteeship, or (f) dissolution, constitutes a cause for disciplinary action.

This section shall not apply to an individual settlement of the obligation of a licensee by the licensee with a creditor that is not a part of or in connection with a settlement with other creditors of the licensee.

No disciplinary action shall be commenced against a licensee for discharge of or settling in bankruptcy under federal law, the licensee's lawful obligations incurred as a contractor for less than the full amount of the obligations, so long as the licensee satisfies all of those lawful obligations, to the extent the obligations are not discharged under federal law.

Added Stats 1959 ch 1361 § 1. Amended Stats 1961 ch 1636 § 7, operative October 1, 1962; Stats 1963 ch 991 § 1; Stats 1975 ch 818 § 2; Stats 1980 ch 135 § 1; Stats 2006 ch 123 § 2 (AB 2658), effective January 1, 2007; Stats 2009. Ch. 500 (AB 1059).

§ 7114. Aiding, abetting, or conspiring with unlicensed person to evade law

(a) Aiding or abetting an unlicensed person to evade the provisions of this chapter or combining or conspiring with an unlicensed person, or allowing one's license to be used by an unlicensed person, or acting as agent or partner or associate, or otherwise, of an unlicensed person with the intent to evade the provisions of this chapter constitutes a cause for disciplinary action.

(b) A licensee who is found by the registrar to have violated subdivision (a) shall, in accordance with the provisions of this article, be subject to the registrar's authority pursuant to Section 7099 to order payment of a specified sum to an injured party, including, but not limited to, payment for any injury resulting from the acts of the unlicensed person.

Added Stats 1939 ch 37 § 1. Amended Stats 1975 ch 329 § 2; Stats 2007 ch 299 § 1 (SB 354), effective January 1, 2008.

§ 7114.1. False certification of qualifications

Any licensee whose signature appears on a falsified certificate in support of an examinee's experience qualifications, or otherwise certifying to false or misleading experience claims by an applicant, which have been submitted to obtain a contractor's license shall be subject to disciplinary action.

Added Stats 1983 ch 891 § 26.

§ 7115. Material failure to comply with chapter, rules, or regulations

Failure in any material respect to comply with the provisions of this chapter, or any rule or regulation adopted pursuant to this chapter, or to comply with the provisions of Section 7106 of the Public Contract Code, constitutes a cause for disciplinary action.

Added Stats 1939 ch 37 § 1. Amended Stats 1983 ch 891 § 27; Stats 1984 ch 1174 § 9; Stats 1990 ch 485 § 1 (SB 2290); Stats 1991 ch 1160 § 34 (AB 2190).

Section VI

§ 7116. Wilful or fraudulent act injuring another

The doing of any wilful or fraudulent act by the licensee as a contractor in consequence of which another is substantially injured constitutes a cause for disciplinary action.

Added Stats 1939 ch 37 § 1.

§ 7116.5. Causes for discipline

It is a cause for discipline for a licensee to do any of the following:

(a) Engage in any conduct that subverts or attempts to subvert an investigation of the board.

(b) Threaten or harass any person or licensee for providing evidence in any possible or actual disciplinary action, arbitration, or other legal action.

(c) Discharge an employee primarily because of the employee's attempt to comply with or aid in compliance with the provisions of this chapter.

Added Stats 2003 ch 607 § 33 (SB 1077).

§ 7117. Acting as contractor under unlicensed name or personnel

Acting in the capacity of a contractor under any license issued hereunder except: (a) in the name of the licensee as set forth upon the license, or (b) in accordance with the personnel of the licensee as set forth in the application for such license, or as later changed as provided in this chapter, constitutes a cause for disciplinary action.

Added Stats 1939 ch 37 § 1.

§ 7117.5. Acting as contractor under inactive or suspended license

(a) Acting in the capacity of a contractor under any license which has been made inactive, as provided in Section 7076.5, constitutes a cause for disciplinary action.

(b) Acting in the capacity of a contractor under any license that has been suspended for any reason constitutes a cause for disciplinary action.

(c) Acting in the capacity of a contractor under any license that has expired constitutes a cause for disciplinary action if the license is subject to renewal pursuant to Section 7141. The actions authorized under this section shall be separate from, and in addition to, all other remedies either civil or criminal.

Added Stats 1961 ch 2099 § 2. Amended Stats 1984 ch 1174 § 10; Stats 1995 ch 467 § 15 (SB 1061).

§ 7117.6. Acting as contractor in unauthorized classification

Acting in the capacity of a contractor in a classification other than that currently held by the licensee constitutes a cause for disciplinary action.

Added Stats 1983 ch 891 § 28.

§ 7118. Entering into contract with unlicensed contractor

Entering into a contract with a contractor while such contractor is not licensed as provided in this chapter constitutes a cause for disciplinary action.

Added Stats 1939 ch 37 § 1. Amended Stats 1975 ch 329 § 3.

§ 7118.4. Asbestos inspections; Disclosure requirements

(a) If a contractor has made an inspection for the purpose of determining the presence of asbestos or the need for related remedial action with knowledge that the report has been required by a person as a condition of making a loan of money secured by the property, or is required by a public entity as a condition of issuing a permit concerning the property, the contractor shall disclose orally and in writing if it is owned or has any common ownership, or any financial relationship whatsoever, including, but not limited to, commissions or referral fees, with an entity in the business of performing the corrective work.

(b) This section does not prohibit a contractor that has contracted to perform corrective work after the report of another company has indicated the presence of asbestos or the need for related remedial action from making its own inspection prior to performing that corrective work or from making an inspection to determine whether the corrective measures were successful and, if not, thereafter performing additional corrective work.

(c) A violation of this section is grounds for disciplinary action.

(d) A violation of this section is a misdemeanor punishable by a fine of not less than three thousand dollars ($3,000) and not more than five thousand dollars ($5,000), or by imprisonment in the county jail for not more than one year, or both.

(e) For the purpose of this section, "asbestos" has the meaning set forth in Section 6501.7 of the Labor Code.

Added Stats 1988 ch 1491 § 1.

§ 7118.5. Sanctions against contractor hiring uncertified person to perform asbestos-related work

Any contractor, applicant for licensure, or person required to be licensed, who, either knowingly or negligently, or by reason of a failure to inquire, enters into a contract with another person who is required to be, and is not, certified pursuant to Section 7058.5 to engage in asbestos-related work, as defined in Section 6501.8 of the Labor Code, is subject to the following penalties:

(a) Conviction of a first offense is an infraction punishable by a fine of not less than one thousand dollars ($1,000) or more than three thousand dollars ($3,000), and by possible revocation or suspension of any contractor's license.

(b) Conviction of a subsequent offense is a misdemeanor requiring revocation or suspension of any contractor's license, and a fine of not less than three thousand dollars ($3,000) or more than five thousand dollars ($5,000), or imprisonment in the county jail for not more than one year, or both the fine and imprisonment.

Added Stats 1988 ch 1003 § 4, operative July 1, 1989. Amended Stats 1991 ch 1160 § 35 (AB 2190).

§ 7118.6. Sanctions for contracting with uncertified person to perform removal or remedial action

Any contractor who, either knowingly or negligently, or by reason of a failure to inquire, enters into a contract with another person who is required to be, and is not certified pursuant to Section 7058.7 to engage in a removal or remedial action, as defined in Section 7058.7, is subject to the following penalties:

(a) Conviction of a first offense is an infraction punishable by a fine of not less than one thousand dollars ($1,000) or more than three thousand dollars ($3,000), and by possible revocation or suspension of any contractor's license.

(b) Conviction of a subsequent offense is a misdemeanor requiring revocation or suspension of any contractor's license, and a fine of not less than three thousand dollars ($3,000) or more than five thousand dollars ($5,000), or imprisonment in the county jail for not more than one year, or both the fine and imprisonment.

Added Stats 1986 ch 1443 § 3, effective September 30, 1986. Amended Stats 1991 ch 1160 § 36 (AB 2190).

§ 7119. Failure to prosecute work diligently

Wilful failure or refusal without legal excuse on the part of a licensee as a contractor to prosecute a construction project or operation with reasonable diligence causing material injury to another constitutes a cause for disciplinary action.

Added Stats 1939 ch 37 § 1.

§ 7120. Failure to pay for materials or services; False denial of liability

Wilful or deliberate failure by any licensee or agent or officer thereof to pay any moneys, when due for any materials or services rendered in connection with his operations as a contractor, when he has the capacity to pay or when he has received sufficient funds therefor as payment for the particular construction work, project, or operation for which the services or materials were rendered or purchased constitutes a cause for disciplinary action, as does the false denial of any such amount due or the validity of the claim thereof with intent to secure for himself, his employer, or other person, any discount upon such indebtedness or with intent to hinder, delay, or defraud the person to whom such indebtedness is due.

Added Stats 1939 ch 37 § 1.

§ 7121. Participation in certain acts as disqualification from employment, election or association by licensee; Disciplinary action

A person who has been denied a license for a reason other than failure to document sufficient satisfactory experience for a supplemental classification for an existing license, or who has had his or her license revoked, or whose license is under suspension, or who has failed to renew his or her license while it was under suspension, or who has been a partner, officer, director, manager, or associate of any partnership, corporation, limited liability company, firm, or association whose application for a license has been denied for a reason other than failure to document sufficient satisfactory experience for a supplemental classification for an existing license, or whose license has been revoked, or whose license is under suspension, or who has failed to renew a license while it was under suspension, and while acting as a partner, officer, director, manager, or associate had knowledge of or participated in any of the prohibited acts for which the license was denied, suspended, or revoked, shall be prohibited from serving as an officer, director, associate, partner, manager, qualifying individual, or member of the personnel of record of a licensee, and the employment, election, or association of this type of person by a licensee in any capacity other than as a nonsupervising bona fide employee shall constitute grounds for disciplinary action.

Added Stats 1941 ch 971 § 18. Amended Stats 1983 ch 891 § 29; Stats 2003 ch 363 § 6 (AB 1382); Stats 2004 ch 865 § 15 (SB 1914); Stats 2010 ch 698 § 28 (SB 392), effective January 1, 2011.

§ 7121.1. Responsibility of disassociated partner, officer, director, manager, or associate for compliance with citation

Notwithstanding any other provision of this chapter, the disassociation of a partner, officer, director, manager, or associate from the license of a partnership, corporation, limited liability company, firm, or association whose license has been cited pursuant to Section 7099 shall not relieve the partner, officer, director, manager, or associate from responsibility for complying with the citation if he or she had knowledge of, or participated in, any of the prohibited acts for which the citation was issued. Section 7121 shall apply to a partner, officer, director, manager, or associate of a licensee that fails to comply with a citation after it is final.

Added Stats 1994 ch 192 § 2 (AB 3475). Amended Stats 2010 ch 698 § 29 (SB 392), effective January 1, 2011.

§ 7121.5. Effect of participation by qualifying individual in acts for which license suspended, revoked, or not renewed

A person who was the qualifying individual on a revoked license, or of a license under suspension, or of a license that was not renewed while it was under suspension, shall be prohibited from serving as an officer, director, associate, partner, manager, or qualifying individual of a licensee, whether or not the individual had knowledge of or participated in the prohibited acts or omissions for which the license was revoked, or suspended, and the employment, election, or association of that person by a licensee shall constitute grounds for disciplinary action.

Added Stats 1983 ch 891 § 30. Amended Stats 2010 ch 698 § 30 (SB 392), effective January 1, 2011.

§ 7121.6. Restricted activities for specified individuals

(a) An individual who meets all of the following criteria shall not perform any act regulated under this chapter for or on behalf of a licensee, other than as a bona fide nonsupervising employee:

(1) The individual was listed as an officer, director, owner, manager, partner, or associate of a license that was revoked.

(2) The individual had knowledge of or participated in any act or omission for which the license was revoked.

(3) The individual is not eligible for reinstatement for licensure under Section 7102.

(b) An individual who meets all of the following criteria shall not perform any act regulated under this chapter for or on behalf of a licensee, other than as a bona fide nonsupervising employee:

(1) The individual furnished the qualifications for licensure, as set forth under Section 7068, and that license was revoked.

(2) The individual served in the capacity of the qualifying individual during the commission or omission of any of the acts that resulted in the revocation of the license, whether or not he or she had knowledge of or participated in those acts.

(3) The individual is not eligible for reinstatement for licensure under Section 7102.

(c) A violation of this section is a misdemeanor punishable by a fine of not less than four thousand five hundred dollars ($4,500), by imprisonment in a county jail for not less than 90 days nor more than one year, or by both the fine and imprisonment. The penalty provided by this subdivision is cumulative to the penalties available under other laws of this state.

(d) Notwithstanding any other provision of law to the contrary, an indictment for any violation of this section shall be found or an information or complaint filed within four years from the performance of any act that is prohibited under this section.

Added Stats 2006 ch 171 § 1 (AB 2897), effective January 1, 2007. Amended Stats 2010 ch 698 § 31 (SB 392), effective January 1, 2011.

§ 7121.65. Notification of license revocation required

Prior to becoming employed in any capacity by an entity that is subject to licensure under this chapter, an individual who is described in subdivision (a) or (b) of Section 7121.6 shall provide the prospective employer with written notice of the license revocation.

Added Stats 2006 ch 171 § 2 (AB 2897), effective January 1, 2007.

§ 7121.7. Employment of individuals with revoked licenses

(a) A qualifying individual, officer, partner, or other person named on a license shall not knowingly employ an individual who is described in subdivision (a) or (b) of Section 7121.6, except as a bona fide nonsupervising employee.

(b) A violation of this section is a misdemeanor punishable by a fine of not less than four thousand five hundred dollars ($4,500), by imprisonment in a county jail for not less than 30 days nor more than one year, or by both the fine and imprisonment.

(c) Notwithstanding any other provision of law to the contrary, an indictment for any violation of this section shall be found or an information or complaint filed within four years from the performance of any act that is prohibited under this section.

Added Stats 2006 ch 171 § 3 (AB 2897), effective January 1, 2007.

§ 7121.8. "Bona fide nonsupervising employee"

For purposes of this article, "bona fide nonsupervising employee" means a person who is exempt from the provisions of this chapter un-

Section VI

der Section 7053, and who does not otherwise meet the test of an independent contractor, as set forth under Section 2750.5 of the Labor Code.

Added Stats 2006 ch 171 § 4 (AB 2897), effective January 1, 2007.

§ 7122. When act or omission of individual or business entity constitutes cause for disciplinary action against licensee

The performance by an individual, partnership, corporation, limited liability company, firm, or association of an act or omission constituting a cause for disciplinary action, likewise constitutes a cause for disciplinary action against a licensee other than the individual qualifying on behalf of the individual or entity, if the licensee was a partner, officer, director, manager, or associate of that individual, partnership, corporation, limited liability company, firm, or association at the time the act or omission occurred, and had knowledge of or participated in the prohibited act or omission.

Added Stats 1947 ch 1285. Amended Stats 1959 ch 407 § 5; Stats 2010 ch 698 § 32 (SB 392), effective January 1, 2011.

§ 7122.1. Responsibility of disassociated qualifying individual for compliance with citation; Applicability of § 7122.5

Notwithstanding Section 7068.2 or any other provision of this chapter, the disassociation of a qualifying individual from a license after the act or omission has occurred that resulted in a citation pursuant to Section 7099 shall not relieve the qualifying individual from responsibility for complying with the citation. Section 7122.5 shall apply to a qualifying individual of a licensee that fails to comply with a citation after it is final.

Added Stats 1994 ch 192 § 3 (AB 3475). Amended Stats 2003 ch 363 § 7 (AB 1382); Stats 2010 ch 698 § 33 (SB 392), effective January 1, 2011.

§ 7122.2. Responsibility for compliance with arbitration award following disassociation

(a) Notwithstanding Section 7068.2 or any other provisions of this chapter, the disassociation of a qualifying individual from a license that has been referred to arbitration pursuant to Section 7085 shall not relieve the qualifying individual from the responsibility of complying with an arbitration award rendered as a result of acts or omissions committed while acting as the qualifying individual for the license as provided under Sections 7068 and 7068.1.

(b) Section 7122.5 shall apply to a qualifying individual of a licensee that fails to comply with an arbitration award once it is rendered.

Added Stats 2002 ch 312 § 4 (AB 728). Amended Stats 2005 ch 385 § 1 (AB 316), effective January 1, 2006; Stats 2010 ch 698 § 34 (SB 392), effective January 1, 2011.

§ 7122.5. Immateriality of licensee's knowledge or participation

The performance by an individual, partnership, corporation, limited liability company, firm, or association of an act or omission constituting a cause for disciplinary action, likewise constitutes a cause for disciplinary action against a licensee who at the time that the act or omission occurred was the qualifying individual of that individual, partnership, corporation, limited liability company, firm, or association, whether or not he or she had knowledge of or participated in the prohibited act or omission.

Added Stats 1959 ch 407 § 6. Amended Stats 2010 ch 698 § 35 (SB 392), effective January 1, 2011.

§ 7123. Criminal conviction as cause for discipline

A conviction of a crime substantially related to the qualifications, functions and duties of a contractor constitutes a cause for disciplinary action. The record of the conviction shall be conclusive evidence thereof.

Added Stats 1955 ch 1532 § 2. Amended Stats 1978 ch 1161 § 365.

§ 7123.5. Disciplinary action for violation of overpricing following emergency or major disaster

If a contractor is convicted of violating Section 396 of the Penal Code or any substantially similar local ordinance in connection with the sale, or offer for sale, of repair or reconstruction services, as defined in Section 396 of the Penal Code, the Contractors' State License Board shall take disciplinary action against the contractor, which shall include a suspension of at least six months or the permanent revocation of the contractor's license.

Added Stats 1993–94 1st Ex Sess ch 52 § 1 (AB 36 X), effective November 30, 1994.

—See Penal Code Section 396, Unlawful Price Increase Following a Declared State of Emergency, in Appendix.

§ 7124. What constitutes conviction; When license may be ordered suspended or revoked, or issuance refused

A plea or verdict of guilty or a conviction following a plea of nolo contendere is deemed to be a conviction within the meaning of this article. The board may order the license suspended or revoked, or may decline to issue a license, when the time for appeal has elapsed, or the judg-

Section VI

ment of conviction has been affirmed on appeal or when an order granting probation is made suspending the imposition of sentence, irrespective of a subsequent order under the provisions of Section 1203.4 of the Penal Code allowing such person to withdraw his plea of guilty and to enter a plea of not guilty, or setting aside the verdict of guilty, or dismissing the accusation, information or indictment.

Added Stats 1955 ch 1532 § 3.

§ 7124.5.   [Section repealed 2004.]

Added Stats 1979 ch 188 § 2, effective June 29, 1979. Repealed Stats 2004 ch 865 § 16 (SB 1914). The repealed section related to public disclosure of complaints against licensees.

§ 7124.6.   Public access to complaints against licensees; Disclaimer; Limitations of disclosure

(a) The registrar shall make available to members of the public the date, nature, and status of all complaints on file against a licensee that do either of the following:

(1) Have been referred for accusation.

(2) Have been referred for investigation after a determination by board enforcement staff that a probable violation has occurred, and have been reviewed by a supervisor, and regard allegations that if proven would present a risk of harm to the public and would be appropriate for suspension or revocation of the contractor's license or criminal prosecution.

(b) The board shall create a disclaimer that shall accompany the disclosure of a complaint that shall state that the complaint is an allegation. The disclaimer may also contain any other information the board determines would be relevant to a person evaluating the complaint.

(c) A complaint resolved in favor of the contractor shall not be subject to disclosure.

(d) Except as described in subdivision (e), the registrar shall make available to members of the public the date, nature, and disposition of all legal actions.

(e) Disclosure of legal actions shall be limited as follows:

(1) Citations shall be disclosed from the date of issuance and for five years after the date of compliance if no additional disciplinary actions have been filed against the licensee during the five-year period. If additional disciplinary actions were filed against the licensee during the five-year period, all disciplinary actions shall be disclosed for as long as the most recent disciplinary action is subject to disclosure under this section. At the end of the specified time period, those citations shall no longer be disclosed.

(2) Accusations that result in suspension, stayed suspension, or stayed revocation of the contractor's license shall be disclosed from the date the accusation is filed and for seven years after the accusation has been settled, including the terms and conditions of probation if no additional disciplinary actions have been filed against the licensee during the seven-year period. If additional disciplinary actions were filed against the licensee during the seven-year period, all disciplinary actions shall be posted for as long as the most recent disciplinary action is subject to disclosure under this section. At the end of the specified time period, those accusations shall no longer be disclosed.

(3) All revocations that are not stayed shall be disclosed indefinitely from the effective date of the revocation.

Added Stats 2001 ch 494 § 2 (SB 135), operative July 1, 2002. Amended Stats 2003 ch 607 § 34 (SB 1077).

Article 7.5
Workers' Compensation Insurance Reports

§ 7125. Reports to registrar; Exemptions (First of two; Repealed January 1, 2013)

(a) Except as provided in subdivision (b), the board shall require as a condition precedent to the issuance, reinstatement, reactivation, renewal, or continued maintenance of a license, that the applicant or licensee have on file at all times a current and valid Certificate of Workers' Compensation Insurance or Certification of Self-Insurance. A Certificate of Workers' Compensation Insurance shall be issued and filed, electronically or otherwise, by one or more insurers duly licensed to write workers' compensation insurance in this state. A Certification of Self-Insurance shall be issued and filed by the Director of Industrial Relations. If reciprocity conditions exist, as defined in Section 3600.5 of the Labor Code, the registrar shall require the information deemed necessary to ensure compliance with this section.

(b) This section does not apply to an applicant or licensee who meets both of the following conditions:

(1) Has no employees provided that he or she files a statement with the board on a form prescribed by the registrar prior to the issuance, reinstatement, reactivation, or continued maintenance of a license, certifying that he or she does not employ any person in any manner so as to become subject to the workers' compensation laws of California or is not otherwise required to provide for workers' compensation insurance coverage under California law.

(2) Does not hold a C-39 license, as defined in Section 832.39 of Title 16 of the California Code of Regulations.

Section VI

(c) No Certificate of Workers' Compensation Insurance, Certification of Self-Insurance, or exemption certificate is required of a holder of a license that has been inactivated on the official records of the board during the period the license is inactive.

(d) (1) The insurer, including the State Compensation Insurance Fund, shall report to the registrar the following information for any policy required under this section: name, license number, policy number, dates that coverage is scheduled to commence and lapse, and cancellation date if applicable.

(2) A workers' compensation insurer shall also report to the registrar a licensee whose workers' compensation insurance policy is canceled by the insurer if all of the following conditions are met:

(A) The insurer has completed a premium audit or investigation.

(B) A material misrepresentation has been made by the insured that results in financial harm to the insurer.

(C) No reimbursement has been paid by the insured to the insurer.

(3) Willful or deliberate disregard and violation of workers' compensation insurance laws constitutes a cause for disciplinary action by the registrar against the licensee.

(e) (1) For any license that, on January 1, 2011, is active and includes a C-39 classification in addition to any other classification, the registrar shall, in lieu of the automatic license suspension otherwise required under this article, remove the C-39 classification from the license unless a valid Certificate of Workers' Compensation Insurance or Certification of Self-Insurance is received by the registrar.

(2) For any licensee whose license, after January 1, 2011, is active and has had the C-39 classification removed as provided in paragraph (1), and who is found by the registrar to have employees and to lack a valid Certificate of Workers' Compensation Insurance or Certification of Self-Insurance, that license shall be automatically suspended as required under this article.

(f) The information reported pursuant to paragraph (2) of subdivision (d) shall be confidential, and shall be exempt from disclosure under the California Public Records Act (Chapter 3.5 (commencing with Section 6250) of Division 7 of Title 1 of the Government Code).

(g) This section shall remain in effect only until January 1, 2013, and as of that date is repealed, unless a later enacted statute, that is enacted before January 1, 2013, deletes or extends that date.

Added Stats 1943 ch 132 § 1. Amended Stats 1990 ch 1386 § 3 (AB 2282); Stats 1991 ch 1160 § 38 (AB 2190); Stats 1995 ch 467 § 16 (SB 1061); Stats 1996 ch 331 § 1 (AB 3355); Stats 2002 ch 311 § 4 (AB 264); Stats 2006 ch 38 § 1 (AB 881), effective January 1, 2007, repealed January 1, 2011; Stats 2010 ch 423 § 1 (AB 2305), effective January 1, 2011, repealed January 1, 2013; Stats 2011 ch 686 § 1 (AB 878), effective January 1, 2012, repealed January 1, 2013.

§ 7125. Reports to registrar; Exemptions (Second of two; Operative January 1, 2013)

(a) The board shall require as a condition precedent to the issuance, reinstatement, reactivation, renewal, or continued maintenance of a license, that the applicant or licensee have on file at all times a current and valid Certificate of Workers' Compensation Insurance or Certification of Self-Insurance. A Certificate of Workers' Compensation Insurance shall be issued and filed, electronically or otherwise, by one or more insurers duly licensed to write workers' compensation insurance in this state. A Certification of Self-Insurance shall be issued and filed by the Director of Industrial Relations. If reciprocity conditions exist, as defined in Section 3600.5 of the Labor Code, the registrar shall require the information deemed necessary to ensure compliance with this section.

(b) This section does not apply to an applicant or licensee who has no employees provided that he or she files a statement with the board on a form prescribed by the registrar prior to the issuance, reinstatement, reactivation, or continued maintenance of a license, certifying that he or she does not employ any person in any manner so as to become subject to the workers' compensation laws of California or is not otherwise required to provide for workers' compensation insurance coverage under California law.

(c) No Certificate of Workers' Compensation Insurance, Certification of Self-Insurance, or exemption certificate is required of a holder of a license that has been inactivated on the official records of the board during the period the license is inactive.

(d) (1) The insurer, including the State Compensation Insurance Fund, shall report to the registrar the following information for any policy required under this section: name, license number, policy number, dates that coverage is scheduled to commence and lapse, and cancellation date, if applicable.

(2) A workers' compensation insurer shall also report to the registrar a licensee whose workers' compensation insurance policy is canceled by the insurer if all of the following conditions are met:

(A) The insurer has completed a premium audit or investigation.

(B) A material misrepresentation has been made by the insured that results in financial harm to the insurer.

(C) No reimbursement has been paid by the insured to the insurer.

(3) Willful or deliberate disregard and violation of workers' compensation insurance laws constitutes a cause for disciplinary action by the registrar against the licensee.

(e) The information reported pursuant to paragraph (2) of subdivision (d) shall be confidential, and shall be exempt from disclosure under the California Public Records Act (Chapter 3.5 (commencing with Section 6250) of Division 7 of Title 1 of the Government Code).

(f) This section shall become operative on January 1, 2013.

Added Stats 2006 ch 38 § 2 (AB 881), effective January 1, 2007. Amended Stats 2010 ch 423 § 2 (AB 2305), effective January 1, 2011; Stats 2011 ch 686 § 2 (AB 878), effective January 1, 2012, operative January 1, 2013.

§ 7125.1. Time limit for acceptance of certificate

(a) The registrar shall accept a certificate required by Section 7125 as of the effective date shown on the certificate, if the certificate is received by the registrar within 90 days after that date, and shall reinstate the license to which the certificate pertains, if otherwise eligible, retroactive to the effective date of the certificate.

(b) Notwithstanding subdivision (a), the registrar shall accept the certificate as of the effective date shown on the certificate, even if the certificate is not received by the registrar within 90 days after that date, upon a showing by the licensee, on a form acceptable to the registrar, that the failure to have a certificate on file was due to circumstances beyond the control of the licensee. The registrar shall reinstate the license to which the certificate pertains, if otherwise eligible, retroactive to the effective date of the certificate.

Added Stats 1995 ch 467 § 18 (SB 1061).

§ 7125.2. Suspension of license for failure to maintain workers' compensation insurance

The failure of a licensee to obtain or maintain workers' compensation insurance coverage, if required under this chapter, shall result in the automatic suspension of the license by operation of law in accordance with the provisions of this section, but this suspension shall not affect, alter, or limit the status of the licensee as an employer for purposes of Section 3716 of the Labor Code.

(a) The license suspension imposed by this section is effective upon the earlier of either of the following:

(1) On the date that the relevant workers' compensation insurance coverage lapses.

(2) On the date that workers' compensation coverage is required to be obtained.

(b) A licensee who is subject to suspension under paragraph (1) of subdivision (a) shall be provided a notice by the registrar that includes all of the following:

(1) The reason for the license suspension and the effective date.

(2) A statement informing the licensee that a pending suspension will be posted to the license record for not more than 45 days prior to the posting of any license suspension periods required under this article.

(3) The procedures required to reinstate the license.

(c) Reinstatement may be made at any time following the suspension by showing proof of compliance as specified in Sections 7125 and 7125.1.

(d) In addition, with respect to an unlicensed individual acting in the capacity of a contractor who is not otherwise exempted from the provisions of this chapter, a citation may be issued by the registrar under Section 7028.7 for failure to comply with this article and to maintain workers' compensation insurance. An opportunity for a hearing as specified in Section 7028.10 will be granted if requested within 15 working days after service of the citation.

Added Stats 1995 ch 467 § 20 (SB 1061). Amended Stats 2002 ch 311 § 5 (AB 264).

§ 7125.3. Periods of licensure

A contractor shall be considered duly licensed during all periods in which the registrar is required to accept the certificate prescribed by Section 7125, provided the licensee has otherwise complied with the provisions of this chapter.

Added Stats 2002 ch 311 § 6 (AB 264).

§ 7125.4. Causes for disciplinary action; Misdemeanor

(a) The filing of the exemption certificate prescribed by this article that is false, or the employment of a person subject to coverage under the workers' compensation laws after the filing of an exemption certificate without first filing a Certificate of Workers' Compensation Insurance or Certification of Self-Insurance in accordance with the provisions of this article, or the employment of a person subject to coverage under the workers' compensation laws without maintaining coverage for that person, constitutes cause for disciplinary action.

(b) Any qualifier for a license who, under Section 7068.1 is responsible for assuring that a licensee complies with the provisions of this chapter, is also guilty of a misdemeanor for committing or failing to prevent the commission of any of the acts that are cause for disciplinary action under this section.

Added Stats 2002 ch 311 § 7 (AB 264). Amended Stats 2005 ch 205 § 2 (SB 488), effective January 1, 2006.

§ 7125.5. Renewal of license; Exemption for workers' compensation insurance; Recertification; Retroactive renewal

(a) At the time of renewal, all active licensees with an exemption for workers' compensation insurance on file with the board, submitted pursuant to subdivision (b) of Section 7125, shall either recertify the licensee's exemption by completing a recertification statement on the license renewal form, as provided by the board, or shall provide a current and valid Certificate of Workers' Compensation Insurance or Certificate of Self-Insurance, whichever is applicable.

(b) The license shall not be renewed unless a licensee with an exemption for workers' compensation insurance on file with the board recertifies the exemption status or provides a current and valid Cer-

Section VI

tificate of Workers' Compensation Insurance or Certificate of Self-Insurance in conjunction with the license renewal.

(c) If the documentation required by subdivision (a) is not provided with the license renewal but is received within 30 days after notification by the board of the renewal rejection, the registrar shall grant a retroactive renewal pursuant to Section 7141.5 back to the date of the postmark of the otherwise acceptable renewal. A renewal that is still incomplete for any reason after 30 days after notification of rejection shall not be eligible for retroactive renewal under this subdivision.

Added Stats 2011 ch 546 § 1 (AB 397), effective January 1, 2012.

§ 7126. Violation of article; Misdemeanor

Any licensee or agent or officer thereof, who violates, or omits to comply with, any of the provisions of this article is guilty of a misdemeanor.

Added Stats 1943 ch 132 § 1.

—See Labor Code Section 3899, Building Permits; Requirement for Verification of Workers Compensation in Appendix.

—See also Health and Safety Code Section 19825, Declaration of Worker's Compensation Required on Building Permits, in Appendix

§ 7127. Stop order; Failure to observe; Protest

(a)(1) If an employer subject to licensure under this chapter has failed to secure the payment of compensation as required by Section 3700 of the Labor Code, and whether that employer is or is not licensed under this chapter, the registrar may, in addition to any other administrative remedy, issue and serve on that employer a stop order prohibiting the use of employee labor. The stop order shall become effective immediately upon service. An employee affected by the work stoppage shall be paid by the employer for his or her time lost, not exceeding 10 days, pending compliance by the employer.

(2) Failure of any employer, officer, or any person having direction, management, or control of any place of employment or of employees to observe a stop order issued and served upon him or her pursuant to this section is a misdemeanor punishable by imprisonment in the county jail not exceeding 60 days or by a fine not exceeding ten thousand dollars ($10,000), or both.

(b) An employer who is subject to this section may protest the stop order by making and filing with the registrar a written request for a hearing within 20 days after service of the stop order. The hearing shall be held within five days from the date of filing the request. The registrar shall notify the employer of the time and place of the hearing by mail. At the conclusion of the hearing, the stop order shall be immediately affirmed or dismissed, and within 24 hours thereafter the registrar shall issue and serve on all parties to the hearing by registered or certified mail a written notice of findings and findings. A writ of mandate may be taken from the findings to the appropriate superior court. Such writ must be taken within 45 days after the mailing of the notice of findings and findings.

Added Stats 2010 ch 643 § 1 (SB 1254), effective January 1, 2011.

Article 8
Revenue

§ 7135. Disposition of fees and penalties; Appropriation

(a) The fees and civil penalties received under this chapter shall be deposited in the Contractors' License Fund. All moneys in the fund are hereby appropriated for the purposes of this chapter.

(b) It is the intent of the Legislature that the board shall use moneys appropriated from the fund to improve its administrative and investigative oversight activities and capacity.

Added Stats 1939 ch 37 § 1. Amended Stats 1979 ch 1013 § 28; Stats 1986 ch 137 § 1.

§ 7135.1. Funds to enforce unlicensed activity provisions

It is the intent of the Legislature that, each fiscal year the board shall designate, if appropriated in the Budget Act and to the extent that it does not conflict with the control language of the Budget Act, no less than 20 percent of the annual amount collected as a result of the fees increased by statutes enacted during the 1993 portion of the 1993–94 Regular Session to be used to enforce the provision of this chapter relative to unlicensed activity.

Added Stats 1993 ch 1188 § 1 (SB 148).

§ 7136. Percentage to be transferred to Consumer Affairs Fund

The director shall designate a sum not to exceed 10 percent of the total income of the Contractors' State License Board for each fiscal year to be transferred to the Consumer Affairs Fund as the board's share of the cost of administration of the department.

Added Stats 1939 ch 37 § 1. Amended Stats 1971 ch 716 § 105; Stats 1984 ch 193 § 2.

§ 7137. Fee schedule

The board shall set fees by regulation. These fees shall not exceed the following schedule:

(a) The application fee for an original license in a single classification shall not be more than three hundred dollars ($300).

The application fee for each additional classification applied for in connection with an original license shall not be more than seventy-five dollars ($75).

The application fee for each additional classification pursuant to Section 7059 shall not be more than seventy-five dollars ($75).

The application fee to replace a responsible managing officer, responsible managing manager, responsible managing member, or responsible managing employee pursuant to Section 7068.2 shall not be more than seventy-five dollars ($75).

(b) The fee for rescheduling an examination for an applicant who has applied for an original license, additional classification, a change of responsible managing officer, responsible managing manager, responsible managing member, or responsible managing employee, or for an asbestos certification or hazardous substance removal certification, shall not be more than sixty dollars ($60).

(c) The fee for scheduling or rescheduling an examination for a licensee who is required to take the examination as a condition of probation shall not be more than sixty dollars ($60).

(d) The initial license fee for an active or inactive license shall not be more than one hundred eighty dollars ($180).

(e) The renewal fee for an active license shall not be more than three hundred sixty dollars ($360).

The renewal fee for an inactive license shall not be more than one hundred eighty dollars ($180).

(f) The delinquency fee is an amount equal to 50 percent of the renewal fee, if the license is renewed after its expiration.

(g) The registration fee for a home improvement salesperson shall not be more than seventy-five dollars ($75).

(h) The renewal fee for a home improvement salesperson registration shall not be more than seventy-five dollars ($75).

(i) The application fee for an asbestos certification examination shall not be more than seventy-five dollars ($75).

(j) The application fee for a hazardous substance removal or remedial action certification examination shall not be more than seventy-five dollars ($75).

(k) In addition to any other fees charged to C-10 and C-7 contractors, the board may charge a fee not to exceed twenty dollars ($20), which shall be used by the board to enforce provisions of the Labor Code related to electrician certification.

Added Stats 1941 ch 971 § 19.5. Amended Stats 1949 ch 750 § 1; Stats 1958 ch 2 § 1; Stats 1961 ch 1636 § 8, operative October 1, 1962, ch 2099 § 3, operative October 1, 1962; Stats 1966 ch 4 § 5; Stats 1972 ch 1138 § 4.5; Stats 1974 ch 423 § 1; Stats 1978 ch 1161 § 366; Stats 1982 ch 1615 § 1, effective September 30, 1982; Stats 1984 ch 329 § 1; Stats 1985 ch 1587 § 5.5, effective October 2, 1985; Stats 1986 ch 951 § 4, ch 1443 § 4, effective September 30, 1986; Stats 1987 ch 875 § 2; Stats 1993 ch 1188 § 2 (SB 148); Stats 1999 ch 982 § 3.7 (AB 1678); Stats 2002 ch 744 § 8 (SB 1953); Stats 2004 ch 865

§ 17 (SB 1914); Stats 2008 ch 716 § 1 (SB 1362), effective January 1, 2009; Stats 2010 ch 698 § 36 (SB 392), effective January 1, 2011.

§ 7137.5. Transfer of funds for use of Uniform Construction Cost Accounting Commission; Recommendation; Reimbursement

The sum of ten thousand dollars ($10,000) shall be transferred from the Contractors' License Fund to the Controller for the exclusive use of the California Uniform Construction Cost Accounting Commission.

The commission shall prepare a recommendation to the Legislature for a local public agency source to fund the commission beginning July 1, 1991, which will provide revenue supported by the contract activities represented by the commission's authority.

Upon adoption of this funding program, the commission shall reimburse the Contractors' License Fund in the amount of ten thousand dollars ($10,000).

Added Stats 1990 ch 1326 § 8 (AB 3480), effective September 25, 1990.

§ 7138. Earned fee; Nonrefundability when application is filed

Notwithstanding any other provision of law, a fee paid in connection with a service or application covered by Section 7137 shall accrue to the Contractors' License Fund as an earned fee and shall not be refunded.

Added Stats 1963 ch 160 § 3. Amended Stats 1966 ch 4 § 6; Stats 1974 ch 423 § 2; Stats 1982 ch 1615 § 3, effective September 30, 1982; Stats 2003 ch 607 § 35 (SB 1077); Stats 2010 ch 698 § 37 (SB 392), effective January 1, 2011.

—See *Unemployment Insurance Code Section 10501, Job Training Program: Waiver of Fees, in Appendix.*

§ 7138.1. Reserve fund level

Notwithstanding Section 7137, the board shall fix fees to be collected pursuant to that section in order to generate revenues sufficient to maintain the board's reserve fund at a level not to exceed approximately six months of annual authorized board expenditures.

Added Stats 1996 ch 528 § 1 (SB 1597). Amended Stats 2002 ch 744 § 9 (SB 1953).

Section VI

Article 8.5

The Construction Management Education Sponsorship Act of 1991

§ 7139. Title of article

This article shall be known as the Construction Management Education Sponsorship Act of 1991.

Added Stats 1991 ch 1158 § 1 (AB 2158).

§ 7139.1. Legislative findings and declarations

The Legislature hereby finds and declares all of the following:

(a) There is a demand and increasing need for construction management education programs and resources within the postsecondary education system that prepare graduates for the management of construction operations and companies regulated by the Contractors' State License Law and enforced by the Contractors' State License Board.

(b) Although construction management programs do exist within the state university system, these programs are woefully underfunded and insufficiently funded to provide training on state-of-the-art management information systems for either graduates or extension programs for continuing education of licensed contractors. Construction industry associations have provided some assistance through direct grants and scholarships, but the industrywide service of these programs and the need for additional assistance mandates broad based industrywide support.

(c) It is the intent of the Legislature that by enabling contractors to designate a portion of their licensure fee and providing a format for contractors to contribute funds to construction management education, this article will receive broad based industry support. In addition, this article allows the contractor to demonstrate the importance of construction management education. This assistance will enable greater development of construction management curricula and will improve the overall quality of construction by providing construction management training to California licensed contractors and their current and future management personnel.

Added Stats 1991 ch 1158 § 1 (AB 2158).

§ 7139.2. Creation of account

(a) There is hereby created the Construction Management Education Account (CMEA) as a separate account in the Contractors' License Fund for the purposes of construction management education. Funds in the account shall be available for the purposes of this article upon appropriation by the Legislature.

(b) The Contractors' State License Board shall allow a contractor to make a contribution to the Construction Management Education Account at the time of the contractor license fee payment. The license fee form shall clearly display this alternative on its face and shall clearly inform the licensee that this provision is a contribution to the Construction Management Education Account and is in addition to the fees.

(c) The board may accept grants from federal, state, or local public agencies, or from private foundations or individuals, in order to assist it in carrying out its duties, functions, and powers under this article. Grant moneys shall be deposited into the Construction Management Education Account.

Added Stats 1991 ch 1158 § 1 (AB 2158). Amended Stats 2003 ch 807 § 15 (SB 1080).

§ 7139.3. Grant awards

(a) The board may award grants to qualified public postsecondary educational institutions for the support of courses of study in construction management.

(b) Any organization of contractors, or organization of contractor organizations, incorporated under Division 2 (commencing with Section 5000) of the Corporations Code may request the board to award grants pursuant to subdivision (a) directly to qualified public postsecondary educational institutions of its choice. However, the total amount of money that may be awarded to one public postsecondary educational institution pursuant to subdivision (a) may not exceed an amount equal to 25 percent of the total funds available under this article.

(c) The board shall establish an advisory committee to recommend grant awards. The advisory committee shall be known as the Construction Management Education Account Advisory Committee and shall consist of 11 members, with at least one representative from each of the following: Associated General Contractors of California, Associated Builders and Contractors, California Building Industry Association, National Electrical Contractors Association, Plumbing-Heating-Cooling Contractor's Association, Southern California Contractor's Association, Associated General Contractors of San Diego, Engineering and Utility Contractors Association, Engineering Contractors Association, California Sheet Metal and Air Conditioning Contractor's Association, and one member representing the California State University and University of California construction management programs accredited by the American Council for Construction Education. Advisory committee member terms shall be for three years and the representatives shall be appointed by each identified group. Members of the advisory committee shall not receive per diem or reimbursement for traveling and other expenses pursuant to Section 103.

Section VI

(d) The mission of the Construction Management Education Account Advisory Committee is to maintain, and increase the quality and availability of, education programs for the construction industry. The primary focus is to provide financial resources not now available to accredited construction management programs in California colleges and universities to maintain and upgrade facilities and provide greater access by the industry to modern construction standards and management practices. The advisory committee shall do all of the following:

(1) Confirm the qualifications of programs applying for grants.

(2) Award less than full grants when the account has insufficient funds to award full grants to all qualifying programs.

(3) Receive and review year-end reports of use and impact of funds.

(4) Affirm applications for American Council for Construction Education accreditation and, when funds are available, award grants to complete the accreditation process.

(5) Promote close ties between feeder junior colleges and four-year construction management programs.

(6) Support development of new educational programs with specific emphasis on outreach to the construction industry at large.

Added Stats 1991 ch 1158 § 1 (AB 2158). Amended Stats 1994 ch 647 § 1 (AB 2934).

§ 7139.4.   Postsecondary programs; Qualifications

Qualified public postsecondary educational institutions shall provide postsecondary construction management programs at the baccalaureate or higher level that either award or provide one of the following:

(a) A bachelor of science construction management degree accredited by the American Council for Construction Education.

(b) A degree with an American Council for Construction Education accredited option, including, but not limited to, engineering technology and industrial technology.

(c) A bachelor of science or higher degree program documenting placement of more than 50 percent of their graduates with California licensed contractors. The placement of a person who holds a master or doctorate degree in the faculty of a construction program shall be counted as though placed with a California licensed contractor.

(d) The development of a construction management curriculum to meet the American Council for Construction Education criteria.

Added Stats 1991 ch 1158 § 1 (AB 2158).

§ 7139.5.   Amounts of grants

Grants shall be made pursuant to this article to public postsecondary educational institutions that meet the qualifications specified in Section 7139.4 in the following amounts:

(a) Three thousand dollars ($3,000) per graduate during the past academic year for institutions qualifying under subdivision (a) of Section 7139.4.

(b) Three thousand dollars ($3,000) per graduate during the past academic year for institutions qualifying under subdivision (b) of Section 7139.4.

(c) Three thousand dollars ($3,000) per graduate placed with California licensed contractors during the past academic year for institutions qualifying under subdivision (c) of Section 7139.4. These funds shall be used for the purpose of becoming accredited by the American Council for Construction Education and shall be available for up to three years. The board may continue to provide this grant to an institution that in its judgment is meeting the intent of this act and is continuing its development towards accreditation.

(d) Institutions qualifying under subdivision (d) of Section 7139.4 may receive a grant in an amount up to twenty-five thousand dollars ($25,000) per year for up to two years. Thereafter, these institutions may receive grants based upon the criteria described in subdivisions (a) to (c), inclusive. The board may continue to award a grant to an institution that in its judgment is meeting the intent of this article and is continuing its development towards accreditation.

Added Stats 1991 ch 1158 § 1 (AB 2158).

§ 7139.6.   Purposes for which grants may be used

(a) The grants issued pursuant to Sections 7139.3 and 7139.5 may be used for all of the following:

(1) Instructional materials and support, equipment, curriculum development, and delivery.

(2) Support and development of outreach, continuing education, and cooperative education or internship programs.

(3) Administrative and clerical support positions.

(4) Faculty recruitment and development, to include support for postgraduate work leading to advanced degrees, visiting lecturer compensation and expenses, teaching assistant positions, and faculty positions.

(b) Grant moneys may also be used to support general classroom and laboratory operating expenses and related administrative supplies, including, but not limited to, reference materials, testing equipment, and equipment maintenance. The list of support items in this subdivision and subdivision (a) are intended to be descriptive rather than limiting. "Support" does not include faculty salary supplements.

Added Stats 1991 ch 1158 § 1 (AB 2158).

Section VI

§ 7139.7. Report by board

The board shall report to the Legislature annually on the condition of the grant program and shall include in the report the names of the public postsecondary educational institutions involved, the amount of funds granted to each of those educational institutions, the purposes for which the funds were granted to each of those recipients, the number of students involved, the number of placements made to the construction industry for the previous academic year, and any other information the board considers relevant to the program.

Added Stats 1991 ch 1158 § 1 (AB 2158).

§ 7139.8. Report by president of institution receiving grant

The president of each public postsecondary educational institution receiving a grant under this article shall submit, with its respective request for a grant each year following the initial year for which grants are issued, a report to the board delineating the amount of the past grant awarded from the Construction Management Education Account to that institution and the utilization of those funds. The report shall include, but not be limited to, the following:

(a) The number of graduates placed with the California licensed contractors during the previous academic year.

(b) The expected enrollment in construction management courses in the upcoming academic year.

(c) Continuing education and extension courses offered during the previous academic year and their enrollments.

Added Stats 1991 ch 1158 § 1 (AB 2158).

§ 7139.9. Allocation for administration

The board may allocate up to fifteen thousand dollars ($15,000) per year from the Construction Management Education Account for the administration of this article.

Added Stats 1991 ch 1158 § 1 (AB 2158).

§ 7139.10. Intent of Legislature

It is the intent of the Legislature that state funding for the grants authorized to be awarded under this section be provided only from the Contractors' License Fund to the extent that funds are available in that fund and that no other state funding be provided for those grants.

Added Stats 1991 ch 1158 § 1 (AB 2158).

Article 9
Renewal of Licenses

§ 7140. Expiration of licenses; Renewal of unexpired licenses

All licenses issued under the provisions of this chapter shall expire two years from the last day of the month in which the license is issued, or two years from the date on which the renewed license last expired.

To renew a license which has not expired, the licensee shall, before the time at which the license would otherwise expire, apply for renewal on a form prescribed by the registrar and pay the renewal fee prescribed by this chapter. Renewal of an unexpired license shall continue the license in effect for the two-year period following the expiration date of the license, when it shall expire if it is not again renewed.

Added stats 1941 ch 971 § 20; Amended Stats 1961 ch 1636 § 9, operative October 1, 1962; Stats 1978 ch 1161 § 367; Stats 1981 ch 583 § 1; Stats 1991 ch 1160 § 39 (AB 2190).

§ 7141. Time for renewal; Effect; Failure to renew

Except as otherwise provided in this chapter, a license that has expired may be renewed at any time within five years after its expiration by filing an application for renewal on a form prescribed by the registrar, and payment of the appropriate renewal fee. Renewal under this section shall be effective on the date an acceptable renewal application is filed with the board. The licensee shall be considered unlicensed and there will be a break in the licensing time between the expiration date and the date the renewal becomes effective. If the license is renewed after the expiration date, the licensee shall also pay the delinquency fee prescribed by this chapter. If so renewed, the license shall continue in effect through the date provided in Section 7140 which next occurs after the effective date of the renewal, when it shall expire if it is not again renewed.

If a license is not renewed within five years, the licensee shall make application for a license pursuant to Section 7066.

Added Stats 1941 ch 971 § 20. Amended Stats 1961 ch 1636 § 10, operative October 1, 1962; Stats 1970 ch 856 § 1; Stats 1972 ch 1138 § 4.7; Stats 1983 ch 891 § 31; Stats 1999 ch 982 § 3.9 (AB 1678); Stats 2002 ch 1013 § 62 (SB 2026); Stats 2003 ch 607 § 36 (SB 1077).

§ 7141.5. Retroactive issuance of license after failure to renew

The registrar may grant the retroactive renewal of a license if the licensee requests the retroactive renewal in a petition to the registrar, files an application for renewal on a form prescribed by the registrar, and pays the appropriate renewal fee and delinquency fee prescribed by this chapter. This section shall only apply for a period not to exceed 90 days from the due date and only upon a showing by the contractor that the failure to renew was due to circumstances beyond the control of the licensee.

Added Stats 1972 ch 1138 § 5. Amended Stats 1975 ch 329 § 4; Stats 1983 ch 891 § 32; Stats 1984 ch 1174 § 11.

§ 7143. Renewal of suspended license

A license that is suspended for any reason which constitutes a basis for suspension under this chapter, is subject to expiration and shall be renewed as provided in this chapter, but this renewal does not entitle the licensee, while the license remains suspended, and until it is reinstated, to engage in any activity to which the license relates, or in any other activity or conduct in violation of the order or judgment by which the license was suspended.

Added Stats 1941 ch 971 § 20. Amended Stats 1961 ch 1636 § 12, operative October 1, 1962; Stats 1972 ch 1138 § 7; Stats 1987 ch 930 § 8, effective September 22, 1987; Stats 2003 ch 363 § 8 (AB 1382).

§ 7143.5. Application for new license by person prohibited from renewing

A person who, by reason of the provisions of Section 7141, is not entitled to renew his license, may apply for and obtain a new license only if he pays all of the fees and meets all of the qualifications and requirements set forth in this chapter for obtaining an original license.

Added Stats 1961 ch 1636 § 13, operative October 1, 1962. Amended Stats 1972 ch 1138 § 8.

§ 7144. Reinstatement of revoked license

A revoked license shall be considered as having expired as of the date of revocation and shall not be renewed. To reinstate a revoked license a licensee may apply for reinstatement of the license only if he pays all of the fees and meets all of the qualifications and requirements set forth in this chapter for obtaining an original license.

Added Stats 1941 ch 971 § 20. Amended Stats 1961 ch 1636 § 14, operative October 1, 1962; Stats 1974 ch 433 § 3.

§ 7145. Incompleteness of application as grounds for refusal to renew license; Abandonment of application; Petition

The registrar may refuse to renew a license for the failure or refusal by the licensee to complete the renewal application prescribed by the registrar. If a licensee fails to return an application for renewal which was rejected for insufficiency or incompleteness within 90 days from the original date of rejection, the application and fee shall be deemed abandoned. Any application abandoned may not be reinstated. However, the applicant may file another application accompanied by the required fee.

The registrar may review and accept the petition of a licensee who disputes the invalidation of his or her application for renewal upon a showing of good cause. This petition shall be received within 90 days from the date the renewal application is deemed abandoned.

Added Stats 1941 ch 971 § 20. Amended Stats 1970 ch 524 § 2; Stats 1984 ch 1174 § 12.

§ 7145.5. Failure to resolve outstanding liabilities as grounds for refusal to renew license

(a) The registrar may refuse to issue, reinstate, reactivate, or renew a license or may suspend a license for the failure of a licensee to resolve all outstanding final liabilities, which include taxes, additions to tax, penalties, interest, and any fees that may be assessed by the board, the Department of Industrial Relations, the Employment Development Department, the Franchise Tax Board, or the State Board of Equalization.

(1) Until the debts covered by this section are satisfied, the qualifying person and any other personnel of record named on a license that has been suspended under this section shall be prohibited from serving in any capacity that is subject to licensure under this chapter, but shall be permitted to act in the capacity of a nonsupervising bona fide employee.

(2) The license of any other renewable licensed entity with any of the same personnel of record that have been assessed an outstanding liability covered by this section shall be suspended until the debt has been satisfied or until the same personnel of record disassociate themselves from the renewable licensed entity.

(b) The refusal to issue a license or the suspension of a license as provided by this section shall be applicable only if the registrar has mailed a notice preliminary to the refusal or suspension that indicates that the license will be refused or suspended by a date certain. This preliminary notice shall be mailed to the licensee at least 60 days before the date certain.

(c) In the case of outstanding final liabilities assessed by the Franchise Tax Board, this section shall be operative within 60 days after the Contractors' State License Board has provided the Franchise Tax Board with the information required under Section 30, relating to licensing information that includes the federal employee identification number or social security number.

(d) All versions of the application for contractors' licenses shall include, as part of the application, an authorization by the applicant, in the form and manner mutually agreeable to the Franchise Tax Board and the board, for the Franchise Tax Board to disclose the tax information that is required for the registrar to administer this section. The Franchise Tax Board may from time to time audit these authorizations.

(e) In the case of outstanding final liabilities assessed by the State Board of Equalization, this section shall not apply to any outstanding final liability if the licensee has entered into an installment payment agreement for that liability with the State Board of Equalization and is in compliance with the terms of that agreement.

Added Stats 1990 ch 1386 § 6 (AB 2282). Amended Stats 2006 ch 122 § 1 (AB 2456), effective January 1, 2007; Stats 2007 ch 130 § 29 (AB 299), effective January 1, 2008; Stats 2011 ch 734 § 1 (AB 1307), effective January 1, 2012.

Article 10
Home Improvement Business

§ 7150. "Person"

"Person" as used in this article is limited to natural persons, notwithstanding the definition of person in Section 7025.

Added Stats 1961 ch 1021 § 1. Amended Stats 1972 ch 1138 § 9.

§ 7150.1. "Home improvement contractor"

A home improvement contractor, including a swimming pool contractor, is a contractor as defined and licensed under this chapter who is engaged in the business of home improvement either full time or part time. A home improvement contractor shall satisfy all requirements imposed by this article.

Added Stats 1969 ch 1583 § 1 as § 7026.2. Amended and renumbered Stats 1972 ch 1138 § 1.1. Amended Stats 1991 ch 1160 § 40 (AB 2190). Amended Stats 1997 ch 888 § 1 (AB 1213).

§ 7150.2. [Section repealed 2004.]

Added Stats 1997 ch 888 § 2 (AB 1213). Repealed, operative January 1, 2004, by its own terms. The repealed section related to certification for home improvement contractors.

§ 7150.3. [Section repealed 2004.]

Added Stats 1997 ch 888 § 3 (AB 1213). Repealed, operative January 1, 2004, by its own terms. The repealed section related to qualification for home improvement contractor.

§ 7151. "Home improvement"; "Home improvement goods or services"

"Home improvement" means the repairing, remodeling, altering, converting, or modernizing of, or adding to, residential property and shall include, but not be limited to, the construction, erection, replacement, or improvement of driveways, swimming pools, including spas and hot tubs, terraces, patios, awnings, storm windows, landscaping, fences, porches, garages, fallout shelters, basements, and other improvements of the structures or land which is adjacent to a dwelling house. "Home improvement" shall also mean the installation of home improvement goods or the furnishing of home improvement services.

For purposes of this chapter, "home improvement goods or services" means goods and services, as defined in Section 1689.5 of the Civil Code, which are bought in connection with the improvement of real property. Such home improvement goods and services include, but are not limited to, carpeting, texture coating, fencing, air conditioning or heating equipment, and termite extermination. Home improvement goods include goods which are to be so affixed to real property as to become a part of real property whether or not severable therefrom.

Added Stats 1961 ch 1021 § 1. Amended Stats 1969 ch 1583 § 10; Stats 1979 ch 1012 § 2; Stats 1980 ch 138 § 3, effective May 30, 1980; Stats 1981 ch 916 § 2; Stats 1982 ch 1210 § 2; Stats 1991 ch 1160 § 41 (AB 2190).

§ 7151.2. "Home improvement contract"

"Home improvement contract" means an agreement, whether oral or written, or contained in one or more documents, between a contractor and an owner or between a contractor and a tenant, regardless of the number of residence or dwelling units contained in the building in which the tenant resides, if the work is to be performed in, to, or upon the residence or dwelling unit of the tenant, for the performance of a home improvement as defined in Section 7151, and includes all labor, services, and materials to be furnished and performed thereunder. "Home improvement contract" also means an agreement, whether oral or written, or contained in one or more documents, between a salesperson, whether or not he or she is a home improvement salesperson, and (a) an owner or (b) a tenant, regardless of the number of residence or dwelling units contained in the building in which the tenant resides, which provides for the sale, installation, or furnishing of home improvement goods or services.

Added Stats 1969 ch 1583 § 11. Amended Stats 1979 ch 1012 § 3; Stats 1991 ch 1160 § 42 (AB 2190).

Section VI

—See Civil Code Sections 1689.5, Home Solicitation Contract;1689.6, Cancellation of Home Solicitation Contract;1689.7, Form of Notice of Cancellation; 1689.8 Contract which provides for Lien; 1689.9, Exemptions: 1689.10, After Cancellation, Seller to Return Downpayment; 1689.11, Buyer to Return Goods; 1689.12, Invalidity of Waiver of Statute; 1689.13, Notice Not Required for Emergency Situations; 1689.14, Void Contracts, in Appendix.

§ 7152.   "Home improvement salesperson"

(a) "Home improvement salesperson" is a person employed by a home improvement contractor licensed under this chapter to solicit, sell, negotiate, or execute contracts for home improvements, for the sale, installation or furnishing of home improvement goods or services, or of swimming pools, spas, or hot tubs.

(b) The following shall not be required to be registered as home improvement salespersons:

(1) An officer of record of a corporation licensed pursuant to this chapter, or a manager of record of a limited liability company licensed pursuant to this chapter.

(2) A general partner listed on the license record of a partnership licensed pursuant to this chapter.

(3) A qualifying person, as defined in Section 7025.

(4) A salesperson whose sales are all made pursuant to negotiations between the parties if the negotiations are initiated by the prospective buyer at or with a general merchandise retail establishment that operates from a fixed location where goods or services are offered for sale.

(5) A person who contacts the prospective buyer for the exclusive purpose of scheduling appointments for a registered home improvement salesperson.

(6) A bona fide service repairperson who is in the employ of a licensed contractor and whose repair or service call is limited to the service, repair, or emergency repair initially requested by the buyer of the service.

(c) The exemption to registration provided under paragraphs (1), (2), and (3) of subdivision (b) shall apply only to those individuals who, at the time of the sales transaction, are listed as personnel of record for the licensee responsible for soliciting, negotiating, or contracting for a service or improvement that is subject to regulation under this article.

Added Stats 1972 ch 1138 § 11. Amended Stats 1973 ch 115 § 1, effective June 26, 1973; Stats 1979 ch 1012 § 4; Stats 1980 ch 138 § 4, effective May 30, 1980; Stats 1982 ch 585 § 1; Stats 1985 ch 1281 § 4; Stats 1991 ch 1160 § 43 (AB 2190); Stats 2006 ch 106 § 4 (AB 2457), effective January 1, 2007; Stats 2010 ch 698 § 38 (SB 392), effective January 1, 2011.

—*See Civil Code Sections 1804.3, Security Interest in Goods Paid For Not Sold; Security Interest unreal Property for Sale of Unattached Goods; 1805.6, Undelivered Goods; 1810.10, Finance Charge, in Appendix.*

§ 7153. Selling without registration

(a) It is a misdemeanor for any person to engage in the occupation of salesperson for one or more home improvement contractors within this state without having a registration issued by the registrar for each of the home improvement contractors by whom he or she is employed as a home improvement salesperson. If, upon investigation, the registrar has probable cause to believe that a salesperson is in violation of this section, the registrar may issue a citation pursuant to Section 7028.7.

It is a misdemeanor for any person to engage in the occupation of salesperson of home improvement goods or services within this state without having a registration issued by the registrar.

(b) Any security interest taken by a contractor, to secure any payment for the performance of any act or conduct described in Section 7151 that occurs on or after January 1, 1995, is unenforceable if the person soliciting the act or contract was not a duly registered salesperson or was not exempt from registration pursuant to Section 7152 at the time the homeowner signs the home improvement contract solicited by the salesperson.

Added Stats 1972 ch 1138 § 13. Amended Stats 1979 ch 1012 § 5; Stats 1994 ch 888 § 1 (AB 3269); Stats 2001 ch 728 § 63 (SB 724).

§ 7153.1. Salesperson's application for registration; Grounds for denial; Fingerprints of applicants; Criminal history and subsequent arrest information

(a) The home improvement salesperson shall submit to the registrar an application in writing containing the statement that he or she desires the issuance of a registration under the terms of this article.

The application shall be made on a form prescribed by the registrar and shall be accompanied by the fee fixed by this chapter.

(b) The registrar may refuse to register the applicant under the grounds specified in Section 480.

(c) As part of an application for a home improvement salesperson, the board shall require an applicant to furnish a full set of fingerprints for purposes of conducting criminal history record checks. Fingerprints furnished pursuant to this subdivision shall be submitted in an electronic format where readily available. Requests for alternative methods of furnishing fingerprints are subject to the approval of the registrar. The board shall use the fingerprints furnished by an applicant to obtain criminal history information on the applicant from the

Section VI

Department of Justice and the United States Federal Bureau of Investigation, including any subsequent arrest information available.

Added Stats 1972 ch 1138 § 14. Amended Stats 1978 ch 1161 § 368; Stats 2002 ch 744 § 10 (SB 1953); Stats 2003 ch 789 § 18 (SB 364); Stats 2004 ch 909 § 27.5 (SB 136), effective September 30, 2004; Stats 2007 ch 240 § 3 (AB 936), effective January 1, 2008.

§ 7153.2.   Expiration of registrations

All registrations issued under the provisions of this article shall expire on a date established pursuant to Section 152.6.

Added Stats 1972 ch 1138 § 15. Amended Stats 1983 ch 891 § 33; Stats 1991 ch 1160 § 44 (AB 2190).

§ 7153.3.   Renewal of registration; Delinquent renewal penalty; Abandonment of application; Petition

(a) To renew a registration, the registrant shall before the time at which the registration would otherwise expire, apply for renewal on a form prescribed by the registrar and pay a renewal fee prescribed by this chapter.

(b) An application for renewal of registration is delinquent if the application is not postmarked by the date on which the registration would otherwise expire. A registration may, however, still be renewed at any time within three years after its expiration upon the filing of an application for renewal on a form prescribed by the registrar and the payment of the renewal fee prescribed by this chapter and a delinquent renewal penalty in the amount of twenty-five dollars ($25). If a registration is not renewed within three years, the person shall make application for registration pursuant to Section 7153.1.

(c) The registrar may refuse to renew a registration for failure by the registrant to complete the application for renewal of registration. If a registrant fails to return the application rejected for insufficiency or incompleteness within 90 days from the original date of rejection, the application and fee shall be deemed abandoned. Any application abandoned may not be reinstated. However, the person may file a new application for registration pursuant to Section 7153.1.

The registrar may review and accept the petition of a person who disputes the abandonment of his or her renewal application upon a showing of good cause. This petition shall be received within 90 days of the date the application for renewal is deemed abandoned.

Added Stats 1972 ch 1138 § 16. Amended Stats 1984 ch 1174 § 13.

§ 7154.   Discipline for employment of unregistered salesman

A home improvement contractor who employs a person to sell home improvement contracts while such person is not registered by the registrar as a home improvement salesman as provided in this article, is subject to disciplinary action by the registrar.

Added Stats 1972 ch 1138 § 18.

§ 7155. Discipline of salesman

Violation of any provision of this chapter by a home improvement salesperson constitutes cause for disciplinary action. The registrar may suspend or revoke the registration of the home improvement salesperson if he or she is found to be in violation. The disciplinary proceedings shall be conducted in accordance with Chapter 5 (commencing with Section 11500) of Part 1 of Division 3 of Title 2 of the Government Code.

Added Stats 1972 ch 1138 § 20. Amended Stats 2011 ch 296 § 16 (AB 1023), effective January 1, 2012.

§ 7155.5. Discipline of contractor for salesman's violations

Violations of any provisions of this chapter by a home improvement salesperson, likewise constitutes a cause for disciplinary action against the contractor, whether or not he or she had knowledge of or participated in the act or omission constituting violations of this chapter.

Added Stats 1972 ch 1138 § 21. Amended Stats 1997 ch 812 § 5 (SB 857), ch 813 § 3 (SB 825).

§ 7156. Misdemeanors; Grounds for discipline

It shall be a misdemeanor and a cause for disciplinary action to commit any of the following acts:

(a) For any salesperson to fail to account for or to remit to his or her employing contractor any payment received in connection with any home improvement transaction or any other transaction involving a work of improvement.

(b) For any person to use a contract form in connection with any home improvement transaction or any other transaction involving a work of improvement if the form fails to disclose the name of the contractor principal by whom he or she is employed.

Added Stats 1969 ch 1583 § 2 as § 7026.8. Amended and Renumbered Stats 1972 ch 1138 § 1.2; Stats 1997 ch 812 § 6 (SB 857), ch 813 § 4 (SB 825).

§ 7157. Prohibited inducements

(a) Except as otherwise provided in subdivision (b), as a part of or in connection with the inducement to enter into any home improvement contract or other contract, which may be performed by a contractor, no person may promise or offer to pay, credit, or allow to any owner, compensation or reward for the procurement or placing of home improvement business with others.

(b) A contractor or his or her agent or salesperson may give tangible items to prospective customers for advertising or sales promotion purposes where the gift is not conditioned upon obtaining a contract for home improvement work if the gift does not exceed a value of five dollars ($5) and only one such gift is given in connection with any one transaction.

(c) No salesperson or contractor's agent may accept any compensation of any kind, for or on account of a home improvement transaction, or any other transaction involving a work of improvement, from any person other than the contractor whom he or she represents with respect to the transaction, nor shall the salesperson or agent make any payment to any person other than his or her employer on account of the sales transaction.

(d) No contractor shall pay, credit, or allow any consideration or compensation of any kind to any other contractor or salesperson other than a licensee for or on account of the performance of any work of improvement or services, including, but not limited to, home improvement work or services, except: (1) where the person to or from whom the consideration is to be paid is not subject to or is exempted from the licensing requirements of this chapter, or (2) where the transaction is not subject to the requirements of this chapter.

As used in this section "owners" shall also mean "tenant."

Commission of any act prohibited by this section is a misdemeanor and constitutes a cause for disciplinary action.

Added Stats 1969 ch 1583 § 3, as B & P C § 7026.9. Renumbered by Stats 1972 ch 1138 § 1.3. Amended Stats 1997 ch 812 § 7 (SB 857), ch 813 § 5 (SB 825).

§ 7158. False completion certificates

(a) Any person who shall accept or receive a completion certificate or other evidence that performance of a contract for a work of improvement, including but not limited to a home improvement, is complete or satisfactorily concluded, with knowledge thatthe document is false and that the performance is not substantially completed, and who shall utter, offer, or use the document in connection with the making or accepting of any assignment or negotiation of the right to receive any payment from the owner, under or in connection with a contract, or for the purpose of obtaining or granting any credit or loan on the security of the right to receive any payment shall be guilty of a misdemeanor and subject to a fine of not less than five hundred dollars ($500) nor more than five thousand dollars ($5,000), or to imprisonment in the county jail for a term of not less than one month nor more than one year, or both.

(b) Any person who violates this section as part of a plan or scheme to defraud an owner of a residential or nonresidential structure, including a mobilehome or manufactured home, in connection with the offer or performance of repairs to the structure for damage caused by a natural disaster, shall be ordered by the court to make full restitution to the victim based on the person's ability to pay, as defined in subdivision (e) of Section 1203.1b of the Penal Code. In addition to full restitution, and imprisonment authorized by subdivision (a), the court may impose a fine of not less than five hundred dollars ($500) nor more than twenty-five thousand dollars ($25,000), based upon the defendant's ability to pay. This subdivision applies to natural disasters for which a state of emergency is proclaimed by the Governor pursuant to Section 8625 of the Government Code or for which an emergency or major disaster is declared by the President of the United States.

Added Stats 1969 ch 1583 § 5 as § 7028.1. Amended and renumbered Stats 1972 ch 1138 § 1.4. Amended Stats 1994 ch 175 § 2 (SB 634), effective July 9, 1994.

—See Penal Code Section 532e, Rebates, in Appendix.

§ 7159. Requirements for home improvement contracts (First of two; Operative until July 1, 2012)

(a) (1) This section identifies the projects for which a home improvement contract is required, outlines the contract requirements, and lists the items that shall be included in the contract, or may be provided as an attachment.

(2) This section does not apply to service and repair contracts that are subject to Section 7159.10, if the contract for the applicable services complies with Sections 7159.10 to 7159.14, inclusive.

(3) This section does not apply to the sale, installation, and servicing of a fire alarm sold in conjunction with an alarm system, as defined in subdivision (n) of Section 7590.1, if all costs attributable to making the fire alarm system operable, including sale and installation costs, do not exceed five hundred dollars ($500), and the licensee complies with the requirements set forth in Section 7159.9.

(4) This section does not apply to any costs associated with monitoring a burglar or fire alarm system.

(5) Failure by the licensee, his or her agent or salesperson, or by a person subject to be licensed under this chapter, to provide the specified information, notices, and disclosures in the contract, or to otherwise fail to comply with any provision of this section, is cause for discipline.

(b) For purposes of this section, "home improvement contract" means an agreement, whether oral or written, or contained in one or more documents, between a contractor and an owner or between a contractor and a tenant, regardless of the number of residence or dwelling units contained in the building in which the tenant resides, if the work is to be performed in, to, or upon the residence or dwelling unit of the tenant, for the performance of a home improvement, as defined in Section 7151, and includes all labor, services, and materials to be furnished and performed thereunder, if the aggregate contract price specified in one or more improvement contracts, including all labor, services, and materials to be furnished by the contractor, exceeds five hundred dollars ($500). "Home improvement contract" also means an agreement, whether oral or written, or contained in one or more documents, between a salesperson, whether or not he or she is a home improvement salesperson, and an owner or a tenant, regardless of the number of residence or dwelling units contained in the building in which the tenant resides, which provides for the sale, installation, or furnishing of home improvement goods or services.

(c) In addition to the specific requirements listed under this section, every home improvement contract and any person subject to licensure under this chapter or his or her agent or salesperson shall comply with all of the following:

(1) The writing shall be legible.

(2) Any printed form shall be readable. Unless a larger typeface is specified in this article, text in any printed form shall be in at least 10-point typeface and the headings shall be in at least 10-point boldface type.

(3) (A) Before any work is started, the contractor shall give the buyer a copy of the contract signed and dated by both the contractor and the buyer. The buyer's receipt of the copy of the contract initiates the buyer's rights to cancel the contract pursuant to Sections 1689.5 to 1689.14, inclusive, of the Civil Code.

(B) The contract shall contain on the first page, in a typeface no smaller than that generally used in the body of the document, both of the following:

(i) The date the buyer signed the contract.

(ii) The name and address of the contractor to which the applicable "Notice of Cancellation" is to be mailed, immediately preceded by a statement advising the buyer that the "Notice of Cancellation" may be sent to the contractor at the address noted on the contract.

(4) The contract shall include a statement that, upon satisfactory payment being made for any portion of the work performed, the contractor, prior to any further payment being made, shall furnish to the person contracting for the home improvement or swimming pool work a full and unconditional release from any potential lien claimant claim or mechanic's lien authorized pursuant to Section 3110 of the Civil Code for that portion of the work for which payment has been made.

(5) A change-order form for changes or extra work shall be incorporated into the contract and shall become part of the contract only if it

is in writing and signed by the parties prior to the commencement of any work covered by a change order.

(6) The contract shall contain, in close proximity to the signatures of the owner and contractor, a notice stating that the owner or tenant has the right to require the contractor to have a performance and payment bond.

(7) If the contract provides for a contractor to furnish joint control, the contractor shall not have any financial or other interest in the joint control.

(8) The provisions of this section are not exclusive and do not relieve the contractor from compliance with any other applicable provision of law.

(d) A home improvement contract and any changes to the contract shall be in writing and signed by the parties to the contract prior to the commencement of work covered by the contract or an applicable change order and, except as provided in paragraph (8) of subdivision (a) of Section 7159.5, shall include or comply with all of the following:

(1) The name, business address, and license number of the contractor.

(2) If applicable, the name and registration number of the home improvement salesperson that solicited or negotiated the contract.

(3) The following heading on the contract form that identifies the type of contract in at least 10-point boldface type: "Home Improvement."

(4) The following statement in at least 12-point boldface type: "You are entitled to a completely filled in copy of this agreement, signed by both you and the contractor, before any work may be started."

(5) The heading: "Contract Price," followed by the amount of the contract in dollars and cents.

(6) If a finance charge will be charged, the heading: "Finance Charge," followed by the amount in dollars and cents. The finance charge is to be set out separately from the contract amount.

(7) The heading: "Description of the Project and Description of the Significant Materials to be Used and Equipment to be Installed," followed by a description of the project and a description of the significant materials to be used and equipment to be installed. For swimming pools, the project description required under this paragraph also shall include a plan and scale drawing showing the shape, size, dimensions, and the construction and equipment specifications.

(8) If a downpayment will be charged, the details of the downpayment shall be expressed in substantially the following form, and shall include the text of the notice as specified in subparagraph (C):

(A) The heading: "Downpayment."

(B) A space where the actual downpayment appears.

(C) The following statement in at least 12-point boldface type:

"THE DOWNPAYMENT MAY NOT EXCEED $1,000 OR 10 PERCENT OF THE CONTRACT PRICE, WHICHEVER IS LESS."

(9) If payments, other than the downpayment, are to be made before the project is completed, the details of these payments, known as progress payments, shall be expressed in substantially the following form, and shall include the text of the statement as specified in subparagraph (C):

(A) A schedule of progress payments shall be preceded by the heading: "Schedule of Progress Payments."

(B) Each progress payment shall be stated in dollars and cents and specifically reference the amount of work or services to be performed and materials and equipment to be supplied.

(C) The section of the contract reserved for the progress payments shall include the following statement in at least 12-point boldface type:

"The schedule of progress payments must specifically describe each phase of work, including the type and amount of work or services scheduled to be supplied in each phase, along with the amount of each proposed progress payment. IT IS AGAINST THE LAW FOR A CONTRACTOR TO COLLECT PAYMENT FOR WORK NOT YET COMPLETED, OR FOR MATERIALS NOT YET DELIVERED. HOWEVER, A CONTRACTOR MAY REQUIRE A DOWNPAYMENT."

(10) The contract shall address the commencement of work to be performed in substantially the following form:

(A) A statement that describes what constitutes substantial commencement of work under the contract.

(B) The heading: "Approximate Start Date."

(C) The approximate date on which work will be commenced.

(11) The estimated completion date of the work shall be referenced in the contract in substantially the following form:

(A) The heading: "Approximate Completion Date."

(B) The approximate date of completion.

(12) If applicable, the heading: "List of Documents to be Incorporated into the Contract," followed by the list of documents incorporated into the contract.

(13) The heading: "Note About Extra Work and Change Orders," followed by the following statement:

"Extra Work and Change Orders become part of the contract once the order is prepared in writing and signed by the parties prior to the commencement of work covered by the new change order. The order must describe the scope of the extra work or change, the cost to be added or subtracted from the contract, and the effect the order will have on the schedule of progress payments."

(e) Except as provided in paragraph (8) of subdivision (a) of Section 7159.5, all of the following notices shall be provided to the owner as part of the contract form as specified or, if otherwise authorized under this subdivision, may be provided as an attachment to the contract:

(1) A notice concerning commercial general liability insurance. This notice may be provided as an attachment to the contract if the contract includes the following statement: "A notice concerning commercial general liability insurance is attached to this contract." The notice shall include the heading "Commercial General Liability Insurance (CGL)," followed by whichever of the following statements is both relevant and correct:

(A) "(The name on the license or 'This contractor') does not carry commercial general liability insurance."

(B) "(The name on the license or 'This contractor') carries commercial general liability insurance written by (the insurance company). You may call (the insurance company) at _____ _____ to check the contractor's insurance coverage."

(C) "(The name on the license or 'This contractor') is self-insured."

(D) "(The name on the license or 'This contractor') is a limited liability company that carries liability insurance or maintains other security as required by law. You may call (the insurance company or trust company or bank) at _____ _____ to check on the contractor's insurance coverage or security."

(2) A notice concerning workers' compensation insurance. This notice may be provided as an attachment to the contract if the contract includes the statement: "A notice concerning workers' compensation insurance is attached to this contract." The notice shall include the heading "Workers' Compensation Insurance" followed by whichever of the following statements is correct:

(A) "(The name on the license or 'This contractor') has no employees and is exempt from workers' compensation requirements."

(B) "(The name on the license or 'This contractor') carries workers' compensation insurance for all employees."

(3) A notice that provides the buyer with the following information about the performance of extra or change-order work:

(A) A statement that the buyer may not require a contractor to perform extra or change-order work without providing written authorization prior to the commencement of work covered by the new change order.

(B) A statement informing the buyer that extra work or a change order is not enforceable against a buyer unless the change order also identifies all of the following in writing prior to the commencement of work covered by the new change order:

(i) The scope of work encompassed by the order.

(ii) The amount to be added or subtracted from the contract.

(iii) The effect the order will make in the progress payments or the completion date.

(C) A statement informing the buyer that the contractor's failure to comply with the requirements of this paragraph does not preclude the recovery of compensation for work performed based upon legal or equitable remedies designed to prevent unjust enrichment.

(4) A notice with the heading "Mechanics' Lien Warning" written as follows:

"MECHANICS LIEN WARNING:

Anyone who helps improve your property, but who is not paid, may record what is called a mechanics' lien on your property. A mechanics' lien is a claim, like a mortgage or home equity loan, made against your property and recorded with the county recorder.

Even if you pay your contractor in full, unpaid subcontractors, suppliers, and laborers who helped to improve your property may record mechanics' liens and sue you in court to foreclose the lien. If a court finds the lien is valid, you could be forced to pay twice or have a court officer sell your home to pay the lien. Liens can also affect your credit.

To preserve their right to record a lien, each subcontractor and material supplier must provide you with a document called a '20-day Preliminary Notice.' This notice is not a lien. The purpose of the notice is to let you know that the person who sends you the notice has the right to record a lien on your property if he or she is not paid.

BE CAREFUL. The Preliminary Notice can be sent up to 20 days after the subcontractor starts work or the supplier provides material. This can be a big problem if you pay your contractor before you have received the Preliminary Notices.

You will not get Preliminary Notices from your prime contractor or from laborers who work on your project. The law assumes that you already know they are improving your property.

PROTECT YOURSELF FROM LIENS. You can protect yourself from liens by getting a list from your contractor of all the subcontractors and material suppliers that work on your project. Find out from your contractor when these subcontractors started work and when these suppliers delivered goods or materials. Then wait 20 days, paying attention to the Preliminary Notices you receive.

PAY WITH JOINT CHECKS. One way to protect yourself is to pay with a joint check. When your contractor tells you it is time to pay for the work of a subcontractor or supplier who has provided you with a Preliminary Notice, write a joint check payable to both the contractor and the subcontractor or material supplier.

For other ways to prevent liens, visit CSLB's Internet Web site at www.cslb.ca.gov or call CSLB at 800-321-CSLB (2752).

REMEMBER, IF YOU DO NOTHING, YOU RISK HAVING A LIEN PLACED ON YOUR HOME. This can mean that you may have

to pay twice, or face the forced sale of your home to pay what you owe."

(5) The following notice shall be provided in at least 12-point typeface:

"Information about the Contractors' State License Board (CSLB): CSLB is the state consumer protection agency that licenses and regulates construction contractors.

Contact CSLB for information about the licensed contractor you are considering, including information about disclosable complaints, disciplinary actions, and civil judgments that are reported to CSLB.

Use only licensed contractors. If you file a complaint against a licensed contractor within the legal deadline (usually four years), CSLB has authority to investigate the complaint. If you use an unlicensed contractor, CSLB may not be able to help you resolve your complaint. Your only remedy may be in civil court, and you may be liable for damages arising out of any injuries to the unlicensed contractor or the unlicensed contractor's employees.

For more information:

Visit CSLB's Internet Web site at www.cslb.ca.gov

Call CSLB at 800-321-CSLB (2752)

Write CSLB at P.O. Box 26000, Sacramento, CA 95826."

(6) (A) The notice set forth in subparagraph (B) and entitled "Three-Day Right to Cancel," shall be provided to the buyer unless the contract is:

(i) Negotiated at the contractor's place of business.

(ii) Subject to the "Seven-Day Right to Cancel," as set forth in paragraph (7).

(iii) Subject to licensure under the Alarm Company Act (Chapter 11.6 (commencing with Section 7590)), provided the alarm company licensee complies with Sections 1689.5, 1689.6, and 1689.7 of the Civil Code, as applicable.

(B) "Three-Day Right to Cancel

You, the buyer, have the right to cancel this contract within three business days. You may cancel by e-mailing, mailing, faxing, or delivering a written notice to the contractor at the contractor's place of business by midnight of the third business day after you received a signed and dated copy of the contract that includes this notice. Include your name, your address, and the date you received the signed copy of the contract and this notice.

If you cancel, the contractor must return to you anything you paid within 10 days of receiving the notice of cancellation. For your part, you must make available to the contractor at your residence, in substantially as good condition as you received them, goods delivered to you under this contract or sale. Or, you may, if you wish, comply with the contractor's instructions on how to return the goods at the contractor's expense and risk. If you do make the goods available to the contractor and the contractor does not pick them up within 20 days of the date of your notice of cancellation, you may keep them without any further obligation. If you fail to make the goods available to the contractor, or if you agree to return the goods to the contractor and fail to do so, then you remain liable for performance of all obligations under the contract."

(C) The "Three-Day Right to Cancel" notice required by this paragraph shall comply with all of the following:

(i) The text of the notice is at least 12-point boldface type.

(ii) The notice is in immediate proximity to a space reserved for the owner's signature.

(iii) The owner acknowledges receipt of the notice by signing and dating the notice form in the signature space.

(iv) The notice is written in the same language, e.g., Spanish, as that principally used in any oral sales presentation.

(v) The notice may be attached to the contract if the contract includes, in at least 12-point boldface type, a checkbox with the following statement: "The law requires that the contractor give you a notice explaining your right to cancel. Initial the checkbox if the contractor has given you a 'Notice of the Three-Day Right to Cancel.'"

(vi) The notice shall be accompanied by a completed form in duplicate, captioned "Notice of Cancellation," which also shall be attached to the agreement or offer to purchase and be easily detachable, and which shall contain the following statement written in the same language, e.g., Spanish, as used in the contract:

"Notice of Cancellation"

_____
/enter date of transaction/
(Date)

"You may cancel this transaction, without any penalty or obligation, within three business days from the above date.

If you cancel, any property traded in, any payments made by you under the contract or sale, and any negotiable instrument executed by you will be returned within 10 days following receipt by the seller of your cancellation notice, and any security interest arising out of the transaction will be canceled.

If you cancel, you must make available to the seller at your residence, in substantially as good condition as when received, any goods delivered to you under this contract or sale, or you may, if you wish, comply with the instructions of the seller regarding the return shipment of the goods at the seller's expense and risk.

If you do make the goods available to the seller and the seller does not pick them up within 20 days of the date of your notice of cancellation, you may retain or dispose of the goods without any further obligation. If you fail to make the goods available to the seller, or if you agree to return the goods to the seller and fail to do so, then you remain liable for performance of all obligations under the contract."

To cancel this transaction, mail or deliver a signed and dated copy of this cancellation notice, or any other written notice, or send a telegram to _____,

/name of seller/

at _____

/address of seller's place of business/

not later than midnight of _____.

(Date)

I hereby cancel this transaction. _____

(Date)

_____

(Buyer's signature)

(7) (A) The following notice entitled "Seven-Day Right to Cancel" shall be provided to the buyer for any contract that is written for the repair or restoration of residential premises damaged by any sudden or catastrophic event for which a state of emergency has been declared by the President of the United States or the Governor, or for which a local emergency has been declared by the executive officer or governing body of any city, county, or city and county:

"Seven-Day Right to Cancel

You, the buyer, have the right to cancel this contract within seven business days. You may cancel by e-mailing, mailing, faxing, or delivering a written notice to the contractor at the contractor's place of business by midnight of the seventh business day after you received a signed and dated copy of the contract that includes this notice. Include your name, your address, and the date you received the signed copy of the contract and this notice.

If you cancel, the contractor must return to you anything you paid within 10 days of receiving the notice of cancellation. For your part, you must make available to the contractor at your residence, in substantially as good condition as you received them, goods delivered to you under this contract or sale. Or, you may, if you wish, comply with the contractor's instructions on how to return the goods at the contractor's expense and risk. If you do make the goods available to the contractor and the contractor does not pick them up within 20 days of the date of your notice of cancellation, you may keep them without any further obligation. If you fail to make the goods available to the contractor, or if you agree to return the goods to the contractor and fail to do so, then you remain liable for performance of all obligations under the contract."

(B) The "Seven-Day Right to Cancel" notice required by this subdivision shall comply with all of the following:

(i) The text of the notice is at least 12-point boldface type.

(ii) The notice is in immediate proximity to a space reserved for the owner's signature.

(iii) The owner acknowledges receipt of the notice by signing and dating the notice form in the signature space.

(iv) The notice is written in the same language, e.g., Spanish, as that principally used in any oral sales presentation.

(v) The notice may be attached to the contract if the contract includes, in at least 12-point boldface type, a checkbox with the following statement: "The law requires that the contractor give you a notice explaining your right to cancel. Initial the checkbox if the contractor has given you a 'Notice of the Seven-Day Right to Cancel.'"

(vi) The notice shall be accompanied by a completed form in duplicate, captioned "Notice of Cancellation," which shall also be attached to the agreement or offer to purchase and be easily detachable, and which shall contain the following statement written in the same language, e.g., Spanish, as used in the contract:

"Notice of Cancellation"

_____
/enter date of transaction/
(Date)

"You may cancel this transaction, without any penalty or obligation, within seven business days from the above date.

If you cancel, any property traded in, any payments made by you under the contract or sale, and any negotiable instrument executed by you will be returned within 10 days following receipt by the seller of your cancellation notice, and any security interest arising out of the transaction will be canceled.

If you cancel, you must make available to the seller at your residence, in substantially as good condition as when received, any goods delivered to you under this contract or sale, or you may, if you wish, comply with the instructions of the seller regarding the return shipment of the goods at the seller's expense and risk.

If you do make the goods available to the seller and the seller does not pick them up within 20 days of the date of your notice of cancellation, you may retain or dispose of the goods without any further obligation. If you fail to make the goods available to the seller, or if you agree to return the goods to the seller and fail to do so, then you remain liable for performance of all obligations under the contract."

To cancel this transaction, mail or deliver a signed and dated copy of this cancellation notice, or any other written notice, or send a telegram to _____,

/name of seller/

at _____
/address of seller's place of business/

not later than midnight of _____.
(Date)
I hereby cancel this transaction. _____
(Date)

_____
(Buyer's signature)

Added Stats 2005 ch 48 § 7 (SB 1113), effective July 18, 2005, operative January 1,
2006. Amended Stats 2005 ch 385 § 2 (AB 316), effective January 1, 2006; Stats 2006
ch 114 § 1 (AB 2073), effective January 1, 2007; Stats 2007 ch 130 § 30 (AB 299), effective January 1, 2008, Stats 2007 ch 230 § 1 (AB 244), effective January 1, 2008, (ch 230
prevails); Stats 2008 ch 179 § 18 (SB 1498), effective January 1, 2009; Stats 2009 ch
307 § 74 (SB 821), effective January 1, 2010; Stats 2010 ch 697 § 4 (SB 189), effective
January 1, 2011, operative July 1, 2012, ch 698 § 39 (SB 392) (ch 698 prevails), effective January 1, 2011.

§ 7159. Requirements for home improvement contracts (Second of two; Operative July 1, 2012)

(a) (1) This section identifies the projects for which a home improvement contract is required, outlines the contract requirements,
and lists the items that shall be included in the contract, or may be
provided as an attachment.

(2) This section does not apply to service and repair contracts that
are subject to Section 7159.10, if the contract for the applicable services complies with Sections 7159.10 to 7159.14, inclusive.

(3) This section does not apply to the sale, installation, and servicing of a fire alarm sold in conjunction with an alarm system, as defined in subdivision (n) of Section 7590.1, if all costs attributable to
making the fire alarm system operable, including sale and installation costs, do not exceed five hundred dollars ($500), and the licensee
complies with the requirements set forth in Section 7159.9.

(4) This section does not apply to any costs associated with monitoring a burglar or fire alarm system.

(5) Failure by the licensee, his or her agent or salesperson, or by a
person subject to be licensed under this chapter, to provide the specified information, notices, and disclosures in the contract, or to otherwise fail to comply with any provision of this section, is cause for discipline.

(b) For purposes of this section, "home improvement contract"
means an agreement, whether oral or written, or contained in one or
more documents, between a contractor and an owner or between a
contractor and a tenant, regardless of the number of residence or
dwelling units contained in the building in which the tenant resides,

Section VI

if the work is to be performed in, to, or upon the residence or dwelling unit of the tenant, for the performance of a home improvement, as defined in Section 7151, and includes all labor, services, and materials to be furnished and performed thereunder, if the aggregate contract price specified in one or more improvement contracts, including all labor, services, and materials to be furnished by the contractor, exceeds five hundred dollars ($500). "Home improvement contract" also means an agreement, whether oral or written, or contained in one or more documents, between a salesperson, whether or not he or she is a home improvement salesperson, and an owner or a tenant, regardless of the number of residence or dwelling units contained in the building in which the tenant resides, which provides for the sale, installation, or furnishing of home improvement goods or services.

(c) In addition to the specific requirements listed under this section, every home improvement contract and any person subject to licensure under this chapter or his or her agent or salesperson shall comply with all of the following:

(1) The writing shall be legible.

(2) Any printed form shall be readable. Unless a larger typeface is specified in this article, text in any printed form shall be in at least 10-point typeface and the headings shall be in at least 10-point boldface type.

(3) (A) Before any work is started, the contractor shall give the buyer a copy of the contract signed and dated by both the contractor and the buyer. The buyer's receipt of the copy of the contract initiates the buyer's rights to cancel the contract pursuant to Sections 1689.5 to 1689.14, inclusive, of the Civil Code.

(B) The contract shall contain on the first page, in a typeface no smaller than that generally used in the body of the document, both of the following:

(i) The date the buyer signed the contract.

(ii) The name and address of the contractor to which the applicable "Notice of Cancellation" is to be mailed, immediately preceded by a statement advising the buyer that the "Notice of Cancellation" may be sent to the contractor at the address noted on the contract.

(4) The contract shall include a statement that, upon satisfactory payment being made for any portion of the work performed, the contractor, prior to any further payment being made, shall furnish to the person contracting for the home improvement or swimming pool work a full and unconditional release from any potential lien claimant claim or mechanics lien authorized pursuant to Sections 8400 and 8404 of the Civil Code for that portion of the work for which payment has been made.

(5) A change-order form for changes or extra work shall be incorporated into the contract and shall become part of the contract only if it

is in writing and signed by the parties prior to the commencement of any work covered by a change order.

(6) The contract shall contain, in close proximity to the signatures of the owner and contractor, a notice stating that the owner or tenant has the right to require the contractor to have a performance and payment bond.

(7) If the contract provides for a contractor to furnish joint control, the contractor shall not have any financial or other interest in the joint control.

(8) The provisions of this section are not exclusive and do not relieve the contractor from compliance with any other applicable provision of law.

(d) A home improvement contract and any changes to the contract shall be in writing and signed by the parties to the contract prior to the commencement of work covered by the contract or an applicable change order and, except as provided in paragraph (8) of subdivision (a) of Section 7159.5, shall include or comply with all of the following:

(1) The name, business address, and license number of the contractor.

(2) If applicable, the name and registration number of the home improvement salesperson that solicited or negotiated the contract.

(3) The following heading on the contract form that identifies the type of contract in at least 10-point boldface type: "Home Improvement."

(4) The following statement in at least 12-point boldface type: "You are entitled to a completely filled in copy of this agreement, signed by both you and the contractor, before any work may be started."

(5) The heading: "Contract Price," followed by the amount of the contract in dollars and cents.

(6) If a finance charge will be charged, the heading: "Finance Charge," followed by the amount in dollars and cents. The finance charge is to be set out separately from the contract amount.

(7) The heading: "Description of the Project and Description of the Significant Materials to be Used and Equipment to be Installed," followed by a description of the project and a description of the significant materials to be used and equipment to be installed. For swimming pools, the project description required under this paragraph also shall include a plan and scale drawing showing the shape, size, dimensions, and the construction and equipment specifications.

(8) If a downpayment will be charged, the details of the downpayment shall be expressed in substantially the following form, and shall include the text of the notice as specified in subparagraph (C):

(A) The heading: "Downpayment."

(B) A space where the actual downpayment appears.

(C) The following statement in at least 12-point boldface type:

"THE DOWNPAYMENT MAY NOT EXCEED $1,000 OR 10 PER-
CENT OF THE CONTRACT PRICE, WHICHEVER IS LESS."

(9) If payments, other than the downpayment, are to be made before the project is completed, the details of these payments, known as
progress payments, shall be expressed in substantially the following
form, and shall include the text of the statement as specified in subparagraph (C):

(A) A schedule of progress payments shall be preceded by the heading: "Schedule of Progress Payments."

(B) Each progress payment shall be stated in dollars and cents and
specifically reference the amount of work or services to be performed
and materials and equipment to be supplied.

(C) The section of the contract reserved for the progress payments
shall include the following statement in at least 12-point boldface
type:

"The schedule of progress payments must specifically describe each
phase of work, including the type and amount of work or services
scheduled to be supplied in each phase, along with the amount of
each proposed progress payment. IT IS AGAINST THE LAW FOR A
CONTRACTOR TO COLLECT PAYMENT FOR WORK NOT YET
COMPLETED, OR FOR MATERIALS NOT YET DELIVERED.
HOWEVER, A CONTRACTOR MAY REQUIRE A DOWNPAY-
MENT."

(10) The contract shall address the commencement of work to be
performed in substantially the following form:

(A) A statement that describes what constitutes substantial commencement of work under the contract.

(B) The heading: "Approximate Start Date."

(C) The approximate date on which work will be commenced.

(11) The estimated completion date of the work shall be referenced
in the contract in substantially the following form:

(A) The heading: "Approximate Completion Date."

(B) The approximate date of completion.

(12) If applicable, the heading: "List of Documents to be Incorporated into the Contract," followed by the list of documents incorporated into the contract.

(13) The heading: "Note About Extra Work and Change Orders," followed by the following statement:

"Extra Work and Change Orders become part of the contract once
the order is prepared in writing and signed by the parties prior to the
commencement of work covered by the new change order. The order
must describe the scope of the extra work or change, the cost to be
added or subtracted from the contract, and the effect the order will
have on the schedule of progress payments."

(e) Except as provided in paragraph (8) of subdivision (a) of Section
7159.5, all of the following notices shall be provided to the owner as

part of the contract form as specified or, if otherwise authorized under this subdivision, may be provided as an attachment to the contract:

(1) A notice concerning commercial general liability insurance. This notice may be provided as an attachment to the contract if the contract includes the following statement: "A notice concerning commercial general liability insurance is attached to this contract." The notice shall include the heading "Commercial General Liability Insurance (CGL)," followed by whichever of the following statements is both relevant and correct:

(A) "(The name on the license or 'This contractor') does not carry commercial general liability insurance."

(B) "(The name on the license or 'This contractor') carries commercial general liability insurance written by (the insurance company). You may call (the insurance company) at _____ _____ to check the contractor's insurance coverage."

(C) "(The name on the license or 'This contractor') is self-insured."

(D) "(The name on the license or 'This contractor') is a limited liability company that carries liability insurance or maintains other security as required by law. You may call (the insurance company or trust company or bank) at _____ _____ to check on the contractor's insurance coverage or security."

(2) A notice concerning workers' compensation insurance. This notice may be provided as an attachment to the contract if the contract includes the statement: "A notice concerning workers' compensation insurance is attached to this contract." The notice shall include the heading "Workers' Compensation Insurance" followed by whichever of the following statements is correct:

(A) "(The name on the license or 'This contractor') has no employees and is exempt from workers' compensation requirements."

(B) "(The name on the license or 'This contractor') carries workers' compensation insurance for all employees."

(3) A notice that provides the buyer with the following information about the performance of extra or change-order work:

(A) A statement that the buyer may not require a contractor to perform extra or change-order work without providing written authorization prior to the commencement of work covered by the new change order.

(B) A statement informing the buyer that extra work or a change order is not enforceable against a buyer unless the change order also identifies all of the following in writing prior to the commencement of work covered by the new change order:

(i) The scope of work encompassed by the order.

(ii) The amount to be added or subtracted from the contract.

(iii) The effect the order will make in the progress payments or the completion date.

(C) A statement informing the buyer that the contractor's failure to comply with the requirements of this paragraph does not preclude the recovery of compensation for work performed based upon legal or equitable remedies designed to prevent unjust enrichment.

(4) A notice with the heading "Mechanics Lien Warning" written as follows:

"MECHANICS LIEN WARNING:

Anyone who helps improve your property, but who is not paid, may record what is called a mechanics lien on your property. A mechanics lien is a claim, like a mortgage or home equity loan, made against your property and recorded with the county recorder.

Even if you pay your contractor in full, unpaid subcontractors, suppliers, and laborers who helped to improve your property may record mechanics liens and sue you in court to foreclose the lien. If a court finds the lien is valid, you could be forced to pay twice or have a court officer sell your home to pay the lien. Liens can also affect your credit.

To preserve their right to record a lien, each subcontractor and material supplier must provide you with a document called a 'Preliminary Notice.' This notice is not a lien. The purpose of the notice is to let you know that the person who sends you the notice has the right to record a lien on your property if he or she is not paid.

BE CAREFUL. The Preliminary Notice can be sent up to 20 days after the subcontractor starts work or the supplier provides material. This can be a big problem if you pay your contractor before you have received the Preliminary Notices.

You will not get Preliminary Notices from your prime contractor or from laborers who work on your project. The law assumes that you already know they are improving your property.

PROTECT YOURSELF FROM LIENS. You can protect yourself from liens by getting a list from your contractor of all the subcontractors and material suppliers that work on your project. Find out from your contractor when these subcontractors started work and when these suppliers delivered goods or materials. Then wait 20 days, paying attention to the Preliminary Notices you receive.

PAY WITH JOINT CHECKS. One way to protect yourself is to pay with a joint check. When your contractor tells you it is time to pay for the work of a subcontractor or supplier who has provided you with a Preliminary Notice, write a joint check payable to both the contractor and the subcontractor or material supplier.

For other ways to prevent liens, visit CSLB's Internet Web site at www.cslb.ca.gov or call CSLB at 800-321-CSLB (2752).

REMEMBER, IF YOU DO NOTHING, YOU RISK HAVING A LIEN PLACED ON YOUR HOME. This can mean that you may have

to pay twice, or face the forced sale of your home to pay what you owe."

(5) The following notice shall be provided in at least 12-point typeface:

"Information about the Contractors' State License Board (CSLB): CSLB is the state consumer protection agency that licenses and regulates construction contractors.

Contact CSLB for information about the licensed contractor you are considering, including information about disclosable complaints, disciplinary actions, and civil judgments that are reported to CSLB.

Use only licensed contractors. If you file a complaint against a licensed contractor within the legal deadline (usually four years), CSLB has authority to investigate the complaint. If you use an unlicensed contractor, CSLB may not be able to help you resolve your complaint. Your only remedy may be in civil court, and you may be liable for damages arising out of any injuries to the unlicensed contractor or the unlicensed contractor's employees.

For more information:

Visit CSLB's Internet Web site at www.cslb.ca.gov

Call CSLB at 800-321-CSLB (2752)

Write CSLB at P.O. Box 26000, Sacramento, CA 95826."

(6) (A) The notice set forth in subparagraph (B) and entitled "Three-Day Right to Cancel," shall be provided to the buyer unless the contract is:

(i) Negotiated at the contractor's place of business.

(ii) Subject to the "Seven-Day Right to Cancel," as set forth in paragraph (7).

(iii) Subject to licensure under the Alarm Company Act (Chapter 11.6 (commencing with Section 7590)), provided the alarm company licensee complies with Sections 1689.5, 1689.6, and 1689.7 of the Civil Code, as applicable.

(B) "Three-Day Right to Cancel

You, the buyer, have the right to cancel this contract within three business days. You may cancel by e-mailing, mailing, faxing, or delivering a written notice to the contractor at the contractor's place of business by midnight of the third business day after you received a signed and dated copy of the contract that includes this notice. Include your name, your address, and the date you received the signed copy of the contract and this notice.

If you cancel, the contractor must return to you anything you paid within 10 days of receiving the notice of cancellation. For your part, you must make available to the contractor at your residence, in substantially as good condition as you received them, goods delivered to you under this contract or sale. Or, you may, if you wish, comply with the contractor's instructions on how to return the goods at the contractor's expense and risk. If you do make the goods available to the contractor and the contractor does not pick them up within 20 days of the date of your notice of cancellation, you may keep them without any further obligation. If you fail to make the goods available to the contractor, or if you agree to return the goods to the contractor and fail to do so, then you remain liable for performance of all obligations under the contract."

(C) The "Three-Day Right to Cancel" notice required by this paragraph shall comply with all of the following:

(i) The text of the notice is at least 12-point boldface type.

(ii) The notice is in immediate proximity to a space reserved for the owner's signature.

(iii) The owner acknowledges receipt of the notice by signing and dating the notice form in the signature space.

(iv) The notice is written in the same language, e.g., Spanish, as that principally used in any oral sales presentation.

(v) The notice may be attached to the contract if the contract includes, in at least 12-point boldface type, a checkbox with the following statement: "The law requires that the contractor give you a notice explaining your right to cancel. Initial the checkbox if the contractor has given you a 'Notice of the Three-Day Right to Cancel.'"

(vi) The notice shall be accompanied by a completed form in duplicate, captioned "Notice of Cancellation," which also shall be attached to the agreement or offer to purchase and be easily detachable, and which shall contain the following statement written in the same language, e.g., Spanish, as used in the contract:

"Notice of Cancellation"

_____

/enter date of transaction/

(Date)

"You may cancel this transaction, without any penalty or obligation, within three business days from the above date.

If you cancel, any property traded in, any payments made by you under the contract or sale, and any negotiable instrument executed by you will be returned within 10 days following receipt by the seller of your cancellation notice, and any security interest arising out of the transaction will be canceled.

If you cancel, you must make available to the seller at your residence, in substantially as good condition as when received, any goods delivered to you under this contract or sale, or you may, if you wish, comply with the instructions of the seller regarding the return shipment of the goods at the seller's expense and risk.

If you do make the goods available to the seller and the seller does not pick them up within 20 days of the date of your notice of cancellation, you may retain or dispose of the goods without any further obligation. If you fail to make the goods available to the seller, or if you agree to return the goods to the seller and fail to do so, then you remain liable for performance of all obligations under the contract."

To cancel this transaction, mail or deliver a signed and dated copy of this cancellation notice, or any other written notice, or send a telegram to _____,

/name of seller/

at _____

/address of seller's place of business/

not later than midnight of _____.

(Date)

I hereby cancel this transaction. _____

(Date)

_____

(Buyer's signature)

(7) (A) The following notice entitled "Seven-Day Right to Cancel" shall be provided to the buyer for any contract that is written for the repair or restoration of residential premises damaged by any sudden or catastrophic event for which a state of emergency has been declared by the President of the United States or the Governor, or for which a local emergency has been declared by the executive officer or governing body of any city, county, or city and county:

"Seven-Day Right to Cancel

You, the buyer, have the right to cancel this contract within seven business days. You may cancel by e-mailing, mailing, faxing, or delivering a written notice to the contractor at the contractor's place of business by midnight of the seventh business day after you received a signed and dated copy of the contract that includes this notice. Include your name, your address, and the date you received the signed copy of the contract and this notice.

If you cancel, the contractor must return to you anything you paid within 10 days of receiving the notice of cancellation. For your part, you must make available to the contractor at your residence, in substantially as good condition as you received them, goods delivered to you under this contract or sale. Or, you may, if you wish, comply with the contractor's instructions on how to return the goods at the contractor's expense and risk. If you do make the goods available to the contractor and the contractor does not pick them up within 20 days of the date of your notice of cancellation, you may keep them without any further obligation. If you fail to make the goods available to the contractor, or if you agree to return the goods to the contractor and fail to do so, then you remain liable for performance of all obligations under the contract."

(B) The "Seven-Day Right to Cancel" notice required by this subdivision shall comply with all of the following:

(i) The text of the notice is at least 12-point boldface type.

(ii) The notice is in immediate proximity to a space reserved for the owner's signature.

(iii) The owner acknowledges receipt of the notice by signing and dating the notice form in the signature space.

(iv) The notice is written in the same language, e.g., Spanish, as that principally used in any oral sales presentation.

(v) The notice may be attached to the contract if the contract includes, in at least 12-point boldface type, a checkbox with the following statement: "The law requires that the contractor give you a notice explaining your right to cancel. Initial the checkbox if the contractor has given you a 'Notice of the Seven-Day Right to Cancel.'"

(vi) The notice shall be accompanied by a completed form in duplicate, captioned "Notice of Cancellation," which shall also be attached to the agreement or offer to purchase and be easily detachable, and which shall contain the following statement written in the same language, e.g., Spanish, as used in the contract:

"Notice of Cancellation"

_____
/enter date of transaction/
(Date)

"You may cancel this transaction, without any penalty or obligation, within seven business days from the above date.

If you cancel, any property traded in, any payments made by you under the contract or sale, and any negotiable instrument executed by you will be returned within 10 days following receipt by the seller of your cancellation notice, and any security interest arising out of the transaction will be canceled.

If you cancel, you must make available to the seller at your residence, in substantially as good condition as when received, any goods delivered to you under this contract or sale, or you may, if you wish, comply with the instructions of the seller regarding the return shipment of the goods at the seller's expense and risk.

If you do make the goods available to the seller and the seller does not pick them up within 20 days of the date of your notice of cancellation, you may retain or dispose of the goods without any further obligation. If you fail to make the goods available to the seller, or if you agree to return the goods to the seller and fail to do so, then you remain liable for performance of all obligations under the contract."

To cancel this transaction, mail or deliver a signed and dated copy of this cancellation notice, or any other written notice, or send a telegram to _____,
/name of seller/

at _____
/address of seller's place of business/

not later than midnight of _____.
                                                    (Date)

I hereby cancel this transaction. _____

                                                    (Date)

_____

(Buyer's signature)

Added Stats 2005 ch 48 § 7 (SB 1113), effective July 18, 2005, operative January 1, 2006. Amended Stats 2005 ch 385 § 2 (AB 316), effective January 1, 2006; Stats 2006 ch 114 § 1 (AB 2073), effective January 1, 2007; Stats 2007 ch 130 § 30 (AB 299), effective January 1, 2008, Stats 2007 ch 230 § 1 (AB 244), effective January 1, 2008, (ch 230 prevails); Stats 2008 ch 179 § 18 (SB 1498), effective January 1, 2009; Stats 2009 ch 307 § 74 (SB 821), effective January 1, 2010; Stats 2010 ch 697 § 4 (SB 189), effective January 1, 2011, operative July 1, 2012, ch 698 § 39 (SB 392) (ch 698 prevails), effective January 1, 2011; Stats 2011 ch 44 § 1 (SB 190), effective January 1, 2012, operative July 1, 2012.

§ 7159.1. Notice in sale of home improvement goods or services (First of two; Operative until July 1, 2012)

In any contract for the sale of home improvement goods or services offered by door-to-door sale that contains or is secured by a lien on real property, the contract shall be accompanied by the following notice in 18-point boldfaced type:

"WARNING TO BUYER: IF YOU SIGN THE CONTRACT WHICH ACCOMPANIES THIS NOTICE, YOU WILL BE PUTTING UP YOUR HOME AS SECURITY. THIS MEANS THAT YOUR HOME COULD BE SOLD WITHOUT YOUR PERMISSION AND WITHOUT ANY COURT ACTION IF YOU MISS ANY PAYMENT REQUIRED BY THIS CONTRACT."

This notice shall be written in the same language as the rest of the contract. It shall be on a separate piece of paper from the rest of the contract and shall be signed and dated by the buyer. The home improvement contractor or home improvement salesperson shall deliver to the buyer at the time of the buyer' s signing and dating of the notice a legible copy of the signed and dated notice. A security interest created in any contract described in this section that does not provide the notice as required by this section shall be void and unenforceable.

This section shall not apply to any of the following:

(a) Any contract that is subject to Chapter 1 (commencing with Section 1801) of Title 2 of Part 4 of Division 3 of the Civil Code.

(b) A mechanic's lien established pursuant to Chapter 2 (commencing with Section 3109) of Title 15 of Part 4 of Division 3 of the Civil Code.

(c) Any contract that is subject to subdivision (a) of Section 7159.2.

Added Stats 1998 ch 571 § 1 (AB 2301).

§ 7159.1. Notice in sale of home improvement goods or services (Second of two; Operative July 1, 2012)

(a) In any contract for the sale of home improvement goods or services offered by door-to-door sale that contains or is secured by a lien on real property, the contract shall be accompanied by the following notice in 18-point boldfaced type:
"WARNING TO BUYER: IF YOU SIGN THE CONTRACT WHICH ACCOMPANIES THIS NOTICE, YOU WILL BE PUTTING UP YOUR HOME AS SECURITY. THIS MEANS THAT YOUR HOME COULD BE SOLD WITHOUT YOUR PERMISSION AND WITHOUT ANY COURT ACTION IF YOU MISS ANY PAYMENT REQUIRED BY THIS CONTRACT."
This notice shall be written in the same language as the rest of the contract. It shall be on a separate piece of paper from the rest of the contract and shall be signed and dated by the buyer. The home improvement contractor or home improvement salesperson shall deliver to the buyer at the time of the buyer's signing and dating of the notice a legible copy of the signed and dated notice. A security interest created in any contract described in this section that does not provide the notice as required by this section shall be void and unenforceable.

(b) This section shall not apply to any of the following:

(1) Any contract that is subject to Chapter 1 (commencing with Section 1801) of Title 2 of Part 4 of Division 3 of the Civil Code.

(2) A mechanics lien established pursuant to Chapter 4 (commencing with Section 8400) of Title 2 of Part 6 of Division 4 of the Civil Code.

(3) Any contract that is subject to subdivision (a) of Section 7159.2.

Added Stats 1998 ch 571 § 1 (AB 2301). Amended Stats 2010 ch 697 § 5 (SB 189), effective January 1, 2011, operative July 1, 2012.

§ 7159.2. Security interest for home improvement goods or services

(a) No home improvement goods or services contract of a value of five thousand dollars ($5,000) or less shall provide for a security interest in real property, except for a mechanic's lien or other interest in property that arises by operation of law. Any lien in violation of this subdivision is void and unenforceable.

(b) When the proceeds of a loan secured by a mortgage on real property are used to fund goods or services pursuant to a home improvement goods or services contract of more than five thousand dollars ($5,000), the person or entity making the loan shall only pay a contractor under the home improvement goods or services contract from the proceeds of the loan by either of the following methods:

(1) By an instrument payable to the borrower or jointly to the borrower and the contractor.

(2) At the election of the borrower, through a third-party escrow agent pursuant to the terms of a written agreement signed by the borrower, the person or entity making the loan, and the contractor prior to the disbursement.

(c) Any person or entity who violates any provision of this section shall be liable for actual damages suffered by the borrower for damages that proximately result from the violation.

(d) Any person or entity who intentionally or as a pattern or practice violates any provision of this section shall be additionally liable for three times the contract price for the home improvement.

(e) Any person who is a senior citizen or disabled person, as defined in subdivisions (f) and (g) of Section 1761 of the Civil Code, as part of any action for a violation of this section, may seek and be awarded, in addition to the remedies provided in this section, up to five thousand dollars ($5,000) as provided in subdivision (b) of Section 1780 of the Civil Code.

(f) The court shall award court costs and attorney's fees to a prevailing plaintiff in an action brought pursuant to this section. Reasonable attorney's fees may be awarded to a prevailing defendant upon a finding by the court that the plaintiff's prosecution of the action was not in good faith.

Added Stats 1998 ch 571 § 2 (AB 2301). Amended Stats 1999 ch 512 § 1 (SB 187).

§ 7159.5. Contract amount; Finance charges; Down payment; Violations; Restitution and punishment (First of two; Operative until July 1, 2012)

This section applies to all home improvement contracts, as defined in Section 7151.2, between an owner or tenant and a contractor, whether a general contractor or a specialty contractor, who is licensed or subject to be licensed pursuant to this chapter with regard to the transaction.

(a) Failure by the licensee or a person subject to be licensed under this chapter, or by his or her agent or salesperson, to comply with the following provisions is cause for discipline:

(1) The contract shall be in writing and shall include the agreed contract amount in dollars and cents. The contract amount shall include the entire cost of the contract, including profit, labor, and materials, but excluding finance charges.

(2) If there is a separate finance charge between the contractor and the person contracting for home improvement, the finance charge shall be set out separately from the contract amount.

(3) If a downpayment will be charged, the downpayment may not exceed one thousand dollars ($1,000) or 10 percent of the contract amount, whichever is less.

(4) If, in addition to a downpayment, the contract provides for payments to be made prior to completion of the work, the contract shall include a schedule of payments in dollars and cents specifically referencing the amount of work or services to be performed and any materials and equipment to be supplied.

(5) Except for a downpayment, the contractor may neither request nor accept payment that exceeds the value of the work performed or material delivered.

(6) Upon any payment by the person contracting for home improvement, and prior to any further payment being made, the contractor shall, if requested, obtain and furnish to the person a full and unconditional release from any potential lien claimant claim or mechanic's lien authorized pursuant to Section 3110 of the Civil Code for any portion of the work for which payment has been made. The person contracting for home improvement may withhold all further payments until these releases are furnished.

(7) If the contract provides for a payment of a salesperson's commission out of the contract price, that payment shall be made on a pro rata basis in proportion to the schedule of payments made to the contractor by the disbursing party in accordance with paragraph (4).

(8) A contractor furnishing a performance and payment bond, lien and completion bond, or a bond equivalent or joint control approved by the registrar covering full performance and payment is exempt from paragraphs (3), (4), and (5), and need not include, as part of the contract, the statement regarding the downpayment specified in subparagraph (C) of paragraph (8) of subdivision (d) of Section 7159, the details and statement regarding progress payments specified in paragraph (9) of subdivision (d) of Section 7159, or the Mechanics' Lien Warning specified in paragraph (4) of subdivision (e) of Section 7159. A contractor furnishing these bonds, bond equivalents, or a joint control approved by the registrar may accept payment prior to completion. If the contract provides for a contractor to furnish joint control, the contractor shall not have any financial or other interest in the joint control.

(b) A violation of paragraph (1), (3), or (5) of subdivision (a) by a licensee or a person subject to be licensed under this chapter, or by his or her agent or salesperson, is a misdemeanor punishable by a fine of not less than one hundred dollars ($100) nor more than five thousand dollars ($5,000), or by imprisonment in a county jail not exceeding one year, or by both that fine and imprisonment.

(1) An indictment or information against a person who is not licensed but who is required to be licensed under this chapter shall be brought, or a criminal complaint filed, for a violation of this section,

in accordance with paragraph (4) of subdivision (d) of Section 802 of the Penal Code, within four years from the date of the contract or, if the contract is not reduced to writing, from the date the buyer makes the first payment to the contractor.

(2) An indictment or information against a person who is licensed under this chapter shall be brought, or a criminal complaint filed, for a violation of this section, in accordance with paragraph (2) of subdivision (d) of Section 802 of the Penal Code, within two years from the date of the contract or, if the contract is not reduced to writing, from the date the buyer makes the first payment to the contractor.

(3) The limitations on actions in this subdivision shall not apply to any administrative action filed against a licensed contractor.

(c) Any person who violates this section as part of a plan or scheme to defraud an owner or tenant of a residential or nonresidential structure, including a mobilehome or manufactured home, in connection with the offer or performance of repairs to the structure for damage caused by a natural disaster, shall be ordered by the court to make full restitution to the victim based on the person's ability to pay, as defined in subdivision (e) of Section 1203.1b of the Penal Code. In addition to full restitution, and imprisonment authorized by this section, the court may impose a fine of not less than five hundred dollars ($500) nor more than twenty-five thousand dollars ($25,000), based upon the defendant's ability to pay. This subdivision applies to natural disasters for which a state of emergency is proclaimed by the Governor pursuant to Section 8625 of the Government Code, or for which an emergency or major disaster is declared by the President of the United States.

Added Stats 2004 ch 566 § 8 (SB 30), operative July 1, 2005. Amended Stats 2005 ch 48 § 11 (SB 1113), effective July 18, 2005, operative January 1, 2006; ch 385 § 5 (AB 316); Stats 2007 ch 230 § 2 (AB 244), effective January 1, 2008; Stats 2009 ch 307 § 75 (SB 821), effective January 1, 2010.

§ 7159.5. Contract amount; Finance charges; Down payment; Violations; Restitution and punishment (Second of two; Operative July 1, 2012)

This section applies to all home improvement contracts, as defined in Section 7151.2, between an owner or tenant and a contractor, whether a general contractor or a specialty contractor, that is licensed or subject to be licensed pursuant to this chapter with regard to the transaction.

(a) Failure by the licensee or a person subject to be licensed under this chapter, or by his or her agent or salesperson, to comply with the following provisions is cause for discipline:

(1) The contract shall be in writing and shall include the agreed contract amount in dollars and cents. The contract amount shall in-

clude the entire cost of the contract, including profit, labor, and materials, but excluding finance charges.

(2) If there is a separate finance charge between the contractor and the person contracting for home improvement, the finance charge shall be set out separately from the contract amount.

(3) If a downpayment will be charged, the downpayment may not exceed one thousand dollars ($1,000) or 10 percent of the contract amount, whichever is less.

(4) If, in addition to a downpayment, the contract provides for payments to be made prior to completion of the work, the contract shall include a schedule of payments in dollars and cents specifically referencing the amount of work or services to be performed and any materials and equipment to be supplied.

(5) Except for a downpayment, the contractor may neither request nor accept payment that exceeds the value of the work performed or material delivered.

(6) Upon any payment by the person contracting for home improvement, and prior to any further payment being made, the contractor shall, if requested, obtain and furnish to the person a full and unconditional release from any potential lien claimant claim or mechanics lien authorized pursuant to Sections 8400 and 8404 of the Civil Code for any portion of the work for which payment has been made. The person contracting for home improvement may withhold all further payments until these releases are furnished.

(7) If the contract provides for a payment of a salesperson's commission out of the contract price, that payment shall be made on a pro rata basis in proportion to the schedule of payments made to the contractor by the disbursing party in accordance with paragraph (4).

(8) A contractor furnishing a performance and payment bond, lien and completion bond, or a bond equivalent or joint control approved by the registrar covering full performance and payment is exempt from paragraphs (3), (4), and (5), and need not include, as part of the contract, the statement regarding the downpayment specified in subparagraph (C) of paragraph (8) of subdivision (d) of Section 7159, the details and statement regarding progress payments specified in paragraph (9) of subdivision (d) of Section 7159, or the Mechanics Lien Warning specified in paragraph (4) of subdivision (e) of Section 7159. A contractor furnishing these bonds, bond equivalents, or a joint control approved by the registrar may accept payment prior to completion. If the contract provides for a contractor to furnish joint control, the contractor shall not have any financial or other interest in the joint control.

(b) A violation of paragraph (1), (3), or (5) of subdivision (a) by a licensee or a person subject to be licensed under this chapter, or by his or her agent or salesperson, is a misdemeanor punishable by a fine of not less than one hundred dollars ($100) nor more than five thousand dollars ($5,000), or by imprisonment in a county jail not exceeding one year, or by both that fine and imprisonment.

(1) An indictment or information against a person who is not licensed but who is required to be licensed under this chapter shall be brought, or a criminal complaint filed, for a violation of this section, in accordance with paragraph (4) of subdivision (d) of Section 802 of the Penal Code, within four years from the date of the contract or, if the contract is not reduced to writing, from the date the buyer makes the first payment to the contractor.

(2) An indictment or information against a person who is licensed under this chapter shall be brought, or a criminal complaint filed, for a violation of this section, in accordance with paragraph (2) of subdivision (d) of Section 802 of the Penal Code, within two years from the date of the contract or, if the contract is not reduced to writing, from the date the buyer makes the first payment to the contractor.

(3) The limitations on actions in this subdivision shall not apply to any administrative action filed against a licensed contractor.

(c) Any person who violates this section as part of a plan or scheme to defraud an owner or tenant of a residential or nonresidential structure, including a mobilehome or manufactured home, in connection with the offer or performance of repairs to the structure for damage caused by a natural disaster, shall be ordered by the court to make full restitution to the victim based on the person's ability to pay, as defined in subdivision (e) of Section 1203.1b of the Penal Code. In addition to full restitution, and imprisonment authorized by this section, the court may impose a fine of not less than five hundred dollars ($500) nor more than twenty-five thousand dollars ($25,000), based upon the defendant's ability to pay. This subdivision applies to natural disasters for which a state of emergency is proclaimed by the Governor pursuant to Section 8625 of the Government Code, or for which an emergency or major disaster is declared by the President of the United States.

Added Stats 2004 ch 566 § 8 (SB 30), operative July 1, 2005. Amended Stats 2005 ch 48 § 11 (SB 1113), effective July 18, 2005, operative January 1, 2006; ch 385 § 5 (AB 316); Stats 2007 ch 230 § 2 (AB 244), effective January 1, 2008; Stats 2009 ch 307 § 75 (SB 821), effective January 1, 2010; Stats 2010 ch 697 § 6 (SB 189), effective January 1, 2011, operative July 1, 2012; Stats 2011 ch 44 § 2 (SB 190), effective January 1, 2012, operative July 1, 2012.

§ 7159.6. Work or change order

(a) An extra work or change order is not enforceable against a buyer unless the change order sets forth all of the following:

(1) The scope of work encompassed by the order.

(2) The amount to be added or subtracted from the contract.

(3) The effect the order will make in the progress payments or the completion date.

Section VI

(b) The buyer may not require a contractor to perform extra or change-order work without providing written authorization.

(c) Failure to comply with the requirements of this section does not preclude the recovery of compensation for work performed based upon legal or equitable remedies designed to prevent unjust enrichment.

(d) This section shall become operative on January 1, 2006.

Added Stats 2004 ch 566 § 9 (SB 30), operative July 1, 2005. Amended Stats 2005 ch 48 § 12 (SB 1113), effective July 18, 2005, operative January 1, 2006.

§ 7159.9. Requirements for home improvement contracts, exemption for fire alarm system

(a) Section 7159 does not apply to the sale, installation, and servicing of a fire alarm sold in conjunction with an alarm system, as defined in subdivision (n) of Section 7590.1 of the Alarm Company Act (Chapter 11.6 (commencing with Section 7590)), provided the licensee does all of the following:

(1) Complies with the contract requirements set forth in Section 7599.54.

(2) Complies with Sections 1689.5, 1689.6, and 1689.7 of the Civil Code, as applicable.

(3) Executes the following certification statement in the contract or in a separate certification document signed by all parties to the contract:

"All costs attributable to making the fire alarm system operable for the residence identified by this document, including sale and installation costs, do not exceed five hundred dollars ($500)."

(4) Certifies to the following if the certification statement described in paragraph (3) is in a separate document:

"I certify that all statements and representations made by me in this document are true and accurate."

(b) The contract or separate certification document shall also include both of the following:

(1) The physical address of the residence for which the certification is applicable.

(2) The name, business address, and license number of the contractor as contained in the official records of the board.

(c) The licensee shall give an exact copy of all documents required pursuant to this section to the party who is contracting to have the alarm system installed.

(d) All documents required pursuant to this section shall be retained by the licensee for a period of five years in accordance with the provisions of Section 7111, and shall be made available to the board within 30 days of a written request.

(e) Failure by the contractor to provide the board with the certification or contract within 30 days of a written request is cause for discipline.

(f) Failure by the licensee to provide the board with the certification or contract within 30 days of a written request creates a presumption that the licensee has violated the provisions of Section 7159, unless evidence to the contrary is presented within the timeframe specified by the board.

Added Stats 2006 ch 114 (AB 2073), effective January 1, 2007. Amended Stats 2007 ch 130 § 31 (AB 299), effective January 1, 2008.

§ 7159.10. Service and repair contract defined

(a)(1) "Service and repair contract" means an agreement between a contractor or salesperson for a contractor, whether a general contractor or a specialty contractor, who is licensed or subject to be licensed pursuant to this chapter with regard to the transaction, and a homeowner or a tenant, for the performance of a home improvement as defined in Section 7151, that conforms to the following requirements:

(A) The contract amount is seven hundred fifty dollars ($750) or less.

(B) The prospective buyer initiated contact with the contractor to request the work.

(C) The contractor does not sell the buyer goods or services beyond those reasonably necessary to take care of the particular problem that caused the buyer to contact the contractor.

(D) No payment is due, or accepted by the contractor, until the work is completed.

(2) As used in this subdivision, "the work is completed" means that all of the conditions that caused the buyer to contact the contractor for service and repairs have been fully corrected and, if applicable, the building department has accepted and approved the corrective work.

(b) For any contract written pursuant to subdivision (a) or otherwise presented to the buyer as a service and repair contract, unless all of the conforming requirements for service and repair contracts specified in subdivision (a) are met, the contract requirements for home improvements set forth in subdivisions (c), (d), and (e) of Section 7159 shall be applicable, including any rights to rescind the contract as set forth in Section 1689.6 or 1689.7 of the Civil Code, regardless of the aggregate contract price.

(c) If all of the requirements of subdivision (a) are met, only those notices and other requirements set forth in this section are applicable to the contract.

(d) Every service and repair contract described in subdivision (a) shall include, or otherwise comply with, all of the following:

(1) The contract, any changes to the contract, and any attachments shall be in writing and signed or acknowledged by the parties as set forth in this section, and shall be written in the same language (for example Spanish) as principally used in the oral sales presentation.

(2) The writing shall be legible.

(3) Any printed form shall be readable. Unless a larger typeface is specified in this article, the text shall be in at least 10-point typeface and the headings shall be in at least 10-point boldface type.

(4) Before any work is started, the contractor shall give the buyer a copy of the contract signed and dated by the buyer and by the contractor or the contractor's representative.

(5) The name, business address, and license number of the contractor.

(6) The date the contract was signed.

(7) A notice concerning commercial general liability insurance. This notice may be provided as an attachment to the contract if the contract includes the statement, "A notice concerning commercial general liability insurance is attached to this contract." The notice shall include the heading "Commercial General Liability Insurance (CGL)" followed by whichever of the following statements is both relevant and correct:

(A) "(The name on the license or 'This contractor') does not carry commercial general liability insurance."

(B) "(The name on the license or 'This contractor') carries commercial general liability insurance written by (the insurance company). You may call the (insurance company) at _____ to check the contractor's insurance coverage."

(C) "(The name on the license or 'This contractor') is self-insured."

(D) "(The name on the license or 'This contractor') is a limited liability company that carries liability insurance or maintains other security as required by law. You may call (the insurance company or trust company or bank) at _____ to check on the contractor's insurance coverage or security."

(8) A notice concerning workers' compensation insurance. This notice may be provided as an attachment to the contract if the contract includes the statement "A notice concerning workers' compensation insurance is attached to this contract." The notice shall include the heading "Workers' Compensation Insurance" followed by whichever of the following statements is both relevant and correct:

(A) "(The name on the license or 'This contractor') has no employees and is exempt from workers' compensation requirements."

(B) "(The name on the license or 'This contractor') carries workers' compensation insurance for all employees."

(e) Every service and repair contract described in subdivision (a) shall provide the following information, notices, and disclosures in the contract:

(1) Notice of the type of contract in at least 10-point boldface type: "Service and Repair."

(2) A notice in at least 12-point boldface type, signed and dated by the buyer: "Notice to the Buyer: The law requires that service and repair contracts must meet all of the following requirements:

(A) The price must be no more than seven hundred and fifty dollars ($750).

(B) You, the buyer, must have initiated contact with the contractor to request the work.

(C) The contractor must not sell you goods or services beyond those reasonably necessary to take care of the particular problem that caused you to contact the contractor.

(D) No payment is due and the contractor may not accept any payment until the work is completed."

(3) The notice in at least 12-point boldface type: "Notice to the Buyer: You are entitled to a completely filled in and signed copy of this agreement before any work may be started."

(4) If applicable, the heading "List of Documents to be Incorporated into the Contract," followed by the list of documents to be incorporated into the contract.

(5) Where the contract is a fixed contract amount, the heading: "Contract Price" followed by the amount of the contract in dollars and cents.

(6) If a finance charge will be charged, the heading: "Finance Charge" followed by the amount in dollars and cents. The finance charge is to be set out separately from the contract amount.

(7) Where the contract is estimated by a time and materials formula, the heading "Estimated Contract Price" followed by the estimated contract amount in dollars and cents. The contract must disclose the set rate and the estimated cost of materials. The contract must also disclose how time will be computed, for example, in increments of quarter hours, half hours, or hours, and the statement: "The actual contract amount of a time and materials contract may not exceed the estimated contract amount without written authorization from the buyer."

(8) The heading: "Description of the Project and Materials to be Used and Equipment to be Installed" followed by a description of the project and materials to be used and equipment to be installed.

(9) The statement: "The law requires that the contractor offer you any parts that were replaced during the service call. If you do not want the parts, initial the checkbox labeled 'OK for contractor to take replaced parts." '

(10) A checkbox labeled "OK for contractor to take replaced parts."

(11) If a service charge is charged, the heading "Amount of Service Charge" followed by the service charge, and the statement "You may

be charged only one service charge, including any trip charge or inspection fee."

(12)(A) The contract, or an attachment to the contract as specified under subparagraph (C) of this paragraph, must include, in immediate proximity to the space reserved for the buyer's signature, the following statement, in at least 12-point boldface type, which shall be dated and signed by the buyer:

"YOUR RIGHTS TO CANCEL BEFORE WORK BEGINS

(A) You, the buyer, have the right to cancel this contract until:

1. You receive a copy of this contract signed and dated by you and the contractor; and

2. The contractor starts work.

(B) However, even if the work has begun you, the buyer, may still cancel the contract for any of the reasons specified in items 1 through 4 of this paragraph. If any of these reasons occur, you may cancel the contract within three business days of signing the contract for normal service and repairs, or within seven business days of signing a contract to repair or correct conditions resulting from any sudden or catastrophic event for which a state of emergency has been declared by the President of the United States or the Governor, or for which a local emergency has been declared by the executive officer or governing body of any city, county, or city and county:

1. You may cancel the contract if the price, including all labor and materials, is more than seven hundred fifty dollars ($750).

2. You may cancel the contract if you did not initiate the contact with the contractor to request the work.

3. You may cancel the contract if the contractor sold you goods or services beyond those reasonably necessary to take care of the particular problem that caused you to contact the contractor.

4. You may cancel the contract if the payment was due or the contractor accepted any money before the work was complete.

(C) If any of these reasons for canceling occurred, you may cancel the contract as specified under paragraph (B) above by e-mailing, mailing, faxing, or delivering a written notice to the contractor at the contractor's place of business within three business days or, if applicable, seven business days of the date you received a signed and dated copy of this contract. Include your name, your address, and the date you received a signed copy of the contract and this notice.

If you cancel, the contractor must return to you anything you paid within 10 days of receiving the notice of cancellation. For your part, you must make available to the contractor at your residence, in substantially as good condition as you received it, any goods delivered to you under this contract. Or, you may, if you wish, comply with the contractor's instructions on how to return the goods at the contractor's expense and risk. If you make the goods available to the contractor and the contractor does not pick them up within 20 days of the date of your notice of cancellation, you may keep them without any further obligation. If you fail to make the goods available to the contractor, or if you agree to return the goods to the contractor and fail to do so, then you remain liable for performance of all obligations under the contract."

(B) This paragraph does not apply to home improvement contracts entered into by a person who holds an alarm company operator's license issued pursuant to Chapter 11.6 (commencing with Section 7590), provided the person complies with Sections 1689.5, 1689.6, and 1689.7 of the Civil Code, as applicable.

(C) The notice required in this paragraph may be incorporated as an attachment to the contract if the contract includes a checkbox and whichever statement is relevant in at least 12-point boldface type:

(i) "The law requires that the contractor give you a notice explaining your right to cancel. Initial the checkbox if the contractor has given you a 'Notice of Your Right to Cancel.' '

(ii) "The law requires that the contractor give you a notice explaining your right to cancel contracts for the repair or restoration of residential premises damaged by a disaster. Initial the checkbox if the contractor has given you a 'Notice of Your Right to Cancel.' '

(f) A bona fide service repairperson employed by a licensed contractor or subcontractor hired by a licensed contractor may enter into a service and repair contract on behalf of that contractor.

(g) The provisions of this section are not exclusive and do not relieve the contractor from compliance with any other applicable provision of law.

Added Stats 2004 ch 566 § 10 (SB 30), operative July 1, 2005. Amended Stats 2005 ch 48 § 13 (SB 1113), effective July 18, 2005, operative January 1, 2006, ch 385 § 6 (AB 316); Stats 2010 ch 698 § 40 (SB 392), effective January 1, 2011.

§ 7159.11. Discipline for violation

A violation of any provision of Section 7159.10 by a licensee, or a person subject to be licensed under this chapter, or by his or her agent or salesperson, is cause for discipline.

Added Stats 2004 ch 566 § 11 (SB 30), operative July 1, 2005. Amended Stats 2005 ch 48 § 14 (SB 1113), effective July 18, 2005, operative January 1, 2006, ch 385 § 7 (AB 316).

§ 7159.14. Further requirements; Statement of agreed amount; Payment due; Punishment for violations; Restitution (First of two; Operative until July 1, 2012)

(a) This section applies to a service and repair contract as defined in Section 7159.10. A violation of this section by a licensee or a person subject to be licensed under this chapter, or by his or her agent or salesperson, is cause for discipline.

(1) The contract may not exceed seven hundred fifty dollars ($750).

(2) The contract shall be in writing and shall state the agreed contract amount, which may be stated as either a fixed contract amount in dollars and cents or, if a time and materials formula is used, as an estimated contract amount in dollars and cents.

(3) The contract amount shall include the entire cost of the contract including profit, labor, and materials, but excluding finance charges.

(4) The actual contract amount of a time and materials contract may not exceed the estimated contract amount without written authorization from the buyer.

(5) The prospective buyer must have initiated contact with the contractor to request work.

(6) The contractor may not sell the buyer goods or services beyond those reasonably necessary to take care of the particular problem that caused the buyer to contact the contractor.

(7) No payment may be due before the project is completed.

(8) A service and repair contractor may charge only one service charge. For purposes of this chapter, a service charge includes such charges as a service or trip charge, or an inspection fee.

(9) A service and repair contractor charging a service charge must disclose in all advertisements that there is a service charge and, when the customer initiates the call for service, must disclose the amount of the service charge.

(10) The service and repair contractor must offer to the customer any parts that were replaced.

(11) Upon any payment by the buyer, the contractor shall, if requested, obtain and furnish to the buyer a full and unconditional release from any potential lien claimant claim or mechanic's lien authorized pursuant to Section 3110 of the Civil Code for any portion of the work for which payment has been made.

(b) A violation of paragraph (1), (2), (3), (4), (5), (6), or (8) of subdivision (a) by a licensee or a person subject to be licensed under this chapter, or by his or her agent or salesperson, is a misdemeanor punishable by a fine of not less than one hundred dollars ($100) nor more than five thousand dollars ($5,000), or by imprisonment in a county jail not exceeding one year, or by both that fine and imprisonment.

(1) An indictment or information against a person who is not licensed but who is required to be licensed under this chapter shall be brought, or a criminal complaint filed, for a violation of this section, in accordance with paragraph (4) of subdivision (d) of Section 802 of the Penal Code, within four years from the date of the contract or, if the contract is not reduced to writing, from the date the buyer makes the first payment to the contractor.

(2) An indictment or information against a person who is licensed under this chapter shall be brought, or a criminal complaint filed, for a violation of this section, in accordance with paragraph (2) of subdivision (d) of Section 802 of the Penal Code, within two years from the date of the contract or, if the contract is not reduced to writing, from the date the buyer makes the first payment to the contractor.

(3) The limitations on actions in this subdivision shall not apply to any administrative action filed against a licensed contractor.

(c) Any person who violates this section as part of a plan or scheme to defraud an owner or tenant of a residential or nonresidential structure, including a mobilehome or manufactured home, in connection with the offer or performance of repairs to the structure for damage caused by a natural disaster, shall be ordered by the court to make full restitution to the victim based on the person's ability to pay, as defined in subdivision (e) of Section 1203.1b of the Penal Code. In addition to full restitution, and imprisonment authorized by this section, the court may impose a fine of not less than five hundred dollars ($500) nor more than twenty-five thousand dollars ($25,000), based upon the defendant's ability to pay. This subdivision applies to natural disasters for which a state of emergency is proclaimed by the Governor pursuant to Section 8625 of the Government Code, or for which an emergency or major disaster is declared by the President of the United States.

Added Stats 2004 ch 566 § 14 (SB 30), operative July 1, 2005. Amended Stats 2005 ch 48 § 17 (SB 1113), effective July 18, 2005, operative January 1, 2006; Stats 2007 ch 230 § 3 (AB 244), effective January 1, 2008; Stats 2009 ch 307 § 76 (SB 821), effective January 1, 2010.

§ 7159.14. Further requirements; Statement of agreed amount; Payment due; Punishment for violations; Restitution (Second of two; Operative July 1, 2012)

(a) This section applies to a service and repair contract as defined in Section 7159.10. A violation of this section by a licensee or a person subject to be licensed under this chapter, or by his or her agent or salesperson, is cause for discipline.

(1) The contract may not exceed seven hundred fifty dollars ($750).

(2) The contract shall be in writing and shall state the agreed contract amount, which may be stated as either a fixed contract amount in dollars and cents or, if a time and materials formula is used, as an estimated contract amount in dollars and cents.

(3) The contract amount shall include the entire cost of the contract including profit, labor, and materials, but excluding finance charges.

(4) The actual contract amount of a time and materials contract may not exceed the estimated contract amount without written authorization from the buyer.

(5) The prospective buyer must have initiated contact with the contractor to request work.

(6) The contractor may not sell the buyer goods or services beyond those reasonably necessary to take care of the particular problem that caused the buyer to contact the contractor.

(7) No payment may be due before the project is completed.

(8) A service and repair contractor may charge only one service charge. For purposes of this chapter, a service charge includes such charges as a service or trip charge, or an inspection fee.

(9) A service and repair contractor charging a service charge must disclose in all advertisements that there is a service charge and, when the customer initiates the call for service, must disclose the amount of the service charge.

(10) The service and repair contractor must offer to the customer any parts that were replaced.

(11) Upon any payment by the buyer, the contractor shall, if requested, obtain and furnish to the buyer a full and unconditional release from any potential lien claimant claim or mechanics lien authorized pursuant to Sections 8400 and 8404 of the Civil Code for any portion of the work for which payment has been made.

(b) A violation of paragraph (1), (2), (3), (4), (5), (6), or (8) of subdivision (a) by a licensee or a person subject to be licensed under this chapter, or by his or her agent or salesperson, is a misdemeanor punishable by a fine of not less than one hundred dollars ($100) nor more than five thousand dollars ($5,000), or by imprisonment in a county jail not exceeding one year, or by both that fine and imprisonment.

(1) An indictment or information against a person who is not licensed but who is required to be licensed under this chapter shall be brought, or a criminal complaint filed, for a violation of this section, in accordance with paragraph (4) of subdivision (d) of Section 802 of the Penal Code, within four years from the date of the contract or, if the contract is not reduced to writing, from the date the buyer makes the first payment to the contractor.

(2) An indictment or information against a person who is licensed under this chapter shall be brought, or a criminal complaint filed, for a violation of this section, in accordance with paragraph (2) of subdivision (d) of Section 802 of the Penal Code, within two years from the date of the contract or, if the contract is not reduced to writing, from the date the buyer makes the first payment to the contractor.

(3) The limitations on actions in this subdivision shall not apply to any administrative action filed against a licensed contractor.

(c) Any person who violates this section as part of a plan or scheme to defraud an owner or tenant of a residential or nonresidential structure, including a mobilehome or manufactured home, in connection with the offer or performance of repairs to the structure for damage caused by a natural disaster, shall be ordered by the court to make full restitution to the victim based on the person's ability to pay, as defined in subdivision (e) of Section 1203.1b of the Penal Code. In addition to full restitution, and imprisonment authorized by this section, the court may impose a fine of not less than five hundred dollars ($500) nor more than twenty-five thousand dollars ($25,000), based upon the defendant's ability to pay. This subdivision applies to natural disasters for which a state of emergency is proclaimed by the Governor pursuant to Section 8625 of the Government Code, or for which an emergency or major disaster is declared by the President of the United States.

Added Stats 2004 ch 566 § 14 (SB 30), operative July 1, 2005. Amended Stats 2005 ch 48 § 17 (SB 1113), effective July 18, 2005, operative January 1, 2006; Stats 2007 ch 230 § 3 (AB 244), effective January 1, 2008; Stats 2009 ch 307 § 76 (SB 821), effective January 1, 2010; Stats 2010 ch 697 § 7 (SB 189), effective January 1, 2011, operative July 1, 2012; Stats 2011 ch 44 § 3 (SB 190), effective January 1, 2012, operative July 1, 2012.

§ 7160. Penalty for fraudulent misrepresentation

Any person who is induced to contract for a work of improvement, including but not limited to a home improvement, in reliance on false or fraudulent representations or false statements knowingly made, may sue and recover from such contractor or solicitor a penalty of five hundred dollars ($500), plus reasonable attorney's fees, in addition to any damages sustained by him by reason of such statements or representations made by the contractor or solicitor.

Added Stats 1969 ch 1583 § 6 as § 7028.2. Renumbered Stats 1972 ch 1138 § 1.5.

§ 7161. Specification of prohibited acts; Misdemeanor

It is a misdemeanor for any person to engage in any of the following acts, the commission of which shall be cause for disciplinary action against any licensee or applicant:

(a) Using false, misleading, or deceptive advertising as an inducement to enter into any contract for a work of improvement, including, but not limited to, any home improvement contract, whereby any member of the public may be misled or injured.

(b) Making any substantial misrepresentation in the procurement of a contract for a home improvement or other work of improvement or making any false promise of a character likely to influence, persuade or, induce any person to enter into the contract.

(c) Any fraud in the execution of, or in the material alteration , any contract, trust deed, mortgage, promissory note, or other document incident to a home improvement transaction or other transaction involving a work of improvement.

(d) Preparing or accepting any trust deed, mortgage, promissory note, or other evidence of indebtedness upon the obligations of a home improvement transaction or other transaction for a work of improvement with knowledge that it specifies a greater monetary obligation than the consideration for the improvement work, which consideration may be a time sale price.

(e) Directly or indirectly publishing any advertisement relating to home improvements or other works of improvement that contains an assertion, representation, or statement of fact that is false, deceptive, or misleading, or by any means advertising or purporting to offer to the general public this improvement work with the intent not to accept contracts for the particular work or at the price that is advertised or offered to the public, except that any advertisement that is subject to and complies with the existing rules, regulations, or guides of the Federal Trade Commission shall not be deemed false, deceptive, or misleading.

(f) Any person who violates subdivision (b), (c), (d), or (e) as part of a plan or scheme to defraud an owner of a residential or nonresidential structure, including a mobilehome or manufactured home, in connection with the offer or performance of repairs to the structure for damage caused by a natural disaster, shall be ordered by the court to make full restitution to the victim based on the person's ability to pay, as defined in subdivision (e) of Section 1203.1b of the Penal Code. In addition to full restitution and imprisonment as authorized by this section, the court may impose a fine of not less than five hundred dollars ($500) nor more than twenty-five thousand dollars ($25,000), based upon the defendant's ability to pay. This subdivision applies to natural disasters for which a state of emergency is proclaimed by the Governor pursuant to Section 8625 of the Government Code or for which an emergency or major disaster is declared by the President of the United States.

Added Stats 1969 ch 1583 § 9 as § 7116.2. Renumbered Stats 1972 ch 1138 § 4. Amended Stats 1994 ch 175 § 4 (SB 634), effective July 9, 1994; Stats 2006 ch 538 § 13 (SB 1852), effective January 1, 2007.

§ 7162. Contents of contract; Representations as to goods and materials

(a) Notwithstanding any other provision of law, any representation by a person licensed pursuant to this chapter with respect to a trademark or brand name, quality, or size of any goods or materials, in reference to bathroom fixtures, a sink, stove, refrigerator, lighting, carpeting and other floor surfaces, burglar and smoke alarms, paints, textured coatings, siding and other wall surfaces, insulation, roofing, air conditioning and heating systems, and appliances, to be provided by the person pursuant to a home improvement contract, as defined in Section 7151.2, shall set forth, in writing, in the contract or specifications and shall include a description of the goods or materials, including any brand name, model number, or similar designation.

(b) Failure to install the specific goods or materials as represented as required by this section constitutes a cause for disciplinary action under this chapter.

Added Stats 1981 ch 916 § 3.

§ 7163. Enforceability of contract prior to buyer obtaining loan

(a) No contract for home improvement shall be enforceable against the buyer if the obtaining of a loan for all or a portion of the contract price is a condition precedent to the contract or if the contractor provides financing, or in any manner assists the buyer to obtain a loan or refers the buyer to any person who may loan or arrange a loan for all or a portion of the contract price unless all of the following requirements are satisfied:

(1) The third party, if any, agrees to make the loan.

(2) The buyer agrees to accept the loan or financing.

(3) The buyer does not rescind the loan or financing transaction, within the period prescribed for rescission, pursuant to the federal Truth in Lending Act (15 U.S.C. Sec. 1601 et seq.) or Regulation Z, if applicable.

(b) Until the requirements of paragraphs (1), (2), and (3) of subdivision (a) are satisfied, it shall be unlawful for the contractor to do any of the following:

(1) Deliver any property or perform any services other than obtaining building permits or other similar services preliminary to the commencement of the home improvement for which no mechanic's lien can be claimed.

(2) Represent in any manner that the contract is enforceable or that the buyer has any obligation thereunder.

Any violation of this subdivision shall render the contract unenforceable.

(c) If the contract is unenforceable pursuant to subdivision (a) or subdivision (b), the contractor shall immediately and without condition return all money, property, and other consideration given by the buyer. If the buyer gave any property as consideration and the contractor does not or cannot return it for whatever reason, the contractor shall immediately return the fair market value of the property or its value as designated in the contract, whichever is greater. Nothing herein shall prohibit a contractor from receiving a downpayment otherwise permitted by law provided the contractor returns the downpayment as herein required if the contract is unenforceable pursuant to subdivision (a) or (b).

Section VI

(d)(1) Except as provided in paragraph (2), the buyer may retain without obligation in law or equity any services or property provided pursuant to a contract that is unenforceable pursuant to subdivision (a) or subdivision (b).

(2) If the contractor has delivered any property to the buyer pursuant to a contract which is unenforceable pursuant to subdivision (a) or subdivision (b), the buyer shall make the property available to the contractor for return provided that all of the following requirements are satisfied:

(A) The property can be practically returned to the contractor without causing any damage to the buyer.

(B) The contractor, at the contractor's expense, first returns to the buyer any money, property, and other consideration taken by the contractor provided that the property is returned in the condition that it was in immediately prior to its taking. If applicable, the contractor shall also, at its expense, reinstall any property taken in the manner in which the property had been installed prior to its taking.

(C) The contractor, at the contractor's expense, picks up the property within 60 days of the execution of the contract.

(e) For the purpose of this section, "home improvement" means "home improvement" as defined in Section 7151. Goods are included within the definition notwithstanding whether they are to be attached to real property or to be so affixed to real property as to become a part thereof whether or not severable therefrom.

(f) The rights and remedies provided the buyer under this section are nonexclusive and cumulative to all other rights and remedies under other laws.

(g) Any waiver of this section shall be deemed contrary to public policy and shall be void and unenforceable. However, the buyer may waive subdivisions (a) and (b) to the extent that the contract is executed in connection with the making of emergency repairs or services that are necessary for the immediate protection of persons or real or personal property. The buyer's waiver for emergency repairs or services shall be in a dated written statement that describes the emergency, states that the contractor has informed the buyer of subdivisions (a) and (b) and that the buyer waives those provisions, and is signed by each owner of the property. Waivers made on printed forms are void and unenforceable.

Added Stats 1985 ch 989 § 1. Amended Stats 1986 ch 1404 § 1, effective September 30, 1986; Stats 1991 ch 1160 § 46 (AB 2190); Stats 1993 ch 589 § 13 (AB 2211).

§ 7164. Contract and changes to be in writing; Requirements (First of two; Operative until July 1, 2012)

(a) Notwithstanding Section 7044, every contract and any changes in a contract, between an owner and a contractor, for the construction of a single-family dwelling to be retained by the owner for at least one year shall be evidenced in writing signed by both parties.

(b) The writing shall contain the following:

(1) The name, address, and license number of the contractor.

(2) The approximate dates when the work will begin and be substantially completed.

(3) A legal description of the location where the work will be done.

(4) A statement with the heading "Mechanics' Lien Warning" as follows:

"MECHANICS LIEN WARNING:

Anyone who helps improve your property, but who is not paid, may record what is called a mechanics' lien on your property. A mechanics' lien is a claim, like a mortgage or home equity loan, made against your property and recorded with the county recorder.

Even if you pay your contractor in full, unpaid subcontractors, suppliers, and laborers who helped to improve your property may record mechanics' liens and sue you in court to foreclose the lien. If a court finds the lien is valid, you could be forced to pay twice or have a court officer sell your home to pay the lien. Liens can also affect your credit.

To preserve their right to record a lien, each subcontractor and material supplier must provide you with a document called a '20-day Preliminary Notice.' This notice is not a lien. The purpose of the notice is to let you know that the person who sends you the notice has the right to record a lien on your property if he or she is not paid.

BE CAREFUL. The Preliminary Notice can be sent up to 20 days after the subcontractor starts work or the supplier provides material. This can be a big problem if you pay your contractor before you have received the Preliminary Notices.

You will not get Preliminary Notices from your prime contractor or from laborers who work on your project. The law assumes that you already know they are improving your property.

PROTECT YOURSELF FROM LIENS. You can protect yourself from liens by getting a list from your contractor of all the subcontractors and material suppliers that work on your project. Find out from your contractor when these subcontractors started work and when these suppliers delivered goods or materials. Then wait 20 days, paying attention to the Preliminary Notices you receive.

PAY WITH JOINT CHECKS. One way to protect yourself is to pay with a joint check. When your contractor tells you it is time to pay for the work of a subcontractor or supplier who has provided you with a Preliminary Notice, write a joint check payable to both the contractor and the subcontractor or material supplier.

For other ways to prevent liens, visit CSLB's Web site at www.cslb.ca.gov or call CSLB at 800-321-CSLB (2752).

REMEMBER, IF YOU DO NOTHING, YOU RISK HAVING A LIEN PLACED ON YOUR HOME. This can mean that you may have

to pay twice, or face the forced sale of your home to pay what you owe."

(5)(A) A statement prepared by the board through regulation that emphasizes the value of commercial general liability insurance and encourages the owner to verify the contractor's insurance coverage and status.

(B) A check box indicating whether or not the contractor carries commercial general liability insurance, and if that is the case, the name and the telephone number of the insurer.

(c) The writing may also contain other matters agreed to by the parties to the contract. The writing shall be legible and shall clearly describe any other document which is to be incorporated into the contract. Prior to commencement of any work, the owner shall be furnished a copy of the written agreement, signed by the contractor. The provisions of this section are not exclusive and do not relieve the contractor from compliance with all other applicable provisions of law.

(d) Every contract subject to the provisions of this section shall contain, in close proximity to the signatures of the owner and contractor, a notice in at least 10-point bold type or in all capital letters, stating that the owner has the right to require the contractor to have a performance and payment bond and that the expense of the bond may be borne by the owner.

(e) The requirements in paragraphs (5) of subdivision (b) shall become operative three months after the board adopts the regulations referenced in subparagrah (A) of paragraph (5) of subdivision (b).

(f) This section shall become operative on January 1, 2006.

Added Stats 2005 ch 48 § 19 (SB 1113), effective July 18, 2005, operative January 1, 2006.

§ 7164. Contract and changes to be in writing; Requirements (Second of two; Operative July 1, 2012)

(a) Notwithstanding Section 7044, every contract and any changes in a contract, between an owner and a contractor, for the construction of a single-family dwelling to be retained by the owner for at least one year shall be evidenced in writing signed by both parties.

(b) The writing shall contain the following:

(1) The name, address, and license number of the contractor.

(2) The approximate dates when the work will begin and be substantially completed.

(3) A legal description of the location where the work will be done.

(4) A statement with the heading "Mechanics Lien Warning" as follows:

"MECHANICS LIEN WARNING:

Anyone who helps improve your property, but who is not paid, may record what is called a mechanics lien on your property. A mechanics lien is a claim, like a mortgage or home equity loan, made against your property and recorded with the county recorder.

Even if you pay your contractor in full, unpaid subcontractors, suppliers, and laborers who helped to improve your property may record mechanics liens and sue you in court to foreclose the lien. If a court finds the lien is valid, you could be forced to pay twice or have a court officer sell your home to pay the lien. Liens can also affect your credit.

To preserve their right to record a lien, each subcontractor and material supplier must provide you with a document called a 'Preliminary Notice.' This notice is not a lien. The purpose of the notice is to let you know that the person who sends you the notice has the right to record a lien on your property if he or she is not paid.

BE CAREFUL. The Preliminary Notice can be sent up to 20 days after the subcontractor starts work or the supplier provides material. This can be a big problem if you pay your contractor before you have received the Preliminary Notices.

You will not get Preliminary Notices from your prime contractor or other persons you contract with directly or from laborers who work on your project. The law assumes that you already know they are improving your property.

PROTECT YOURSELF FROM LIENS. You can protect yourself from liens by getting a list from your contractor of all the subcontractors and material suppliers that work on your project. Find out from your contractor when these subcontractors started work and when these suppliers delivered goods or materials. Then wait 20 days, paying attention to the Preliminary Notices you receive.

PAY WITH JOINT CHECKS. One way to protect yourself is to pay with a joint check. When your contractor tells you it is time to pay for the work of a subcontractor or supplier who has provided you with a Preliminary Notice, write a joint check payable to both the contractor and the subcontractor or material supplier.

For other ways to prevent liens, visit CSLB's Web site at www.cslb.ca.gov or call CSLB at 800-321-CSLB (2752).

REMEMBER, IF YOU DO NOTHING, YOU RISK HAVING A LIEN PLACED ON YOUR HOME. This can mean that you may have to pay twice, or face the forced sale of your home to pay what you owe."

(5)(A) A statement prepared by the board through regulation that emphasizes the value of commercial general liability insurance and encourages the owner to verify the contractor's insurance coverage and status.

(B) A check box indicating whether or not the contractor carries commercial general liability insurance, and if that is the case, the name and the telephone number of the insurer.

(c) The writing may also contain other matters agreed to by the parties to the contract. The writing shall be legible and shall clearly describe any other document which is to be incorporated into the contract. Prior to commencement of any work, the owner shall be furnished a copy of the written agreement, signed by the contractor. The provisions of this section are not exclusive and do not relieve the contractor from compliance with all other applicable provisions of law.

(d) Every contract subject to the provisions of this section shall contain, in close proximity to the signatures of the owner and contractor, a notice in at least 10-point boldface type or in all capital letters, stating that the owner has the right to require the contractor to have a performance and payment bond and that the expense of the bond may be borne by the owner.

(e) The requirements in paragraph (5) of subdivision (b) shall become operative three months after the board adopts the regulations referenced in subparagraph (A) of paragraph (5) of subdivision (b).

(f) This section shall become operative on January 1, 2006.

Added Stats 2005 ch 48 § 19 (SB 1113), effective July 18, 2005, operative January 1, 2006. Amended Stats 2010 ch 697 § 8 (SB 189), effective January 1, 2011, operative July 1, 2012.

§ 7165.   Conditions under which swimming pool contract financed by third-party lender is enforceable

The requirements of this section may be substituted for the requirements of paragraphs (1), (2), and (3) of subdivision (a) of Section 7163 if a swimming pool contract is to be financed by a third-party lender and if all the following conditions are met:

(a) The lender has agreed, in writing, to provide financing to the buyer for the maximum estimated construction cost of the swimming pool.

(b) The lender has provided the buyer a written copy of the terms and conditions of the loan for the maximum estimated construction cost of the swimming pool, including the following terms disclosed in the manner required by the federal Truth in Lending Act and Regulation Z: the annual percentage rate, the finance charge, the amount financed, the total number of payments, the payment schedule, and a description of the security interest to be taken by the lender.

(c) The lender has agreed in writing to the following:

(1) To offer to loan the maximum estimated construction cost on the terms and conditions disclosed pursuant to subdivision (b).

(2) If the construction cost of the swimming pool is determined after the completion of excavation to be less than the maximum estimated construction cost, to offer to loan the lesser amount needed to complete the construction of the swimming pool on the same security as, and at an annual percentage rate and monthly payment amount not to exceed, that disclosed in subdivision (b).

The lender's written agreement shall state the duration of the offer, which shall not be less than 15 days following the completion of the excavation of the swimming pool.

(d) The buyer acknowledges receipt of the writings required by subdivisions (a), (b), and (c) and, no sooner than three business days after receiving all of these writings, requests on the form prescribed in subdivision (e) that the contractor begin performance of the swimming pool contract prior to the expiration of any rescission period applicable to the loan.

(e) The request of a buyer, described in subdivision (d), shall be set forth on a document separate and apart from the swimming pool contract and shall contain the following notice in at least 10-point type unless otherwise stated:

"NOTICE

Under the law, this contract is not enforceable until:

(1) A third party agrees to make a loan to finance the construction cost of the swimming pool;

(2) You agree to accept the loan; and

(3) You do not cancel the loan within the period prescribed for cancellation under the federal Truth in Lending Act or Regulation Z (usually three business days after the loan is consummated).

Until the cancellation period is over, the contractor cannot deliver any materials or perform any services except preliminary services for which no mechanic's lien can be claimed.

However, as an alternative to the above, you can ask the contractor to start work and deliver materials before the cancellation period on the loan is over if all of the following have occurred:

(1) The lender has agreed, in writing, to provide you with financing for up to the maximum estimated construction cost of the swimming pool.

(2) The lender has provided you with a written copy of the terms and conditions of a loan for the maximum estimated cost, including the annual percentage rate, the finance charge, the amount financed, the total of payments, the payment schedule, and a description of the security interest to be taken by the lender.

(3) The lender has agreed in writing to offer these terms and conditions for a period not less than 15 days following completion of the excavation of the swimming pool.

(4) Three business days have passed since you received the writing mentioned in paragraphs (1), (2), and (3), and you then sign a copy of this form to request that the contractor begin construction of the swimming pool before the cancellation period on your loan is over.

The first day you can sign the request for the contractor to begin construction of the swimming pool is

Section VI

(contractor to insert third business day after buyer receives writings described in subdivisions (a), (b), and (c))

If you sign this request, the contractor will be permitted to immediately begin performance of the contract, and if the contractor is not paid in accordance with the terms of the contract, he or she may file a lien against your property for the value of the labor and materials provided. [This paragraph shall be printed in 12-point type.]

REQUEST

I/we request that the contractor immediately start construction of the swimming pool.

_____
Date

Buyer(s)"

(f) The contractor shall provide the buyer a copy of the buyer's signed request at the time of signature.

(g) This section applies to each buyer who signs the swimming pool contract or the promissory note, other evidence of indebtedness, or security instrument incident to the loan for swimming pool construction.

(h) For the purpose of this section, "business day" has the meaning provided in Section 9 of the Civil Code.

Added Stats 1986 ch 1404 § 2, effective September 30, 1986, as § 7167.5. Renumbered by Stats 1991 ch 1160 § 51 (AB 2190).

—*See Health and Safety Code Section 115920, Citations; 115921, Definitions; 115922, Safety Features; 115923, Enclosure; 115924, Consumer Notice; 15925, Inapplicability, in Appendix.*

§ 7166. Application of article to contracts for construction of specified swimming pools

The provisions of Article 10 shall not apply to contracts for the construction of swimming pools to be built for the use and enjoyment of other than a single-family unit upon or contiguous to premises occupied only by a single-family unit, nor shall they apply to the construction of swimming pools built as part of an original building plan by the same contractor who builds a single-family dwelling unit on the premises.

Added Stats 1979 ch 747 § 2 as § 7170. Amended Stats 1980 ch 138 § 8, effective May 30, 1980. Amended and renumbered Stats 1991 ch 1160 § 54 (AB 2190).

§ 7167. Certain contracts for construction of swimming pool void; Recovery for work performed

(a) Any contract, the primary purpose of which is the construction of a swimming pool, that does not substantially comply with paragraph (4) or (5) of subdivision (c) or paragraph (7), (8), or (9) of subdivision (d) of Section 7159, shall be void and unenforceable by the contractor as contrary to public policy.

(b) Failure by the contractor to comply with paragraph (5) of subdivision (c) of Section 7159 as set forth in subdivision (a) of this section does not preclude the recovery of compensation for work performed based on quasi-contract, quantum meruit, restitution, or other similar legal or equitable remedies designed to prevent unjust enrichment.

Added Stats 2005 ch 48 § 21 (SB 1113), effective July 18, 2005, operative January 1, 2006. Amended Stats 2005 ch 385 § 10 (AB 316), effective January 1, 2006.

§ 7168. Reasonable attorney's fees

In any action between a person contracting for construction of a swimming pool and a swimming pool contractor arising out of a contract for swimming pool construction, the court shall award reasonable attorney's fees to the prevailing party.

Added Stats 1979 ch 747 § 2 as § 7169. Amended and renumbered Stats 1991 ch 1160 § 53 (AB 2190).

Article 11
Asbestos Consultants

§ 7180. Requirement of certification

(a) No person shall, on or after July 1, 1992, engage in the practice of an asbestos consultant as defined in Section 7181, or as a site surveillance technician as defined in Section 7182, unless he or she is certified by the Division of Occupational Safety and Health pursuant to regulations required by subdivision (b) of Section 9021.5 of the Labor Code.

(b) Certification as an asbestos consultant or site surveillance technician shall not be required when a licensed contractor or registered asbestos abatement contractor takes no more than 12 bulk samples of suspected asbestos-containing material that is required to be removed, repaired, or disturbed as part of a construction project in a residential dwelling solely for any of the following purposes: (1) bid preparation for asbestos abatement; (2) evaluating exposure to its own employees during construction or asbestos abatement; or (3) determining for its own purposes or for the purpose of communicating whether or not a contract for asbestos abatement has been satisfactorily completed. Persons taking samples for the purposes described in this section shall be certified building inspectors under the Asbestos Hazard Emergency Response Act, as specified in Section 763 of Title 40 of the Code of Federal Regulations, appendix (c) to subpart (e). No licensed contractor or asbestos abatement contractor may provide professional health and safety services or perform any asbestos risk assessment. A bid for asbestos abatement may communicate the results and location of sampling for the presence of asbestos and how the asbestos will be abated. This section does not affect the requirement that asbestos abatement contractors be registered under Section 6501.5 of the Labor Code, nor does it permit a licensed contractor or asbestos abatement contractor to perform clearance air monitoring following asbestos abatement, unless otherwise permitted by law.

Added Stats 1990 ch 1255 § 1 (SB 732). Amended Stats 1996 ch 526 § 1 (SB 1486).

§ 7180.5. Requirement of certification for building owner or operator contracts

When a building owner or operator engages the services of a person to perform asbestos consulting or site surveillance technician activities as defined in Sections 7181 and 7182 after July 1, 1992, the building owner or operator shall contract with a person who is certified by the Division of Occupational Safety and Health pursuant to the regulations required by subdivision (b) of Section 9021.5 of the Labor Code.

Added Stats 1990 ch 1255 § 1 (SB 732).

§ 7181. "Asbestos consultant"

An "asbestos consultant," as used in this chapter, means any person who contracts to provide professional health and safety services relating to asbestos-containing material, as defined in subdivision (b) of Section 6501.8 of the Labor Code, including building inspections, abatement project design, contract administration, supervision of site surveillance technicians as defined in Section 7182, sample collections, preparation of asbestos management plans, and clearance air monitoring.

Added Stats 1990 ch 1255 § 1 (SB 732).

§ 7182. "Site surveillance technician"

A "site surveillance technician" means any person who acts as an independent onsite representative of an asbestos consultant who monitors the asbestos abatement activities of others, provides asbestos air monitoring services for area and personnel samples, and performs building surveys and contract administration at the direction of an asbestos consultant.

Added Stats 1990 ch 1255 § 1 (SB 732).

§ 7183. Notice of complete application; Issuance of certificate; Provisional certification card

(a) Within 15 days of receipt of an application for certification pursuant to this article, the division shall inform the applicant in writing either (1) that the application is complete and accepted, or (2) that it is deficient and that additional information, documentation, or examination, specified in the notification, is required to complete the application. Within 45 days of the date of filing of a completed application, the division shall issue to each person who qualifies for certification pursuant to this article, a certification card which shall identify the holder thereof and the type of certification for which he or she has qualified. If the division cannot comply with the notification deadlines specified in this section, the division shall issue a provisional certification card until all procedures specified in this section are completed.

(b) The certification required by this article shall satisfy all certification requirements of the division for asbestos consultants and site surveillance technicians.

Added Stats 1990 ch 1255 § 1 (SB 732).

§ 7183.5. Enforcement by division

The division shall enforce this article. In the event the division determines that a certified asbestos consultant or site surveillance technician obtained certification under false pretenses, or that a certified asbestos consultant or site surveillance technician acted in a grossly negligent or fraudulent manner, or engaged in repeated acts of negligence, the division shall revoke that person's certification. The division shall only revoke a certification after complying with all of the procedural requirements of Chapter 5 (commencing with Section 11500) of Division 3 of Part 1 of Title 2 of the Government Code.

Added Stats 1990 ch 1255 § 1 (SB 732).

§ 7184. Requirements for qualification as certified asbestos consultant

A person shall qualify as a certified asbestos consultant by meeting all of the following requirements:

(a) Having any one of the following:

(1) One year of asbestos-related experience, and a bachelor of science degree in engineering, architecture, industrial hygiene, construction management, or a related biological or physical science.

Section VI

(2) Two years of asbestos-related experience, and a bachelor's degree.

(3) Three years of asbestos-related experience, and an associate of arts degree in engineering, architecture, industrial hygiene, construction management, or a related biological or physical science.

(4) Four years of asbestos-related experience and a high school diploma or its equivalent.

(b) Possession of a valid federal Asbestos Hazard Emergency Response Act (Subchapter II (commencing with Section 2641) of Chapter 53 of Title 15 of the United States Code) certificate for the type of work being performed, or its equivalent, as determined by the division.

(c) Demonstration of proficiency by achieving a passing score as determined by the division on an examination approved or administered by the division including, but not limited to, the following subjects:

(1) Physical characteristics of asbestos.

(2) Health effects of asbestos.

(3) Federal Occupational Safety and Health Administration, Division of Occupational Safety and Health, Environmental Protection Agency, air quality management districts, and State Department of Health Services regulatory requirements, including protective clothing, respiratory protection, exposure limits, personal hygiene, medical monitoring, disposal, and general industry safety hazards.

(4) State-of-the-art asbestos abatement and control work procedures. The division shall define and incorporate into the certification standards the term "state-of-the-art" for purposes of this article, in the regulations required by subdivision (b) of Section 9021.5 of the Labor Code.

(5) Federal Asbestos Hazard Emergency Response Act training information and procedures for inspectors, management planners, and supervisors, as provided for under Subchapter II (commencing with Section 2641) of Chapter 53 of Title 15 of the United States Code, or the equivalent, as determined by the division.

(6) Information concerning industrial hygiene sampling methodology, including asbestos sampling and analysis techniques and recordkeeping.

Added Stats 1990 ch 1255 § 1 (SB 732).

§ 7185. Requirements for qualification as certified site surveillance technician

A person shall qualify as a certified site surveillance technician by meeting all of the following requirements:

(a) Having six months of asbestos-related experience under the supervision of an asbestos consultant.

(b) Possession of a high school diploma or equivalent.

(c) Possession of a valid federal Asbestos Hazard Emergency Response Act (Subchapter II (commencing with Section 2641) of Chapter 53 of Title 15 of the United States Code) certificate for the type of work being performed, or its equivalent, as determined by the division.

(d) Demonstration of proficiency by achieving a passing score, as determined by the division, on an examination approved or administered by the division covering the following subjects:

(1) Physical characteristics of asbestos.

(2) Health effects of asbestos.

(3) Federal Occupational Safety and Health Administration, Division of Occupational Safety and Health, Environmental Protection Agency, air quality management districts, and State Department of Health Services regulatory requirements, including protective clothing, respiratory protection, exposure limits, personal hygiene, medical monitoring, and general industry safety hazards.

(4) State-of-the-art asbestos abatement and control work procedures.

(5) Industrial hygiene sampling methodology, including sampling techniques and recordkeeping.

Added Stats 1990 ch 1255 § 1 (SB 732).

§ 7187. Financial conflict of interest; Legislative intent

When a building owner or operator contracts with an asbestos consultant or site surveillance technician for performance of the activities described in Sections 7181 and 7182, that asbestos consultant or site surveillance technician shall not have any financial or proprietary interest in an asbestos abatement contractor hired for the same project. However, this section shall not preclude the hiring of a consultant by a contractor for the purpose of providing health and safety services for the personnel of the contractor. This section shall not apply when a licensed contractor or registered asbestos abatement contractor takes no more than 12 bulk samples of suspected asbestos-containing material that is required to be removed, repaired, or disturbed as part of a construction project in a residential dwelling solely for any of the following purposes: (1) bid preparation for asbestos abatement; (2) evaluating exposure to its own employees during construction or asbestos abatement; or (3) determining for its own purposes or for the purpose of communicating whether or not a contract for asbestos abatement has been satisfactorily completed. Persons taking samples for the purposes described in this section shall be certified building inspectors under the Asbestos Hazard Emergency Response Act, as specified in Section 763 of Title 40 of the Code of Federal Regulations, appendix (c) to subpart (e). No licensed contractor or asbestos abatement contractor may provide professional health and safety services or perform any asbestos risk assessment. A licensed contractor or asbestos abatement contractor may seek compensation

Section VI

for bid preparation, including the cost of laboratory analysis of asbestos-containing material.

It is the intent of the Legislature in enacting this section to make certain that the asbestos-related work performed by a consultant, including, but not limited to, clearance air monitoring, project design, and contract administration, is performed in a manner which provides for independent professional judgment undertaken without consideration of the financial or beneficial interest of the contractor.

Added Stats 1990 ch 1255 § 1 (SB 732). Amended Stats 1996 ch 526 § 2 (SB 1486).

§ 7189. Penalties for violation

Any person who engages in the practices of an asbestos consultant or a site surveillance technician, who is not certified pursuant to this article, or who violates Section 7187, is subject to one of the following penalties:

(a) Conviction of a first offense is an infraction punishable by a fine of not less than one thousand dollars ($1,000) or more than three thousand dollars ($3,000).

(b) Conviction of a subsequent offense is a misdemeanor requiring revocation or suspension of any asbestos consultant's or site surveillance technician's certification, and a fine not not less than three thousand dollars ($3,000) or more than five thousand dollars ($5,000), or imprisonment in the county jail not exceeding one year, or both the fine and imprisonment.

The division shall only impose these penalties after complying with all of the procedural requirements of Chapter 5 (commencing with Section 11500) of Division 3 of Part 1 of Title 2 of the Government Code.

Added Stats 1990 ch 1255 § 1 (SB 732).

§ 7189.5. Application of article

This article shall apply to asbestos abatement projects within the meaning of asbestos-related work as defined in Section 6501.8 of the Labor Code, and which involves 100 square feet or more of surface area of asbestos containing material.

Added Stats 1990 ch 1255 § 1 (SB 732).

§ 7189.7. Construction of article

(a) Nothing in this article shall be construed to require agencies of the state to contract with asbestos consultants or site surveillance technicians who are not employees of the state as long as employees of the state who are assigned to perform the activities described in Sections 7181 and 7182 have been certified by the division pursuant to the regulations required by subdivision (b) of Section 9021.5 of the Labor Code. Where feasible, the state shall assign a state civil service classification of associate industrial hygienist or senior industrial hygienist to carry out asbestos consultation activities as described in Section 7181 for state-owned and leased buildings. The individuals in the classification assigned shall be certified as required in this article before performing these activities.

(b) Nothing in this article shall be construed to require attorneys who provide legal advice on asbestos-related matters to building owners or operators to be certified by the division pursuant to the regulations required by subdivision (b) of Section 9021.5 of the Labor Code.

Added Stats 1990 ch 1255 § 1 (SB 732).

Article 12

Prohibitions

§ 7190. Use of name or position of public official in advertisement or promotional material; Disclaimer

(a) The name or position of a public official may not be used in an advertisement or any promotional material by a person licensed under this chapter, without the written authorization of the public official. A printed advertisement or promotional material that uses the name or position of a public official with that public official's written authorization, shall also include a disclaimer in at least 10-point roman boldface type, that shall be in a color or print which contrasts with the background so as to be easily legible, and set apart from any other printed matter. The disclaimer shall consist of a statement that reads "The name of (specify name of public official) does not imply that (specify name of public official) endorses this product or service in (his or her) official capacity and does not imply an endorsement by any governmental entity." If the advertisement is broadcast, this statement shall be read in a clearly audible tone of voice.

(b) For purposes of this section, "public official" means a member, officer, employee, or consultant of a local government agency, as defined in Section 82041 of the Government Code, or state agency, as defined in Section 82049 of the Government Code.

Added Stats 1994 ch 1135 § 5 (AB 3302).

—See Civil Code Section 1770, Unfair Practices, in Appendix.

§ 7191. Title of provision for arbitration of disputes in contract for work on specified residential property

(a) If a contract for work on residential property with four or fewer units contains a provision for arbitration of a dispute between the principals in the transaction, the provision shall be clearly titled "ARBITRATION OF DISPUTES."

If a provision for arbitration is included in a printed contract, it shall be set out in at least 10-point roman boldface type or in contrasting red print in at least 8-point roman boldface type, and if the provision is included in a typed contract, it shall be set out in capital letters.

(b) Immediately before the line or space provided for the parties to indicate their assent or nonassent to the arbitration provision described in subdivision (a), and immediately following that arbitration provision, the following shall appear:

"NOTICE: BY INITIALING IN THE SPACE BELOW YOU ARE AGREEING TO HAVE ANY DISPUTE ARISING OUT OF THE MATTERS INCLUDED IN THE 'ARBITRATION OF DISPUTES' PROVISION DECIDED BY NEUTRAL ARBITRATION AS PROVIDED BY CALIFORNIA LAW AND YOU ARE GIVING UP ANY RIGHTS YOU MIGHT POSSESS TO HAVE THE DISPUTE LITIGATED IN A COURT OR JURY TRIAL. BY INITIALING IN THE SPACE BELOW YOU ARE GIVING UP YOUR JUDICIAL RIGHTS TO DISCOVERY AND APPEAL, UNLESS THOSE RIGHTS ARE SPECIFICALLY INCLUDED IN THE 'ARBITRATION OF DISPUTES' PROVISION. IF YOU REFUSE TO SUBMIT TO ARBITRATION AFTER AGREEING TO THIS PROVISION, YOU MAY BE COMPELLED TO ARBITRATE UNDER THE AUTHORITY OF THE BUSINESS AND PROFESSIONS CODE OR OTHER APPLICABLE LAWS. YOUR AGREEMENT TO THIS ARBITRATION PROVISION IS VOLUNTARY." "WE HAVE READ AND UNDERSTAND THE FOREGOING AND AGREE TO SUBMIT DISPUTES ARISING OUT OF THE MATTERS INCLUDED IN THE 'ARBITRATION OF DISPUTES' PROVISION TO NEUTRAL ARBITRATION."

If the above provision is included in a printed contract, it shall be set out either in at least 10-point roman boldface type or in contrasting red print in at least 8-point roman boldface type, and if the provision is included in a typed contract, it shall be set out in capital letters.

(c) A provision for arbitration of a dispute between a principal in a contract for work on a residential property with four or fewer units that does not comply with this section may not be enforceable against any person other than the licensee.

(d) This section does not limit the board's authority to investigate complaints or to discipline a licensee for violations of this code.

Added Stats 1994 ch 1135 § 5 (AB 3302).

Chapter 9.3

Home Inspectors

§ 7195. Definitions

For purposes of this chapter, the following definitions apply:

(a)(1) "Home inspection" is a noninvasive, physical examination, performed for a fee in connection with a transfer, as defined in subdivision (e), of real property, of the mechanical, electrical, or plumbing systems or the structural and essential components of a residential dwelling of one to four units designed to identify material defects in those systems, structures and components. "Home inspection" includes any consultation regarding the property that is represented to be a home inspection or any confusingly similar term.

(2) "Home inspection," if requested by the client, may include an inspection of energy efficiency. Energy efficiency items to be inspected may include the following:

(A) A noninvasive inspection of insulation R-values in attics, roofs, walls, floors, and ducts.

(B) The number of window glass panes and frame types.

(C) The heating and cooling equipment and water heating systems.

(D) The age and fuel type of major appliances.

(E) The exhaust and cooling fans.

(F) The type of thermostat and other systems.

(G) The general integrity and potential leakage areas of walls, window areas, doors, and duct systems.

(H) The solar control efficiency of existing windows.

(b) A "material defect" is a condition that significantly affects the value, desirability, habitability, or safety of the dwelling. Style or aesthetics shall not be considered in determining whether a system, structure, or component is defective.

(c) A "home inspection report" is a written report prepared for a fee and issued after a home inspection. The report clearly describes and identifies the inspected systems, structures, or components of the dwelling, any material defects identified, and any recommendations regarding the conditions observed or recommendations for evaluation by appropriate persons.

(d) A "home inspector" is any individual who performs a home inspection.

(e) "Transfer" is a transfer by sale, exchange, installment land sales contract, as defined in Section 2985 of the Civil Code, lease with an option to purchase, any other option to purchase, or ground lease coupled with improvements, of real property or residential stock cooperative, improved with or consisting of not less than one nor more than four dwelling units.

Added Stats 1996 ch 338 § 2 (SB 258). Amended Stats 2001 ch 773 § 2 (AB 1574).

§ 7196. Duties

It is the duty of a home inspector who is not licensed as a general contractor, structural pest control operator, or architect, or registered as a professional engineer to conduct a home inspection with the degree of care that a reasonably prudent home inspector would exercise.

Added Stats 1996 ch 338 § 2 (SB 258).

§ 7196.1.   Application

(a) Nothing in this chapter shall be construed to allow home inspectors who are not registered engineers to perform any analysis of the systems, components, or structural integrity of a dwelling that would constitute the practice of civil, electrical, or mechanical engineering, or to exempt a home inspector from Chapter 3 (commencing with Section 5500), Chapter 7 (commencing with Section 6700), Chapter 9 (commencing with Section 7000), or Chapter 14 (commencing with Section 8500) of Division 3.

(b) This chapter does not apply to a registered engineer, licensed land surveyor, or licensed architect acting pursuant to his or her professional registration or license, nor does it affect the obligations of a real estate licensee or transferor under Article 1.5 (commencing with Section 1102) of Chapter 2 of Title 4 of Part 3 of Division 2 of, or Article 2 (commencing with Section 2079) of Chapter 3 of Title 6 of Part 4 of Division 3 of, the Civil Code.

Added Stats 1996 ch 338 § 2 (SB 258).

§ 7197.   Unfair practices

(a) It is an unfair business practice for a home inspector, a company that employs the inspector, or a company that is controlled by a company that also has a financial interest in a company employing a home inspector, to do any of the following:

(1) To perform or offer to perform, for an additional fee, any repairs to a structure on which the inspector, or the inspector's company, has prepared a home inspection report in the past 12 months.

(2) Inspect for a fee any property in which the inspector, or the inspector's company, has any financial interest or any interest in the transfer of the property.

(3) To offer or deliver any compensation, inducement, or reward to the owner of the inspected property, the broker, or agent, for the referral of any business to the inspector or the inspection company.

(4) Accept an engagement to make an inspection or to prepare a report in which the employment itself or the fee payable for the inspection is contingent upon the conclusions in the report, preestablished findings, or the close of escrow.

(5) A home protection company that is affiliated with or that retains the home inspector does not violate this section if it performs repairs pursuant to claims made under the home protection contract.

(b) This section shall not affect the ability of a structural pest control operator to perform repairs pursuant to Section 8505 as a result of a structural pest control inspection.

Added Stats 1996 ch 338 § 2 (SB 258). Amended Stats 2004 ch 443 § 1 (AB 1725).

§ 7198. Public policy

Contractual provisions that purport to waive the duty owed pursuant to Section 7196, or limit the liability of the home inspector to the cost of the home inspection report, are contrary to public policy and invalid.

Added Stats 1996 ch 338 § 2 (SB 258).

§ 7199. Statute of limitation

The time for commencement of a legal action for breach of duty arising from a home inspection report shall not exceed four years from the date of the inspection.

Added Stats 1996 ch 338 § 2 (SB 258).

Chapter 9.4

Home Energy Rating System (HERS) Home Inspections

§ 7199.5. HERS California home energy audit

(a) All home inspections, including those defined in paragraph (1) of subdivision (a) of Section 7195, may, if requested by the client, be accompanied by a Home Energy Rating System (HERS) California home energy audit pursuant to regulations adopted by the Energy Commission in compliance with Section 25942 of the Public Resources Code.

(b) If the client requests a HERS California home energy audit, the HERS California home inspection report accompanying any home inspection report defined in subdivision (c) of Section 7195 shall comply with the standards and requirements established by the Energy Commission for HERS California home energy audits as specified in Article 8 (commencing with Section 1670) of Chapter 4 of Division 2 of Title 20 of the California Code of Regulations, implementing the California Home Energy Rating System Program.

Added Stats 2010 ch 453 § 1 (AB 1809), effective January 1, 2011.

§ 7199.7. Legislative intent

It is the intent of the Legislature that a Home Energy Rating System (HERS) California home energy audit may, at the request of the client, be performed by a home inspector who meets the requirements of Article 8 (commencing with Section 1670) of Chapter 4 of Division 2 of Title 20 of the California Code of Regulations.

Added Stats 2010 ch 453 § 1 (AB 1809), effective January 1, 2011.

Section VI

Chapter 13.

Contractors State License Board
Rules and Regulations

Rules and regulations serve to interpret or make laws specific. The laws provide the authority for rules and regulations. Laws take precedence and are in effect, even if the affected rules and regulations have not been corrected to reflect any changes in the law.

If you have questions concerning a particular regulation, refer to the sections of the Business and Professions Code cited in the note after the particular regulation.

What follows is the statute text, history notes for current rules and regulations, and history notes for repealed rules and regulations. You can follow the progress of proposed regulatory actions on CSLB's website at *http://www.cslb.ca.gov/laws/default.asp*.

LIST OF CURRENT BOARD RULES AND REGULATIONS

465

Article 4. Examinations

Article 5. Renewal of License

Article 6. Bonds

Section VI

CALIFORNIA CODE OF REGULATIONS

TITLE 16. DIVISION 8. CONTRACTORS STATE LICENSE BOARD

ARTICLE 1. DEFINITIONS

810. Definitions.

For the purposes of this chapter, "Board" means the Contractors State License Board and "Code," unless otherwise defined, means the Business and Professions Code.

(Authority cited: Section 7008, Business and Professions Code. Reference: Section 7008, Business and Professions Code.)

ARTICLE 1.5. REVENUE

811. Fees.

(a) Prior to July 1, 2011, the fee for:

(1) An application for an original license in a single classification is $250.

(2) An application for each additional classification is $50.

(3) An application to replace a responsible managing officer or employee is $50.

(4) Rescheduling an examination is $50.

(5) Scheduling or rescheduling an examination pursuant to Business and Professions Code Section 7137(c) is $50.

(6) Initial license of an active or inactive license is $150.

(7) Renewal of an active license that expires on or before June 30, 2011, is $300.

(8) Renewal of an inactive license that expires on or before June 30, 2011, is $150.

(9) An application for a home improvement salesperson registration is $50.

(10) Renewal of a home improvement salesperson registration is $75.

(11) An application for an asbestos certification examination is $50.

(12) An application for a hazardous substance removal or remedial action certification examination is $50.

(b) As of July 1, 2011, the fee for:

(1) An application for an original license in a single classification is $300.

(2) An application for each additional classification is $75.

(3) An application to replace a responsible managing officer or employee is $75.

(4) Rescheduling an examination is $60.

(5) Scheduling or rescheduling an examination pursuant to Business and Professions Code Section 7137(c) is $60.

(6) Initial license of an active or inactive license is $180.

(7) Renewal of an active license that expires on or after July 1, 2011, is $360.

(8) Renewal of an inactive license that expires on or after July 1, 2011, is $180.

(9) Reactivation of an inactive license is the full amount of the renewal fee for an active license.

(10) An application for a home improvement salesperson registration is $75.

(11) Renewal of a home improvement salesperson registration is $75.

(12) An application for an asbestos certification examination is $75.

(13) An application for a hazardous substance removal or remedial action certification examination is $75.

Note: Authority cited: Section 7008, Business and Professions Code. Reference: Sections 7076.5 and 7137, Business and Professions Code.

812. Dishonored Check Service Charge

The dishonored check service charge authorized by Section 6157 of the Government Code is $10.00 for each check.

(Authority cited: Section 7008, Business and Professions Code. Reference: Section 7008, Business and Professions Code; and Section 6157, Government Code.)

813. Abandonment of Application

(a) An application, other than a renewal application, shall be deemed abandoned whenever an applicant fails to return an application rejected for insufficiency or incompleteness within 90 days from date of original notice of rejection. This 90-day period may be extended by the Registrar for good cause.

Section VI

(b) Any application so abandoned may not be reinstated; however, the applicant may file a new application accompanied by the required fee.

(Authority cited: Section 7008, Business and Professions Code. Reference: Section 7067, Business and Professions Code.)

ARTICLE 2. APPLICATION FOR LICENSE

816. Application Form for Original License

(a) The license application form prescribed by the Registrar shall seek from each member of the personnel of the applicant the following information:

(1) All information required by Section 7067.5 of the Code.

(2) A record of the previous experience in the field of construction of the member of applicant's personnel who will qualify for the classification requested.

(3) Whether the applicant or a member of applicant's personnel or whether to his or her knowledge anyone with whom he/she has been associated in the contracting field has ever been licensed or had a professional or vocational license refused or revoked.

(b) The application shall be signed, under penalty of perjury, by each member of the personnel of the applicant.

(c) Nothing in this Rule shall be interpreted to limit the Registrar's authority to require an applicant to provide any other information necessary to determine the applicant's qualifications, or to exempt the applicant therefrom, or to enforce the provisions of the Contractors License Law, except as otherwise required by law.

The Registrar may exempt applicants who are eligible for waiver of examination, pursuant to Section 7065.1 of the Code, or who are not required to take the examination, pursuant to Section 7065 of the Code, from the requirement to submit information described in subsection (a)(2).

(Authority cited: Section 7008, Business and Professions Code. Reference: Sections 7066, 7067.5, 7067.6 and 7070, Business and Professions Code.)

817. Operating Capital Defined

(a) For purposes of Section 7067.5 of the Code, the term "operating capital" means the difference between current assets and current liabilities as defined in subsections (b) and (c), respectively.

(b) For accounting purposes, "current assets" means cash and other assets or resources commonly identified as those which are reasonably expected to be realized in cash or sold or consumed during the normal operating cycle of the business. Thus, the term comprehends in general such resources as

(1) cash available for current operations and items which are the equivalent of cash;

(2) inventories of merchandise, raw materials, goods in process, finished goods, operating supplies, and ordinary maintenance material and parts;

(3) trade accounts, notes, and acceptances receivable;

(4) receivables from officers, employees, affiliates, and others, if collectible in the ordinary course of business within a year;

(5) installment or deferred accounts and notes receivable if they conform generally to normal trade practices and terms within the business;

(6) marketable securities representing the investment of cash available for current operations; and

(7) prepaid expenses such as insurance, interest, rents, taxes, unused royalties, current paid advertising service not yet received, and operating supplies. Prepaid expenses are not current assets in the sense that they will be converted into cash but in the sense that, if not paid in advance, they would require the use of current assets during the operating cycle.

(c) For accounting purposes, current liabilities include those obligations whose liquidation is reasonably expected to require the use of existing resources properly classifiable as current assets, or the creation of other current liabilities. As a balance-sheet category, the classification is intended to include obligations for items which have entered into the operating cycle, such as payables incurred in the acquisition of materials and supplies to be used in the production of goods or in providing services to be offered for sale; collections received in advance of the delivery of goods or performance of services; and debts which arise from operations directly related to the operating cycle, such as accruals for wages, salaries, commissions, rentals, royalties, and income and other taxes. Other liabilities whose regular and ordinary liquidation is expected to occur within a relatively short period of time, usually twelve months, are also intended for inclusion, such as short-term debts arising from the acquisition of capital assets, serial maturities of long-term obligations, amounts required to be expended within one year under sinking fund provisions, and agency obligations arising from the collection or acceptance of cash or other assets for the account of third persons.

(Authority cited: Section 7008, Business and Professions Code. Reference: Section 7067.5, Business and Professions Code.)

819. Requirement of Corporations

A foreign or domestic corporation, applying for a license, shall complete a certification as prescribed by the Registrar, showing that it has fulfilled the filing requirements of the California Secretary of State as set out in Sections 200 and 2105 of the Corporations Code.

(Authority cited: Section 7008, Business and Professions Code. Reference: Section 7067, Business and Professions Code.)

823. Definitions: Bona Fide Employee; Direct Supervision and Control

(a) For purposes of Section 7068 of the Code, "bona fide employee" of the applicant means an employee who is permanently employed by the applicant and is actively engaged in the operation of the applicant's contracting business for at least 32 hours or 80% of the total hours per week such business is in operation, whichever is less.

(b) For purposes of Section 7068.1 of the Code, "direct supervision and control" includes any one or any combination of the following activities: supervising construction, managing construction activities by making technical and administrative decisions, checking jobs for proper workmanship, or direct supervision on construction job sites.

(Authority cited: Section 7008, Business and Professions Code. Reference: Sections 7068 and 7068.1, Business and Professions Code.)

824. Application Investigation Required

In addition to a review and verification of all applications for licensure, the Registrar shall conduct a comprehensive field investigation of a minimum of 3% of all such applications. Such investigation shall include those areas of experience claimed and such other areas as the Registrar deems appropriate for the protection of the public.

All claimed experience shall be supportable by documentation satisfactory to the Board. The Registrar shall provide to the Board, for its approval, acceptable forms of such documentation and shall inform the applicant in the application form that such documentation may be requested by the Board.

(Authority cited: Section 7008, Business and Professions Code. Reference: Section 7068, Business and Professions Code.)

825. Experience Requirement of Applicant

(a) Every applicant for a contractor's license must have had, within the last 10 years immediately preceding the filing of the application, not less than four years experience as a journeyman, foreman, supervising employee or contractor in the particular class within which the applicant intends to engage as a contractor. For purposes of this section, "journeyman" means an experienced worker in the trade who is fully qualified, as opposed to a trainee, and is able to perform the trade without supervision; or one who has completed an apprenticeship program.

(b) An applicant who was formerly a qualifier on a license in the same classification applied for may compute experience without regard to the ten-year limitation.

(c) An applicant shall not be jeopardized in computing time for service in the armed forces of the United States during a National Emergency and the length of service may be added to the 10 years mentioned above.

(d) Acceptable training in an accredited school or completion of an approved apprenticeship program in accordance with the California Labor Code (commencing with Section 3070 of the Labor Code, Chapter 4, of Division 3) or its equivalent, as approved by the Registrar, in the construction trade for which application is made will be counted as experience. In no case, however, will such training or completion of an approved apprenticeship program count for more than 3 years of the experience.

(e) The required experience shall be possessed by one member of the applicant entity or by a responsible managing employee therefore, and the member or responsible managing employee shall be required to take the examination.

(Authority cited: Section 7008, Business and Professions Code. Reference: Section 7068, Business and Professions Code.)

826. Registrar to Pass on Experience

The Registrar may determine that an applicant who does not have the specific experience required in Section 825 has some comparable knowledge, training, and/or experience which is equivalent to the required experience.

Section VI

827. Review of Application for Original License, Additional Classification, or Replacement of Qualifying Person

(a) Application Requiring Examination:

(1) The Board shall inform an applicant in writing within 60 days of receipt whether the application is complete and has been referred for examination or is deficient and what specific information is required. An application is "complete" when an acceptable application and fee have been filed by the applicant.

(2) When an application is returned which was previously rejected for deficiencies, the Board shall decide within 5 days of receipt whether the application is complete and accepted for filing.

(3) The Board shall decide within 115 days after a complete application has been referred for examination whether an applicant meets the requirements for licensure, provided that the examination has been successfully completed and the applicant has filed the bond(s), fee and other documents required by Division 3 of the Business and Professions Code.

(4) If an applicant has not successfully completed the examination as scheduled in subsection (3), or met the other requirements of that subsection (subject to the limitations of Business and Professions Code Section 7074), the Board shall decide within 45 days of the successful completion of a subsequently scheduled examination and the filing of acceptable bond(s), fee and other documents required by Division 3 of the Business and Professions Code, whether the applicant meets the requirements for licensure.

(5) The periods specified in subsection (3) and (4) shall be extended by a period of 60 days, if the application must be investigated.

(6) The minimum, median and maximum times for an application requiring examination for licensure as a contractor, for an additional classification, or for replacement of the qualifying person from the time of receipt of the application until the Board decided to issue the license, grant the additional classification or the replacement of the qualifying person, based on the Board's past two years performance, were:

(A) Application for Original License, with Examination:

Minimum......... 11 days

Median........... 253 days

Maximum ...... 726 days

(B) Application for Additional Classification, with Examination:

Minimum......... 20 days

Median............. 96 days

Maximum ...... 617 days

(C) Application for Replacement of the Qualifying Person, with Examination:

Minimum......... 20 days

Median............. 78 days

Maximum ...... 428 days

These periods include not only the Board's processing time, but also the time for which the applicant is responsible: e.g., the return of a rejected application, failure of and/or failure to appear at examinations, filing of the required bond(s) and fee.

(b) Applications Not Requiring Examination:

(1) The Board shall inform an applicant for licensure, without examination, as a contractor, for an additional classification, or for replacement of the qualifying person pursuant to Sections 7065 or 7065.1 of the Business and Professions Code within 50 days of receipt whether the application is complete and what the issuance or granting requirements are or that the application is deficient and what specific information is required.

(2) When an application is returned which was previously rejected for deficiencies, the Board shall decide within 5 days of receipt if the application is now complete and accepted for filing.

(3) Once the applicant has filed acceptable bond(s) and other documents required by Division 3 of the Business and Professions Code, the Board shall decide within 15 days whether the applicant meets the requirements for licensure.

(4) The period outlined in subsection (1) may be extended by 60 days if the application must be investigated.

(5) The minimum, median and maximum times for an application for licensure, without examination, as a contractor, for an additional classification, or for replacement of the qualifying person from the time of receipt of the application until the Board decided to issue the license, grant the additional classification or the replacement of the qualifying person, based on the Board's past two years performance were:

(A) Application for Original License, without Examination:

Minimum............. 1 day

Median............. 48 days

Section VI

Maximum ...... 349 days

(B) Application for Additional Classification, without Examination:

Minimum .... 24 days

Median .... 58.5 days

Maximum ...... 358 days

(C) Application for Replacement of the Qualifying Person, without Examination:

Minimum .... 1 day

Median .... 29 days

Maximum ...... 253 days

These periods include not only the Board's processing time, but also the time for which the applicant is responsible: e.g., return of a rejected application and filing of the required bond(s) and fee.

(Authority cited: Section 7008, Business and Professions Code; and Section 15376, Government Code. Reference: Section 15376, Government Code; and Sections 7065, 7065.1 and 7074, Business and Professions Code.)

828. Review of Application for Home Improvement Salesman Registration

(a) The Board shall inform, in writing, an applicant for registration as home improvement salesman within 30 days of receipt whether the application is deficient and what specific information is required or whether the registration has been issued.

(b) When an application is returned which was previously rejected for deficiencies, the Board shall decide whether the applicant meets the requirements for registration within 5 days after return of the completed application. A "completed application" means that an acceptable application form together with all required information, documentation and fee has been filed by the applicant.

(c) The time periods outlined in (a) and (b) may be extended by 5 weeks if the fee is in the form of a personal or company check, or by 60 days if an application requires investigation to determine if a statement of issues must be filed.

(d) The minimum, median and maximum processing times for an application for registration as a home improvement salesman from the time of receipt of the initial application until the Board makes a final decision on the application, based on the Board's past two years performance, are:

Minimum:............1 day

Median:..............8 days

Maximum: ....53 days

(Authority cited: Section 7008, Business and Professions Code. Reference: Section 15376, Government Code; and Section 7153.1, Business and Professions Code.)

ARTICLE 3. CLASSIFICATION

830. Classification Policy

(a) All contractors to whom licenses are issued shall be classified by the Registrar as a specialty contractor, as defined in this article; a general engineering contractor (Class A), as defined in Section 7056 of the Code; or a general building contractor (Class B), as defined in Section 7057 of the Code.

(b) Contractors licensed in one classification shall be prohibited from contracting in the field of any other classification unless they are also licensed in that classification or are permitted to do so by Section 831.

(Authority cited: Section 7008, Business and Professions Code. Reference: Section 7059, Business and Professions Code.)

831. Incidental and Supplemental Defined

For purposes of Section 7059, work in other classifications is "incidental and supplemental" to the work for which a specialty contractor is licensed if that work is essential to accomplish the work in which the contractor is classified. A specialty contractor may use subcontractors to complete the incidental and supplemental work, or he may use his own employees to do so.

(Authority cited: Sections 7008 and 7059, Business and Professions Code. Reference: Section 7059, Business and Professions Code.)

832. Specialty Contractors Classified

Specialty contractors shall perform their trade using the art, experience, science and skill necessary to satisfactorily organize, administer, construct and complete projects under their classification, in accordance with the standards of their trade.

They are classified into the following sub-classifications:

Classification	Code	Section
Boiler, Hot Water Heating and Steam Fitting	C-4	832.04
Building Moving and Demolition	C-21	832.21

Section VI

Classification	Code	Section
Cabinet, Millwork and Finish Carpentry	C-6	832.06
Ceramic and Mosaic Tile	C-54	832.54
Concrete	C-8	832.08
Construction Zone Traffic Control	C-31	832.31
Drywall	C-9	832.09
Earthwork and Paving	C-12	832.12
Electrical (General)	C-10	832.10
Electrical Sign	C-45	832.45
Elevator	C-11	832.11
Fencing	C-13	832.13
Fire Protection	C-16	832.16
Flooring and Floor Covering	C-15	832.15
Framing and Rough Carpentry	C-5	832.05
General Manufactured Housing	C-47	832.47
Glazing	C-17	832.17
Insulation and Acoustical	C-2	832.02
Landscaping	C-27	832.27
Lathing and Plastering	C-35	832.35
Limited Specialty	C-61	832.61
Lock and Security Equipment	C-28	832.28
Low Voltage Systems	C-7	832.07
Masonry	C-29	832.29
Ornamental Metal	C-23	832.23
Painting and Decorating	C-33	832.33
Parking and Highway Improvement	C-32	832.32
Pipeline	C-34	832.34
Plumbing	C-36	832.36
Refrigeration	C-38	832.38
Roofing	C-39	832.39

Classification	Code	Section
Sanitation System	C-42	832.42
Sheet Metal	C-43	832.43
Solar	C-46	832.46
Steel, Reinforcing	C-50	832.50
Steel, Structural	C-51	832.51
Swimming Pool	C-53	832.53
Warm-Air Heating, Ventilating and Air Conditioning	C-20	832.20
Water Conditioning	C-55	832.55
Welding	C-60	832.60
Well Drilling	C-57	832.57

(Authority cited: Sections 7008 and 7059, Business and Professions Code. Reference: Sections 7058 and 7059, Business and Professions Code.)

832.02. Class C-2—Insulation and Acoustical Contractor

An insulation and acoustical contractor installs any insulating media and preformed architectural acoustical materials for the purpose of temperature and/or sound control.

(Authority cited: Sections 7008 and 7059, Business and Professions Code. Reference: Sections 7058 and 7059, Business and Professions Code.)

832.04. Class C-4—Boiler, Hot-Water Heating and Steam Fitting Contractor

A boiler, hot-water heating and steam fitting contractor installs, services and repairs power boiler installations, hot-water heating systems and steam fitting, including fire-tube and water-tube steel power boilers and hot-water heating low pressure boilers, steam fitting and piping, fittings, valves, gauges, pumps, radiators, convectors, fuel oil tanks, fuel oil lines, chimneys, flues, heat insulation and all other equipment, including solar heating equipment, associated with these systems.

(Authority cited: Sections 7008 and 7059, Business and Professions Code. Reference: Sections 7058 and 7059, Business and Professions Code.)

832.05. Class C-5—Framing and Rough Carpentry Contractor

A framing and rough carpentry contractor performs any form work, framing or rough carpentry necessary to construct framed structures; installs or repairs individual components of framing systems and performs any rough carpentry or associated work, including but not limited to the construction or installation of: sub-flooring, siding, exterior staircases and railings, overhead doors, roof decking, truss members, and sheathing.

The amendments made to this section in 2002 shall become operative January 1, 2003, or as soon thereafter as administratively feasible, whereupon any licensee who has passed the C-5 Carpentry, Cabinet and Millwork trade examination on or after January 10, 2000, up to the effective date of this section, shall have the C-6 Cabinet, Millwork and Finish Carpentry classification added to the applicable license.

832.06. Class C-6—Cabinet, Millwork and Finish Carpentry Contractor

A cabinet, millwork and finish carpentry contractor makes cabinets, cases, sashes, doors, trims, nonbearing partitions and other items of "finish carpentry" by cutting, surfacing, joining, gluing and fabricating wood or other products to provide a functional surface. This contractor also places, erects, and finishes such cabinets and millwork in structures.

The amendments made to this section in 2002 shall become operative January 1, 2003, or as soon thereafter as administratively feasible, whereupon the C-6 Cabinet, Millwork and Finish Carpentry classification shall replace the C-5 Carpentry, Cabinet and Millwork classification on any license unless the qualifier for the license has passed the C-5 Carpentry, Cabinet and Millwork trade exam on or after January 10, 2000, or held the C-5 classification prior to that date.

(Authority cited: Sections 7008 and 7059, Business and Professions Code. Reference: Sections 7058 and 7059, Business and Professions Code.)

832.07. Class C-7—Low Voltage Systems Contractor

A communication and low voltage contractor installs, services and maintains all types of communication and low voltage systems which are energy limited and do not exceed 91 volts. These systems include, but are not limited to telephone systems, sound systems, cable television systems, closed-circuit video systems, satellite dish antennas, instrumentation and temperature controls, and low voltage landscape lighting. Low voltage fire alarm systems are specifically not included in this section.

(Authority cited: Sections 7008 and 7059, Business and Professions Code. Reference: Sections 7058 and 7059, Business and Professions Code.)

832.08. Class C-8—Concrete Contractor

A concrete contractor forms, pours, places, finishes and installs specified mass, pavement, flat and other concrete work; and places and sets screeds for pavements or flatwork. This class shall not include contractors whose sole contracting business is the application of plaster coatings or the placing and erecting of steel or bars for the reinforcing of mass, pavement, flat and other concrete work.

(Authority cited: Sections 7008 and 7059, Business and Professions Code. Reference: Sections 7058 and 7059, Business and Professions Code.)

832.09. Class C-9—Drywall Contractor

A drywall contractor lays out and installs gypsum wall board and gypsum wallboard assemblies, including nonstructural metal framing members, and performs the taping and texturing operations including the applications of compounds that adhere to wall board to produce a continuous smooth or textured surface.

(Authority cited: Sections 7008 and 7059, Business and Professions Code. Reference: Sections 7058 and 7059, Business and Professions Code.)

832.10. Class C-10—Electrical Contractor

An electrical contractor places, installs, erects or connects any electrical wires, fixtures, appliances, apparatus, raceways, conduits, solar photovoltaic cells or any part thereof, which generate, transmit, transform or utilize electrical energy in any form or for any purpose.

(Authority cited: Sections 7008 and 7059, Business and Professions Code. Reference: Sections 7058 and 7059, Business and Professions Code.)

832.11. Class C-11—Elevator Contractor

An elevator contractor fabricates, erects, installs and repairs elevators, including sheave beams, motors, sheaves, cable and wire rope, guides, cab, counterweights, doors (including sidewalk elevator doors), automatic and manual controls, signal systems, and all other devices and equipment associated with the safe and efficient installation and operation of electrical, hydraulic and manually operated elevators.

(Authority cited: Sections 7008 and 7059, Business and Professions Code. Reference: Sections 7058 and 7059, Business and Professions Code.)

832.12. Class C-12—Earthwork and Paving Contractors

An earthwork and paving contractor digs, moves, and places material forming the surface of the earth, other than water, in such a manner that a cut, fill, excavation, grade, trench, backfill, or tunnel (if incidental thereto) can be executed, including the use of explosives for these purposes. This classification includes the mixing, fabricating and placing of paving and any other surfacing materials.

(Authority cited: Sections 7008 and 7059, Business and Professions Code. Reference: Sections 7058 and 7059, Business and Professions Code.)

832.13. Class C-13—Fencing Contractor

A fencing contractor constructs, erects, alters, or repairs all types of fences, corrals, runs, railings, cribs, game court enclosures, guard rails and barriers, playground game equipment, backstops, posts, flagpoles, and gates, excluding masonry walls.

(Authority cited: Sections 7008 and 7059, Business and Professions Code. Reference: Sections 7058 and 7059, Business and Professions Code.)

832.14. Class C-14—Metal Roofing Contractor

(a) Effective July 1, 1998, the C-14 (Metal Roofing Contractor) classification shall be abolished, and a C-14 license cannot be renewed. On July 1, 1998, contractors who hold a C-14 and a C-39 (Roofing Contractor) license will hold only a C-39 license. On July 1, 1998, contractors who hold a C-14 and a C-43 (Sheet Metal Contractor) license will hold only a C-43 license. On July 1, 1998, contractors holding only a C-14 license will be granted a C-39 license.

(b) No application for the C-14 classification will be accepted by the board after the effective date of this regulatory proposal.

(Authority cited: Sections 7008 and 7059, Business and Professions Code. Reference: Sections 7058 and 7059, Business and Professions Code.)

832.15. Class C-15—Flooring and Floor Covering Contractors

A flooring and floor covering contractor prepares any surface for the installation of flooring and floor coverings, and installs carpet, resilient sheet goods, resilient tile, wood floors and flooring (including the finishing and repairing thereof), and any other materials established as flooring and floor covering material, except ceramic tile.

(Authority cited: Sections 7008 and 7059, Business and Professions Code. Reference: Sections 7058 and 7059, Business and Professions Code.)

832.16. Class C-16—Fire Protection Contractor

A Fire protection contractor lays out, fabricates and installs all types of fire protection systems; including all the equipment associated with these systems, excluding electrical alarm systems.

(Authority cited: Section 7008 and 7059 of the Business and Professions Code. Reference: Sections 7058 and 7059, Business and Professions Code.)

832.17. Class C-17—Glazing Contractor

A glazing contractor selects, cuts, assembles and/or installs all makes and kinds of glass, glass work, mirrored glass, and glass substitute materials for glazing; executes the fabrication and glazing of frames, panels, sashes and doors; and/or installs these items in any structure.

(Authority cited: Sections 7008 and 7059, Business and Professions Code. Reference: Sections 7058 and 7059, Business and Professions Code.)

832.20. Class C-20—Warm-Air Heating, Ventilating and Air-Conditioning Contractor

A warm-air heating, ventilating and air-conditioning contractor fabricates, installs, maintains, services and repairs warm-air heating systems and water heating heat pumps, complete with warm-air appliances; ventilating systems complete with blowers and plenum chambers; air-conditioning systems complete with air-conditioning unit; and the ducts, registers, flues, humidity and thermostatic controls and air filters in connection with any of these systems. This classification shall include warm-air heating, ventilating and air-conditioning systems which utilize solar energy.

(Authority cited: Sections 7008 and 7059, Business and Professions Code. Reference: Sections 7026.1, 7058 and 7059, Business and Professions Code.)

832.21. Class C-21—Building Moving/Demolition Contractor

A building moving/demolition contractor raises, lowers, cribs, underpins, demolishes and moves or removes structures, including their foundations. This classification does not include the alterations, additions, repairs or rehabilitation of the permanently retained portions of such structures.

(Authority cited: Sections 7008 and 7059, Business and Professions Code. Reference: Sections 7058 and 7059, Business and Professions Code.)

832.23. Class C-23—Ornamental Metal Contractor

An ornamental metals contractor assembles, casts, cuts, shapes, stamps, forges, welds, fabricates and installs, sheet, rolled and cast, brass, bronze, copper, cast iron, wrought iron, monel metal, stainless steel, steel, and/or any other metal for the architectural treatment and ornamental decoration of structures. This classification does not include the work of a sheet metal contractor.

(Authority cited: Sections 7008 and 7059, Business and Professions Code. Reference: Sections 7058 and 7059, Business and Professions Code.)

832.27. Class C-27—Landscaping Contractor

A landscape contractor constructs, maintains, repairs, installs, or subcontracts the development of landscape systems and facilities for public and private gardens and other areas which are designed to aesthetically, architecturally, horticulturally, or functionally improve the grounds within or surrounding a structure or a tract or plot of land. In connection therewith, a landscape contractor prepares and grades plots and areas of land for the installation of any architectural, horticultural and decorative treatment or arrangement.

(Authority cited: Sections 7008 and 7059, Business and Professions Code. Reference: Sections 7058 and 7059, Business and Professions Code.)

832.28. Class C-28—Lock and Security Equipment Contractor

A lock and security equipment contractor evaluates, sets up, installs, maintains and repairs all doors and door assemblies, gates, locks and locking devices, panic and fire rated exit devices, manual and automatic operated gate and door closures and releases, jail and prison locking devices and permanently installed or built in safes and vaults. This classification includes but is not limited to master key systems, metal window guards, security doors, card activated and electronic access control systems for control equipment, motion and other types of detectors and computer systems for control and audit of control systems and other associated equipment. Fire alarm systems are specifically not included in this section.

(Authority Cited: Sections 7008 and 7059, Business and Professions Code. Reference: Sections 7058 and 7059, Business and Professions Code.)

832.29. Class C-29—Masonry Contractor

A masonry contractor installs concrete units and baked clay products; concrete, glass and clay block; natural and manufactured stone; terra cotta; and fire brick or other material for refractory work. This classification includes the fabrication and installation of masonry component units for structural load bearing and non-load bearing walls for structures and fences installed with or without mortar; ceramic veneer (not tile) and thin brick that resembles full brick for facing; paving; and clear waterproofing, cleaning and caulking incidental to masonry construction.

(Authority cited: Sections 7008 and 7059, Business and Professions Code. Reference: Sections 7058 and 7059, Business and Professions Code.)

832.31. Class C-31—Construction Zone Traffic Control Contractor

A construction zone traffic control contractor prepares or removes lane closures, flagging or traffic diversions, utilizing portable devices, such as cones, delineators, barricades, sign stands, flashing beacons, flashing arrow trailers, and changeable message signs, on roadways, including, but not limited to, public streets, highways, or any public conveyance.

(Authority cited: Sections 7008 and 7059, Business and Professions Code. Reference: Sections 7058 and 7059, Business and Professions Code.)

832.32. Class C-32—Parking and Highway Improvement Contractor

A parking and highway improvement contractor applies and installs protective coatings, vehicle stops, guard rails and mechanical devices, directional lines, buttons, markers, signs and arrows on the horizontal surface of any game court, parking facility, airport, highway or roadway constructed of concrete, asphalt or similar material. This classification includes the surface preparatory work necessary for the application of protective coatings but does not include the re-paving of these surfaces.

(Authority cited: Sections 7008 and 7059, Business and Professions Code. Reference: Sections 7058 and 7059, Business and Professions Code.)

832.33. Class C-33—Painting and Decorating Contractors

A painting and decorating contractor prepares by scraping, sandblasting or other means and applies any of the following: paints, papers, textures, fabrics, pigments, oils, turpentines, japans, driers, thinners, varnishes, shellacs, stains, fillers, waxes, adhesives, water and any other vehicles, mediums and materials which adhere by evaporation and may be mixed, used and applied to the surfaces of structures and the appurtenances thereto for purposes of decorating, protecting, fireproofing and waterproofing.

(Authority cited: Sections 7008 and 7059, Business and Professions Code. Reference: Sections 7058 and 7059, Business and Professions Code.)

832.34. Class C-34—Pipeline Contractor

A pipeline contractor fabricates and installs pipelines for the conveyance of fluids, such as water, gas, or petroleum, or for the containment or protection of any other material, including the application of protective coatings or systems and the trenching, boring, shoring, backfilling, compacting, paving and surfacing necessary to complete the installation of such pipelines.

(Authority cited: Sections 7008 and 7059, Business and Professions Code. Reference: Sections 7058 and 7059, Business and Professions Code.)

832.35. Class C-35—Lathing and Plastering Contractor

(a) A lathing and plastering contractor coats surfaces with a mixture of sand, gypsum plaster, quick-lime or hydrated lime and water, or sand and cement and water, or a combination of such other materials that create a permanent surface coating, including coatings for the purpose of soundproofing and fireproofing. These coatings are applied with a plasterer's trowel or sprayed over any surface which offers a mechanical means for the support of such coating, and will adhere by suction. This contractor also installs lath (including metal studs) or any other material prepared or manufactured to provide a base or bond for such coating.

(b) A lathing and plastering contractor also applies and affixes wood and metal lath, or any other material prepared or manufactured to provide key or suction bases for the support of plaster coatings. This classification includes the channel work and metal studs for the

Section VI

support of metal or any other lathing material and for solid plaster partitions.

(c) Effective January 1, 1998, or as soon thereafter as administratively feasible, all C-26 licensees will be merged into the C-35 Lathing and Plastering classification. On and after January 1, 1998, no application for the C-26 classification will be accepted and no new C-26 Lathing licenses will be issued.

(Authority cited: Sections 7008 and 7059, Business and Professions Code. Reference: Sections 7058 and 7059, Business and Professions Code.)

832.36. Class C-36—Plumbing Contractor

A plumbing contractor provides a means for a supply of safe water, ample in volume and of suitable temperature for the purpose intended and the proper disposal of fluid waste from the premises in all structures and fixed works. This classification includes but is not limited to:

(a) Complete removal of waste from the premises or the construction and connection of on-site waste disposal systems;

(b) Piping, storage tanks and venting for a safe and adequate supply of gases and liquids for any purpose, including vacuum, compressed air and gases for medical, dental, commercial and industrial uses;

(c) All gas appliances, flues and gas connections for all systems including suspended space heating units. This does not include forced warm air units;

(d) Water and gas piping from the property owner's side of the utility meter to the structure or fixed works;

(e) Installation of any type of equipment to heat water, or fluids, to a temperature suitable for the purposes listed in this section, including the installation of solar equipment for this purpose; and

(f) The maintenance and replacement of all items described above and all health and safety devices such as, but not limited to, gas earthquake valves, gas control valves, back flow preventors, water conditioning equipment and regulating valves.

(Authority Cited: Sections 7008 and 7059, Business and Professions Code. Reference: Sections 7058 and 7059, Business and Professions Code.)

832.38. Class C-38—Refrigeration Contractor

A refrigeration contractor constructs, fabricates, erects, installs, maintains, services and repairs refrigerators, refrigerated rooms, and insulated refrigerated spaces, temperature insulation, air-conditioning units, ducts, blowers, registers, humidity and thermostatic controls for the control of air, liquid, and/or gas temperatures below fifty degrees Fahrenheit (50▢), or ten degrees Celsius (10▢).

(Authority cited: Sections 7008 and 7059, Business and Professions Code. Reference: Sections 7026.1, 7058 and 7059, Business and Professions Code.)

832.39. Class C-39—Roofing Contractor

A roofing contractor installs products and repairs surfaces that seal, waterproof and weatherproof structures. This work is performed to prevent water or its derivatives, compounds or solids from penetrating such protection and gaining access to material or space beyond. In the course of this work, the contractor examines and/or prepares surfaces and uses the following material: asphaltum, pitch, tar, felt, glass fabric, urethane foam, metal roofing systems, flax, shakes, shingles, roof tile, slate or any other roofing, waterproofing, weatherproofing or membrane material(s) or a combination thereof.

(Authority cited: Sections 7008 and 7059, Business and Professions Code. Reference: Sections 7058 and 7059, Business and Professions Code.)

832.42. Class C-42—Sanitation System Contractor

A sanitation system contractor fabricates and installs cesspools, septic tanks, storm drains, and other sewage disposal and drain structures. This classification includes the laying of cast-iron, steel, concrete, vitreous and non-vitreous pipe and any other hardware associated with these systems.

(Authority cited: Sections 7008 and 7059, Business and Professions Code. Reference: Sections 7058 and 7059, Business and Professions Code.)

832.43. Class C-43—Sheet Metal Contractor

A sheet metal contractor selects, cuts, shapes, fabricates and installs sheet metal such as cornices, flashings, gutters, leaders, pans, kitchen equipment, duct work (including insulation, patented chimneys, metal flues, metal roofing systems and any other installations requiring sheet metal).

(Authority cited: Sections 7008 and 7059, Business and Professions Code. Reference: Sections 7058 and 7059, Business and Professions Code.)

832.45. Class C-45—Sign Contractor

A sign contractor fabricates, installs, and erects electrical signs, including the wiring of such electrical signs, and non-electrical signs, including but not limited to: post or pole supported signs, signs attached to structures, painted wall signs, and modifications to existing signs.

(Authority cited: Sections 7008 and 7059, Business and Professions Code. Reference: Sections 7058 and 7059, Business and Professions Code.)

Section VI

832.46. Class C-46—Solar Contractor

A solar contractor installs, modifies, maintains, and repairs thermal and photovoltaic solar energy systems.

A licensee classified in this section shall not undertake or perform building or construction trades, crafts, or skills, except when required to install a thermal or photovoltaic solar energy system.

(Authority cited: Sections 7008 and 7059, Business and Professions Code. Reference: Sections 7058 and 7059, Business and Professions Code.)

<u>Note:</u> Development of the examination is complete and in effect.

832.47. Class C-47—General Manufactured Housing Contractor

(a) A general manufactured housing contractor installs, alters, repairs, or prepares for moving any type of manufactured home as defined in Section 18007 of the Health and Safety Code, any; type of mobilehome as defined in Section 18008 of the Health and Safety Code, and any type of multifamily manufactured home as defined in Section 18008.7 of the Health and Safety Code, including the accessory buildings or structures, and the foundations. A manufactured home does not include any recreational vehicle, commercial coach, or factory-built housing as defined in Section 19971 of the Health and Safety Code.

(b) A general manufactured housing contractor may provide utility services on a single-family individual site placement. Utility services mean the connection of gas, water, sewer, and electrical utilities to the home.

(Authority cited: Sections 7008 and 7059, Business and Professions Code. Reference: Sections 7026.11, 7058 and 7059, Business and Professions Code.)

832.50. Class C-50—Reinforcing Steel Contractor

A reinforcing steel contractor fabricates, places and ties steel mesh or steel reinforcing bars (rods), of any profile, perimeter, or cross-section, that are or may be used to reinforce concrete structures.

(Authority cited: Sections 7008 and 7059, Business and Professions Code. Reference: Sections 7058 and 7059, Business and Professions Code.)

832.51. Class C-51—Structural Steel Contractor

A structural steel contractor fabricates and erects structural steel shapes and plates, of any profile, perimeter or cross-section, that are or may be used as structural members for buildings and structures, including the riveting, welding, rigging, and metal roofing systems necessary to perform this work.

(Authority cited: Sections 7008 and 7059, Business and Professions Code. Reference: Sections 7058 and 7059, Business and Professions Code.)

832.53. Class C-53—Swimming Pool Contractor

A swimming pool contractor constructs swimming pools, spas or hot tubs, including installation of solar heating equipment using those trades or skills necessary for such construction.

(Authority cited: Sections 7008 and 7059, Business and Professions Code. Reference: Sections 7058 and 7059, Business and Professions Code.)

832.54. Class C-54—Ceramic and Mosaic Tile Contractors

A ceramic and mosaic tile contractor prepares surfaces as necessary and installs glazed wall, ceramic, mosaic, quarry, paver, faience, glass mosaic and stone tiles; thin tile that resembles full brick, natural or simulated stone slabs for bathtubs, showers and horizontal surfaces inside of buildings, or any tile units set in the traditional or innovative tile methods, excluding hollow or structural partition tile.

(Authority cited: Sections 7008 and 7059, Business and Professions Code. Reference: Sections 7058 and 7059, Business and Professions Code.)

832.55. Class C-55—Water Conditioning Contractor

A water conditioning contractor installs water conditioning equipment with the use of only such pipe and fittings as are necessary to connect the water conditioning equipment to the water supply system and to by-pass all those parts of the water supply system within the premises from which conditioned water is to be excluded.

(Authority cited: Sections 7008 and 7059, Business and Professions Code. Reference: Sections 7058 and 7059, Business and Professions Code.)

832.57. Class C-57—Well Drilling Contractor

A well drilling contractor installs and repairs water wells and pumps by boring, drilling, excavating, casing, cementing and cleaning to provide a supply of uncontaminated water.

(Authority cited: Sections 7008 and 7059, Business and Professions Code. Reference: Sections 7026.3, 7058 and 7059, Business and Professions Code.)

832.60. Class C-60—Welding Contractor

A welding contractor causes metals to become permanently attached, joined and fabricated by the use of gases and electrical energy, which creates temperatures of sufficient heat to perform this work.

(Authority cited: Sections 7008 and 7059, Business and Professions Code. Reference: Sections 7058 and 7059, Business and Professions Code.)

Section VI

832.61. Classification C-61—Limited Specialty

(a) Limited specialty is a specialty contractor classification limited to a field and scope of operations of specialty contracting for which an applicant is qualified other than any of the specialty contractor classifications listed and defined in this article.

(b) An applicant classified and licensed in the classification Limited Specialty shall confine activities as a contractor to that field or fields and scope of operations set forth in the application and accepted by the Registrar or to that permitted by Section 831.

(c) Upon issuance of a C-61 license, the Registrar shall endorse upon the face of the original license certificate the field and scope of operations in which the licensee has demonstrated qualifications.

(d) A specialty contractor, other than a C-61 contractor, may perform work within the field and scope of the operations of Classification C-61, provided the work is consistent with established usage and procedure in the construction industry and is related to the specialty contractor's classification.

(Authority cited: Sections 7008 and 7059, Business and Professions Code. Reference: Sections 7058 and 7059, Business and Professions Code.)

832.62. Solar System Work Within Scope of Class A, Class B, and Class C-61 (Swimming Pool Maintenance)

(a) The phrase "in connection with fixed works requiring specialized engineering knowledge and skill" in Section 7056 of the Business and Professions Code shall include but not be limited to an active solar energy system.

(b) An active solar energy system constitutes use of more than two unrelated building trades or crafts within the meaning of Section 7057 of the Business and Professions Code.

(c) C-61 (Swimming Pool Maintenance Contractors) currently holding the SC-44 supplemental solar classification may continue to perform solar work authorized by Class SC-44 until one year after the implementation of the C-46 Solar Classification. Thereafter, classification C-61 (Swimming Pool Maintenance) is authorized to repair active solar heating systems for swimming pools.

(Authority cited: Sections 7008 and 7059, Business and Professions Code. Reference: Sections 7056, 7057 and 7058, Business and Professions Code.)

834. Limitation of Classification

(a) A licensee classified as a general engineering contractor shall operate only within those areas defined in Section 7056 of the Code.

(b) A licensee classified as a general building contractor, as defined in Section 7057 of the Code, shall take a prime contract or subcontract only as authorized by Section 7057.

(c) A licensee classified as a specialty contractor, as defined in Section 7058 of the Code, shall not act in the capacity of a contractor in any classification other than one in which he/she is classified except on work incidental or supplemental to the performance of a contract in a classification in which any contractor is licensed by the Board.

(Authority cited: Sections 7008 and 7059, Business and Professions Code. Reference: Sections 7056, 7057, 7058 and 7059, Business and Professions Code.)

ARTICLE 4. EXAMINATIONS

840. Written Examinations Required of All Applicants

Except as provided in Section 7065.1 of the Code, an applicant, including an applicant for an additional classification or classifications, must pass the written examination prescribed by the Registrar. No oral examination shall be given to any applicant. The reading of the examination instructions or questions or the explanation of the wording or intent of any of the questions to an examinee by any Board personnel authorized to conduct examinations, or by any duly sworn translators, shall not be considered an oral examination.

(Authority cited: Section 7008, Business and Professions Code. Reference: Sections 7065 and 7068, Business and Professions Code.)

841. Elimination and Revision of Examination Questions

The Registrar shall, under the Board's direction, prepare and revise the written examinations for contractors' licenses.

The Registrar shall replace, eliminate or change any examination question or answer thereto brought to his/her attention if, in the Registrar's opinion, the question is misleading or unfair, or the approved answer is incorrect.

(Authority cited: Section 7008, Business and Professions Code. Reference: Sections 7011, 7065, 7065.05 and 7068, Business and Professions Code.)

ARTICLE 5. RENEWAL OF LICENSE

853. Renewal Application Form

(a) The Registrar shall mail to each licensee, prior to the expiration of the license, a renewal form with complete instructions for renewal of the license.

Section VI

(b) A renewal application is delinquent if not postmarked by the expiration date.

(c) An incomplete renewal application shall be returned to the licensee by the Registrar with an explanation of the reasons for its rejection. If the renewal application is not returned before the expiration date of the license, the license shall expire as provided in Section 7140 of the Code.

(d) An expired license shall not be renewed until any accrued delinquency fee has been paid.

(Authority cited: Section 7008, Business and Professions Code. Reference: Section 7140, Business and Professions Code.)

854. Renewal Fee and Reactivation Credit

A $100 credit will be applied to active license renewals and license reactivations within the renewal period of July 1, 1997 through June 30, 1999.

(Authority cited: Section 7008, Business and Professions Code. Reference: Section 7076.5, 7137 and 7138.1.)

ARTICLE 6. BONDS

856. Security in Lieu of Bond

(a) A certificate of deposit, submitted pursuant to Section 7071.12(a) of the code, shall:

(1) When filed in lieu of a contractor's bond

(A) by an applicant, show the name style as set out on page one of the application.

(B) by a licensee, show the name style as currently recorded in the official files of the Board.

(2) When filed in lieu of a bond of qualifying individual, show the name style as in (1) above and the name of the responsible managing individual.

(3) Be made payable to the Contractors State License Board. The word "trustee" shall not be included.

(4) Be issued for a period of not less than one year.

(5) Be automatically renewable at each maturity date.

(6) Provide that any interest earned shall be paid to the depositor.

(b) Assignment of a savings and loan association investment certificate or share account, or of a credit union certificate for funds or share account shall be upon a form prescribed and approved by the Registrar.

(1) The form shall show:

(A) The assignment of the account to the board.

(B) The name style as prescribed in subsection (a) above.

(C) The current address of the applicant or licensee.

(D) The name and address of the savings and loan association or credit union having custody of such funds.

(E) A declaration signed by an officer of the savings and loan association or the credit union that it received written notice of the assignment. This declaration shall include the title of the officer signing it.

(F) A receipt for the assignment from the Board with direction to the savings and loan association or the credit union that the earnings on the assigned account or certificate shall be paid to the assignor.

(2) The assignment form shall be accompanied by the savings and loan association pass book or investment certificate, the credit union certificate for funds or share account pass book of the assignor which shall show the name of the depositor-investor, that of the licensee or applicant, and the responsible managing individual, if applicable, and the amount of the assignment required by law.

(c) Eligible bearer bonds submitted pursuant to Section 7071.12(c) of the code shall be delivered to a bank in Sacramento, California, which shall act as agent for the applicant, licensee or responsible managing employee. The bank shall deliver the bonds to the Treasurer of the State of California only on order of the Registrar or an employee designated by the Registrar.

(1) The Registrar shall prescribe and approve the forms for the deposit or withdrawal of bearer bonds.

(2) Interest coupons shall remain attached to bearer bonds deposited with the Treasurer until such bonds are permanently withdrawn from the depository, not be resubmitted for deposit.

(3) In order to insure that sufficient security is on deposit, the bid price of bearer bonds, as recorded in the bond securities listed on the Pacific Coast Stock Exchange or some other authoritative source on the first day of the month in which such bonds are submitted for deposit, shall be at least 25% in excess of the amount of the surety bond or cash deposit required to be submitted.

Section VI

The Registrar shall prescribe such procedures and forms, and issue such orders as necessary to accept and process any cash deposit submitted pursuant to Section 7071.12(d) of the code. Personal checks shall not be accepted as cash.

(Authority cited: Section 7008, Business and Professions Code. Reference: Sections 7071.5, 7071.6, 7071.8, 7071.9, 7071.10 and 7071.12, Business and Professions Code.)

858. Blanket Performance and Payment Bond Defined

(a) The purpose of these sections is to establish requirements for contractors seeking to obtain approval from the Registrar for a blanket performance and payment bond (hereafter referred to as "blanket bond") as specified under the provisions of paragraph (a)(8) of Section 7159.5 of the Code.

(b) For the purposes of this Article, the term "blanket bond" means a single surety instrument, executed by an admitted surety that is conditioned for the payment in full of all claims that arise from the obligations created by a licensee under any contract that is subject to the provisions of Section 7159 of the Code (hereafter referred to as "home improvement contract") and as set forth in Section 858.1 of this Article.

(c) For the purposes of this Article, the term "obligation" has the same meaning as set forth under Section 1427 of the Civil Code: "An obligation is a legal duty, by which a person is bound to do or not to do a certain thing."

(Authority cited: Section 7008, Business and Professions Code. Reference: Sections 7151, 7159 and 7159.5, Business and Professions Code.)

858.1. Blanket Performance and Payment Bond Requirements

(a) A blanket bond that is filed on behalf of a licensee to satisfy the provisions of Section 858 shall be underwritten for a dollar amount that is sufficient to cover one-hundred percent (100%) of the home improvement contracts for which the licensee has an obligation.

(b) Upon written request by a licensee, the Registrar is authorized to approve a blanket bond that is capped according to the schedule listed under subsection (c) provided the following conditions are met:

(1) The licensee, or the parent company of the licensee, is required to submit annual reports (Form 10-K) to the United States Securities and Exchange Commission (U.S. SEC).

(2) Upon the filing of a request that the blanket bond be capped, a copy of the most recently filed Form 10-K shall be submitted to the Registrar. Thereafter, a copy of any Form 10-K report shall be submitted to the Registrar within 10 days of filing with the U.S. SEC.

(3) The net worth of the applicable firm shall, initially and annually thereafter, be not less than 10 times the sum of the blanket bond as determined by the Registrar. Each net worth calculation shall be applicable to the period for which the most recent Form 10-K report was submitted to the U.S. SEC.

(c) The blanket bonds for which a request has been submitted under subsection (b) shall comply with the following schedule:

(1) If a licensee, or the parent company of a licensee, is classified as a "large accelerated filer" by the U.S. SEC, the amount of the blanket bond shall be $10 million.

(2) If a licensee, or the parent company of a licensee, is classified as an "accelerated filer" by the U.S. SEC, the amount of the blanket bond shall be $5 million.

(3) If a licensee, or the parent company of a licensee, is classified as a "non-accelerated filer" by the U.S. SEC, the amount of the blanket bond shall be $1 million.

(d) A licensee who is granted approval of a blanket bond pursuant to subsections (b) and (c) is not subject to the biennial financial reporting requirement specified under Section 858.4(a)(2). However, the qualifier's certification statement must be submitted biennially as specified under that section.

(e) For the purpose of executing the qualifier's certification statement required under Section 858.2(a)(4), the provisions of subsections (a), (b), and (c) of Section 858.1 shall be referenced collectively as "the 100% rule."

On the date that this section becomes effective, any licensee that has a blanket bond on file with the Board that fails to comply with the 100% rule shall achieve compliance not later than 90 days after the effective date of the section. The Registrar is authorized to rescind the approval of the blanket bond in accordance with the provisions of Section 858.8 of this Article if the licensee fails to comply with any provision of this section.

(f) The form of the blanket bond specified under this section is subject to the approval of the Registrar and shall conform to the following with regard to content:

This bond shall be filed with the Registrar of Contractors
State of California
Contractors State License Board

Surety Code: _____
Bond No.: _____

License No.: _____

BLANKET PERFORMANCE AND PAYMENT BOND
13B-39 (Rev. 08/11)
(Business and Professions Code Section 7159.5)

The term of this bond is _____ to _____.

KNOW ALL BY THESE PRESENTS: That _____

(Business Name as Shown on the License)

whose address for service is

_____

(Street Address)   (City)   (State)   (Zip Code)

as Principal, and _____

(Name of Surety)

a corporation organized under the laws of the State of _____ and authorized to transact a general surety business in the State of California, as Surety, are held and firmly bound unto each owner or tenant of a residence or dwelling unit as the beneficiaries with whom the Principal, as of the date of this bond and thereafter, enters into a home improvement contract as defined in Section 7151.2 of the Business & Professions Code for repairing, remodeling, altering, converting, or modernizing such building or structure; and the aggregate contract price specified in one or more improvement contracts including all labor services and materials to be furnished by the Principal as the contractor exceeds _____ Dollars ( ) in the just and full sum of the amount of each individual contract for which sum, well and truly to be paid, we bind ourselves, our heirs, executors, successors, and assigns, jointly and severally, firmly by these presents.

THE CONDITION OF THE OBLIGATION IS SUCH, That, WHEREAS, Sections 7159 and 7159.5 of the Business & Professions Code provide for bonding requirements for contractors entering into contracts covered by these provisions of law, AND, WHEREAS, the Principal desires to file a blanket guarantee to operate as security in accordance with Section 995.020 of the Code of Civil Procedure, to cover the performance and payment of all obligations resultant from such contracts in order to conduct business under the exemptions specified under paragraph (8) of subdivision (a) of Section 7159.5 of the Business & Professions Code.

NOW THEREFORE, if the Principal shall well and truly perform and fulfill all the understandings, covenants, terms, conditions, and agreements of said contracts, and shall also well and truly perform and fulfill all the undertakings, covenants, terms, conditions, and agreements of any and all duly authorized modifications of said contracts; and if the Principal shall promptly make payments to all persons, whether or not in direct contractual relationship with Principal, supplying labor or material or both for the prosecution of the work provided in said contracts, then this obligation is to be void; otherwise, it is to remain in full force and effect as though separate bonds in the full amount of the contract price had been written on the individual contracts.

PROVIDED, HOWEVER, this bond is issued subject to the following express conditions:

1. This bond may be cancelled by the surety in accordance with the provisions of Sections 996.310 et seq. of the Code of Civil Procedure.

2. This bond shall be deemed continuous in form and shall remain in full force and effect and shall run concurrently with the license period for which the license is granted and shall continue beyond that period and every succeeding license period or periods for which said Principal may hold this license or until the effective date of rescission of the Registrar's approval of the bond, after which liability hereunder shall cease in accordance with provisions of Section 996.360 of the Code of Civil Procedure.

3. This bond to become effective _____
                                              (Date)

4. Even though this bond may be in effect for more than one year, the surety's aggregate liability for all contracts covered hereunder shall in no event exceed the amount set forth above.

5. The surety signing this bond is jointly and severally liable on the obligations of the bond, the obligations of the statutes providing for this bond, and the applicable provisions of the Code of Civil Procedure regarding bonds.

_____   _____
(Name of Surety)   (Address for Service)

I declare under penalty of perjury under the laws of the State of California that I have executed the foregoing bond under an unrevoked power of attorney. I further declare that I have relied upon the "Qualifier's Certification Statement" to determine that, as of the date of execution, the penal sum of this bond is a good faith valuation of the funds required to safeguard the financial interests of the beneficiaries relative to the obligations for which this bond is posted.

Executed in _____, _____ on _____,
                 (City and State)   (Date)

Section VI

under the laws of the State of California.
Certificate of Authority # _____
Signature of Attorney-in-Fact _____
Printed or Typed Name of Attorney-in-Fact _____
Address of Attorney-in-Fact _____
Telephone Number of Attorney-in-Fact (   ) _____
Signature of Principal (Qualifier for the License) _____

(Authority cited: Section 7008, Business and Professions Code. Reference: Sections 7151.2, 7159 and 7159.5, Business and Professions Code.)

858.2. Application for Approval of Blanket Performance and Payment Bond

(a) A licensee seeking approval of a blanket bond shall meet the applicable conditions specified under this Article and submit to the Board an Application for Approval of Blanket Performance and Payment Bond, form 13B-35 (11/2011), that includes the following information:

(1) The name and address of the licensee as listed on the license record and the license number.

(2) The name of every person listed on the license record of the applicant who, as specified under Section 7068 of the Code, is acting as a qualifier for the license.

(3) The reviewed year-end financial statements and a report prepared by a certified public accountant (CPA) duly licensed by the California Board of Accountancy or licensed by another state board of accountancy. The reviewed financial statements shall include supplemental information related to the liquidity ratios of the licensee's business and shall particularly include the current ratio and the quick ratio, the calculations for which are specified under subparagraphs (A) and (B) below. The review report, or a separate supplementary report, shall include an explanation that the information has been subject to the review of the CPA. The review report shall cover the two fiscal years immediately preceding application for approval of the blanket bond, and should be prepared in accordance with the current Statements of Standards for Accounting and Review Services issued by the American Institute of Certified Public Accounts.

(A) Current ratio calculation: current assets; divided by current liabilities.

(B) Quick ratio calculation: current assets minus inventory; divided by current liabilities.

(4) A certification statement, signed under penalty of perjury by the qualifier for the license, which shall conform to the following language:

QUALIFIER'S CERTIFICATION STATEMENT

(Unless otherwise noted, all section references are to the California Business & Professions Code.)

The undersigned declares that, in accordance with Sections 7068 and 7068.1 of the Code, he or she is a qualifier for the licensee identified below (hereafter referred to as "licensee") and is responsible for exercising the direct supervision and control of the licensee's operations as is necessary to secure full compliance with the laws and regulations that are under the jurisdiction of the Contractors State License Board. As a qualifier of the licensee, the undersigned has reviewed sufficient financial information to execute this certification as it pertains to the licensee's home improvement sales and services that are subject to the home improvement contract requirements specified under Section 7159 of the Code. As of close of business on _____ the blanket performance and payment bond

     (Date)

(bond) number _____ issued by _____

     (Bond Number)   (Name of Surety Company)

as surety is, according to my comprehension of the data derived from the licensee, in an aggregate amount that is sufficient to comply with the "100% rule" as specified in the provisions of Section 858.1 of Title 16, Division 8 of the California Code of Regulations. The undersigned also certifies that he or she will monitor the relevant business activity of the licensee; exercise due diligence to secure ongoing compliance with the 100% rule; and notify the Registrar within 30 days of the licensee's refusal, failure, or inability to comply with the 100% rule.

The undersigned also certifies that, upon approval of the blanket bond by the Registrar, the contract forms that will be used by the licensee for all transactions which are subject to Section 7159 of the Code will contain a notice which informs the property owner that a blanket performance and payment bond is on file with the Registrar of Contractors, or in lieu thereof, a notice that clearly identifies the name and address of the surety that has issued the blanket performance and payment bond.

As a qualifying individual for the licensee, I declare under penalty of perjury under the laws of the State of California that the foregoing is true and correct and that this declaration was executed on _____ at _____

     (Date)   (City and State)

_____

(Name of Licensee as it Appears on the License)   (License Number)

_____

(Printed Name of Qualifier)   (Signature of Qualifier)

(b) A licensee shall be licensed in this state in an active status for not less than five years prior to submitting the application provided for by this section.

(c) Except as otherwise provided under this subsection, an application for approval of a blanket bond shall not be accepted for consideration if any member of the personnel of record of the licensee, or any home improvement salespersons registered to the licensee, was found to have been responsible for, participated in, or otherwise culpable relative to any legal action that is subject to disclosure under Section 7124.6(e)(2) or 7124.6 (e)(3) of the Code, or is named on a license that is suspended pursuant to Section 7071.17 of the Code.

(1) Any person who, after the effective date of the most recent disciplinary order applicable to that individual, is listed on an active license for three consecutive years with no violations resulting in disciplinary action may make application as provided under this Article.

(d) The application shall be signed by the person qualifying on behalf of the licensee who has executed the qualifier's certification statement required under this section. In the case of a responsible managing employee qualifier, the application shall also be signed by the owner, partner, or current corporate officer.

(e) The application shall be accompanied by a blanket bond that complies with the provisions of Section 858.1 of this Article and is underwritten by a surety that has been admitted in the State of California.

(Authority cited: Section 7008, Business and Professions Code. Reference: Sections 7068, 7068.1, 7124.6, 7159 and 7159.5, Business and Professions Code.)

858.3. Minimum Standards for Blanket Performance and Payment Bond Approval—Cause for Denial

(a) For each of the year-end financial statements for which a report is required under Section 858.2, the following standards must be met in order to qualify for blanket bond approval:

(1) The quick ratio shall not be less than 1:1, or, in lieu thereof, the current ratio shall not be less than 2:1.

(b) In addition to any other cause for denial, the Registrar may deny or rescind approval of the blanket bond based on information in the reviewed report or the information contained in the supplemental information required under subparagraph (a)(3) of Section 858.2 if the information demonstrates the licensee will be unable to meet current liabilities.

(Authority cited: Section 7008, Business and Professions Code. Reference: Section 7159.5, Business and Professions Code.)

858.4. Blanket Performance and Payment Bond Biennial Certification and Financial Reporting Requirements

(a) Except as otherwise provided under this Article, a licensee that maintains a blanket bond under this Article shall comply with the following:

(1) A certification statement as specified in Section 858.2 of this Article, signed under penalty of perjury by the member of the personnel of record who is listed as the qualifier for the license in accordance with Section 7068 of the Code, shall be submitted biennially to the Registrar as specified under subsection (b).

(2) With each application to renew the license for which the blanket bond has been posted, reviewed year-end financial statements and a report prepared in accordance with the provisions of Section 858.2(a)(3) shall be submitted to the Registrar as follows:

(A) If it has been one calendar year or more since the Registrar's approval of the blanket bond, the licensee shall submit a copy of a review report and the accompanying financial statements covering the entire period that is subsequent to the approval, but not more than the two fiscal years immediately preceding the license renewal date.

(B) If it has been less than one calendar year since the Registrar's initial approval of the blanket bond, the reviewed report required by this subsection shall be submitted at next renewal period that is more than one calendar year subsequent to the initial approval of the blanket bond.

(b) The due date for the qualifier's certification statement and any reports required under this section shall coincide with the license renewal period of the license for which blanket bond approval has been granted. For each subsequent renewal cycle, the certification statement and reports of financial statements shall be submitted to the Registrar no later than the date the license is due to expire.

(c) The Registrar may rescind approval of the blanket bond based on information in the reviewed report or in the supplemental information that demonstrates the licensee's business may not be able to meet its current liabilities.

Section VI

(d) If a licensee fails to submit the certification statement or comply with the financial reporting requirements as specified by this section, the Registrar may rescind approval of the blanket bond in accordance with the provisions of Section 858.8 of this Article.

(Authority cited: Section 7008, Business and Professions Code. Reference: Sections 7068, 7068.1 and 7159.5, Business and Professions Code.)

858.5. Blanket Performance and Payment Bond Audit Authorization and Procedures

(a) The Registrar may order an audit of a licensee that has an approved blanket bond on file if he or she deems an audit is necessary to ensure that the sum for which the blanket bond has been filed is sufficient to protect the public.

(1) The Registrar shall provide a licensee with not less than 30 days written notification that an audit is to be conducted pursuant to this section. The notice shall specify the period to be covered by the audit and set a date for the audit to begin. The audit period shall not exceed the period that is specified for the retention of licensee records under Section 7111 of the Code. Delivery of the notice shall be by certified mail to the current business address of record listed on the license record. Upon written request, the Registrar may grant the licensee an additional 30 days to prepare for the audit.

(2) For any audit conducted pursuant to this section, the licensee shall, pursuant to the receipt of the audit notice, provide access to the licensee's books, business records, and documents in accordance with the provisions of Section 7111 of the Code.

(b) Upon completion and review of the audit and all relevant information, the Registrar shall determine if the licensee is in compliance with the 100% rule specified under Section 858.1.

(Authority cited: Section 7008, Business and Professions Code. Reference: Sections 7111 and 7159.5, Business and Professions Code.)

858.6. Authorization and Procedures for Ordering the Amount of Blanket Performance and Payment Bond to Be Increased

(a) Pursuant to an audit conducted in accordance with Section 858.5 of this Article, the Registrar is authorized to order an increase in the dollar amount of the blanket bond to an amount that meets the requirements specified in Section 858.1 of this Article. The adjustment determination shall be based on the information contained in records of the licensee that are required to be made available for an audit as specified under this Article.

(b) An order to increase the sum of the blanket bond pursuant to this section shall be sent by certified and regular mail to the licensee's address of record. The order shall include a notice that failure to increase the dollar amount of the blanket bond within 30 days of the date of the order is cause for rescission of approval of the blanket bond.

(c) If a licensee fails to comply within 30 days of the date of an order that is issued pursuant to this section, the Registrar shall rescind approval of the blanket bond in accordance with the provisions of Section 858.8 of this Article.

(Authority cited: Section 7008, Business and Professions Code. Reference: Section 7159.5, Business and Professions Code.)

858.7. Maintenance of the Blanket Performance and Payment Bond

(a) In order for any licensee to maintain the Registrar's approval of a blanket bond in accordance with this Article, all provisions of this section are applicable:

(1) No member of the personnel of record of the licensee, nor home improvement salesperson registered to the licensee, shall have been found to have been responsible for, participated in, or otherwise culpable relative to any acts or omissions that resulted in any discipline that is subject to disclosure under Section 7124.6(e)(2) or 7124.6(e)(3) of the Code. The approval of the blanket bond posted by a licensee found to be in violation of this section is subject to rescission in accordance with the provisions of Section 858.8 of this Article. In determining whether or not to rescind approval of the blanket bond for violations of this section, the Registrar shall give due consideration to protection of the public as set forth in Section 7000.6 of the Code.

(2) No member of the personnel of record of the licensee, nor home improvement salespersons registered to the licensee, shall be named on a license that is suspended pursuant to Section 7071.17 of the Code. The approval of the blanket bond posted by a licensee found to be in violation of this section is subject to rescission in accordance with the provisions of Section 858.8 of this Article. In determining whether or not to rescind approval of the blanket bond for violations of this section, the Registrar shall give due consideration to protection of the public as set forth in Section 7000.6 of the Code.

(3) Whenever any qualifier who has executed and filed the qualifier's certification statement required under this Article disassociates from the licensee, a subsequent qualifier for the licensee shall complete, execute, and file the qualifier's certification statement contained in the application form specified under Section 858.2 of this Article. The qualifier's certification statement required by this paragraph must be

Section VI

filed within 90 days of the date that the former qualifier who executed the qualifier's certification statement disassociated from the license, as noted on the official license record of the Board.

(4) The failure to file an acceptable qualifier's certification statement within 90 days as specified under subdivision (3) of this subsection is cause for rescission of approval of the bond in accordance with the provisions of Section 858.8 of this Article. If a licensee files a written request prior to the date the qualifier's certification statement is due, the Registrar may grant an additional 30 days within which to file the certification statement. The licensee's request shall clearly state the reason(s) why additional time is needed to file the qualifier's certification statement.

(Authority cited: Section 7008, Business and Professions Code. Reference: Sections 7000.6, 7071.17, 7124.6 and 7159.5, Business and Professions Code.)

858.8. Rescission of Blanket Performance and Payment Bond Approval

(a) The Registrar may rescind the approval of any blanket bond (also referenced as "approval rescission" under this section) if any provision or condition specified under this Article is not satisfied.

(b) To rescind the approval of a blanket bond, the Registrar shall send written notice by certified and regular mail to the licensee's address of record that specifies the date of and the reasons for the Registrar's decision to rescind approval of the blanket bond. When appropriate, the notice shall also contain the conditions that must be met to prevent the rescission.

(c) The rescission shall, as of the date specified, extinguish the licensee's authorization to use the blanket bond in satisfaction of the provisions under subsection (a)(8) of Section 7159.5 of the Code.

(d) The licensee shall be given not less than 30 days notice prior to the effective date of the rescission of the blanket bond. Prior to the effective date of the rescission, the licensee may file a written appeal of the rescission of the blanket bond with the Registrar. A written appeal is considered timely if it is postmarked prior to the date the rescission would otherwise become effective. Where a rescission is not appealed timely, the blanket bond shall be rescinded on the effective date specified by the Registrar. If the rescission is appealed timely, the effective date of the rescission shall be delayed until a decision on the appeal is issued, and a notice regarding the appeal and the pending decision of the Registrar shall be posted as specified under subsection (b) of Section 858.9.

(e) Upon cancellation of the blanket bond, the Registrar's approval shall be automatically rescinded effective on the date of the cancellation.

(f) Upon the effective date of the Registrar's approval rescission, the licensee shall be subject to and comply with the provisions of subsections (a)(3), (4), and (5) of Section 7159.5 of the Code and shall, in addition to complying with all other requirements specified under Section 7159 of the Code, include the Mechanics' Lien Warning disclosure as part of all home improvement contracts that are subject to that section.

(Authority cited: Section 7008, Business and Professions Code. Reference: Sections 7159 and 7159.5, Business and Professions Code.)

858.9. Posting of Blanket Performance and Payment Bond Information to License Records

(a) Upon approval of a blanket bond by the Registrar, regardless of the effective date of the blanket bond, the following information shall be posted to the public license record of the licensee named as principal on the blanket bond:

(1) A statement indicating that the licensee has an approved blanket performance and payment bond on file with the Board.

(2) The date that the blanket bond was approved.

(3) The number of the blanket bond.

(4) The dollar amount for which the blanket bond has been filed.

(5) The name and address of the surety company on the blanket bond.

(b) Whenever a licensee is notified of a decision to rescind the approval of the licensee's blanket bond, the Registrar shall post a notice on the public license record indicating that the rescission is pending. The notice shall be posted to the license record no earlier than 5 calendar days and no later than 10 calendar days after the date that written notification of the rescission is sent to the licensee. If the rescission is appealed timely by the licensee, the Registrar shall also post a notice that an appeal has been filed and indicate that the decision to rescind the approval of the blanket bond is delayed pending the outcome of the licensee's appeal.

(c) Upon rescission of approval of a blanket bond or its cancellation, the statement specified in paragraph (1) of subsection (a) shall be changed to indicate the disposition of the blanket bond and the effective date thereof. The information in paragraphs (2), (3), (4), and (5) of subsection (a) shall remain on the license record for not less

Section VI

than five years after the date the blanket bond was rescinded or cancelled.

(Authority cited: Section 7008, Business and Professions Code. Reference: Section 7159.5, Business and Professions Code.)

ARTICLE 7. SPECIAL PROVISIONS

860. Penalty for Failure to Comply with Rules

Licensees and applicants for licenses shall comply with all rules and regulations of the Board and regulations issued by the Registrar. Violation of such rules and regulations shall constitute grounds for disciplinary action, or for the denial of a license.

(Authority cited: Section 7008, Business and Professions Code. Reference: Section 7008, Business and Professions Code.)

861. "Advertising" Defined

As used in Section 7030.5 of the Code, the term "advertising" includes but is not limited to the following: any card, contract proposal, sign, billboard, lettering on vehicles registered in this or any other state, brochure, pamphlet, circular, newspaper, magazine, airwave or any electronic transmission, and any form of directory under any listing denoting "Contractor" or any word or words of a similar import or meaning requesting any work for which a license is required by the Contractors License Law.

(Authority cited: Section 7008, Business and Professions Code. Reference: Section 7030.5, Business and Professions Code.)

861.5. Definition of "Structural Defect"

For the purpose of subdivision (b) of Section 7091 of the Code, "structural defect" is defined as meaning:

(1) A failure or condition that would probably result in a failure in the load bearing portions of a structure,

(2) which portions of the structure are not constructed in compliance with the codes in effect at the time for the location of the structure, provided that,

(3) such failure or condition results in the inability to reasonably use the affected portion of the structure for the purpose for which it was intended.

(Authority cited: Sections 7008, 7091, Business and Professions Code. Reference: Section 7091, Business and Professions Code.)

863. Public Access to Information

The Registrar shall establish a system whereby members of the public may obtain from board records information regarding complaints made against licensed contractors, their history of legal actions taken by the board, and license status, as hereafter specified. For purposes of this section, "complaint" means a written allegation which has been investigated and has been referred for legal action against the licensee. For purposes of this section, "legal action" means referral of the complaint for the issuance of a citation, accusation, statement of issues, or for the initiation of criminal action or injunctive proceedings.

(a) The Registrar shall maintain records showing the complaints received against licensees and, with respect to such complaints, shall make available to members of the public, upon request, the following information:

(1) The nature of all complaints on file against a licensee which have been investigated by a Deputy Registrar and referred for legal action against the licensee by the District Office. Information regarding complaints which are in the process of being screened, mediated, arbitrated or investigated shall not be disclosed.

(2) Such general cautionary statements as may be considered appropriate regarding the usefulness of complaint information to individual consumers in their selection of a contractor.

(3) Whenever complaint information is requested, the information disclosable under subsections (c) and (d) below shall also be released.

(b) If a complaint results in a legal action and is subsequently determined by the registrar, the Office of the Attorney General or a court of competent jurisdiction not to have merit, it shall be deleted from the complaint disclosure system.

(c) The Registrar shall maintain records showing a history of any legal actions taken by the board against all current license holders and shall make available to members of the public, upon request, all the following information:

(1) Whether any current license holder has ever been disciplined by the registrar and, if so, when and for what offense; and

(2) Whether any current licensee has ever been cited, and, if so, when and for what offense, and, whether such citation is on appeal or has been complied with;

(3) Whether any current license holder is named as a respondent in any currently pending disciplinary or legal action.

(d) The Registrar shall maintain records showing certain licensing and bonding information for all current license holders and shall make available to members of the public, upon request, all the following information regarding current license holders:

(1) The name of the licensee as it appears in the board's records; and

(2) The license number; and

(3) The classification(s) held; and

(4) The address of record; and

(5) The personnel of the licensee; and

(6) The date of original licensure; and

(7) Whether a bond or cash deposit is maintained and, if so, its amount; and

(8) If the licensee maintains a bond, the name and address of the bonding company and the bond's identification number, if any.

(e) Limitation of access to information. Further, the Registrar may set reasonable limits upon the number of requests for information responded per month from any one requestor.

(Authority cited: Section 7008, Business and Professions Code. Reference: Sections 7124.5 and 7124.6, Business and Professions Code.)

864. Continuance of License under Section 7068.2

When a notice of disassociation of the responsible managing officer or responsible managing employee is given within the time and in the manner prescribed by Section 7068.2 of the code, the license shall remain in force for a period of 90 days from the date of such disassociation.

(Authority cited: Section 7008, Business and Professions Code. Reference: Section 7068.2, Business and Professions Code.)

865. Continuance of License under Section 7076

(a) An application for the continuation of a business under an existing license may be submitted to the Registrar within 90 days of:

(1) the death of a person licensed as an individual,

(2) the death or the disassociation of a partner of a licensed partnership, or

(3) the death of an individual member or the disassociation of any entity of a licensed joint venture. If the application is approved by the Registrar, the license shall remain in force for a period of up to one year from the date of death or disassociation.

(b) The Registrar may approve an extension to the one-year provision outlined in subsection (a) if additional time is necessary to complete projects contracted for or commenced before the disassociation or death.

(c) A license so extended is subject to all the provisions of the Contractors License Law including those relating to renewal and bond requirements.

(Authority cited: Section 7008, Business and Professions Code. Reference: Section 7076, Business and Professions Code.)

867. Procedure to Reactivate an Inactive License

(a) A reactivation of an inactive license shall be effective on the date on which an acceptable form is received by the Registrar, on the date on which the full renewal fee provided for in Section 7137(d) of the code is paid, or on the date, if any, requested by the licensee, whichever last occurs.

(b) When an inactive license is reactivated, the Registrar shall issue to the licensee an active pocket license.

(c) The name, address, license number and classification of the reactivated licensee shall be posted publicly as prescribed by the Registrar.

(Authority cited: Section 7008, Business and Professions Code. Reference: Section 7076.5, Business and Professions Code.)

868. Criteria to Aid in Determining if Crimes or Acts Are Substantially Related to Contracting Business

For the purposes of denial, suspension, or revocation of a license pursuant to Division 1.5 (commencing with Section 475) of the code, a crime or act, as defined in Section 480 of the code, shall be considered to be substantially related to the qualifications, functions, or duties of a licensee (under Division 3, Chapter 9 of the code) if it evidences present or potential unfitness of an applicant or licensee to perform the functions authorized by the license in a manner consistent with the public health, safety, and welfare. The crimes or acts shall include, but not be limited to, the following:

(a) Any violation of the provisions of Chapter 9 of Division 3 of the code.

(b) Failure to comply with the provisions of the California Administrative Code, Chapter 8, Title 16.

(c) Crimes or acts involving dishonesty, fraud, deceit, or theft with the intent to substantially benefit oneself or another or to substantially harm another.

(d) Crimes or acts involving physical violence against persons.

(e) Crimes or acts that indicate a substantial or repeated disregard for the health, safety, or welfare of the public.

(Authority cited: Sections 481 and 7008, Business and Professions Code. Reference: Sections 480, 481, 490, 7066,, 7069, 7073, 7090, 7123, and 7124, Business and Professions Code.)

869. Criteria for Rehabilitation

(a) When considering the denial, suspension, or revocation of a license pursuant to Division 1.5 (commencing with Section 475) of the code, the Board in evaluating the applicant's or licensee's rehabilitation and present eligibility for a license will consider the following criteria:

(1) Subject to the provisions of subsection (a)(2), an applicant or licensee may be determined to be rehabilitated if he or she meets the following criteria:

(A) For felony convictions that are substantially related to the qualifications, functions, or duties of a licensee as defined in Section 868, seven (7) years have passed from the time of release from incarceration or completion of probation if no incarceration was imposed, without the occurrence of additional criminal activity or substantially-related acts.

(B) For misdemeanor convictions that are substantially related to the qualifications, functions, or duties of a licensee as defined in Section 868, three (3) years have passed from the time of release from incarceration or completion of probation if no incarceration was imposed, without the occurrence of additional criminal activity or substantially-related acts.

(C) For acts that are substantially related to the qualifications, functions, or duties of a licensee as defined in Section 868, three (3) years have passed from the time of commission of the act(s), without the occurrence of criminal activity or additional substantially-related acts.

(2) The amount of time needed to demonstrate rehabilitation under subsection (a)(1) may be increased or decreased by taking into account the following:

(A) The nature and severity of the crime(s) or act(s) that are under consideration as, or that were, the grounds for denial, suspension, or revocation.

(B) Evidence of any crime(s) or act(s) committed subsequent to the crime(s) or act(s) that are under consideration as, or that were, the grounds for denial, suspension, or revocation, which also could be considered as grounds for denial, suspension, or revocation.

(C) The time that has elapsed since commission of the crime(s) or act(s) that are under consideration as, or that were, the grounds for denial, suspension, or revocation.

(D) The extent to which the applicant or licensee has complied with any terms of parole, probation, restitution, or any other sanctions lawfully imposed against the applicant or licensee.

(E) Consistent work history subsequent to the release from incarceration, or the completion of probation if no incarceration was imposed, or subsequent to the time of commission of the act(s).

(F) Documents or testimony from credible individuals who have personal knowledge of the applicant's or licensee's life and activities subsequent to the time of commission of the crime(s) or act(s) who can attest to the applicant's or licensee's present fitness for licensure.

(G) If applicable, evidence of expungement proceedings pursuant to Section 1203.4 of the Penal Code.

(H) Other relevant evidence, if any, of rehabilitation submitted by the applicant or licensee. For example, relevant evidence may include evidence of recovery from drug and/or alcohol addiction or abuse or completion of a drug and/or alcohol aversion program if the crime(s) or act(s) related to or involved drug and/or alcohol use; or evidence of completion of an anger management program if the crime(s) or act(s) demonstrated the applicant's or licensee's inability to control one's temper.

(b) When considering a petition for reinstatement of the license of a contractor, the Board shall evaluate evidence of rehabilitation submitted by the petitioner, considering those criteria specified in subsection (a).

(Authority cited: Sections 482 and 7008, Business and Professions Code. Reference: Sections 480, 482, 490, 496, 7066, 7069, 7073, 7123, and 7124, Business and Professions Code.)

869.1. Applicant Defined

(a) All applicants for licensure shall furnish a full set of fingerprints for purposes of the board conducting a criminal history record check. The fingerprints will be used to allow the California Department of Justice and the Federal Bureau of Investigation to provide criminal history to the Board.

(b) For purposes of fingerprinting, "applicant" means any individual applying to be a member of the personnel of record.

(c) For purposes of fingerprinting, "applicant" means an individual applying for a home improvement registration.

(Authority cited: Section 7008, Business and Professions Code. Reference: Sections 7069 and 7153.1, Business and Professions Code.)

869.2. Exemptions

(a) Applicants for a joint venture license who hold a current active license in good standing are not subject to fingerprinting.

(b) Individuals already fingerprinted as required by Section 869.1 and for whom subsequent arrest information remains available at the Board need not submit fingerprints when submitting a subsequent application.

(Authority cited: Section 7008, Business and Professions Code. Reference: Sections 7069 and 7153.1, Business and Professions Code.)

869.3. Methods for Submitting Fingerprints

(a) Applicants residing inside the State of California shall submit their fingerprints through the electronic format certified by the California Department of Justice but, with approval of the Registrar, may submit their fingerprints on hard copy forms provided by the Registrar.

(b) Applicants residing outside the State of California may submit their fingerprints using the electronic format certified by the California Department of Justice but also may submit their fingerprints on hard copy forms provided by the Registrar.

(Authority cited: Section 7008, Business and Professions Code. Reference: Sections 7069 and 7153.1, Business and Professions Code.)

869.4. Subsequent Arrest History

(a) Once an applicant has been fingerprinted, the Board will maintain access to the applicant's subsequent arrest history until such time as the individual's license is cancelled, revoked or no longer renewable.

(b) Once the Board no longer receives subsequent arrest information, an individual seeking to apply for a license must be fingerprinted as required in Section 869.1.

(Authority cited: Section 7008, Business and Professions Code. Reference: Sections 7069 and 7153.1, Business and Professions Code.)

869.5. Inquiry into Criminal Convictions

The Board may conduct an inquiry into the circumstances surrounding the commission of a crime in order to fix the degree of discipline or to determine if the crime is substantially related to the qualifications, functions, and duties of an applicant or licensee by requiring the applicant or licensee to provide documents including, but not limited to, certified court documents, certified court orders or sentencing documents.

(Authority cited: Section 7008, Business and Professions Code. Reference: Sections 7069 and 7153.1, Business and Professions Code.)

869.9. Criteria to Aid in Determining Earliest Date a Denied Applicant May Reapply for Licensure

(a) For an applicant who is denied licensure pursuant to subdivision (a) of Section 480 of the Business and Professions Code, the date of reapplication shall be set by the registrar at not less than one year nor more than five years after the denial. When computing the date for reapplication, the time shall commence from the effective date of the decision if an appeal is made or from the service of the notice under Section 485(b) if a request for hearing is not made. The registrar will consider the following criteria when setting the reapplication date of an individual who was denied a license:

(1) For felony convictions that are substantially related to the qualifications, functions, or duties of a licensee as defined in Section 868, seven (7) years have passed from the time of release from incarceration or completion of probation if no incarceration was imposed, without the occurrence of additional criminal activity or substantially-related acts.

(2) For misdemeanor convictions that are substantially related to the qualifications, functions, or duties of a licensee as defined in Section 868, three (3) years have passed from the time of release from incarceration or completion of probation if no incarceration was imposed, without the occurrence of additional criminal activity or substantially-related acts.

(3) For acts that are substantially related to the qualifications, functions, or duties of a licensee as defined in Section 868, three (3) years have passed from the time of commission of the act(s), without the occurrence of criminal activity or additional substantially-related acts.

(4) The nature and severity of the crime(s) or act(s) that were the grounds for denial.

(5) Evidence of any crime(s) or act(s) committed subsequent to the crime(s) or act(s) that were the grounds for denial, which also could be considered as grounds for denial.

(6) The time that has elapsed since commission of the crime(s) or act(s) that were the grounds for denial.

(7) The extent to which the applicant or licensee has complied with any terms of parole, probation, restitution, or any other sanctions lawfully imposed against the applicant.

(8) Consistent work history subsequent to the release from incarceration, or the completion of probation if no incarceration was imposed, or subsequent to the time of commission of the act(s).

(9) Documents or testimony from credible individuals who have personal knowledge of the applicant's life and activities subsequent to the time of commission of the crime(s) or act(s) who can attest to the applicant's present fitness for licensure.

(10) If applicable, evidence of expungement proceedings pursuant to Section 1203.4 of the Penal Code.

(11) Other relevant evidence, if any, of eligibility for reapplication submitted by the applicant. For example, relevant evidence may include evidence of recovery from drug and/or alcohol addiction or abuse or completion of a drug and/or alcohol aversion program if the crime(s) or act(s) related to or involved drug and/or alcohol use; or evidence of completion of an anger management program if the crime(s) or act(s) demonstrated the applicant's or licensee's inability to control one's temper.

(b) Nothing in this section shall preclude the registrar from denying the license of an applicant who was previously denied a license and who is eligible for reapplication in accordance with this section.

(Authority cited: Sections 482, 7008 and 7073, Business and Professions Code. Reference: Sections 480, 482, 486, 496, 7066, 7069, 7073 and 7124, Business and Professions Code.)

870. Factors to Apply in Determining Earliest Date a Revoked Licensee May Apply for Licensure

(a) The Registrar shall have exclusive authority in setting the earliest date a revoked licensee may reapply for reissuance or reinstatement of a license.

(b) when extending the minimum one year period, the Registrar shall give due consideration to the gravity of the violation, the history of previous violations and criminal convictions and evaluate the application based on the following criteria:

Reapplication Dates:

5 years—   License has been revoked:

> (1) One or more times; or

> (2) For committing fraudulent acts; or

> (3) Committing acts which have seriously endangered the public welfare and safety; or

> (4) For being convicted of a construction-related crime. (For the purposes of determining if a crime is

construction-related, CCR Title 16, Chapter 8, Section 868 shall apply.)

4 years— License has been revoked:

(1) For committing violations on multiple construction projects; or

(2) For committing multiple violations of law for reasons other than fraud, danger to the public welfare and safety and for conviction of a construction-related crime.

3 years— License has been revoked and revoked licensee:

(1) Has been issued more than one citation which has become final within one year immediately preceding the date of revocation or

(2) Has been previously suspended by the Registrar as the result of a disciplinary action.

2 years— License has been revoked and revoked licensee has been issued a citation, which has become final within one year immediately preceding the date of revocation.

1 year— Licensee has been revoked for the first time and revoked licensee has no previous legal action history with the Board.

(Authority cited: Sections 7008 and 7059, Business and Professions Code. Reference: Sections 7058 and 7059, Business and Professions Code.)

871. Disciplinary Guidelines

In reaching a decision on a disciplinary action under the Administrative Procedure Act (Government Code Section 11400 et seq.), the board shall consider the disciplinary guidelines entitled "Disciplinary Guidelines" (rev. 12/11/96) which are hereby incorporated by reference. Deviation from these guidelines and orders, including the standard terms of probation, is appropriate where the board in its sole discretion determines that the facts of the particular case warrant such a deviation—for example, the presence of mitigating factors such as the age of the case; evidentiary problems.

(Authority cited: Section 7008, Business and Professions Code; and Sections 11400.20 and 11400.21, Government Code. Reference: Sections 7090 and 7095, Business and Professions Code; and Section 11425.50(e), Government Code.)

Section VI

DISCIPLINARY GUIDELINES
(Rev. 12/11/96)

In assessing a disciplinary penalty against a person who has not had a previous citation, revocation, suspension nor denial of application, as the result of the filing of an accusation or a statement of issues, the Registrar shall give due consideration to the following guidelines. In addition to any penalties imposed, all persons that have had a license disciplined, whether or not the disciplinary action has been stayed, will be required to post a disciplinary bond pursuant to Section 7071.8. Unless otherwise specified, all references are to the Business and Professions Code.

Factors To Be Considered

In determining whether revocation, suspension or probation is to be imposed in a given case, factors such as the following should be considered:

1. Nature and severity of the act(s), offenses, or crime(s) under consideration.

2. Actual or potential harm to the public.

3. Performed work that was potentially hazardous to the health, safety, or general welfare of the public.

4. Prior disciplinary record.

5. Number and/or variety of current violations.

6. Mitigation evidence.

7. Rehabilitation evidence.

8. In case of a criminal conviction, compliance with terms of sentence and/or court-ordered probation.

Sections and Disciplinary Guidelines

125. Conspiracy with an Unlicensed Person

Minimum Penalty: Revocation, stayed, 3 years probation

Maximum Penalty: Revocation

If warranted:

1. Actual suspension of 5 days or more.

2. Standard terms and conditions in cases of probation. *(See page 547.)*

3. Submit copies of construction contracts to the Registrar upon demand during the probation period.

4. If not taken within the past 5 years, take and pass the CSLB law and business examination.

5. Take and pass a course in Contractors License Law or a course related to construction law at an accredited community college. All courses must be approved in advance by the Registrar.

6. Community Service time as determined by the Registrar; 5-21 days.

7. Pay CSLB investigation and enforcement costs.

141. Disciplinary Action by Foreign Jurisdiction

Minimum Penalty: Revocation, stayed, 3 years probation

Maximum Penalty: Revocation

If warranted:

1. Actual suspension of 5 days or more.

2. Standard terms and conditions in cases of probation. (*See page 547.*)

3. Pay CSLB investigation and enforcement costs.

4. Community Service as determined by the Registrar; 5-21 days.

490. Conviction of a Crime—Substantial Relationship Required

Minimum Penalty: Revocation, stayed, 3 years probation

Maximum Penalty: Revocation

If warranted:

1. Absent compelling mitigating circumstances, conviction of a crime related to the functions of a contractor is a serious offense that warrants an outright revocation.

2. Actual suspension of at least 30 days.

3. Standard terms and conditions in cases of probation. (*See page 547.*)

4. Make restitution.

5. If not taken within the past 5 years, take and pass the CSLB law and business examination.

6. Prohibit receipt of down payments.

Section VI

7. Community Service as determined by the Registrar; 5-21 days.

8. Pay CSLB investigation and enforcement costs.

496. Violation of Section 123—Subversion of Licensee Examinations

Minimum Penalty: Revocation

Maximum Penalty: Revocation

If warranted:

1. Pay CSLB investigation and enforcement costs.

498. Securing a License through Fraud, Deceit or Knowing Misrepresentation

Minimum Penalty: Revocation

Maximum Penalty: Revocation

If warranted:

1. Pay CSLB investigation and enforcement costs.

499. False Statement in Support of Application

Minimum Penalty: Revocation, stayed, 3 years probation

If warranted:

1. Absent compelling mitigating circumstances, making a false statement in support of an application of another person, is a serious offense that warrants an outright revocation.

2. Actual suspension of at least 30 days.

3. Standard terms and conditions in cases of probation. (*See page 547.*)

4. If not taken within the past 5 years, take and pass the CSLB law and business examination.

5. Take and pass a course in Contractors License Law or a course related to construction law at an accredited community college. All courses must be approved in advance by the Registrar.

6. Community Service as determined by CSLB; 5-21 days.

7. Pay CSLB investigation and enforcement costs.

860. (CCR) Penalty for Failure to Comply with Rules

Minimum Penalty: 5 day suspension, stayed, 1 year probation

Maximum Penalty: Revocation

If warranted:

1. Actual suspension of 5 days or more.

2. Standard terms and conditions in cases of probation. (*See page 547.*)

3. If not taken within the past 5 years, take and pass the CSLB law and business examination.

4. Take and pass a course in Contractors License Law or a course related to construction law at an accredited community college. All courses must be approved in advance by the Registrar.

5. Pay CSLB investigation and enforcement costs.

7018.5. Notice to Owner; Mechanics' Lien Law

Minimum Penalty: 5 day suspension, stayed, 1 year probation

Maximum Penalty: 60 day suspension, 1 year probation

If warranted:

1. Standard terms and conditions in cases of probation. (*See page 547.*)

2. Submit copies of construction contracts to the Registrar upon demand during the probation period.

3. If not taken within the past 5 years, take and pass the CSLB law and business examination.

4. Take and pass a course in Contractors License Law or a course related to construction law at an accredited community college. All courses must be approved in advance by the Registrar.

5. Pay CSLB investigation and enforcement costs.

7027.3. Fraudulent Use of a License Number

Minimum Penalty: Revocation

Maximum Penalty: Revocation

If warranted:

1. Pay CSLB investigation and enforcement costs.

7029.1. Contracting Jointly Without a Joint Venture License

Minimum Penalty: 5 day suspension, stayed, 1 year probation

Maximum Penalty: 60 day suspension, 1 year probation

Section VI

If warranted:

1. Actual suspension of 5 days or more.

2. Standard terms and conditions in cases of probation. (*See page 547.*)

3. If not taken within the past 5 years, take and pass the CSLB law and business examination.

4. Take and pass a course in Contractors License Law or a course related to construction law at an accredited community college. All courses must be approved in advance by the Registrar.

5. Pay CSLB investigation and enforcement costs.

7029.5. Identification on Vehicle, Plumbing, Electrical Sign, and Well-drilling

Minimum Penalty: 5 day suspension, stayed, 1 year probation

Maximum Penalty: 60 suspension, 1 year probation

If warranted:

1. Standard terms and conditions in cases of probation. (*See page 547.*)

2. Pay CSLB investigation and enforcement costs.

7068.2. Failure to Notify; Disassociation of RMO/RME

Minimum Penalty: 60 day suspension, stayed, 1 year probation

Maximum Penalty: Revocation

If warranted:

1. Standard terms and conditions in cases of probation. (*See page 547.*)

2. If not taken within the past 5 years, take and pass the CSLB law and business examination.

3. Take and pass a course in Contractors License Law or a course related to construction law at an accredited community college. All courses must be approved in advance by the Registrar.

4. Pay CSLB investigation and enforcement costs.

7071.11. Judgment, Admitted Claim or Good Faith Payment on Bond

Minimum Penalty: 60 day suspension, stayed, 1 year probation

Maximum Penalty: Revocation

If warranted:

1. Actual suspension of 5 days or more.

2. Standard terms and conditions in cases of probation. (*See page 547.*)

3. Make restitution.

4. Pay CSLB investigation and enforcement costs.

7071.13. Reference in Advertising; Contractors Bond

Minimum Penalty: 5 day suspension, stayed, 1 year probation

Maximum Penalty: 60 day suspension, 1 year probation

If warranted:

1. Standard terms and conditions in cases of probation. *(See page 547.)*

2. Submit copies of advertisements relating to contracting business to the Registrar prior to their being displayed or published during the probation period.

3. If not taken within the past 5 years, take and pass the CSLB law and business examination.

4. Take and pass a course in Contractors License Law or a course related to construction law at an accredited community college. All courses must be approved in advance by the Registrar.

5. Pay CSLB investigation and enforcement costs.

7071.15. Failure to Maintain a Sufficient Bond

Minimum Penalty: 60 day suspension, stayed, 1 year probation

Maximum Penalty: Revocation

If warranted:

1. Actual suspension of 5 days or more.

2. Standard terms and conditions in cases of probation. (*See page 547.*)

3. If not taken within the past 5 years, take and pass the CSLB law and business examination.

4. Take and pass a course in Contractors License Law or a course related to construction law at an accredited community college. All courses must be approved in advance by the Registrar.

5. Pay CSLB investigation and enforcement costs.

Section VI

7076. Failure to Notify; Death or Disassociation of Licensee Personnel

Minimum Penalty: 60 day suspension, stayed, 1 year probation

Maximum Penalty: Revocation

If warranted:

1. Standard terms and conditions in cases of probation. (*See page 547.*)

2. If not taken within the past 5 years, take and pass the CSLB law and business examination.

3. Take and pass a course in Contractors License Law or a course related to construction law at an accredited community college. All courses must be approved in advance by the Registrar.

4. Pay CSLB investigation and enforcement costs.

7083. Failure to Notify, Changes of Personnel, Business Name, Address, Bond Exemption, and Multiple License Exemption

Minimum Penalty: 60 day suspension, stayed, 1 year probation

Maximum Penalty: Revocation

If warranted:

1. Standard terms and conditions in cases of probation. (*See page 547.*)

2. If not taken within the past 5 years, take and pass the CSLB law and business examination.

3. Take and pass a course in Contractors License Law or a course related to construction law at an accredited community college. All courses must be approved in advance by the Registrar.

4. Pay CSLB investigation and enforcement costs.

7090. Failure to Obtain Building Permits

Minimum Penalty: 60 day suspension, stayed, 1 year probation

Maximum Penalty: Revocation

If warranted:

1. Actual suspension of 5 days or more.

2. Standard terms and conditions in cases of probation. (*See page 547.*)

3. Make restitution.

4. Submit copies of building permits to the Registrar upon demand for projects undertaken during the probation period.

5. If not taken within the past 5 years, take and pass the CSLB trade examination.

6. Take and pass a course in Contractors License Law or a course related to construction law at an accredited community college. All courses must be approved in advance by the Registrar.

7. Pay CSLB investigation and enforcement costs.

7090.5. Fraud and Repeated Acts, Despite Corrections of Conditions

Minimum Penalty: Revocation, stayed, 3 years probation

Maximum Penalty: revocation

If warranted:

1. Actual suspension of 5 days or more.

2. Standard terms and conditions in cases of probation. (*See page 547.*)

3. Take and pass a course in accounting, bookkeeping and/or business management at an accredited community college. All courses must be approved in advance by the Registrar.

4. Submit copies of building permits to the Registrar upon demand for projects undertaken during the probation period.

5. Submit copies of construction contracts to the Registrar upon demand during the probation period.

6. Prohibit receipt of down payments.

7. Submit to the Registrar a detailed plan setting forth the procedure to be used to provide for direct supervising and control by the qualifying individual.

8. If not taken within the past 5 years, take and pass the CSLB law and business examination.

9. Take and pass a course in Contractors License Law or a course related to business law at an accredited community college. All courses must be approved in advance by the Registrar.

10. If not taken within the past 5 years, take and pass the CSLB trade examination.

Section VI

11. Take and pass a vocational course(s) related to the trade(s) employed on the project. All courses must be approved in advance by the Registrar.

12. Pay CSLB investigation and enforcement costs.

7099.6. Failure to Comply with a Citation

Minimum Penalty: Revocation, stayed, 1 year probation

Maximum Penalty: Revocation

If warranted:

1. Actual suspension of 5 days or more.

2. Standard terms and conditions in cases of probation. (*See page 547.*)

3. Make restitution.

4. Take and pass a course in Contractors License Law or a course related to construction law at an accredited community college. All courses must be approved in advance by the Registrar.

5. Pay CSLB investigation and enforcement costs.

7103. Disciplinary Action by Another State

Minimum Penalty: Revocation, stayed, 3 years probation.

Maximum Penalty: Revocation

If warranted:

1. Actual suspension of 5 days or more.

2. Standard terms and conditions in cases of probation. (*See page 547.*)

3. Pay CSLB investigation and enforcement costs.

7107. Abandonment

Minimum Penalty: Revocation, stayed, 3 years probation

Maximum Penalty: Revocation

If warranted:

1. Absent compelling mitigating circumstances, abandonment of a project is a serious offense that warrants an actual period of suspension of at least 30 days.

2. Standard terms and conditions in cases of probation. (*See page 547.*)

3. Make restitution.

4. Submit copies of building permits to the Registrar upon demand for projects undertaken during the probation period.

5. Submit copies of construction contracts to the Registrar upon demand during the probation period.

6. Submit to the Registrar a detailed plan setting forth the procedure to be used to provide for direct supervision and control by the qualifying individual.

7. If not taken within the past 5 years, take and pass the CSLB law and business examination.

8. Take and pass a course in Contractors License Law or a course related to construction law at an accredited community college. All courses must be approved in advance by the Registrar.

9. If not taken within the past 5 years, take and pass the CSLB trade examination.

10. Take and pass a vocational course(s) related to the trade(s) employed on the project. All courses must be approved in advance by the Registrar.

11. During the period of probation, provide lien releases to project owners as soon as payment is received.

12. Pay CSLB investigation and enforcement costs.

7108. Misuse of Funds

Minimum Penalty: Revocation, stayed, 3 years probation

Maximum Penalty: Revocation

If warranted:

1. Absent compelling mitigating circumstances, misuse of funds is a serious offense that warrants an actual period of suspension of at least 30 days.

2. If diversion or misuse of funds is for personal use not related to construction work, outright revocation is appropriate.

3. Standard terms and conditions in cases of probation. (*See page 547.*)

4. Make restitution.

5. Take and pass a course in accounting, bookkeeping and/or business management at an accredited community college. All courses must be approved in advance by the Registrar.

6. Submit copies of construction contracts to the Registrar upon demand during the probation period.

7. If not taken within the past 5 years, take and pass the CSLB law and business examination.

8. Take and pass a course in Contractors License Law or course related to construction law at an accredited community college. All courses must be approved in advance by the Registrar.

9. Community Service as determined by CSLB; 5-21 days.

10. Pay CSLB investigation and enforcement costs.

7108.5. Prime Contractors and Subcontractors; Payment Required

Minimum Penalty: 60 day suspension, stayed, 1 year probation

Maximum Penalty: Revocation

If warranted:

1. Actual suspension of 5 days or more.

2. Standard terms and conditions in cases of probation. (*See page 547.*)

3. Make restitution.

4. Take and pass a course in accounting, bookkeeping and/or business management at an accredited community college. All courses must be approved in advance by the Registrar.

5. If not taken within the past 5 years, take and pass the CSLB law and business examination.

6. Take and pass a course in Contractors License Law or a course related to construction law at an accredited community college. All courses must be approved in advance by the Registrar.

7. Pay CSLB investigation and enforcement costs.

7109(a). Departure from Accepted Trade Standards for Workmanship

Minimum Penalty: Revocation, stayed, 2 years probation

Maximum Penalty: Revocation

If warranted:

1. Actual suspension of 5 days or more. If the departure from trade standards is substantial, actual suspension of at least 30 days.

2. Standard terms and conditions in cases of probation. (*See page 547.*)

3. Make restitution.

4. Submit copies of building permits to the Registrar upon demand for projects undertaken during the probationary period.

5. Submit copies of construction contracts to the Registrar upon demand during the probation period.

6. Submit to the Registrar a detailed plan setting forth the procedure to be used to provide for direct supervising and control by the qualifying individual.

7. If not taken within the last 5 years, take and pass the CSLB law and business examination.

8. Take and pass a course in Contractors License Law or a course related to construction law at an accredited community college. All courses must be approved in advance by the Registrar.

9. If not taken within the past 5 years, take and pass the CSLB trade examination.

10. Take and pass a vocational course(s) related to the trade(s) employed on the project. All courses must be approved in advance by the Registrar.

11. Pay CSLB investigation and enforcement costs.

7109(b). Departure from Plans and/or Specifications

Minimum Penalty: Revocation, stayed, 2 years probation

Maximum Penalty: Revocation

If warranted:

1. Actual suspension of 5 days or more. If the departure from plans and/or specifications is substantial, actual suspension of at least 30 days.

2. Standard terms and conditions in cases of probation. (*See page 547.*)

3. Make restitution.

4. Submit copies of building permits to the Registrar upon demand for all projects undertaken during the probationary period.

5. Submit copies of construction contracts to the Registrar upon demand during the probation period.

6. Submit to the Registrar a detailed plan setting forth the procedure to be used to provide for direct supervising and control by the qualifying individual.

7. If not taken within the past 5 years, take and pass the CSLB law and business examination.

8. Take and pass a course in Contractors License Law or a course related to construction law at an accredited community college. All courses must be approved in advance by the Registrar.

9. If not taken within the past 5 years, take and pass the CSLB trade examination.

10. Take and pass a vocational course(s) related to the trade(s) employed on the project. All courses must be approved in advance by the Registrar.

11. Pay CSLB investigation and enforcement costs.

7109.5. Violation of Safety Orders

Minimum Penalty: Revocation, stayed, 2 years probation

Maximum Penalty: Revocation

If warranted:

1. Actual suspension of 5 days or more.

2. Standard terms and conditions in cases of probation. (*See page 547.*)

3. If not taken within the past 5 years, take and pass the CSLB law and business examination.

4. Take and pass a course in Contractors License Law or a course related to construction law at an accredited community college. All courses must be approved in advance by the Registrar.

5. Establish a safety program.

6. Pay CSLB investigation and enforcement costs.

7110. Violations of Other Laws; Disciplinary Action

Minimum Penalty: Revocation, stayed, 2 years probation

Maximum Penalty: Revocation

If warranted:

1. Actual suspension of 5 days or more.

2. Standard terms and conditions in cases of probation. (*See page 547.*)

3. Make restitution.

4. Comply with orders or assessments of relevant agency.

5. If not taken within the past 5 years, take and pass the CSLB law and business examination.

6. Take and pass a course in Contractors License Law or a course related to construction law at an accredited community college. All courses must be approved in advance by the Registrar.

7. Submit copies of building permits to the Registrar upon demand for projects undertaken during the probation period.

8. Establish a safety program.

9. Pay CSLB investigation and enforcement costs.

7110.1. Violation of Labor Code Section 206.5; Requiring Release of Claim for Wages

Minimum Penalty: 60 day suspension, stayed, 1 year probation

Maximum Penalty: Revocation

If warranted:

1. Actual suspension of 5 days or more.

2. Standard terms and conditions in cases of probation. (*See page 547.*)

3. If not taken within the past 5 years, take and pass the CSLB law and business examination.

4. Take and pass a course in Contractors License Law or a course related to construction law at an accredited community college. All courses must be approved in advance by the Registrar.

5. Pay CSLB investigation and enforcement costs.

7110.5. Violation Pursuant to Section 98.9 of the Labor Code

Minimum Penalty: 60 day suspension, stayed, 1 year probation

Maximum Penalty: Revocation

If warranted:

1. Actual suspension of 5 days or more.

2. Standard terms and conditions in cases of probation. (*See page 547.*)

3. If not taken within the past 5 years, take and pass the CSLB law and business examination.

Section VI

4. Take and pass a course in Contractors License Law or a course related to construction law at an accredited community college. All courses must be approved in advance by the Registrar.

5. Pay CSLB investigation and enforcement costs.

7111. Preservation of Records

Minimum Penalty: 60 day suspension, stayed, 1 year probation

Maximum Penalty: Revocation

If warranted:

1. Actual suspension of 5 days or more.

2. Standard terms and conditions in cases of probation. (*See page 547.*)

3. Take and pass a course in accounting, bookkeeping and/or business management at an accredited community college. All courses must be approved in advance by the Registrar.

4. If not taken within the past 5 years, take and pass the CSLB law and business examination.

5. Take and pass a course in Contractors License Law or a course related to construction law at an accredited community college. All courses must be approved in advance by the Registrar.

6. Pay CSLB investigation and enforcement costs.

7111.1. Failure of Licensee To Cooperate in an Investigation of a Complaint

Minimum Penalty: 60 day suspension, stayed, 1 year probation

Maximum Penalty: revocation

If warranted:

1. Actual suspension of 5 days or more.

2. Standard terms and conditions in cases of probation. (*See page 547.*)

3. If not taken within the past 5 years, take and pass CSLB law and business examination.

4. Take and pass a course in Contractors License Law or a course related to construction law at an accredited community college. All courses must be approved in advance by the Registrar.

5. Pay CSLB investigation and enforcement costs.

7112. Misrepresentation on an Application

Minimum Penalty: Revocation, stayed, 3 years probation

Maximum Penalty: Revocation

If warranted:

1. Absent compelling mitigating circumstances, misrepresentation is a serious offense that warrants an outright revocation.

2. Actual suspension of at least 30 days.

3. Standard terms and conditions in cases of probation. (*See page 547.*)

4. Community Service as determined by CSLB; 5-21 days.

5. Pay CSLB investigation and enforcement costs.

7113. Failure to Complete Project for Contract Price

Minimum Penalty: Revocation, stayed, 2 years probation

Maximum Penalty: Revocation

If warranted:

1. Actual suspension of 5 days or more. If injury is substantial, actual suspension of at least 30 days.

2. Standard terms and conditions in cases of probation. (*See page 547.*)

3. Make restitution.

4. Complete an education course in estimating construction costs or a related course in the field of construction science. All courses must be approved in advance by the Registrar.

5. Prohibit receipt of down payments.

6. If not taken within the past 5 years, take and pass the CSLB law and business examination.

7. Take and pass a course in Contractors License Law or a course related to construction law at an accredited community college. All courses must be approved in advance by the Registrar.

8. Pay CSLB investigation and enforcement costs.

7113.5. Settlement of Lawful Obligations

Minimum Penalty: Revocation, stayed, 2 years probation

Maximum Penalty: Revocation

Section VI

If warranted:

1. Actual suspension of 5 days or more.

2. Standard terms and conditions in cases of probation. (*See page 547.*)

3. Make restitution.

4. Take and pass a course in accounting, bookkeeping and/or business management at an accredited community college. All courses must be approved in advance by the Registrar.

5. Submit a list of all subcontractors used on construction projects to the Registrar upon demand during the probation period.

6. Submit a list of all material suppliers used on construction projects to the Registrar upon demand during the probation period.

7. Pay CSLB investigation and enforcement costs.

7114. Aiding and Abetting an Unlicensed Person

Minimum Penalty: Revocation, stayed, 2 years probation

Maximum Penalty: Revocation

If warranted:

1. Actual suspension of 5 days or more.

2. Standard terms and conditions in cases of probation. (*See page 547.*)

3. If not taken within the past 5 years, take and pass the CSLB law and business examination.

4. Take and pass a course in Contractors License Law or a course related to construction law at an accredited community college. All courses must be approved in advance by the Registrar.

5. Submit a list of all subcontractors used on construction projects to the Registrar upon demand during the probation period.

6. Pay CSLB investigation and enforcement costs.

7114.1. Certifying to False Experience

Minimum Penalty: Revocation, stayed, 3 years probation

Maximum Penalty: Revocation

If warranted:

1. Absent compelling mitigating circumstances, certifying false experience is a serious offense that warrants an outright revocation.

2. Standard terms and conditions in cases of probation. (*See page 547.*)

3. Community Service as determined by CSLB; 5-21 days.

4. Pay CSLB investigation and enforcement costs.

7115. Violation of the Contractors License Law

Minimum Penalty: 5 day suspension, stayed, 1 year probation

Maximum Penalty: Revocation

If warranted:

1. Actual suspension of 5 days or more.

2. Standard terms and conditions in case of probation. (*See page 547.*)

3. Pay CSLB investigation and enforcement costs.

7116. Any Willful or Fraudulent Act

Minimum Penalty: Revocation, stayed, 3 years probation

Maximum Penalty: revocation

If warranted:

1. Absent compelling circumstances, fraud is a serious offense that warrants an actual suspension of at least 60 days.

2. If the injury is substantial, outright revocation is appropriate.

3. Standard terms and conditions in case of probation. (*See page 547.*)

4. Make restitution.

5. If not taken within the past 5 years, take and pass the CSLB law and business examination.

6. Take and pass a course in Contractors License Law or a course related to construction law at an accredited community college. All courses must be approved in advance by the Registrar.

7. Community Service as determined by CSLB; 5-21 days.

8. Pay CSLB investigation and enforcement costs.

Section VI

7117. Variance from License as to Name or Personnel

Minimum Penalty: 5 day suspension, stayed, 1 year probation

Maximum Penalty: 364 day suspension, 2 years probation

If warranted:

1. Standard terms and conditions in case of probation. (*See page 547.*)

2. If not taken within the past 5 years, take and pass the CSLB law and business examination.

3. Take and pass a course in Contractors License Law or a course related to construction law at an accredited community college. All courses must be approved in advance by the Registrar.

4. Pay CSLB investigation and enforcement costs.

7117.5. Contracting with an Inactive, Suspended or Expired License

Minimum Penalty: Revocation, stayed, 2 years probation

Maximum Penalty: Revocation

If warranted:

1. Actual suspension of 5 days or more.

2. Standard terms and conditions in case of probation. (*See page 547.*)

3. If not taken within the past 5 years, take and pass the CSLB law and business examination.

4. Take and pass a course in Contractors License Law or a course related to construction law at an accredited community college. All courses must be approved in advance by the Registrar.

5. Pay CSLB investigation and enforcement costs.

7117.6. Contracting Out of Classification

Minimum Penalty: 60 day suspension, stayed, 1 year probation

Maximum Penalty: Revocation

If warranted:

1. Actual suspension of 5 days or more.

2. Standard terms and conditions in case of probation. (*See page 547.*)

3. Submit copies of construction contracts to the Registrar upon demand during the probation period.

4. Submit copies of all advertisements relating to contracting business to the Registrar prior to their being displayed or published during the probation period.

5. Pay CSLB investigation and enforcement costs.

7118. Contracting with an Unlicensed Person

Minimum Penalty: Revocation, stayed, 2 years probation
Maximum Penalty: Revocation
If warranted:
1. Actual suspension of 5 days or more.

2. Standard terms and conditions in cases of probation . (*See page 547.*)

3. If not taken within the past 5 years, take and pass the CSLB law and business examination.

4. Take and pass a course in Contractors License Law or a course related to construction law at an accredited community college. All courses must be approved in advance by the Registrar.

5. Submit a list of all subcontractors used on construction projects to the Registrar upon demand during the probation period.

6. Community Service as determined by CSLB; 5-21 days.

7. Pay CSLB investigation and enforcement costs.

7118.4. Asbestos Related Inspection with Knowledge of Report being Required for Loan; Disclosure Required

Minimum Penalty: 60 day suspension, stayed, 1 year probation

Maximum Penalty: Revocation

If warranted:

1. Absent compelling mitigating circumstances, conducting an asbestos related inspection while maintaining a financial relationship with an entity which performs corrective work without disclosing this fact is a serious offense that warrants an actual suspension of 60 days.

2. Standard terms and conditions in cases of probation. (*See page 547.*)

3. If not taken within the past 5 years, take and pass the CSLB law and business examination.

Section VI

4. Take and pass a course in Contractors License Law or a course related to construction law at an accredited community college. All courses must be approved in advance by the Registrar.

5. Community Service as determined by CSLB; 5-21 days.

6. Pay CSLB investigation and enforcement costs.

7118.5. Asbestos-related Work; Contracting with Uncertified Contractor

Minimum Penalty: 60 day suspension, stayed, 1 year probation

Maximum Penalty: Revocation

If warranted:

1. Absent compelling mitigating circumstances, contracting with an uncertified asbestos contractor to perform asbestos related work is a serious offense that warrants an actual suspension of 60 days.

2. Standard terms and conditions in cases of probation. (*See page 547.*)

3. Submit a list of all subcontractors used on construction projects to the Registrar upon demand during the probation period.

4. Community Service as determined by CSLB; 5-21 days.

5. Pay CSLB investigation and enforcement costs.

7118.6. Asbestos-contracting with an Uncertified Person for Removal or Remedial Action

Minimum Penalty: 60 day suspension, stayed, 1 year probation

Maximum Penalty: Revocation

If warranted:

1. Absent compelling mitigating circumstances, contracting with an uncertified person for removal or remedial asbestos work is a serious offense that warrants an actual suspension of 60 days.

2. Standard terms and conditions in cases of probation. (*See page 547.*)

3. Submit a list of all subcontractors used on construction projects to the Registrar upon demand during the probation period.

4. Community Service as determined by CSLB; 5-21 days.

5. Pay CSLB investigation and enforcement costs.

7119. Lack of Reasonable Diligence

Minimum Penalty: 60 day suspension, stayed, 1 year probation

Maximum Penalty: Revocation

If warranted:

1. Actual suspension of 5 days or more.

2. Standard terms and conditions in cases of probation. (*See page 547.*)

3. Make restitution.

4. Prohibit receipt of down payments.

5. Pay CSLB investigation and enforcement costs.

7120. Failure to Pay Money

Minimum Penalty: 60 day suspension, stayed, 1 year probation

Maximum Penalty: Revocation

If warranted:

1. Actual suspension of 5 days or more.

2. Standard terms and conditions in cases of probation. (*See page 547.*)

3. Take and pass a course in accounting, bookkeeping and/or business management at an accredited community college. All courses must be approved in advance by the Registrar.

4. If not taken within the past 5 years, take and pass the CSLB law and business examination.

5. Take and pass a course in Contractors License Law or a course related to construction law at an accredited community college. All courses must be approved in advance by the Registrar.

6. Submit a list of all subcontractors used on construction projects to the Registrar upon demand during the probation period.

7. Submit a list of all material suppliers used on construction projects to the Registrar upon demand during the probation period.

8. Prohibit the receipt of down payments.

9. Provide lien releases to project owners on all future construction projects upon receipt of payments.

10. Pay CSLB investigation and enforcement costs.

7121. Prohibition against Association

Minimum Penalty: Revocation, stayed, 2 years probation

Maximum Penalty: Revocation

If warranted:

1. Actual suspension of 5 days or more.

2. Standard terms and conditions in cases of probation. (*See page 547.*)

3. Make restitution.

4. If not taken within the past 5 years, take and pass the CSLB law and business examination.

5. Take and pass a course in Contractors License Law or a course related to construction law at an accredited community college. All courses must be approved in advance by the Registrar.

6. Pay CSLB investigation and enforcement costs.

7123. Conviction of a Crime

Minimum Penalty: Revocation, stayed, 3 years probation

Maximum Penalty; Revocation

If warranted:

1. Absent compelling mitigating circumstances, conviction of a crime related to the functions of a contractor is a serious offense and warrants an outright revocation.

2. Actual suspension of at least 30 days.

3. Standard terms and conditions in cases of probation. (*See page 547.*)

4. Make restitution.

5. If not taken within the past 5 years, take and pass the CSLB law and business examination.

6. Take and pass a course in Contractors License Law or a course related to construction law at an accredited community college. All courses must be approved in advance by the Registrar.

7. Prohibit the receipt of down payments.

8. Community Service as determined by CSLB; 5-21 days.

9. Pay CSLB investigation and enforcement costs.

7123.5. Violation of Prohibition against Overpricing Following an Emergency or Disaster (Penal Code Section 396)

Minimum Penalty: 6 month suspension, 3 years probation

Maximum Penalty: Revocation

If warranted:

1. Absent compelling mitigating circumstances, overpricing following an emergency or disaster is a serious offense and warrants an outright revocation.
2. Actual suspension of 6 months.
3. Standard terms and conditions in cases of probation. (*See page 547.*)
4. Make restitution.
5. If not taken within the past 5 years, take and pass the CSLB law and business examination.
6. Take and pass a course in Contractors License Law or a course related to construction law at an accredited community college. All courses must be approved in advance by the Registrar.
7. Prohibit the receipt of down payments.
8. Community Service as determined by CSLB; 5-21 days.
9. Pay CSLB investigation and enforcement costs.

7125(b). Filing False Workers' Compensation Exemption Reports

Minimum Penalty: Revocation, stayed, 2 years probation

Maximum Penalty: Revocation

If warranted:

1. Actual suspension of 5 days or more.
2. Standard terms and conditions in cases of probation. (*See page 547.*)
3. If not taken within the past 5 years, take and pass the CSLB law and business examination.
4. Take and pass a course in Contractors License Law or a course related to construction law at an accredited community college. All courses must be approved in advance by the Registrar.

Section VI

5. Submit a list of persons employed on construction related projects to the Registrar upon demand during the probation period.

6. Make restitution.

7. Pay CSLB investigation and enforcement costs.

7154. Employment of a Nonregistered Home Improvement Salesperson

Minimum Penalty: 60 day suspension, stayed, 1 year probation

Maximum Penalty: Revocation

If warranted:

1. Actual suspension of 5 days or more.

2. Standard terms and conditions in cases of probation. (*See page 547.*)

3. If not taken within the past 5 years, take and pass the CSLB law and business examination.

4. Take and pass a course in Contractors License Law or a course related to construction law at an accredited community college. All courses must be approved in advance by the Registrar.

5. Pay CSLB investigation and enforcement costs.

7155. Violation of Contractors License Law by Home Improvement Salesperson

Minimum Penalty: 60 day suspension, stayed, 1 year probation

Maximum Penalty: Revocation

If warranted:

1. Actual suspension of 5 days or more.

2. Standard terms and conditions in cases of probation. (*See page 547.*)

3. Submit copies of construction contracts to the Registrar upon demand during the probation period.

4. If not taken within the past 5 years, take and pass the CSLB law and business examination.

5. Take and pass a course in Contractors License Law or a course related to construction law at an accredited community college. All courses must be approved in advance by the Registrar.

6. Pay CSLB investigation and enforcement costs.

7155.5. Liability of a Contractor for a Home Improvement Salesperson

Minimum Penalty: Suspension, stayed, 1 year probation

Maximum Penalty: Revocation

If warranted:

1. Actual suspension of 5 days or more.

2. Standard terms and conditions in cases of probation. (*See page 547.*)

3. If not taken within the past 5 years, take and pass the CSLB law and business examination.

4. Take and pass a course in Contractors License Law or a course related to construction law at an accredited community college. All courses must be approved in advance by the Registrar.

5. Submit copies of construction contracts to the Registrar upon demand during the probation period.

6. Prohibit the receipt of down payments.

7. Pay CSLB investigation and enforcement costs

7156. Registered Salespersons Violations

Minimum Penalty: 60 day suspension, stayed, 1 year probation

Maximum Penalty: Revocation

If warranted:

1. Actual suspension of 5 days or more.

2. Standard terms and conditions in cases of probation. (*See page 547.*)

3. Submit copies of construction contracts to the Registrar upon demand during the probation period.

4. Pay CSLB investigation and enforcement costs.

7157. Home Improvement Inducements

Minimum Penalty: 60 day suspension, stayed, 1 year probation

Maximum Penalty: Revocation

If warranted:

1. Actual suspension of at least 5 days.

Section VI

2. Standard terms and conditions in cases of probation. (*See page 547.*)

3. If not taken within the past 5 years, take and pass the CSLB law and business examination.

4. Take and pass a course in Contractors License Law or a course related to construction law at an accredited community college. All courses must be approved in advance by the Registrar.

5. Submit copies of advertisements relating to contracting business to the Registrar prior to their being displayed or published during the probation period.

6. Prohibit the receipt of down payments.

7. Pay CSLB investigation and enforcement costs.

7158. False Completion Certificate

Minimum Penalty: Revocation, stayed, 3 years probation

Maximum Penalty: Revocation

If warranted:

1. Absent compelling circumstances, knowingly using a false certificate is a serious offense that warrants an actual suspension of at least 30 days.

2. Standard terms and conditions in cases of probation. (*See page 547.*)

3. If not taken within the past 5 years, take and pass the CSLB law and business examination.

4. Take and pass a course in Contractors License Law or a course related to construction law at an accredited community college. All courses must be approved in advance by the Registrar.

5. Make restitution.

6. Submit copies of construction contracts to the Registrar upon demand during the probation period.

7. Prohibit receipt of down payments.

8. Community Service as determined by CSLB; 5-21 days.

9. Pay CSLB investigation and enforcement costs.

7159. Home Improvement Contract Requirements

Minimum Penalty: 60 day suspension, stayed, 1 year probation

Maximum Penalty: Revocation

If warranted:

1. If any injuries are involved, actual suspension of at least 30 days.

2. Standard terms and conditions in cases of probation. (*See page 547.*)

3. If not taken within the past 5 years, take and pass the CSLB law and business examination.

4. Take and pass a course in Contractors License Law or a course related to construction law at an accredited community college. All courses must be approved in advance by the Registrar.

5. Submit copies of construction contracts to the Registrar upon demand during the probation period.

6. Prohibit receipt of down payments.

7. Community Service as determined by CSLB; 5-21 days.

8. Pay CSLB investigation and enforcement costs.

7161. Misrepresentation; False Advertisement

Minimum Penalty: Revocation, stayed, 3 years probation

Maximum Penalty: Revocation

If warranted:

1. Absent compelling mitigating circumstances, misrepresentation and false or deceptive advertising are serious offenses that warrant an actual period of suspension of at least 30 days.

2. If injury is substantial, outright revocation is appropriate.

3. Standard terms and conditions in cases of probation. (*See page 547.*)

4. If not taken within the past 5 years, take and pass the CSLB law and business examination.

5. Take and pass a course in Contractors License Law or a course related to construction law at an accredited community college. All courses must be approved in advance by the Registrar.

6. Submit copies of construction contracts to the Registrar upon demand during the probation period.

7. Submit copies of advertisements relating to contracting business to the Registrar prior to their being displayed or published during the probation period.

8. Prohibit the receipt of down payments.

Section VI

9. Community Service as determined by CSLB; 5-21 days.

10. Pay CSLB investigation and enforcement costs.

7162. Representation with Respect to Trademark or Brand Name; Quantity or Size

Minimum Penalty: Revocation, stayed, 2 years probation

Maximum Penalty: Revocation

If warranted:

1. Actual suspension of 5 days or more.

2. Standard terms and conditions in cases of probation. (*See page 547.*)

3. If not taken within the past 5 years, take and pass the CSLB law and business examination.

4. Take and pass a course in Contractors License Law or a course related to construction law at an accredited community college. All courses must be approved in advance by the Registrar.

5. Make restitution.

6. Submit copies of construction contracts to the Registrar upon demand during the probation period.

7. Submit copies of advertisements relating to contracting business to the Registrar prior to their being displayed or published during the probation period.

8. Prohibit the receipt of down payments.

9. Pay CSLB investigation and enforcement costs.

7164. Contract Form for Single Family Dwelling

Minimum Penalty: 60 day suspension, stayed, 1 year probation

Maximum Penalty: Revocation

If warranted:

1. Actual suspension of 5 days or more.

2. Standard terms and conditions in cases of probation. (*See page 547.*)

3. If not taken within the past 5 years, take and pass the CSLB law and business examination.

4. Take and pass a course in Contractors License Law or a course related to construction law at an accredited community college. All courses must be approved in advance by the Registrar.

5. Submit copies of construction contracts to the Registrar upon demand during the probation period.

6. Pay CSLB investigation and enforcement costs.

7165. Swimming Pool Construction Contract

Minimum Penalty: 60 day suspension, stayed, 1 year probation

Maximum Penalty: Revocation

If warranted:

1. Actual suspension of 5 days or more.

2. Standard terms and conditions in cases of probation. (*See page 547.*)

3. If not taken within the past 5 years, take and pass the CSLB law and business examination.

4. Take and pass a course in Contractors License Law or a course related to construction law at an accredited community college. All courses must be approved in advance by the Registrar.

5. Submit copies of construction contracts to the Registrar upon demand during the probation period.

6. Pay CSLB investigation and enforcement costs.

7183.5. Asbestos; Certification Obtained under False Pretenses

Minimum Penalty: Revocation, stayed, 3 years probation

Maximum Penalty: Revocation

If warranted:

1. Absent compelling mitigating circumstances, obtaining an asbestos certification under false pretenses is a serious offense and warrants an outright revocation.

2. Actual suspension of at least 30 days.

3. Standard terms and conditions in cases of probation. (*See page 547.*)

4. Community Service as determined by CSLB; 5-21 days.

5. Pay CSLB investigation and enforcement costs.

7189. Asbestos Certification; Conflicts of Interest

Minimum Penalty: 60 day suspension, stayed, 1 year probation

Maximum Penalty: Revocation

Section VI

If warranted:

1. Absent compelling circumstances, a person defined as an "asbestos consultant" or a "site surveillance technician," having financial or proprietary interest in an asbestos contractor's company is a serious offense that warrants an actual suspension period of at least 30 days.

2. Standard terms and conditions in cases of probation. (*See page 547.*)

3. Submit copies of construction contracts to the Registrar upon demand during the probation period.

4. Prohibit the receipt of down payments.

5. Community Service as determined by CSLB; 5-21 days.

6. Pay CSLB investigation and enforcement costs.

All Other Violations

Minimum Penalty: 5 day suspension, stayed, 1 year probation

Maximum Penalty: Revocation

If warranted:

1. Actual suspension of 5 days or more.

2. Standard terms and conditions in cases of probation. (*See page 547.*)

3. If not taken within the past 5 years, take and pass the CSLB law and business examination.

4. Take and pass a course in Contractors License Law or a course related to construction law at an accredited community college. All courses must be approved in advance by the Registrar.

5. If not taken within the past 5 years, take and pass the CSLB trade examination.

6. Take and pass a vocational course(s) related to the trade(s) employed on the project. All courses must be approved in advance by the Registrar.

7. Submit copies of construction contracts to the Registrar upon demand during the probation period.

8. Make restitution

9. Pay CSLB investigation and enforcement costs.

Standard Terms and Conditions to Be Included in all Cases of Probation

1. Obey All Laws:

   Respondent shall comply with all federal, state and local laws governing the activities of a licensed contractor in California.

2. Interviews With Regional Deputy:

   Respondent and any of respondent's personnel of record shall appear in person for interviews with the Regional Deputy or designee upon request and reasonable notice.

3. Completion Of Probation:

   Upon successful completion of probation, the contractor's license will be fully restored.

4. Violation Of Probation:

   If respondent violates probation in any respect, the Registrar, after giving notice and opportunity to be heard, may revoke probation and impose the disciplinary order that was stayed. If the decision contains an order to make restitution, the Registrar may impose the disciplinary order without giving the respondent an opportunity to be heard should the respondent fail to comply with the restitution order.

5. Respondent shall submit copies of documents directly related to the person's construction operations to the Registrar upon demand during the probation period.

872. Disclosure of General Liability Insurance

(a) As used in this regulation, "home improvement contract" is defined in Code Section 7151.2 The following statement, must accompany every estimate (bid) intended to result in a home improvement contract and every home improvement contract. The heading shall be printed in at least 14-point type, the questions in at least 12-point type, and the comments in italics of at least 11-point type. The text should be bold where indicated. **This is 14-point type**. **This is 12-point type.** *This is 11-point type in italics.*

Information About Commercial General Liability Insurance Home Improvement

Pursuant to California Business & Professions Code § 7159.3 (SB 2029), home improvement contractors must provide this notice and disclose whether or not they carry commercial general liability insurance.

Did your contractor tell you whether he or she carries Commercial General Liability Insurance?

Home improvement contractors are required by law to tell you whether or not they carry Commercial General Liability Insurance. This written statement must accompany the bid, if there is one, and the contract.

What does this insurance cover?

Commercial General Liability Insurance can protect against third-party bodily injury and accidental property damage. It is not intended to cover the work the contractor performs.

Is this insurance required?

No. But the Contractors State License Board strongly recommends that all contractors carry it. The Board cautions you to evaluate the risk to your family and property when you hire a contractor who is not insured. Ask yourself, if something went wrong, would this contractor be able to cover losses ordinarily covered by insurance?

How can you make sure the contractor is insured?

If he or she is insured, your contractor is required to provide you with the name and telephone number of the insurance company. Check with the insurance company to verify that the contractor's insurance coverage will cover your project.

What about a contractor who is self-insured?

A self-insured contractor has made a business decision to be personally responsible for losses that would ordinarily be covered by insurance. Before contracting with a self-insured contractor, ask yourself, if something went wrong, would this contractor be able to cover losses ordinarily covered by insurance?

■ _____ does not carry Commercial General Liability
 (CONTRACTOR'S NAME)

Insurance.

■ _____ carries Commercial General Liability
 (CONTRACTOR'S NAME)

Insurance.

The insurance company is _____
(COMPANY NAME)

You may call the insurance company at _____
(TELEPHONE NUMBER)

to verify coverage.

For more information about Commercial General Liability Insurance, contact the Contractors State License Board at www.cslb.ca.gov or call 800-321-CSLB (2752).

(This form meets the requirements of Rule 872 and Sections 7159.3 and 7164, Business and Professions Code.)

(b) The following statement must accompany every contract described in Code Section 7164. The heading shall be printed in at least 14-point type, the questions in at least 12-point type, and the comments in italics of at least 11-point type. The text should be bold where indicated. **This is 14-point type. This is 12-point type.** *This is 11-point type in italics.*

Information About Commercial General Liability Insurance Single Family Home

Pursuant to California Business & Professions Code §7164 (SB 2029), contractors building single-family residences for owners who intend to occupy the home for at least a year must provide this notice and disclose whether or not they carry commercial general liability insurance.

Did your contractor tell you whether he or she carries Commercial General Liability Insurance?

Contractors building single-family residences for owners who intend to occupy the home for at least a year are required by law to tell you whether or not they carry Commercial General Liability Insurance. This written statement must accompany the contract.

What does this insurance cover?

Commercial General Liability Insurance can protect against third-party bodily injury and accidental property damage. It is not intended to cover the work the contractor performs.

Is this insurance required?

No. But the Contractors State License Board strongly recommends that all contractors carry it. The Board cautions you to evaluate the risk to your family and property when you hire a contractor who is not insured. Ask yourself, if something went wrong, would this contractor be able to cover losses ordinarily covered by insurance?

How can you make sure the contractor is insured?

If he or she is insured, your contractor is required to provide you with the name and telephone number of the insurance company. Check with the insurance company to verify that the contractor's insurance coverage will cover your project.

What about a contractor who is self-insured?

A self-insured contractor has made a business decision to be personally responsible for losses that would ordinarily be covered by insurance. Before contracting with a self-insured contractor, ask yourself, if something went wrong, would this contractor be able to cover losses ordinarily covered by insurance?

■ _____ does not carry Commercial General Liability
   (CONTRACTOR'S NAME)

Insurance.

■ _____ carries Commercial General Liability
   (CONTRACTOR'S NAME)

Insurance.

   The insurance company is _____
                                  (COMPANY NAME)

   You may call the insurance company at _____
                                              (TELEPHONE NUMBER)

to verify coverage.

For more information about Commercial General Liability Insurance, contact the Contractors State License Board at *www.cslb.ca.gov* or call 800-321-CSLB (2752).

(This form meets the requirements of Rule 872 and Sections 7159.3 and 7164, Business and Professions Code.)

872.1. Checklist for Homeowners

(a) As used in this regulation, home improvement is defined in Code Section 7151.2.

(b) The following statement, must accompany every estimate (bid) intended to result in a home improvement contract and every home improvement contract that does not include a swimming pool. The heading shall be printed in at least 14-point type, the questions in a least 12-point type, and the comments in italics of at least 11-point type. The text should be bold where indicated. This is 14-point type. **This is 12-point type.** *This is 11-point type in italics.*

Checklist for Homeowners
Home Improvement

Pursuant to California Business & Professions Code § 7159.3 (SB 2029), home improvement contractors must provide this notice.

Section VI

- **Check Out Your Contractor**

  ☐ Did you contact the Contractors State License Board (CSLB) to check the status of the contractor's license?

  *Contact the **CSLB at 1-800-321-CSLB (2752)** or visit our **web site: www.cslb.ca.gov**.*

  ☐ Did you get at least 3 local references from the contractors you are considering?

  Did you call them?

  ☐ Building Permits—will the contractor get a permit before the work starts?

- **Check Out the Contract**

  ☐ Did you read and do you understand your contract?

☐ Does the 3-day right to cancel a contract apply to you?

Contact the CSLB if you don't know.

☐ Does the contract tell you when work will start and end?

☐ Does the contract include a detailed description of the work to be done, the material to be used, and equipment to be installed?

This description should include brand names, model numbers, quantities and colors. Specific descriptions now will prevent disputes later.

☐ Are you required to pay a down payment?

If you are, the down payment should never be more than 10% of the contract price or $1,000, whichever is less.

☐ Is there a schedule of payments?

If there is a schedule of payments, you should pay only as work is completed and not before. There are some exceptions—contact the CSLB to find out what they are.

☐ Did your contractor give you a "Notice to Owner," a warning notice describing liens and ways to prevent them?

Even if you pay your contractor, a lien can be placed on your home by unpaid laborers, subcontractors, or material suppliers. A lien can result in you paying twice or, in some cases, losing your home in a foreclosure. Check the "Notice to Owner" for ways to protect yourself.

☐ Did you know changes or additions to your contract must all be in writing?

Putting changes in writing reduces the possibility of a later dispute.

(This form meets the requirements of Rule 872.1 and Sections 7159.3 and 7164, Business and Professions Code.)

(c) The following statement, must accompany every estimate (bid) intended to result in a home improvement contract and every home improvement contract that includes a swimming pool. The heading shall be printed in at least 14-point type, the questions in at least 12-point type, and the comments in italics of at least 11-point type. The text should be bold where indicated. **This is 14-point type. This is 12-point type.** *This is 11-point type in italics.*

Checklist for Homeowners
Swimming Pool

Pursuant to California Business & Professions Code § 7159.3 (SB 2029), home improvement contractors building swimming pools must provide this notice.

- **Check Out Your Contractor**
  - ☐ Did you contact the Contractors State License Board (CSLB) to check the status of the contractor's license?

    Contact the **CSLB at 1-800-321-CSLB (2752)** *or visit our* **web site: www.cslb.ca.gov.**

  - ☐ Did you get at least 3 local references from the contractors you are considering?
  - ☐ *Did you call them?*
  - ☐ Building Permits—will the contractor get a permit before the work starts?

  - ☐ **Check Out the Contract**
  - ☐ Did you read and do you understand your contract?
  - ☐ Does the 3-day right to cancel a contract apply to you?
  - ☐ Contact the CSLB if you don't know.
  - ☐ Does the contract tell you when work will start and end?

☐ Does the contract include a detailed description of the work to be done, the material that will be used and equipment to be installed?

This description should include a plan and scale drawing showing the shape, size, dimensions and specifications. It should include brand names, model numbers, quantities and colors. Specific descriptions now will prevent disputes later.

☐ Are you required to pay a down payment?

The down payment for swimming pools should never be more than 10% of the contract price or $1,000, whichever is less.

☐ Is there a schedule of payments?

If there is a schedule of payments, you should pay only as work is completed and not before. There are some exceptions—contact the CSLB to find out what they are.

☐ Did your contractor give you a "Notice to Owner," a warning notice describing liens and ways to prevent them?

*Even if you pay your contractor, a lien can be placed on your home by unpaid laborers, subcontractors, or material suppliers. A lien can result in you paying twice or, in some cases, losing your home in a foreclosure. Check the **"Notice to Owner"** for ways to protect yourself.*

☐ Did you know changes or additions to your contract **must** all be in writing?

Putting changes in writing reduces the possibility of a later dispute.

(This form meets the requirements of Rule 872.1 and Sections 7159.3 and 7164, Business and Professions Code.)

ARTICLE 8. CITATION

880. Order of Correction—Practical Feasibility

Before including an order of correction in a citation, due consideration shall be given to the practical feasibility of correction in accordance with, but not limited to, the following criteria:

(a) An order of correction is appropriate where it would not result in excessive destruction of or substantial waste of existing acceptable construction.

(b) An order of correction is appropriate where the owner of the construction project is willing to allow the cited licensee to correct.

(c) An order of correction is appropriate where it appears to the Registrar that the cited licensee has competence or ability to correct.

(Authority cited: Sections 7008 and 7099.1, Business and Professions Code. Reference: Sections 7099 and 7099.1, Business and Professions Code.)

881. Order of Correction—Alternative Compliance

A cited licensee may comply with an order of correction by having and paying for another licensee to do the corrective work. The cited licensee remains responsible, however, for any failure to fully comply with the order of correction.

An order of correction may, but need not, contain the alternative that the cited person may pay a specified sum to the owner of the construction project in lieu of correcting.

(Authority cited: Sections 7008 and 7099.1, Business and Professions Code. Reference: Sections 7099 and 7099.1, Business and Professions Code.)

882. Order of Correction—Time Required to Correct

Where an order of correction is included in a citation, due consideration shall be given to the time required to correct in accordance with, but not limited to, the following criteria:

(a) Accepted industry practice in that area relating to performance of such work under certain climate or weather conditions.

(b) A reasonable time in which to obtain necessary materials.

(c) The number of working days the construction project will be made accessible by the owner for corrections.

(Authority cited: Sections 7008 and 7099.1, Business and Professions Code. Reference: Sections 7099 and 7099.1, Business and Professions Code.)

883. Order of Correction—Extension of Time to Correct

If the cited person, after exercising substantial efforts ad reasonable diligence, is unable to complete the correction within the time allowed

Section VI

because of conditions beyond his control, he may request an extension of time in which to correct. Such request must be made in writing, and must be made prior to the expiration of the time allowed in the order of correction. An extension may be granted upon showing of good cause which determination is within the discretion of the Registrar. If a request for extension of time is not made prior to the expiration of time allowed in the order of correction, failure to correct within the time allowed shall constitute a violation of the order of correction whether or not good cause for an extension of time existed.

(Authority cited: Sections 7008 and 7099.1, Business and Professions Code. Reference: Sections 7099 and 7099.1, Business and Professions Code.)

884. Assessments of Civil Penalties

(a) Civil penalties against persons who have been cited for violation of the Contractors License Law shall be assessed in accordance with the following ranges of penalties.

Section Violated	Minimum Civil Penalty	Maximum Civil Penalty
7027.1	100	1,000
7028	200	5,000
7028.1	1,000	5,000
7028.5	200	5,000
7028.7	200	15,000
7029.1	200	2,500
7029.5	100	500
7029.6	100	500
7030	500	1,500
7030.1	1,000	5,000
7030.5	100	1,000
7031.5	100	500
7034	100	1,000
7058.7	500	5,000
7068.1	100	5,000
7068.2	100	1,000
7071.11	100	1,000
7071.13	100	500
7075	100	500
7076	100	1,000
7083	100	1,000
7083.1	100	1,000
7099.10	100	1,500

Section Violated	Minimum Civil Penalty	Maximum Civil Penalty
7099.11	100	1,500
7107	200	5,000
7108	200	5,000
7108.5	200	2,000
7108.6	200	2,000
7109	200	5,000
7109.5	500	5,000
7110	200	5,000
7110.1	100	1,000
7111	100	1,000
7111.1	100	1,500
7113	200	5,000
7114	500	15,000
7114.1	200	2,000
7115	100	5,000
7116	100	5,000
7117	100	1,000
7117.5	200	5,000
7117.6	200	5,000
7118	500	15,000
7118.4	3,000	5,000
7118.5	1,000	5,000
7118.6	1,000	5,000
7119	200	2,000
7120	200	2,000
7123	500	5,000
7125	100	500
7125.4	200	5,000
7154	100	1,000
7157	100	1,000
7158	500	5,000
7159	100	1,000
7159.5(a)(1), (a)(3), and (a)(5),	100	5,000
7159.5(a)(2), (a)(4), (a)(6), (a)(7), and (a)(8)	100	1,000
7159.10	100	500

Section Violated	Minimum Civil Penalty	Maximum Civil Penalty
7159.14	100	5,000
7161	100	5,000
7162	100	1,500
7164	100	1,000

(b) When determining the amount of assessed civil penalty, the Registrar shall take into consideration whether one or more of the following or similar circumstances apply:

1. the citation includes multiple violations;

2. the cited person has a history of violations of the same or similar sections of the Contractors License Law;

3. in the judgment of the Registrar, a person has exhibited bad faith;

4. in the judgment of the Registrar, the violation is serious or harmful;

5. the citation involves a violation or violations perpetrated against a senior citizen or disabled person; and/or

6. the citation involves a violation or violations involving a construction project in connection with repairs for damages caused by a natural disaster as described in Section 7158 of the code.

(c) Where a citation lists more than one violation and each of the violations relates to the same construction project, the total penalty assessment in each citation shall not exceed $5,000, except as provided for violations of Sections 7028.7, 7114, or 7118.

(d) Where a citation lists more than one violation, the amount of assessed civil penalty shall be stated separately for each section violated.

(Authority cited: Sections 7008, 7099.2 and 7115, Business and Professions Code. Reference: Sections 7099, 7099.1 and 7115, Business and Professions Code.)

885. Appeal of Citation

Any person served with a citation pursuant to Section 7099 of the Business and Professions Code may contest the citation by appealing to the Registrar within 15 working days from the receipt of such citation. The 15 day period may be extended upon showing of good cause which determination is within the discretion of the Registrar.

The cited person may contest any or all of the following aspects of the citation:

1. The occurrence of a violation of the Contractors License Law;

2.   The reasonableness of the order of correction, if an order of correction is included in the citation;

3.   The period of time allowed for correction, if an order of correction is included in the citation;

4.   The amount of the civil penalty, if a civil penalty is assessed in the citation.

(Authority cited: Section 7008, Business and Professions Code. Reference: Sections 7099.3, 7099.4 and 7099.5, Business and Professions Code.)

886. Service of Citation

Service of a citation shall be made in accordance with the provisions of Section 11505(c) of the Government Code, and, further, that a copy of the citation be sent by regular mail.

(Authority cited: Section 7008, Business and Professions Code. Reference: Sections 7099.3, 7099.4 and 7099.5, Business and Professions Code.)

887. Criteria to Evaluate the Gravity of a Violation of Business and Professions Code Section 7028.7

Before assessing a civil penalty under Section 7028.7 of the Business and Professions Code, the Registrar shall give due consideration to the gravity of the violation, including, but not limited to, a consideration of whether the cited person did one or more of the following:

1.   Falsely represented that he/she was licensed.

2.   Failed to perform work for which money was received.

3.   Executed or used any false or misleading documents in order to induce a person to enter into a contract or to pay money.

4.   Made false or misleading statements in order to induce a person to enter into a contract or pay money.

5.   Failed to apply funds which were received for the purpose of obtaining or paying for services, labor, materials, or equipment.

6.   Performed work that was potentially hazardous to the health, safety, or general welfare of the public.

7.   Performed work in violation of the building laws, safety laws, labor laws, compensation insurance laws, or unemployment insurance laws.

8.   Performed work that did not meet acceptable trade standards for good and workmanlike construction.

9.   Was convicted of a crime in connection with the violation.

Section VI

10. Committed any act which would be cause for disciplinary action against a licensee.

11. Committed numerous or repeated violations.

(Authority cited: Sections 7008 and 7028.7, Business and Professions Code. Reference: Section 7028.7, Business and Professions Code.)

ARTICLE 9. ARBITRATION

890. Minimum Qualification Standards for Arbitrators

For the purposes of Section 7085.5 of the Code, regardless of the method of appointment or selection, arbitrators shall possess the following minimum qualifications:

(a) (1) Five (5) years of experience in the construction industry as a licensed contractor or a professional in a construction related field, such as an architect or engineer, or

(2) Five (5) years of experience as an attorney, judge, administrative law judge, arbitrator, or a combination thereof, handling a minimum of 8 construction related matters.

(b) Completion of an arbitrator's course on construction arbitration within the last 5 years including, but not limited to, training on the process, the ethics and the laws relating to arbitration. The training on the process of arbitration may include such topics as the role of the arbitrator, the use of effective questioning techniques, and the role of an expert in an arbitration proceeding.

(c) Completion of 8 hours of continuing education on construction arbitration every 5 years, including, but not limited to, the topics set forth in subsection (b).

(d) Completion of a training program related specifically to the Board's arbitration procedures, laws and policies.

(Authority cited: Sections 7008 and 7085.5(b)(3), Business and Professions Code. Reference: Section 7085 et seq., Business and Professions Code.)

HISTORY NOTES FOR
CURRENT BOARD RULES AND REGULATIONS

(History notes for repealed rules and regulations appear at the end of this section.)

810. DEFINITIONS

1. *Repealer of Article 1 (Sections 700 and 701) and new Article 1 (Section 700) filed 5-25-83; effective thirtieth day thereafter (Register 83, No. 22).*

2. *Section renumbered from 700 to 810, filed 2-27-84; effective upon filing pursuant to Government Code Section 11346.2(d) (Register 84, No. 9).*

811. FEES

1. *New section filed 12-31-2002 as an emergency; operative 1-1-2003 (Register 2003. No.1).*

2. *Certificate of Compliance as to 12-31-2002 order, including new subsection (e), subsection relettering and amendment of Note, transmitted to OAL 4-25-2003 and filed 6-5-2003 Register 2003, 23).*

3. *Amendment of section and Note filed 11-18-2010; operative 12-18-2010 (Register 2010, No. 47).*

812. DISHONORED CHECK SERVICE CHARGE

1. *New section filed 9-30-82; effective thirtieth day thereafter (Register 82, No. 40).*

2. *Section renumbered from 703 to 812, filed 2-27-84; effective upon filing pursuant to Government Code Section 11346.2(d) (Register 84, No. 9).*

813. ABANDONMENT OF APPLICATION

1. *New section filed 8-25-83; effective upon filing pursuant to Government Code Section 11346.2(d) (Register 83, No. 35).*

2. *Section renumbered from 705 to 813, filed 2-27-84; effective upon filing pursuant to Government Code Section 11346.2(d) (Register 84, No. 9).*

816. APPLICATION FORM FOR ORIGINAL LICENSE

1. *Amendment filed 9-8-77; effective thirtieth day thereafter (Register 77, No. 37).*

2. *Editorial correction of subsection (c) (Register 77, No. 52).*

3. *Amendment filed 8-25-83; effective upon filing pursuant to Government Code Section 11346.2(d) (Register 83, No. 35).*

4. *Section renumbered from 706 to 816, filed 2-27-84; effective upon filing pursuant to Government Code Section 11346.2(d) (Register 84, No. 9).*

5. *Amendment of subsection (a)(1) and (c) filed 6-6-86; effective thirtieth day thereafter (Register 86, No. 23).*

817. OPERATING CAPITAL DEFINED

1. *New section filed 1-24-80; effective thirtieth day thereafter (Register 80, No. 4).*

2. *Amendment filed 8-25-83; effective upon filing pursuant to Government Code Section 11346.2(d) (Register 83, No. 35).*

3. *Section renumbered from 707.1 to 817, filed 2-27-84; effective upon filing pursuant to Government Code Section 11346.2(d) (Register 84, No. 9).*

819. REQUIREMENT OF CORPORATIONS

1. *Amendment filed 7-19-74; effective thirtieth day thereafter (Register 74, No. 29).*

2. *Amendment filed 8-25-83; effective upon filing pursuant to Government Code Section 11346.2(d) (Register 83, No. 35).*

3. *Section renumbered from 714 to 819, filed 2-27-84; effective upon filing pursuant to Government Code Section 11346.2(d) (Register 84, No. 9).*

823. DEFINITIONS: BONA FIDE EMPLOYEE; DIRECT SUPERVISION AND CONTROL

1. *New section filed 1-24-80; effective thirtieth day thereafter (Register 80, No. 4). For prior history, see Registers 53, No. 13; 57, No. 6; and 57, No. 18.*

2. *Amendment filed 1-27-84; effective upon filing pursuant to Government Code Section 11346.2(d) (Register 84, No. 4).*

3. *Section renumbered from 795 to 823, filed 2-27-84; effective upon filing pursuant to Government Code Section 11346.2(d) (Register 84, No. 9).*

4. *Editorial correction filed 7-19-84 (Register 84, No. 29).*

824. APPLICATION INVESTIGATION REQUIRED

1. *New section filed 1-24-80; effective thirtieth day thereafter (Register 80, No. 4).*
2. *Amendment filed 8-25-83; effective upon filing pursuant to Government Code Section 11346.2(d) (Register 83, No. 35).*
3. *Section renumbered from 723.1 to 824, filed 2-27-84; effective upon filing pursuant to Government Code Section 11346.2(d) (Register 84, No. 9).*

825. EXPERIENCE REQUIREMENT OF APPLICANT

1. *Amendment filed 9-8-77; effective thirtieth day thereafter (Register 77, No. 37). For prior history, see Register 74, No. 29.*
2. *Editorial correction (Register 77, No. 52).*
3. *Amendment filed 8-25-83; effective upon filing pursuant to Government Code Section 11346.2(d) (Register 83, No. 35).*
4. *Section renumbered from 724 to 825, filed 2-27-84; effective upon filing, pursuant to Government Code Section 11346.2(d) (Register 84, No. 9).*
5. *Amendment of subsection (a) filed 4-12-84; effective upon filing pursuant to Government Code Section 11346.2(d) Register 84, No. 15).*

826. REGISTRAR TO PASS ON EXPERIENCE

1. *Amendment filed 9-8-77; effective thirtieth day thereafter (Register 77, No. 37).*
2. *Amendment filed 8-25-83; effective upon filing pursuant to Government Code Section 11346.2(d) (Register 83, No. 35).*
3. *Section renumbered from 725 to 826, filed 2-27-84; effective upon filing pursuant to Government Code Section 11346.2(d) (Register 84, No. 9).*

827. REVIEW OF APPLICATION FOR ORIGINAL LICENSE, ADDITIONAL CLASSIFICATION, OR REPLACEMENT OF QUALIFYING PERSON

1. *New section filed 12-3-85; effective thirtieth day thereafter (Register 85, No. 49).*

828. REVIEW OF APPLICATION FOR HOME IMPROVEMENT SALESMAN REGISTRATION

1. *New section filed 10-26-84; effective thirtieth day thereafter (Register 84, No. 43).*

830. CLASSIFICATION POLICY

1. *Amendment filed 9-8-77; effective thirtieth day thereafter (Register 77, No. 37).*
2. *Amendment filed 8-19-83; effective thirtieth day thereafter (Register 83, No. 35).*
3. *Section renumbered from 730 to 830, filed 2-27-84; effective upon filing pursuant to Government Code Section 11346.2(d) (Register 84, No. 9).*

831. INCIDENTAL AND SUPPLEMENTAL DEFINED

1. *New section filed 8-19-83; effective thirtieth day thereafter (Register 83, No. 35).*
2. *Section renumbered from 730.1 to 831, filed 2-27-84; effective upon filing pursuant to Government Code Section 11346.2(d) (Register 84, No. 9).*

832. SPECIALTY CONTRACTORS CLASSIFIED

1. *Amendment filed 4-29-64; effective thirtieth day thereafter (Register 64, No. 9). For prior history see Register 55, No. 11 and Register 61, No. 19.*
2. *Amendment filed 7-18-68; designated effective 10-15-68 (Register 68, No. 27).*
3. *Amendment filed 5-8-73; effective thirtieth day thereafter (Register 73, No. 19).*
4. *Amendment filed 4-16-74 as procedural and organizational; designated effective 5-16-74 (Register 74, No. 16).*

5. *Amendment filed 8-19-83; effective thirtieth day thereafter (Register 83, No. 35).*

6. *Section renumbered from 732 to 832, filed 2-27-84; effective upon filing pursuant to Government Code Section 11346.2(d) (Register 84, No. 9).*

7. *Amendment filed 6-6-86; effective thirtieth day thereafter (Register 86, No. 23).*

8. *Amendment filed 10-22-86; effective thirtieth day thereafter (Register 86, No. 43).*

9. *Amendment filed 9-15-88; operative 10-15-88 Register 88, No. 39).*

10. *Amendment filed 11-9-95; effective thirtieth day thereafter (Register 95, No. 45).*

832.02. CLASS C-2—INSULATION AND ACOUSTICAL CONTRACTOR

1. *New section filed 9-18-47 as an emergency; effective upon filing (Register 9).*

2. *Amendment filed 4-12-61; effective 30th day thereafter (Register 61, No. 8).*

3. *Amendment filed 8-19-83; effective thirtieth day thereafter (Register 83, No. 35).*

4. *Section renumbered from 754.8 to 832.02, filed 2-27-84; effective upon filing pursuant to Government Code Section 11346.2(d) (Register 84, No. 9).*

832.04. CLASS C-4—BOILER, HOT-WATER HEATING AND STEAM FITTING CONTRACTOR

1. *New section filed 9-18-47 as an emergency; effective upon filing (Register 9).*

2. *Amendment filed 5-4-72; effective thirtieth day thereafter (Register 72, No. 19).*

3. *Amendment filed 4-28-82; effective thirtieth day thereafter (Register 82, No. 18).*

4. *Amendment filed 8-25-83; effective upon filing pursuant to Government Code Section 11346.2(d) (Register 83, No. 35).*

5. *Section renumbered from 754.1 to 832.04, filed 2-27-84; effective upon filing pursuant to Government Code Section 11346.2(d) (Register 84, No. 9).*

832.05. CLASS C-5—FRAMING AND ROUGH CARPENTRY CONTRACTOR

1. *New section filed 10-26-93; operative 11-25-93 (Register 93, No. 44).*

2. *Amendment filed 12-18-97; effective 01-01-98 (Register 97, No. 172)*

3. *Amendment of section heading, section and Note filed 5-24-2002; operative 1-1-2003 Register 2002, No.21).*

832.06. CLASS C-6—CABINET, MILLWORK AND FINISH CARPENTRY CONTRACTOR

1. *New section filed 5-24-2002; operative 1-1-2003 (Register 97, No. 51).*

832.07. CLASS C-7—LOW VOLTAGE SYSTEMS CONTRACTOR

1. *New section filed 9-15-88; operative 10-15-88 (Register 88, No. 39).*

2. *Amendment filed 5-17-95; operative 6-16-95 (Register 95, No. 20).*

832.08. CLASS C-8—CONCRETE CONTRACTOR

1. *Amendment filed 10-12-72; effective thirtieth day thereafter (Register 72, No. 42).*

2. *Amendment filed 8-25-83; effective upon filing pursuant to Government Code Section 11346.2(d) (Register 83, No. 35).*

3. *Section renumbered from 739 to 832.08, filed 2-27-84; effective upon filing pursuant to Government Code Section 11346.2(d) (Register 84, No. 9).*

832.09. CLASS C-9—DRYWALL CONTRACTOR

1. *New section filed 4-29-64; effective thirtieth day thereafter (Register 64, No. 9).*

2. *Amendment filed 10-14-65; effective thirtieth day thereafter (Register 65, No. 19).*

3. *Amendment filed 8-19-83; effective thirtieth day thereafter (Register 83, No. 34).*

4. *Section renumbered from 754.13 to 832.09, filed 2-27-84; effective upon filing pursuant to Government Code Section 11346.2(d) (Register 84, No. 9).*

5. *Amendment filed 5-8-2002; operative 6-7-2002 (Register 2002, No.19).*

832.10. CLASS C-10—ELECTRICAL CONTRACTOR

1. *Amendment filed 4-28-82; effective thirtieth day thereafter (Register 82, No. 18).*

2. *Amendment filed 8-19-83; effective thirtieth day thereafter (Register 83, No. 34).*

3. *Section renumbered from 733 to 832.10, filed 2-27-84, effective upon filing pursuant to Government Code Section 11346.2(d) (Register 84, No. 9).*

832.11. CLASS C-11—ELEVATOR CONTRACTOR

1. *New section filed 9-18-47 as an emergency; effective upon filing (Register 9).*

2. *Amendment filed 8-25-83; effective upon filing pursuant to Government Code Section 11346.2(d) (Register 83, No. 35).*

3. *Section renumbered from 754.3 to 832.11, filed 2-27-84; effective upon filing pursuant to Government Code Section 11346.2(d) (Register 84, No. 9).*

832.12. CLASS C-12—EARTHWORK AND PAVING CONTRACTORS

1. *Originally published 12-5-46 (Title 16).*

2. *Amendment filed 9-18-47 as an emergency; effective upon filing (Register 9).*

3. *Amendment filed 8-3-72; effective thirtieth day thereafter (Register 72, No. 32).*

4. *Amendment filed 8-25-83; effective upon filing pursuant to Government Code Section 11346.2(d) (Register 83, No. 35).*

5. *Section renumbered from 745 to 832.12, filed 2-27-84; effective upon filing pursuant to Government Code Section 11346.2(d) (Register 84, No. 9).*

832.13. CLASS C-13—FENCING CONTRACTOR

1. *New section filed 4-16-74; effective thirtieth day thereafter (Register 74, No. 16).*

2. *Amendment filed 8-25-83; effective upon filing pursuant to Government Code Section 11346.2(d) (Register 83, No. 35).*

3. *Section renumbered from 754.15 to 832.13, filed 2-27-84; effective upon filing pursuant to Government Code Section 11346.2(d) (Register 84, No. 9).*

832.14. CLASS C-14—METAL ROOFING CONTRACTOR

1. *New section filed 10-22-86; effective thirtieth day thereafter (Register 86, No. 43).*

2. *Repealer and new section filed 6-22-98; operative 7-1-98 pursuant to Government Code section 11343.4(d) (Register 98, No. 26).*

832.15. CLASS C-15—FLOORING AND FLOOR COVERING CONTRACTORS

1. *Originally published 12-5-46 (Title 16).*

2. *Amendment filed 9-18-47 as an emergency; effective upon filing (Register 9).*

3. *Amendment filed 8-3-72; effective thirtieth day thereafter (Register 72, No. 32).*

4. *Amendment filed 8-25-83; effective upon filing pursuant to Government Code Section 11346.2(d) (Register 83, No. 35).*

5. *Section renumbered from 741 to 832.15, filed 2-27-84; effective upon filing pursuant to Government Code Section 11346.2(d) (Register 84, No. 9).*

832.16. CLASS C-16—FIRE PROTECTION CONTRACTOR

1. *New section filed 4-27-49 (Register 16, No. 2).*

2. *Amendment filed 8-12-83; effective thirtieth day thereafter (Register 83, No. 33).*

3. *Section renumbered from 754.9 to 832.16, filed 2-27-84; effective upon filing pursuant to Government Code Section 11346.2(d) (Register 84, No. 9).*

4. *Amendment filed 8-21-90; operative 9-20-90 (Register 90, No. 41).*

832.17. CLASS C-17—GLAZING CONTRACTOR

1. *Amendment filed 10-29-69; effective thirtieth day thereafter (Register 69, No. 44).*
2. *Amendment filed 8-25-83; effective upon filing pursuant to Government Code Section 11346.2(d) (Register 83, No. 35).*
3. *Section renumbered from 750 to 832.17, filed 2-27-84; effective upon filing pursuant to Government Code Section 11346.2(d) (Register 84, No. 9).*

832.20. CLASS C-20—WARM-AIR HEATING, VENTILATING AND AIR-CONDITIONING CONTRACTOR

1. *Originally published 12-5-46 (Title 16).*
2. *Amendment filed 9-18-47 as an emergency; effective upon filing (Register 9).*
3. *Amendment filed 5-4-72; effective thirtieth day thereafter (Register 72, No. 19).*
4. *Amendment filed 4-28-82; effective thirtieth day thereafter (Register 82, No. 18).*
5. *Amendment filed 11-1-83; effective upon filing pursuant to Government Code Section 11346.2(d) (Register 83, No. 45).*
6. *Section renumbered from 746 to 832.20, filed 2-27-84; effective upon filing pursuant to Government Code Section 11346.2(d) (Register 84, No. 9).*
7. *Editorial correction filed 7-19-84 (Register 84, No. 29).*

832.21. CLASS C-21–BUILDING MOVING/DEMOLITION CONTRACTOR

1. *Amendment filed 1-31-72; effective thirtieth day thereafter (Register 72, No. 6). For prior history see Register 55, No. 11.*
2. *Amendment filed 8-3-72; effective thirtieth day thereafter (Register 72, No. 32).*
3. *Amendment filed 8-25-83; effective upon filing pursuant to Government Code Section 11346.2(d) (Register 83, No. 35).*
4. *Section renumbered from 752 to 832.21, filed 2-27-84; effective upon filing pursuant to Government Code Section 11346.2(d) (Register 84, No. 9).*

832.23. CLASS C-23—ORNAMENTAL METAL CONTRACTOR

1. *Amendment filed 8-25-83; effective upon filing pursuant to Government Code Section 11346.2(d) (Register 83, No. 35).*
2. *Section renumbered from 749 to 832.23, filed 2-27-84; effective upon filing pursuant to Government Code Section 11346.2(d) (Register 84, No. 9).*

832.27. CLASS C-27—LANDSCAPING CONTRACTOR

1. *Amendment filed 10-14-68; effective thirtieth day thereafter (Register 68, No. 39).*
2. *Amendment filed 8-19-83; effective thirtieth day thereafter (Register 83, No. 34).*
3. *Section renumbered from 747 to 832.27, filed 2-27-84; effective upon filing pursuant to Government Code Section 11346.2(d) (Register 84, No. 9).*
4. *Amendment filed 6-1-88; operative 7-1-88 (Register 88, No. 23).*

832.28. CLASS C-28—LOCK AND SECURITY EQUIPMENT CONTRACTOR

1. *New section filed 1-31-95; operative 3-1-95 (Register 95, No.6Z).*

832.29. CLASS C-29—MASONRY CONTRACTOR

1. *Amendment filed 8-25-83; effective upon filing pursuant to Government Code Section 11346.2(d) (Register 83, No. 35).*
2. *Section renumbered from 740 to 832.29, filed 2-27-84; effective upon filing pursuant to Government Code Section 11346.2(d) (Register 84, No. 9).*

Section VI

832.31. CLASS C-31—CONSTRUCTION ZONE TRAFFIC CONTROL CONTRACTOR

1. *New section filed 9-18-2000; operative 9-18-2000 pursuant to Government Code Section 11343.4 (d) (Register 2000, No.38).*

832.32. CLASS C-32—PARKING AND HIGHWAY IMPROVEMENT CONTRACTOR

1. *New section filed 7-18-68; designated effective 10-15-68 (Register 68, No. 27).*
2. *Amendment filed 8-19-83; effective thirtieth day thereafter (Register 83, No. 34).*
3. *Section renumbered from 754.14 to 832.32, filed 2-27-84; effective upon filing pursuant to Government Code Section 11346.2(d) (Register 84, No. 9).*

832.33. CLASS C-33—PAINTING AND DECORATING CONTRACTORS

1. *Amendment filed 8-19-83; effective thirtieth day thereafter (Register 83, No. 34).*
2. *Section renumbered from 735 to 832.33, filed 2-27-84; effective upon filing pursuant to Government Code Section 11346.2(d) (Register 84, No. 9).*

832.34. CLASS C-34—PIPELINE CONTRACTOR

1. *New section filed 7-24-56; designated effective sixtieth day thereafter (Register 56, No. 14).*
2. *Amendment filed 8-19-83; effective thirtieth day thereafter (Register 83, No. 34).*
3. *Section renumbered from 754.11 to 832.34, filed 2-27-84; effective upon filing pursuant to Government Code Section 11346.2(d) (Register 84, No. 9).*

832.35. CLASS C-35—LATHING AND PLASTERING CONTRACTOR

1. *Amendment filed 9-23-83; effective upon filing pursuant to Government Code Section 11346.2(d) (Register 83, No. 39).*
2. *Editorial correction of paging error in Register 83, No. 39 (Register 83, No. 43).*
3. *Section renumbered from 736 to 832.35, filed 2-27-84; effective upon filing pursuant to Government Code Section 11346.2(d) (Register 84, No. 9).*
4. *Amendment filed 12-18-97; effective 01-01-98 (Register 97, No. 172).*

832.36. CLASS C-36—PLUMBING CONTRACTOR

1. *Amendment filed 4-29-64; effective thirtieth day thereafter (Register 64, No. 9).*
2. *Amendment filed 4-28-82; effective thirtieth day thereafter (Register 82, No. 18).*
3. *Amendment filed 8-12-83; effective thirtieth day thereafter (Register 83, No. 33).*
4. *Section renumbered from 734 to 832.36, filed 2-27-84; effective upon filing pursuant to Government Code Section 11346.2(d) (Register 84, No. 9).*
5. *Amendment filed 5-25-89; operative 6-24-89 (Register 89, No. 22). 2. Editorial correction of printing error and restoration of History 1. (Register 92, No. 29).*
6. *Amendment filed 12-1-94; operative 12-31-94 (Register 94, No. 50Z).*

832.38. CLASS C-38—REFRIGERATION CONTRACTOR

1. *Amendment filed 5-4-72; effective thirtieth day thereafter (Register 72, No. 19).*
2. *Amendment filed 8-19-83; effective thirtieth day thereafter (Register 83, No. 34).*
3. *Section renumbered from 748 to 832.38, filed 2-27-84; effective upon filing pursuant to Government Code Section 11346.2(d) (Register 84, No. 9).*

832.39. CLASS C-39—ROOFING CONTRACTOR

1. *Amendment filed 8-25-83; effective upon filing pursuant to Government Code Section 11346.2(d) (Register 83, No. 35).*
2. *Section renumbered from 737 to 832.39, filed 2-27-84; effective upon filing pursuant to Government Code Section 11346.2(d) (Register 84, No. 9).*

3. *Amendment filed 6-22-98; operative 7-1-98 pursuant to Government Code section 11343.4 (d) (Register 98, No. 26).*

832.42. CLASS C-42—SANITATION SYSTEM CONTRACTOR

1. *New section filed 9-18-47 as an emergency; effective upon filing (Register 9).*
2. *Amendment filed 8-3-72; effective thirtieth day thereafter (Register 72, No. 32).*
3. *Amendment filed 8-19-83; effective thirtieth day thereafter (Register 83, No. 34).*
4. *Section renumbered from 754.4 to 832.42, filed 2-27-84; effective upon filing pursuant to Government Code Section 11346.2(d) (Register 84, No. 9).*

832.43. CLASS C-43—SHEET METAL CONTRACTOR

1. *Originally published 12-5-46 (Title 16).*
2. *Amendment filed 9-18-47 as an emergency; effective upon filing (Register 9).*
3. *Amendment filed 8-19-83; effective thirtieth day thereafter (Register 83, No. 34).*
4. *Section renumbered from 742 to 832.43, filed 2-27-84; effective upon filing pursuant to Government Code Section 11346.2(d) (Register 84, No. 9).*
5. *Amendment filed 6-22-98; operative 7-1-98 pursuant to Government Code section 11343.4 (d) (Register 98, No. 26).*

832.45. CLASS C-45—ELECTRICAL SIGN CONTRACTOR

1. *New section filed 9-18-47 as an emergency; effective upon filing (Register 9).*
2. *Amendment filed 8-25-83; effective upon filing pursuant to Government Code Section 11346.2(d) (Register 83, No. 35).*
3. *Section renumbered from 754.2 to 832.45, filed 2-27-84; effective upon filing pursuant to Government Code Section 11346.2(d) (Register 84, No. 9).*
4. *Amendment of section heading and section filed 11-30-2009; operative 12-30-2009 (Register 2009, No. 49).*

832.46. CLASS C-46—SOLAR CONTRACTOR

1. *New section filed 10-20-78; effective thirtieth day thereafter (Register 78, No. 42).*
2. *Amendment filed 4-28-82; effective thirtieth day thereafter (Register 82, No. 18).*
3. *Amendment filed 8-25-83; effective upon filing pursuant to Government Code Section 11346.2(d) (Register 83, No. 35).*
4. *Section renumbered from 754.16 to 832.46, filed 2-27-84; effective upon filing pursuant to Government Code Section 11346.2(d) (Register 84, No. 9).*
5. *Amendment filed 11-30-2009; operative 12-30-2009 (Register 2009, No. 49).*

832.47. CLASS C-47—GENERAL MANUFACTURED HOUSING CONTRACTOR

1. *New section filed 3-15-83; effective thirtieth day thereafter (Register 83, No. 12).*
2. *Section renumbered from 754.18 to 832.47, filed 2-27-84; effective upon filing pursuant to Government Code Section 11346.2(d) (Register 84, No. 9).*
3. *Amendment of section and Note filed 10-7-2008; operative 11-6-2008 (Register 2008, No. 41).*

832.50. CLASS C-50—REINFORCING STEEL CONTRACTOR

1. *New section filed 9-18-47 as an emergency; effective upon filing (Register 9).*
2. *Amendment filed 8-19-83; effective thirtieth day thereafter (Register 83, No. 34).*
3. *Section renumbered from 754.5 to 832.50, filed 2-27-84; effective upon filing pursuant to Government Code Section 11346.2(d) (Register 84, No. 9).*
4. *Amendment filed 6-1-88; operative 7-1-88 (Register 88, No. 23).*

Section VI

832.51. CLASS C-51—STRUCTURAL STEEL CONTRACTOR

1. *New section filed 9-18-47 as an emergency; effective upon filing (Register 9).*
2. *Amendment filed 8-19-83; effective thirtieth day thereafter (Register 83, No. 34).*
3. *Section renumbered from 754.6 to 832.51, filed 2-27-84; effective upon filing pursuant to Government Code Section 11346.2(d) (Register 84, No. 9).*
4. *Amendment filed 11-30-98; effective thirtieth day thereafter (Register 98, No. 49).*

832.53. CLASS C-53—SWIMMING POOL CONTRACTOR

1. *New section filed 5-3-55; effective thirtieth day thereafter (Register 55, No. 7).*
2. *Amendment filed 4-28-82; effective thirtieth day thereafter (Register 82, No. 18).*
3. *Amendment filed 8-19-83; effective thirtieth day thereafter (Register 83, No. 34).*
4. *Section renumbered from 754.10 to 832.53, filed 2-27-84; effective upon filing pursuant to Government Code Section 11346.2(d) (Register 84, No. 9).*

832.54. CLASS C-54—TILE CONTRACTORS (CERAMIC AND MOSAIC)

1. *Originally published 12-5-46 (Title 16).*
2. *Amendment filed 9-18-47 as an emergency; effective upon filing (Register 9).*
3. *Amendment filed 8-25-83; effective upon filing pursuant to Government Code Section 11346.2(d) (Register 83, No. 35).*
4. *Section renumbered from 738 to 832.54, filed 2-27-84; effective upon filing pursuant to Government Code Section 11346.2(d) (Register 84, No. 9).*
5. *Amendment filed 5-16-2002; operative 5-16-2002 pursuant to Government Code section 11343.4 (Register 2002, No. 20).*

832.55. CLASS C-55—WATER CONDITIONING CONTRACTOR

1. *New section filed 5-24-61; designated effective 8-22-61 (Register 61, No. 10).*
2. *Amendment filed 8-19-83; effective thirtieth day thereafter (Register 83, No. 34).*
3. *Section renumbered from 754.12 to 832.55, filed 2-27-84; effective upon filing pursuant to Government Code Section 11346.2(d) (Register 84, No. 9).*

832.57. CLASS C-57—WELL DRILLING CONTRACTOR

1. *Originally published 12-5-46 (Title 16).*
2. *Amendment filed 10-19-48 as an emergency (Register 14, No. 3).*
3. *Amendment filed 8-25-83; effective upon filing pursuant to Government Code Section 11346.2(d) (Register 83, No. 35).*
4. *Section renumbered from 751 to 832.57, filed 2-27-84; effective upon filing pursuant to Government Code Section 11346.2(d) (Register 84, No. 9).*

832.60. CLASS C-60—WELDING CONTRACTOR

1. *New section filed 9-18-47 as an emergency; effective upon filing (Register 9).*
2. *Amendment filed 8-19-83; effective thirtieth day thereafter (Register 83, No. 34).*
3. *Section renumbered from 754.7 to 832.60, filed 2-27-84; effective upon filing pursuant to Government Code Section 11346.2(d) (Register 84, No. 9).*

832.61. CLASSIFICATION C-61, LIMITED SPECIALTY

1. *New section filed 9-5-61; effective thirtieth day thereafter (Register 61, No. 19).*
2. *Amendment filed 4-29-64; effective thirtieth day thereafter (Register 64, No. 9).*
3. *Amendment filed 9-8-77; effective thirtieth day thereafter (Register 77, No. 37).*
4. *Editorial correction (Register 77, No. 52).*
5. *Amendment filed 8-19-83; effective thirtieth day thereafter (Register 83, No. 34).*

6. *Section renumbered from 732.1 to 832.61, filed 2-27-84, effective upon filing pursuant to Government Code Section 11346.2(d) (Register 84, No. 9).*

832.62. SOLAR SYSTEM WORK WITHIN SCOPE OF CLASS A, CLASS B, AND CLASS C-61 (SWIMMING POOL MAINTENANCE)

1. *New section filed 4-28-82; effective thirtieth day thereafter (Register 82, No. 18).*
2. *Section renumbered from 754.17 to 832.62, filed 2-27-84, effective upon filing pursuant to Government Code Section 11346.2(d) (Register 84, No. 9).*

834. LIMITATION OF CLASSIFICATION

1. *New section filed 7-17-47 as an emergency (Register 9).*
2. *Amendment filed 4-29-64; effective thirtieth day thereafter (Register 64, No. 9).*
3. *Amendment filed 9-8-77; effective thirtieth day thereafter (Register 77, No. 37).*
4. *Editorial correction (Register 77, No. 52).*
5. *Amendment filed 11-1-83; effective upon filing pursuant to Government Code Section 11346.2(d) (Register 83, No. 45).*
6. *Section renumbered from 760 to 834, filed 2-27-84; effective upon filing pursuant to Government Code Section 11346.2(d) (Register 84, No. 9).*
7. *Editorial correction filed 7-19-84 (Register 84, No. 29).*
8. *Amendment of subsection (b) filed 8-10-99; effective thirtieth day thereafter (Register 99, No. 33).*

840. WRITTEN EXAMINATIONS REQUIRED OF ALL APPLICANTS

1. *Amendment filed 9-8-77; effective thirtieth day thereafter (Register 77, No. 37).*
2. *Editorial correction (Register 77, No. 52).*
3. *Amendment filed 5-6-83; effective thirtieth day thereafter (Register 83, No. 19).*
4. *Section renumbered from 765 to 840, filed 2-27-84; effective upon filing pursuant to Government Code Section 11346.2(d) (Register 84, No. 9).*
5. *Amendment filed 6-6-86; effective thirtieth day thereafter (Register 89, No. 23).*

841. ELIMINATION AND REVISION OF EXAMINATION QUESTIONS

1. *Amendment filed 9-8-77; effective thirtieth day thereafter (Register 77, No. 37).*
2. *Editorial correction (Register 77, No. 52).*
3. *Amendment filed 5-6-83; effective thirtieth day thereafter (Register 83, No. 19).*
4. *Section renumbered from 768 to 841, filed 2-27-84; effective upon filing pursuant to Government Code Section 11346.2(d) (Register 84, No. 9).*

853. RENEWAL APPLICATION FORM

1. *Amendment filed 10-8-64; effective thirtieth day thereafter (Register 64, No. 20).*
2. *Amendment filed 9-8-77; effective thirtieth day thereafter (Register 77, No. 37).*
3. *Amendment filed 5-25-83; effective thirtieth day thereafter (Register 83, No. 22).*
4. *Section renumbered from 781 to 853, filed 2-27-84; effective upon filing pursuant to Government Code Section 11346.2(d) (Register 84, No. 9).*

854. RENEWAL FEE AND REACTIVATION CREDIT

1. *New section filed 6-3-97; operative 6-3-97 pursuant to Government Code section 11343.4(d) (Register 97, No. 23).*

856. SECURITY IN LIEU OF BOND

1. *Amendment filed 11-23-71; effective thirtieth day thereafter (Register 71, No. 48). For prior history see Register 67, No. 17.*
2. *Amendment filed 1-28-77; effective thirtieth day thereafter (Register 77, No. 5).*

3. Amendment filed 5-25-83; effective thirtieth day thereafter (Register 83, No. 22).

4. Section renumbered from 791 to 856, filed 2-27-84; effective upon filing pursuant to Government Code Section 11346.2(d) (Register 84, No. 9).

5. Amendment filed 11-9-95; effective thirtieth day thereafter (Register 95, No. 45).

858. BLANKET PERFORMANCE AND PAYMENT BOND DEFINED

1. New section filed 11-22-2011; operative 12-22-2011 (Register 2011, No. 47).

858.1. BLANKET PERFORMANCE AND PAYMENT BOND REQUIREMENTS

1. New section filed 11-22-2011; operative 12-22-2011 (Register 2011, No. 47).

858.2. APPLICATION FOR APPROVAL OF BLANKET PERFORMANCE AND PAYMENT BOND

1. New section filed 11-22-2011; operative 12-22-2011 (Register 2011, No. 47).

858.3. MINIMUM STANDARDS FOR BLANKET PERFORMANCE AND PAYMENT BOND APPROVAL—CAUSE FOR DENIAL

1. New section filed 11-22-2011; operative 12-22-2011 (Register 2011, No. 47).

858.4. BLANKET PERFORMANCE AND PAYMENT BOND BIENNIAL CERTIFICATION AND FINANCIAL REPORTING REQUIREMENTS

1. New section filed 11-22-2011; operative 12-22-2011 (Register 2011, No. 47).

858.5. BLANKET PERFORMANCE AND PAYMENT BOND AUDIT AUTHORIZATION AND PROCEDURES

1. New section filed 11-22-2011; operative 12-22-2011 (Register 2011, No. 47).

858.6. AUTHORIZATION AND PROCEDURES FOR ORDERING THE AMOUNT OF BLANKET PERFORMANCE AND PAYMENT BOND TO BE INCREASED

1. New section filed 11-22-2011; operative 12-22-2011 (Register 2011, No. 47).

858.7. MAINTENANCE OF THE BLANKET PERFORMANCE AND PAYMENT BOND

1. New section filed 11-22-2011; operative 12-22-2011 (Register 2011, No. 47).

858.8. RESCISSION OF BLANKET PERFORMANCE AND PAYMENT BOND APPROVAL

1. New section filed 11-22-2011; operative 12-22-2011 (Register 2011, No. 47).

858.9. POSTING OF BLANKET PERFORMANCE AND PAYMENT BOND INFORMATION TO LICENSE RECORDS

1. New section filed 11-22-2011; operative 12-22-2011 (Register 2011, No. 47).

860. PENALTY FOR FAILURE TO COMPLY WITH RULES

1. Amendment filed 5-25-83; effective thirtieth day thereafter (Register 83, No. 22).

2. Section renumbered from 794 to 860, filed 2-27-84; effective upon filing pursuant to Government Code Section 11346.2(d) (Register 84, No. 9).

861. LICENSE NUMBER REQUIRED IN ADVERTISING

1. New section filed 10-20-78; effective thirtieth day thereafter (Register 78, No. 42).

2. Amendment filed 10-21-83; effective thirtieth day thereafter (Register 83, No. 43).

3. *Section renumbered from 794.1 to 861, filed 2-27-84; effective upon filing pursuant to Government Code Section 11346.2(d) (Register 84, No. 9).*

4. *Editorial correction filed 7-19-84 (Register 84, No. 29).*

5. *Amendment of section heading and section filed 11-30-2009; operative 12-30-2009 (Register 2009, No. 49).*

861.5 DEFINITION OF "STRUCTURAL DEFECT"

1. *New section filed 08-28-96; effective thirtieth day thereafter (Register 96, No. 35).*

863. PUBLIC ACCESS TO INFORMATION

1. *Repealer filed 8-1-62; effective thirtieth day thereafter (Register 62, No. 16).*

2. *New section filed 5-15-80; designated effective July 1, 1980 (Register 80, No. 20).*

3. *Amendment filed 10-24-83; effective thirtieth day thereafter (Register 83, No. 43).*

4. *Section renumbered from 722 to 863, filed 2-27-84; effective upon filing pursuant to Government Code Section 11346.2(d) (Register 84, No. 9).*

5. *Editorial correction filed 7-19-84 (Register 84, No. 29).*

6. *Amendment filed 4-10-92; operative 5-11-92 (Register 92, No. 18).*

864. CONTINUANCE OF LICENSE UNDER SECTION 7068.2

1. *Originally published 12-5-46 (Title 16).*

2. *Amendment filed 5-5-48 as an emergency (Register 12, No. 6).*

3. *Amendment filed 10-14-65; effective thirtieth day thereafter (Register 65, No. 19).*

4. *Amendment filed 5-25-83; effective thirtieth day thereafter (Register 83, No. 22).*

5. *Section renumbered from 796 to 864, filed 2-27-84; effective upon filing pursuant to Government Code Section 11346.2(d) (Register 84, No. 9).*

865. CONTINUANCE OF LICENSE UNDER SECTION 7076

1. *Amendment filed 10-14-68; effective thirtieth day thereafter (Register 68, No. 39). For prior history, see Section 65, No. 19.*

2. *Amendment filed 5-25-83; effective thirtieth day thereafter (Register 83, No. 22).*

3. *Section renumbered from 796.5 to 865, filed 2-27-84; effective upon filing pursuant to Government Code Section 11346.2(d) (Register 84, No. 9).*

4. *Amendment of subsections (a) and (b) filed 6-6-86; effective thirtieth day thereafter (Register 86, No. 23).*

867. PROCEDURE TO REINSTATE INACTIVE LICENSE

1. *New section filed 8-1-62; designated effective 10-1-62 (Register 62, No. 16).*

2. *Amendment filed 5-25-83; effective thirtieth day thereafter (Register 83, No. 22).*

3. *Section renumbered from 799 to 867, filed 2-27-84; effective upon filing pursuant to Government Code Section 11346.2(d) (Register 84, No. 9).*

4. *Amendment filed 6-6-86; effective thirtieth day thereafter (Register 86, No. 23).*

868. CRITERIA TO AID IN DETERMINING IF CRIMES OR ACTS ARE SUBSTANTIALLY RELATED TO CONTRACTING BUSINESS

1. *Amendment filed 9-8-77; effective thirtieth day thereafter (Register 77, No. 37). For prior history, see Register 75, No. 6.*

2. *Amendment filed 5-25-83; effective thirtieth day thereafter (Register 83, No. 22).*

3. *Section renumbered from 800 to 868, filed 2-27-84; effective upon filing pursuant to Government Code Section 11346.2(d) (Register 84, No. 9).*

4. *Amendment of section heading, section and Note filed 5-31-2006; operative 6-30-2006 (Register 2006, No. 22).*

869. CRITERIA FOR REHABILITATION

1. *Amendment filed 9-8-77; effective thirtieth day thereafter (Register 77, No. 37). For prior history, see Register 75, No. 6.*
2. *Amendment filed 5-25-83; effective thirtieth day thereafter (Register 83, No. 22).*
3. *Section renumbered from 801 to 869, filed 2-27-84; effective upon filing pursuant to Government Code Section 11346.2(d) (Register 84, No. 9).*
4. *Amendment of section and Note filed 5-31-2006; operative 6-30-2006 (Register 2006, No. 22).*

869.1. APPLICANT DEFINED

1. *New section filed 3-17-2005; operative 4-16-2005 (Register 2005, No. 11).*

869.2. EXEMPTIONS

1. *New section filed 3-17-2005; operative 4-16-2005 (Register 2005, No. 11).*

869.3. METHODS FOR SUBMITTING FINGERPRINTS

1. *New section filed 3-17-2005; operative 4-16-2005 (Register 2005, No. 11).*

869.4. SUBSEQUENT ARREST HISTORY

1. *New section filed 3-17-2005; operative 4-16-2005 (Register 2005, No. 11).*

869.5. INQUIRY INTO CRIMINAL CONVICTIONS

1. *New section filed 3-17-2005; operative 4-16-2005 (Register 2005, No. 11).*

869.9. CRITERIA TO AID IN DETERMINING EARLIEST DATE A DENIED APPLICANT MAY REAPPLY FOR LICENSURE

1. *New section filed 5-31-2006; operative 6-30-2006 (Register 2006, No. 22).*

870. FACTORS TO APPLY IN DETERMINING EARLIEST DATE A REVOKED LICENSEE MAY APPLY FOR LICENSURE

1. *New section filed 5-11-89; operative 6-10-89 (Register 89, No. 19).*

871. DISCIPLINARY GUIDELINES

1. *New section filed 5-29-97; operative 5-29-97 pursuant to Government Code 11343.4(d) (Register 97, No. 22).*

872. DISCLOSURE OF GENERAL LIABILITY INSURANCE

1. *New section filed 11-28-2001; operative 2-26-2002 (Register 2001, No. 48).*

872.1. CHECKLIST FOR HOMEOWNERS

1. *New section filed 11-28-2001; operative 2-26-2002 (Register 2001, No. 48).*

880. ORDER OF CORRECTION—PRACTICAL FEASIBILITY

1. *New Article 8 (Sections 803-806.1) filed 4-7-81; effective thirtieth day thereafter (Register 81, No. 15).*
2. *Section renumbered from 803 to 880, filed 2-27-84; effective upon filing pursuant to Government Code Section 11346.2(d) (Register 84, No. 9).*

881. ORDER OF CORRECTION—ALTERNATIVE COMPLIANCE

1. *New section filed 4-7-81; effective thirtieth day thereafter (Register 81, No. 15).*
2. *Section renumbered from 803.1 to 881, filed 2-27-84; effective upon filing pursuant to Government Code Section 11346.2(d) (Register 84, No. 9).*

882. ORDER OF CORRECTION—TIME REQUIRED TO CORRECT

1. *New section filed 4-7-81; effective thirtieth day thereafter (Register 81, No. 15).*
2. *Section renumbered from 804 to 882, filed 2-27-84; effective upon filing pursuant to Government Code Section 11346.2(d) (Register 84, No. 9).*

883. ORDER OF CORRECTION—EXTENSION OF TIME TO CORRECT

1. *New section filed 4-7-81; effective thirtieth day thereafter (Register 81, No. 15).*
2. *Section renumbered from 804.1 to 883, filed 2-27-84; effective upon filing pursuant to Government Code Section 11346.2(d) (Register 84, No. 9).*

884. RECOMMENDED ASSESSMENTS OF CIVIL PENALTIES

1. *New section filed 4-7-81; effective thirtieth day thereafter (Register 81, No. 15).*
2. *Section renumbered from 805 to 884, filed 2-27-84; effective upon filing pursuant to Government Code Section 11346.2(d) (Register 84, No. 9).*
3. *Amendment filed 5-23-94; operative 6-22-94 (Register 94, No. 21).*
4. *Amendment of section and Note filed 1-31-2007; operative 3-2-2007 (Register 2007, No. 5).*

885. APPEAL OF CITATION

1. *New Section filed 4-7-81; effective thirtieth day thereafter (Register 81, No. 15).*
2. *Section renumbered from 806 to 885, filed 2-27-84; effective upon filing pursuant to Government Code Section 11346.2(d) (Register 84, No. 9).*

886. SERVICE OF CITATION

1. *New Section filed 4-7-81; effective thirtieth day thereafter (Register 81, No. 15).*
2. *Section renumbered from 806.1 to 886, filed 2-27-84; effective upon filing pursuant to Government Code Section 11346.2(d) (Register 84, No. 9).*

887. CRITERIA TO EVALUATE THE GRAVITY OF A VIOLATION OF BUSINESS AND PROFESSIONS CODE SECTION 7028.7

1. *New section filed 5-13-82; effective thirtieth day thereafter (Register 82, No. 20).*
2. *Section renumbered from 807 to 887, filed 2-27-84; effective upon filing pursuant to Government Code Section 11346.2(d) (Register 84, No. 9).*

890. MINIMUM QUALIFICATION STANDARDS FOR ARBITRATORS

1. *New article 9 (section 890) and section filed 10-31-2001; operative 11-30-2001 (Register 2001, No. 44).*

HISTORY NOTES FOR
REPEALED BOARD RULES AND REGULATIONS

701. PURPOSE OF LAW—PROTECTION, HEALTH AND SAFETY OF PUBLIC

1. *Repealer filed 5-25-83; effective thirtieth day thereafter (Register 83, No. 22).*

702. FEES

1. *New Article 1.5 (Section 702) filed 12-21-81; designated effective 2-1-82 (Register 81, No. 52).*
2. *Repealer filed 3-15-83; effective thirtieth day thereafter (Register 83, No. 12).*

707. ALL MEMBERS OF APPLICANT TO FURNISH INFORMATION

1. *Repealer filed 8-25-83; effective upon filing pursuant to Government Code Section 11346.2(d) (Register 83, No. 35).*

708. SIGNING AND VERIFICATION OF APPLICATION

1. Amendment filed 7-19-74; effective thirtieth day thereafter (Register 74, No. 29).

2. Repealer filed 8-25-83; effective upon filing pursuant to Government Code Section 11346.2(d) (Register 83, No. 35).

709. FURNISHING REFERENCES

1. Repealer filed 3-3-53; effective thirtieth day thereafter (Register 53, No. 4).

710. POWER OF REGISTRAR TO DENY INSUFFICIENT APPLICATIONS

1. Amendment filed 9-8-77; effective thirtieth day thereafter (Register 77, No. 37).

2. Repealer filed 8-25-83; effective upon filing pursuant to Government Code Section 11346.2(d) (Register 83, No. 35).

711.1. ABANDONMENT OF APPLICATION

1. New section filed 1-22-76; effective thirtieth day thereafter (Register 76, No. 4).

2. Repealer filed 8-25-83; effective upon filing pursuant to Government Code Section 11346.2(d) (Register 83, No. 35).

712. POWER OF REGISTRAR TO WAIVE FORMAL REQUIREMENTS

1. Amendment filed 9-8-77; effective thirtieth day thereafter (Register 77, No. 37).

2. Repealer filed 8-25-83; effective upon filing pursuant to Government Code Section 11346.2(d) (Register 83, No. 35).

713. TENDER OF FEE

1. Originally published 12-5-46 (Title 16).

2. Amendment filed 9-18-47 as an emergency (Register 9).

3. Repealer filed 1-23-50 (Register 19, No. 2).

716. POWER IN REGISTRAR TO WAIVE POSTING

1. Originally published 12-5-46 (Title 16).

2. Amendment filed 9-18-47 as an emergency (Register 9).

3. Repealer filed 1-27-71; effective thirtieth day thereafter (Register 71, No. 5).

719. BOND REQUIREMENT OF APPLICANTS

1. Repealer filed 8-1-62; effective thirtieth day thereafter (Register 62, No. 16).

720. POSTING OF BOND AS CONDITION OF REINSTATEMENT

1. Repealer filed 8-1-62; effective thirtieth day thereafter (Register 62, No. 16).

721. REGISTRAR MAY WAIVE BOND

1. Repealer filed 8-1-62; effective thirtieth day thereafter (Register 62, No. 16).

723. POLICY OF THE BOARD REGARDING EXPERIENCE

1. Amendment filed 9-8-77; effective thirtieth day thereafter (Register 77, No. 37).

2. Editorial correction (Register 77, No. 52).

3. Repealer filed 12-22-82; effective thirtieth day thereafter (Register 82, No. 52).

726. CREDIT FOR ADDITIONAL EXPERIENCE

1. Originally published 12-5-48 (Title 16).

2. Amendment filed 3-12-47 (Register 8).

3. Repealer filed 2-28-80; effective thirtieth day thereafter (Register 80, No. 9).

731. ALL CONTRACTORS TO BE CLASSIFIED

1. Repealer filed 12-22-82; effective thirtieth day thereafter (Register 82, No. 52).

753. CLASS C-22—STRUCTURAL PEST CONTROL CONTRACTOR

1. Repealer filed 10-18-55; effective thirtieth day thereafter (Register 55, No. 16).

754. CLASS C-56—WATERPROOFING, WEATHERPROOFING AND DAMP-PROOFING CONTRACTORS

1. Originally published 12-5-46 (Title 16).

2. Repealer filed 9-18-47 as an emergency; effective upon filing (Register 9).

755. PRIMARY AND SUPPLEMENTAL CLASSIFICATIONS

1. Amendment filed 9-8-77; effective thirtieth day thereafter (Register 77, No. 37).

2. Editorial correction (Register 77, No. 52).

3. Repealer filed 12-22-82; effective thirtieth day thereafter (Register 82, No. 52).

756. ASSIGNMENT OF PRIMARY CLASSIFICATION

1. Amendment filed 2-7-75; effective thirtieth day thereafter (Register 75, No. 6).

2. Amendment filed 9-8-77; effective thirtieth day thereafter (Register 77, No. 37).

3. Repealer filed 12-22-82; effective thirtieth day thereafter (Register 82, No. 52).

756.1. ASSIGNMENT OF SUPPLEMENTAL SOLAR CLASSIFICATION

1. New section filed 10-20-78; effective thirtieth day thereafter (Register 78, No. 42).

2. Repealer filed 3-15-83; effective thirtieth day thereafter (Register 83, No. 12).

756.2. QUALIFICATION FOR SUPPLEMENTAL SOLAR CLASSIFICATION

1. New section filed 10-20-78; effective thirtieth day thereafter (Register 78, No. 42).

2. Repealer filed 4-28-82; effective thirtieth day thereafter (Register 82, No. 18).

756.3. SOLAR PROJECT REPORTING REQUIREMENTS

1. New section filed 10-20-78; effective thirtieth day thereafter (Register 78, No. 42).

2. Repealer filed 4-28-82; effective thirtieth day thereafter (Register 82, No. 18).

756.4. EFFECTIVE DATE OF REGULATION

1. New section filed 10-20-78; effective thirtieth day thereafter (Register 78, No. 42).

2. Repealer filed 4-28-82; effective thirtieth day thereafter (Register 82, No. 18).

757. NO "SUPPLEMENTAL" CLASSIFICATION WHERE NO SPECIAL EXAMINATION

1. Originally published 12-5-46 (Title 16).

2. Repealer filed 9-18-47 as an emergency; effective upon filing (Register 9).

759. WAIVER OF RECLASSIFICATION EXAMINATIONS

1. Amendment filed 9-8-77; effective thirtieth day thereafter (Register 77, No. 37).

2. Repealer filed 2-28-80; effective thirtieth day thereafter (Register 80, No. 9).

764. POLICY OF THE BOARD REGARDING EXAMINATIONS

1. Amendment filed 9-8-77; effective thirtieth day thereafter (Register 77, No. 37).

2. Editorial correction (Register 77, No. 52).

3. Repealer filed 12-22-82; effective thirtieth day thereafter (Register 82, No. 52).

Section VI

766. TYPES OF EXAMINATIONS

1. Repealer filed 5-6-83; effective thirtieth day thereafter (Register 83, No. 19).

767. "SPECIFIC" AND "BLANKET" EXAMINATIONS APPROVED

1. Originally published 12-5-46 (Title 16).

2. Repealer filed 9-18-47 as an emergency; effective upon filing (Register 9).

769. REGISTRAR TO REQUIRE EXAMINATION OF APPLICANTS

1. Repealer filed 12-22-82; effective thirtieth day thereafter (Register 82, No. 52).

770. REGISTRAR MAY CHANGE WRITTEN EXAMINATIONS

1. Amendment filed 9-8-77; effective thirtieth day thereafter (Register 77, No. 37).

2. Repealer filed 5-6-83; effective thirtieth day thereafter (Register 83, No. 19).

772. GRADING OF EXAMINATIONS

1. Originally published 12-5-46 (Title 16).

2. Amendment filed 3-17-47 (Register 8).

3. Amendment filed 2-28-80; effective thirtieth day thereafter (Register 80, No. 9).

4. Repealer filed 4-15-83; effective upon filing pursuant to Government Code Section 11346.2(d) (Register 83, No. 16).

773. REGISTRAR MAY MAKE RULES ON EXAMINATION PROCEDURE

1. Amendment filed 9-8-77; effective thirtieth day thereafter (Register 77, No. 37).

2. Editorial correction (Register 77, No. 52).

3. Repealer filed 5-6-83; effective thirtieth day thereafter (Register 83, No. 19).

774. NO EXAMINATION REQUIRED

1. Sections 774 and 775 originally published 12-5-46 (Title 16).

2. Amendments to same filed 10-19-48 as emergencies (Register 14, No. 3).

3. Amendment filed 8-6-64; effective thirtieth day thereafter (Register 64, No. 17).

4. Repealer filed 8-25-83; effective upon filing pursuant to Government Code Section 11346.2(d) (Register 83, No. 35).

818. INSUFFICIENT OR INCOMPLETE APPLICATIONS—REJECTION

1. Amendment filed 2-7-75; effective thirtieth day thereafter (Register 75, No. 6).

2. Amendment filed 8-25-83; effective upon filing pursuant to Government Code Section 11346.2(d) (Register 83, No. 35).

3. Section renumbered from 711 to 818, filed 2-27-84; effective upon filing pursuant to Government Code Section 11346.2(d) (Register 84, No. 9).

4. Repealer filed 11-9-95; effective thirtieth day thereafter (Register 95, No. 45).

820. POSTING OF NAMES OF APPLICANTS

1. Originally published 12-5-46 (Title 16).

2. Amendment filed 7-31-50 as a procedural rule; effective upon filing (Register 21, No. 4).

3. Amendment filed 1-27-71; effective thirtieth day thereafter (Register 71, No. 5).

4. Amendment filed 2-7-75; effective thirtieth day thereafter (Register 75, No. 6).

5. Amendment filed 8-25-83; effective upon filing pursuant to Government Code Section 11346.2(d) (Register 83, No. 35).

6. Section renumbered from 715 to 820, filed 2-27-84; effective upon filing pursuant to Government Code Section 11346.2(d) (Register 84, No. 9).

7. Repealer filed 11-9-95; effective thirtieth day thereafter (Register 95, No.45).

821. JOINT VENTURE LICENSE DEFINED

1. *Originally published 12-5-46 (Title 16).*

2. *Amendment filed 10-18-49 as an emergency (Register 18, No. 3).*

3. *Amendment filed 12-16-63; effective thirtieth day thereafter (Register 63, No. 25).*

4. *Amendment filed 8-25-83; effective upon filing pursuant to Government Code Section 11346.2(d) (Register 83, No. 35).*

5. *Section renumbered from 717 to 821, filed 2-27-84; effective upon filing pursuant to Government Code Section 11346.2(d) (Register 84, No. 9).*

6. *Repealer filed 11-9-95; effective thirtieth day thereafter (Register 95, No.45).*

822. LICENSING REQUIREMENTS FOR JOINT VENTURE LICENSE

1. *Amendment filed 9-8-77; effective thirtieth day thereafter (Register 77, No. 37). For prior history, see Register 71, No. 5.*

2. *Amendment filed 8-25-83; effective upon filing pursuant to Government Code Section 11346.2(d) (Register 83, No. 35).*

3. *Section renumbered from 718 to 822, filed 2-27-84; effective upon filing pursuant to Government Code Section 11346.2(d) (Register 84, No. 9).*

4. *Repealer filed 11-9-95; effective thirtieth day thereafter (Register 95, No.45).*

829. CREDIT FOR EXPERIENCE

1. *New section filed 5-30-90; operative 6-29-90 (Register 90, No. 29).*

2. *Repealer filed 8-10-2006; operative 9-9-2006 (Register 2006, No. 32).*

832.06. CLASS C-6—CABINET AND MILLWORK CONTRACTORS

1. *Amendment filed 8-25-83; effective upon filing pursuant to Government Code Section 11346.2(d) (Register 83, No. 35).*

2. *Section renumbered from 744 to 832.06, filed 2-27-84; effective upon filing pursuant to Government Code Section 11346.2(d) (Register 84, No. 9).*

3. *Repealer filed 12-18-97; effective 01-01-98 (Register 97, No.172).*

832.26. CLASS C-26—LATHING CONTRACTORS

1. *Amendment filed 9-23-83; effective upon filing pursuant to Government Code Section 11346.2(d) (Register 83, No. 39).*

2. *Section renumbered from 743 to 832.26, filed 2-27-84; effective upon filing pursuant to Government Code Section 11346.2(d) (Register 84, No. 9).*

3. *Repealer filed 12-18-97; effective 01-01-98 (Register 97, No.172).*

833. ADDITIONAL CLASSIFICATIONS

1. *Sections 758 and 759 originally published 12-5-46 (Title 16).*

2. *Amendments to same filed 10-19-48 as emergencies (Register 14, No. 3).*

3. *Amendment filed 9-8-77; effective thirtieth day thereafter (Register 77, No. 37).*

4. *Amendment filed 8-19-83; effective thirtieth day thereafter (Register 83, No. 35).*

5. *Section renumbered from 758 to 833, filed 2-27-84; effective upon filing pursuant to Government Code Section 11346.2(d) (Register 84, No. 9).*

6. *Repealer filed 6-6-86; effective thirtieth day thereafter (Register 86, No. 23).*

842. APPLICANTS MAY BE RE-EXAMINED

1. *Amendment filed 7-19-66; effective thirtieth day thereafter (Register 66, No. 23).*

2. *Amendment filed 9-8-77; effective thirtieth day thereafter (Register 77, No. 37).*

3. *Amendment filed 5-6-83; effective thirtieth day thereafter (Register 83, No. 19).*

4. *Section renumbered from 771 to 842, filed 2-27-84; effective upon filing pursuant to Government Code Section 11346.2(d) (Register 84, No. 9).*

5. *Amendment filed 6-6-86; effective thirtieth day thereafter (Register 86, No. 23).*

6. *Repealer filed 11-30-2009; operative 12-30-2009 (Register 2009, No. 49).*

843. WAIVER OF EXAMINATION

1. *New section filed 7-2-81; effective thirtieth day thereafter (Register 81, No. 27). For history of former section, see Registers 80, No. 9; 77, No. 52; 77, No. 37; 62, No. 1 and 57, No. 6.*

2. *Section renumbered from 775 to 843, filed 2-27-84; effective upon filing pursuant to Government Code Section 11346.2(d) (Register 84, No. 9).*

3. *Repealer filed 6-6-86; effective thirtieth day thereafter (Register 86, No. 23).*

844. FAILURE TO APPEAR FOR EXAMINATION

1. *Originally filed 12-5-46 (Title 16).*

2. *Amendment filed 4-30-47 (Register 8).*

3. *Amendment filed 9-8-77; effective thirtieth day thereafter (Register 77, No. 37).*

4. *Amendment filed 8-25-83; effective upon filing pursuant to Government Code Section 11346.2(d) (Register 83, No. 35).*

5. *Section renumbered from 776 to 844, filed 2-27-84; effective upon filing pursuant to Government Code Section 11346.2(d) (Register 84, No. 9).*

6. *Repealer filed 6-6-86; effective thirtieth day thereafter (Register 86, No. 23).*

852. RENEWAL OF LICENSES

1. *New section filed 6-22-78; effective thirtieth day thereafter (Register 78, No. 25). For history of prior section 780, see Register 66, No. 23.*

2. *Amendment filed 5-25-83; effective thirtieth day thereafter (Register 83, No. 22).*

3. *Section renumbered from 780 to 852, filed 2-27-84; effective upon filing pursuant to Government Code Section 11346.2(d) (Register 84, No. 9).*

4. *Change without regulatory effect repealing section filed 11-9-95 pursuant to section 100, title 1, California Code of Regulations (Register 95, No. 45).*

862. NOTICE TO OWNER

1. *New section filed 6-5-80; effective thirtieth day thereafter (Register 80, No. 23).*

2. *Amendment filed 3-26-82; effective thirtieth day thereafter (Register 82, No. 13).*

3. *Section renumbered from 794.2 to 862, filed 2-27-84; effective upon filing pursuant to Government Code Section 11346.2(d) (Register 84, No. 9).*

4. *Amendment filed 3-6-84; effective upon filing pursuant to Government Code Section 11346.2(d) (Register 84, No. 9).*

5. *Change without regulatory effect repealing section filed 11-9-95 pursuant to section 100, title 1, California Code of Regulations (Register 95, No. 45).*

866. PROCEDURE TO INACTIVATE LICENSE

1. *New section filed 8-1-62; designated effective 10-1-62 (Register 62, No. 16).*

2. *Amendment filed 5-25-83; effective thirtieth day thereafter (Register 83, No. 22).*

3. *Section renumbered from 798 to 866, filed 2-27-84; effective upon filing pursuant to Government Code Section 11346.2(d) (Register 84, No. 9).*

4. *Repealer filed 6-6-86; effective thirtieth day thereafter (Register 86, No. 23).*

APPENDIX

Extracts from Laws Related to
CSLB Laws & Regulations

CALIFORNIA CONSTITUTION

Article XIV

LABOR RELATIONS

§ 3. Mechanics' liens

Mechanics, persons furnishing materials, artisans, and laborers of every class, shall have a lien upon the property upon which they have bestowed labor or furnished material for the value of such labor done and material furnished; and the Legislature shall provide, by law, for the speedy and efficient enforcement of such liens.

Adopted June 8, 1976.

BUSINESS AND PROFESSIONS CODE

DIVISION 3

PROFESSIONS AND VOCATIONS GENERALLY

Chapter 3

Architecture

Article 3

Application of Chapter

§ 5537. When plans and drawings by uncertificated persons permitted

(a) This chapter does not prohibit any person from preparing plans, drawings, or specifications for any of the following:

(1) Single–family dwellings of woodframe construction not more than two stories and basement in height.

(2) Multiple dwellings containing no more than four dwelling units of woodframe construction not more than two stories and basement in height. However, this paragraph shall not be construed as allowing an unlicensed person to design multiple clusters of up to four dwelling units each to form apartment or condominium complexes where the total exceeds four units on any lawfully divided lot.

(3) Garages or other structures appurtenant to buildings described under subdivision (a), of woodframe construction not more than two stories and basement in height.

(4) Agricultural and ranch buildings of woodframe construction, unless the building official having jurisdiction deems that an undue risk to the public health, safety, or welfare is involved.

(b) If any portion of any structure exempted by this section deviates from substantial compliance with conventional framing requirements for woodframe construction found in the most recent edition of Title 24 of the California Code of Regulations or tables of limitation for woodframe construction, as defined by the applicable building code duly adopted by the local jurisdiction or the state, the building official having jurisdiction shall require the preparation of plans, drawings, specifications, or calculations for that portion by, or under the responsible control of, a licensed architect or registered engineer. The documents for that portion shall bear the stamp and signature of the licensee who is responsible for their preparation. Substantial compliance for purposes of this section is not intended to restrict the ability of the building officials to approve plans pursuant to existing law and is only intended to clarify the intent of Chapter 405 of the Statutes of 1985.

Added Stats 1939 ch 33 § 1. Amended Stats 1963 ch 2133 § 17; Stats 1984 ch 1405 § 6; Stats 1985 ch 1327 § 4.5; Stats 1986 ch 204 § 1; Stats 1987 ch 589 § 2; Stats 1990 ch 94 § 5 (AB 1005); Stats 1996 ch 184 § 8 (SB 1607).

§ 5537.2. Application of chapter to contractors

This chapter shall not be construed as authorizing a licensed contractor to perform design services beyond those described in Section 5537 or in Chapter 9 (commencing with Section 7000), unless those services are performed by or under the direct supervision of a person licensed to practice architecture under this chapter, or a professional or civil engineer licensed pursuant to Chapter 7 (commencing with Section 6700) of Division 3, insofar as the professional or civil engineer practices the profession for which he or she is registered under that chapter.

However, this section does not prohibit a licensed contractor from performing any of the services permitted by Chapter 9 (commencing with Section 7000) of Division 3 within the classification for which the license is issued. Those services may include the preparation of shop and field drawings for work which he or she has contracted or offered to perform, and designing systems and facilities which are necessary to the completion of contracting services which he or she has contracted or offered to perform.

However, a licensed contractor may not use the title "architect," unless he or she holds a license as required in this chapter.

Added Stats 1963 ch 2133 § 19. Amended Stats 1984 ch 1405 § 7; Stats 1985 ch 1327 § 6.

Chapter 7

Professional Engineers

Article 3

Application of Chapter

§ 6737.3. Exemption of contractors

A contractor licensed under Chapter 9 (commencing with Section 7000) of Division 3 is exempt from the provisions of this chapter relating to the practice of electrical or mechanical engineering so long as the services he or she holds himself or herself out as able to perform or does perform, which services are subject to the provisions of this chapter, are performed by, or under the responsible charge of a registered electrical or mechanical engineer insofar as the electrical or mechanical engineer practices the branch of engineering for which he or she is registered.

This section shall not prohibit a licensed contractor, while engaged in the business of contracting for the installation of electrical or mechanical systems or facilities, from designing those systems or facilities in accordance with applicable construction codes and standards for work to be performed and supervised by that contractor within the classification for which his or her license is issued, or from preparing electrical or mechanical shop or field drawings for work which he or she has contracted to perform. Nothing in this section is intended to imply that a licensed contractor may design work which is to be installed by another person.

Added Stats 1967 ch 1463 § 10. Amended Stats 1994 ch 26 § 201 (AB 1807), effective March 30, 1994; Stats 2003 ch 607 § 28 (SB 1077).

Appendix

Chapter 11.6

Alarm Companies

Article 1

General Provisions

§ 7590.1. Definitions

The following terms as used in this chapter have the meaning expressed in this article:

(a) "Person" means any individual, firm, company, association, organization, partnership, limited liability company, or corporation.

(b) "Department" means the Department of Consumer Affairs.

(c) "Director" means the Director of Consumer Affairs.

(d) "Bureau" means the Bureau of Security and Investigative Services.

(e) "Chief" means the Chief of the Bureau of Security and Investigative Services.

(f) "Employer" means a person who employs an individual for wages or salary, lists the individual on the employer's payroll records, and withholds all legally required deductions and contributions.

(g) "Employee" means an individual who works for an employer, is listed on the employer's payroll records, and is under the employer's direction and control.

(h) "Employer–employee relationship" means an individual who works for another and where the individual's name appears on the payroll records of the employer.

(i) "Licensee" means a business entity, whether an individual, partnership, or corporation licensed under this chapter.

(j) "Qualified manager" means an individual who is in active control, management, and direction of the licensee's business, and who is in possession of a current and valid qualified manager's certificate pursuant to this chapter.

(k) "Registrant" means any person registered or who has applied for registration under this chapter.

(*l*) "Branch office" means any location, other than the principal place of business of the licensee, which is licensed as set forth in Article 11 (commencing with Section 7599.20).

(m) "Branch office manager" means an individual designated by the qualified manager to manage the licensee's branch office and who has met the requirements as set forth in Article 11 (commencing with Section 7599.20).

(n) "Alarm system" means an assembly of equipment and devices arranged to signal the presence of a hazard requiring urgent attention and to which police are expected to respond.

(o) "Alarm agent" means a person employed by an alarm company operator whose duties include selling on premises, altering, installing, maintaining, moving, repairing, replacing, servicing, responding, or monitoring an alarm system, or a person who manages or supervises a person employed by an alarm company to perform any of the duties described in this subdivision or any person in training for any of the duties described in this subdivision.

(p) "Deadly weapon" means and includes any instrument or weapon of the kind commonly known as a blackjack, slungshot, billy, sandclub, sandbag, metal knuckles; any dirk, dagger, pistol, revolver, or any other firearm; any knife having a blade longer than five inches; any razor with an unguarded blade; or any metal pipe or bar used or intended to be used as a club.

(q) "Firearms permit" means a permit issued by the bureau, pursuant to Article 6 (commencing with Section 7596), to a licensee, a qualified manager, or an alarm agent, to carry an exposed firearm while on duty.

(r)(1) "Advertisement" means:

(A) Any written or printed communication for the purpose of soliciting, describing, or promoting the licensed business of the licensee, including a brochure, letter, pamphlet, newspaper, periodical, publication, or other writing.

(B) A directory listing caused or permitted by the licensee which indicates his or her licensed activity.

(C) A radio, television, or similar airwave transmission which solicits or promotes the licensed business of the licensee.

(2) "Advertisement" does not include any of the following:

(A) Any printing or writing used on buildings, vehicles, uniforms, badges, or other property where the purpose of the printing or writing is identification.

(B) Any printing or writing on communications, memoranda, or any other writings used in the ordinary course of business where the sole purpose of the writing is other than the solicitation or promotion of business.

(C) Any printing or writing on novelty objects used in the promotion of the licensee's business where the printing of the information required by this chapter would be impractical due to the available area or surface.

(s) "Residential sales agreement" means and includes an agreement between an alarm company operator and an owner or tenant for the purchase of an alarm system to be utilized in the personal residence of the owner or tenant.

(t) "Firearm permit" means and includes "firearms permit," "firearms qualification card," "firearms qualification," and "firearms qualification permit."

Added Stats 1982 ch 1210 § 12. Amended Stats 1986 ch 1168 § 1; Stats 1989 ch 1104 § 32; Stats 1993 ch 1263 § 12 (AB 936); Stats 1994 ch 1010 § 13 (SB 2053).

Chapter 14

Structural Pest Control Operators

Article 1

General Provisions

§ 8513. Mechanics' lien; Notice to owner; Release (First of two; Operative until July 1, 2012)

(a) The board shall prescribe a form entitled "Notice to Owner" that shall describe, in nontechnical language and in a clear and coherent manner using words with common and everyday meaning, the pertinent provisions of this state's mechanics' lien laws and the rights and responsibilities of an owner of property and a registered pest control company thereunder. Each company registered under this chapter, prior to entering into a contract with an owner for work for which a company registration is required, shall give a copy of this "Notice to Owner" to the owner, his or her agent, or the payer.

(b) No company that is required to be registered under this chapter shall require or request a waiver of lien rights from any subcontractor, employee, or supplier.

(c) Each company registered under this chapter that acts as a subcontractor for another company registered under this chapter shall, within 20 days of commencement of any work for which a company registration is required, give the preliminary 20-day notice (private work) in accordance with the provisions of Section 3097 of the Civil Code, to the owner, his or her agent, or the payer.

(d) Each company registered under this chapter that acts as a prime contractor for work for which a company registration is required shall, prior to accepting payment for the work, furnish to the owner, his or her agent, or the payer a full and unconditional release from any claim of mechanics' lien by any subcontractor entitled to enforce a mechanics' lien pursuant to Section 3114 of the Civil Code.

(e) Each company registered under this chapter that subcontracts to another company registered under this chapter work for which a company registration is required shall furnish to the subcontractor the name of the owner, his or her agent, or the payer.

(f) The provisions of this section shall be applicable only to those registered companies, as defined in Section 8506.1, operating pursuant to a Branch 1 or Branch 3 registration.

(g) A violation of the provisions of this section is a ground for disciplinary action.

Added Stats 1982 ch 770 § 1. Amended Stats 1985 ch 1348 § 18, operative January 1, 1987; Stats 1994 ch 844 § 8 (SB 2070); Stats 2001 ch 306 § 12 (AB 446).

§ 8513. Mechanics' lien; Notice to owner; Release (Second of two; Operative July 1, 2012)

(a) The board shall prescribe a form entitled "Notice to Owner" that shall describe, in nontechnical language and in a clear and coherent manner using words with common and everyday meaning, the pertinent provisions of this state's mechanics lien laws and the rights and responsibilities of an owner of property and a registered pest control company thereunder. Each company registered under this chapter, prior to entering into a contract with an owner for work for which a company registration is required, shall give a copy of this "Notice to Owner" to the owner, his or her agent, or the payer.

(b) No company that is required to be registered under this chapter shall require or request a waiver of lien rights from any subcontractor, employee, or supplier.

(c) Each company registered under this chapter that acts as a subcontractor for another company registered under this chapter shall, within 20 days of commencement of any work for which a company registration is required, give the preliminary notice in accordance with Chapter 2 (commencing with Section 8200) of Title 2 of Part 6 of Division 4 of the Civil Code, to the owner, his or her agent, or the payer.

(d) Each company registered under this chapter that acts as a prime contractor for work for which a company registration is required shall, prior to accepting payment for the work, furnish to the owner, his or her agent, or the payer a full and unconditional release from any claim of mechanics lien by any subcontractor entitled to enforce a mechanics lien pursuant to Section 8410 of the Civil Code.

(e) Each company registered under this chapter that subcontracts to another company registered under this chapter work for which a company registration is required shall furnish to the subcontractor the name of the owner, his or her agent, or the payer.

(f) The provisions of this section shall be applicable only to those registered companies, as defined in Section 8506.1, operating pursuant to a Branch 1 or Branch 3 registration.

(g) A violation of the provisions of this section is a ground for disciplinary action.

Added Stats 1982 ch 770 § 1. Amended Stats 1985 ch 1348 § 18, operative January 1, 1987; Stats 1994 ch 844 § 8 (SB 2070); Stats 2001 ch 306 § 12 (AB 446); Stats 2010 ch 697 § 9 (SB 189), effective January 1, 2011, operative July 1, 2012; Stats 2011 ch 44 § 4 (SB 190), effective January 1, 2012, operative July 1, 2012.

Article 3

Application of the Chapter

§ 8556. Removal and replacement of damaged areas; Application of wood preservative; Contracting for performance of soil treatment pest control work

(a) Licensed contractors acting in their capacity as such, may remove and replace any structure or portions of a structure damaged by wood destroying pests or organisms if that work is incidental to other work being performed on the structure involved or if that work has been identified by a structural pest control inspection report. Licensed contractors acting in their capacity as such may apply wood preservatives directly to end cuts and drill holes of pressure treated wood, and to foundation wood as required by building codes, as well as to fencing and decking, by brush, dip, or spray method and need not obtain a license under this chapter for performance of that work, provided a disclosure in the following form is submitted to the customer in writing: "The application of a wood preservative is intended to prevent the establishment and flourishing of organisms which can deteriorate wood. If you suspect pest infestation or infection, contact a registered structural pest control company prior to the application of a wood preservative."

These exemptions do not authorize the performance of any other acts defined in Section 8505.

(b) A licensed contractor may contract for the performance of any soil treatment pest control work to eliminate, exterminate, control, or prevent infestations or infections of pests or organisms in the ground beneath or adjacent to any existing building or structure or in or upon any site upon which any building or structure is to be constructed, but the actual performance of any such work must be done by a registered structural pest control company.

Added Stats 1941 ch 1163 § 1. Amended Stats 1953 ch 1163 § 1; Stats 1957 ch 1686 § 2; Stats 1968 ch 804 § 1; Stats 1979 ch 687 § 2; Stats 1985 ch 1348 § 33, operative January 1, 1987; Stats 1989 ch 1401 § 3; Stats 1998 ch 970 § 94 (AB 2802); Stats 1999 ch 983 § 10.4 (SB 1307).

CIVIL CODE

DIVISION 1
PERSONS

PART 2

PERSONAL RIGHTS

§ 43.99. Liability of person or entity under contract with residential building permit applicant for quality review of compliance with State Housing Law

(a) There shall be no monetary liability on the part of, and no cause of action for damages shall arise against, any person or other legal entity that is under contract with an applicant for a residential building permit to provide independent quality review of the plans and specifications provided with the application in order to determine compliance with all applicable requirements imposed pursuant to the State Housing Law (Part 1.5 (commencing with Section 17910) of Division 13 of the Health and Safety Code), or any rules or regulations adopted pursuant to that law, or under contract with that applicant to provide independent quality review of the work of improvement to determine compliance with these plans and specifications, if the person or other legal entity meets the requirements of this section and one of the following applies:

(1) The person, or a person employed by any other legal entity, performing the work as described in this subdivision, has completed not less than five years of verifiable experience in the appropriate field and has obtained certification as a building inspector, combination inspector, or combination dwelling inspector from the International Conference of Building Officials (ICBO) and has successfully passed the technical written examination promulgated by ICBO for those certification categories.

(2) The person, or a person employed by any other legal entity, performing the work as described in this subdivision, has completed not less than five years of verifiable experience in the appropriate field and is a registered professional engineer, licensed general contractor, or a licensed architect rendering independent quality review of the work of improvement or plan examination services within the scope of his or her registration or licensure.

(3) The immunity provided under this section does not apply to any action initiated by the applicant who retained the qualified person.

(4) A "qualified person" for purposes of this section means a person holding a valid certification as one of those inspectors.

(b) Except for qualified persons, this section shall not relieve from, excuse, or lessen in any manner, the responsibility or liability of any person, company, contractor, builder, developer, architect, engineer, designer, or other individual or entity who develops, improves, owns, operates, or manages any residential building for any damages to persons or property caused by construction or design defects. The fact that an inspection by a qualified person has taken place may not be introduced as evidence in a construction defect action, including any reports or other items generated by the qualified person. This subdivision shall not apply in any action initiated by the applicant who retained the qualified person.

(c) Nothing in this section, as it relates to construction inspectors or plans examiners, shall be construed to alter the requirements for licensure, or the jurisdiction, authority, or scope of practice, of architects pursuant to Chapter 3 (commencing with Section 5500) of Division 3 of the Business and Professions Code, professional engineers pursuant to Chapter 7 (commencing with Section 6700) of Division 3 of the Business and Professions Code, or general contractors pursuant to Chapter 9 (commencing with Section 7000) of Division 3 of the Business and Professions Code.

(d) Nothing in this section shall be construed to alter the immunity of employees of the Department of Housing and Community Development under the Tort Claims Act (Division 3.6 (commencing with Section 810) of Title 1 of the Government Code) when acting pursuant to Section 17965 of the Health and Safety Code.

(e) The qualifying person shall engage in no other construction, design, planning, supervision, or activities of any kind on the work of improvement, nor provide quality review services for any other party on the work of improvement.

(f) The qualifying person, or other legal entity, shall maintain professional errors and omissions insurance coverage in an amount not less than two million dollars ($2,000,000).

(g) The immunity provided by subdivision (a) does not inure to the benefit of the qualified person for damages caused to the applicant solely by the negligence or willful misconduct of the qualified person resulting from the provision of services under the contract with the applicant.

Added Stats 2002 ch 722 § 2 (SB 800).

DIVISION 2
PROPERTY

PART 2
REAL OR IMMOVABLE PROPERTY

TITLE 7
Requirements for Actions for Construction Defects

Chapter 1
Definitions

§ 895. Definitions

(a) "Structure" means any residential dwelling, other building, or improvement located upon a lot or within a common area.

(b) "Designed moisture barrier" means an installed moisture barrier specified in the plans and specifications, contract documents, or manufacturer's recommendations.

(c) "Actual moisture barrier" means any component or material, actually installed, that serves to any degree as a barrier against moisture, whether or not intended as such.

(d) "Unintended water" means water that passes beyond, around, or through a component or the material that is designed to prevent that passage.

(e) "Close of escrow" means the date of the close of escrow between the builder and the original homeowner. With respect to claims by an association, as defined in subdivision (a) of Section 1351, "close of escrow" means the date of substantial completion, as defined in Section 337.15 of the Code of Civil Procedure, or the date the builder relinquishes control over the association's ability to decide whether to initiate a claim under this title, whichever is later.

(f) "Claimant" or "homeowner" includes the individual owners of single–family homes, individual unit owners of attached dwellings and, in the case of a common interest development, any association as defined in subdivision (a) of Section 1351.

Added Stats 2002 ch 722 § 3 (SB 800).

Appendix

Chapter 2

Actionable Defects

§ 896. Standards for residential construction

In any action seeking recovery of damages arising out of, or related to deficiencies in, the residential construction, design, specifications, surveying, planning, supervision, testing, or observation of construction, a builder, and to the extent set forth in Chapter 4 (commencing with Section 910), a general contractor, subcontractor, material supplier, individual product manufacturer, or design professional, shall, except as specifically set forth in this title, be liable for, and the claimant's claims or causes of action shall be limited to violation of, the following standards, except as specifically set forth in this title. This title applies to original construction intended to be sold as an individual dwelling unit. As to condominium conversions, this title does not apply to or does not supersede any other statutory or common law.

(a) With respect to water issues:

(1) A door shall not allow unintended water to pass beyond, around, or through the door or its designed or actual moisture barriers, if any.

(2) Windows, patio doors, deck doors, and their systems shall not allow water to pass beyond, around, or through the window, patio door, or deck door or its designed or actual moisture barriers, including, without limitation, internal barriers within the systems themselves. For purposes of this paragraph, "systems" include, without limitation, windows, window assemblies, framing, substrate, flashings, and trim, if any.

(3) Windows, patio doors, deck doors, and their systems shall not allow excessive condensation to enter the structure and cause damage to another component. For purposes of this paragraph, "systems" include, without limitation, windows, window assemblies, framing, substrate, flashings, and trim, if any.

(4) Roofs, roofing systems, chimney caps, and ventilation components shall not allow water to enter the structure or to pass beyond, around, or through the designed or actual moisture barriers, including, without limitation, internal barriers located within the systems themselves. For purposes of this paragraph, "systems" include, without limitation, framing, substrate, and sheathing, if any.

(5) Decks, deck systems, balconies, balcony systems, exterior stairs, and stair systems shall not allow water to pass into the adjacent structure. For purposes of this paragraph, "systems" include, without limitation, framing, substrate, flashing, and sheathing, if any.

(6) Decks, deck systems, balconies, balcony systems, exterior stairs, and stair systems shall not allow unintended water to pass within the systems themselves and cause damage to the systems. For purposes

of this paragraph, "systems" include, without limitation, framing, substrate, flashing, and sheathing, if any.

(7) Foundation systems and slabs shall not allow water or vapor to enter into the structure so as to cause damage to another building component.

(8) Foundation systems and slabs shall not allow water or vapor to enter into the structure so as to limit the installation of the type of flooring materials typically used for the particular application.

(9) Hardscape, including paths and patios, irrigation systems, landscaping systems, and drainage systems, that are installed as part of the original construction, shall not be installed in such a way as to cause water or soil erosion to enter into or come in contact with the structure so as to cause damage to another building component.

(10) Stucco, exterior siding, exterior walls, including, without limitation, exterior framing, and other exterior wall finishes and fixtures and the systems of those components and fixtures, including, but not limited to, pot shelves, horizontal surfaces, columns, and plant-ons, shall be installed in such a way so as not to allow unintended water to pass into the structure or to pass beyond, around, or through the designed or actual moisture barriers of the system, including any internal barriers located within the system itself. For purposes of this paragraph, "systems" include, without limitation, framing, substrate, flashings, trim, wall assemblies, and internal wall cavities, if any.

(11) Stucco, exterior siding, and exterior walls shall not allow excessive condensation to enter the structure and cause damage to another component. For purposes of this paragraph, "systems" include, without limitation, framing, substrate, flashings, trim, wall assemblies, and internal wall cavities, if any.

(12) Retaining and site walls and their associated drainage systems shall not allow unintended water to pass beyond, around, or through its designed or actual moisture barriers including, without limitation, any internal barriers, so as to cause damage. This standard does not apply to those portions of any wall or drainage system that are designed to have water flow beyond, around, or through them.

(13) Retaining walls and site walls, and their associated drainage systems, shall only allow water to flow beyond, around, or through the areas designated by design.

(14) The lines and components of the plumbing system, sewer system, and utility systems shall not leak.

(15) Plumbing lines, sewer lines, and utility lines shall not corrode so as to impede the useful life of the systems.

(16) Sewer systems shall be installed in such a way as to allow the designated amount of sewage to flow through the system.

(17) Showers, baths, and related waterproofing systems shall not leak water into the interior of walls, flooring systems, or the interior of other components.

(18) The waterproofing system behind or under ceramic tile and tile countertops shall not allow water into the interior of walls, flooring systems, or other components so as to cause damage. Ceramic tile systems shall be designed and installed so as to deflect intended water to the waterproofing system.

(b) With respect to structural issues:

(1) Foundations, load bearing components, and slabs, shall not contain significant cracks or significant vertical displacement.

(2) Foundations, load bearing components, and slabs shall not cause the structure, in whole or in part, to be structurally unsafe.

(3) Foundations, load bearing components, and slabs, and underlying soils shall be constructed so as to materially comply with the design criteria set by applicable government building codes, regulations, and ordinances for chemical deterioration or corrosion resistance in effect at the time of original construction.

(4) A structure shall be constructed so as to materially comply with the design criteria for earthquake and wind load resistance, as set forth in the applicable government building codes, regulations, and ordinances in effect at the time of original construction.

(c) With respect to soil issues:

(1) Soils and engineered retaining walls shall not cause, in whole or in part, damage to the structure built upon the soil or engineered retaining wall.

(2) Soils and engineered retaining walls shall not cause, in whole or in part, the structure to be structurally unsafe.

(3) Soils shall not cause, in whole or in part, the land upon which no structure is built to become unusable for the purpose represented at the time of original sale by the builder or for the purpose for which that land is commonly used.

(d) With respect to fire protection issues:

(1) A structure shall be constructed so as to materially comply with the design criteria of the applicable government building codes, regulations, and ordinances for fire protection of the occupants in effect at the time of the original construction.

(2) Fireplaces, chimneys, chimney structures, and chimney termination caps shall be constructed and installed in such a way so as not to cause an unreasonable risk of fire outside the fireplace enclosure or chimney.

(3) Electrical and mechanical systems shall be constructed and installed in such a way so as not to cause an unreasonable risk of fire.

(e) With respect to plumbing and sewer issues:

Plumbing and sewer systems shall be installed to operate properly and shall not materially impair the use of the structure by its inhabitants. However, no action may be brought for a violation of this subdivision more than four years after close of escrow.

(f) With respect to electrical system issues:

Electrical systems shall operate properly and shall not materially impair the use of the structure by its inhabitants. However, no action shall be brought pursuant to this subdivision more than four years from close of escrow.

(g) With respect to issues regarding other areas of construction:

(1) Exterior pathways, driveways, hardscape, sidewalls, sidewalks, and patios installed by the original builder shall not contain cracks that display significant vertical displacement or that are excessive. However, no action shall be brought upon a violation of this paragraph more than four years from close of escrow.

(2) Stucco, exterior siding, and other exterior wall finishes and fixtures, including, but not limited to, pot shelves, horizontal surfaces, columns, and plant-ons, shall not contain significant cracks or separations.

(3)(A) To the extent not otherwise covered by these standards, manufactured products, including, but not limited to, windows, doors, roofs, plumbing products and fixtures, fireplaces, electrical fixtures, HVAC units, countertops, cabinets, paint, and appliances shall be installed so as not to interfere with the products' useful life, if any.

(B) For purposes of this paragraph, "useful life" means a representation of how long a product is warranted or represented, through its limited warranty or any written representations, to last by its manufacturer, including recommended or required maintenance. If there is no representation by a manufacturer, a builder shall install manufactured products so as not to interfere with the product's utility.

(C) For purposes of this paragraph, "manufactured product" means a product that is completely manufactured offsite.

(D) If no useful life representation is made, or if the representation is less than one year, the period shall be no less than one year. If a manufactured product is damaged as a result of a violation of these standards, damage to the product is a recoverable element of damages. This subparagraph does not limit recovery if there has been damage to another building component caused by a manufactured product during the manufactured product's useful life.

(E) This title does not apply in any action seeking recovery solely for a defect in a manufactured product located within or adjacent to a structure.

(4) Heating, if any, shall be installed so as to be capable of maintaining a room temperature of 70 degrees Fahrenheit at a point three feet above the floor in any living space.

(5) Living space air-conditioning, if any, shall be provided in a manner consistent with the size and efficiency design criteria specified in Title 24 of the California Code of Regulations or its successor.

(6) Attached structures shall be constructed to comply with interunit noise transmission standards set by the applicable government building codes, ordinances, or regulations in effect at the time of the

original construction. If there is no applicable code, ordinance, or regulation, this paragraph does not apply. However, no action shall be brought pursuant to this paragraph more than one year from the original occupancy of the adjacent unit.

(7) Irrigation systems and drainage shall operate properly so as not to damage landscaping or other external improvements. However, no action shall be brought pursuant to this paragraph more than one year from close of escrow.

(8) Untreated wood posts shall not be installed in contact with soil so as to cause unreasonable decay to the wood based upon the finish grade at the time of original construction. However, no action shall be brought pursuant to this paragraph more than two years from close of escrow.

(9) Untreated steel fences and adjacent components shall be installed so as to prevent unreasonable corrosion. However, no action shall be brought pursuant to this paragraph more than four years from close of escrow.

(10) Paint and stains shall be applied in such a manner so as not to cause deterioration of the building surfaces for the length of time specified by the paint or stain manufacturers' representations, if any. However, no action shall be brought pursuant to this paragraph more than five years from close of escrow.

(11) Roofing materials shall be installed so as to avoid materials falling from the roof.

(12) The landscaping systems shall be installed in such a manner so as to survive for not less than one year. However, no action shall be brought pursuant to this paragraph more than two years from close of escrow.

(13) Ceramic tile and tile backing shall be installed in such a manner that the tile does not detach.

(14) Dryer ducts shall be installed and terminated pursuant to manufacturer installation requirements. However, no action shall be brought pursuant to this paragraph more than two years from close of escrow.

(15) Structures shall be constructed in such a manner so as not to impair the occupants' safety because they contain public health hazards as determined by a duly authorized public health official, health agency, or governmental entity having jurisdiction. This paragraph does not limit recovery for any damages caused by a violation of any other paragraph of this section on the grounds that the damages do not constitute a health hazard.

Added Stats 2002 ch 722 § 3 (SB 800). Amended Stats 2003 ch 762 § 1 (AB 903); Stats 2006 ch 567 § 2 (AB 2303), effective January 1, 2007.

§ 897. Intent of standards

The standards set forth in this chapter are intended to address every function or component of a structure. To the extent that a function or component of a structure is not addressed by these standards, it shall be actionable if it causes damage.

Added Stats 2002 ch 722 § 3 (SB 800).

Chapter 3

Obligations

§ 900. Warranty covering fit and finish items

As to fit and finish items, a builder shall provide a homebuyer with a minimum one–year express written limited warranty covering the fit and finish of the following building components. Except as otherwise provided by the standards specified in Chapter 2 (commencing with Section 896), this warranty shall cover the fit and finish of cabinets, mirrors, flooring, interior and exterior walls, countertops, paint finishes, and trim, but shall not apply to damage to those components caused by defects in other components governed by the other provisions of this title. Any fit and finish matters covered by this warranty are not subject to the provisions of this title. If a builder fails to provide the express warranty required by this section, the warranty for these items shall be for a period of one year.

Added Stats 2002 ch 722 § 3 (SB 800).

§ 901. Enhanced protection agreement

A builder may, but is not required to, offer greater protection or protection for longer time periods in its express contract with the homeowner than that set forth in Chapter 2 (commencing with Section 896). A builder may not limit the application of Chapter 2 (commencing with Section 896) or lower its protection through the express contract with the homeowner. This type of express contract constitutes an "enhanced protection agreement."

Added Stats 2002 ch 722 § 3 (SB 800).

§ 902. Effect of enhanced protection agreement

If a builder offers an enhanced protection agreement, the builder may choose to be subject to its own express contractual provisions in place of the provisions set forth in Chapter 2 (commencing with Section 896). If an enhanced protection agreement is in place, Chapter 2 (commencing with Section 896) no longer applies other than to set forth minimum provisions by which to judge the enforceability of the particular provisions of the enhanced protection agreement.

Added Stats 2002 ch 722 § 3 (SB 800).

§ 903. Written copy of enhanced protection agreement

If a builder offers an enhanced protection agreement in place of the provisions set forth in Chapter 2 (commencing with Section 896), the election to do so shall be made in writing with the homeowner no later than the close of escrow. The builder shall provide the homeowner with a complete copy of Chapter 2 (commencing with Section 896) and advise the homeowner that the builder has elected not to be subject to its provisions. If any provision of an enhanced protection agreement is later found to be unenforceable as not meeting the minimum standards of Chapter 2 (commencing with Section 896), a builder may use this chapter in lieu of those provisions found to be unenforceable.

Added Stats 2002 ch 722 § 3 (SB 800).

§ 904. Enforcement of construction standards in lieu of particular enhanced protection agreement provision

If a builder has elected to use an enhanced protection agreement, and a homeowner disputes that the particular provision or time periods of the enhanced protection agreement are not greater than, or equal to, the provisions of Chapter 2 (commencing with Section 896) as they apply to the particular deficiency alleged by the homeowner, the homeowner may seek to enforce the application of the standards set forth in this chapter as to those claimed deficiencies. If a homeowner seeks to enforce a particular standard in lieu of a provision of the enhanced protection agreement, the homeowner shall give the builder written notice of that intent at the time the homeowner files a notice of claim pursuant to Chapter 4 (commencing with Section 910).

Added Stats 2002 ch 722 § 3 (SB 800).

§ 905. Responsive pleading in action to enforce construction standards of this chapter in lieu of enhanced protection agreement

If a homeowner seeks to enforce Chapter 2 (commencing with Section 896), in lieu of the enhanced protection agreement in a subsequent litigation or other legal action, the builder shall have the right to have the matter bifurcated, and to have an immediately binding determination of his or her responsive pleading within 60 days after the filing of that pleading, but in no event after the commencement of discovery, as to the application of either Chapter 2 (commencing with Section 896) or the enhanced protection agreement as to the deficiencies claimed by the homeowner. If the builder fails to seek that determination in the timeframe specified, the builder waives the right to do so and the standards set forth in this title shall apply. As to any nonoriginal homeowner, that homeowner shall be deemed in privity for purposes of an enhanced protection agreement only to the extent that the builder has recorded the enhanced protection agreement on title or provided actual notice to the nonoriginal homeowner of the enhanced protection agreement. If the enhanced protection agreement is not recorded on title or no actual notice has been provided, the standards set forth in this title apply to any nonoriginal homeowners' claims.

Added Stats 2002 ch 722 § 3 (SB 800).

§ 906. Effect of election of enhanced protection agreement on provisions of prelitigation procedures

A builder's election to use an enhanced protection agreement addresses only the issues set forth in Chapter 2 (commencing with Section 896) and does not constitute an election to use or not use the provisions of Chapter 4 (commencing with Section 910). The decision to use or not use Chapter 4 (commencing with Section 910) is governed by the provisions of that chapter.

Added Stats 2002 ch 722 § 3 (SB 800).

§ 907. Obligation of homeowner to follow reasonable maintenance obligations

A homeowner is obligated to follow all reasonable maintenance obligations and schedules communicated in writing to the homeowner by the builder and product manufacturers, as well as commonly accepted maintenance practices. A failure by a homeowner to follow these obligations, schedules, and practices may subject the homeowner to the affirmative defenses contained in Section 944.

Added Stats 2002 ch 722 § 3 (SB 800).

Chapter 4

Prelitigation Procedure

§ 910. Procedures required prior to filing action for violation of construction standards

Prior to filing an action against any party alleged to have contributed to a violation of the standards set forth in Chapter 2 (commencing with Section 896), the claimant shall initiate the following prelitigation procedures:

(a) The claimant or his or her legal representative shall provide written notice via certified mail, overnight mail, or personal delivery to the builder, in the manner prescribed in this section, of the claimant's claim that the construction of his or her residence violates any of the standards set forth in Chapter 2 (commencing with Section 896). That notice shall provide the claimant's name, address, and preferred method of contact, and shall state that the claimant alleges a violation pursuant to this part against the builder, and shall describe the claim in reasonable detail sufficient to determine the nature and location, to the extent known, of the claimed violation. In the case of a group of homeowners or an association, the notice may identify the claimants solely by address or other description sufficient to apprise the builder of the locations of the subject residences. That document shall have the same force and effect as a notice of commencement of a legal proceeding.

(b) The notice requirements of this section do not preclude a homeowner from seeking redress through any applicable normal customer service procedure as set forth in any contractual, warranty, or other builder–generated document; and, if a homeowner seeks to do so, that request shall not satisfy the notice requirements of this section.

Added Stats 2002 ch 722 § 3 (SB 800).

§ 911. "Builder" defined

(a) For purposes of this title, except as provided in subdivision (b), "builder" means any entity or individual, including, but not limited to a builder, developer, general contractor, contractor, or original seller, who, at the time of sale, was also in the business of selling residential units to the public for the property that is the subject of the homeowner's claim or was in the business of building, developing, or constructing residential units for public purchase for the property that is the subject of the homeowner's claim.

(b) For the purposes of this title, "builder" does not include any entity or individual whose involvement with a residential unit that is the subject of the homeowner's claim is limited to his or her capacity as general contractor or contractor and who is not a partner, member of, subsidiary of, or otherwise similarly affiliated with the builder. For purposes of this title, these nonaffiliated general contractors and nonaffiliated contractors shall be treated the same as subcontractors, material suppliers, individual product manufacturers, and design professionals.

Added Stats 2002 ch 722 § 3 (SB 800). Amended Stats 2003 ch 762 § 2 (AB 903).

§ 912. Builder's duties

A builder shall do all of the following:

(a) Within 30 days of a written request by a homeowner or his or her legal representative, the builder shall provide copies of all relevant plans, specifications, mass or rough grading plans, final soils reports, Department of Real Estate public reports, and available engineering calculations, that pertain to a homeowner's residence specifically or as part of a larger development tract. The request shall be honored if it states that it is made relative to structural, fire safety, or soils provisions of this title. However, a builder is not obligated to provide a copying service, and reasonable copying costs shall be borne by the requesting party. A builder may require that the documents be copied onsite by the requesting party, except that the homeowner may, at his or her option, use his or her own copying service, which may include an offsite copy facility that is bonded and insured. If a builder can show that the builder maintained the documents, but that they later became unavailable due to loss or destruction that was not the fault of the builder, the builder may be excused from the requirements of this subdivision, in which case the builder shall act with reasonable diligence to assist the homeowner in obtaining those documents from any applicable government authority or from the source that generated the document. However, in that case, the time limits specified by this section do not apply.

(b) At the expense of the homeowner, who may opt to use an offsite copy facility that is bonded and insured, the builder shall provide to the homeowner or his or her legal representative copies of all maintenance and preventative maintenance recommendations that pertain to his or her residence within 30 days of service of a written request for those documents. Those documents shall also be provided to the homeowner in conjunction with the initial sale of the residence.

(c) At the expense of the homeowner, who may opt to use an offsite copy facility that is bonded and insured, a builder shall provide to the homeowner or his or her legal representative copies of all manufactured products maintenance, preventive maintenance, and limited warranty information within 30 days of a written request for those documents. These documents shall also be provided to the homeowner in conjunction with the initial sale of the residence.

(d) At the expense of the homeowner, who may opt to use an offsite copy facility that is bonded and insured, a builder shall provide to the homeowner or his or her legal representative copies of all of the builder's limited contractual warranties in accordance with this part in effect at the time of the original sale of the residence within 30 days of a written request for those documents. Those documents shall also be provided to the homeowner in conjunction with the initial sale of the residence.

(e) A builder shall maintain the name and address of an agent for notice pursuant to this chapter with the Secretary of State or, alternatively, elect to use a third party for that notice if the builder has

Appendix

notified the homeowner in writing of the third party's name and address, to whom claims and requests for information under this section may be mailed. The name and address of the agent for notice or third party shall be included with the original sales documentation and shall be initialed and acknowledged by the purchaser and the builder's sales representative.

This subdivision applies to instances in which a builder contracts with a third party to accept claims and act on the builder's behalf. A builder shall give actual notice to the homeowner that the builder has made such an election, and shall include the name and address of the third party.

(f) A builder shall record on title a notice of the existence of these procedures and a notice that these procedures impact the legal rights of the homeowner. This information shall also be included with the original sales documentation and shall be initialed and acknowledged by the purchaser and the builder's sales representative.

(g) A builder shall provide, with the original sales documentation, a written copy of this title, which shall be initialed and acknowledged by the purchaser and the builder's sales representative.

(h) As to any documents provided in conjunction with the original sale, the builder shall instruct the original purchaser to provide those documents to any subsequent purchaser.

(i) Any builder who fails to comply with any of these requirements within the time specified is not entitled to the protection of this chapter, and the homeowner is released from the requirements of this chapter and may proceed with the filing of an action, in which case the remaining chapters of this part shall continue to apply to the action.

Added Stats 2002 ch 722 § 3 (SB 800). Amended Stats 2003 ch 762 § 3 (AB 903).

§ 913. Acknowledgement of receipt of notice

A builder or his or her representative shall acknowledge, in writing, receipt of the notice of the claim within 14 days after receipt of the notice of the claim. If the notice of the claim is served by the claimant's legal representative, or if the builder receives a written representation letter from a homeowner's attorney, the builder shall include the attorney in all subsequent substantive communications, including, without limitation, all written communications occurring pursuant to this chapter, and all substantive and procedural communications, including all written communications, following the commencement of any subsequent complaint or other legal action, except that if the builder has retained or involved legal counsel to assist the builder in this process, all communications by the builder's counsel shall only be with the claimant's legal representative, if any.

Added Stats 2002 ch 722 § 3 (SB 800).

§ 914. Nonadversarial procedure established

(a) This chapter establishes a nonadversarial procedure, including the remedies available under this chapter which, if the procedure does not resolve the dispute between the parties, may result in a subsequent action to enforce the other chapters of this title. A builder may attempt to commence nonadversarial contractual provisions other than the nonadversarial procedures and remedies set forth in this chapter, but may not, in addition to its own nonadversarial contractual provisions, require adherence to the nonadversarial procedures and remedies set forth in this chapter, regardless of whether the builder's own alternative nonadversarial contractual provisions are successful in resolving the dispute or ultimately deemed enforceable.

At the time the sales agreement is executed, the builder shall notify the homeowner whether the builder intends to engage in the nonadversarial procedure of this section or attempt to enforce alternative nonadversarial contractual provisions. If the builder elects to use alternative nonadversarial contractual provisions in lieu of this chapter, the election is binding, regardless of whether the builder's alternative nonadversarial contractual provisions are successful in resolving the ultimate dispute or are ultimately deemed enforceable.

(b) Nothing in this title is intended to affect existing statutory or decisional law pertaining to the applicability, viability, or enforceability of alternative dispute resolution methods, alternative remedies, or contractual arbitration, judicial reference, or similar procedures requiring a binding resolution to enforce the other chapters of this title or any other disputes between homeowners and builders. Nothing in this title is intended to affect the applicability, viability, or enforceability, if any, of contractual arbitration or judicial reference after a nonadversarial procedure or provision has been completed.

Added Stats 2002 ch 722 § 3 (SB 800).

§ 915. Actions resulting in nonapplication of chapter

If a builder fails to acknowledge receipt of the notice of a claim within the time specified, elects not to go through the process set forth in this chapter, or fails to request an inspection within the time specified, or at the conclusion or cessation of an alternative nonadversarial proceeding, this chapter does not apply and the homeowner is released from the requirements of this chapter and may proceed with the filing of an action. However, the standards set forth in the other chapters of this title shall continue to apply to the action.

Added Stats 2002 ch 722 § 3 (SB 800).

Appendix

§ 916. Inspection of claimed unmet standards by builder

(a) If a builder elects to inspect the claimed unmet standards, the builder shall complete the initial inspection and testing within 14 days after acknowledgment of receipt of the notice of the claim, at a mutually convenient date and time. If the homeowner has retained legal representation, the inspection shall be scheduled with the legal representative's office at a mutually convenient date and time, unless the legal representative is unavailable during the relevant time periods. All costs of builder inspection and testing, including any damage caused by the builder inspection, shall be borne by the builder. The builder shall also provide written proof that the builder has liability insurance to cover any damages or injuries occurring during inspection and testing. The builder shall restore the property to its pretesting condition within 48 hours of the testing. The builder shall, upon request, allow the inspections to be observed and electronically recorded, video recorded, or photographed by the claimant or his or her legal representative.

(b) Nothing that occurs during a builder's or claimant's inspection or testing may be used or introduced as evidence to support a spoliation defense by any potential party in any subsequent litigation.

(c) If a builder deems a second inspection or testing reasonably necessary, and specifies the reasons therefor in writing within three days following the initial inspection, the builder may conduct a second inspection or testing. A second inspection or testing shall be completed within 40 days of the initial inspection or testing. All requirements concerning the initial inspection or testing shall also apply to the second inspection or testing.

(d) If the builder fails to inspect or test the property within the time specified, the claimant is released from the requirements of this section and may proceed with the filing of an action. However, the standards set forth in the other chapters of this title shall continue to apply to the action.

(e) If a builder intends to hold a subcontractor, design professional, individual product manufacturer, or material supplier, including an insurance carrier, warranty company, or service company, responsible for its contribution to the unmet standard, the builder shall provide notice to that person or entity sufficiently in advance to allow them to attend the initial, or if requested, second inspection of any alleged unmet standard and to participate in the repair process. The claimant and his or her legal representative, if any, shall be advised in a reasonable time prior to the inspection as to the identity of all persons or entities invited to attend. This subdivision does not apply to the builder's insurance company. Except with respect to any claims involving a repair actually conducted under this chapter, nothing in this subdivision shall be construed to relieve a subcontractor, design professional, individual product manufacturer, or material supplier of any liability under an action brought by a claimant.

Added Stats 2002 ch 722 § 3 (SB 800). Amended Stats 2003 ch 762 § 4 (AB 903); Stats. 2009, Ch. 140 (AB 176).

§ 917. Offer to repair

Within 30 days of the initial or, if requested, second inspection or testing, the builder may offer in writing to repair the violation. The offer to repair shall also compensate the homeowner for all applicable damages recoverable under Section 944, within the timeframe for the repair set forth in this chapter. Any such offer shall be accompanied by a detailed, specific, step–by–step statement identifying the particular violation that is being repaired, explaining the nature, scope, and location of the repair, and setting a reasonable completion date for the repair. The offer shall also include the names, addresses, telephone numbers, and license numbers of the contractors whom the builder intends to have perform the repair. Those contractors shall be fully insured for, and shall be responsible for, all damages or injuries that they may cause to occur during the repair, and evidence of that insurance shall be provided to the homeowner upon request. Upon written request by the homeowner or his or her legal representative, and within the timeframes set forth in this chapter, the builder shall also provide any available technical documentation, including, without limitation, plans and specifications, pertaining to the claimed violation within the particular home or development tract. The offer shall also advise the homeowner in writing of his or her right to request up to three additional contractors from which to select to do the repair pursuant to this chapter.

Added Stats 2002 ch 722 § 3 (SB 800).

§ 918. Authorization to proceed with repair

Upon receipt of the offer to repair, the homeowner shall have 30 days to authorize the builder to proceed with the repair. The homeowner may alternatively request, at the homeowner's sole option and discretion, that the builder provide the names, addresses, telephone numbers, and license numbers for up to three alternative contractors who are not owned or financially controlled by the builder and who regularly conduct business in the county where the structure is located. If the homeowner so elects, the builder is entitled to an additional noninvasive inspection, to occur at a mutually convenient date and time within 20 days of the election, so as to permit the other proposed contractors to review the proposed site of the repair. Within 35 days after the request of the homeowner for alternative contractors, the builder shall present the homeowner with a choice of contractors. Within 20 days after that presentation, the homeowner shall authorize the builder or one of the alternative contractors to perform the repair.

Added Stats 2002 ch 722 § 3 (SB 800).

§ 919. Offer to mediate dispute

The offer to repair shall also be accompanied by an offer to mediate the dispute if the homeowner so chooses. The mediation shall be limited to a four–hour mediation, except as otherwise mutually agreed before a nonaffiliated mediator selected and paid for by the builder. At the homeowner's sole option, the homeowner may agree to split the cost of the mediator, and if he or she does so, the mediator shall be selected jointly. The mediator shall have sufficient availability such that the mediation occurs within 15 days after the request to mediate is received and occurs at a mutually convenient location within the county where the action is pending. If a builder has made an offer to repair a violation, and the mediation has failed to resolve the dispute, the homeowner shall allow the repair to be performed either by the builder, its contractor, or the selected contractor.

Added Stats 2002 ch 722 § 3 (SB 800).

§ 920. Actions resulting in filing of an action by homeowner; Applicable standards

If the builder fails to make an offer to repair or otherwise strictly comply with this chapter within the times specified, the claimant is released from the requirements of this chapter and may proceed with the filing of an action. If the contractor performing the repair does not complete the repair in the time or manner specified, the claimant may file an action. If this occurs, the standards set forth in the other chapters of this part shall continue to apply to the action.

Added Stats 2002 ch 722 § 3 (SB 800).

§ 921. Procedure when resolution involves repair by builder

(a) In the event that a resolution under this chapter involves a repair by the builder, the builder shall make an appointment with the claimant, make all appropriate arrangements to effectuate a repair of the claimed unmet standards, and compensate the homeowner for all damages resulting therefrom free of charge to the claimant. The repair shall be scheduled through the claimant's legal representative, if any, unless he or she is unavailable during the relevant time periods. The repair shall be commenced on a mutually convenient date within 14 days of acceptance or, if an alternative contractor is selected by the homeowner, within 14 days of the selection, or, if a mediation occurs, within seven days of the mediation, or within five days after a permit is obtained if one is required. The builder shall act with reasonable diligence in obtaining any such permit.

(b) The builder shall ensure that work done on the repairs is done with the utmost diligence, and that the repairs are completed as soon as reasonably possible, subject to the nature of the repair or some unforeseen event not caused by the builder or the contractor performing the repair. Every effort shall be made to complete the repair within 120 days.

Added Stats 2002 ch 722 § 3 (SB 800).

§ 922. Observation and electronic recording, videotaping, or photographing of repair allowed

The builder shall, upon request, allow the repair to be observed and electronically recorded, video recorded, or photographed by the claimant or his or her legal representative. Nothing that occurs during the repair process may be used or introduced as evidence to support a spoliation defense by any potential party in any subsequent litigation.

Added Stats 2002 ch 722 § 3 (SB 800). Amended Stats. 2009, Ch. 88 (AB 176).

§ 923. Availability to homeowner of correspondence, photographs and other material pertaining to repairs

The builder shall provide the homeowner or his or her legal representative, upon request, with copies of all correspondence, photographs, and other materials pertaining or relating in any manner to the repairs.

Added Stats 2002 ch 722 § 3 (SB 800).

§ 924. Offer to repair some, but not all, of claimed unmet standards

If the builder elects to repair some, but not all of, the claimed unmet standards, the builder shall, at the same time it makes its offer, set forth with particularity in writing the reasons, and the support for those reasons, for not repairing all claimed unmet standards.

Added Stats 2002 ch 722 § 3 (SB 800).

§ 925. Failure to timely complete repairs

If the builder fails to complete the repair within the time specified in the repair plan, the claimant is released from the requirements of this chapter and may proceed with the filing of an action. If this occurs, the standards set forth in the other chapters of this title shall continue to apply to the action.

Added Stats 2002 ch 722 § 3 (SB 800).

Appendix

§ 926. Release or waiver in exchange for repair work prohibited

The builder may not obtain a release or waiver of any kind in exchange for the repair work mandated by this chapter. At the conclusion of the repair, the claimant may proceed with filing an action for violation of the applicable standard or for a claim of inadequate repair, or both, including all applicable damages available under Section 944.

Added Stats 2002 ch 722 § 3 (SB 800).

§ 927. Statute of limitations

If the applicable statute of limitations has otherwise run during this process, the time period for filing a complaint or other legal remedies for violation of any provision of this title, or for a claim of inadequate repair, is extended from the time of the original claim by the claimant to 100 days after the repair is completed, whether or not the particular violation is the one being repaired. If the builder fails to acknowledge the claim within the time specified, elects not to go through this statutory process, or fails to request an inspection within the time specified, the time period for filing a complaint or other legal remedies for violation of any provision of this title is extended from the time of the original claim by the claimant to 45 days after the time for responding to the notice of claim has expired. If the builder elects to attempt to enforce its own nonadversarial procedure in lieu of the procedure set forth in this chapter, the time period for filing a complaint or other legal remedies for violation of any provision of this part is extended from the time of the original claim by the claimant to 100 days after either the completion of the builder's alternative nonadversarial procedure, or 100 days after the builder's alternative nonadversarial procedure is deemed unenforceable, whichever is later.

Added Stats 2002 ch 722 § 3 (SB 800).

§ 928. Mediation procedure

If the builder has invoked this chapter and completed a repair, prior to filing an action, if there has been no previous mediation between the parties, the homeowner or his or her legal representative shall request mediation in writing. The mediation shall be limited to four hours, except as otherwise mutually agreed before a nonaffiliated mediator selected and paid for by the builder. At the homeowner's sole option, the homeowner may agree to split the cost of the mediator and if he or she does so, the mediator shall be selected jointly. The mediator shall have sufficient availability such that the mediation will occur within 15 days after the request for mediation is received and shall occur at a mutually convenient location within the county where the action is pending. In the event that a mediation is used at this point, any applicable statutes of limitations shall be tolled from the date of the request to mediate until the next court day after the mediation is completed, or the 100–day period, whichever is later.

Added Stats 2002 ch 722 § 3 (SB 800).

§ 929.   Cash offer in lieu of repair

(a) Nothing in this chapter prohibits the builder from making only a cash offer and no repair. In this situation, the homeowner is free to accept the offer, or he or she may reject the offer and proceed with the filing of an action. If the latter occurs, the standards of the other chapters of this title shall continue to apply to the action.

(b) The builder may obtain a reasonable release in exchange for the cash payment. The builder may negotiate the terms and conditions of any reasonable release in terms of scope and consideration in conjunction with a cash payment under this chapter.

Added Stats 2002 ch 722 § 3 (SB 800).

§ 930.   Strict construction of requirements; Failure of claimant to conform

(a) The time periods and all other requirements in this chapter are to be strictly construed, and, unless extended by the mutual agreement of the parties in accordance with this chapter, shall govern the rights and obligations under this title. If a builder fails to act in accordance with this section within the timeframes mandated, unless extended by the mutual agreement of the parties as evidenced by a postclaim written confirmation by the affected homeowner demonstrating that he or she has knowingly and voluntarily extended the statutory timeframe, the claimant may proceed with filing an action. If this occurs, the standards of the other chapters of this title shall continue to apply to the action.

(b) If the claimant does not conform with the requirements of this chapter, the builder may bring a motion to stay any subsequent court action or other proceeding until the requirements of this chapter have been satisfied. The court, in its discretion, may award the prevailing party on such a motion, his or her attorney's fees and costs in bringing or opposing the motion.

Added Stats 2002 ch 722 § 3 (SB 800).

§ 931.   Claim combined with other causes of action

If a claim combines causes of action or damages not covered by this part, including, without limitation, personal injuries, class actions, other statutory remedies, or fraud–based claims, the claimed unmet standards shall be administered according to this part, although evidence of the property in its unrepaired condition may be introduced to support the respective elements of any such cause of action. As to any fraud–based claim, if the fact that the property has been repaired under this chapter is deemed admissible, the trier of fact shall be informed that the repair was not voluntarily accepted by the homeowner. As to any class action claims that address solely the incorporation of a defective component into a residence, the named and unnamed class members need not comply with this chapter.

Added Stats 2002 ch 722 § 3 (SB 800).

§ 932. Subsequent discovered claims of unmet standards

Subsequently discovered claims of unmet standards shall be administered separately under this chapter, unless otherwise agreed to by the parties. However, in the case of a detached single family residence, in the same home, if the subsequently discovered claim is for a violation of the same standard as that which has already been initiated by the same claimant and the subject of a currently pending action, the claimant need not reinitiate the process as to the same standard. In the case of an attached project, if the subsequently discovered claim is for a violation of the same standard for a connected component system in the same building as has already been initiated by the same claimant, and the subject of a currently pending action, the claimant need not reinitiate this process as to that standard.

Added Stats 2002 ch 722 § 3 (SB 800).

§ 933. Evidence of repair work

If any enforcement of these standards is commenced, the fact that a repair effort was made may be introduced to the trier of fact. However, the claimant may use the condition of the property prior to the repair as the basis for contending that the repair work was inappropriate, inadequate, or incomplete, or that the violation still exists. The claimant need not show that the repair work resulted in further damage nor that damage has continued to occur as a result of the violation.

Added Stats 2002 ch 722 § 3 (SB 800).

§ 934. Evidence of parties' conduct

Evidence of both parties' conduct during this process may be introduced during a subsequent enforcement action, if any, with the exception of any mediation. Any repair efforts undertaken by the builder, shall not be considered settlement communications or offers of settlement and are not inadmissible in evidence on such a basis.

Added Stats 2002 ch 722 § 3 (SB 800).

§ 935. Similar requirements of Civil Code § 1375

To the extent that provisions of this chapter are enforced and those provisions are substantially similar to provisions in Section 1375 of the Civil Code, but an action is subsequently commenced under Section 1375 of the Civil Code, the parties are excused from performing the substantially similar requirements under Section 1375 of the Civil Code.

Added Stats 2002 ch 722 § 3 (SB 800).

§ 936. Applicability of title to other entities involved in construction process

Each and every provision of the other chapters of this title apply to general contractors, subcontractors, material suppliers, individual product manufacturers, and design professionals to the extent that the general contractors, subcontractors, material suppliers, individual product manufacturers, and design professionals caused, in whole or in part, a violation of a particular standard as the result of a negligent act or omission or a breach of contract. In addition to the affirmative defenses set forth in Section 945.5, a general contractor, subcontractor, material supplier, design professional, individual product manufacturer, or other entity may also offer common law and contractual defenses as applicable to any claimed violation of a standard. All actions by a claimant or builder to enforce an express contract, or any provision thereof, against a general contractor, subcontractor, material supplier, individual product manufacturer, or design professional is preserved. Nothing in this title modifies the law pertaining to joint and several liability for builders, general contractors, subcontractors, material suppliers, individual product manufacturer, and design professionals that contribute to any specific violation of this title. However, the negligence standard in this section does not apply to any general contractor, subcontractor, material supplier, individual product manufacturer, or design professional with respect to claims for which strict liability would apply.

Added Stats 2002 ch 722 § 3 (SB 800). Amended Stats 2003 ch 762 § 5 (AB 903).

§ 937. Claims and damages not covered by this title

Nothing in this title shall be interpreted to eliminate or abrogate the requirement to comply with Section 411.35 of the Code of Civil Procedure or to affect the liability of design professionals, including architects and architectural firms, for claims and damages not covered by this title.

Added Stats 2002 ch 722 § 3 (SB 800).

Appendix

§ 938. Date of sale for applicability of title

This title applies only to new residential units where the purchase agreement with the buyer was signed by the seller on or after January 1, 2003.

Added Stats 2002 ch 722 § 3 (SB 800). Amended Stats 2003 ch 762 § 6 (AB 903).

Chapter 5

Procedure

§ 941. Time limit for bringing action

(a) Except as specifically set forth in this title, no action may be brought to recover under this title more than 10 years after substantial completion of the improvement but not later than the date of recordation of a valid notice of completion.

(b) As used in this section, "action" includes an action for indemnity brought against a person arising out of that person's performance or furnishing of services or materials referred to in this title, except that a cross–complaint for indemnity may be filed pursuant to subdivision (b) of Section 428.10 of the Code of Civil Procedure in an action which has been brought within the time period set forth in subdivision (a).

(c) The limitation prescribed by this section may not be asserted by way of defense by any person in actual possession or the control, as owner, tenant or otherwise, of such an improvement, at the time any deficiency in the improvement constitutes the proximate cause for which it is proposed to make a claim or bring an action.

(d) Sections 337.15 and 337.1 of the Code of Civil Procedure do not apply to actions under this title.

(e) Existing statutory and decisional law regarding tolling of the statute of limitations shall apply to the time periods for filing an action or making a claim under this title, except that repairs made pursuant to Chapter 4 (commencing with Section 910), with the exception of the tolling provision contained in Section 927, do not extend the period for filing an action, or restart the time limitations contained in subdivision (a) or (b) of Section 7091 of the Business and Professions Code. If a builder arranges for a contractor to perform a repair pursuant to Chapter 4 (commencing with Section 910), as to the builder the time period for calculating the statute of limitation in subdivision (a) or (b) of Section 7091 of the Business and Professions Code shall pertain to the substantial completion of the original construction and not to the date of repairs under this title. The time limitations established by this title do not apply to any action by a claimant for a contract or express contractual provision. Causes of action and damages to which this chapter does not apply are not limited by this section.

Added Stats 2002 ch 722 § 3 (SB 800). Amended Stats 2003 ch 62 § 12 (SB 600), ch 762 § 7 (AB 903) (ch 762 prevails).

§ 942. Showing required for claim

In order to make a claim for violation of the standards set forth in Chapter 2 (commencing with Section 896), a homeowner need only demonstrate, in accordance with the applicable evidentiary standard, that the home does not meet the applicable standard, subject to the affirmative defenses set forth in Section 945.5. No further showing of causation or damages is required to meet the burden of proof regarding a violation of a standard set forth in Chapter 2 (commencing with Section 896), provided that the violation arises out of, pertains to, or is related to, the original construction.

Added Stats 2003 ch 762 § 9 (AB 903).

§ 943. Other causes of action; Claims involving detached single–family home

(a) Except as provided in this title, no other cause of action for a claim covered by this title or for damages recoverable under Section 944 is allowed. In addition to the rights under this title, this title does not apply to any action by a claimant to enforce a contract or express contractual provision, or any action for fraud, personal injury, or violation of a statute. Damages awarded for the items set forth in Section 944 in such other cause of action shall be reduced by the amounts recovered pursuant to Section 944 for violation of the standards set forth in this title.

(b) As to any claims involving a detached single–family home, the homeowner's right to the reasonable value of repairing any nonconformity is limited to the repair costs, or the diminution in current value of the home caused by the nonconformity, whichever is less, subject to the personal use exception as developed under common law.

Added Stats 2002 ch 722 § 3 (SB 800), as CC § 942. Renumbered by Stats 2003 ch 762 § 8 (AB 903).

§ 944. Damages

If a claim for damages is made under this title, the homeowner is only entitled to damages for the reasonable value of repairing any violation of the standards set forth in this title, the reasonable cost of repairing any damages caused by the repair efforts, the reasonable cost of repairing and rectifying any damages resulting from the failure of the home to meet the standards, the reasonable cost of removing and replacing any improper repair by the builder, reasonable relocation and storage expenses, lost business income if the home was used as a principal place of a business licensed to be operated from the home, reasonable investigative costs for each established violation, and all other costs or fees recoverable by contract or statute.

Added Stats 2002 ch 722 § 3 (SB 800).

Appendix

§ 945. Original purchasers and successors–in–interest

The provisions, standards, rights, and obligations set forth in this title are binding upon all original purchasers and their successors-in-interest. For purposes of this title, associations and others having the rights set forth in Sections 1368.3 and 1368.4 shall be considered to be original purchasers and shall have standing to enforce the provisions, standards, rights, and obligations set forth in this title.

Added Stats 2002 ch 722 § 3 (SB 800). Amended Stats 2005 ch 37 § 1 (SB 853), effective January 1, 2006.

§ 945.5. Affirmative defenses

A builder, general contractor, subcontractor, material supplier, individual product manufacturer, or design professional, under the principles of comparative fault pertaining to affirmative defenses, may be excused, in whole or in part, from any obligation, damage, loss, or liability if the builder, general contractor, subcontractor, material supplier, individual product manufacturer, or design professional, can demonstrate any of the following affirmative defenses in response to a claimed violation:

(a) To the extent it is caused by an unforeseen act of nature which caused the structure not to meet the standard. For purposes of this section an "unforeseen act of nature" means a weather condition, earthquake, or manmade event such as war, terrorism, or vandalism, in excess of the design criteria expressed by the applicable building codes, regulations, and ordinances in effect at the time of original construction.

(b) To the extent it is caused by a homeowner's unreasonable failure to minimize or prevent those damages in a timely manner, including the failure of the homeowner to allow reasonable and timely access for inspections and repairs under this title. This includes the failure to give timely notice to the builder after discovery of a violation, but does not include damages due to the untimely or inadequate response of a builder to the homeowner's claim.

(c) To the extent it is caused by the homeowner or his or her agent, employee, general contractor, subcontractor, independent contractor, or consultant by virtue of their failure to follow the builder's or manufacturer's recommendations, or commonly accepted homeowner maintenance obligations. In order to rely upon this defense as it relates to a builder's recommended maintenance schedule, the builder shall show that the homeowner had written notice of these schedules and recommendations and that the recommendations and schedules were reasonable at the time they were issued.

(d) To the extent it is caused by the homeowner or his or her agent's or an independent third party's alterations, ordinary wear and tear, misuse, abuse, or neglect, or by the structure's use for something other than its intended purpose.

(e) To the extent that the time period for filing actions bars the claimed violation.

(f) As to a particular violation for which the builder has obtained a valid release.

(g) To the extent that the builder's repair was successful in correcting the particular violation of the applicable standard.

(h) As to any causes of action to which this statute does not apply, all applicable affirmative defenses are preserved.

Added Stats 2002 ch 722 § 3 (SB 800). Amended Stats 2003 ch 762 § 10 (AB 903).

TITLE 8
Reconstruction of Homes Lost in Cedar Fire, October 2003

§ 945.6. [Section repealed 2008.]

Added Stats 2005 ch 40 § 2 (AB 662), effective July 11, 2005, repealed January 1, 2008. Repealed, operative January 1, 2008, by its own terms.

DIVISION 3
OBLIGATIONS

PART 2
CONTRACTS

TITLE 5
Extinction of Contracts

Chapter 2
Rescission

§ 1689.5. Definitions

As used in Sections 1689.6 to 1689.11, inclusive, and in Section 1689.14:

(a) "Home solicitation contract or offer" means any contract, whether single or multiple, or any offer which is subject to approval, for the sale, lease, or rental of goods or services or both, made at other than appropriate trade premises in an amount of twenty-five dollars ($25) or more, including any interest or service charges. "Home solicitation contract" does not include any contract under which the buyer has the right to rescind pursuant to Title 1, Chapter 2, Section 125 of the Federal Consumer Credit Protection Act (P.L. 90-321) and the regulations promulgated pursuant thereto.

(b) "Appropriate trade premises," means premises where either the owner or seller normally carries on a business, or where goods are normally offered or exposed for sale in the course of a business carried on at those premises.

(c) "Goods" means tangible chattels bought for use primarily for personal, family, or household purposes, including certificates or coupons exchangeable for these goods, and including goods that, at the time of the sale or subsequently, are to be so affixed to real property as to become a part of the real property whether or not severable therefrom, but does not include any vehicle required to be registered under the Vehicle Code, nor any goods sold with this vehicle if sold under a contract governed by Section 2982, and does not include any mobilehome, as defined in Section 18008 of the Health and Safety Code, nor any goods sold with this mobilehome if either are sold under a contract subject to Section 18036.5 of the Health and Safety Code.

(d) "Services" means work, labor and services, including, but not limited to, services furnished in connection with the repair, restoration, alteration, or improvement of residential premises, or services furnished in connection with the sale or repair of goods as defined in Section 1802.1, and courses of instruction, regardless of the purpose for which they are taken, but does not include the services of attorneys, real estate brokers and salesmen, securities dealers or investment counselors, physicians, optometrists, or dentists, nor financial services offered by banks, savings institutions, credit unions, industrial loan companies, personal property brokers, consumer finance lenders, or commercial finance lenders, organized pursuant to state or federal law, that are not connected with the sale of goods or services, as defined herein, nor the sale of insurance that is not connected with the sale of goods or services as defined herein, nor services in connection with the sale or installation of mobilehomes or of goods sold with a mobilehome if either are sold or installed under a contract subject to Section 18036.5 of the Health and Safety Code, nor services for which the tariffs, rates, charges, costs, or expenses, including in each instance the time sale price, is required by law to be filed with and approved by the federal government or any official, department, division, commission, or agency of the United States or of the state.

(e) "Business day" means any calendar day except Sunday, or the following business holidays: New Year's Day, Washington's Birthday, Memorial Day, Independence Day, Labor Day, Columbus Day, Veterans' Day, Thanksgiving Day, and Christmas Day.

(f) This section shall become operative on January 1, 2006.

Added Stats 2005 ch 48 § 23 (SB 1113), effective July 18, 2005, operative January 1, 2006.

§ 1689.6. Right to cancel home solicitation contract or offer

(a)(1) Except for a contract written pursuant to Section 7151.2 or 7159.10 of the Business and Professions Code, in addition to any other right to revoke an offer, the buyer has the right to cancel a home solicitation contract or offer until midnight of the third business day after the day on which the buyer signs an agreement or offer to purchase which complies with Section 1689.7.

(2) In addition to any other right to revoke an offer, the buyer has the right to cancel a home solicitation contract written pursuant to Section 7151.2 of the Business and Professions Code until midnight of the third business day after the buyer receives a signed and dated copy of the contract or offer to purchase that complies with Section 1689.7 of this code.

(3)(A) In addition to any other right to revoke an offer, the buyer has the right to cancel a home solicitation contract or offer to purchase written pursuant to Section 7159.10 of the Business and Professions Code, until the buyer receives a signed and dated copy of a service and repair contract that complies with the contract requirements specified in Section 7159.10 of the Business and Professions Code and the work commences.

(B) For any contract written pursuant to Section 7159.10 of the Business and Professions Code, or otherwise presented to the buyer as a service and repair contract, unless all of the conforming requirements listed under subdivision (a) of that section are met, the requirements set forth under Section 7159 of the Business and Professions Code shall be applicable, regardless of the aggregate contract price, including the right to cancel as set forth under this section.

(b) In addition to any other right to revoke an offer, any buyer has the right to cancel a home solicitation contract or offer for the purchase of a personal emergency response unit until midnight of the seventh business day after the day on which the buyer signs an agreement or offer to purchase which complies with Section 1689.7. This subdivision shall not apply to a personal emergency response unit installed with, and as part of, a home security alarm system subject to the Alarm Company Act (Chapter 11.6 (commencing with Section 7590) of Division 3 of the Business and Professions Code) which has two or more stationary protective devices used to enunciate an intrusion or fire and is installed by an alarm company operator operating under a current license issued pursuant to the Alarm Company Act, which shall instead be subject to subdivision (a).

Appendix

(c) In addition to any other right to revoke an offer, a buyer has the right to cancel a home solicitation contract or offer for the repair or restoration of residential premises damaged by a disaster that was not void pursuant to Section 1689.14, until midnight of the seventh business day after the buyer signs and dates the contract unless the provisions of Section 1689.15 are applicable.

(d) Cancellation occurs when the buyer gives written notice of cancellation to the seller at the address specified in the agreement or offer.

(e) Notice of cancellation, if given by mail, is effective when deposited in the mail properly addressed with postage prepaid.

(f) Notice of cancellation given by the buyer need not take the particular form as provided with the contract or offer to purchase and, however expressed, is effective if it indicates the intention of the buyer not to be bound by the home solicitation contract or offer.

(g) "Personal emergency response unit," for purposes of this section, means an in-home radio transmitter device or two-way radio device generally, but not exclusively, worn on a neckchain, wrist strap, or clipped to clothing, and connected to a telephone line through which a monitoring station is alerted of an emergency and emergency assistance is summoned.

Added Stats 2005 ch 48 § 25 (SB 1113), effective July 18, 2005, operative January 1, 2006. Amended Stats 2005 ch 385 § 11 (AB 316).

§ 1689.7. Form of home solicitation contract or offer; Notice of cancellation

(a)(1) Except for contracts written pursuant to Sections 7151.2 and 7159.10 of the Business and Professions Code, in a home solicitation contract or offer, the buyer's agreement or offer to purchase shall be written in the same language, e.g., Spanish, as principally used in the oral sales presentation, shall be dated, shall be signed by the buyer, and except as provided in paragraph (2), shall contain in immediate proximity to the space reserved for his or her signature, a conspicuous statement in a size equal to at least 10-point boldface type, as follows: "You, the buyer, may cancel this transaction at any time prior to midnight of the third business day after the date of this transaction. See the attached notice of cancellation form for an explanation of this right."

(2) The statement required pursuant to this subdivision for a home solicitation contract or offer for the purchase of a personal emergency response unit, as defined in Section 1689.6, that is not installed with and as part of a home security alarm system subject to the Alarm Company Act (Chapter 11.6 (commencing with Section 7590) of Division 3 of the Business and Professions Code) that has two or more stationary protective devices used to enunciate an intrusion or fire and is installed by an alarm company operator operating under a current license issued pursuant to the Alarm Company Act, is as follows:

"You, the buyer, may cancel this transaction at any time prior to midnight of the seventh business day after the date of this transaction. See the attached notice of cancellation form for an explanation of this right."

(3) Except for contracts written pursuant to Sections 7151.2 and 7159.10 of the Business and Professions Code, the statement required pursuant to this subdivision for the repair or restoration of residential premises damaged by a disaster pursuant to subdivision (c) of Section 1689.6 is as follows: "You, the buyer, may cancel this transaction at any time prior to midnight of the seventh business day after the date of this transaction. See the attached notice of cancellation form for an explanation of this right."

(4) A home solicitation contract written pursuant to Section 7151.2 of the Business and Professions Code shall be written in the same language, e.g., Spanish, as principally used in the oral sales presentation. The contract, or an attachment to the contract that is subject to Section 7159 of the Business and Professions Code shall include in immediate proximity to the space reserved for his or her signature, the following statement in a size equal to at least 12-point boldface type, which shall be dated and signed by the buyer:

"Three-Day Right to Cancel

You, the buyer, have the right to cancel this contract within three business days. You may cancel by e-mailing, mailing, faxing, or delivering a written notice to the contractor at the contractor's place of business by midnight of the third business day after you received a signed and dated copy of the contract that includes this notice. Include your name, your address, and the date you received the signed copy of the contract and this notice.

If you cancel, the contractor must return to you anything you paid within 10 days of receiving the notice of cancellation. For your part, you must make available to the contractor at your residence, in substantially as good condition as you received it, any goods delivered to you under this contract or sale. Or, you may, if you wish, comply with the contractor's instructions on how to return the goods at the contractor's expense and risk. If you do make the goods available to the contractor and the contractor does not pick them up within 20 days of the date of your notice of cancellation, you may keep them without any further obligation. If you fail to make the goods available to the contractor, or if you agree to return the goods to the contractor and fail to do so, then you remain liable for performance of all obligations under the contract."

(b) The agreement or offer to purchase shall contain on the first page, in a type size no smaller than that generally used in the body of the document, the following: (1) the name and address of the seller to which the notice is to be mailed, and (2) the date the buyer signed the agreement or offer to purchase.

(c) Except for contracts written pursuant to Sections 7151.2 and 7159.10 of the Business and Professions Code, or except as provided in subdivision (d), the agreement or offer to purchase shall be accompanied by a completed form in duplicate, captioned "Notice of Cancellation" which shall be attached to the agreement or offer to purchase and be easily detachable, and which shall contain in type of at least 10-point the following statement written in the same language, e.g., Spanish, as used in the contract:

"Notice of Cancellation"

/enter date of transaction/
(Date)

"You may cancel this transaction, without any penalty or obligation, within three business days from the above date.

If you cancel, any property traded in, any payments made by you under the contract or sale, and any negotiable instrument executed by you will be returned within 10 days following receipt by the seller of your cancellation notice, and any security interest arising out of the transaction will be canceled.

If you cancel, you must make available to the seller at your residence, in substantially as good condition as when received, any goods delivered to you under this contract or sale, or you may, if you wish, comply with the instructions of the seller regarding the return shipment of the goods at the seller's expense and risk.

If you do make the goods available to the seller and the seller does not pick them up within 20 days of the date of your notice of cancellation, you may retain or dispose of the goods without any further obligation. If you fail to make the goods available to the seller, or if you agree to return the goods to the seller and fail to do so, then you remain liable for performance of all obligations under the contract."

To cancel this transaction, mail or deliver a signed and dated copy of this cancellation notice, or any other written notice, or send a telegram

to _____,

/name of seller/

at _____

/address of seller's place of business/

at _____

(Date)

I hereby cancel this transaction._____

(Date)

_____

(Buyer's signature)

(d) Any agreement or offer to purchase a personal emergency response unit, as defined in Section 1689.6, which is not installed with and as part of a home security alarm system subject to the Alarm Company Act which has two or more stationary protective devices used to enunciate an intrusion or fire and is installed by an alarm company operator operating under a current license issued pursuant to the Alarm Company Act, shall be subject to the requirements of subdivision (c), and shall be accompanied by the "Notice of Cancellation" required by subdivision (c), except that the first paragraph of that notice shall be deleted and replaced with the following paragraph:

You may cancel this transaction, without any penalty or obligation, within seven business days from the above date.

(e) A home solicitation contract written pursuant to Section 7151.2 of the Business and Professions Code for the repair or restoration of residential premises damaged by a disaster that is subject to subdivision (c) of Section 1689.6, shall be written in the same language, e.g., Spanish, as principally used in the oral sales presentation. The contract, or an attachment to the contract that is subject to Section 7159 of the Business and Professions Code shall include, in immediate proximity to the space reserved for his or her signature, the following statement in a size equal to at least 12-point boldface type, which shall be signed and dated by the buyer:

"Seven-Day Right to Cancel

You, the buyer, have the right to cancel this contract within three business days. You may cancel by e-mailing, mailing, faxing, or delivering a written notice to the contractor at the contractor's place of business by midnight of the third business day after you received a signed and dated copy of the contract that includes this notice. Include your name, your address, and the date you received the signed copy of the contract and this notice.

If you cancel, the contractor must return to you anything you paid within 10 days of receiving the notice of cancellation. For your part, you must make available to the contractor at your residence, in substantially as good condition as you received it, any goods delivered to you under this contract or sale. Or, you may, if you wish, comply with the contractor's instructions on how to return the goods at the contractor's expense and risk. If you do make the goods available to the contractor and the contractor does not pick them up within 20 days of the date of your notice of cancellation, you may keep them without any further obligation. If you fail to make the goods available to the contractor, or if you agree to return the goods to the contractor and fail to do so, then you remain liable for performance of all obligations under the contract."

(f) The seller shall provide the buyer with a copy of the contract or offer to purchase and the attached notice of cancellation, and shall inform the buyer orally of his or her right to cancel and the requirement that cancellation be in writing, at the time the home solicitation contract or offer is executed.

(g) Until the seller has complied with this section the buyer may cancel the home solicitation contract or offer.

(h) "Contract or sale" as used in subdivision (c) means "home solicitation contract or offer" as defined by Section 1689.5.

Added Stats 2005 ch 48 § 27 (SB 1113), effective July 18, 2005, operative January 1, 2006. Amended Stats 2005 ch 385 § 12 (AB 316), effective January 1, 2006.

§ 1689.8. Home solicitation contract or offer for home improvements which provides for lien on real property

(a) Every home solicitation contract or offer for home improvement goods or services which provides for a lien on real property is subject to the provisions of Chapter 1 (commencing with Section 1801) of Title 2 of Part 4 of Division 3.

(b) For purposes of this section, "home improvement goods or services" means goods and services, as defined in Section 1689.5, which are bought in connection with the improvement of real property. Such home improvement goods and services include, but are not limited to, burglar alarms, carpeting, texture coating, fencing, air conditioning or heating equipment, and termite extermination. Home improvement goods include goods which, at the time of sale or subsequently, are to be so affixed to real property as to become a part of real property whether or not severable therefrom.

Added Stats 1979 ch 1012 § 6.

§ 1689.9. Absence of buyer's right to cancel home solicitation contract or offer if goods affixed to sold or encumbered real property

Where the goods sold under any home solicitation contract are so affixed to real property as to become a part thereof, whether or not severable therefrom, the buyer shall not have the right to cancel as provided in Section 1689.6 or Section 1689.7 if, subsequent to his signing such contract, he has sold or encumbered such real property to a bona fide purchaser or encumbrancer who was not a party to such sale of goods or to any loan agreement in connection therewith.

Added Stats 1971 ch 375 § 5.

§ 1689.10. Tender of payments to buyer upon cancellation of home solicitation contract or offer

(a) Except as provided in Sections 1689.6 to 1689.11, inclusive, within 10 days after a home solicitation contract or offer has been canceled, the seller must tender to the buyer any payments made by the buyer and any note or other evidence of indebtedness.

(b) If the downpayment includes goods traded in, the goods must be tendered in substantially as good condition as when received.

(c) Until the seller has complied with the obligations imposed by Sections 1689.7 to 1689.11, inclusive, the buyer may retain possession of goods delivered to him by the seller and has a lien on the goods for any recovery to which he is entitled.

Added Stats 1971 ch 375 § 6. Amended Stats 1973 ch 554 § 5.

§ 1689.11. Tender of goods by buyer upon cancellation of home solicitation contract or offer

(a) Except as provided in subdivision (c) of Section 1689.10, within 20 days after a home solicitation contract or offer has been canceled, the buyer, upon demand, must tender to the seller any goods delivered by the seller pursuant to the sale or offer, but he is not obligated to tender at any place other than his own address. If the seller fails to demand possession of goods within 20 days after cancellation, the goods become the property of the buyer without obligation to pay for them.

(b) The buyer has a duty to take reasonable care of the goods in his possession both prior to cancellation and during the 20–day period following. During the 20–day period after cancellation, except for the buyer's duty of care, the goods are at the seller's risk.

(c) If the seller has performed any services pursuant to a home solicitation contract or offer prior to its cancellation, the seller is entitled to no compensation. If the seller's services result in the alteration of property of the buyer, the seller shall restore the property to substantially as good condition as it was at the time the services were rendered.

Added Stats 1971 ch 375 § 7. Amended Stats 1973 ch 554 § 6.

§ 1689.12. Waiver or confession of judgment invalid

Any waiver or confession of judgment of the provisions of Sections 1689.5 to 1689.11, inclusive, shall be deemed contrary to public policy and shall be void and unenforceable.

Added Stats 1971 ch 375 § 8. Amended Stats 1973 ch 554 § 7.

§ 1689.13. Applicability to emergency repairs or services

Sections 1689.5, 1689.6, 1689.7, 1689.10, 1689.12, and 1689.14 do not apply to a contract that meets all of the following requirements:

(a) The contract is initiated by the buyer or his or her agent or insurance representative.

(b) The contract is executed in connection with making of emergency or immediately necessary repairs that are necessary for the immediate protection of persons or real or personal property.

(c) The buyer gives the seller a separate statement that is dated and signed that describes the situation that requires immediate remedy, and expressly acknowledges and waives the right to cancel the sale within three or seven business days, whichever applies.

(d) This section shall become operative on January 1, 2006.

Added Stats 2005 ch 48 § 29 (SB 1113), effective July 18, 2005, operative January 1, 2006.

§ 1689.14. Home solicitation contract or offer for repair signed following disaster; Void as specified

(a) Any home solicitation contract or offer for the repair or restoration of residential premises signed by the buyer on or after the date on which a disaster causes damage to the residential premises, but not later than midnight of the seventh business day after this date, shall be void, unless the buyer or his or her agent or insurance representative solicited the contract or offer at the appropriate trade premises of the seller. Any contract covered by this subdivision shall not be void if solicited by the buyer or his or her agent or insurance representative regardless of where the contract is made. For purposes of this section, buyer solicitation includes a telephone call from the buyer to the appropriate trade premises of the seller whether or not the call is in response to a prior home solicitation.

(b) As used in this section and Section 1689.6, "disaster" means an earthquake, flood, fire, hurricane, riot, storm, tidal wave, or other similar sudden or catastrophic occurrence for which a state of emergency has been declared by the President of the United States or the Governor or for which a local emergency has been declared by the executive officer or governing body of any city, county, or city and county.

Added Stats 1st Ex Sess 1993–94 ch 51 § 5 (AB 57 X). Amended Stats 1995 ch 123 § 1 (AB 1610), effective July 18, 1995.

§ 1689.15. Commencment of work; Right of cancellation

Notwithstanding any other provision of law, a contractor who is duly licensed pursuant to Chapter 9 (commencing with Section 7000) of Division 3 of the Business and Professions Code may commence work on a service and repair project as soon as the buyer receives a signed and dated copy of a service and repair contract that meets all of the contract requirements specified in Section 7159.10 of the Business and Professions Code. The buyer retains any right of cancellation applicable to home solicitations under Sections 1689.5 to 1689.14, inclusive, until such time as the buyer receives a signed and dated copy of a service and repair contract that meets all of the contract requirements specified in Section 7159.10 of the Business and Professions Code and the licensee in fact commences that project, at which time any cancellation rights provided in Sections 1689.5 to 1689.14, inclusive, are extinguished by operation of law.

Added Stats 2004 ch 566 § 20 (SB 30), operative July 1, 2005. Amended Stats 2005 ch 48 § 30 (SB 1113), effective July 18, 2005, operative January 1, 2006, ch 385 § 13 (AB 316).

PART 4

OBLIGATIONS ARISING FROM PARTICULAR TRANSACTIONS

TITLE 1.5
Consumers Legal Remedies Act

Chapter 3

Deceptive Practices

§ 1770. Unlawful practices

(a) The following unfair methods of competition and unfair or deceptive acts or practices undertaken by any person in a transaction intended to result or which results in the sale or lease of goods or services to any consumer are unlawful:

(1) Passing off goods or services as those of another.

(2) Misrepresenting the source, sponsorship, approval, or certification of goods or services.

(3) Misrepresenting the affiliation, connection, or association with, or certification by, another.

(4) Using deceptive representations or designations of geographic origin in connection with goods or services.

(5) Representing that goods or services have sponsorship, approval, characteristics, ingredients, uses, benefits, or quantities which they do not have or that a person has a sponsorship, approval, status, affiliation, or connection which he or she does not have.

(6) Representing that goods are original or new if they have deteriorated unreasonably or are altered, reconditioned, reclaimed, used, or secondhand.

(7) Representing that goods or services are of a particular standard, quality, or grade, or that goods are of a particular style or model, if they are of another.

(8) Disparaging the goods, services, or business of another by false or misleading representation of fact.

(9) Advertising goods or services with intent not to sell them as advertised.

(10) Advertising goods or services with intent not to supply reasonably expectable demand, unless the advertisement discloses a limitation of quantity.

(11) Advertising furniture without clearly indicating that it is unassembled if that is the case.

(12) Advertising the price of unassembled furniture without clearly indicating the assembled price of that furniture if the same furniture is available assembled from the seller.

(13) Making false or misleading statements of fact concerning reasons for, existence of, or amounts of price reductions.

(14) Representing that a transaction confers or involves rights, remedies, or obligations which it does not have or involve, or which are prohibited by law.

(15) Representing that a part, replacement, or repair service is needed when it is not.

(16) Representing that the subject of a transaction has been supplied in accordance with a previous representation when it has not.

(17) Representing that the consumer will receive a rebate, discount, or other economic benefit, if the earning of the benefit is contingent on an event to occur subsequent to the consummation of the transaction.

(18) Misrepresenting the authority of a salesperson, representative, or agent to negotiate the final terms of a transaction with a consumer.

(19) Inserting an unconscionable provision in the contract.

(20) Advertising that a product is being offered at a specific price plus a specific percentage of that price unless (A) the total price is set forth in the advertisement, which may include, but is not limited to, shelf tags, displays, and media advertising, in a size larger than any other price in that advertisement, and (B) the specific price plus a specific percentage of that price represents a markup from the seller's costs or from the wholesale price of the product. This subdivision shall not apply to in-store advertising by businesses which are open only to members or cooperative organizations organized pursuant to Division 3 (commencing with Section 12000) of Title 1 of the Corporations Code where more than 50 percent of purchases are made at the specific price set forth in the advertisement.

(21) Selling or leasing goods in violation of Chapter 4 (commencing with Section 1797.8) of Title 1.7.

(22) (A) Disseminating an unsolicited prerecorded message by telephone without an unrecorded, natural voice first informing the person answering the telephone of the name of the caller or the organization being represented, and either the address or the telephone number of the caller, and without obtaining the consent of that person to listen to the prerecorded message.

(B) This subdivision does not apply to a message disseminated to a business associate, customer, or other person having an established relationship with the person or organization making the call, to a call for the purpose of collecting an existing obligation, or to any call generated at the request of the recipient.

(23) The home solicitation, as defined in subdivision (h) of Section 1761, of a consumer who is a senior citizen where a loan is made encumbering the primary residence of that consumer for the purposes of paying for home improvements and where the transaction is part of a pattern or practice in violation of either subsection (h) or (i) of Section 1639 of Title 15 of the United States Code or subsection (e) of Section 226.32 of Title 12 of the Code of Federal Regulations.

A third party shall not be liable under this subdivision unless (A) there was an agency relationship between the party who engaged in home solicitation and the third party or (B) the third party had actual knowledge of, or participated in, the unfair or deceptive transaction. A third party who is a holder in due course under a home solicitation transaction shall not be liable under this subdivision.

(24) (A) Charging or receiving an unreasonable fee to prepare, aid, or advise any prospective applicant, applicant, or recipient in the procurement, maintenance, or securing of public social services.

(B) For purposes of this paragraph, the following definitions shall apply:

(i) "Public social services" means those activities and functions of state and local government administered or supervised by the State Department of Health Care Services, the State Department of Public Health, or the State Department of Social Services, and involved in providing aid or services, or both, including health care services, and medical assistance, to those persons who, because of their economic circumstances or social condition, are in need of that aid or those services and may benefit from them.

(ii) "Public social services" also includes activities and functions administered or supervised by the United States Department of Veterans Affairs or the California Department of Veterans Affairs involved in providing aid or services, or both, to veterans, including pension benefits.

(iii) "Unreasonable fee" means a fee that is exorbitant and disproportionate to the services performed. Factors to be considered, when appropriate, in determining the reasonableness of a fee, are based on the circumstances existing at the time of the service and shall include, but not be limited to, all of the following:

(I) The time and effort required.

(II) The novelty and difficulty of the services.

(III) The skill required to perform the services.

(IV) The nature and length of the professional relationship.

(V) The experience, reputation, and ability of the person providing the services.

(C) This paragraph shall not apply to attorneys licensed to practice law in California, who are subject to the California Rules of Professional Conduct and to the mandatory fee arbitration provisions of Article 13 (commencing with Section 6200) of Chapter 4 of Division 3 of the Business and Professions Code, when the fees charged or received are for providing representation in administrative agency appeal proceedings or court proceedings for purposes of procuring, maintaining, or securing public social services on behalf of a person or group of persons.

(b) (1) It is an unfair or deceptive act or practice for a mortgage broker or lender, directly or indirectly, to use a home improvement contractor to negotiate the terms of any loan that is secured, whether in whole or in part, by the residence of the borrower and which is used to finance a home improvement contract or any portion thereof. For purposes of this subdivision, "mortgage broker or lender" includes a finance lender licensed pursuant to the California Finance Lenders Law (Division 9 (commencing with Section 22000) of the Financial Code), a residential mortgage lender licensed pursuant to the California Residential Mortgage Lending Act (Division 20 (commencing with Section 50000) of the Financial Code), or a real estate broker licensed under the Real Estate Law (Division 4 (commencing with Section 10000) of the Business and Professions Code).

(2) This section shall not be construed to either authorize or prohibit a home improvement contractor from referring a consumer to a mortgage broker or lender by this subdivision. However, a home improvement contractor may refer a consumer to a mortgage lender or broker if that referral does not violate Section 7157 of the Business and Professions Code or any other provision of law. A mortgage lender or broker may purchase an executed home improvement contract if that purchase does not violate Section 7157 of the Business and Professions Code or any other provision of law. Nothing in this paragraph shall have any effect on the application of Chapter 1 (commencing with Section 1801) of Title 2 to a home improvement transaction or the financing thereof.

Added Stats 1970 ch 1550 § 1. Amended Stats 1975 ch 379 § 1; Stats 1979 ch 819 § 4, effective September 19, 1979; Stats 1984 ch 1171 § 1; Stats 1986 ch 1497 § 1; Stats 1990 ch 1641 § 1 (AB 4084); Stats 1995 ch 255 § 2 (SB 320); Stats 1996 ch 684 § 1 (SB 2045); Stats 2008 ch 479 § 1 (SB 1136), effective January 1, 2009; Stats 2009 ch 140 § 26 (AB 1164), effective January 1, 2010; Stats 2011 ch 79 § 1 (SB 180), effective January 1, 2012.

TITLE 1.7
Consumer Warranties

Chapter 5
Home Roof Warranties

§ 1797.90. Application of chapter

This chapter shall apply to all contracts and warranties for roofing materials used on a residential structure, including, but not limited to, a manufactured home or mobilehome, and to all contracts and warranties for the installation, repair, or replacement of all or any portion of the roof of a residential structure, including, but not limited to, a manufactured home or mobilehome.

Added Stats 1993 ch 835 § 1 (SB 409).

§ 1797.91. Necessity for written contract

Any contract for roofing materials, or for the installation, repair, or replacement of all or any portion of the roof of a residential structure, including, but not limited to, a manufactured home or mobilehome, shall be in writing if the contract includes any warranty of the materials or workmanship that extends for any period of time beyond completion of the work.

Added Stats 1993 ch 835 § 1 (SB 409).

§ 1797.92. Beneficiaries of warranty

For any contract subject to this chapter that is entered into on or after January 1, 1994, the warranty obligations shall inure to the benefit of, and shall be directly enforceable by, all subsequent purchasers and transferees of the residential structure, without limitation, unless the contract contains a clear and conspicuous provision limiting transferability of the warranty.

Added Stats 1993 ch 835 § 1 (SB 409).

§ 1797.93. Lifetime warranties

If any warranty subject to this chapter, uses the term "lifetime," "life," or a similar representation to describe the duration of the warranty, then the warranty shall disclose with such clarity and prominence as will be noticed and understood by prospective purchasers, the life to which the representation refers.

Added Stats 1993 ch 835 § 1 (SB 409).

Appendix

TITLE 2
Credit Sales

Chapter 1
Retail Installment Sales

Article 4

Restrictions on Retail Installment Contracts

§ 1804.3. Security interests

(a) No contract other than one for services shall provide for a security interest in any goods theretofore fully paid for or which have not been sold by the seller.

(b) Any contract for goods which provides for a security interest in real property where the primary goods sold are not to be attached to the real property shall be a violation of this chapter and subject to the penalties set forth in Article 12.2 (commencing with Section 1812.6).

(c) This section shall become operative October 1, 1982.

Added Stats 1980 ch 1380 § 11, effective October 1, 1980, operative July 1, 1981. Amended Stats 1981 ch 107 § 4, effective June 29, 1981, operative April 1, 1982; Stats 1982 ch 129 § 4, effective March 25, 1982, operative October 1, 1982.

Article 5

Finance Charge Limitation

§ 1805.6. Undelivered goods; Home improvement contract

(a) Notwithstanding the provisions of any contract to the contrary, except as provided in subdivision (b) or (c), no retail seller shall assess any finance charge for goods purchased under a retail installment contract until the goods are in the buyer's possession.

(b) A finance charge may be assessed for such undelivered goods, as follows:

(1) From the date when such goods are available for pickup by the buyer and the buyer is notified of their availability, or

(2) From the date of purchase, when such goods are delivered or available for pickup by the buyer within 10 days of the date of purchase.

(c) In the case of a home improvement contract as defined in Section 7151.2 of the Business and Professions Code, a finance charge may be assessed from the approximate date of commencement of the work as set forth in the home improvement contract.

Added Stats 1975 ch 1041 § 1. Amended Stats 1976 ch 1271 § 3, effective September 28, 1976; Stats 1977 ch 868 § 3; Stats 1979 ch 1000 § 4; Stats 1980 ch 1380 § 15, effective October 1, 1980; Stats 1981 ch 1075 § 8, operative October 1, 1982.

Article 10

Retail Installment Accounts

§ 1810.10.   Charge for undelivered goods

(a) Notwithstanding the provision of any contract to the contrary, except as provided in subdivision (b) or (c), no retail seller shall assess any finance charge against the outstanding balance for goods purchased under a retail installment account until the goods are in the buyer's possession.

(b) A finance charge may be assessed against the outstanding balance for such undelivered goods, as follows:

(1) From the date when such goods are available for pickup by the buyer and the buyer is notified of their availability, or

(2) From the date of purchase, when such goods are delivered or available for pickup by the buyer within 10 days of the date of purchase.

(c) In the case of a home improvement contract as defined in Section 7151.2 of the Business and Professions Code, a finance charge may be assessed against the amount financed from the approximate date of commencement of the work as set forth in the home improvement contract.

Added Stats 1975 ch 1041 § 2. Amended Stats 1976 ch 1271 § 5, effective September 28, 1976; Stats 1977 ch 868 § 5; Stats 1979 ch 1000 § 6.

TITLE 12

Indemnity

§ 2782.   Construction contracts; Agreements indemnifying promisee or relieving public agency from liability as void; Subcontractor's defense or indemnity obligation; Builder's or general contractor's rights to damages; Equitable indemnity

(a) Except as provided in Sections 2782.1, 2782.2, 2782.5, and 2782.6, provisions, clauses, covenants, or agreements contained in, collateral to, or affecting any construction contract and that purport to indemnify the promisee against liability for damages for death or bodily injury to persons, injury to property, or any other loss, damage or expense arising from the sole negligence or willful misconduct of the promisee or the promisee's agents, servants, or independent contractors who are directly responsible to the promisee, or for defects in design furnished by those persons, are against public policy and are void and unenforceable; provided, however, that this section shall not affect the validity of any insurance contract, workers' compensation, or agreement issued by an admitted insurer as defined by the Insurance Code.

(b) (1) Except as provided in Sections 2782.1, 2782.2, and 2782.5, provisions, clauses, covenants, or agreements contained in, collateral to, or affecting any construction contract with a public agency entered into before January 1, 2013, that purport to impose on the contractor, or relieve the public agency from, liability for the active negligence of the public agency are void and unenforceable.

(2) Except as provided in Sections 2782.1, 2782.2, and 2782.5, provisions, clauses, covenants, or agreements contained in, collateral to, or affecting any construction contract with a public agency entered into on or after January 1, 2013, that purport to impose on any contractor, subcontractor, or supplier of goods or services, or relieve the public agency from, liability for the active negligence of the public agency are void and unenforceable.

(c) (1) Except as provided in subdivision (d) and Sections 2782.1, 2782.2, and 2782.5, provisions, clauses, covenants, or agreements contained in, collateral to, or affecting any construction contract entered into on or after January 1, 2013, with the owner of privately owned real property to be improved and as to which the owner is not acting as a contractor or supplier of materials or equipment to the work, that purport to impose on any contractor, subcontractor, or supplier of goods or services, or relieve the owner from, liability are unenforceable to the extent of the active negligence of the owner, including that of its employees.

(2) For purposes of this subdivision, an owner of privately owned real property to be improved includes the owner of any interest therein, other than a mortgage or other interest that is held solely as security for performance of an obligation.

(3) This subdivision shall not apply to a homeowner performing a home improvement project on his or her own single family dwelling.

(d) For all construction contracts, and amendments thereto, entered into after January 1, 2009, for residential construction, as used in Title 7 (commencing with Section 895) of Part 2 of Division 2, all provisions, clauses, covenants, and agreements contained in, collateral to, or affecting any construction contract, and amendments thereto, that purport to insure or indemnify, including the cost to defend, the builder, as defined in Section 911, or the general contractor or contractor not affiliated with the builder, as described in subdivision (b) of Section 911, by a subcontractor against liability for claims of construction defects are unenforceable to the extent the claims arise out of, pertain to, or relate to the negligence of the builder or contractor or the builder's or contractor's other agents, other servants, or other independent contractors who are directly responsible to the builder, or for defects in design furnished by those persons, or to the extent the claims do not arise out of, pertain to, or relate to the scope of work in the written agreement between the parties. This section shall not be waived or modified by contractual agreement, act, or omission of the parties. Contractual provisions, clauses, covenants, or agreements not expressly prohibited herein are reserved to the agreement of the parties. Nothing in this subdivision shall prevent any party from exercising its rights under subdivision (a) of Section 910. This subdivision shall not affect the obligations of an insurance carrier under the holding of Presley Homes, Inc. v. American States Insurance Company (2001) 90 Cal.App.4th 571. Nor shall this subdivision affect the obligations of a builder or subcontractor pursuant to Title 7 (commencing with Section 895) of Part 2 of Division 2.

(e) Subdivision (d) does not prohibit a subcontractor and builder or general contractor from mutually agreeing to the timing or immediacy of the defense and provisions for reimbursement of defense fees and costs, so long as that agreement does not waive or modify the provisions of subdivision (d) subject, however, to paragraphs (1) and (2). A subcontractor shall owe no defense or indemnity obligation to a builder or general contractor for a construction defect claim unless and until the builder or general contractor provides a written tender of the claim, or portion thereof, to the subcontractor which includes all of the information provided to the builder or general contractor by the claimant or claimants, including, but not limited to, information provided pursuant to subdivision (a) of Section 910, relating to claims caused by that subcontractor's scope of work. This written tender shall have the same force and effect as a notice of commencement of a legal proceeding. If a builder or general contractor tenders a claim for construction defects, or a portion thereof, to a subcontractor in the manner specified by this provision, the subcontractor shall elect to perform either of the following, the performance of which shall be deemed to satisfy the subcontractor's defense obligation to the builder or general contractor:

(1) Defend the claim with counsel of its choice, and the subcontractor shall maintain control of the defense for any claim or portion of claim to which the defense obligation applies. If a subcontractor elects to defend under this paragraph, the subcontractor shall provide written notice of the election to the builder or general contractor within a reasonable time period following receipt of the written tender, and in no event later than 90 days following that receipt. Consistent with subdivision (d), the defense by the subcontractor shall be a complete defense of the builder or general contractor of all claims or portions thereof to the extent alleged to be caused by the subcontractor, including any vicarious liability claims against the builder or general contractor resulting from the subcontractor's scope of work, but not including claims resulting from the scope of work, actions, or omissions of the builder, general contractor, or any other party. Any vicarious liability imposed upon a builder or general contractor for claims caused by the subcontractor electing to defend under this paragraph

shall be directly enforceable against the subcontractor by the builder, general contractor, or claimant.

(2) Pay, within 30 days of receipt of an invoice from the builder or general contractor, no more than a reasonable allocated share of the builder's or general contractor's defense fees and costs, on an ongoing basis during the pendency of the claim, subject to reallocation consistent with subdivision (d), and including any amounts reallocated upon final resolution of the claim, either by settlement or judgment. The builder or general contractor shall allocate a share to itself to the extent a claim or claims are alleged to be caused by its work, actions, or omissions, and a share to each subcontractor to the extent a claim or claims are alleged to be caused by the subcontractor's work, actions, or omissions, regardless of whether the builder or general contractor actually tenders the claim to any particular subcontractor, and regardless of whether that subcontractor is participating in the defense. Any amounts not collected from any particular subcontractor may not be collected from any other subcontractor.

(f) Notwithstanding any other provision of law, if a subcontractor fails to timely and adequately perform its obligations under paragraph (1) of subdivision (e), the builder or general contractor shall have the right to pursue a claim against the subcontractor for any resulting compensatory damages, consequential damages, and reasonable attorney's fees. If a subcontractor fails to timely perform its obligations under paragraph (2) of subdivision (e), the builder or general contractor shall have the right to pursue a claim against the subcontractor for any resulting compensatory and consequential damages, as well as for interest on defense and indemnity costs, from the date incurred, at the rate set forth in subdivision (g) of Section 3260, and for the builder's or general contractor's reasonable attorney's fees incurred to recover these amounts. The builder or general contractor shall bear the burden of proof to establish both the subcontractor's failure to perform under either paragraph (1) or (2) of subdivision (e) and any resulting damages. If, upon request by a subcontractor, a builder or general contractor does not reallocate defense fees to subcontractors within 30 days following final resolution of the claim as described above, the subcontractor shall have the right to pursue a claim against the builder or general contractor for any resulting compensatory and consequential damages, as well as for interest on the fees, from the date of final resolution of the claim, at the rate set forth in subdivision (g) of Section 3260, and the subcontractor's reasonable attorney's fees incurred in connection therewith. The subcontractor shall bear the burden of proof to establish both the failure to reallocate the fees and any resulting damages. Nothing in this section shall prohibit the parties from mutually agreeing to reasonable contractual provisions for damages if any party fails to elect for or perform its obligations as stated in this section.

(g) A builder, general contractor, or subcontractor shall have the right to seek equitable indemnity for any claim governed by this section.

(h) Nothing in this section limits, restricts, or prohibits the right of a builder, general contractor, or subcontractor to seek equitable indemnity against any supplier, design professional, or product manufacturer.

(i) As used in this section, "construction defect" means a violation of the standards set forth in Sections 896 and 897.

(h) Nothing in this section limits, restricts, or prohibits the right of a builder, general contractor, or subcontractor to seek equitable indemnity against any supplier, design professional, or product manufacturer.

(i) As used in this section, "construction defect" means a violation of the standards set forth in Sections 896 and 897.

Added Stats 1967 ch 1327 § 1. Amended Stats 1980 ch 211 § 1; Stats 1982 ch 386 § 1; Stats 1985 ch 567 § 1; Stats 1990 ch 814 § 1 (SB 1922); Stats 2005 ch 394 § 1 (AB 758), effective January 1, 2006; Stats 2007 ch 32 § 1 (SB 138), effective January 1, 2008; Stats 2008 ch 467 § 1 (AB 2738), effective January 1, 2009; Stats 2011 ch 707 § 2 (SB 474), effective January 1, 2012.

§ 2782.6. Exception for professional engineer or geologist; "Hazardous materials"

(a) Nothing in subdivision (a) of Section 2782 prevents an agreement to indemnify a professional engineer or geologist or the agents, servants, independent contractors, subsidiaries, or employees of that engineer or geologist from liability as described in Section 2782 in providing hazardous materials identification, evaluation, preliminary assessment, design, remediation services, or other services of the types described in Sections 25322 and 25323 of the Health and Safety Code or the federal National Oil and Hazardous Substances Pollution Contingency Plan (40 C.F.R. Sec. 300.1 et seq.), if all of the following criteria are satisfied:

(1) The services in whole or in part address subterranean contamination or other concealed conditions caused by the hazardous materials.

(2) The promisor is responsible, or potentially responsible, for all or part of the contamination.

(b) The indemnification described in this section is valid only for damages arising from, or related to, subterranean contamination or concealed conditions, and is not applicable to the first two hundred fifty thousand dollars ($250,000) of liability or such greater amount as is agreed by the parties.

(c) This section does not authorize contracts for indemnification, by promisors specified in paragraph (2) of subdivision (a), of any liability

Appendix

of a promisee arising from the gross negligence or willful misconduct of the promisee.

(d) "Hazardous materials," as used in this section, means any hazardous or toxic substance, material, or waste which is or becomes subject to regulation as such by any agency of the state, any municipality or political subdivision of the state, or the United States. "Hazardous materials" includes, but is not limited to, any material or substance that is any of the following:

(1) A hazardous substance, as defined in Section 25316 of the Health and Safety Code.

(2) Hazardous material, as defined in subdivision (j) of Section 25501 of the Health and Safety Code.

(3) Acutely hazardous material, as defined in subdivision (a) of Section 25532 of the Health and Safety Code.

(4) Hazardous waste, as defined in Section 25117 of the Health and Safety Code.

(5) Extremely hazardous waste, as defined in Section 25115 of the Health and Safety Code.

(6) Petroleum.

(7) Asbestos.

(8) Designated as a hazardous substance for purposes of Section 311 of the Federal Water Pollution Control Act, as amended (33 U.S.C. Sec. 1321).

(9) Hazardous waste, as defined by subsection (5) of Section 1004 of the federal Resource Conservation and Recovery Act of 1976, as amended (42 U.S.C. Sec. 6903).

(10) A hazardous substance, as defined by subsection (14) of Section 101 of the federal Comprehensive Environmental Response, Compensation, and Liability Act of 1980, as amended (42 U.S.C. Sec. 9601).

(11) A regulated substance, as defined by subsection (2) of Section 9001 of the federal Solid Waste Disposal Act, as amended (42 U.S.C. Sec. 6991).

(e) Nothing in this section shall be construed to alter, modify, or otherwise affect the liability of the promisor or promisee, under an indemnity agreement meeting the criteria of this section, to third parties for damages for death or bodily injury to persons, injury to property, or any other loss, damage, or expense.

(f) This section does not apply to public entities, as defined by Section 811.2 of the Government Code.

Added Stats 1990 ch 814 § 2 (SB 1922).

§ 2782.8.   Contracts for design professional services; Agreements indemnifying public agency from liability as void

(a) For all contracts, and amendments thereto, entered into on or after January 1, 2007, with a public agency for design professional services, all provisions, clauses, covenants, and agreements contained in, collateral to, or affecting any such contract, and amendments thereto, that purport to indemnify, including the duty and the cost to defend, the public agency by a design professional against liability for claims against the public agency, are unenforceable, except for claims that arise out of, pertain to, or relate to the negligence, recklessness, or willful misconduct of the design professional. The duty to indemnify, including the duty and the cost to defend, is limited as provided in this section. This section shall not be waived or modified by contractual agreement, act, or omission of the parties. Contractual provisions, clauses, covenants, or agreements not expressly prohibited herein are reserved to the agreement of the parties.

(b) All contracts and all solicitation documents, including requests for proposal, invitations for bid, and other solicitation documents, between a public agency and a design professional, are deemed to incorporate by reference the provisions of this section.

(c) For purposes of this section, the following definitions apply:

(1) "Public agency" includes any county, city, city and county, district, school district, public authority, municipal corporation, or other political subdivision, joint powers authority, or public corporation in the state. Public agency does not include the State of California.

(2) "Design professional" includes all of the following:

(A) An individual licensed as an architect pursuant to Chapter 3 (commencing with Section 5500) of Division 3 of the Business and Professions Code, and a business entity offering architectural services in accordance with that chapter.

(B) An individual licensed as a landscape architect pursuant to Chapter 3.5 (commencing with Section 5615) of Division 3 of the Business and Professions Code, and a business entity offering landscape architectural services in accordance with that chapter.

(C) An individual registered as a professional engineer pursuant to Chapter 7 (commencing with Section 6700) of Division 3 of the Business and Professions Code, and a business entity offering professional engineering services in accordance with that chapter.

(D) An individual licensed as a professional land surveyor pursuant to Chapter 15 (commencing with Section 8700) of Division 3 of the Business and Professions Code, and a business entity offering professional land surveying services in accordance with that chapter.

(d) This section shall only apply to a professional service contract, or any amendment thereto, entered into on or after January 1, 2007.

(e) The amendments made to this section by the act adding this subdivision shall apply to services offered pursuant to a design professional contract, or any amendment thereto, entered into on or after January 1, 2011.

(f) Nothing in this section shall abrogate the provisions of Section 1104 of the Public Contract Code.

Added Stats 2006 ch 455 § 1 (AB 573), effective January 1, 2007. Amended Stats 2010 ch 510 § 1 (SB 972), effective January 1, 2011.

§ 2782.9.   Construction contracts on which wrap-up insurance policy applicable; Agreements indemnifying another from liability void; Equitable indemnity; Waiver or modification

(a) All contracts, provisions, clauses, amendments, or agreements contained therein entered into after January 1, 2009, for a residential construction project on which a wrap-up insurance policy, as defined in subdivision (b) of Section 11751.82 of the Insurance Code, or other consolidated insurance program, is applicable, that require an enrolled and participating subcontractor or other participant to indemnify, hold harmless, or defend another for any claim or action covered by that program, arising out of that project are unenforceable.

(b) To the extent any contractual provision is deemed unenforceable pursuant to this section, any party may pursue an equitable indemnity claim against another party for a claim or action unless there is coverage for the claim or action under the wrap-up policy or policies. Nothing in this section shall prohibit a builder or general contractor from requiring a reasonably allocated contribution from a subcontractor or other participant to the self-insured retention or deductible required under the wrap-up policy or other consolidated insurance program, if the maximum amount and method of collection of the participant's contribution is disclosed in the contract with the participant and the contribution is reasonably limited so that each participant may have some financial obligation in the event of a claim alleged to be caused by that participant's scope of work. The contribution shall only be collected when and as any such self-insured retention or deductible is incurred by the builder or general contractor and in an amount that bears a reasonable and proportionate relationship to the alleged liability arising from the claim or claims alleged to be caused by the participant's scope of work, when viewed in the context of the entirety of the alleged claim or claims. Any contribution shall only be collected from a participant after written notice to the participant of the amount of and basis for the contribution. In no event shall the total amount of contributions collected from participants exceed the amount of any self-insured retention or deductible due and payable by the builder or general contractor for the claim or claims. However, this requirement does not prohibit any legally permissible recovery of costs and legal fees to collect a participant's contribution if the contribution satisfies the requirements of this subdivision and is not paid by the participant when due.

(c) This section shall not be waived or modified by contractual agreement, act, or omission of the parties.

Added Stats 2008 ch 467 § 2 (AB 2738), effective January 1, 2009.

§ 2782.95. Provisions governing construction where wrap-up insurance policy covers private residential improvement; Disclosure; Bidding

For any wrap-up insurance policy or other consolidated insurance program that insures a private residential (as that term is used in Title 7 (commencing with Section 895) of Part 2 of Division 2) work of improvement that first commences construction after January 1, 2009, the following shall apply:

(a) The owner, builder, or general contractor obtaining the wrap-up insurance policy or other consolidated insurance program shall disclose the total amount or method of calculation of any credit or compensation for premium required from a subcontractor or other participant for that wrap-up policy in the contract documents.

(b) The contract documents shall disclose, if and to the extent known:

(1) The policy limits.

(2) The scope of policy coverage.

(3) The policy term.

(4) The basis upon which the deductible or occurrence is triggered by the insurance carrier.

(5) If the policy covers more than one work of improvement, the number of units, if any, indicated on the application for the insurance policy.

(6) A good faith estimate of the amount of available limits remaining under the policy as of a date indicated in the disclosure obtained from the insurer.

(7) Disclosures made pursuant to paragraphs (5) and (6) are recognized to be based upon information at a given moment in time and may not accurately reflect the actual number of units covered by the policy nor the amount of insurance available, if any, when a later claim is made. These disclosures are presumptively made in good faith if the disclosure pursuant to paragraph (5) is the same as that contained in the application to the wrap-up insurer and the disclosure pursuant to paragraph (6) was obtained from the wrap-up insurer or broker. The presumptions stated above shall be overcome only by a showing that the insurer, broker, builder, or general contractor intentionally misrepresented the facts identified in paragraphs (5) or (6).

(c) Upon the written request of any participant, a copy of the insurance policy shall be provided, if available, that shows the coverage terms and items in paragraphs (1) to (4), inclusive, of subdivision (b) above. If the policy is not available at the time of the request, a copy of the insurance binder or declaration of coverage may be provided in lieu of the actual policy. Paragraphs (1) to (4), inclusive, of subdivi-

Appendix

sion (b) may be satisfied by providing the participant with a copy of the binder or declaration. Any party receiving a copy of the policy, binder, or declaration shall not disclose it to third parties other than the participant's insurance broker or attorney unless required to do so by law. The participant's insurance broker or attorney may not disclose the policy, binder, or declaration to any third party unless required to do so by law.

(d) If the owner, builder, or general contractor obtaining the wrap-up insurance policy or other consolidated insurance program does not disclose the total amount or method of calculation of the premium credit or compensation to be charged to the participant prior to the time the participant submits its bid, the participant shall not be legally bound by the bid unless that participant has the right to increase the bid up to the amount equal to the difference between the amount the participant included, if any, for insurance in the original bid and the amount of the actual bid credit required by the owner, builder, or general contractor obtaining the wrap-up insurance policy or other consolidated insurance program. This subdivision shall not apply if the owner, builder, or general contractor obtaining the wrap-up insurance policy or other consolidated insurance program did not require the subcontractor to offset the original bid amount with a deduction for the wrap-up insurance policy or program.

Added Stats 2008 ch 467 § 3 (AB 2738), effective January 1, 2009.

§ 2782.96. Provisions governing construction where wrap-up insurance policy covers public work; Calculations to be clearly delineated in bid document; Disclosure

If an owner, builder, or general contractor obtains a wrap-up insurance policy or other consolidated insurance program for a public work as defined in Section 1720 of the Labor Code or any other project other than residential construction, as that term is used in Title 7 (commencing with Section 895) of Part 2 of Division 2, that is put out for bid after January 1, 2009, the following shall apply:

(a) The total amount or method of calculation of any credit or compensation for premium required from a subcontractor or other participant for that policy shall be clearly delineated in the bid documents.

(b) The named insured, to the extent known, shall disclose to the subcontractor or other participant in the contract documents the policy limits, known exclusions, and the length of time the policy is intended to remain in effect. In addition, upon written request, once available, the named insured shall provide copies of insurance policies to all those who are covered by the policy. Until such time as the policies are available, the named insured may also satisfy the disclosure requirements of this subdivision by providing the subcontractor or other participant with a copy of the insurance binder or declaration of coverage. Any party receiving a copy of the policy, binder, or declaration shall not disclose it to third parties other than the participant's insurance broker or attorney unless required to do so by law. The participant's insurance broker or attorney may not disclose the policy, binder, or declaration to any third party unless required to do so by law.

(c) The disclosure requirements in subdivisions (a) and (b) do not apply to an insurance policy purchased by an owner, builder, or general contractor that provides additional coverage beyond what was contained in the original wrap-up policy or other consolidated insurance program if no credit or compensation for premium is required of the subcontractor for the additional insurance policy.

Added Stats 2008 ch 467 § 4 (AB 2738), effective January 1, 2009. Amended Stats. 2009, Ch. 140 (AB 1164).

TITLE 15
Works of Improvement

Chapter 1
General Definitions

§ 3084. "Claim of lien" or "mechanic's lien"; Recordation; Service of mechanics lien (Repealed July 1, 2012)

(a) "Claim of lien" or "mechanics lien" means a written statement, signed and verified by the claimant or by the claimant's agent, containing all of the following:

(1) A statement of the claimant's demand after deducting all just credits and offsets.

(2) The name of the owner or reputed owner, if known.

(3) A general statement of the kind of labor, services, equipment, or materials furnished by the claimant.

(4) The name of the person by whom the claimant was employed or to whom the claimant furnished the labor, services, equipment, or materials.

(5) A description of the site sufficient for identification.

(6) A proof of service affidavit completed and signed by the person serving the Notice of Mechanics Lien pursuant to subdivision (c). A "proof of service affidavit" is an affidavit of the person making the service, showing the date, place, and manner of service and facts showing that the service was made in accordance with this section. The affidavit shall show the name and address of the owner or reputed owner upon whom a copy of the mechanics lien and the Notice of Mechanics Lien was served pursuant to paragraphs (1) or (2) of

subdivision (c), and the title or capacity in which the person or entity was served.

(7) The following statement, printed in at least 10-point boldface type. The letters of the last sentence shall be printed in uppercase type, excepting the Internet Web site address of the Contractors' State License Board, which shall be printed in lowercase type:

"NOTICE OF MECHANICS LIEN

ATTENTION!

Upon the recording of the enclosed MECHANICS LIEN with the county recorder's office of the county where the property is located, your property is subject to the filing of a legal action seeking a court-ordered foreclosure sale of the real property on which the lien has been recorded. That legal action must be filed with the court no later than 90 days after the date the mechanics lien is recorded.

The party identified in the mechanics lien may have provided labor or materials for improvements to your property and may not have been paid for these items. You are receiving this notice because it is a required step in filing a mechanics lien foreclosure action against your property. The foreclosure action will seek a sale of your property in order to pay for unpaid labor, materials, or improvements provided to your property. This may affect your ability to borrow against, re-finance, or sell the property until the mechanics lien is released.

BECAUSE THE LIEN AFFECTS YOUR PROPERTY, YOU MAY WISH TO SPEAK WITH YOUR CONTRACTOR IMMEDIATELY, OR CONTACT AN ATTORNEY, OR FOR MORE INFORMATION ON MECHANICS LIENS GO TO THE CONTRACTORS' STATE LICENSE BOARD WEB SITE AT www.cslb.ca.gov."

(b) A mechanics lien or claim of lien in otherwise proper form, verified and containing the information required by this section, shall be accepted by the recorder for recording and shall be deemed duly recorded without acknowledgment.

(c) (1) The mechanics lien and the Notice of Mechanics Lien described in this section shall be served on the owner or reputed owner. Service shall be made as follows:

(A) For an owner or reputed owner to be notified who resides in or outside this state, by registered mail, certified mail, or first-class mail, evidenced by a certificate of mailing, postage prepaid, addressed to the owner or reputed owner at the owner's or reputed owner's residence or place of business address or at the address shown by the building permit on file with the authority issuing a building permit for the work, or as otherwise provided in subdivision (j) of Section 3097.

(B) If the owner or reputed owner cannot be served by this method, then the notice may be given by registered mail, certified mail, or first-class mail, evidenced by a certificate of mailing, postage prepaid, addressed to the construction lender or to the original contractor.

(2) Service by registered mail, certified mail, or first-class mail, evidenced by a certificate of mailing, postage prepaid, is complete at the time of the deposit of that first-class certified or registered mail.

(d) Failure to serve the mechanics lien, including the Notice of Mechanics Lien, as prescribed by this section, shall cause the mechanics lien to be unenforceable as a matter of law.

Added Stats 1969 ch 1362 § 2 p 2752, operative January 1, 1971. Amended Stats 1981 ch 321 § 1; Stats 2009 ch 109 § 1 (AB 457), effective January 1, 2010, operative January 1, 2011. Repealed Stats 2010 ch 697 § 16 (SB 189), effective January 1, 2011, operative July 1, 2012; Stats 2011 ch 673 § 1 (AB 456), effective January 1, 2012.

§ 3097. "Preliminary 20–day notice (private work)"; Procedure (Repealed July 1, 2012)

"Preliminary 20–day notice (private work)" means a written notice from a claimant that is given prior to the recording of a mechanic's lien, prior to the filing of a stop notice, and prior to asserting a claim against a payment bond, and is required to be given under the following circumstances:

(a) Except one under direct contract with the owner or one performing actual labor for wages as described in subdivision (a) of Section 3089, or a person or entity to whom a portion of a laborer's compensation is paid as described in subdivision (b) of Section 3089, every person who furnishes labor, service, equipment, or material for which a lien or payment bond otherwise can be claimed under this title, or for which a notice to withhold can otherwise be given under this title, shall, as a necessary prerequisite to the validity of any claim of lien, payment bond, and of a notice to withhold, cause to be given to the owner or reputed owner, to the original contractor, or reputed contractor, and to the construction lender, if any, or to the reputed construction lender, if any, a written preliminary notice as prescribed by this section.

(b) Except the contractor, or one performing actual labor for wages as described in subdivision (a) of Section 3089, or a person or entity to whom a portion of a laborer's compensation is paid as described in subdivision (b) of Section 3089, all persons who have a direct contract with the owner and who furnish labor, service, equipment, or material for which a lien or payment bond otherwise can be claimed under this title, or for which a notice to withhold can otherwise be given under this title, shall, as a necessary prerequisite to the validity of any claim of lien, claim on a payment bond, and of a notice to withhold, cause to be given to the construction lender, if any, or to the reputed construction lender, if any, a written preliminary notice as prescribed by this section.

(c) The preliminary notice referred to in subdivisions (a) and (b) shall contain the following information:

Appendix

(1) A general description of the labor, service, equipment, or materials furnished, or to be furnished, and an estimate of the total price thereof.

(2) The name and address of the person furnishing that labor, service, equipment, or materials.

(3) The name of the person who contracted for purchase of that labor, service, equipment, or materials.

(4) A description of the jobsite sufficient for identification.

(5) The following statement in boldface type:

NOTICE TO PROPERTY OWNER

If bills are not paid in full for the labor, services, equipment, or materials furnished or to be furnished, a mechanic's lien leading to the loss, through court foreclosure proceedings, of all or part of your property being so improved may be placed against the property even though you have paid your contractor in full. You may wish to protect yourself against this consequence by (1) requiring your contractor to furnish a signed release by the person or firm giving you this notice before making payment to your contractor, or (2) any other method or device that is appropriate under the circumstances. Other than residential homeowners of dwellings containing fewer than five units, private project owners must notify the original contractor and any lien claimant who has provided the owner with a preliminary 20–day lien notice in accordance with Section 3097 of the Civil Code that a notice of completion or notice of cessation has been recorded within 10 days of its recordation. Notice shall be by registered mail, certified mail, or first–class mail, evidenced by a certificate of mailing. Failure to notify will extend the deadlines to record a lien.

(6) If the notice is given by a subcontractor who has failed to pay all compensation due to his or her laborers on the job, the notice shall also contain the identity and address of any laborer and any express trust fund to whom employer payments are due.

If an invoice for materials or certified payroll contains the information required by this section, a copy of the invoice, transmitted in the manner prescribed by this section shall be sufficient notice.

A certificated architect, registered engineer, or licensed land surveyor who has furnished services for the design of the work of improvement and who gives a preliminary notice as provided in this section not later than 20 days after the work of improvement has commenced shall be deemed to have complied with subdivisions (a) and (b) with respect to architectural, engineering, or surveying services furnished, or to be furnished.

(d) The preliminary notice referred to in subdivisions (a) and (b) shall be given not later than 20 days after the claimant has first furnished labor, service, equipment, or materials to the jobsite. If labor, service, equipment, or materials have been furnished to a jobsite by a claimant who did not give a preliminary notice, that claimant shall not be precluded from giving a preliminary notice at any time thereafter. The claimant shall, however, be entitled to record a lien, file a stop notice, and assert a claim against a payment bond only for labor, service, equipment, or material furnished within 20 days prior to the service of the preliminary notice, and at any time thereafter.

(e) Any agreement made or entered into by an owner, whereby the owner agrees to waive the rights or privileges conferred upon the owner by this section shall be void and of no effect.

(f) The notice required under this section may be served as follows:

(1) If the person to be notified resides in this state, by delivering the notice personally, or by leaving it at his or her address of residence or place of business with some person in charge, or by first–class registered or certified mail, postage prepaid, addressed to the person to whom notice is to be given at his or her residence or place of business address or at the address shown by the building permit on file with the authority issuing a building permit for the work, or at an address recorded pursuant to subdivision (j).

(2) If the person to be notified does not reside in this state, by any method enumerated in paragraph (1) of this subdivision. If the person cannot be served by any of these methods, then notice may be given by first–class certified or registered mail, addressed to the construction lender or to the original contractor.

(3) If service is made by first–class certified or registered mail, service is complete at the time of the deposit of that registered or certified mail.

(g) A person required by this section to give notice to the owner, to an original contractor, and to a person to whom a notice to withhold may be given, need give only one notice to the owner, to the original contractor, and to the person to whom a notice to withhold may be given with respect to all materials, services, labor, or equipment he or she furnishes for a work of improvement, that means the entire structure or scheme of improvements as a whole, unless the same is furnished under contracts with more than one subcontractor, in which event, the notice requirements shall be met with respect to materials, services, labor, or equipment furnished to each contractor.

If a notice contains a general description required by subdivision (a) or (b) of the materials, services, labor, or equipment furnished to the date of notice, it is not defective because, after that date, the person giving notice furnishes materials, services, labor, or equipment not within the scope of this general description.

(h) If the contract price to be paid to any subcontractor on a particular work of improvement exceeds four hundred dollars ($400), the failure of that contractor, licensed under Chapter 9 (commencing with Section 7000) of Division 3 of the Business and Professions Code, to give the notice provided for in this section, constitutes grounds for disciplinary action by the Registrar of Contractors.

Appendix

If the notice is required to contain the information set forth in paragraph (6) of subdivision (c), a failure to give the notice, including that information, that results in the filing of a lien, claim on a payment bond, or the delivery of a stop notice by the express trust fund to which the obligation is owing constitutes grounds for disciplinary action by the Registrar of Contractors against the subcontractor if the amount due the trust fund is not paid.

(i) Every city, county, city and county, or other governmental authority issuing building permits shall, in its application form for a building permit, provide space and a designation for the applicant to enter the name, branch, designation, if any, and address of the construction lender and shall keep the information on file open for public inspection during the regular business hours of the authority.

If there is no known construction lender, that fact shall be noted in the designated space. Any failure to indicate the name and address of the construction lender on the application, however, shall not relieve any person from the obligation to give to the construction lender the notice required by this section.

(j) A mortgage, deed of trust, or other instrument securing a loan, any of the proceeds of which may be used for the purpose of constructing improvements on real property, shall bear the designation "Construction Trust Deed" prominently on its face and shall state all of the following: (1) the name and address of the lender, and the name and address of the owner of the real property described in the instrument, and (2) a legal description of the real property that secures the loan and, if known, the street address of the property. The failure to be so designated or to state any of the information required by this subdivision shall not affect the validity of the mortgage, deed of trust, or other instrument.

Failure to provide this information on this instrument when recorded shall not relieve persons required to give preliminary notice under this section from that duty.

The county recorder of the county in which the instrument is recorded shall indicate in the general index of the official records of the county that the instrument secures a construction loan.

(k) Every contractor and subcontractor employing laborers as described in subdivision (a) of Section 3089 who has failed to pay those laborers their full compensation when it became due, including any employer payments described in Section 1773.1 of the Labor Code and regulations adopted thereunder shall, without regard to whether the work was performed on a public or private work, cause to be given to those laborers, their bargaining representatives, if any, and to the construction lender, if any, or to the reputed construction lender, if any, not later than the date the compensation became delinquent, a written notice containing all of the following:

(1) The name of the owner and the contractor.

(2) A description of the jobsite sufficient for identification.

(3) The identity and address of any express trust fund described in Section 3111 to which employer payments are due.

(4) The total number of straight time and overtime hours on each job.

(5) The amount then past due and owing.

Failure to give this notice shall constitute grounds for disciplinary action by the Registrar of Contractors.

(*l*) Every written contract entered into between a property owner and an original contractor shall provide space for the owner to enter his or her name, residence address, and place of business if any. The original contractor shall make available the name and address of residence of the owner to any person seeking to serve the notice specified in subdivision (c).

(m) Every written contract entered into between a property owner and an original contractor, except home improvement contracts and swimming pool contracts subject to Article 10 (commencing with Section 7150) of Chapter 9 of Division 3 of the Business and Professions Code, shall provide space for the owner to enter the name and address of the construction lender or lenders. The original contractor shall make available the name and address of the construction lender or lenders to any person seeking to serve the notice specified in subdivision (c). Every contract entered into between an original contractor and subcontractor, and between subcontractors, shall provide a space for the name and address of the owner, original contractor, and any construction lender.

(n) If one or more construction loans are obtained after commencement of construction, the property owner shall provide the name and address of the construction lender or lenders to each person who has given the property owner the notice specified in subdivision (c).

(o)(1) Each person who has served a preliminary 20-day notice pursuant to subdivision (f) may file the preliminary 20-day notice with the county recorder in the county in which any portion of the property is located. A preliminary 20-day notice filed pursuant to this section shall contain all of the following:

(A) The name and address of the person furnishing the labor, service, equipment, or materials.

(B) The name of the person who contracted for purchase of the labor, services, equipment, or materials.

(C) The common street address of the jobsite.

(2) Upon the acceptance for recording of a notice of completion or notice of cessation the county recorder shall mail to those persons who have filed a preliminary 20-day notice, notification that a notice of completion or notice of cessation has been recorded on the property, and shall affix the date that the notice of completion or notice of cessation was recorded with the county recorder.

Appendix

(3) The failure of the county recorder to mail the notification to the person who filed a preliminary 20–day notice, or the failure of those persons to receive the notification or to receive complete notification, shall not affect the period within which a claim of lien is required to be recorded. However, the county recorder shall make a good faith effort to mail notification to those persons who have filed the preliminary 20–day notice under this section and to do so within five days after the recording of a notice of completion or notice of cessation.

(4) This new function of the county recorder shall not become operative until July 1, 1988. The county recorder may cause to be destroyed all documents filed pursuant to this section, two years after the date of filing.

(5) The preliminary 20–day notice that a person may file pursuant to this subdivision is for the limited purpose of facilitating the mailing of notice by the county recorder of recorded notices of completion and notices of cessation. The notice that is filed is not a recordable document and shall not be entered into those official records of the county which by law impart constructive notice. Notwithstanding any other provision of law, the index maintained by the recorder of filed preliminary 20–day notices shall be separate and distinct from those indexes maintained by the county recorder of those official records of the county which by law impart constructive notice. The filing of a preliminary 20–day notice with the county recorder does not give rise to any actual or constructive notice with respect to any party of the existence or contents of a filed preliminary 20–day notice nor to any duty of inquiry on the part of any party as to the existence or contents of that notice.

(p)(1) The change made to the statement described in subdivision (c) by Chapter 974 of the Statutes of 1994 shall have no effect upon the validity of any notice that otherwise meets the requirements of this section. The failure to provide, pursuant to Chapter 974 of the Statutes of 1994, a written preliminary notice to a subcontractor with whom the claimant has contracted shall not affect the validity of any preliminary notice provided pursuant to this section.

(2)(A) The inclusion of the language added to paragraph (5) of subdivision (c) by Chapter 795 of the Statutes of 1999, shall not affect the validity of any preliminary notice given on or after January 1, 2000, and prior to the operative date of the amendments to this section enacted at the 2000 portion of the 1999–2000 Regular Session, that otherwise meets the requirements of that subdivision.

(B) A preliminary notice given on or after January 1, 2000, and prior to the operative date of the amendments to this section enacted at the 2000 portion of the 1999–2000 Regular Session, shall not be invalid because of the failure to include the language added to paragraph (5) of subdivision (c) by Chapter 795 of the Statutes of 1999, if the notice otherwise complies with that subdivision.

(C) The failure to provide an affidavit form or notice of rights, or both, pursuant to the requirements of Chapter 795 of the Statutes of 1999, shall not affect the validity of any preliminary notice pursuant to this section.

Added Stats 1969 ch 1362 § 1, operative January 1, 1971. Amended Stats 1969 ch 1364 § 2, operative January 1, 1971, ch 1468 § 4, operative January 1, 1971; Stats 1971 ch 1284 § 2; Stats 1975 ch 46 § 1; Stats 1976 ch 396 § 1, ch 839 §§ 2, 3, operative January 1, 1978; Stats 1979 ch 375 § 1; Stats 1986 ch 545 § 1; Stats 1987 ch 716 § 1; Stats 1994 ch 974 § 3 (AB 3357); Stats 1995 ch 225 § 1 (AB 901), effective July 31, 1995; Stats 1999 ch 795 § 5 (SB 914); Stats 2000 ch 13 § 1 (AB 576), effective April 17, 2000; Stats 2001 ch 159 § 37 (SB 662); Stats 2003 ch 54 § 1 (SB 134). Repealed Stats 2010 ch 697 § 16 (SB 189), effective January 1, 2011, operative July 1, 2012.

Chapter 2

Mechanics' Liens

Article 7

Enforcement of Lien

§ 3146. Time and place for recording notice of lis pendens; Effect of notice on purchaser or encumbrancer

After the filing of the complaint in the proper court to foreclose on the mechanic's lien, the plaintiff shall record in the office of the county recorder of the county, or of the several counties in which the property is situated, a notice of the pendency of the proceedings, as provided in Title 4.5 (commencing with Section 405) of Part 2 of the Code of Civil Procedure on or before 20 days after the filing of the mechanic's lien foreclosure action. Only from the time of recording that notice shall a purchaser or encumbrancer of the property affected thereby be deemed to have constructive notice of the pendency of the action, and in that event only of its pendency against parties designated by their real names.

Added Stats 1969 ch 1362 § 2 p 2752, operative January 1, 1971. Amended Stats ch 109.

Chapter 8

Miscellaneous Provisions

§ 3260. Disbursement of retention proceeds; Penalty for failure to comply (Repealed July 1, 2012)

(a) This section is applicable with respect to all contracts entered into on or after July 1, 1991, relating to the construction of any private work of improvement. However, the amendments made to this section during the 1992 portion of the 1991–92 Regular Session of the Legislature are applicable only with respect to contracts entered into on or after January 1, 1993, relating to the construction of any private work of improvement. Moreover, the amendments made to this section during the 1993 portion of the 1993–94 Regular Session of the Legislature are applicable only with respect to contracts entered into on or after January 1, 1994, relating to the construction of any private work of improvement.

(b) The retention proceeds withheld from any payment by the owner from the original contractor, or by the original contractor from any subcontractor, shall be subject to this section.

(c) Within 45 days after the date of completion, the retention withheld by the owner shall be released. "Date of completion," for purposes of this section, means any of the following:

(1) The date of issuance of any certificate of occupancy covering the work by the public agency issuing the building permit.

(2) The date of completion indicated on a valid notice of completion recorded pursuant to Section 3093.

(3) The date of completion as defined in Section 3086.

However, release of retentions withheld for any portion of the work of improvement which ultimately will become the property of a public agency, may be conditioned upon the acceptance of the work by the public agency. In the event of a dispute between the owner and the original contractor, the owner may withhold from the final payment an amount not to exceed 150 percent of the disputed amount.

(d) Subject to subdivision (e), within 10 days from the time that all or any portion of the retention proceeds are received by the original contractor, the original contractor shall pay each of its subcontractors from whom retention has been withheld, each subcontractor's share of the retention received. However, if a retention payment received by the original contractor is specifically designated for a particular subcontractor, payment of the retention shall be made to the designated subcontractor, if the payment is consistent with the terms of the subcontract.

(e) If a bona fide dispute exists between a subcontractor and the original contractor, the original contractor may withhold from that subcontractor with whom the dispute exists its portion of the retention proceeds. The amount withheld from the retention payment shall not exceed 150 percent of the estimated value of the disputed amount.

(f) Within 10 days of receipt of written notice by the owner from the original contractor or by the original contractor from the subcontractor, as the case may be, that any work in dispute has been completed in accordance with the terms of the contract, the owner or original contractor shall advise the notifying party of the acceptance or rejection of the disputed work. Within 10 days of acceptance of the disputed work, the owner or original contractor, as the case may be, shall release the retained portion of the retention proceeds.

(g) In the event that retention payments are not made within the time periods required by this section, the owner or original contractor withholding the unpaid amounts shall be subject to a charge of 2 percent per month on the improperly withheld amount, in lieu of any interest otherwise due. Additionally, in any action for the collection of funds wrongfully withheld, the prevailing party shall be entitled to his or her attorney's fees and costs.

(h) It shall be against public policy for any party to require any other party to waive any provision of this section.

(i) This section shall not be construed to apply to retentions withheld by a lender in accordance with the construction loan agreement.

Added Stats 1990 ch 1536 § 1 (SB 2515). Amended Stats 1992 ch 387 § 1 (AB 1352); Stats 1993 ch 271 § 1 (AB 138); Stats 1994 ch 1046 § 1 (AB 2962). Repealed Stats 2010 ch 697 § 16 (SB 189), effective January 1, 2011, operative July 1, 2012.

§ 3260.1.   Payment of progress payments (Repealed July 1, 2012)

(a) This section is applicable with respect to all contracts entered into on or after January 1, 1992, relating to the construction of any private work of improvement.

(b) Except as otherwise agreed in writing, the owner shall pay to the contractor, within 30 days following receipt of a demand for payment in accordance with the contract, any progress payment due thereunder as to which there is no good faith dispute between the parties. In the event of a dispute between the owner and the contractor, the owner may withhold from the progress payment an amount not to exceed 150 percent of the disputed amount. If any amount is wrongfully withheld in violation of this subdivision, the contractor shall be entitled to the penalty specified in subdivision (g) of Section 3260.

(c) Nothing in this section shall be deemed to supersede any requirement of Section 3260 respecting the withholding of retention proceeds.

Added Stats 1991 ch 368 § 1 (AB 1608). Amended Stats 1999 ch 982 § 5 (AB 1678). Repealed Stats 2010 ch 697 § 16 (SB 189), effective January 1, 2011, operative July 1, 2012.

§ 3260.2.   Original contractor's right to serve 10–day stop work order on owner in case of nonpayment; Liability for damages from cessation of work; Service of order (Repealed July 1, 2012)

(a) If an original contractor is not paid all moneys which are owed pursuant to a written contract for a private work of improvement

Appendix

within 35 days from the date payment is due pursuant to the written contract, and there is no dispute as to the satisfactory performance of that original contractor, the original contractor shall have a right to serve upon the owner a "10–day stop work order" that states that unless all amounts then due the original contractor are paid within 10 days from the date notice is provided under this section, the original contractor will stop work on the project. At least five days before service upon the owner of a "10–day stop work order," the contractor shall post, in a conspicuous location at the job site and at the main office, if one exists, of the job site, a notice that the original contractor intends to file a 10–day stop work order pursuant to this section. A copy of the written notice shall also be served upon all subcontractors with whom the original contractor has a direct contractual relationship on the project at the same time the notice is served upon the owner. Within five days of receipt of written notice by an original contractor pursuant to this section, the owner shall forward to the construction lender, if any, at the address provided in the construction loan agreement, a copy of the notice by first–class mail.

Upon resolution of the dispute or cancellation of the 10–day notice by the original contractor, the original contractor shall post, in a conspicuous location at the job site and at the main office, and serve a notice to inform the subcontractors with whom the original contractor has a direct contractual relationship of this resolution or cancellation.

(b) The original contractor's right to stop work pursuant to this section is in addition to any and all other rights the original contractor may have under the law.

(c) Notwithstanding any other provision, the original contractor or his or her surety, or subcontractor or his or her surety, shall not be liable for any delays or damages that the owner or contractor of a subcontractor may suffer as a result of the original contractor serving the owner with a 10–day stop work order, and subsequently stopping work for nonpayment if all of the posting and notice requirements described in subdivision (a) are met. An original contractor's or original subcontractor's liability to a subcontractor or material supplier resulting from the cessation of work under this section shall be limited to the amount of monetary damages the subcontractor or material supplier could recover under the mechanic's lien law for goods and services provided up to the date the subcontractor ceases work, provided that (1) liability shall continue for work performed and materials supplied up to and including the 10–day notice period and not beyond, and (2) this provision does not apply to limit monetary damages for custom work, including materials which have been fabricated, manufactured, or ordered to specifications that are unique to the job.

(d) If the payment is not made within 10 days from the date the notice was served, the original contractor or his or her surety, may seek a judicial determination of liability for the amount not paid for work performed in an expedited proceeding in the superior court in the county in which the private work improvement is located.

(e) It shall be against public policy to waive the provisions of this section in any written contract for private work of improvement.

(f) This section shall apply to any contract entered into on or after January 1, 1999. However, nothing in this section shall be construed to apply to retentions withheld by a lender in accordance with the construction loan agreement.

(g) The stop work order specified in this section for private works of improvement may be served as follows:

(1) If the person to be notified resides in this state, by delivering the stop work order personally, or by leaving it at his or her address of residence or place of business with some person in charge, or by first–class registered or certified mail, postage prepaid, addressed to the person to whom notice is to be given at his or her residence or place of business address or at the address shown by the building permit on file with the authority issuing a building permit for the work, or at an address recorded pursuant to subdivision (j) of Section 3097.

(2) If the person to be notified of the stop work order does not reside in this state, by any method enumerated in paragraph (1) of this subdivision. If the person cannot be served by any of these methods, then notice may be given by first–class certified or registered mail, addressed to the construction lender.

(3) Service pursuant to this paragraph by certified mail is effective upon receipt. Service by registered mail is effective five days after mailing.

Added Stats 1998 ch 986 § 1 (AB 2627). Repealed Stats 2010 ch 697 § 16 (SB 189), effective January 1, 2011, operative July 1, 2012.

PART 6

WORKS OF IMPROVEMENT

TITLE 1
Works of Improvement Generally

Chapter 1

General Provisions

Article 1

Definitions

§ 8000.   Definitions as governing construction of part (Operative July 1, 2012)

Unless the provision or context otherwise requires, the definitions in this article govern the construction of this part.

Added Stats 2010 ch 697 § 20 (SB 189), effective January 1, 2011, operative July 1, 2012.

Law Revision Commission Comments:

2010—Section 8000 continues former Section 3082 without substantive change.

§ 8002.   "Admitted surety insurer" (Operative July 1, 2012)

"Admitted surety insurer" has the meaning provided in Section 995.120 of the Code of Civil Procedure.

Added Stats 2010 ch 697 § 20 (SB 189), effective January 1, 2011, operative July 1, 2012.

Law Revision Commission Comments:

2010—Section 8002 is new. It is included for drafting convenience. "Admitted surety insurer" replaces references in former law to a corporate surety authorized to write or issue surety bonds in the State of California.

See Sections 8424 (lien claim release bond), 8510 (stop payment notice release bond), 8534 (construction lender objection to bonded stop payment notice), 8604 (lending institution objection to surety on payment bond), 8606 (payment bond).

§ 8004.   "Claimant" (Operative July 1, 2012)

"Claimant" means a person that has a right under this part to record a claim of lien, give a stop payment notice, or assert a claim against a payment bond, or do any combination of the foregoing.

Added Stats 2010 ch 697 § 20 (SB 189), effective January 1, 2011, operative July 1, 2012.

Law Revision Commission Comments:

2010—Section 8004 restates former Section 3085 without substantive change.

See also Sections 8026 ("lien"), 8030 ("payment bond"), 8032 ("person"), 8044 ("stop payment notice").

§ 8006. "Construction lender" (Operative July 1, 2012)

"Construction lender" means either of the following:

(a) A mortgagee or beneficiary under a deed of trust lending funds with which the cost of all or part of a work of improvement is to be paid, or the assignee or successor in interest of the mortgagee or beneficiary.

(b) An escrow holder or other person holding funds provided by an owner, lender, or another person as a fund for with which the cost of all or part of a work of improvement is to be paid.

Added Stats 2010 ch 697 § 20 (SB 189), effective January 1, 2011, operative July 1, 2012.

Law Revision Commission Comments:

2010—Section 8006 restates former Section 3087 without substantive change.

See also Section 14 (present includes future).

See also Sections 8032 ("person"), 8050 ("work of improvement").

§ 8008. "Contract" (Operative July 1, 2012)

"Contract" means an agreement that provides for all or part of a work of improvement.

Added Stats 2010 ch 697 § 20 (SB 189), effective January 1, 2011, operative July 1, 2012.

Law Revision Commission Comments:

2010—Section 8008 broadens the definition of "contract" in former Section 3088. There are instances in this part where the term is not used in its defined sense. See, e.g., Section 8444(d)(2). See also Section 8000 (application of definitions).

An agreement between an owner and a direct contractor that provides for all or part of a work of improvement is a "direct contract." See Section 8016.

See also Section 8050 ("work of improvement").

§ 8010. "Contract price" (Operative July 1, 2012)

"Contract price" means the price agreed to in a direct contract for a work of improvement.

Added Stats 2010 ch 697 § 20 (SB 189), effective January 1, 2011, operative July 1, 2012.

Appendix

Law Revision Commission Comments:

> **2010**—Section 8010 is new. It is included for drafting convenience.
> See also Sections 8016 ("direct contract"), 8050 ("work of improvement").

§ 8012. "Contractor" (Operative July 1, 2012)

"Contractor" includes a direct contractor, subcontractor, or both. This section does not apply to Sections 8018 and 8046.

Added Stats 2010 ch 697 § 20 (SB 189), effective January 1, 2011, operative July 1, 2012.

Law Revision Commission Comments:

> **2010**—Section 8012 is new. It is included for drafting convenience.
> See also Sections 8018 ("direct contractor"), 8046 ("subcontractor").

§ 8014. "Design professional" (Operative July 1, 2012)

"Design professional" means a person licensed as an architect pursuant to Chapter 3 (commencing with Section 5500) of Division 3 of the Business and Professions Code, licensed as a landscape architect pursuant to Chapter 3.5 (commencing with Section 5615) of Division 3 of the Business and Professions Code, registered as a professional engineer pursuant to Chapter 7 (commencing with Section 6700) of Division 3 of the Business and Professions Code, or licensed as a land surveyor pursuant to Chapter 15 (commencing with Section 8700) of Division 3 of the Business and Professions Code.

Added Stats 2010 ch 697 § 20 (SB 189), effective January 1, 2011, operative July 1, 2012.

Law Revision Commission Comments:

> **2010**—Section 8014 generalizes the first paragraph of former Section 3081.1, and adds a licensed landscape architect to the persons included within the definition of "design professional."
> See also Sections 8032 ("person"), 8050 ("work of improvement").

§ 8016. "Direct contract" (Operative July 1, 2012)

"Direct contract" means a contract between an owner and a direct contractor that provides for all or part of a work of improvement.

Added Stats 2010 ch 697 § 20 (SB 189), effective January 1, 2011, operative July 1, 2012.

Law Revision Commission Comments:

> **2010**—Section 8016 restates former Section 3088 without substantive change.
> See also Sections 8008 ("contract"), 8018 ("direct contractor"), 8050 ("work of improvement").

§ 8018. "Direct contractor" (Operative July 1, 2012)

"Direct contractor" means a contractor that has a direct contractual relationship with an owner. A reference in another statute to a "prime contractor" in connection with the provisions in this part means a "direct contractor."

Added Stats 2010 ch 697 § 20 (SB 189), effective January 1, 2011, operative July 1, 2012.

Law Revision Commission Comments:

2010—Section 8018 supersedes former Section 3095 ("original contractor"). A direct contractor within the meaning of this section is one that contracts directly with the owner, as opposed to one that contracts with another contractor (i.e., a subcontractor).

A direct contractor is at times referred to in other code sections as a "prime contractor." See e.g., Pub. Cont. Code § 4113.

§ 8020. "Funds" (Operative July 1, 2012)

For the purposes of Title 3 (commencing with Section 9000), "funds" means warrant, check, money, or bonds (if bonds are to be issued in payment of the public works contract).

Added Stats 2010 ch 697 § 20 (SB 189), effective January 1, 2011, operative July 1, 2012.

Law Revision Commission Comments:

2010—Section 8020 is new. It is included for drafting convenience. It generalizes provisions of former Sections 3186, 3187, and 3196.

See also Section 8038 ("public works contract").

§ 8022. "Labor, service, equipment, or material" (Operative July 1, 2012)

"Labor, service, equipment, or material" includes, but is not limited to, labor, skills, services, material, supplies, equipment, appliances, power, and surveying, provided for a work of improvement.

Added Stats 2010 ch 697 § 20 (SB 189), effective January 1, 2011, operative July 1, 2012.

Law Revision Commission Comments:

2010—Section 8022 is new. It is included for drafting convenience. The phrase is intended to replace various phrases used throughout the former law, including "labor or material," "labor, services, equipment, or materials," "appliances, teams, or power," and the like, and is not intended to effect any change in the law. The definition applies to variant grammatical forms of the phrase used in this part, such as "labor, service, equipment, and material."

See also Section 8050 ("work of improvement").

§ 8024. "Laborer"; Standing to enforce rights or claims of laborer; Public policy (Operative July 1, 2012)

(a) "Laborer" means a person who, acting as an employee, performs labor upon, or bestows skill or other necessary services on, a work of improvement.

(b) "Laborer" includes a person or entity to which a portion of a laborer's compensation for a work of improvement, including, but not limited to, employer payments described in Section 1773.1 of the Labor Code and implementing regulations, is paid by agreement with that laborer or the collective bargaining agent of that laborer.

(c) A person or entity described in subdivision (b) that has standing under applicable law to maintain a direct legal action, in its own name or as an assignee, to collect any portion of compensation owed for a laborer for a work of improvement, shall have standing to enforce any rights or claims of the laborer under this part, to the extent of the compensation agreed to be paid to the person or entity for labor on that improvement. This subdivision is intended to give effect to the longstanding public policy of this state to protect the entire compensation of a laborer on a work of improvement, regardless of the form in which that compensation is to be paid.

Added Stats 2010 ch 697 § 20 (SB 189), effective January 1, 2011, operative July 1, 2012.

Law Revision Commission Comments:

2010—Subdivision (a) of Section 8024 continues former Section 3089(a) without substantive change.

Subdivision (b) restates the first sentence of former Section 3089(b) and a part of former Section 3111 without substantive change.

Subdivision (c) restates the second and third sentences of former Section 3089(b) and a part of former Section 3111 without substantive change.

See also Sections 8032 ("person"), 8050 ("work of improvement").

§ 8026. "Lien" (Operative July 1, 2012)

"Lien" means a lien under Title 2 (commencing with Section 8160) and includes a lien of a design professional under Section 8302, a lien for a work of improvement under Section 8400, and a lien for a site improvement under Section 8402.

Added Stats 2010 ch 697 § 20 (SB 189), effective January 1, 2011, operative July 1, 2012.

Law Revision Commission Comments:

2010—Section 8026 is new. It is included for drafting convenience. There are instances in this part where the term is not used in its defined sense. See Section 8000 (application of definitions).

Note that the application of this part to a design professionals lien is limited. See Section 8308 (application of part).

See also Sections 8014 ("design professional"), 8042 ("site improvement"), 8050 ("work of improvement").

§ 8028. "Material supplier" (Operative July 1, 2012)

"Material supplier" means a person that provides material or supplies to be used or consumed in a work of improvement.

Added Stats 2010 ch 697 § 20 (SB 189), effective January 1, 2011, operative July 1, 2012.

Law Revision Commission Comments:

2010—Section 8028 continues former Section 3090 without substantive change. It replaces the term "materialman" with the term "material supplier" to conform to contemporary usage under this part.

See also Sections 8032 ("person"), 8050 ("work of improvement").

§ 8030. "Payment bond" (Operative July 1, 2012)

(a) For the purposes of Title 2 (commencing with Section 8160), "payment bond" means a bond given under Section 8600.

(b) For the purposes of Title 3 (commencing with Section 9000), "payment bond" means a bond required by Section 9550.

Added Stats 2010 ch 697 § 20 (SB 189), effective January 1, 2011, operative July 1, 2012.

Law Revision Commission Comments:

2010—Section 8030 supersedes former Section 3096. There are instances in this part where the term is not used in its defined sense. See, e.g., Sections 8452 (payment bond obtained by holder of mortgage or deed of trust), 8720-8722 (payment bond as security for large project).

See also Section 8000 (application of definitions).

§ 8032. "Person" (Operative July 1, 2012)

"Person" means an individual, corporation, public entity, business trust, estate, trust, partnership, limited liability company, association, or other entity.

Added Stats 2010 ch 697 § 20 (SB 189), effective January 1, 2011, operative July 1, 2012.

Law Revision Commission Comments:

2010—Section 8032 is a new definition. It is included for drafting convenience. It supplements Section 14 ("person" includes corporation as well as natural person).

See also Section 8036 ("public entity").

§ 8034. "Preliminary notice" (Operative July 1, 2012)

(a) For the purposes of Title 2 (commencing with Section 8160), "preliminary notice" means the notice provided for in Chapter 2 (commencing with Section 8200) of Title 2.

(b) For the purposes of Title 3 (commencing with Section 9000), "preliminary notice" means the notice provided for in Chapter 3 (commencing with Section 9300) of Title 3.

Added Stats 2010 ch 697 § 20 (SB 189), effective January 1, 2011, operative July 1, 2012.

Law Revision Commission Comments:

2010—Section 8034 supersedes parts of former Sections 3097 and 3098. The substantive requirements for preliminary notice on a private work are relocated to Section 8200 et seq. The substantive requirements for preliminary notice on a public work are relocated to Section 9300 *et seq.*

§ 8036. "Public entity" (Operative July 1, 2012)

"Public entity" means the state, Regents of the University of California, a county, city, district, public authority, public agency, and any other political subdivision or public corporation in the state.

Added Stats 2010 ch 697 § 20 (SB 189), effective January 1, 2011, operative July 1, 2012.

Law Revision Commission Comments:

2010—Section 8036 continues former Section 3099 without change.
See also Section 14 ("county" includes city and county).

§ 8038. "Public works contract" (Operative July 1, 2012)

"Public works contract" has the meaning provided in Section 1101 of the Public Contract Code.

Added Stats 2010 ch 697 § 20 (SB 189), effective January 1, 2011, operative July 1, 2012.

Law Revision Commission Comments:

2010—Section 8038 supersedes former Section 3100 ("public work"). Under Public Contract Code Section 1101, "public works contract" means an agreement for the erection, construction, alteration, repair, or improvement of any public structure, building, road, or other public improvement of any kind.

§ 8040. "Site" (Operative July 1, 2012)

"Site" means the real property on which a work of improvement is situated or planned.

Added Stats 2010 ch 697 § 20 (SB 189), effective January 1, 2011, operative July 1, 2012.

Law Revision Commission Comments:

2010—Section 8040 continues former Section 3101 without substantive change, except to add a reference to a planned work of improvement. See Section 8302 (design professionals lien).

See also Section 8050 ("work of improvement").

§ 8042. "Site improvement" (Operative July 1, 2012)

"Site improvement" means any of the following work on real property:

(a) Demolition or removal of improvements, trees, or other vegetation.

(b) Drilling test holes.

(c) Grading, filling, or otherwise improving the real property or a street, highway, or sidewalk in front of or adjoining the real property.

(d) Construction or installation of sewers or other public utilities.

(e) Construction of areas, vaults, cellars, or rooms under sidewalks.

(f) Any other work or improvements in preparation of the site for a work of improvement.

Added Stats 2010 ch 697 § 20 (SB 189), effective January 1, 2011, operative July 1, 2012.

Law Revision Commission Comments:

2010—Section 8042 continues former Section 3102 without substantive change, except that subdivision (f) makes clear that the reference in former law to "making any improvements" means preparatory work, and does not include construction of a structure.

See also Sections 8040 ("site"), 8048 ("work"), 8050 ("work of improvement").

§ 8044. "Stop payment notice"; "Bonded stop payment notice"; "Stop notice" (Operative July 1, 2012)

(a)(1) For the purposes of Title 2 (commencing with Section 8160), "stop payment notice" means the notice given by a claimant under Chapter 5 (commencing with Section 8500) of Title 2.

(2) A stop payment notice given under Title 2 (commencing with Section 8160) may be bonded or unbonded. A "bonded stop payment notice" is a notice given with a bond under Section 8532. An "unbonded stop payment notice" is a notice not given with a bond under Section 8532.

(3) Except to the extent Title 2 (commencing with Section 8160) distinguishes between a bonded and an unbonded stop payment notice, a reference in that title to a stop payment notice includes both a bonded and an unbonded notice.

(b) For the purposes of Title 3 (commencing with Section 9000), "stop payment notice" means the notice given by a claimant under Chapter 4 (commencing with Section 9350) of Title 3.

Appendix

(c) A reference in another statute to a "stop notice" in connection with the remedies provided in this part means a stop payment notice.

Added Stats 2010 ch 697 § 20 (SB 189), effective January 1, 2011, operative July 1, 2012.

Law Revision Commission Comments:

2010—Section 8044 supersedes former Section 3103. The term "stop payment notice" replaces the term "stop notice" used in former law.
See also Section 8004 ("claimant").

§ 8046. "Subcontractor" (Operative July 1, 2012)

"Subcontractor" means a contractor that does not have a direct contractual relationship with an owner. The term includes a contractor that has a contractual relationship with a direct contractor or with another subcontractor.

Added Stats 2010 ch 697 § 20 (SB 189), effective January 1, 2011, operative July 1, 2012.

Law Revision Commission Comments:

2010—The first sentence of Section 8046 continues former Section 3104 without substantive change. The second sentence is new; it makes clear that the term "subcontractor" includes a subcontractor of a subcontractor.
See also Section 8018 ("direct contractor").

§ 8048. "Work" (Operative July 1, 2012)

"Work" means labor, service, equipment, or material provided to a work of improvement.

Added Stats 2010 ch 697 § 20 (SB 189), effective January 1, 2011, operative July 1, 2012.

Law Revision Commission Comments:

2010—Section 8048 is new. It is included for drafting convenience.
See also Sections 8022 ("labor, service, equipment, or material"), 8050 ("work of improvement").

§ 8050. "Work of improvement" (Operative July 1, 2012)

(a) "Work of improvement" includes, but is not limited to:
(1) Construction, alteration, repair, demolition, or removal, in whole or in part, of, or addition to, a building, wharf, bridge, ditch, flume, aqueduct, well, tunnel, fence, machinery, railroad, or road.
(2) Seeding, sodding, or planting of real property for landscaping purposes.
(3) Filling, leveling, or grading of real property.

(b) Except as otherwise provided in this part, "work of improvement" means the entire structure or scheme of improvement as a whole, and includes site improvement.

Added Stats 2010 ch 697 § 20 (SB 189), effective January 1, 2011, operative July 1, 2012.

Law Revision Commission Comments:

2010—Section 8050 restates former Section 3106. The section is revised to reorganize and tabulate the different types of work falling within the definition, to expand the coverage of the definition, and to make various technical, nonsubstantive revisions. The term "real property" replaces "lot or tract of land."

A site improvement is treated under this part in the same manner as a work of improvement, except as specifically provided in this part. See e.g., Sections 8450 (priority of lien), 8458 (priority of site improvement lien).

See also Section 8042 ("site improvement").

Article 2

Miscellaneous Provisions

§ 8052. Operative date; Effectiveness of notice on work of improvement; Provisions construed as restatements and continuations (Operative July 1, 2012)

(a) This part is operative on July 1, 2012.

(b) Notwithstanding subdivision (a), the effectiveness of a notice given or other action taken on a work of improvement before July 1, 2012, is governed by the applicable law in effect before July 1, 2012, and not by this part.

(c) A provision of this part, insofar as it is substantially the same as a previously existing provision relating to the same subject matter, shall be construed as a restatement and continuation thereof and not as a new enactment.

Added Stats 2010 ch 697 § 20 (SB 189), effective January 1, 2011, operative July 1, 2012.

Law Revision Commission Comments:

2010—Section 8052 is new. Although this part applies generally to all works of improvement on or after July 1, 2012, it does not govern notices given or actions taken prior to July 1, 2012, on a work of improvement. Such notices or actions are governed by former law.

Subdivision (c) states the relationship between a provision of this part and a provision of former law that the provision of this part continues or restates. See also Section 107 of Chapter 697 of the Statutes of 2010.

See also Section 8050 ("work of improvement").

§ 8054. Applicability of part (Operative July 1, 2012)

(a) This part does not apply to a transaction governed by the Oil and Gas Lien Act (Chapter 2.5 (commencing with Section 1203.50) of Title 4 of Part 3 of the Code of Civil Procedure).

(b) This part does not apply to or change improvement security under the Subdivision Map Act (Division 2 (commencing with Section 66410) of Title 7 of the Government Code).

(c) This part does not apply to a transaction governed by Sections 20457 to 20464, inclusive, of the Public Contract Code.

Added Stats 2010 ch 697 § 20 (SB 189), effective January 1, 2011, operative July 1, 2012.

Law Revision Commission Comments:

2010—Subdivision (a) of Section 8054 restates former Section 3266(a).

Subdivision (b) is new. It clarifies the interrelation between this part and the Subdivision Map Act. For relevant provisions of that act, see Government Code Sections 66499-66499.10 (improvement security).

Subdivision (c) restates former Section 3266(b). This provision updates the former cross-reference to Streets and Highways Code Sections 5290-5297, which were repealed in 1982 when the Public Contract Code was created. See 1982 Cal. Stat. ch. 465, § 56. The repealed sections were superseded by Public Contract Code Sections 20457-20464. See 1982 Cal. Stat. ch. 465, § 11. The new sections apply to bonds in "street work" projects under Division 2 (commencing with Section 1600) of the Public Contract Code. See Pub. Cont. Code § 20457.

§ 8056. Applicable Code of Civil Procedure provisions (Operative July 1, 2012)

Except as otherwise provided in this part, Part 2 (commencing with Section 307) of the Code of Civil Procedure provides the rules of practice in proceedings under this part.

Added Stats 2010 ch 697 § 20 (SB 189), effective January 1, 2011, operative July 1, 2012.

Law Revision Commission Comments:

2010—Section 8056 continues the first sentence of former Section 3259 without substantive change. The second sentence of former Section 3259 is not continued; this part does not include special provisions relating to new trials or appeals.

Section 8056 makes former Section 3149, relating to joinder and consolidation of actions, unnecessary. Part 2 of the Code of Civil Procedure enables persons claiming liens on the same property to join in the same action to enforce their liens. See Code Civ. Proc. § 378 (permissive joinder). If separate actions are commenced, the court may consolidate them. See Code Civ. Proc. § 1048 (consolidation of actions).

§ 8058. "Day" (Operative July 1, 2012)

For purposes of this part, "day" means a calendar day.

Added Stats 2010 ch 697 § 20 (SB 189), effective January 1, 2011, operative July 1, 2012.

Law Revision Commission Comments:

2010—Section 8058 is new. A reference to the term "day" in a statute typically means a calendar day, unless otherwise specifically indicated. Iverson v. Superior Court, 167 Cal. App. 3d 544, 548, 213 Cal. Rptr. 399 (1985).)

See also Sections 10 (computing time), 11 (holidays).

§ 8060. Filing documents with county recorder; Duties of county recorder (Operative July 1, 2012)

(a) If this part provides for filing a contract, plan, or other paper with the county recorder, the provision is satisfied by filing the paper in the office of the county recorder of the county in which the work of improvement or part of it is situated.

(b) If this part provides for recording a notice, claim of lien, release of lien, payment bond, or other paper, the provision is satisfied by filing the paper for record in the office of the county recorder of the county in which the work of improvement or part of it is situated.

(c) The county recorder shall number, index, and preserve a contract, plan, or other paper presented for filing under this part, and shall number, index, and transcribe into the official records, in the same manner as a conveyance of real property, a notice, claim of lien, payment bond, or other paper recorded under this part.

(d) The county recorder shall charge and collect the fees provided in Article 5 (commencing with Section 27360) of Chapter 6 of Part 3 of Division 2 of Title 3 of the Government Code for performing duties under this section.

Added Stats 2010 ch 697 § 20 (SB 189), effective January 1, 2011, operative July 1, 2012.

Law Revision Commission Comments:

2010—Subdivisions (a) and (b) of Section 8060 are new. They generalize a number of provisions of former law. See also Section 1170 (recordation), Gov't Code §§ 27280, 27287 (recordation of documents).

Subdivisions (c) and (d) continue former Section 3258 without substantive change.

See also Sections 8008 ("contract"), 8024 ("lien"), 8030 ("payment bond"), 8050 ("work of improvement").

§ 8062. Construction of acts of owner; Exoneration of surety on performance or payment bond (Operative July 1, 2012)

No act of an owner in good faith and in compliance with a provision of this part shall be construed to prevent a direct contractor's performance of the contract, or exonerate a surety on a performance or payment bond.

Added Stats 2010 ch 697 § 20 (SB 189), effective January 1, 2011, operative July 1, 2012.

Law Revision Commission Comments:

> **2010**—Section 8062 restates former Section 3263 without substantive change.
> See also Section 8152 (no release of surety from liability).
> See also Sections 8008 ("contract"), 8018 ("direct contractor"), 8030 ("payment bond").

§ 8064. Acts on behalf of co-owner; Requirements (Operative July 1, 2012)

An owner may give a notice or execute or file a document under this part on behalf of a co-owner if the owner acts on the co-owner's behalf and includes in the notice or document the name and address of the co-owner on whose behalf the owner acts.

Added Stats 2010 ch 697 § 20 (SB 189), effective January 1, 2011, operative July 1, 2012.

Law Revision Commission Comments:

> **2010**—Section 8064 is new. It generalizes provisions found in former Sections 3092 (notice of cessation) and 3093 (notice of completion).

§ 8066. Acts within scope of agent's authority (Operative July 1, 2012)

An act that may be done by or to a person under this part may be done by or to the person's agent to the extent the act is within the scope of the agent's authority.

Added Stats 2010 ch 697 § 20 (SB 189), effective January 1, 2011, operative July 1, 2012.

Law Revision Commission Comments:

> **2010**—Section 8066 is a specific application of Section 2305. This section makes clear that an agent's authority is limited to the scope of the agency. Thus, to the extent a direct contractor is deemed to be the agent of an owner for the purpose of engaging a subcontractor, the scope of the agency does not include other acts, such as compromise of litigation.
> For provisions relating to the agency authority of co-owners, see Section 8064 (co-owners).
> See also Section 8032 ("person").

Chapter 2

Notice

§ 8100.   Form of notice; "Writings" (Operative July 1, 2012)

Notice under this part shall be in writing. Writing includes printing and typewriting.

Added Stats 2010 ch 697 § 20 (SB 189), effective January 1, 2011, operative July 1, 2012.

Law Revision Commission Comments:

2010—Section 8100 generalizes various provisions of former law. See, e.g., former Sections 3092 (notice of cessation), 3093 (notice of completion), 3094 (notice of nonresponsibility), 3097 (preliminary notice (private work)), 3103 (stop notice).
See also Evid. Code § 250 ("writing").

§ 8102.   Contents of notice; Sufficiency (Operative July 1, 2012)

(a) Notice under this part shall, in addition to any other information required by statute for that type of notice, include all of the following information to the extent known to the person giving the notice:

(1) The name and address of the owner or reputed owner.

(2) The name and address of the direct contractor.

(3) The name and address of the construction lender, if any.

(4) A description of the site sufficient for identification, including the street address of the site, if any. If a sufficient legal description of the site is given, the effectiveness of the notice is not affected by the fact that the street address is erroneous or is omitted.

(5) The name, address, and relationship to the parties of the person giving the notice.

(6) If the person giving the notice is a claimant:

(A) A general statement of the work provided.

(B) The name of the person to or for whom the work is provided.

(C) A statement or estimate of the claimant's demand, if any, after deducting all just credits and offsets.

(b) Notice is not invalid by reason of any variance from the requirements of this section if the notice is sufficient to substantially inform the person given notice of the information required by this section and other information required in the notice.

Added Stats 2010 ch 697 § 20 (SB 189), effective January 1, 2011, operative July 1, 2012.

Law Revision Commission Comments:

2010—Section 8102 is new. It generalizes and standardizes provisions found throughout former law. See, e.g., former Sections 3092 (notice of cessation), 3093 (notice of completion), 3097 (preliminary notice), 3103 (stop notice).

See also Sections 8004 ("claimant"), 8006 ("construction lender"), 8018 ("direct contractor"), 8032 ("person"), 8040 ("site"), 8048 ("work").

§ 8104.   Failure to pay full compensation to laborer; Notice required; Contents; Grounds for disciplinary action (Operative July 1, 2012)

(a) A direct contractor or subcontractor on a work of improvement governed by this part that employs a laborer and fails to pay the full compensation due the laborer, including any employer payments described in Section 1773.1 of the Labor Code and implementing regulations, shall not later than the date the compensation became delinquent, give the laborer, the laborer's bargaining representative, if any, the construction lender or reputed construction lender, if any, and the owner or reputed owner, notice that includes all of the following information, in addition to the information required by Section 8102:

(1) The name and address of the laborer, and of any person or entity described in subdivision (b) of Section 8024 to which employer payments are due.

(2) The total number of straight time and overtime hours worked by the laborer on each job.

(3) The amount then past due and owing.

(b) Failure to give the notice required by subdivision (a) constitutes grounds for disciplinary action under the Contractors' State License Law, Chapter 9 (commencing with Section 7000) of Division 3 of the Business and Professions Code.

Added Stats 2010 ch 697 § 20 (SB 189), effective January 1, 2011, operative July 1, 2012.

Law Revision Commission Comments:

2010—Section 8104 restates former Section 3097(k), with the additional requirement that the information provided be given to the owner or reputed owner, and include the name and address of the unpaid laborer. See also Sections 8100-8118 (notice).

The reference to the Registrar of Contractors in the final sentence of former Section 3097(k) is revised to refer to the Contractors' State License Law. This is a technical, nonsubstantive change.

The information required in this notice is in addition to the information required by Section 8102 (contents of notice).

Compliance with this section does not excuse compliance with Section 8202(b), if applicable. See Section 8202 (contents of preliminary notice).

See also Sections 8006 ("construction lender"), 8018 ("direct contractor"), 8024 ("laborer"), 8032 ("person"), 8046 ("subcontractor"), 8050 ("work of improvement").

§ 8106. Manner of giving notice (Operative July 1, 2012)

Except as otherwise provided by statute, notice under this part shall be given by any of the following means:

(a) Personal delivery.

(b) Mail in the manner provided in Section 8110.

(c) Leaving the notice and mailing a copy in the manner provided in Section 415.20 of the Code of Civil Procedure for service of summons and complaint in a civil action.

Added Stats 2010 ch 697 § 20 (SB 189), effective January 1, 2011, operative July 1, 2012.

Law Revision Commission Comments:

2010—Section 8106 is new. It generalizes and standardizes provisions found throughout former law. See, e.g., former Sections 3097 (preliminary notice), 3103 (stop notice), 3144.5 (notice of release bond), 3227 (notice to principal and surety), 3259.5 (notice of recordation of notice of completion), 3260.2 (stop work notice).

Under subdivision (c), when notice is given in the manner provided in Code of Civil Procedure Section 415.20 for service of summons and complaint, the notice is complete five days after mailing the notice. See Section 8116 (when notice complete). The 10 day delay provided in the Code of Civil Procedure for completion of service under that code is inapplicable.

This part may prescribe a different or more limited manner of giving a particular notice. See, e.g., Section 8486 (service of petition for order releasing lien).

§ 8108. Person to be notified at person's residence, place of business, or specified addresses (Operative July 1, 2012)

Except as otherwise provided by this part, notice under this part shall be given to the person to be notified at the person's residence, the person's place of business, or at any of the following addresses:

(a) If the person to be notified is an owner other than a public entity, the owner's address shown on the direct contract, the building permit, or a construction trust deed.

(b) If the person to be notified is a public entity, the office of the public entity or another address specified by the public entity in the contract or elsewhere for service of notices, papers, and other documents.

(c) If the person to be notified is a construction lender, the construction lender's address shown on the construction loan agreement or construction trust deed.

(d) If the person to be notified is a direct contractor or a subcontractor, the contractor's address shown on the building permit, on the contractor's contract, or on the records of the Contractors' State License Board.

(e) If the person to be notified is a claimant, the claimant's address shown on the claimant's contract, preliminary notice, claim of lien, stop payment notice, or claim against a payment bond, or on the records of the Contractors' State License Board.

(f) If the person to be notified is a surety on a bond, the surety's address shown on the bond for service of notices, papers, and other documents, or on the records of the Department of Insurance.

Added Stats 2010 ch 697 § 20 (SB 189), effective January 1, 2011, operative July 1, 2012.

Law Revision Commission Comments:

2010—Section 8108 is new. It generalizes and standardizes provisions found throughout former law. For an example of a more particularized notice provision, see Section 8506.

Subdivision (f) does not continue the unique provisions found in former Section 3227 for notice to alternate persons in the case of a personal surety or admitted surety insurer. The bond and undertaking law requires every bond to include the address at which the principal and sureties may be served with notices, papers, and other documents. See Code Civ. Proc. § 995.320.

See also Sections 8004 ("claimant"), 8006 ("construction lender"), 8008 ("contract"), 8012 ("contractor"), 8016 ("direct contract"), 8018 ("direct contractor"), 8026 ("lien"), 8030 ("payment bond"), 8032 ("person"), 8034 ("preliminary notice"), 8036 ("public entity"), 8044 ("stop payment notice"), 8046 ("subcontractor").

§ 8110. Registered or certified mail, express mail, or overnight delivery by express service carrier (Operative July 1, 2012)

Except as otherwise provided by this part, notice by mail under this part shall be given by registered or certified mail, express mail, or overnight delivery by an express service carrier.

Added Stats 2010 ch 697 § 20 (SB 189), effective January 1, 2011, operative July 1, 2012.

Law Revision Commission Comments:

2010—Section 8110 is a new provision included for drafting convenience. It generalizes a number of provisions of former law, and expands the methods of giving notice to include delivery by express service carrier.

For an example of a more particularized notice provision, see Section 8486.

§ 8114. Posting of notice (Operative July 1, 2012)

A notice required by this part to be posted shall be displayed in a conspicuous location at the site.

Added Stats 2010 ch 697 § 20 (SB 189), effective January 1, 2011, operative July 1, 2012.

Law Revision Commission Comments:

2010—Section 8114 is new. It generalizes provisions found in former law. See, e.g., former Sections 3094 (notice of nonresponsibility), 3260.2 (stop work notice).

See also Section 8040 ("site").

§ 8116. When notice is complete and deemed to have been given at specified times (Operative July 1, 2012)

Notice under this part is complete and deemed to have been given at the following times:

(a) If given by personal delivery, when delivered.

(b) If given by mail, when deposited in the mail or with an express service carrier in the manner provided in Section 1013 of the Code of Civil Procedure.

(c) If given by leaving the notice and mailing a copy in the manner provided in Section 415.20 of the Code of Civil Procedure for service of summons in a civil action, five days after mailing.

(d) If given by posting, when displayed.

(e) If given by recording, when recorded in the office of the county recorder.

Added Stats 2010 ch 697 § 20 (SB 189), effective January 1, 2011, operative July 1, 2012.

Law Revision Commission Comments:

2010—Section 8116 is new. It generalizes and standardizes provisions found in former law. See, e.g., former Section 3097(f)(3) (service of preliminary notice).

Under subdivision (b), when notice is given in the manner provided in Code of Civil Procedure Section 1013, the notice is complete when deposited in the mail or with an express service carrier. The 10 and 20 day delays provided in the Code of Civil Procedure for completion of service under that code are inapplicable. For an exception to this rule, see Section 8486 (notice of hearing on lien release petition).

Under subdivision (c), when notice is given in the manner provided in Code of Civil Procedure Section 415.20 for service of summons and complaint, the notice is complete five days after mailing of the notice. The 10 day delay provided in the Code of Civil Procedure for completion of service under that code is inapplicable.

See also Sections 1170 (recordation), 8058 (calculation of time), 8060 (filing and re-cordation of papers), 8110 (mailed notice), 8114 (posting of notice).

§ 8118. Proof that notice was given; Proof of notice declaration; Contents (Operative July 1, 2012)

(a) Proof that notice was given to a person in the manner required by this part shall be made by a proof of notice declaration that states all of the following:

(1) The type or description of the notice given.

(2) The date, place, and manner of notice, and facts showing that notice was given in the manner required by statute.

(3) The name and address of the person to which notice was given, and, if appropriate, the title or capacity in which the person was given notice.

(b) If the notice is given by mail, the declaration shall be accompanied by one of the following:

(1) Documentation provided by the United States Postal Service showing that payment was made to mail the notice using registered or certified mail, or express mail.

(2) Documentation provided by an express service carrier showing that payment was made to send the notice using an overnight delivery service.

(3) A return receipt, delivery confirmation, signature confirmation, tracking record, or other proof of delivery or attempted delivery provided by the United States Postal Service, or a photocopy of the record of delivery and receipt maintained by the United States Postal Service, showing the date of delivery and to whom delivered, or in the event of nondelivery, by the returned envelope itself.

(4) A tracking record or other documentation provided by an express service carrier showing delivery or attempted delivery of the notice.

Added Stats 2010 ch 697 § 20 (SB 189), effective January 1, 2011, operative July 1, 2012.

Law Revision Commission Comments:

2010—Section 8118 is new. It generalizes and standardizes provisions found throughout former law, and expands the methods of proof to include documentation of the mailing provided by the United States Postal Service or an express service carrier. See, e.g., former Sections 3097 (preliminary notice), 3260.2 (stop work notice). Subdivision (b) specifies the documentation that must be attached to a proof of notice declaration when notice is given by mail. Documentation establishing proof of delivery or attempted delivery of the notice as specified in subdivision (b)(3)-(4) is sufficient, but not necessary, to satisfy the requirement of the subdivision. Proof that payment was made to the United States Postal Service or an express service carrier for an approved method of delivery is also sufficient. See subdivision (b)(1)-(2).See also Section 8110 (mailed notice).See also Section 8032 ("person").

Chapter 3

Waiver and Release

§ 8120. Applicability of chapter (Operative July 1, 2012)

The provisions of this chapter apply to a work of improvement governed by this part.

Added Stats 2010 ch 697 § 20 (SB 189), effective January 1, 2011, operative July 1, 2012.

Law Revision Commission Comments:

2010—Section 8120 is new. It provides the scope of applicability of the provisions of Chapter 3 of Title 1.See also Section 8050 ("work of improvement").

§ 8122. Affecting claimant's rights; Exception (Operative July 1, 2012)

An owner, direct contractor, or subcontractor may not, by contract or otherwise, waive, affect, or impair any other claimant's rights under this part, whether with or without notice, and any term of a contract that purports to do so is void and unenforceable unless and until the claimant executes and delivers a waiver and release under this article.

Added Stats 2010 ch 697 § 20 (SB 189), effective January 1, 2011, operative July 1, 2012.

Law Revision Commission Comments:

2010—Section 8122 continues the first and second sentences of former Section 3262(a) without substantive change, except to add a reference to a subcontractor. See also Sections 8004 ("claimant"), 8008 ("contract"), 8018 ("direct contractor"), 8046 ("subcontractor").

§ 8124. Effect of claimant's waiver and release on payment bond from lien or claim; Conditions (Operative July 1, 2012)

A claimant's waiver and release does not release the owner, construction lender, or surety on a payment bond from a lien or claim unless both of the following conditions are satisfied:

(a) The waiver and release is in substantially the form provided in this article and is signed by the claimant.

(b) If the release is a conditional release, there is evidence of payment to the claimant. Evidence of payment may be either of the following:

(1) The claimant's endorsement on a single or joint payee check that has been paid by the financial institution on which it was drawn.

(2) Written acknowledgment of payment by the claimant.

Added Stats 2010 ch 697 § 20 (SB 189), effective January 1, 2011, operative July 1, 2012.

Law Revision Commission Comments:

2010—Section 8124 continues the third and fourth sentences of former Section 3262(a) without substantive change. The term "financial institution" replaces "bank" in subdivision (b) and in the forms provided in this article.

The waiver and release may be signed by the claimant's agent. See Section 8066 (agency).

See also Sections 8004 ("claimant"), 8006 ("construction lender"), 8026 ("lien"), 8030 ("payment bond").

Appendix

§ 8126. Validity and enforceability of oral or written statement (Operative July 1, 2012)

An oral or written statement purporting to waive, release, impair or otherwise adversely affect a lien or claim is void and unenforceable and does not create an estoppel or impairment of the lien or claim unless either of the following conditions is satisfied:

(a) The statement is pursuant to a waiver and release under this article.

(b) The claimant has actually received payment in full for the claim.

Added Stats 2010 ch 697 § 20 (SB 189), effective January 1, 2011, operative July 1, 2012.

Law Revision Commission Comments:

2010—Section 8126 continues former Section 3262(b)(1) without substantive change. See also Section 8004 ("claimant"), 8026 ("lien").

§ 8128. Reduction or release of stop payment notice; Writing; Effect (Operative July 1, 2012)

(a) A claimant may reduce the amount of, or release in its entirety, a stop payment notice. The reduction or release shall be in writing and may be given in a form other than a waiver and release form provided in this article.

(b) The writing shall identify whether it is a reduction of the amount of the stop payment notice, or a release of the notice in its entirety. If the writing is a reduction, it shall state the amount of the reduction, and the amount to remain withheld after the reduction.

(c) A claimant's reduction or release of a stop payment notice has the following effect:

(1) The reduction or release releases the claimant's right to enforce payment of the claim stated in the notice to the extent of the reduction or release.

(2) The reduction or release releases the person given the notice from the obligation to withhold funds pursuant to the notice to the extent of the reduction or release.

(3) The reduction or release does not preclude the claimant from giving a subsequent stop payment notice that is timely and proper.

(4) The reduction or release does not release any right of the claimant other than the right to enforce payment of the claim stated in the stop payment notice to the extent of the reduction or release.

Added Stats 2010 ch 697 § 20 (SB 189), effective January 1, 2011, operative July 1, 2012.

Law Revision Commission Comments:

2010—Subdivisions (a) and (c) of Section 8128 generalize former Section 3262(b)(2), so as to apply to a stop payment notice given to a construction lender as well as to a stop payment notice given to an owner.

Subdivision (b) is new.

See also Sections 8004 ("claimant"), 8032 ("person"), 8044 ("stop payment notice").

§ 8130. Enforceability of accord and satisfaction or agreement and settlement; Effect of article (Operative July 1, 2012)

This article does not affect the enforceability of either an accord and satisfaction concerning a good faith dispute or an agreement made in settlement of an action pending in court if the accord and satisfaction or agreement and settlement make specific reference to the lien or claim.

Added Stats 2010 ch 697 § 20 (SB 189), effective January 1, 2011, operative July 1, 2012.

Law Revision Commission Comments:

2010—Section 8130 continues former Section 3262(c) without substantive change. See also Section 8026 ("lien").

§ 8132. Conditional waiver and release in exchange for progress payment; Form (Operative July 1, 2012)

If a claimant is required to execute a waiver and release in exchange for, or in order to induce payment of, a progress payment and the claimant is not, in fact, paid in exchange for the waiver and release or a single payee check or joint payee check is given in exchange for the waiver and release, the waiver and release shall be null, void, and unenforceable unless it is in substantially the following form:

CONDITIONAL WAIVER AND RELEASE ON PROGRESS

PAYMENT NOTICE: THIS DOCUMENT WAIVES THE CLAIMANT'S LIEN, STOP PAYMENT NOTICE, AND PAYMENT BOND RIGHTS EFFECTIVE ON RECEIPT OF PAYMENT. A PERSON SHOULD NOT RELY ON THIS DOCUMENT UNLESS SATISFIED THAT THE CLAIMANT HAS RECEIVED PAYMENT.

Identifying Information

Name of Claimant: _____

Name of Customer: _____

Job Location: _____

Owner: _____

Through Date: _____

Appendix

Conditional Waiver and Release

This document waives and releases lien, stop payment notice, and payment bond rights the claimant has for labor and service provided, and equipment and material delivered, to the customer on this job through the Through Date of this document. Rights based upon labor or service provided, or equipment or material delivered, pursuant to a written change order that has been fully executed by the parties prior to the date that this document is signed by the claimant, are waived and released by this document, unless listed as an Exception below. This document is effective only on the claimant's receipt of payment from the financial institution on which the following check is drawn:

Maker of Check: _____

Amount of Check: $ _____

Check Payable to: _____

Exceptions

This document does not affect any of the following:

(1) Retentions.

(2) Extras for which the claimant has not received payment.

(3) The following progress payments for which the claimant has previously given a conditional waiver and release but has not received payment:

Date(s) of waiver and release: _____

Amount(s) of unpaid progress payment(s): $ _____

(4) Contract rights, including (A) a right based on rescission, abandonment, or breach of contract, and (B) the right to recover compensation for work not compensated by the payment.

Signature

Claimant's Signature: _____

Claimant's Title: _____

Date of Signature:_____

Added Stats 2010 ch 697 § 20 (SB 189), effective January 1, 2011, operative July 1, 2012.

Law Revision Commission Comments:

2010—Section 8132 restates former Section 3262(d)(1) without substantive change, except to add language relating to progress payments covered by previous releases that have not been paid. The statutory form is recast for clarity.See also Sections 8004 ("claimant"), 8008 ("contract"), 8026 ("lien"), 8030 ("payment bond"), 8032 ("person"), 8044 ("stop payment notice"), 8048 ("work").

§ 8134. Unconditional waiver and release in exchange for progress payment; Form (Operative July 1, 2012)

If the claimant is required to execute a waiver and release in exchange for, or in order to induce payment of, a progress payment and the claimant asserts in the waiver that the claimant has, in fact, been paid the progress payment, the waiver and release shall be null, void, and unenforceable unless it is in substantially the following form, with the text of the "Notice to Claimant" in at least as large a type as the largest type otherwise in the form:

UNCONDITIONAL WAIVER AND RELEASE ON PROGRESS

PAYMENT NOTICE TO CLAIMANT: THIS DOCUMENT WAIVES AND RELEASES LIEN, STOP PAYMENT NOTICE, AND PAYMENT BOND RIGHTS UNCONDITIONALLY AND STATES THAT YOU HAVE BEEN PAID FOR GIVING UP THOSE RIGHTS. THIS DOCUMENT IS ENFORCEABLE AGAINST YOU IF YOU SIGN IT, EVEN IF YOU HAVE NOT BEEN PAID. IF YOU HAVE NOT BEEN PAID, USE A CONDITIONAL WAIVER AND RELEASE FORM.

Identifying Information

Name of Claimant: _____

Name of Customer: _____

Job Location: _____

Owner: _____

Through Date: _____

Unconditional Waiver and Release

This document waives and releases lien, stop payment notice, and payment bond rights the claimant has for labor and service provided, and equipment and material delivered, to the customer on this job through the Through Date of this document. Rights based upon labor or service provided, or equipment or material delivered, pursuant to a written change order that has been fully executed by the parties prior to the date that this document is signed by the claimant, are waived and released by this document, unless listed as an Exception below. The claimant has received the following progress payment:

$ _____

Exceptions

This document does not affect any of the following:

(1) Retentions.

(2) Extras for which the claimant has not received payment.

(3) Contract rights, including (A) a right based on rescission, abandonment, or breach of contract, and (B) the right to recover compensation for work not compensated by the payment.

Signature

Claimant's Signature: _____

Claimant's Title: _____

Date of Signature:_____

Added Stats 2010 ch 697 § 20 (SB 189), effective January 1, 2011, operative July 1, 2012.

Law Revision Commission Comments:

2010—Section 8134 restates former Section 3262(d)(2) without substantive change. The statutory form is recast for clarity.See also Sections 8004 ("claimant"), 8008 ("contract"), 8026 ("lien"), 8030 ("payment bond"), 8044 ("stop payment notice"), 8048 ("work").

§ 8136. Conditional waiver and release in exchange for final payment; Form (Operative July 1, 2012)

If the claimant is required to execute a waiver and release in exchange for, or in order to induce payment of, a final payment and the claimant is not, in fact, paid in exchange for the waiver and release or a single payee check or joint payee check is given in exchange for the waiver and release, the waiver and release shall be null, void, and unenforceable unless it is in substantially the following form:

CONDITIONAL WAIVER AND RELEASE ON FINAL PAYMENT

NOTICE: THIS DOCUMENT WAIVES THE CLAIMANT'S LIEN, STOP PAYMENT NOTICE, AND PAYMENT BOND RIGHTS EFFECTIVE ON RECEIPT OF PAYMENT. A PERSON SHOULD NOT RELY ON THIS DOCUMENT UNLESS SATISFIED THAT THE CLAIMANT HAS RECEIVED PAYMENT.

Identifying Information
Name of Claimant: _____
Name of Customer: _____
Job Location: _____
Owner: _____
Conditional Waiver and Release

This document waives and releases lien, stop payment notice, and payment bond rights the claimant has for labor and service provided, and equipment and material delivered, to the customer on this job. Rights based upon labor or service provided, or equipment or material delivered, pursuant to a written change order that has been fully executed by the parties prior to the date that this document is signed by the claimant, are waived and released by this document, unless listed as an Exception below. This document is effective only on the claimant's receipt of payment from the financial institution on which the following check is drawn:

Maker of Check: _____
Amount of Check: $ _____
Check Payable to: _____
Exceptions
This document does not affect any of the following:
Disputed claims for extras in the amount of: $ _____
Signature
Claimant's Signature: _____
Claimant's Title: _____
Date of Signature:_____

Added Stats 2010 ch 697 § 20 (SB 189), effective January 1, 2011, operative July 1, 2012.

Law Revision Commission Comments:

2010—Section 8136 restates former Section 3262(d)(3) without substantive change, except to add a line for identification of the waivant's customer. The statutory form is recast for clarity.

See also Sections 8004 ("claimant"), 8026 ("lien"), 8030 ("payment bond"), 8032 ("person"), 8044 ("stop payment notice").

§ 8138. Unconditional waiver and release in exchange for final payment; Form (Operative July 1, 2012)

If the claimant is required to execute a waiver and release in exchange for, or in order to induce payment of, a final payment and the claimant asserts in the waiver that the claimant has, in fact, been paid the final payment, the waiver and release shall be null, void, and unenforceable unless it is in substantially the following form, with the text of the "Notice to Claimant" in at least as large a type as the largest type otherwise in the form:

UNCONDITIONAL WAIVER AND RELEASE ON FINAL PAYMENT

NOTICE TO CLAIMANT: THIS DOCUMENT WAIVES AND RELEASES LIEN, STOP PAYMENT NOTICE, AND PAYMENT BOND RIGHTS UNCONDITIONALLY AND STATES THAT YOU HAVE BEEN PAID FOR GIVING UP THOSE RIGHTS. THIS DOCUMENT IS ENFORCEABLE AGAINST YOU IF YOU SIGN IT, EVEN IF YOU HAVE NOT BEEN PAID. IF YOU HAVE NOT BEEN PAID, USE A CONDITIONAL WAIVER AND RELEASE FORM.

Identifying Information

Name of Claimant: _____

Name of Customer: _____

Job Location: _____

Owner: _____

Unconditional Waiver and Release

This document waives and releases lien, stop payment notice, and payment bond rights the claimant has for all labor and service provided, and equipment and material delivered, to the customer on this job. Rights based upon labor or service provided, or equipment or material delivered, pursuant to a written change order that has been fully executed by the parties prior to the date that this document is signed by the claimant, are waived and released by this document, unless listed as an Exception below. The claimant has been paid in full.

Exceptions

This document does not affect the following:

Disputed claims for extras in the amount of: $ _____

Signature

Claimant's Signature: _____

Appendix

Claimant's Title: _____

Date of Signature:_____

Added Stats 2010 ch 697 § 20 (SB 189), effective January 1, 2011, operative July 1, 2012.

Law Revision Commission Comments:

2010—Section 8138 restates former Section 3262(d)(4) without substantive change. The statutory form is recast for clarity.

See also Sections 8004 ("claimant"), 8026 ("lien"), 8030 ("payment bond"), 8044 ("stop payment notice").

TITLE 2
Private Works of Improvement

Chapter 4
Mechanics Lien

Article 2

Conditions to Enforcing a Lien

§ 8416. Claim of mechanics lien; Form; Contents; Service; Failure to serve (Operative July 1, 2012)

(a) A claim of mechanics lien shall be a written statement, signed and verified by the claimant, containing all of the following:

(1) A statement of the claimant's demand after deducting all just credits and offsets.

(2) The name of the owner or reputed owner, if known.

(3) A general statement of the kind of work furnished by the claimant.

(4) The name of the person by whom the claimant was employed or to whom the claimant furnished work.

(5) A description of the site sufficient for identification.

(6) The claimant's address.

(7) A proof of service affidavit completed and signed by the person serving a copy of the claim of mechanics lien pursuant to subdivision (c). The affidavit shall show the date, place, and manner of service, and facts showing that the service was made in accordance with this section. The affidavit shall show the name and address of the owner or reputed owner upon whom the copy of the claim of mechanics lien was served pursuant to paragraphs (1) or (2) of subdivision (c), and the title or capacity in which the person or entity was served.

(8) The following statement, printed in at least 10-point boldface type. The letters of the last sentence shall be printed in uppercase

type, excepting the Internet Web site address of the Contractors' State License Board, which shall be printed in lowercase type:

"NOTICE OF MECHANICS LIEN
ATTENTION!

Upon the recording of the enclosed MECHANICS LIEN with the county recorder's office of the county where the property is located, your property is subject to the filing of a legal action seeking a court-ordered foreclosure sale of the real property on which the lien has been recorded. That legal action must be filed with the court no later than 90 days after the date the mechanics lien is recorded.

The party identified in the enclosedmechanics lien may have provided labor or materials for improvements to your property and may not have been paid for these items. You are receiving this notice because it is a required step in filing a mechanics lien foreclosure action against your property. The foreclosure action will seek a sale of your property in order to pay for unpaid labor, materials, or improvements provided to your property. This may affect your ability to borrow against, refinance, or sell the property until the mechanics lien is released.

BECAUSE THE LIEN AFFECTS YOUR PROPERTY, YOU MAY WISH TOSPEAK WITH YOUR CONTRACTOR IMMEDIATELY, OR CONTACT AN ATTORNEY, OR FOR MORE INFORMATION ON MECHANICS LIENS GO TO THE CONTRACTORS' STATE LICENSE BOARD WEB SITE AT www.cslb.ca.gov."

(b) A claim of mechanics lien in otherwise proper form, verified and containing the information required in subdivision (a), shall be accepted by the recorder for recording and shall be deemed duly recorded without acknowledgment.

(c) A copy of the claim of mechanics lien, which includes the Notice of Mechanics Lien required by paragraph (8) of subdivision (a), shall be served on the owner or reputed owner. Service shall be made as follows:

(1) For an owner or reputed owner to be notified who resides in or outside this state, by registered mail, certified mail, or first-class mail, evidenced by a certificate of mailing, postage prepaid, addressed to the owner or reputed owner at the owner's or reputed owner's residence or place of business address or at the address shown by the building permit on file with the authority issuing a building permit for the work, or as otherwise provided in Section 8174.

(2) If the owner or reputed owner cannot be served by this method, then the copy of the claim of mechanics lien may be given by registered mail, certified mail, or first-class mail, evidenced by a certificate of mailing, postage prepaid, addressed to the construction lender or to the original contractor.

(d) Service of the copy of the claim of mechanics lien by registered mail, certified mail, or first-class mail, evidenced by a certificate of mailing, postage prepaid, is complete at the time of the deposit of that first-class, certified, or registered mail.

(e) Failure to serve the copy of the claim of mechanics lien as prescribed by this section, including the Notice of Mechanics Lien required by paragraph (8) of subdivision (a), shall cause the claim of mechanics lien to be unenforceable as a matter of law.

Added Stats 2010 ch 697 § 20 (SB 189), effective January 1, 2011, operative July 1, 2012. Amended Stats 2011 ch 673 § 2 (AB 456), effective January 1, 2012.

§ 8422. Effect of erroneous information (Operative July 1, 2012)

(a) Except as provided in subdivisions (b) and (c), erroneous information contained in a claim of lien relating to the claimant's demand, credits and offsets deducted, the work provided, or the description of the site, does not invalidate the claim of lien.

(b) Erroneous information contained in a claim of lien relating to the claimant's demand, credits and offsets deducted, or the work provided, invalidates the claim of lien if the court determines either of the following:

(1) The claim of lien was made with intent to defraud.

(2) An innocent third party, without notice, actual or constructive, became the bona fide owner of the property after recordation of the claim of lien, and the claim of lien was so deficient that it did not put the party on further inquiry in any manner.

(c) Any person who shall willfully include in a claim of lien labor, services, equipment, or materials not furnished for the property described in the claim, shall thereby forfeit the person's lien.

Added Stats 2010 ch 697 § 20 (SB 189), effective January 1, 2011, operative July 1, 2012. Amended Stats 2011 ch 44 § 5 (SB 190), effective January 1, 2012, operative July 1, 2012.

Chapter 5

Stop Payment Notice

Article 1

General Provisions

§ 8504.   False stop payment notice or information; Forfeiture of rights to participate in distribution of funds (Operative July 1, 2012)

A claimant that willfully gives a false stop payment notice or that willfully includes in the notice a demand to withhold for work that has not been provided forfeits all right to participate in the distribution of the funds withheld and all right to a lien under Chapter 4 (commencing with Section 8400).

Added Stats 2010 ch 697 § 20 (SB 189), effective January 1, 2011, operative July 1, 2012.

Law Revision Commission Comments:

2010— Section 8504 restates former Section 3168 without substantive change.

See also Sections 8004 ("claimant"), 8026 ("lien"), 8044 ("stop payment notice"), 8048 ("work").

Appendix

CODE OF CIVIL PROCEDURE

PART 1

COURTS OF JUSTICE

TITLE 1
Organization and Jurisdiction

Chapter 5.5
Small Claims Court

Article 2

Small Claims Court

§ 116.220. Jurisdiction

(a) The small claims court has jurisdiction in the following actions:

(1) Except as provided in subdivisions (c), (e), and (f), for recovery of money, if the amount of the demand does not exceed five thousand dollars ($5,000).

(2) Except as provided in subdivisions (c), (e), and (f), to enforce payment of delinquent unsecured personal property taxes in an amount not to exceed five thousand dollars ($5,000), if the legality of the tax is not contested by the defendant.

(3) To issue the writ of possession authorized by Sections 1861.5 and 1861.10 of the Civil Code if the amount of the demand does not exceed five thousand dollars ($5,000).

(4) To confirm, correct, or vacate a fee arbitration award not exceeding five thousand dollars ($5,000) between an attorney and client that is binding or has become binding, or to conduct a hearing de novo between an attorney and client after nonbinding arbitration of a fee dispute involving no more than five thousand dollars ($5,000) in controversy, pursuant to Article 13 (commencing with Section 6200) of Chapter 4 of Division 3 of the Business and Professions Code.

(5) For an injunction or other equitable relief only when a statute expressly authorizes a small claims court to award that relief.

(b) In any action seeking relief authorized by paragraphs (1) to (4), inclusive, of subdivision (a), the court may grant equitable relief in the form of rescission, restitution, reformation, and specific performance, in lieu of, or in addition to, money damages. The court may issue a conditional judgment. The court shall retain jurisdiction until full payment and performance of any judgment or order.

(c) Notwithstanding subdivision (a), the small claims court has jurisdiction over a defendant guarantor as follows:

(1) For any action brought by a natural person against the Registrar of the Contractors' State License Board as the defendant guarantor, the small claims jurisdictional limit stated in Section 116.221 shall apply.

(2) For any action against a defendant guarantor that does not charge a fee for its guarantor or surety services, if the amount of the demand does not exceed two thousand five hundred dollars ($2,500).

(3) For any action brought by a natural person against a defendant guarantor that charges a fee for its guarantor or surety services, if the amount of the demand does not exceed six thousand five hundred dollars ($6,500).

(4) For any action brought by an entity other than a natural person against a defendant guarantor that charges a fee for its guarantor or surety services or against the Registrar of the Contractors' State License Board as the defendant guarantor, if the amount of the demand does not exceed four thousand dollars ($4,000).

(d) In any case in which the lack of jurisdiction is due solely to an excess in the amount of the demand, the excess may be waived, but any waiver is not operative until judgment.

(e) Notwithstanding subdivision (a), in any action filed by a plaintiff incarcerated in a Department of Corrections and Rehabilitation facility, the small claims court has jurisdiction over a defendant only if the plaintiff has alleged in the complaint that he or she has exhausted his or her administrative remedies against that department, including compliance with Sections 905.2 and 905.4 of the Government Code. The final administrative adjudication or determination of the plaintiff's administrative claim by the department may be attached to the complaint at the time of filing in lieu of that allegation.

(f) In any action governed by subdivision (e), if the plaintiff fails to provide proof of compliance with the requirements of subdivision (e) at the time of trial, the judicial officer shall, at his or her discretion, either dismiss the action or continue the action to give the plaintiff an opportunity to provide that proof.

(g) For purposes of this section, "department" includes an employee of a department against whom a claim has been filed under this chapter arising out of his or her duties as an employee of that department.

Added Stats 1990 ch 1305 § 3 (SB 2627). Amended Stats 1990 ch 1683 § 3 (AB 3916); Stats 1991 ch 133 § 1 (AB 1827), ch 915 § 3 (SB 771); Stats 1992 ch 8 § 1 (AB 1551), effective February 19, 1992, ch 142 § 2 (SB 1376); Stats 1993 ch 1262 § 5 (AB 1272), ch 1264 § 95 (SB 574); Stats 1994 ch 479 § 10 (AB 3219); Stats 1995 ch 366 § 1 (AB 725); Stats 1998 ch 240 § 2 (AB 771); Stats 1999 ch 982 § 6 (AB 1678); Stats 2006 ch 150 § 1 (AB 2455), effective January 1, 2007; Stats 2008 ch 157 § 4 (SB 1432), effective January 1, 2009; Stats. 2009, Ch. 468 (AB 712).

Appendix

§ 116.221. Additional jurisdiction

In addition to the jurisdiction conferred by Section 116.220, the small claims court has jurisdiction in an action brought by a natural person, if the amount of the demand does not exceed ten thousand dollars ($10,000), except for actions specified in Section 116.224, or otherwise prohibited by subdivision (c) of Section 116.220 or subdivision (a) of Section 116.231.

Added Stats 2005 ch 600 § 2 (SB 422), ch 618 § 2 (AB 1459), effective January 1, 2006. Amended Stats 2011 ch 64 §§ 1, 2 (SB 221), effective January 1, 2012.

PART 2

CIVIL ACTIONS

TITLE 14
Miscellaneous Provisions

Chapter 2
Bonds and Undertakings

Article 1

Preliminary Provisions and Definitions

§ 995.010. Short title

This chapter shall be known and may be cited as the Bond and Undertaking Law.

Added Stats 1982 ch 998 § 1.

§ 995.020. Application of chapter

(a) The provisions of this chapter apply to a bond or undertaking executed, filed, posted, furnished, or otherwise given as security pursuant to any statute of this state, except to the extent the statute prescribes a different rule or is inconsistent.

(b) The provisions of this chapter apply to a bond or undertaking given at any of the following times:

(1) On or after January 1, 1983.

(2) Before January 1, 1983, to the extent another surety is substituted for the original surety on or after January 1, 1983, or to the extent the principal gives a new, additional, or supplemental bond or undertaking on or after January 1, 1983.

Except to the extent provided in this section, the law governing a bond or undertaking given before January 1, 1983, is the law applicable to the bond or undertaking immediately before January 1, 1983, pursuant to Section 414 of Chapter 517 of the Statutes of 1982.

(c) The provisions of this chapter do not apply to a bail bond or an undertaking of bail.

Added Stats 1982 ch 998 § 1. Amended Stats 1983 ch 18 § 18.2, effective April 21, 1983.

§ 995.030. Manner of service

If service of a notice, paper, or other document is required under this chapter, service shall be made in the same manner as service of process in civil actions generally.

Added Stats 1982 ch 998 § 1.

§ 995.040. Affidavits

An affidavit made under this chapter shall conform to the standards prescribed for an affidavit made pursuant to Section 437c.

Added Stats 1982 ch 998 § 1.

§ 995.050. Extensions of time

The times provided in this chapter, or in any other statute relating to a bond given in an action or proceeding, may be extended pursuant to Sections 1054 and 1054.1.

Added Stats 1982 ch 998 § 1.

§ 995.110. Application of definitions

Unless the provision or context otherwise requires, the definitions in this article govern the construction of this chapter.

Added Stats 1982 ch 998 § 1.

§ 995.120. "Admitted surety insurer"

(a) "Admitted surety insurer" means a corporate insurer or a reciprocal or interinsurance exchange to which the Insurance Commissioner has issued a certificate of authority to transact surety insurance in this state, as defined in Section 105 of the Insurance Code.

(b) For the purpose of application of this chapter to a bond given pursuant to any statute of this state, the phrases "admitted surety insurer," "authorized surety company," "bonding company," "corporate surety," and comparable phrases used in the statute mean "admitted surety insurer" as defined in this section.

Added Stats 1982 ch 998 § 1.

Appendix

§ 995.130. "Beneficiary"

(a) "Beneficiary" means the person for whose benefit a bond is given, whether executed to, in favor of, in the name of, or payable to the person as an obligee.

(b) If a bond is given for the benefit of the State of California or the people of the state, "beneficiary" means the court, officer, or other person required to determine the sufficiency of the sureties or to approve the bond.

(c) For the purpose of application of this chapter to a bond given pursuant to any statute of this state, the terms "beneficiary," "obligee," and comparable terms used in the statute mean "beneficiary" as defined in this section.

Added Stats 1982 ch 998 § 1.

§ 995.140. "Bond"

(a) "Bond" includes both of the following:

(1) A surety, indemnity, fiduciary, or like bond executed by both the principal and sureties.

(2) A surety, indemnity, fiduciary, or like undertaking executed by the sureties alone.

(b) A bond provided for or given "in an action or proceeding" does not include a bond provided for, or given as, a condition of a license or permit.

Added Stats 1982 ch 998 § 1.

§ 995.150. "Court"

"Court" means, if a bond is given in an action or proceeding, the court in which the action or proceeding is pending.

Added Stats 1982 ch 998 § 1.

§ 995.160. "Officer"

"Officer" means the sheriff, marshal, clerk of court, judge or magistrate (if there is no clerk), board, commission, department, or other public official or entity to whom the bond is given or with whom a copy of the bond is filed or who is required to determine the sufficiency of the sureties or to approve the bond.

Added Stats 1982 ch 998 § 1. Amended Stats 1996 ch 872 § 19 (AB 3472).

§ 995.170. "Principal"

(a) "Principal" means the person who gives a bond.

(b) For the purpose of application of this chapter to a bond given pursuant to any statute of this state, the terms "obligor," "principal," and comparable terms used in the statute mean "principal" as defined in this section.

Added Stats 1982 ch 998 § 1.

§ 995.180. "Statute"

"Statute" includes administrative regulation promulgated pursuant to statute.

Added Stats 1982 ch 998 § 1.

§ 995.185. "Surety"

(a) "Surety" has the meaning provided in Section 2787 of the Civil Code and includes personal surety and admitted surety insurer.

(b) For the purpose of application of this chapter to a bond given pursuant to any statute of this state, the terms "bail," "guarantor," "bondsman," "surety," and comparable terms used in the statute mean "surety" as defined in this section.

Added Stats 1982 ch 998 § 1.

§ 995.190. "Undertaking"

"Undertaking" means a surety, indemnity, fiduciary, or like undertaking executed by the sureties alone.

Added Stats 1982 ch 998 § 1.

Article 2

General Provisions

§ 995.210. Bonds and undertakings interchangeable

Unless the provision or context otherwise requires:

(a) If a statute provides for a bond, an undertaking that otherwise satisfies the requirements for the bond may be given in its place with the same effect as if a bond were given, and references in the statute to the bond shall be deemed to be references to the undertaking.

(b) If a statute provides for an undertaking, a bond that otherwise satisfies the requirements for the undertaking may be given in its place with the same effect as if an undertaking were given, and references in the statute to the undertaking shall be deemed to be references to the bond.

Added Stats 1982 ch 998 § 1.

Appendix

§ 995.220. Bond not required of public entity or officer

Notwithstanding any other statute, if a statute provides for a bond in an action or proceeding, including but not limited to a bond for issuance of a restraining order or injunction, appointment of a receiver, or stay of enforcement of a judgment on appeal, the following public entities and officers are not required to give the bond and shall have the same rights, remedies, and benefits as if the bond were given:

(a) The State of California or the people of the state, a state agency, department, division, commission, board, or other entity of the state, or a state officer in an official capacity or on behalf of the state.

(b) A county, city, or district, or public authority, public agency, or other political subdivision in the state, or an officer of the local public entity in an official capacity or on behalf of the local public entity.

(c) The United States or an instrumentality or agency of the United States, or a federal officer in an official capacity or on behalf of the United States or instrumentality or agency.

Added Stats 1982 ch 998 § 1.

§ 995.230. Reduction or waiver by beneficiary

The beneficiary of a bond given in an action or proceeding may in writing consent to the bond in an amount less than the amount required by statute or may waive the bond.

Added Stats 1982 ch 998 § 1.

§ 995.240. Waiver in case of indigency

The court may, in its discretion, waive a provision for a bond in an action or proceeding and make such orders as may be appropriate as if the bond were given, if the court determines that the principal is unable to give the bond because the principal is indigent and is unable to obtain sufficient sureties, whether personal or admitted surety insurers. In exercising its discretion the court shall take into consideration all factors it deems relevant, including but not limited to the character of the action or proceeding, the nature of the beneficiary, whether public or private, and the potential harm to the beneficiary if the provision for the bond is waived.

Added Stats 1982 ch 998 § 1.

§ 995.250. Cost of bond recoverable

If a statute allows costs to a party in an action or proceeding, the costs shall include all of the following:

(a) The premium on a bond reasonably paid by the party pursuant to a statute that provides for the bond in the action or proceeding.

(b) The premium on a bond reasonably paid by the party in connection with the action or proceeding, unless the court determines that the bond was unnecessary.

Added Stats 1982 ch 998 § 1.

§ 995.260. Evidence of bond

If a bond is recorded pursuant to statute, a certified copy of the record of the bond with all affidavits, acknowledgments, endorsements, and attachments may be admitted in evidence in an action or proceeding with the same effect as the original, without further proof.

Added Stats 1982 ch 998 § 1.

Article 3

Execution and Filing

§ 995.310. Sureties on bond

Unless the statute providing for the bond requires execution by an admitted surety insurer, a bond shall be executed by two or more sufficient personal sureties or by one sufficient admitted surety insurer or by any combination of sufficient personal sureties and admitted surety insurers.

Added Stats 1982 ch 998 § 1.

§ 995.311. Sureties on bond on public works contract; Status verification procedures

(a) Notwithstanding any other provision of law, any bond required on a public works contract, as defined in Section 1101 of the Public Contract Code, shall be executed by an admitted surety insurer. A public agency approving the bond on a public works contract shall have a duty to verify that the bond is being executed by an admitted surety insurer.

(b) A public agency may fulfill its duty under subdivision (a) by verifying the status of the party executing the bond in one of the following ways:

(1) Printing out information from the website of the Department of Insurance confirming the surety is an admitted surety insurer and attaching it to the bond.

(2) Obtaining a certificate from the county clerk that confirms the surety is an admitted insurer and attaching it to the bond.

Added Stats 2001 ch 181 § 1 (AB 263).

Appendix

§ 995.320. Contents of bond

(a) A bond shall be in writing signed by the sureties under oath and shall include all of the following:

(1) A statement that the sureties are jointly and severally liable on the obligations of the statute providing for the bond.

(2) The address at which the principal and sureties may be served with notices, papers, and other documents under this chapter.

(3) If the amount of the bond is based upon the value of property or an interest in property, a description of the property or interest, and the principal's estimate of the value of the property or interest, or if given pursuant to the estimate of the beneficiary or court, the value as so estimated.

(b) The sureties signing the bond are jointly and severally liable on the obligations of the bond, the provisions of this chapter, and the statute providing for the bond.

Added Stats 1982 ch 998 § 1.

§ 995.330. Form of bond

A bond or undertaking given in an action or proceeding may be in the following form:

"(Title of court. Title of cause.)

Whereas the ... desires to give (a bond) (an undertaking) for (state what) as provided by (state sections of code requiring bond or under-taking); now, therefore, the undersigned (principal and) (sureties) (surety) hereby (obligate ourselves, jointly and severally) (obligates itself) to (name who) under the statutory obligations, in the amount of ... dollars."

Added Stats 1982 ch 998 § 1.

§ 995.340. Filing required

If a bond is given in an action or proceeding:

(a) The bond shall be filed with the court unless the statute providing for the bond requires that the bond be given to another person.

(b) If the statute providing for the bond requires that the bond be given to an officer, the officer shall file the bond with the court unless the statute providing for the bond otherwise provides.

(c) A bond filed with the court shall be preserved in the office of the clerk of the court.

Added Stats 1982 ch 998 § 1.

§ 995.350. Entry in register of actions

(a) Upon the filing of a bond with the court in an action or proceeding, the clerk shall enter in the register of actions the following information:

(1) The date and amount of the bond.

(2) The names of the sureties on the bond.

(b) In the event of the loss of the bond, the entries in the register of actions are prima facie evidence of the giving of the bond in the manner required by statute.

Added Stats 1982 ch 998 § 1.

§ 995.360. Return of bond

A bond given in an action or proceeding may be withdrawn from the file and returned to the principal on order of the court only if one of the following conditions is satisfied:

(a) The beneficiary so stipulates.

(b) The bond is no longer in force and effect and the time during which the liability on the bond may be enforced has expired.

Added Stats 1982 ch 998 § 1.

§ 995.370. Service of copy of bond

At the time a bond is given, the principal shall serve a copy of the bond on the beneficiary. An affidavit of service shall be given and filed with the bond.

Added Stats 1982 ch 998 § 1.

§ 995.380. Defect in bond

(a) If a bond does not contain the substantial matter or conditions required by this chapter or by the statute providing for the bond, or if there are any defects in the giving or filing of the bond, the bond is not void so as to release the principal and sureties from liability.

(b) The beneficiary may, in proceedings to enforce the liability on the bond, suggest the defect in the bond, or its giving or filing, and enforce the liability against the principal and the persons who intended to become and were included as sureties on the bond.

Added Stats 1982 ch 998 § 1.

Appendix

Article 4

Approval and Effect

§ 995.410. Approval of bond

(a) A bond becomes effective without approval unless the statute providing for the bond requires that the bond be approved by the court or officer.

(b) If the statute providing for a bond requires that the bond be approved, the court or officer may approve or disapprove the bond on the basis of the affidavit or certificate of the sureties or may require the attendance of witnesses and the production of evidence and may examine the sureties under oath touching their qualifications.

(c) Nothing shall be construed to preclude approval of a bond in an amount greater than that required by statute.

Added Stats 1982 ch 998 § 1.

§ 995.420. Time bond becomes effective

(a) Unless the statute providing for a bond provides that the bond becomes effective at a different time, a bond is effective at the time it is given or, if the statute requires that the bond be approved, at the time it is approved.

(b) If the statute providing for a bond provides that the bond becomes effective at a time other than the time it is given or approved, the bond is effective at the time provided unless an objection is made to the bond before that time. If an objection is made to a bond before the time provided, the bond becomes effective when the court makes an order determining the sufficiency of the bond.

Added Stats 1982 ch 998 § 1.

§ 995.430. Term of bond

A bond remains in force and effect until the earliest of the following events:

(a) The sureties withdraw from or cancel the bond or a new bond is given in place of the original bond.

(b) The purpose for which the bond was given is satisfied or the purpose is abandoned without any liability having been incurred.

(c) A judgment of liability on the bond that exhausts the amount of the bond is satisfied.

(d) The term of the bond expires. Unless the statute providing for the bond prescribes a fixed term, the bond is continuous.

Added Stats 1982 ch 998 § 1.

§ 995.440. Term of license or permit bond

A bond given as a condition of a license or permit shall be continuous in form, remain in full force and effect, and run concurrently with the license or permit period and any and all renewals, or until cancellation or withdrawal of the surety from the bond.

Added Stats 1982 ch 998 § 1.

Article 5

Personal Sureties

§ 995.510. Qualifications of surety

(a) A personal surety on a bond is sufficient if all of the following conditions are satisfied:

(1) The surety is a person other than the principal. No officer of the court or member of the State Bar shall act as a surety.

(2) The surety is a resident, and either an owner of real property or householder, within the state.

(3) The surety is worth the amount of the bond in real or personal property, or both, situated in this state, over and above all debts and liabilities, exclusive of property exempt from enforcement of a money judgment.

(b) If the amount of a bond exceeds ten thousand dollars ($10,000) and is executed by more than two personal sureties, the worth of a personal surety may be less than the amount of the bond, so long as the aggregate worth of all sureties executing the bond is twice the amount of the bond.

Added Stats 1982 ch 998 § 1.

§ 995.520. Affidavit of surety

(a) A bond executed by personal sureties shall be accompanied by an affidavit of qualifications of each surety.

(b) The affidavit shall contain all of the following information:

(1) The name, occupation, residence address, and business address (if any) of the surety.

(2) A statement that the surety is a resident, and either an owner of real property or householder, within the state.

(3) A statement that the surety is worth the amount of the bond in real or personal property, or both, situated in this state, over and above all debts and liabilities, exclusive of property exempt from enforcement of a money judgment.

(c) If the amount of the bond exceeds five thousand dollars ($5,000), the affidavit shall contain, in addition to the information required by subdivision (b), all of the following information:

(1) A description sufficient for identification of real and personal property of the surety situated in this state and the nature of the surety's interest therein that qualifies the surety on the bond.

(2) The surety's best estimate of the fair market value of each item of property.

(3) A statement of any charge or lien and its amount, known to the surety, whether of public record or not, against any item of property.

(4) Any other impediment or cloud known to the surety on the free right of possession, use, benefit, or enjoyment of the property.

(d) If the amount of the bond exceeds ten thousand dollars ($10,000) and is executed by more than two sureties, the affidavit may state that the surety is worth less than the amount of the bond and the bond may stipulate that the liability of the surety is limited to the worth of the surety stated in the affidavit, so long as the aggregate worth of all sureties executing the bond is twice the amount of the bond.

Added Stats 1982 ch 998 § 1.

Article 6

Admitted Surety Insurers

§ 995.610. Admitted surety insurer in lieu of personal sureties

(a) If a statute provides for a bond with any number of sureties, one sufficient admitted surety insurer may become and shall be accepted as sole surety on the bond.

(b) The admitted surety insurer is subject to all the liabilities and entitled to all the rights of personal sureties.

Added Stats 1982 ch 998 § 1.

§ 995.620. More than one surety

Two or more admitted surety insurers may be sureties on a bond by executing the same or separate bonds for amounts aggregating the required amount of the bond. Each admitted surety insurer is jointly and severally liable to the extent of the amount of the liability assumed by it.

Added Stats 1982 ch 998 § 1.

§ 995.630. Authentication of bond

An admitted surety insurer shall be accepted or approved by the court or officer as surety on a bond without further acknowledgment if the bond is executed in the name of the surety insurer under penalty of perjury or the fact of execution of the bond is duly acknowledged before an officer authorized to take and certify acknowledgments, and either one of the following conditions, at the option of the surety insurer, is satisfied:

(a) A copy of the transcript or record of the unrevoked appointment, power of attorney, bylaws, or other instrument, duly certified by the proper authority and attested by the seal of the insurer entitling or authorizing the person who executed the bond to do so for and in behalf of the insurer, is filed in the office of the clerk of the county in which the court or officer is located.

(b) A copy of a power of attorney is attached to the bond.

Added Stats 1982 ch 998 § 1. Amended Stats 1992 ch 380 § 1 (SB 1521).

§ 995.640. Certificate of authority

Upon review of the Internet Web site of the Department of Insurance, the county clerk of any county shall, upon request of any person, do any of the following:

(a) Issue a certificate stating whether a surety is admitted or if the certificate of authority of an admitted surety insurer issued by the Insurance Commissioner authorizing the insurer to transact surety insurance has been surrendered, revoked, canceled, annulled, or suspended, and, in the event that it has, whether renewed authority has been granted. The county clerk in issuing the certificate shall rely solely upon the information furnished by the Insurance Commissioner pursuant to Article 2 (commencing with Section 12070) of Chapter 1 of Part 4 of Division 2 of the Insurance Code.

(b) Issue a certificate stating whether a copy of the transcript or record of the unrevoked appointment, power of attorney, bylaws, or other instrument, duly certified by the proper authority and attested by the seal of an admitted surety insurer entitling or authorizing the person who executed a bond to do so for and on behalf of the insurer, is filed in the office of the clerk.

Added Stats 1982 ch 998 § 1. Amended Stats 2004 ch 183 § 44 (AB 3082); Stats 2005 ch 22 § 19 (SB 1108), effective January 1, 2006; Stats 2008 ch 351 § 1 (SB 1279), effective January 1, 2009.

§ 995.650. Objection to sufficiency of surety

If an objection is made to the sufficiency of an admitted surety insurer, the person making the objection shall attach to and incorporate in the objection one or both of the following:

(a) The certificate of the county clerk of the county in which the court is located stating that the insurer is not listed as an admitted surety insurer on the department's Internet Web site or that the certificate of authority of the insurer has been surrendered, revoked, canceled, annulled, or suspended and has not been renewed.

Appendix

(b) An affidavit stating facts that establish the insufficiency of the insurer.

Added Stats 1982 ch 998 § 1. Amended Stats 2008 ch 351 § 2 (SB 1279), effective January 1, 2009.

§ 995.660. Determination of sufficiency of surety

(a) If an objection is made to the sufficiency of an admitted surety insurer on a bond or if the bond is required to be approved, the insurer shall submit to the court or officer the following documents:

(1) The original, or a certified copy, of the unrevoked appointment, power of attorney, bylaws, or other instrument entitling or authorizing the person who executed the bond to do so, within 10 calendar days of the insurer's receipt of a request to submit the instrument.

(2) A certified copy of the certificate of authority of the insurer issued by the Insurance Commissioner, within 10 calendar days of the insurer's receipt of a request to submit the copy.

(3) A certificate from the clerk of the county in which the court or officer is located that the certificate of authority of the insurer has not been surrendered, revoked, canceled, annulled, or suspended or, in the event that it has, that renewed authority has been granted, within 10 calendar days of the insurer's receipt of the certificate.

(4) Copies of the insurer's most recent annual statement and quarterly statement filed with the Department of Insurance pursuant to Article 10 (commencing with Section 900) of Chapter 1 of Part 2 of Division 1 of the Insurance Code, within 10 calendar days of the insurer's receipt of a request to submit the statements.

(b) If the admitted surety insurer complies with subdivision (a), and if it appears that the bond was duly executed, that the insurer is authorized to transact surety insurance in the state, and that its assets exceed its liabilities in an amount equal to or in excess of the amount of the bond, the insurer is sufficient and shall be accepted or approved as surety on the bond, subject to Section 12090 of the Insurance Code.

Added Stats 1982 ch 998 § 1. Amended Stats 1992 ch 379 § 1 (SB 1502); Stats 1994 ch 487 § 1 (AB 3493).

§ 995.670. Admitted surety to comply only with specified requirements relating to objections to surety's sufficiency

(a) This section applies to a bond executed, filed, posted, furnished, or otherwise given as security pursuant to any statute of this state or any law or ordinance of a public agency.

No public agency shall require an admitted surety insurer to comply with any requirements other than those in Section 995.660 whenever an objection is made to the sufficiency of the admitted surety insurer on the bond or if the bond is required to be approved.

(b) For the purposes of this section, "public agency" means the state, any agency or authority, any city, county, city and county, district, municipal or public corporation, or any instrumentality thereof.

Added Stats 1992 ch 997 § 1 (AB 2872). Amended Stats 1994 ch 487 § 2 (AB 3493).

§ 995.675. Listing surety insurer

Notwithstanding Sections 995.660 and 995.670, the California Integrated Waste Management Board, the State Water Resources Control Board, and the Department of Toxic Substances Control may require, in order to comply with Subtitle C or Subtitle D of the federal Resource Conservation and Recovery Act of 1976, as amended (42 U.S.C. Sec. 6901 et seq.), an admitted surety insurer to be listed in Circular 570 issued by the United States Treasury.

Added Stats 1998 ch 477 § 1 (AB 2353).

Article 7

Deposit in Lieu of Bond

§ 995.710. Deposit of money, certificates, accounts, bonds, or notes

(a) Except as provided in subdivision (e) or to the extent the statute providing for a bond precludes a deposit in lieu of bond or limits the form of deposit, the principal may instead of giving a bond, deposit with the officer any of the following:

(1) Lawful money of the United States. The money shall be maintained by the officer in an interest–bearing trust account.

(2) Bearer bonds or bearer notes of the United States or the State of California.

(3) Certificates of deposit payable to the officer, not exceeding the federally insured amount, issued by banks or savings associations authorized to do business in this state and insured by the Federal Deposit Insurance Corporation.

(4) Savings accounts assigned to the officer, not exceeding the federally insured amount, together with evidence of the deposit in the savings accounts with banks authorized to do business in this state and insured by the Federal Deposit Insurance Corporation.

(5) Investment certificates or share accounts assigned to the officer, not exceeding the federally insured amount, issued by savings associations authorized to do business in this state and insured by the Federal Deposit Insurance Corporation.

(6) Certificates for funds or share accounts assigned to the officer, not exceeding the guaranteed amount, issued by a credit union, as

Appendix

defined in Section 14002 of the Financial Code, whose share deposits are guaranteed by the National Credit Union Administration or guaranteed by any other agency approved by the Department of Financial Institutions.

(b) The deposit shall be in an amount or have a face value, or in the case of bearer bonds or bearer notes have a market value, equal to or in excess of the amount that would be required to be secured by the bond if the bond were given by an admitted surety insurer. Notwithstanding any other provision of this chapter, in the case of a deposit of bearer bonds or bearer notes other than in an action or proceeding, the officer may, in the officer's discretion, require that the amount of the deposit be determined not by the market value of the bonds or notes but by a formula based on the principal amount of the bonds or notes.

(c) The deposit shall be accompanied by an agreement executed by the principal authorizing the officer to collect, sell, or otherwise apply the deposit to enforce the liability of the principal on the deposit. The agreement shall include the address at which the principal may be served with notices, papers, and other documents under this chapter.

(d) The officer may prescribe terms and conditions to implement this section.

(e) This section may not be utilized after January 1, 1999, for deposits with the Secretary of State. Any principal who made a deposit with the Secretary of State pursuant to this section prior to January 1, 1999, may continue to utilize that deposit in lieu of a bond pursuant to this section and the statute that prescribes a bond; however, the deposit shall not be renewable pursuant to this section.

Added Stats 1982 ch 998 § 1. Amended Stats 1983 ch 18 § 18.5, effective April 21, 1983; Stats 1996 ch 1064 § 6 (AB 3351), operative July 1, 1997; Stats 1998 ch 829 § 16 (SB 1652); Stats 1999 ch 892 § 11 (AB 1672).

§ 995.720.   Valuation of bearer bonds or notes

(a) The market value of bearer bonds or bearer notes shall be agreed upon by stipulation of the principal and beneficiary or, if the bonds or notes are given in an action or proceeding and the principal and beneficiary are unable to agree, the market value shall be determined by court order in the manner prescribed in this section. A certified copy of the stipulation or court order shall be delivered to the officer at the time of the deposit of the bonds or notes.

(b) If the bonds or notes are given in an action or proceeding, the principal may file a written application with the court to determine the market value of the bonds or notes. The application shall be served upon the beneficiary and proof of service shall be filed with the application. The application shall contain all of the following:

(1) A specific description of the bonds or notes.

(2) A statement of the current market value of the bonds or notes as of the date of the filing of the application.

(3) A statement of the amount of the bonds or notes that the principal believes would be equal to the required amount of the deposit.

(c) The application pursuant to subdivision (b) shall be heard by the court not less than five days or more than 10 days after service of the application. If at the time of the hearing no objection is made to the current market value of the bonds or notes alleged in the application, the court shall fix the amount of the bonds or notes on the basis of the market value alleged in the application. If the beneficiary contends that the current market value of the bonds or notes is less than alleged in the application, the principal shall offer evidence in support of the application, and the beneficiary may offer evidence in opposition. At the conclusion of the hearing, the court shall make an order determining the market value of the bonds or notes and shall fix and determine the amount of the bonds or notes to be deposited by the principal.

Added Stats 1982 ch 998 § 1.

§ 995.730. Effect of deposit

A deposit given instead of a bond has the same force and effect, is treated the same, and is subject to the same conditions, liability, and statutory provisions, including provisions for increase and decrease of amount, as the bond.

Added Stats 1982 ch 998 § 1.

§ 995.740. Interest on deposit

If no proceedings are pending to enforce the liability of the principal on the deposit, the officer shall:

(a) Pay quarterly, on demand, any interest on the deposit, when earned in accordance with the terms of the account or certificate, to the principal.

(b) Deliver to the principal, on demand, any interest coupons attached to bearer bonds or bearer notes as the interest coupons become due and payable, or pay annually any interest payable on the bonds or notes.

Added Stats 1982 ch 998 § 1.

§ 995.750. Obligation of principal

(a) The principal shall pay the amount of the liability on the deposit within 30 days after the date on which the judgment of liability becomes final.

(b) If the deposit was given to stay enforcement of a judgment on appeal, the principal shall pay the amount of the liability on the deposit, including damages and costs awarded against the principal on appeal, within 30 days after the filing of the remittitur from the appellate court in the court from which the appeal is taken.

Added Stats 1982 ch 998 § 1.

§ 995.760. Enforcement against deposit

(a) If the principal does not pay the amount of the liability on the deposit within the time prescribed in Section 995.750, the deposit shall be collected, sold, or otherwise applied to the liability upon order of the court that entered the judgment of liability, made upon five days' notice to the parties.

(b) Bearer bonds or bearer notes without a prevailing market price shall be sold at public auction. Notice of sale shall be served on the principal. Bearer bonds or bearer notes having a prevailing market price may be sold at private sale at a price not lower than the prevailing market price.

(c) The deposit shall be distributed in the following order:

(1) First, to pay the cost of collection, sale, or other application of the deposit.

(2) Second, to pay the judgment of liability of the principal on the deposit.

(3) Third, the remainder, if any, shall be returned to the principal.

Added Stats 1982 ch 998 § 1.

§ 995.770. Return of deposit

A deposit given pursuant to this article shall be returned to the principal at the earliest of the following times:

(a) Upon substitution of a sufficient bond for the deposit. The bond shall be in full force and effect for all liabilities incurred, and for acts, omissions, or causes existing or which arose, during the period the deposit was in effect.

(b) The time provided by Section 995.360 for return of a bond.

(c) The time provided by statute for return of the deposit.

Added Stats 1982 ch 998 § 1.

Article 8

Bonds to the State of California

§ 995.810. Application of article

The provisions of this article apply to a bond executed to, in favor of, in the name of, or payable to the State of California or the people of the state, including but not limited to an official bond.

Added Stats 1982 ch 998 § 1.

§ 995.820. Bond by officer of court

Except as otherwise provided by statute, a bond given by an officer of the court for the faithful discharge of the officer's duties and obedience to the orders of the court shall be to the State of California.

Added Stats 1982 ch 998 § 1.

§ 995.830. Bond where no beneficiary provided

If a statute or court order pursuant thereto providing for a bond does not specify the beneficiary of the bond, the bond shall be to the State of California.

Added Stats 1982 ch 998 § 1.

§ 995.840. Court approval of bond

If a bond under this article is given in an action or proceeding:
(a) The bond shall be approved by the court.
(b) Any party for whose benefit the bond is given may object to the bond.

Added Stats 1982 ch 998 § 1.

§ 995.850. Enforcement by or for benefit of persons damaged

(a) The liability on a bond under this article may be enforced by or for the benefit of, and in the name of, any and all persons for whose benefit the bond is given who are damaged by breach of the condition of the bond.
(b) A person described in subdivision (a) may, in addition to any other remedy the person has, enforce the liability on the bond in the person's own name, without assignment of the bond.

Added Stats 1982 ch 998 § 1.

Appendix

Article 9

Objections to Bonds

§ 995.910. Article limited to actions and proceedings

This article governs objections to a bond given in an action or proceeding.

Added Stats 1982 ch 998 § 1.

§ 995.920. Grounds for objection

The beneficiary may object to a bond on any of the following grounds:
(a) The sureties are insufficient.
(b) The amount of the bond is insufficient.
(c) The bond, from any other cause, is insufficient.

Added Stats 1982 ch 998 § 1.

§ 995.930. Manner of making objection

(a) An objection shall be in writing and shall be made by noticed motion. The notice of motion shall specify the precise grounds for the objection. If a ground for the objection is that the amount of the bond is insufficient, the notice of motion shall state the reason for the insufficiency and shall include an estimate of the amount that would be sufficient.

(b) The objection shall be made within 10 days after service of a copy of the bond on the beneficiary or such other time as is required by the statute providing for the bond.

(c) If no objection is made within the time required by statute, the beneficiary is deemed to have waived all objections except upon a showing of good cause for failure to make the objection within the time required by statute or of changed circumstances.

Added Stats 1982 ch 998 § 1. Amended Stats 1984 ch 538 § 33.

§ 995.940. Objection to sufficiency of bond based on market value

If a ground for the objection is that the value of property or an interest in property on which the amount of the bond is based exceeds the value estimated in the bond:
(a) The objection shall state the beneficiary's estimate of the market value of the property or interest in property.
(b) The principal may accept the beneficiary's estimate of the market value of the property or interest in property and immediately file an increased bond based on the estimate. In such case, no hearing

shall be held on that ground for the objection, and the beneficiary is bound by the estimate of the market value of the property or interest in property.

Added Stats 1982 ch 998 § 1.

§ 995.950. Hearing on objection

(a) Unless the parties otherwise agree, the hearing on an objection shall be held not less than two or more than five days after service of the notice of motion.

(b) The hearing shall be conducted in such manner as the court determines is proper. The court may permit witnesses to attend and testify and evidence to be procured and introduced in the same manner as in the trial of a civil case.

(c) If the value of property or an interest in property is a ground for the objection, the court shall estimate its value. The court may appoint one or more disinterested persons to appraise property or an interest in property for the purpose of estimating its value.

Added Stats 1982 ch 998 § 1.

§ 995.960. Determination of sufficiency of bond

(a) Upon the hearing, the court shall make an order determining the sufficiency or insufficiency of the bond.

(b) If the court determines that the bond is insufficient:

(1) The court shall specify in what respect the bond is insufficient and shall order that a bond with sufficient sureties and in a sufficient amount be given within five days. If a sufficient bond is not given within the time required by the court order, all rights obtained by giving the bond immediately cease and the court shall upon ex parte motion so order.

(2) If a bond is in effect, the bond remains in effect until a bond with sufficient sureties and in a sufficient amount is given in its place, or the time in which to give the bond has expired, whichever first occurs. If the time in which to give a sufficient bond expires, the original bond remains in full force and effect for all liabilities incurred before, and for acts, omissions, or causes existing or which arose before, expiration.

(c) If the court determines that a bond is sufficient, no future objection to the bond may be made except upon a showing of changed circumstances.

Added Stats 1982 ch 998 § 1.

Appendix

Article 10

Insufficient and Excessive Bonds

§ 996.010. Bond in action or proceeding

(a) If a bond is given in an action or proceeding, the court may determine that the bond is or has from any cause become insufficient because the sureties are insufficient or because the amount of the bond is insufficient.

(b) The court determination shall be upon motion supported by affidavit or upon the court's own motion. The motion shall be deemed to be an objection to the bond. The motion shall be heard and notice of motion shall be given in the same manner as an objection to the bond.

(c) Upon the determination the court shall order that a sufficient new, additional, or supplemental bond be given within a reasonable time not less than five days. The court order is subject to any limitations in the statute providing for the bond.

(d) If a sufficient bond is not given within the time required by the court order, all rights obtained by giving the original bond immediately cease and the court shall upon ex parte motion so order.

Added Stats 1982 ch 998 § 1.

§ 996.020. Bond other than in action or proceeding

(a) If a bond is given other than in an action or proceeding and it is shown by affidavit of a credible witness or it otherwise comes to the attention of the officer that the bond is or has from any cause become insufficient because the sureties are insufficient or because the amount of the bond is insufficient, the officer may serve an order on the principal to appear and show cause why the officer should not make a determination that the bond is insufficient. The order shall name a day not less than three or more than 10 days after service.

(b) If the principal fails to appear or show good cause on the day named why a determination that the bond is insufficient should not be made, the officer may determine that the bond is insufficient and order a sufficient new, additional, or supplemental bond to be given.

(c) If a sufficient bond is not given within 10 days after the order, the officer shall make an order vacating the rights obtained by giving the original bond, including declaring vacant any office and suspending or revoking any license or certificate for which the bond was given. Any office vacated, license suspended or revoked, or any other rights lost, for failure to give a new, additional, or supplemental bond, shall not be reinstated until a new, additional, or supplemental bond is given.

Added Stats 1982 ch 998 § 1.

§ 996.030. Reduced bond

(a) The court if a bond is given or ordered in an action or proceeding, or the officer if a bond is given or ordered other than in an action or proceeding, may determine that the amount of the bond is excessive and order the amount reduced to an amount that in the discretion of the court or officer appears proper under the circumstances. The order is subject to any limitations in the statute providing for the bond.

(b) The determination shall be made upon motion or affidavit of the principal in the same manner as a motion or affidavit for a determination under this article that a bond is insufficient. The notice of motion or the order to show cause made pursuant to affidavit shall be served on the beneficiary. The determination shall be made in the same manner and pursuant to the same procedures as a determination under this article that the bond is insufficient.

(c) The principal may give a new bond for the reduced amount. The sureties may be the same sureties as on the original bond.

Added Stats 1982 ch 998 § 1. Amended Stats 1988 ch 309 § 1.

Article 11

Release or Substitution of Sureties on Bond Given in Action or Proceeding

§ 996.110. Application for substitution and release

(a) A surety on a bond given in an action or proceeding may at any time apply to the court for an order that the surety be released from liability on the bond.

(b) The principal on a bond may, if a surety applies for release from liability on a bond, apply to the court for an order that another surety be substituted for the original surety.

(c) The applicant shall serve on the principal or surety (other than the applicant) and on the beneficiary a copy of the application and a notice of hearing on the application. Service shall be made not less than 15 days before the date set for hearing.

Added Stats 1982 ch 998 § 1.

§ 996.120. Hearing

Upon the hearing of the application, the court shall determine whether injury to the beneficiary would result from substitution or release of the surety. If the court determines that release would not reduce the amount of the bond or the number of sureties below the minimum required by the statute providing for the bond, substitution of a sufficient surety is not necessary and the court shall order the release of the surety. If the court determines that no injury would result from substitution of the surety, the court shall order the substitution of a sufficient surety within such time as appears reasonable.

Added Stats 1982 ch 998 § 1.

§ 996.130. Substitution and release

(a) If a substitute surety is given, the substitute surety is subject to all the provisions of this chapter, including but not limited to the provisions governing insufficient and excessive bonds.

(b) Upon the substitution of a sufficient surety, the court shall order the release of the original surety from liability on the bond.

Added Stats 1982 ch 998 § 1.

§ 996.140. Failure to give substitute surety

If the principal does not give a sufficient substitute surety within the time ordered by the court or such longer time as the surety consents to, all rights obtained by giving the original bond immediately cease and the court shall upon ex parte motion so order.

Added Stats 1982 ch 998 § 1.

§ 996.150. Liability of released surety

If a surety is ordered released from liability on a bond:

(a) The bond remains in full force and effect for all liabilities incurred before, and for acts, omissions, or causes existing or which arose before, the release. Legal proceedings may be had therefor in all respects as though there had been no release.

(b) The surety is not liable for any act, default, or misconduct of the principal or other breach of the condition of the bond that occurs after, or for any liabilities on the bond that arise after, the release.

(c) The release does not affect the bond as to the remaining sureties, or alter or change their liability in any respect.

Added Stats 1982 ch 998 § 1.

Article 12

New, Additional, and Supplemental Bonds

§ 996.210. When bond given

(a) The principal shall give a new, additional, or supplemental bond if the court or officer orders that a new, additional, or supplemental bond be given.

(b) The principal may give a new bond if a surety withdraws from or cancels the original bond or to obtain the release of sureties from liability on the original bond.

Added Stats 1982 ch 998 § 1.

§ 996.220. Contents of bond

(a) A new, additional, or supplemental bond shall be in the same form and have the same obligation as the original bond and shall be in all other respects the same as the original bond, and shall be in such amount as is necessary for the purpose for which the new, additional, or supplemental bond is given.

(b) A supplemental bond shall, in addition to any other requirements, recite the names of the remaining original sureties, the name of the new surety, and the amount for which the new surety is liable. The supplemental bond shall be for the amount for which the original surety was liable on the original bond.

Added Stats 1982 ch 998 § 1.

§ 996.230. Provisions applicable to bond

A new, additional, or supplemental bond is subject to all the provisions applicable to the original bond and to the provisions of this chapter, including but not limited to the provisions governing giving and objecting to a bond and liabilities and enforcement procedures.

Added Stats 1982 ch 998 § 1.

§ 996.240. Effect of new bond

If a new bond is given in place of the original bond:

(a) The original bond remains in full force and effect for all liabilities incurred before, and for acts, omissions, or causes existing or which arose before, the new bond became effective.

(b) The sureties on the original bond are not liable for any act, default, or misconduct of the principal or other breach of the condition of the bond that occurs after or for any liabilities on the bond that arise after, the new bond becomes effective.

Added Stats 1982 ch 998 § 1.

§ 996.250. Effect of additional or supplemental bond

(a) An additional or supplemental bond does not discharge or affect the original bond. The original bond remains in full force and effect as if the additional or supplemental bond had not been given.

(b) After an additional or supplemental bond is given, the principal and sureties are liable upon either or both bonds for injury caused by breach of any condition of the bonds. Subject to subdivision (c), the beneficiary may enforce the liability on either bond, or may enforce the liability separately on both bonds and recover separate judgments of liability on both.

Appendix

(c) If the beneficiary recovers separate judgments of liability on both bonds for the same cause of action, the beneficiary may enforce both judgments. The beneficiary may collect, by execution or otherwise, the costs of both proceedings to enforce the liability and the amount actually awarded to the beneficiary on the same cause of action in only one of the proceedings, and no double recovery shall be allowed.

(d) If the sureties on either bond have been compelled to pay any sum of money on account of the principal, they are entitled to recover from the sureties on the remaining bond a distributive part of the sum paid, in the proportion the amounts of the bonds bear one to the other and to the sums paid.

Added Stats 1982 ch 998 § 1.

Article 13

Cancellation of Bond or Withdrawal of Sureties

§ 996.310. Application of article

This article governs cancellation of or withdrawal of a surety from a bond given other than in an action or proceeding.

Added Stats 1982 ch 998 § 1.

§ 996.320. Notice of cancellation or withdrawal

A surety may cancel or withdraw from a bond by giving a notice of cancellation or withdrawal to the officer to whom the bond was given in the same manner the bond was given, notwithstanding Section 995.030. The surety shall at the same time mail or deliver a copy of the notice of cancellation or withdrawal to the principal.

Added Stats 1982 ch 998 § 1.

§ 996.330. Effective date of cancellation or withdrawal

Cancellation or withdrawal of a surety is effective at the earliest of the following times:

(a) Thirty days after notice of cancellation or withdrawal is given.

(b) If a new surety is substituted for the original surety, the date the substitution becomes effective.

(c) If a new bond is given, the date the new bond becomes effective.

Added Stats 1982 ch 998 § 1.

§ 996.340. Effect of cancellation or withdrawal

(a) If the principal does not give a new bond within 30 days after notice of cancellation or withdrawal is given, all rights obtained by giving the original bond immediately cease, any office for which the bond is given is vacant, any commission for which the bond is given is revoked, and any license or registration for which the bond is given is suspended.

(b) A person whose license or registration is suspended shall not operate or carry on business pursuant to the license or registration during the period of suspension. A license or registration that is suspended may be revived only by the giving of a new bond during the license or registration period in which the cancellation or withdrawal occurred.

Added Stats 1982 ch 998 § 1. Amended Stats 1983 ch 18 § 19, effective April 21, 1983.

§ 996.350. New bond not required

If the withdrawal of a surety does not reduce the amount of the bond or the number of sureties below the minimum required by the statute providing for the bond, no new bond is required or necessary to maintain the original bond in effect.

Added Stats 1982 ch 998 § 1.

§ 996.360. Liability of surety

If a surety cancels or withdraws from a bond:

(a) The bond remains in full force and effect for all liabilities incurred before, and for acts, omissions, or causes existing or which arose before, the cancellation or withdrawal. Legal proceedings may be had therefor in all respects as though there had been no cancellation or withdrawal.

(b) The surety is not liable for any act, default, or misconduct of the principal or other breach of the condition of the bond that occurs after, or for any liabilities on the bond that arise after, the cancellation or withdrawal.

(c) The cancellation or withdrawal does not affect the bond as to the remaining sureties, or alter or change their liability in any respect.

Added Stats 1982 ch 998 § 1.

Article 14

Liability of Principal and Sureties

§ 996.410. Enforcement of liability on bond

(a) The beneficiary may enforce the liability on a bond against both the principal and sureties.

(b) If the beneficiary is a class of persons, any person in the class may enforce the liability on a bond in the person's own name, without assignment of the bond.

Appendix

Added Stats 1982 ch 998 § 1.

§ 996.420. Surety subject to jurisdiction of court

(a) A surety on a bond given in an action or proceeding submits itself to the jurisdiction of the court in all matters affecting its liability on the bond.

(b) This section does not apply to a bond of a public officer or fiduciary.

Added Stats 1982 ch 998 § 1.

§ 996.430. Action to enforce liability

(a) The liability on a bond may be enforced by civil action. Both the principal and the sureties shall be joined as parties to the action.

(b) If the bond was given in an action or proceeding, the action shall be commenced in the court in which the action or proceeding was pending. If the bond was given other than in an action or proceeding, the action shall be commenced in any court of competent jurisdiction, and the amount of damage claimed in the action, not the amount of the bond, determines the jurisdictional classification of the case.

(c) A cause of action on a bond may be transferred and assigned as other causes of action.

Added Stats 1982 ch 998 § 1. Amended Stats 1998 ch 931 § 105 (SB 2139), effective September 28, 1998.

§ 996.440. Motion to enforce liability

(a) If a bond is given in an action or proceeding, the liability on the bond may be enforced on motion made in the court without the necessity of an independent action.

(b) The motion shall not be made until after entry of the final judgment in the action or proceeding in which the bond is given and the time for appeal has expired or, if an appeal is taken, until the appeal is finally determined. The motion shall not be made or notice of motion served more than one year after the later of the preceding dates.

(c) Notice of motion shall be served on the principal and sureties at least 30 days before the time set for hearing of the motion. The notice shall state the amount of the claim and shall be supported by affidavits setting forth the facts on which the claim is based. The notice and affidavits shall be served in accordance with any procedure authorized by Chapter 5 (commencing with Section 1010).

(d) Judgment shall be entered against the principal and sureties in accordance with the motion unless the principal or sureties serve and file affidavits in opposition to the motion showing such facts as may be deemed by the judge hearing the motion sufficient to present a triable issue of fact. If such a showing is made, the issues to be tried shall be specified by the court. Trial shall be by the court and shall be set for the earliest date convenient to the court, allowing sufficient time for such discovery proceedings as may be requested.

(e) The principal and sureties shall not obtain a stay of the proceedings pending determination of any conflicting claims among beneficiaries.

Added Stats 1982 ch 998 § 1.

§ 996.450. Statute of limitations

No provision in a bond is valid that attempts by contract to shorten the period prescribed by Section 337 or other statute for the commencement of an action on the bond or the period prescribed by Section 996.440 for a motion to enforce a bond. This section does not apply if the principal, beneficiary, and surety accept a provision for a shorter period in a bond.

Added Stats 1982 ch 998 § 1.

§ 996.460. Judgment of liability

(a) Notwithstanding Section 2845 of the Civil Code, a judgment of liability on a bond shall be in favor of the beneficiary and against the principal and sureties and shall obligate each of them jointly and severally.

(b) The judgment shall be in an amount determined by the court.

(c) A judgment that does not exhaust the full amount of the bond decreases the amount of the bond but does not discharge the bond. The liability on the bond may be enforced thereafter from time to time until the amount of the bond is exhausted.

(d) The judgment may be enforced by the beneficiary directly against the sureties. Nothing in this section affects any right of subrogation of a surety against the principal or any right of a surety to compel the principal to satisfy the judgment.

Added Stats 1982 ch 998 § 1.

§ 996.470. Limitation on liability of surety

(a) Notwithstanding any other statute other than Section 996.480, the aggregate liability of a surety to all persons for all breaches of the condition of a bond is limited to the amount of the bond. Except as otherwise provided by statute, the liability of the principal is not limited to the amount of the bond.

(b) If a bond is given in an amount greater than the amount required by statute or by order of the court or officer pursuant to statute, the liability of the surety on the bond is limited to the amount required by statute or by order of the court or officer, unless the amount of the bond has been increased voluntarily or by agreement of the parties to satisfy an objection to the bond made in an action or proceeding.

(c) The liability of a surety is limited to the amount stipulated in any of the following circumstances:

(1) The bond contains a stipulation pursuant to Section 995.520 that the liability of a personal surety is limited to the worth of the surety.

(2) The bond contains a stipulation that the liability of a surety is an amount less than the amount of the bond pursuant to a statute that provides that the liability of sureties in the aggregate need not exceed the amount of the bond.

Added Stats 1982 ch 998 § 1. Amended Stats 1993 ch 527 § 2 (AB 908).

§ 996.475. Liability of surety pursuant to other statute

Nothing in this chapter is intended to limit the liability of a surety pursuant to any other statute. This section is declaratory of, and not a change in, existing law.

Added Stats 1984 ch 538 § 33.3.

§ 996.480. Voluntary payment by surety

(a) If the nature and extent of the liability of the principal is established by final judgment of a court and the time for appeal has expired or, if an appeal is taken, the appeal is finally determined and the judgment is affirmed:

(1) A surety may make payment on a bond without awaiting enforcement of the bond. The amount of the bond is reduced to the extent of any payment made by the surety in good faith.

(2) If the beneficiary makes a claim for payment on a bond given in an action or proceeding after the liability of the principal is so established and the surety fails to make payment, the surety is liable for costs incurred in obtaining a judgment against the surety, including a reasonable attorney's fee, and interest on the judgment from the date of the claim, notwithstanding Section 996.470.

(b) Partial payment of a claim by a surety shall not be considered satisfaction of the claim and the beneficiary may enforce the liability on the bond. If a right is affected or a license is suspended or revoked until payment of a claim, the right continues to be affected and the license continues to be suspended or revoked until the claim is satisfied in full.

Added Stats 1982 ch 998 § 1.

§ 996.490. Effect of payment by surety

(a) Payment by a surety of the amount of a bond constitutes a full discharge of all the liability of the surety on the bond.

(b) Each surety is liable to contribution to cosureties who have made payment in proportion to the amount for which each surety is liable.

Added Stats 1982 ch 998 § 1.

§ 996.495. Enforcement of judgment

A judgment of liability on a bond may be enforced in the same manner and to the same extent as other money judgments.

Added Stats 1982 ch 998 § 1.

Article 15

Enforcement Lien

§ 996.510. Application of article

This article applies to proceedings for the benefit of the state to enforce the liability on a bond executed to, in favor of, or payable to the state or the people of the state, including but not limited to an official bond.

Added Stats 1982 ch 998 § 1.

§ 996.520. Affidavit

The person enforcing the liability may file with the court in the proceedings an affidavit stating the following:

(a) The bond was executed by the defendant or one or more of the defendants (designating whom).

(b) The bond is one to which this article applies.

(c) The defendant or defendants have real property or an interest in real property (designating the county or counties in which the real property is situated).

(d) The liability is being enforced for the benefit of the state.

Added Stats 1982 ch 998 § 1.

§ 996.530. Certification by clerk

The clerk receiving the affidavit shall certify to the recorder of the county in which the real property is situated all of the following:

(a) The names of the parties.

(b) The court in which the proceedings are pending.

(c) The amount claimed.

(d) The date of commencement of the proceedings.

Added Stats 1982 ch 998 § 1.

Appendix

§ 996.540. Recordation of certificate

(a) Upon receiving the certificate the county recorder shall endorse upon it the time of its receipt.

(b) The certificate shall be filed and recorded in the same manner as notice of the pendency of an action affecting real property.

Added Stats 1982 ch 998 § 1.

§ 996.550. Lien of judgment

(a) Any judgment recovered is a lien upon all real property belonging to the defendant situated in any county in which the certificate is filed, from the filing of the certificate.

(b) The lien is for the amount for which the owner of the real property is liable upon the judgment.

Added Stats 1982 ch 998 § 1.

§ 996.560. Specific performance of agreement to sell property

If an agreement to sell real property affected by the lien created by the filing of a certificate was made before the filing of the certificate and the purchase price under the agreement was not due until after the filing of the certificate, and the purchaser is otherwise entitled to specific performance of the agreement:

(a) The court in an action to compel specific performance of the agreement shall order the purchaser to pay the purchase price, or so much of the purchase price as may be due, to the State Treasurer, and to take the State Treasurer's receipt for payment.

(b) Upon payment, the purchaser is entitled to enforcement of specific performance of the agreement. The purchaser takes the real property free from the lien created by the filing of the certificate.

(c) The State Treasurer shall hold the payment pending the proceedings referred to in the certificate. The payment is subject to the lien created by the filing of the certificate.

Added Stats 1982 ch 998 § 1.

FAMILY CODE

DIVISION 17
SUPPORT SERVICES

Chapter 2
Child Support Enforcement

Article 2

Collections and Enforcement

§ 17520. Consolidated lists of persons; License renewals; Review procedures; Report to Legislature; Rules and regulations; Forms; Use of information; Suspension or revocation of driver's license; Severability

(a) As used in this section:

(1) "Applicant" means any person applying for issuance or renewal of a license.

(2) "Board" means any entity specified in Section 101 of the Business and Professions Code, the entities referred to in Sections 1000 and 3600 of the Business and Professions Code, the State Bar, the Department of Real Estate, the Department of Motor Vehicles, the Secretary of State, the Department of Fish and Game, and any other state commission, department, committee, examiner, or agency that issues a license, certificate, credential, permit, registration, or any other authorization to engage in a business, occupation, or profession, or to the extent required by federal law or regulations, for recreational purposes. This term includes all boards, commissions, departments, committees, examiners, entities, and agencies that issue a license, certificate, credential, permit, registration, or any other authorization to engage in a business, occupation, or profession. The failure to specifically name a particular board, commission, department, committee, examiner, entity, or agency that issues a license, certificate, credential, permit, registration, or any other authorization to engage in a business, occupation, or profession does not exclude that board, commission, department, committee, examiner, entity, or agency from this term.

(3) "Certified list" means a list provided by the local child support agency to the Department of Child Support Services in which the local child support agency verifies, under penalty of perjury, that the

names contained therein are support obligors found to be out of compliance with a judgment or order for support in a case being enforced
under Title IV–D of the Social Security Act.

(4) "Compliance with a judgment or order for support" means that,
as set forth in a judgment or order for child or family support, the obligor is no more than 30 calendar days in arrears in making payments
in full for current support, in making periodic payments in full,
whether court ordered or by agreement with the local child support
agency, on a support arrearage, or in making periodic payments in
full, whether court ordered or by agreement with the local child support agency, on a judgment for reimbursement for public assistance,
or has obtained a judicial finding that equitable estoppel as provided
in statute or case law precludes enforcement of the order. The local
child support agency is authorized to use this section to enforce orders for spousal support only when the local child support agency is
also enforcing a related child support obligation owed to the obligee
parent by the same obligor, pursuant to Sections 17400 and 17604.

(5) "License" includes membership in the State Bar, and a certificate, credential, permit, registration, or any other authorization issued by a board that allows a person to engage in a business, occupation, or profession, or to operate a commercial motor vehicle, including appointment and commission by the Secretary of State as a notary public. "License" also includes any driver's license issued by the
Department of Motor Vehicles, any commercial fishing license issued
by the Department of Fish and Game, and to the extent required by
federal law or regulations, any license used for recreational purposes.
This term includes all licenses, certificates, credentials, permits, registrations, or any other authorization issued by a board that allows a
person to engage in a business, occupation, or profession. The failure
to specifically name a particular type of license, certificate, credential,
permit, registration, or other authorization issued by a board that
allows a person to engage in a business, occupation, or profession,
does not exclude that license, certificate, credential, permit, registration, or other authorization from this term.

(6) "Licensee" means any person holding a license, certificate, credential, permit, registration, or other authorization issued by a board,
to engage in a business, occupation, or profession, or a commercial
driver's license as defined in Section 15210 of the Vehicle Code, including an appointment and commission by the Secretary of State as
a notary public. "Licensee" also means any person holding a driver's
license issued by the Department of Motor Vehicles, any person holding a commercial fishing license issued by the Department of Fish
and Game, and to the extent required by federal law or regulations,
any person holding a license used for recreational purposes. This
term includes all persons holding a license, certificate, credential,
permit, registration, or any other authorization to engage in a busi-

ness, occupation, or profession, and the failure to specifically name a particular type of license, certificate, credential, permit, registration, or other authorization issued by a board does not exclude that person from this term. For licenses issued to an entity that is not an individual person, "licensee" includes any individual who is either listed on the license or who qualifies for the license.

(b) The local child support agency shall maintain a list of those persons included in a case being enforced under Title IV–D of the Social Security Act against whom a support order or judgment has been rendered by, or registered in, a court of this state, and who are not in compliance with that order or judgment. The local child support agency shall submit a certified list with the names, social security numbers, and last known addresses of these persons and the name, address, and telephone number of the local child support agency who certified the list to the department. The local child support agency shall verify, under penalty of perjury, that the persons listed are subject to an order or judgment for the payment of support and that these persons are not in compliance with the order or judgment. The local child support agency shall submit to the department an updated certified list on a monthly basis.

(c) The department shall consolidate the certified lists received from the local child support agencies and, within 30 calendar days of receipt, shall provide a copy of the consolidated list to each board that is responsible for the regulation of licenses, as specified in this section.

(d) On or before November 1, 1992, or as soon thereafter as economically feasible, as determined by the department, all boards subject to this section shall implement procedures to accept and process the list provided by the department, in accordance with this section. Notwithstanding any other law, all boards shall collect social security numbers from all applicants for the purposes of matching the names of the certified list provided by the department to applicants and licensees and of responding to requests for this information made by child support agencies.

(e)(1) Promptly after receiving the certified consolidated list from the department, and prior to the issuance or renewal of a license, each board shall determine whether the applicant is on the most recent certified consolidated list provided by the department. The board shall have the authority to withhold issuance or renewal of the license of any applicant on the list.

(2) If an applicant is on the list, the board shall immediately serve notice as specified in subdivision (f) on the applicant of the board's intent to withhold issuance or renewal of the license. The notice shall be made personally or by mail to the applicant's last known mailing address on file with the board. Service by mail shall be complete in accordance with Section 1013 of the Code of Civil Procedure.

(A) The board shall issue a temporary license valid for a period of 150 days to any applicant whose name is on the certified list if the applicant is otherwise eligible for a license.

(B) Except as provided in subparagraph (D), the 150–day time period for a temporary license shall not be extended. Except as provided in subparagraph (D), only one temporary license shall be issued during a regular license term and it shall coincide with the first 150 days of that license term. As this paragraph applies to commercial driver's licenses, "license term" shall be deemed to be 12 months from the date the application fee is received by the Department of Motor Vehicles. A license for the full or remainder of the license term shall be issued or renewed only upon compliance with this section.

(C) In the event that a license or application for a license or the renewal of a license is denied pursuant to this section, any funds paid by the applicant or licensee shall not be refunded by the board.

(D) This paragraph shall apply only in the case of a driver's license, other than a commercial driver's license. Upon the request of the local child support agency or by order of the court upon a showing of good cause, the board shall extend a 150–day temporary license for a period not to exceed 150 extra days.

(3)(A) The department may, when it is economically feasible for the department and the boards to do so as determined by the department, in cases where the department is aware that certain child support obligors listed on the certified lists have been out of compliance with a judgment or order for support for more than four months, provide a supplemental list of these obligors to each board with which the department has an interagency agreement to implement this paragraph. Upon request by the department, the licenses of these obligors shall be subject to suspension, provided that the licenses would not otherwise be eligible for renewal within six months from the date of the request by the department. The board shall have the authority to suspend the license of any licensee on this supplemental list.

(B) If a licensee is on a supplemental list, the board shall immediately serve notice as specified in subdivision (f) on the licensee that his or her license will be automatically suspended 150 days after notice is served, unless compliance with this section is achieved. The notice shall be made personally or by mail to the licensee's last known mailing address on file with the board. Service by mail shall be complete in accordance with Section 1013 of the Code of Civil Procedure.

(C) The 150–day notice period shall not be extended.

(D) In the event that any license is suspended pursuant to this section, any funds paid by the licensee shall not be refunded by the board.

(E) This paragraph shall not apply to licenses subject to annual renewal or annual fee.

(f) Notices shall be developed by each board in accordance with guidelines provided by the department and subject to approval by the department. The notice shall include the address and telephone number of the local child support agency that submitted the name on the certified list, and shall emphasize the necessity of obtaining a release from that local child support agency as a condition for the issuance, renewal, or continued valid status of a license or licenses.

(1) In the case of applicants not subject to paragraph (3) of subdivision (e), the notice shall inform the applicant that the board shall issue a temporary license, as provided in subparagraph (A) of paragraph (2) of subdivision (e), for 150 calendar days if the applicant is otherwise eligible and that upon expiration of that time period the license will be denied unless the board has received a release from the local child support agency that submitted the name on the certified list.

(2) In the case of licensees named on a supplemental list, the notice shall inform the licensee that his or her license will continue in its existing status for no more than 150 calendar days from the date of mailing or service of the notice and thereafter will be suspended indefinitely unless, during the 150–day notice period, the board has received a release from the local child support agency that submitted the name on the certified list. Additionally, the notice shall inform the licensee that any license suspended under this section will remain so until the expiration of the remaining license term, unless the board receives a release along with applications and fees, if applicable, to reinstate the license during the license term.

(3) The notice shall also inform the applicant or licensee that if an application is denied or a license is suspended pursuant to this section, any funds paid by the applicant or licensee shall not be refunded by the board. The Department of Child Support Services shall also develop a form that the applicant shall use to request a review by the local child support agency. A copy of this form shall be included with every notice sent pursuant to this subdivision.

(g)(1) Each local child support agency shall maintain review procedures consistent with this section to allow an applicant to have the underlying arrearage and any relevant defenses investigated, to provide an applicant information on the process of obtaining a modification of a support order, or to provide an applicant assistance in the establishment of a payment schedule on arrearages if the circumstances so warrant.

(2) It is the intent of the Legislature that a court or local child support agency, when determining an appropriate payment schedule for arrearages, base its decision on the facts of the particular case and the priority of payment of child support over other debts. The payment schedule shall also recognize that certain expenses may be essential to enable an obligor to be employed. Therefore, in reaching its

decision, the court or the local child support agency shall consider both of these goals in setting a payment schedule for arrearages.

(h) If the applicant wishes to challenge the submission of his or her name on the certified list, the applicant shall make a timely written request for review to the local child support agency who certified the applicant's name. A request for review pursuant to this section shall be resolved in the same manner and timeframe provided for resolution of a complaint pursuant to Section 17800. The local child support agency shall immediately send a release to the appropriate board and the applicant, if any of the following conditions are met:

(1) The applicant is found to be in compliance or negotiates an agreement with the local child support agency for a payment schedule on arrearages or reimbursement.

(2) The applicant has submitted a request for review, but the local child support agency will be unable to complete the review and send notice of its findings to the applicant within the time specified in Section 17800.

(3) The applicant has filed and served a request for judicial review pursuant to this section, but a resolution of that review will not be made within 150 days of the date of service of notice pursuant to subdivision (f). This paragraph applies only if the delay in completing the judicial review process is not the result of the applicant's failure to act in a reasonable, timely, and diligent manner upon receiving the local child support agency's notice of findings.

(4) The applicant has obtained a judicial finding of compliance as defined in this section.

(i) An applicant is required to act with diligence in responding to notices from the board and the local child support agency with the recognition that the temporary license will lapse or the license suspension will go into effect after 150 days and that the local child support agency and, where appropriate, the court must have time to act within that period. An applicant's delay in acting, without good cause, which directly results in the inability of the local child support agency to complete a review of the applicant's request or the court to hear the request for judicial review within the 150–day period shall not constitute the diligence required under this section which would justify the issuance of a release.

(j) Except as otherwise provided in this section, the local child support agency shall not issue a release if the applicant is not in compliance with the judgment or order for support. The local child support agency shall notify the applicant in writing that the applicant may, by filing an order to show cause or notice of motion, request any or all of the following:

(1) Judicial review of the local child support agency's decision not to issue a release.

(2) A judicial determination of compliance.

(3) A modification of the support judgment or order.

The notice shall also contain the name and address of the court in which the applicant shall file the order to show cause or notice of motion and inform the applicant that his or her name shall remain on the certified list if the applicant does not timely request judicial review. The applicant shall comply with all statutes and rules of court regarding orders to show cause and notices of motion.

Nothing in this section shall be deemed to limit an applicant from filing an order to show cause or notice of motion to modify a support judgment or order or to fix a payment schedule on arrearages accruing under a support judgment or order or to obtain a court finding of compliance with a judgment or order for support.

(k) The request for judicial review of the local child support agency's decision shall state the grounds for which review is requested and judicial review shall be limited to those stated grounds. The court shall hold an evidentiary hearing within 20 calendar days of the filing of the request for review. Judicial review of the local child support agency's decision shall be limited to a determination of each of the following issues:

(1) Whether there is a support judgment, order, or payment schedule on arrearages or reimbursement.

(2) Whether the petitioner is the obligor covered by the support judgment or order.

(3) Whether the support obligor is or is not in compliance with the judgment or order of support.

(4)(A) The extent to which the needs of the obligor, taking into account the obligor's payment history and the current circumstances of both the obligor and the obligee, warrant a conditional release as described in this subdivision.

(B) The request for judicial review shall be served by the applicant upon the local child support agency that submitted the applicant's name on the certified list within seven calendar days of the filing of the petition. The court has the authority to uphold the action, unconditionally release the license, or conditionally release the license.

(C) If the judicial review results in a finding by the court that the obligor is in compliance with the judgment or order for support, the local child support agency shall immediately send a release in accordance with subdivision (*l*) to the appropriate board and the applicant. If the judicial review results in a finding by the court that the needs of the obligor warrant a conditional release, the court shall make findings of fact stating the basis for the release and the payment necessary to satisfy the unrestricted issuance or renewal of the license without prejudice to a later judicial determination of the amount of support arrearages, including interest, and shall specify payment terms, compliance with which are necessary to allow the release to remain in effect.

(*l*) The department shall prescribe release forms for use by local child support agencies. When the obligor is in compliance, the local child support agency shall mail to the applicant and the appropriate board a release stating that the applicant is in compliance. The receipt of a release shall serve to notify the applicant and the board that, for the purposes of this section, the applicant is in compliance with the judgment or order for support. Any board that has received a release from the local child support agency pursuant to this subdivision shall process the release within five business days of its receipt.

If the local child support agency determines subsequent to the issuance of a release that the applicant is once again not in compliance with a judgment or order for support, or with the terms of repayment as described in this subdivision, the local child support agency may notify the board, the obligor, and the department in a format prescribed by the department that the obligor is not in compliance.

The department may, when it is economically feasible for the department and the boards to develop an automated process for complying with this subdivision, notify the boards in a manner prescribed by the department, that the obligor is once again not in compliance. Upon receipt of this notice, the board shall immediately notify the obligor on a form prescribed by the department that the obligor's license will be suspended on a specific date, and this date shall be no longer than 30 days from the date the form is mailed. The obligor shall be further notified that the license will remain suspended until a new release is issued in accordance with subdivision (h). Nothing in this section shall be deemed to limit the obligor from seeking judicial review of suspension pursuant to the procedures described in subdivision (k).

(m) The department may enter into interagency agreements with the state agencies that have responsibility for the administration of boards necessary to implement this section, to the extent that it is cost–effective to implement this section. These agreements shall provide for the receipt by the other state agencies and boards of federal funds to cover that portion of costs allowable in federal law and regulation and incurred by the state agencies and boards in implementing this section. Notwithstanding any other provision of law, revenue generated by a board or state agency shall be used to fund the nonfederal share of costs incurred pursuant to this section. These agreements shall provide that boards shall reimburse the department for the nonfederal share of costs incurred by the department in implementing this section. The boards shall reimburse the department for the nonfederal share of costs incurred pursuant to this section from moneys collected from applicants and licensees.

(n) Notwithstanding any other provision of law, in order for the boards subject to this section to be reimbursed for the costs incurred in administering its provisions, the boards may, with the approval of the appropriate department director, levy on all licensees and applicants a surcharge on any fee or fees collected pursuant to law, or, alternatively, with the approval of the appropriate department director, levy on the applicants or licensees named on a certified list or supplemental list, a special fee.

(o) The process described in subdivision (h) shall constitute the sole administrative remedy for contesting the issuance of a temporary license or the denial or suspension of a license under this section. The procedures specified in the administrative adjudication provisions of the Administrative Procedure Act (Chapter 4.5 (commencing with Section 11400) and Chapter 5 (commencing with Section 11500) of Part 1 of Division 3 of Title 2 of the Government Code) shall not apply to the denial, suspension, or failure to issue or renew a license or the issuance of a temporary license pursuant to this section.

(p) In furtherance of the public policy of increasing child support enforcement and collections, on or before November 1, 1995, the State Department of Social Services shall make a report to the Legislature and the Governor based on data collected by the boards and the district attorneys in a format prescribed by the State Department of Social Services. The report shall contain all of the following:

(1) The number of delinquent obligors certified by district attorneys under this section.

(2) The number of support obligors who also were applicants or licensees subject to this section.

(3) The number of new licenses and renewals that were delayed, temporary licenses issued, and licenses suspended subject to this section and the number of new licenses and renewals granted and licenses reinstated following board receipt of releases as provided by subdivision (h) by May 1, 1995.

(4) The costs incurred in the implementation and enforcement of this section.

(q) Any board receiving an inquiry as to the licensed status of an applicant or licensee who has had a license denied or suspended under this section or has been granted a temporary license under this section shall respond only that the license was denied or suspended or the temporary license was issued pursuant to this section. Information collected pursuant to this section by any state agency, board, or department shall be subject to the Information Practices Act of 1977 (Chapter 1 (commencing with Section 1798) of Title 1.8 of Part 4 of Division 3 of the Civil Code).

(r) Any rules and regulations issued pursuant to this section by any state agency, board, or department may be adopted as emergency regulations in accordance with the rulemaking provisions of the Administrative Procedure Act (Chapter 3.5 (commencing with Section 11340) of Part 1 of Division 3 of Title 2 of the Government Code). The adoption of these regulations shall be deemed an emergency and necessary for the immediate preservation of the public peace, health, and safety, or general welfare. The regulations shall become effective immediately upon filing with the Secretary of State.

(s) The department and boards, as appropriate, shall adopt regulations necessary to implement this section.

(t) The Judicial Council shall develop the forms necessary to implement this section, except as provided in subdivisions (f) and (*l*).

(u) The release or other use of information received by a board pursuant to this section, except as authorized by this section, is punishable as a misdemeanor.

(v) The State Board of Equalization shall enter into interagency agreements with the department and the Franchise Tax Board that will require the department and the Franchise Tax Board to maximize the use of information collected by the State Board of Equalization, for child support enforcement purposes, to the extent it is cost–effective and permitted by the Revenue and Taxation Code.

(w)(1) The suspension or revocation of any driver's license, including a commercial driver's license, under this section shall not subject the licensee to vehicle impoundment pursuant to Section 14602.6 of the Vehicle Code.

(2) Notwithstanding any other provision of law, the suspension or revocation of any driver's license, including a commercial driver's license, under this section shall not subject the licensee to increased costs for vehicle liability insurance.

(x) If any provision of this section or the application thereof to any person or circumstance is held invalid, that invalidity shall not affect other provisions or applications of this section which can be given effect without the invalid provision or application, and to this end the provisions of this section are severable.

(y) All rights to administrative and judicial review afforded by this section to an applicant shall also be afforded to a licensee.

Added Stats 1999 ch 654 § 3.5 (AB 370). Amended Stats 2001 ch 755 § 14 (SB 943), effective October 12, 2001.

GOVERNMENT CODE

TITLE 1
General

DIVISION 4
PUBLIC OFFICERS AND EMPLOYEES

Chapter 4
Resignations and Vacancies

Article 2

Vacancies

§ 1774.   Filling vacancies; Interim appointments; When office deemed vacant

(a) When an office, the appointment to which is vested in the Governor and Senate, either becomes vacant or the term of the incumbent thereof expires, the Governor may appoint a person to the office or reappoint the incumbent after the expiration of the term. Until Senate confirmation of the person appointed or reappointed, that person serves at the pleasure of the Governor. If the term of office of an incumbent subject to this section expires, the Governor shall have 60 days after the expiration date to reappoint the incumbent. If the incumbent is not reappointed within the 60–day period, the office shall be deemed to be vacant as of the first day following the end of the 60–day period.

(b) With respect to the appointment or reappointment by the Governor of a person to an office subject to confirmation by the Senate, the Governor shall submit the name of the person appointed, or the name of the incumbent reappointed, and the effective date of the appointment or reappointment to the Senate or, if the Senate is in recess or has adjourned, to the Secretary of the Senate, within 60 days after the person first began performing the duties of the office, or, as to the reappointment of an incumbent, within 90 days after the expiration date of the term. If the Governor does not provide the required notification within 60 days after the person first began performing the duties of the office, or, as to the reappointment of an incumbent to an office after the expiration date of the term, within 90 days after the expiration of the term, the office shall be deemed to be vacant as of the first day immediately following the end of the applicable period.

(c) If the Senate either refuses to confirm, or fails to confirm within 365 days after the day the person first began performing the duties of the office, or, with respect to an incumbent whose appointment to that office previously had been confirmed by the Senate and who is reappointed to that office, within 365 days after the expiration date of the term, the following shall apply:

(1) If the Senate refuses to confirm, the person may continue to serve in that office until 60 days have elapsed since the refusal to confirm or until 365 days have elapsed since the person first began performing the duties of the office, whichever occurs first, or with respect to an incumbent whose appointment to that office previously had been confirmed by the Senate and who is reappointed to that office, until 60 days have elapsed since refusal or until 365 days after the expiration date of the prior term, and the office for which the appointment was made shall be deemed to be vacant as of the first day immediately following the end of the applicable period.

(2) If the Senate fails to confirm within the applicable 365–day period, the person may not continue to serve in that office, and the office for which the appointment was made shall be deemed to be vacant as of the first day immediately following the end of the 365–day period.

Enacted Stats 1943 ch 134. Amended Stats 1955 ch 1881 § 1; Stats 1973 ch 603 § 1, effective September 18, 1973; Stats 1980 ch 1338 § 1; Stats 1982 ch 801 § 1.

TITLE 2
Government of the State of California

DIVISION 3
EXECUTIVE DEPARTMENT

PART 1
STATE DEPARTMENTS AND AGENCIES

Chapter 2
State Departments

Article 2

Investigations and Hearings

§ 11181. Acts authorized in connection with investigations and actions

In connection with any investigation or action authorized by this article, the department head may do any of the following:

(a) Inspect and copy books, records, and other items described in subdivision (e).

(b) Hear complaints.

(c) Administer oaths.

(d) Certify to all official acts.

(e) Issue subpoenas for the attendance of witnesses and the production of papers, books, accounts, documents, any writing as defined by Section 250 of the Evidence Code, tangible things, and testimony pertinent or material to any inquiry, investigation, hearing, proceeding, or action conducted in any part of the state.

(f) Promulgate interrogatories pertinent or material to any inquiry, investigation, hearing, proceeding, or action.

(g) Divulge information or evidence related to the investigation of unlawful activity discovered from interrogatory answers, papers, books, accounts, documents, and any other item described in subdivision (e), or testimony, to the Attorney General or to any prosecuting attorney of this state, any other state, or the United States who has a responsibility for investigating the unlawful activity investigated or discovered, or to any governmental agency responsible for enforcing laws related to the unlawful activity investigated or discovered, if the Attorney General, prosecuting attorney, or agency to which the information or evidence is divulged agrees to maintain the confidentiality of the information received to the extent required by this article.

(h) Present information or evidence obtained or developed from the investigation of unlawful activity to a court or at an administrative hearing in connection with any action or proceeding.

Added Stats 1945 ch 111 § 3. Amended Stats 1981 ch 778 § 1; Stats 1987 ch 1453 § 8; Stats 2001 ch 74 § 2 (AB 260); Stats 2003 ch 876 § 6 (SB 434).

§ 11183. Divulging information; Offense; Disqualification

Except in a report to the head of the department or when called upon to testify in any court or proceeding at law or as provided in Section 11180.5 or subdivisions (g) and (h) of Section 11181, an officer shall not divulge any information or evidence acquired by the officer from the interrogatory answers or subpoenaed private books, documents, papers, or other items described in subdivision (e) of Section 11181 of any person while acting or claiming to act under any authorization pursuant to this article, in respect to the confidential or private transactions, property or business of any person. An officer who divulges information or evidence in violation of this section is guilty of a misdemeanor and disqualified from acting in any official capacity in the department.

Added Stats 1945 ch 111 § 3. Amended Stats 1981 ch 778 § 2; Stats 2003 ch 876 § 7 (SB 434).

PART 2.8

DEPARTMENT OF FAIR EMPLOYMENT AND HOUSING

Chapter 6

Discrimination Prohibited

Article 1

Unlawful Practices, Generally

§ 12944. Discrimination by "licensing board"

(a) It shall be unlawful for a licensing board to require any examination or establish any other qualification for licensing that has an adverse impact on any class by virtue of its race, creed, color, national origin or ancestry, sex, gender, gender identity, gender expression, age, medical condition, genetic information, physical disability, mental disability, or sexual orientation, unless the practice can be demonstrated to be job related.

Where the commission, after hearing, determines that an examination is unlawful under this subdivision, the licensing board may continue to use and rely on the examination until such time as judicial review by the superior court of the determination is exhausted.

If an examination or other qualification for licensing is determined to be unlawful under this section, that determination shall not void, limit, repeal, or otherwise affect any right, privilege, status, or responsibility previously conferred upon any person by the examination or by a license issued in reliance on the examination or qualification.

(b) It shall be unlawful for a licensing board to fail or refuse to make reasonable accommodation to an individual's mental or physical disability or medical condition.

(c) It shall be unlawful for any licensing board, unless specifically acting in accordance with federal equal employment opportunity guidelines or regulations approved by the commission, to print or circulate or cause to be printed or circulated any publication, or to make any non-job-related inquiry, either verbal or through use of an application form, which expresses, directly or indirectly, any limitation, specification, or discrimination as to race, religious creed, color, national origin, ancestry, physical disability, mental disability, medical condition, genetic information, sex, gender, gender identity, gender expression, age, or sexual orientation or any intent to make any such limitation, specification, or discrimination. Nothing in this subdivision shall prohibit any licensing board from making, in connection with prospective licensure or certification, an inquiry as to, or a request for information regarding, the physical fitness of applicants if that inquiry or request for information is directly related and pertinent to the license or the licensed position the applicant is applying for. Nothing in this subdivision shall prohibit any licensing board, in connection with prospective examinations, licensure, or certification, from inviting individuals with physical or mental disabilities to request reasonable accommodations or from making inquiries related to reasonable accommodations.

(d) It is unlawful for a licensing board to discriminate against any person because the person has filed a complaint, testified, or assisted in any proceeding under this part.

(e) It is unlawful for any licensing board to fail to keep records of applications for licensing or certification for a period of two years following the date of receipt of the applications.

(f) As used in this section, "licensing board" means any state board, agency, or authority in the State and Consumer Services Agency that has the authority to grant licenses or certificates which are prerequisites to employment eligibility or professional status.

TITLE 7
Planning and Land Use

DIVISION 2
SUBDIVISIONS

Chapter 5
Improvement Security

§66499.7. Release of security; Notice of completion (Operative July 1, 2012; Repealed January 1, 2016)

The security furnished by the subdivider shall be released in whole or in part in the following manner:

(a) Security given for faithful performance of any act or agreement shall be released upon the performance of the act or final completion and acceptance of the required work. The legislative body may provide for the partial release of the security upon the partial performance of the act or the acceptance of the work as it progresses, consistent with the provisions of this section. The security may be a surety bond, a cash deposit, a letter of credit, escrow account, or other form of performance guarantee required as security by the legislative body that meets the requirements as acceptable security pursuant to law. If the security furnished by the subdivider is a documentary evidence of security such as a surety bond or a letter of credit, the legislative body shall release the documentary evidence and return the original to the issuer upon performance of the act or final completion and acceptance of the required work. In the event that the legislative body is unable to return the original documentary evidence to the issuer, the security shall be released by written notice sent by certified mail to the subdivider and issuer of the documentary evidence within 30 days of the acceptance of the work. The written notice shall contain a statement that the work for which the security was furnished has been performed or completed and accepted by the legislative body, a description of the project subject to the documentary evidence and the notarized signature of the authorized representative of the legislative body.

(b) At the time that the subdivider believes that the obligation to perform the work for which security was required is complete, the subdivider may notify the local agency in writing of the completed work, including a list of work completed. Upon receipt of the written notice, the local agency shall have 45 days to review and comment or approve the completion of the required work. If the local agency does not agree that all work has been completed in accordance with the plans and specifications for the improvements, it shall supply a list of all remaining work to be completed.

(c) Within 45 days of receipt of the list of remaining work from the local agency, the subdivider may then provide cost estimates for all remaining work for review and approval by the local agency. Upon receipt of the cost estimates, the local agency shall then have 45 days to review, comment, and approve, modify, or disapprove those cost estimates. No local agency shall be required to engage in this process of partial release more than once between the start of work and completion and acceptance of all work; however, nothing in this section prohibits a local agency from allowing for a partial release as it otherwise deems appropriate.

(d) If the local agency approves the cost estimate, the local agency shall release all performance security except for security in an amount up to 200 percent of the cost estimate of the remaining work. The process allowing for a partial release of performance security shall occur when the cost estimate of the remaining work does not exceed 20 percent of the total original performance security unless the local agency allows for a release at an earlier time. Substitute bonds or other security may be used as a replacement for the performance security, subject to the approval of the local agency. If substitute bonds or other security is used as a replacement for the performance security released, the release shall not be effective unless and until the local agency receives and approves that form of replacement security. A reduction in the performance security, authorized under this section, is not, and shall not be deemed to be, an acceptance by the local agency of the completed improvements, and the risk of loss or damage to the improvements and the obligation to maintain the improvements shall remain the sole responsibility of the subdivider until all required public improvements have been accepted by the local agency and all other required improvements have been fully completed in accordance with the plans and specifications for the improvements.

(e) The subdivider shall complete the works of improvement until all remaining items are accepted by the local agency.

(f) Upon the completion of the improvements, the subdivider, or his or her assigns, shall be notified in writing by the local agency within 45 days.

(g) Within 45 days of the issuance of the notification by the local agency, the release of any remaining performance security shall be placed upon the agenda of the legislative body of the local agency for approval of the release of any remaining performance security. If the local agency delegates authority for the release of performance security to a public official or other employee, any remaining performance security shall be released within 60 days of the issuance of the written statement of completion.

(h) Security securing the payment to the contractor, his or her subcontractors and to persons furnishing labor, materials or equipment shall, after passage of the time within which claims of lien are required to be recorded pursuant to Article 2 (commencing with Section 8410) of Chapter 4 of Title 2 of Part 6 of Division 4 of the Civil Code and after acceptance of the work, be reduced to an amount equal to the total claimed by all claimants for whom claims of lien have been recorded and notice thereof given in writing to the legislative body, and if no claims have been recorded, the security shall be released in full.

(i) The release shall not apply to any required guarantee and warranty period required by Section 66499.9 for the guarantee or warranty nor to the amount of the security deemed necessary by the local agency for the guarantee and warranty period nor to costs and reasonable expenses and fees, including reasonable attorney's fees.

(j) The legislative body may authorize any of its public officers or employees to authorize release or reduction of the security in accordance with the conditions hereinabove set forth and in accordance with any rules that it may prescribe.

(k) This section shall remain in effect only until January 1, 2016, and as of that date is repealed, unless a later enacted statute, that is enacted before January 1, 2016, deletes or extends that date.

Added Stats 1974 ch 1536 § 4, operative March 1, 1975. Amended Stats 1982 ch 87 § 24, effective March 1, 1982; Stats 1983 ch 1195 § 2; Stats 1988 ch 1308 § 5; Stats 1997 ch 124 § 1 (SB 562); Stats 2005 ch 411 § 1 (AB 1460), effective January 1, 2006, repealed January 1, 2011; Stats 2006 ch 643 § 22 (SB 1196), effective January 1, 2007; Stats 2010 ch 697 § 36 (SB 189), ch 174 § 1 (SB 1019) (ch 174 prevails), effective January 1, 2011, repealed January 1, 2016; Stats 2011 ch 44 § 6 (SB 189), ch 174 § 1 (SB 190), effective January 1, 2012, operative July 1, 2012, repealed January 1, 2016.

HEALTH AND SAFETY CODE

DIVISION 13
HOUSING

PART 1.5

REGULATION OF BUILDINGS USED FOR HUMAN HABITATION

Chapter 2

Rules and Regulations

§ 17926. Carbon monoxide devices required; Number and placement; Violation; Local ordinance

(a) An owner of a dwelling unit intended for human occupancy shall install a carbon monoxide device, approved and listed by the State Fire Marshal pursuant to Section 13263, in each existing dwelling unit having a fossil fuel burning heater or appliance, fireplace, or an attached garage, within the earliest applicable time period as follows:

(1) For all existing single-family dwelling units intended for human occupancy on or before July 1, 2011.

(2) For all other existing dwelling units intended for human occupancy on or before January 1, 2013.

(b) With respect to the number and placement of carbon monoxide devices, an owner shall install the devices in a manner consistent with building standards applicable to new construction for the relevant type of occupancy or with the manufacturer's instructions, if it is technically feasible to do so.

(c)(1) Notwithstanding Section 17995, and except as provided in paragraph (2), a violation of this section is an infraction punishable by a maximum fine of two hundred dollars ($200) for each offense.

(2) Notwithstanding paragraph (1), a property owner shall receive a 30-day notice to correct. If an owner receiving notice fails to correct within that time period, the owner may be assessed the fine pursuant to paragraph (2).

(d) No transfer of title shall be invalidated on the basis of a failure to comply with this section, and the exclusive remedy for the failure to comply with this section is an award of actual damages not to exceed one hundred dollars ($100), exclusive of any court costs and attorney's fees. This subdivision is not intended to affect any duties, rights, or remedies otherwise available at law.

(e) A local ordinance requiring carbon monoxide devices may be enacted or amended if the ordinance is consistent with this chapter.

Added Stats 2010 ch 19 § 4 (SB 183), effective January 1, 2011.

§ 17926.2. Temporary suspension of enforcement of carbon monoxide device regulations; Effect of change in building standards

(a) If the department, in consultation with the State Fire Marshal, determines that a sufficient amount of tested and approved carbon monoxide devices are not available to property owners to meet the requirements of the Carbon Monoxide Poisoning Prevention Act of 2009 and Sections 17926 and 17926.1, the department may suspend enforcement of the requirements of Sections 17926 and 17926.1 for up to six months. If the department elects to suspend enforcement of these requirements, the department shall notify the Secretary of State of its decision and shall post a public notice that describes its findings and decision on the departmental Internet Web site.

(b) If the California Building Standards Commission adopts or updates building standards relating to carbon monoxide devices, the owner or owner's agent, who has installed a carbon monoxide device as required by Section 17926 or 17926.1, shall not be required to install a new device meeting the requirements of those building standards within an individual dwelling unit until the owner makes application for a permit for alterations, repairs, or additions to that dwelling unit, the cost of which will exceed one thousand dollars ($1,000).

Added Stats 2010 ch 19 § 6 (SB 183), effective January 1, 2011.

Appendix

PART 3

MISCELLANEOUS

Chapter 9

Local Building Permits

Article 1

Contents

§ 19825. Building permit application; Form; Owner-Builder Declaration; Documentation and verification (First of two; Operative until July 1, 2012)

(a) Every city, county, or city and county, whether general law or chartered, that requires the issuance of a permit as a condition precedent to the construction, alteration, improvement, demolition, or repair of any building or structure, shall require the execution of a permit application, in substantially the same form set forth under this subdivision, and require any individual who executes the Owner-Builder Declaration to present documentation sufficient to identify the property owner and, as necessary, verify the signature of the property owner. A city, county, or city and county may require additional information on the permit application.

PERMIT APPLICATION
BUILDING PROJECT IDENTIFICATION

Applicant's Mailing Address   _____

Property Location or Address   _____

Property Owner's Name   _____
Property Owner's Telephone No.   _____

Licensed Design Professional (Architect _____
or Engineer) in charge of the project   _____

Mailing Address of Licensed Design   _____
Professional   _____

                                     _____
                            License No. _____

LICENSED CONTRACTOR'S DECLARATION

I hereby affirm under penalty of perjury that I am licensed under provisions of Chapter 9 (commencing with Section 7000) of Division 3 of the Business and Professions Code, and my license is in full force and effect.

License Class _____ License No. _____

Date _____ Contractor Signature _____

OWNER-BUILDER DECLARATION

I hereby affirm under penalty of perjury that I am exempt from the Contractors' State License Law for the reason(s) indicated below by the checkmark(s) I have placed next to the applicable item(s) (Section 7031.5, Business and Professions Code: Any city or county that requires a permit to construct, alter, improve, demolish, or repair any structure, prior to its issuance, also requires the applicant for the permit to file a signed statement that he or she is licensed pursuant to the provisions of the Contractors' State License Law (Chapter 9 (commencing with Section 7000) of Division 3 of the Business and Professions Code) or that he or she is exempt from licensure and the basis for the alleged exemption. Any violation of Section 7031.5 by any applicant for a permit subjects the applicant to a civil penalty of not more than five hundred dollars ($500).):

(_) I, as owner of the property, or my employees with wages as their sole compensation, will do (_) all of or (_) portions of the work, and the structure is not intended or offered for sale (Section 7044, Business and Professions Code: The Contractors' State License Law does not apply to an owner of property who, through employees' or personal effort, builds or improves the property, provided that the improvements are not intended or offered for sale. If, however, the building or improvement is sold within one year of completion, the Owner-Builder will have the burden of proving that it was not built or improved for the purpose of sale.).

(_) I, as owner of the property, am exclusively contracting with licensed Contractors to construct the project (Section 7044, Business and Professions Code: The Contractors' State License Law does not apply to an owner of property who builds or improves thereon, and who contracts for the projects with a licensed Contractor pursuant to the Contractors' State License Law.).

(_) I am exempt from licensure under the Contractors' State License Law for the following reason:

_____

By my signature below I acknowledge that, except for my personal residence in which I must have resided for at least one year prior to completion of the improvements covered by this permit, I cannot legally sell a structure that I have built as an owner-builder if it has not been constructed in its entirety by licensed contractors. I understand that a copy of the applicable law, Section 7044 of the Business and Professions Code, is available upon request

when this application is submitted or at the following Web site:
http://www.leginfo.ca.gov/calaw.html.

Date _____

Signature of Property Owner or Authorized Agent _____

WORKERS' COMPENSATION DECLARATION

WARNING: FAILURE TO SECURE WORKERS' COMPENSATION
COVERAGE IS UNLAWFUL, AND SHALL SUBJECT AN EMPLOYER TO
CRIMINAL PENALTIES AND CIVIL FINES UP TO ONE HUNDRED
THOUSAND DOLLARS ($100,000), IN ADDITION TO THE COST OF
COMPENSATION, DAMAGES AS PROVIDED FOR IN SECTION 3706 OF
THE LABOR CODE, INTEREST, AND ATTORNEY'S FEES.

I hereby affirm under penalty of perjury one of the following declarations:

_____ I have and will maintain a certificate of consent to self-insure for
workers' compensation, issued by the Director of Industrial Relations as provided for by Section 3700 of the Labor Code, for the performance of the work
for which this permit is issued.

Policy No. _____

_____ I have and will maintain workers' compensation insurance, as required by Section 3700 of the Labor Code, for the performance of the work for
which this permit is issued. My workers' compensation insurance carrier and
policy number are:

Carrier _____ Policy Number _____ Expiration Date _____

Name of Agent _____ Phone #_____

_____ I certify that, in the performance of the work for which this permit is
issued, I shall not employ any person in any manner so as to become subject
to the workers' compensation laws of California, and agree that, if I should
become subject to the workers' compensation provisions of Section 3700 of the
Labor Code, I shall forthwith comply with those provisions.

_____   _____
      Signature of Applicant   Date

DECLARATION REGARDING CONSTRUCTION LENDING AGENCY

I hereby affirm under penalty of perjury that there is a construction lending agency for the performance of the work for which this permit is issued
(Section 3097, Civil Code).

Lender's Name _____

Lender's Address _____

By my signature below, I certify to each of the following:

I am the property owner or authorized to act on the property owner's behalf.

I have read this application and the information I have provided is correct.

I agree to comply with all applicable city and county ordinances and state laws relating to building construction.

I authorize representatives of this city or county to enter the above-identified property for inspection purposes.

Signature of Property Owner or Authorized Agent _____

Date _____

(b) When the Permit Application and the Owner-Builder Declaration have been executed by a person other than the property owner, prior to issuing the permit, the following shall be completed by the property owner and returned to the agency responsible for issuing the permit:

AUTHORIZATION OF AGENT TO ACT ON PROPERTY OWNER'S BEHALF

Excluding the Notice to Property Owner, the execution of which I understand is my personal responsibility, I hereby authorize the following person(s) to act as my agent(s) to apply for, sign, and file the documents necessary to obtain an Owner-Builder Permit for my project.

Scope of Construction Project (or Description of Work):

_____

Project Location or Address: _____

Name of Authorized Agent: _____

Address of Authorized Agent: _____

Phone Number of Authorized Agent: _____

I declare under penalty of perjury that I am the property owner for the address listed above and I personally filled out the above information and certify its accuracy.

Property Owner's Signature: _____ Date: _____

Note: A copy of the owner's driver's license, form notarization, or other verification acceptable to the agency is required to be presented when the permit is issued to verify the property owner's signature.

(c) When the Owner-Builder Declaration required under subdivision (a) is executed, a Notice to Property Owner also shall be executed by the property owner in substantially the same form set forth under this section. The Notice to Property Owner shall appear on the official letterhead of the issuer and shall be provided to the applicant by one of the following methods chosen by the permitting authority: regular mail, electronic format, or given directly to the applicant at the time the application for the permit is made. Except as otherwise provided, the Notice to Property Owner pursuant to this section shall be completed and signed by the property owner and returned prior to issuance of the permit. An agent of the owner shall not execute this notice unless the property owner obtains the prior approval of the permitting authority. A permit shall not be issued unless the property owner complies with this section.

NOTICE TO PROPERTY OWNER

Dear Property Owner:
An application for a building permit has been submitted in your name listing yourself as the builder of the property improvements specified at

_____.
We are providing you with an Owner-Builder Acknowledgment and Information Verification Form to make you aware of your responsibilities and possible risk you may incur by having this permit issued in your name as the Owner-Builder.
We will not issue a building permit until you have read, initialed your understanding of each provision, signed, and returned this form to us at our official address indicated. An agent of the owner cannot execute this notice unless you, the property owner, obtain the prior approval of the permitting authority.

OWNER'S ACKNOWLEDGMENT AND VERIFICATION OF INFORMATION

DIRECTIONS: Read and initial each statement below to signify you understand or verify this information.
_____ 1. I understand a frequent practice of unlicensed persons is to have the property owner obtain an "Owner-Builder" building permit that erroneously implies that the property owner is providing his or her own labor and material personally. I, as an Owner-Builder, may be held liable and subject to serious financial risk for any injuries sustained by an unlicensed person and his or her employees while working on my property. My homeowner's insurance may not provide coverage for those injuries. I am willfully acting as an

Owner-Builder and am aware of the limits of my insurance coverage for injuries to workers on my property.

_____ 2. I understand building permits are not required to be signed by property owners unless they are responsible for the construction and are not hiring a licensed Contractor to assume this responsibility.

_____ 3. I understand as an "Owner-Builder" I am the responsible party of record on the permit. I understand that I may protect myself from potential financial risk by hiring a licensed Contractor and having the permit filed in his or her name instead of my own.

_____ 4. I understand Contractors are required by law to be licensed and bonded in California and to list their license numbers on permits and contracts.

_____ 5. I understand if I employ or otherwise engage any persons, other than California licensed Contractors, and the total value of my construction is at least five hundred dollars ($500), including labor and materials, I may be considered an "employer" under state and federal law.

_____ 6. I understand if I am considered an "employer" under state and federal law, I must register with the state and federal government, withhold payroll taxes, provide workers' compensation disability insurance, and contribute to unemployment compensation for each "employee." I also understand my failure to abide by these laws may subject me to serious financial risk.

_____ 7. I understand under California Contractors' State License Law, an Owner-Builder who builds single-family residential structures cannot legally build them with the intent to offer them for sale, unless all work is performed by licensed subcontractors and the number of structures does not exceed four within any calendar year, or all of the work is performed under contract with a licensed general building Contractor.

_____ 8. I understand as an Owner-Builder if I sell the property for which this permit is issued, I may be held liable for any financial or personal injuries sustained by any subsequent owner(s) that result from any latent construction defects in the workmanship or materials.

_____ 9. I understand I may obtain more information regarding my obligations as an "employer" from the Internal Revenue Service, the United States Small Business Administration, the California Department of Benefit Payments, and the California Division of Industrial Accidents. I also understand I may contact the California Contractors' State License Board (CSLB) at 1-800- 321-CSLB (2752) or www.cslb.ca.gov for more information about licensed contractors.

_____ 10. I am aware of and consent to an Owner-Builder building permit applied for in my name, and understand that I am the party legally and financially responsible for proposed construction activity at the following address:

_____

_____ 11. I agree that, as the party legally and financially responsible for this proposed construction activity, I will abide by all applicable laws and requirements that govern Owner- Builders as well as employers.

_____ 12. I agree to notify the issuer of this form immediately of any additions, deletions, or changes to any of the information I have provided on this form.

Licensed contractors are regulated by laws designed to protect the public. If you contract with someone who does not have a license, the Contractors' State License Board may be unable to assist you with any financial loss you may sustain as a result of a complaint. Your only remedy against unlicensed Contractors may be in civil court. It is also important for you to understand that if an unlicensed Contractor or employee of that individual or firm is injured while working on your property, you may be held liable for damages. If you obtain a permit as Owner-Builder and wish to hire Contractors, you will be responsible for verifying whether or not those Contractors are properly licensed and the status of their workers' compensation insurance coverage.

Before a building permit can be issued, this form must be completed and signed by the property owner and returned to the agency responsible for issuing the permit.

Note: A copy of the property owner's driver's license, form notarization, or other verification acceptable to the agency is required to be presented when the permit is issued to verify the property owner's signature.

Signature of property owner _____   Date: _____

Added Stats 2008 ch 66 § 2 (AB 2335), effective January 1, 2009.

§ 19825. Building permit application; Form; Owner-Builder Declaration; Documentation and verification (Second of two; Operative July 1, 2012)

(a) Every city, county, or city and county, whether general law or chartered, that requires the issuance of a permit as a condition precedent to the construction, alteration, improvement, demolition, or repair of any building or structure, shall require the execution of a permit application, in substantially the same form set forth under this subdivision, and require any individual who executes the Owner-Builder Declaration to present documentation sufficient to identify the property owner and, as necessary, verify the signature of the property owner. A city, county, or city and county may require additional information on the permit application.

PERMIT APPLICATION
BUILDING PROJECT IDENTIFICATION

Applicant's Mailing Address   _____

Property Location or Address   _____

Property Owner's Name   _____
Property Owner's Telephone No.   _____

Licensed Design Professional (Architect _____
or Engineer) in charge of the project   _____

Mailing Address of Licensed Design   _____
Professional   _____

                                         _____
                              License No. _____

LICENSED CONTRACTOR'S DECLARATION

I hereby affirm under penalty of perjury that I am licensed under provisions of Chapter 9 (commencing with Section 7000) of Division 3 of the Business and Professions Code, and my license is in full force and effect.

License Class _____ License No. _____
Date _____ Contractor Signature _____

OWNER-BUILDER DECLARATION

I hereby affirm under penalty of perjury that I am exempt from the Contractors' State License Law for the reason(s) indicated below by the checkmark(s) I have placed next to the applicable item(s) (Section 7031.5, Business and Professions Code: Any city or county that requires a permit to construct, alter, improve, demolish, or repair any structure, prior to its issuance, also requires the applicant for the permit to file a signed statement that he or she is licensed pursuant to the provisions of the Contractors' State License Law (Chapter 9 (commencing with Section 7000) of Division 3 of the Business and Professions Code) or that he or she is exempt from licensure and the basis for the alleged exemption. Any violation of Section 7031.5 by any applicant for a permit subjects the applicant to a civil penalty of not more than five hundred dollars ($500).):

(_) I, as owner of the property, or my employees with wages as their sole compensation, will do (_) all of or (_) portions of the work, and the structure is not intended or offered for sale (Section 7044, Business and Professions Code: The Contractors' State License Law does not apply to an owner of property who, through employees' or personal effort, builds or improves the property, provided that the improvements are not intended or offered for sale. If, however, the building or improvement is sold within one year of completion, the Owner-Builder will have the burden of proving that it was not built or improved for the purpose of sale.).

(_) I, as owner of the property, am exclusively contracting with licensed Contractors to construct the project (Section 7044, Business and Professions Code: The Contractors' State License Law does not apply to an owner of

Appendix

property who builds or improves thereon, and who contracts for the projects with a licensed Contractor pursuant to the Contractors' State License Law.).

(_) I am exempt from licensure under the Contractors' State License Law for the following reason:

_____

By my signature below I acknowledge that, except for my personal residence in which I must have resided for at least one year prior to completion of the improvements covered by this permit, I cannot legally sell a structure that I have built as an owner-builder if it has not been constructed in its entirety by licensed contractors. I understand that a copy of the applicable law, Section 7044 of the Business and Professions Code, is available upon request when this application is submitted or at the following Web site: http://www.leginfo.ca.gov/calaw.html.

Date _____

Signature of Property Owner or Authorized Agent _____

WORKERS' COMPENSATION DECLARATION

WARNING: FAILURE TO SECURE WORKERS' COMPENSATION COVERAGE IS UNLAWFUL, AND SHALL SUBJECT AN EMPLOYER TO CRIMINAL PENALTIES AND CIVIL FINES UP TO ONE HUNDRED THOUSAND DOLLARS ($100,000), IN ADDITION TO THE COST OF COMPENSATION, DAMAGES AS PROVIDED FOR IN SECTION 3706 OF THE LABOR CODE, INTEREST, AND ATTORNEY'S FEES.

I hereby affirm under penalty of perjury one of the following declarations:

_____ I have and will maintain a certificate of consent to self-insure for workers' compensation, issued by the Director of Industrial Relations as provided for by Section 3700 of the Labor Code, for the performance of the work for which this permit is issued.

Policy No. _____

_____ I have and will maintain workers' compensation insurance, as required by Section 3700 of the Labor Code, for the performance of the work for which this permit is issued. My workers' compensation insurance carrier and policy number are:

Carrier _____ Policy Number _____ Expiration Date _____

Name of Agent _____ Phone #_____

_____ I certify that, in the performance of the work for which this permit is issued, I shall not employ any person in any manner so as to become subject to the workers' compensation laws of California, and agree that, if I should become subject to the workers' compensation provisions of Section 3700 of the Labor Code, I shall forthwith comply with those provisions.

—————————————— ——————————————

Signature of Applicant   Date

DECLARATION REGARDING CONSTRUCTION LENDING AGENCY

I hereby affirm under penalty of perjury that there is a construction lending agency for the performance of the work for which this permit is issued (Section 8172, Civil Code).

Lender's Name _____

Branch Designation _____

Lender's Address _____

By my signature below, I certify to each of the following:

I am the property owner or authorized to act on the property owner's behalf.

I have read this application and the information I have provided is correct.

I agree to comply with all applicable city and county ordinances and state laws relating to building construction.

I authorize representatives of this city or county to enter the above-identified property for inspection purposes.

Signature of Property Owner or Authorized Agent _____

Date _____

(b) When the Permit Application and the Owner-Builder Declaration have been executed by a person other than the property owner, prior to issuing the permit, the following shall be completed by the property owner and returned to the agency responsible for issuing the permit:

AUTHORIZATION OF AGENT TO ACT ON PROPERTY OWNER'S BEHALF

Excluding the Notice to Property Owner, the execution of which I understand is my personal responsibility, I hereby authorize the following person(s) to act as my agent(s) to apply for, sign, and file the documents necessary to obtain an Owner-Builder Permit for my project.

Scope of Construction Project (or Description of Work):

_____

Project Location or Address: _____

Name of Authorized Agent: _____

Appendix

Address of Authorized Agent: _____

Phone Number of Authorized Agent: _____

I declare under penalty of perjury that I am the property owner for the address listed above and I personally filled out the above information and certify its accuracy.

Property Owner's Signature: _____   Date: _____

Note: A copy of the owner's driver's license, form notarization, or other verification acceptable to the agency is required to be presented when the permit is issued to verify the property owner's signature.

(c) When the Owner-Builder Declaration required under subdivision (a) is executed, a Notice to Property Owner also shall be executed by the property owner in substantially the same form set forth under this section. The Notice to Property Owner shall appear on the official letterhead of the issuer and shall be provided to the applicant by one of the following methods chosen by the permitting authority: regular mail, electronic format, or given directly to the applicant at the time the application for the permit is made. Except as otherwise provided, the Notice to Property Owner pursuant to this section shall be completed and signed by the property owner and returned prior to issuance of the permit. An agent of the owner shall not execute this notice unless the property owner obtains the prior approval of the permitting authority. A permit shall not be issued unless the property owner complies with this section.

NOTICE TO PROPERTY OWNER

Dear Property Owner:
An application for a building permit has been submitted in your name listing yourself as the builder of the property improvements specified at

_____.

We are providing you with an Owner-Builder Acknowledgment and Information Verification Form to make you aware of your responsibilities and possible risk you may incur by having this permit issued in your name as the Owner-Builder.

We will not issue a building permit until you have read, initialed your understanding of each provision, signed, and returned this form to us at our official address indicated. An agent of the owner cannot execute this notice unless you, the property owner, obtain the prior approval of the permitting authority.

OWNER'S ACKNOWLEDGMENT AND VERIFICATION OF INFORMATION

DIRECTIONS: Read and initial each statement below to signify you understand or verify this information.

_____ 1. I understand a frequent practice of unlicensed persons is to have the property owner obtain an "Owner-Builder" building permit that erroneously implies that the property owner is providing his or her own labor and material personally. I, as an Owner-Builder, may be held liable and subject to serious financial risk for any injuries sustained by an unlicensed person and his or her employees while working on my property. My homeowner's insurance may not provide coverage for those injuries. I am willfully acting as an Owner-Builder and am aware of the limits of my insurance coverage for injuries to workers on my property.

_____ 2. I understand building permits are not required to be signed by property owners unless they are responsible for the construction and are not hiring a licensed Contractor to assume this responsibility.

_____ 3. I understand as an "Owner-Builder" I am the responsible party of record on the permit. I understand that I may protect myself from potential financial risk by hiring a licensed Contractor and having the permit filed in his or her name instead of my own.

_____ 4. I understand Contractors are required by law to be licensed and bonded in California and to list their license numbers on permits and contracts.

_____ 5. I understand if I employ or otherwise engage any persons, other than California licensed Contractors, and the total value of my construction is at least five hundred dollars ($500), including labor and materials, I may be considered an "employer" under state and federal law.

_____ 6. I understand if I am considered an "employer" under state and federal law, I must register with the state and federal government, withhold payroll taxes, provide workers' compensation disability insurance, and contribute to unemployment compensation for each "employee." I also understand my failure to abide by these laws may subject me to serious financial risk.

_____ 7. I understand under California Contractors' State License Law, an Owner-Builder who builds single-family residential structures cannot legally build them with the intent to offer them for sale, unless all work is performed by licensed subcontractors and the number of structures does not exceed four within any calendar year, or all of the work is performed under contract with a licensed general building Contractor.

_____ 8. I understand as an Owner-Builder if I sell the property for which this permit is issued, I may be held liable for any financial or personal injuries sustained by any subsequent owner(s) that result from any latent construction defects in the workmanship or materials.

_____ 9. I understand I may obtain more information regarding my obligations as an "employer" from the Internal Revenue Service, the United States Small Business Administration, the California Department of Benefit Payments, and the California Division of Industrial Accidents. I also understand I may contact the California Contractors' State License Board (CSLB) at 1-800- 321-CSLB (2752) or www.cslb.ca.gov for more information about licensed contractors.

_____ 10. I am aware of and consent to an Owner-Builder building permit applied for in my name, and understand that I am the party legally and financially responsible for proposed construction activity at the following address:

_____

_____ 11. I agree that, as the party legally and financially responsible for this proposed construction activity, I will abide by all applicable laws and requirements that govern Owner- Builders as well as employers.

_____ 12. I agree to notify the issuer of this form immediately of any additions, deletions, or changes to any of the information I have provided on this form.

Licensed contractors are regulated by laws designed to protect the public. If you contract with someone who does not have a license, the Contractors' State License Board may be unable to assist you with any financial loss you may sustain as a result of a complaint. Your only remedy against unlicensed Contractors may be in civil court. It is also important for you to understand that if an unlicensed Contractor or employee of that individual or firm is injured while working on your property, you may be held liable for damages. If you obtain a permit as Owner-Builder and wish to hire Contractors, you will be responsible for verifying whether or not those Contractors are properly licensed and the status of their workers' compensation insurance coverage.

Before a building permit can be issued, this form must be completed and signed by the property owner and returned to the agency responsible for issuing the permit.

Note: A copy of the property owner's driver's license, form notarization, or other verification acceptable to the agency is required to be presented when the permit is issued to verify the property owner's signature.

Signature of property owner _____   Date: _____

Added Stats 2008 ch 66 § 2 (AB 2335), effective January 1, 2009. Amended Stats 2010 ch 697 § 39 (SB 189), effective January 1, 2011, operative July 1, 2012.

DIVISION 20

MISCELLANEOUS HEALTH AND SAFETY PROVISIONS

Chapter 6.7

Underground Storage of Hazardous Substances

§ 25281. Definitions

For purposes of this chapter, the following definitions apply:

(a) "Automatic line leak detector" means any method of leak detection, as determined in regulations adopted by the board, that alerts the owner or operator of an underground storage tank to the presence of a leak. "Automatic line leak detector" includes, but is not limited to, any device or mechanism that alerts the owner or operator of an underground storage tank to the presence of a leak by restricting or shutting off the flow of a hazardous substance through piping, or by triggering an audible or visual alarm, and that detects leaks of three gallons or more per hour at 10 pounds per square inch line pressure within one hour.

(b) "Board" means the State Water Resources Control Board. "Regional board" means a California regional water quality control board.

(c) "Compatible" means the ability of two or more substances to maintain their respective physical and chemical properties upon contact with one another for the design life of the tank system under conditions likely to be encountered in the tank system.

(d)(1) "Certified Unified Program Agency" or "CUPA" means the agency certified by the Secretary for Environmental Protection to implement the unified program specified in Chapter 6.11 (commencing with Section 25404) within a jurisdiction.

(2) "Participating Agency" or "PA" means an agency that has a written agreement with the CUPA pursuant to subdivision (d) of Section 25404.3, and is approved by the secretary to implement or enforce the unified program element specified in paragraph (3) of subdivision (c) of Section 25404, in accordance with Sections 25404.1 and 25404.2.

(3) "Unified Program Agency" or "UPA" means the CUPA, or its participating agencies to the extent each PA has been designated by the CUPA, pursuant to a written agreement, to implement or enforce the unified program element specified in paragraph (3) of subdivision (c) of Section 25404. For purposes of this chapter, a UPA has the responsibility and authority, to the extent provided by this chapter and Sections 25404.1 and 25404.2, to implement and enforce only those requirements of this chapter listed in paragraph (3) of subdivision (c)

Appendix

of Section 25404 and the regulations adopted to implement those requirements. Except as provided in Section 25296.09, after a CUPA has been certified by the secretary, the UPA shall be the only local agency authorized to enforce the requirements of this chapter listed in paragraph (3) of subdivision (c) of Section 25404 within the jurisdiction of the CUPA. This paragraph shall not be construed to limit the authority or responsibility granted to the board and the regional boards by this chapter to implement and enforce this chapter and the regulations adopted pursuant to this chapter.

(e) "Department" means the Department of Toxic Substances Control.

(f) "Facility" means any one, or combination of, underground storage tanks used by a single business entity at a single location or site.

(g) "Federal act" means Subchapter IX (commencing with Section 6991) of Chapter 82 of Title 42 of the United States Code, as added by the Hazardous and Solid Waste Amendments of 1984 (P.L. 98–616), or as it may subsequently be amended or supplemented.

(h) "Hazardous substance" means either of the following:

(1) All of the following liquid and solid substances, unless the department, in consultation with the board, determines that the substance could not adversely affect the quality of the waters of the state:

(A) Substances on the list prepared by the Director of Industrial Relations pursuant to Section 6382 of the Labor Code.

(B) Hazardous substances, as defined in Section 25316.

(C) Any substance or material that is classified by the National Fire Protection Association (NFPA) as a flammable liquid, a class II combustible liquid, or a class III–A combustible liquid.

(2) Any regulated substance, as defined in subsection (2) of Section 6991 of Title 42 of the United States Code, as that section reads on January 1, 1989, or as it may subsequently be amended or supplemented.

(i) "Local agency" means the local agency authorized, pursuant to Section 25283, to implement this chapter.

(j) "Operator" means any person in control of, or having daily responsibility for, the daily operation of an underground storage tank system.

(k) "Owner" means the owner of an underground storage tank.

(l) "Person" means an individual, trust, firm, joint stock company, corporation, including a government corporation, partnership, limited liability company, or association. "Person" also includes any city, county, district, the state, another state of the United States, any department or agency of this state or another state, or the United States to the extent authorized by federal law.

(m) "Pipe" means any pipeline or system of pipelines that is used in connection with the storage of hazardous substances and that is not intended to transport hazardous substances in interstate or intrastate commerce or to transfer hazardous materials in bulk to or from a marine vessel.

(n) "Primary containment" means the first level of containment, such as the portion of a tank that comes into immediate contact on its inner surface with the hazardous substance being contained.

(o) "Product tight" means impervious to the substance that is contained, or is to be contained, so as to prevent the seepage of the substance from the containment.

(p) "Release" means any spilling, leaking, emitting, discharging, escaping, leaching, or disposing from an underground storage tank into or on the waters of the state, the land, or the subsurface soils.

(q) "Secondary containment" means the level of containment external to, and separate from, the primary containment.

(r) "Single walled" means construction with walls made of only one thickness of material. For the purposes of this chapter, laminated, coated, or clad materials are considered single walled.

(s) "Special inspector" means a professional engineer, registered pursuant to Chapter 7 (commencing with Section 6700) of Division 3 of the Business and Professions Code, who is qualified to attest, at a minimum, to structural soundness, seismic safety, the compatibility of construction materials with contents, cathodic protection, and the mechanical compatibility of the structural elements of underground storage tanks.

(t) "Storage" or "store" means the containment, handling, or treatment of hazardous substances, either on a temporary basis or for a period of years. "Storage" or "store" does not include the storage of hazardous wastes in an underground storage tank if the person operating the tank has been issued a hazardous waste facilities permit by the department pursuant to Section 25200 or granted interim status under Section 25200.5.

(u) "Tank" means a stationary device designed to contain an accumulation of hazardous substances which is constructed primarily of nonearthen materials, including, but not limited to, wood, concrete, steel, or plastic that provides structural support.

(v) "Tank integrity test" means a test method capable of detecting an unauthorized release from an underground storage tank consistent with the minimum standards adopted by the board.

(w) "Tank tester" means an individual who performs tank integrity tests on underground storage tanks.

(x) "Unauthorized release" means any release of any hazardous substance that does not conform to this chapter, including an unauthorized release specified in Section 25295.5.

(y)(1) "Underground storage tank" means any one or combination of tanks, including pipes connected thereto, that is used for the storage of hazardous substances and that is substantially or totally beneath

Appendix

the surface of the ground. "Underground storage tank" does not include any of the following:

(A) A tank with a capacity of 1,100 gallons or less that is located on a farm and that stores motor vehicle fuel used primarily for agricultural purposes and not for resale.

(B) A tank that is located on a farm or at the residence of a person, that has a capacity of 1,100 gallons or less, and that stores home heating oil for consumptive use on the premises where stored.

(C) Structures, such as sumps, separators, storm drains, catch basins, oil field gathering lines, refinery pipelines, lagoons, evaporation ponds, well cellars, separation sumps, lined and unlined pits, sumps and lagoons. A sump that is a part of a monitoring system required under Section 25290.1, 25290.2, 25291, or 25292 and sumps or other structures defined as underground storage tanks under the federal act are not exempted by this subparagraph.

(D) A tank holding hydraulic fluid for a closed loop mechanical system that uses compressed air or hydraulic fluid to operate lifts, elevators, and other similar devices.

(2) Structures identified in subparagraphs (C) and (D) of paragraph (1) may be regulated by the board and any regional board pursuant to the Porter–Cologne Water Quality Control Act (Division 7 (commencing with Section 13000) of the Water Code) to ensure that they do not pose a threat to water quality.

(z) "Underground tank system" or "tank system" means an underground storage tank, connected piping, ancillary equipment, and containment system, if any.

(aa)(1) "Unified program facility" means all contiguous land and structures, other appurtenances, and improvements on the land that are subject to the requirements of paragraph (3) of subdivision (c) of Section 25404.

(2) "Unified program facility permit" means a permit issued pursuant to Chapter 6.11 (commencing with Section 25404), and that encompasses the permitting requirements of Section 25284.

(3) "Permit" means a permit issued pursuant to Section 25284 or a unified program facility permit as defined in paragraph (2).

Added Stats 1983 ch 1046 § 3. Amended and renumbered by Stats 1984 ch 1038 § 2. Amended Stats 1986 ch 935 § 1, ch 1390 § 1, effective September 30, 1986, ch 1390 § 2, effective September 30, 1986, operative January 1, 1987; Stats 1987 ch 1372 § 1; Stats 1989 ch 1397 § 3. Supplemented by Governor's Reorganization Plan No. 1 of 1991 § 108, effective July 1, 1991. Amended Stats 1991 ch 1138 § 1 (AB 1954); Stats 1992 ch 654 § 2 (AB 3089), effective September 12, 1992; Stats 1993 ch 432 § 2 (AB 1061), effective September 22, 1993; Stats 1994 ch 1200 § 35 (SB 469), effective September 30, 1994; Stats 1995 ch 639 § 52 (SB 1191); Stats 1999 ch 328 § 1 (SB 665). Amended Stats 2002 ch 999 § 11 (AB 2481); Stats 2003 ch 42 § 4 (AB 1702), effective July 7, 2003; ch 341 § 1 (SB 1002), effective September 8, 2003.

Chapter 10.35

Asbestos and Hazardous Substance Removal Contracts

§ 25914. Legislative findings and declarations

The Legislature hereby finds and declares that it is the public policy of the state to ensure that work performed on behalf of the public or private entity or person be done properly to safeguard the public health and safety when removing asbestos and hazardous substances.

Added Stats 1991 ch 789 § 1 (AB 1639).

§ 25914.1. Definitions

For purposes of this chapter, the following definitions shall apply:

(a) "Asbestos" has the same meaning as defined in Section 6501.7 of the Labor Code.

(b) "Asbestos–related work," is defined in Chapter 6 (commencing with Section 6500) of Part 1 of Division 5 of the Labor Code, including Section 6501.8 of the Labor Code, and involves 100–square feet or more of surface area of asbestos–containing material and is such that it requires that the contractor who performs the work must be certified in accordance with subdivision (a) of Section 7058.5 of the Business and Professions Code.

(c) "Hazardous substance removal" has the same meaning as used in Section 7058.7 of the Business and Professions Code.

Added Stats 1991 ch 789 § 1 (AB 1639).

§ 25914.2. Separate contract for undisclosed presence; Continuance of work in unaffected areas; Emergency condition

(a) All asbestos–related work and hazardous substance removal shall be performed pursuant to a contract separate from any other work to be performed, when the presence of asbestos or hazardous substances is not disclosed in the bid or contract documents.

(b) All asbestos–related and hazardous substance removal work which is disclosed in the bid or contract documents shall not require a separate contract from any other work to be performed.

(c) In the event the contractor encounters on the site materials he or she reasonably believes to be asbestos or a hazardous substance, and the asbestos or hazardous substance has not been rendered harmless, the contractor may continue work in unaffected areas reasonably believed safe, and shall immediately cease work on the area affected and report the condition to the owner, or the owner's representative, or architect in writing.

Appendix

(d) With regard to a public entity, if an emergency condition arises, as defined in Section 10122 or 22035 of the Public Contract Code, then all asbestos–related and hazardous substance removal shall be contracted and performed pursuant to Section 10122 or 22035 of the Public Contract Code, respectively. Contractors performing the work shall have all registration and certificates required pursuant to the Labor Code and the Business and Professions Code.

Added Stats 1991 ch 789 § 1 (AB 1639).

§ 25914.3. Uncertified contractor

Notwithstanding any other provision of law, a contractor who is not certified pursuant to Section 7058.6 of the Business and Professions Code may bid on a project involving asbestos related work so long as the asbestos–related work is performed by a contractor who is registered pursuant to Section 6501.5 of the Labor Code and certified pursuant to Section 7058.6 of the Business and Professions Code.

Added Stats 1991 ch 789 § 1 (AB 1639).

DIVISION 104

ENVIRONMENTAL HEALTH

PART 10

RECREATIONAL SAFETY

Chapter 5

Safe Recreational Water Use

Article 2.5

The Swimming Pool Safety Act

§ 115920. Citation

This act shall be known and may be cited as the Swimming Pool Safety Act.

Added Stats 1996 ch 925 [§ 3] (AB 3305).

§ 115921. Definitions

As used in this article the following terms have the following meanings:

(a) "Swimming pool" or "pool" means any structure intended for swimming or recreational bathing that contains water over 18 inches deep. "Swimming pool" includes in–ground and above–ground structures and includes, but is not limited to, hot tubs, spas, portable spas, and nonportable wading pools.

(b) "Public swimming pool" means a swimming pool operated for the use of the general public with or without charge, or for the use of the members and guests of a private club. Public swimming pool does not include a swimming pool located on the grounds of a private single–family home.

(c) "Enclosure" means a fence, wall, or other barrier that isolates a swimming pool from access to the home.

(d) "Approved safety pool cover" means a manually or power–operated safety pool cover that meets all of the performance standards of the American Society for Testing and Materials (ASTM), in compliance with standard F1346–91.

(e) "Exit alarms" means devices that make audible, continuous alarm sounds when any door or window, that permits access from the residence to the pool area that is without any intervening enclosure, is opened or is left ajar. Exit alarms may be battery operated or may be connected to the electrical wiring of the building.

Added Stats 1996 ch 925 [§ 3] (AB 3305).

§ 115922. Safety features; inspection

(a) Commencing January 1, 2007, except as provided in Section 115925, whenever a building permit is issued for construction of a new swimming pool or spa, or any building permit is issued for remodeling of an existing pool or spa, at a private, single-family home, it shall be equipped with at least one of the following seven drowning prevention safety features:

(1) The pool shall be isolated from access to a home by an enclosure that meets the requirements of Section 115923.

(2) The pool shall incorporate removable mesh pool fencing that meets American Society for Testing and Materials (ASTM) Specifications F 2286 standards in conjunction with a gate that is self-closing and self-latching and can accommodate a key lockable device.

(3) The pool shall be equipped with an approved safety pool cover that meets all requirements of the ASTM Specifications F 1346.

(4) The residence shall be equipped with exit alarms on those doors providing direct access to the pool.

(5) All doors providing direct access from the home to the swimming pool shall be equipped with a self-closing, self-latching device with a release mechanism placed no lower than 54 inches above the floor.

(6) Swimming pool alarms that, when placed in pools, will sound upon detection of accidental or unauthorized entrance into the water. These pool alarms shall meet and be independently certified to the ASTM Standard F 2208 "Standards Specification for Pool Alarms"

Appendix

which includes surface motion, pressure, sonar, laser, and infrared type alarms. For purposes of this article, "swimming pool alarms" shall not include swimming protection alarm devices designed for individual use, such as an alarm attached to a child that sounds when the child exceeds a certain distance or becomes submerged in water.

(7) Other means of protection, if the degree of protection afforded is equal to or greater than that afforded by any of the devices set forth above, and have been independently verified by an approved testing laboratory as meeting standards for those devices established by the ASTM or the American Society of Mechanical Engineers (ASME).

(b) Prior to the issuance of any final approval for the completion of permitted construction or remodeling work, the local building code official shall inspect the drowning safety prevention devices required by this act and if no violations are found, shall give final approval.

Added Stats 1996 ch 925 [§ 3] (AB 3305). Amended Stats 2006 ch 478 § 2 (AB 2977), effective January 1, 2007.

§ 115923. Enclosure

An enclosure shall have all of the following characteristics:

(a) Any access gates through the enclosure open away from the swimming pool, and are self–closing with a self–latching device placed no lower than 60 inches above the ground.

(b) A minimum height of 60 inches.

(c) A maximum vertical clearance from the ground to the bottom of the enclosure of two inches.

(d) Gaps or voids, if any, do not allow passage of a sphere equal to or greater than four inches in diameter.

(e) An outside surface free of protrusions, cavities, or other physical characteristics that would serve as handholds or footholds that could enable a child below the age of five years to climb over.

Added Stats 1996 ch 925 [§ 3] (AB 3305).

§ 115924. Consumer notice; Availability of information on Web site

(a) Any person entering into an agreement to build a swimming pool or spa, or to engage in permitted work on a pool or spa covered by this article, shall give the consumer notice of the requirements of this article.

(b) Pursuant to existing law, the Department of Health Services shall have available on the department's Web site, commencing January 1, 2007, approved pool safety information available for consumers to download. Pool contractors are encouraged to share this information with consumers regarding the potential dangers a pool or spa poses to toddlers. Additionally, pool contractors may provide the consumer with swimming pool safety materials produced from organizations such as the United States Consumer Product Safety Commission, Drowning Prevention Foundation, California Coalition for Children's Safety & Health, Safe Kids Worldwide, Association of Pool and Spa Professionals, or the American Academy of Pediatrics.

Added Stats 1996 ch 925 [§ 3] (AB 3305). Amended Stats 2006 ch 478 § 3 (AB 2977), effective January 1, 2007.

§ 115925. Inapplicability

The requirements of this article shall not apply to any of the following:
(a) Public swimming pools.
(b) Hot tubs or spas with locking safety covers that comply with the American Society for Testing Materials–Emergency Performance Specification (ASTM–ES 13–89).
(c) Any pool within the jurisdiction of any political subdivision that adopts an ordinance for swimming pool safety that includes requirements that are at least as stringent as this article.
(d) An apartment complex, or any residential setting other than a single–family home.

Added Stats 1996 ch 925 [§ 3] (AB 3305).

§ 115926. State social services

This article does not apply to any facility regulated by the State Department of Social Services even if the facility is also used as the private residence of the operator. Pool safety in those facilities shall be regulated pursuant to regulations adopted therefor by the State Department of Social Services.

Added Stats 1996 ch 925 [§ 3] (AB 3305).

§ 115927. Interpretation

Notwithstanding any other provision of law, this article shall not be subject to further modification or interpretation by any regulatory agency of the state, this authority being reserved exclusively to local jurisdictions, as provided for in subdivision (e) of Section 115922 and subdivision (c) of Section 115924.

Added Stats 1996 ch 925 [§ 3] (AB 3305).

§ 115928. Suction outlet and entrapment standards

Whenever a building permit is issued for the construction of a new swimming pool or spa, the pool or spa shall meet all of the following requirements:
(a)(1) The suction outlet of the pool or spa for which the permit is issued shall be equipped to provide circulation throughout the pool or spa as prescribed in paragraph (2).

(2) The swimming pool or spa shall have at least two circulation drains per pump that shall be hydraulically balanced and symmetrically plumbed through one or more "T" fittings, and that are separated by a distance of at least three feet in any dimension between the drains.

(b) Suction outlets that are less than 12 inches across shall be covered with antientrapment grates, as specified in the ASME/ANSI Standard A 112.19.8, that cannot be removed except with the use of tools. Slots or openings in the grates or similar protective devices shall be of a shape, area, and arrangement that would prevent physical entrapment and would not pose any suction hazard to bathers.

(c) Any backup safety system that an owner of a new swimming pool or spa may choose to install in addition to the requirements set forth in subdivisions (a) and (b) shall meet the standards as published in the document, "Guidelines for Entrapment Hazards: Making Pools and Spas Safer," Publication Number 363, March 2005, United States Consumer Product Safety Commission.

Added Stats 2002 ch 679 § 1 (SB 1726). Amended Stats 2003 ch 62 § 194 (SB 600); Stats 2006 ch 478 § 4 (AB 2977), effective January 1, 2007; Stats 2007 ch 596 § 19 (AB 382), effective January 1, 2008.

§ 115928.5. Issuance of building permit for remodeling or modification of an existing swimming pool, toddler pool, or spa

Whenever a building permit is issued for the remodel or modification of an existing swimming pool, toddler pool, or spa, the permit shall require that the suction outlet of the existing swimming pool, toddler pool, or spa be upgraded so as to be equipped with an antientrapment cover meeting current standards of the American Society for Testing and Materials (ASTM) or the American Society of Mechanical Engineers (ASME).

Added Stats 2007 ch 596 § 20 (AB 382), effective January 1, 2008.

Article 5

Swimming Pool Sanitation

§ 116064.1. Legislative findings and declarations

The Legislature finds and declares that the public health interest requires that there be uniform statewide health and safety standards for public swimming pools to prevent physical entrapment and serious injury to children and adults. It is the intent of the Legislature to occupy the whole field of health and safety standards for public swimming pools and the requirements established in this article and the regulations adopted pursuant to this article shall be exclusive of all local health and safety standards relating to public swimming pools.

Added Stats. 2009, Ch. 267 (AB 1020).

§ 116064.2. Anti-entrapment devices or systems as applicable standard; Deadline for installation; Alternative devices or systems; New construction; Retrofitting; Compliance and documentation; Fee

(a) As used in this section, the following words have the following meanings:

(1) "ASME/ANSI performance standard" means a standard that is accredited by the American National Standards Institute and published by the American Society of Mechanical Engineers.

(2) "ASTM performance standard" means a standard that is developed and published by ASTM International.

(3) "Main drain" means a submerged suction outlet typically located at the bottom of a swimming pool that conducts water to a recirculating pump.

(4) "Public swimming pool" means an outdoor or indoor structure, whether in-ground or above-ground, intended for swimming or recreational bathing, including a swimming pool, hot tub, spa, or nonportable wading pool, that is any of the following:

(A) Open to the public generally, whether for a fee or free of charge.

(B) Open exclusively to members of an organization and their guests, residents of a multiunit apartment building, apartment complex, residential real estate development, or other multifamily residential area, or patrons of a hotel or other public accommodations facility.

(C) Located on the premises of an athletic club, or public or private school.

(5) "Qualified individual" means a contractor who holds a current valid license issued by the State of California or a professional engineer licensed in the State of California who has experience working on public swimming pools.

(6) "Safety vacuum release system" means a vacuum release system that ceases operation of the pump, reverses the circulation flow, or otherwise provides a vacuum release at a suction outlet when a blockage is detected.

(7) "Skimmer equalizer line" means a suction outlet located below the waterline and connected to the body of a skimmer that prevents air from being drawn into the pump if the water level drops below the skimmer weir. However, a skimmer equalizer line is not a main drain.

Appendix

(8) "Unblockable drain" means a drain of any size and shape that a human body cannot sufficiently block to create a suction entrapment hazard.

(b) Subject to subdivision (c), an ASME/ANSI or ASTM performance standard relating to antientrapment devices or systems or an amendment or successor to, or later published edition of an ASME/ANSI or ASTM performance standard relating to antientrapment devices or systems shall become the applicable standard in California 90 days after publication by ASME/ANSI or ASTM, respectively, provided that the performance standard or amendment or successor to, or later published edition is approved by the department within 90 days of the publication of the performance standard by ASME/ANSI or ASTM, respectively. Notwithstanding any other law, the department may implement, interpret, or make specific the provisions of this section by means of a policy letter or similar instruction and this action by the department shall not be subject to the rulemaking requirements of the Administrative Procedure Act (Chapter 3.5 (commencing with Section 11340) of Part 1 of Division 3 of Title 2 of the Government Code).

(c) Subject to subdivision (f), every public swimming pool shall be equipped with antientrapment devices or systems that comply with ASME/ANSI performance standard A112.19.8, as in effect December 31, 2009, or any applicable ASME/ANSI performance standard that has been adopted by the department pursuant to subdivision (b).

(d) Subject to subdivisions (e) and (f), every public swimming pool with a single main drain that is not an unblockable drain shall be equipped with at least one or more of the following devices or systems that are designed to prevent physical entrapment by pool drains:

(1) A safety vacuum release system that has been tested by a department-approved independent third party and found to conform to ASME/ANSI performance standard A112.19.17, as in effect on December 31, 2009, or any applicable ASME/ANSI performance standard that has been adopted by the department pursuant to subdivision (b), or ASTM performance standard F2387, as in effect on December 31, 2009, or any applicable ASTM performance standard that has been adopted by the department pursuant to subdivision (b).

(2) A suction-limiting vent system with a tamper-resistant atmospheric opening, provided that it conforms to any applicable ASME/ANSI or ASTM performance standard that has been adopted by the department pursuant to subdivision (b).

(3) A gravity drainage system that utilizes a collector tank, provided that it conforms to any applicable ASME/ANSI or ASTM performance standard that has been adopted by the department pursuant to subdivision (b).

(4) An automatic pump shut-off system tested by a department-approved independent third party and found to conform to any appli-

cable ASME/ANSI or ASTM performance standard that has been adopted by the department pursuant to subdivision (b).

(5) Any other system that is deemed, in accordance with federal law, to be equally effective as, or more effective than, the systems described in paragraphs (1) to (4), inclusive, at preventing or eliminating the risk of injury or death associated with pool drainage systems.

(e) Every public swimming pool constructed on or after January 1, 2010, shall have at least two main drains per pump that are hydraulically balanced and symmetrically plumbed through one or more "T" fittings, and that are separated by a distance of at least three feet in any dimension between the drains. A public swimming pool constructed on or after January 1, 2010, that meets the requirements of this subdivision, shall be exempt from the requirements of subdivision (d).

(f) A public swimming pool constructed prior to January 1, 2010, shall be retrofitted to comply with subdivisions (c) and (d) by no later than July 1, 2010, except that no further retrofitting is required for a public swimming pool that completed a retrofit between December 19, 2007, and January 1, 2010, that complied with the Virginia Graeme Baker Pool and Spa Safety Act (15 U.S.C. Sec. 8001 et seq.) as in effect on the date of issue of the construction permit, or for a nonportable wading pool that completed a retrofit prior to January 1, 2010, that complied with state law on the date of issue of the construction permit. A public swimming pool owner who meets the exception described in this subdivision shall do one of the following prior to September 30, 2010:

(1) File the form issued by the department pursuant to subdivision (g), as otherwise provided in subdivision (i).

(2)(A) File a signed statement attesting that the required work has been completed.

(B) Provide a document containing the name and license number of the qualified individual who completed the required work.

(C) Provide either a copy of the final building permit, if required by the local agency, or a copy of one of the following documents if no permit was required:

(i) A document that describes the modification in a manner that provides sufficient information to document the work that was done to comply with federal law.

(ii) A copy of the final paid invoice. The amount paid for the services may be omitted or redacted from the final invoice prior to submission.

(g) Prior to March 31, 2010, the department shall issue a form for use by an owner of a public swimming pool to indicate compliance with this section. The department shall consult with county health officers and directors of departments of environmental health in developing the form and shall post the form on the department's Internet Web site. The form shall be completed by the owner of a public

Appendix

swimming pool prior to filing the form with the appropriate city, county, or city and county department of environmental health. The form shall include, but not be limited to, the following information:

(1) A statement of whether the pool operates with a single or split main drain.

(2) Identification of the type of antientrapment devices or systems that have been installed pursuant to subdivision (c) and the date or dates of installation.

(3) Identification of the type of devices or systems designed to prevent physical entrapment that have been installed pursuant to subdivision (d) in a public swimming pool with a single main drain that is not an unblockable drain and the date or dates of installation or the reason why the requirement is not applicable.

(4) A signature and license number of a qualified individual who certifies that the factual information provided on the form in response to paragraphs (1) to (3), inclusive, is true to the best of his or her knowledge.

(h) A qualified individual who improperly certifies information pursuant to paragraph (4) of subdivision (g) shall be subject to potential disciplinary action at the discretion of the licensing authority.

(i) Except as provided in subdivision (f), each public swimming pool owner shall file a completed copy of the form issued by the department pursuant to this section with the city, county, or city and county department of environmental health in the city, county, or city and county in which the swimming pool is located. The form shall be filed within 30 days following the completion of the swimming pool construction or installation required pursuant to this section or, if the construction or installation is completed prior to the date that the department issues the form pursuant to this section, within 30 days of the date that the department issues the form. The public swimming pool owner or operator shall not make a false statement, representation, certification, record, report, or otherwise falsify information that he or she is required to file or maintain pursuant to this section.

(j) In enforcing this section, health officers and directors of city, county, or city and county departments of environmental health shall consider documentation filed on or with the form issued pursuant to this section by the owner of a public swimming pool as evidence of compliance with this section. A city, county, or city and county department of environmental health may verify the accuracy of the information filed on or with the form.

(k) To the extent that the requirements for public wading pools imposed by Section 116064 conflict with this section, the requirements of this section shall prevail.

(l)(1) Until January 1, 2014, the department may assess an annual fee on the owners of each public swimming pool, to be collected by the applicable local health department, in an amount not to exceed the amount necessary to defray the department's costs of carrying out its duties under Section 116064.1 and this section but in no case shall this fee exceed six dollars ($6).

(2) The local health department may retain a portion of the fee collected pursuant to paragraph (1) in an amount necessary to cover the administrative costs of collecting the fee, but in no case to exceed one dollar ($1).

(3) The local health department shall bill the owner of each public swimming pool in its jurisdiction for the amount of the state fee. The local health department shall transmit the collected state fee to the Controller for deposit into the Recreational Health Fund, which is hereby created in the State Treasury. The local health department shall not be required to take action to collect an unpaid state fee, but shall submit to the department, every six months, a list containing the name and address of the owner of each public swimming pool who has failed to pay the state fee for more than 90 days after the date that the bill was provided to the owner of the public swimming pool.

(4) Owners that are exempt from local swimming pool permit fees shall also be exempt from the fees imposed pursuant to this subdivision.

(5) Except as provided in paragraph (2), all moneys collected by the department pursuant to this section shall be deposited into the Recreational Health Fund. Notwithstanding Section 16305.7 of the Government Code, interest and dividends on moneys in the Recreational Health Fund shall also be deposited in the fund. Moneys in the fund shall, upon appropriation by the Legislature, be available to the department for carrying out its duties under Section 116064.1 and this section and shall not be redirected for any other purpose.

Added Stats 2009 ch 267 § 3 (AB 1020), effective January 1, 2010. Amended Stats 2010 ch 328 § 135 (SB 1330), effective January 1, 2011.

INSURANCE CODE

PART 3

LIABILITY, WORKERS' COMPENSATION, AND COMMON CARRIER LIABILITY INSURANCE

Chapter 2

Workers' Compensation Policies

Article 2

Policy Provisions

§ 11665. Insurance policy for contractor holding C-39 license (Repealed January 1, 2013)

(a) An insurer who issues a workers' compensation insurance policy to a roofing contractor holding a C-39 license from the Contractors State License Board shall perform an annual payroll audit for the contractor. The insurer may impose a surcharge on each policyholder audited under this subdivision in an amount necessary to recoup the reasonable costs of conducting the annual payroll audits.

(b) The commissioner shall direct the rating organization designated as his or her statistical agent to compile pertinent statistical data on those holding C-39 licenses, as reported by the appropriate state entity, on an annual basis and provide a report to him or her each year. The data shall track the total annual payroll and loss data reported on those holding C-39 licenses in accordance with the standard workers' compensation insurance classifications applicable to roofing operations. The report shall also be provided to the Legislature, in compliance with Section 9795 of the Government Code. Reports required under this section for the 2008 and 2009 calendar years shall be filed by March 1, 2012.

(c) This section shall remain in effect only until January 1, 2013, and as of that date is repealed, unless a later enacted statute, that is enacted before January 1, 2013, deletes or extends that date.

Added Stats 2006 ch 38 § 3 (AB 881), effective January 1, 2007, repealed January 1, 2011. Amended Stats 2010 ch 423 § 3 (AB 2305), effective January 1, 2011, repealed January 1, 2013.

Chapter 3

Regulation of Business of Workers' Compensation Insurance

Article 4

Penalties for Misrepresentation

§ 11760.1. Audit of employer; Failure to provide access to records; Costs

(a) If an employer fails to provide for access by the insurer or its authorized representative to its records, to enable the insurer to perform an audit to determine the remuneration earned by the employer's employees and by any of its uninsured subcontractors and the employees of any of its uninsured subcontractors during the policy period, the employer shall be liable to pay to the insurer a total premium for the policy equal to three times the insurer's then-current estimate of the annual premium on the expiration date of the policy. The employer shall also be liable, in addition to the premium, for costs incurred by the insurer in its attempts to perform an audit, after the insured has failed upon the insurer's third request during at least a 90-day period to provide access, and the insured has provided no compelling business reason for the failure. This section shall only apply if the insurer elects to comply with the conditions set forth in subdivision (d).

(b) "Access" shall mean access at any time during regular business hours during the policy period and within three years after the policy period ends. "Access" may also include any other time mutually agreed upon by the employer and insurer.

(c) The insurer shall have and follow regular and reasonable rules and procedures to notify employers of their duty to provide for access to records, and to contact employers to make appointments during regular business hours for that purpose.

(d) Upon the employer's failure to provide access after the insurer's third request during at least a 90-day period, the insurer may notify the employer through its mailing of a certified, return-receipt, document of the increased premium and the total amount of the costs incurred by the insurer for its attempts to perform an audit as described under subdivision (a). Upon the expiration of 30 days after the delivery of the notice, collection by the insurer of the amount of premium and costs described under subdivision (a), less all premiums previously paid by the employer for the policy, shall be fully enforceable and executable.

(e) If the employer provides for access to its records after having received the notice described in subdivision (d), and if the insurer then succeeds in performing the audit to its satisfaction, the insurer shall revise the total premium and costs payable for the policy by the employer to reflect the results of its audit.

Added Stats 2007 ch 615 § 1 (AB 812), effective January 1, 2008.

LABOR CODE

DIVISION 1

DEPARTMENT OF INDUSTRIAL RELATIONS

Chapter 4

Division of Labor Standards Enforcement

§ 106. Authorization to issue citations and serve penalty assessment orders

(a) The Labor Commissioner may authorize an employee of any of the agencies that participate in the Joint Enforcement Strike Force on the Underground Economy, as defined in Section 329 of the Unemployment Insurance Code, to issue citations pursuant to Sections 226.4 and 1022 and issue and serve a penalty assessment order pursuant to subdivision (a) of Section 3722.

(b) No employees shall issue citations or penalty assessment orders pursuant to this section unless they have been specifically designated, authorized, and trained by the Labor Commissioner for this purpose. Appeals of all citations or penalty assessment orders shall follow the procedures prescribed in Section 226.5, 1023, or 3725, whichever is applicable.

Added Stats 1994 ch 1117 § 1 (SB 1490). Amended Stats 1999 ch 306 § 1 (SB 319); Stats 2004 ch 685 § 1 (AB 3020).

Appendix

DIVISION 2

EMPLOYMENT REGULATION AND SUPERVISION

PART 1

COMPENSATION

Chapter 1

Payment of Wages

Article 1

General Occupations

§ 206.5. Prohibition against, and invalidity of, release of claim for wages; Violation as misdemeanor

(a) An employer shall not require the execution of a release of a claim or right on account of wages due, or to become due, or made as an advance on wages to be earned, unless payment of those wages has been made. A release required or executed in violation of the provisions of this section shall be null and void as between the employer and the employee. Violation of this section by the employer is a misdemeanor.

(b) For purposes of this section, "execution of a release" includes requiring an employee, as a condition of being paid, to execute a statement of the hours he or she worked during a pay period which the employer knows to be false.

Added Stats 1959 ch 1066 § 1. Amended Stats 2008 ch 224 § 1 (AB 2075), effective January 1, 2009.

§ 226.8. Unlawful activities; Penalties; Disciplinary action; Information to be posted on Internet Web site; Enforcement

(a) It is unlawful for any person or employer to engage in any of the following activities:

(1) Willful misclassification of an individual as an independent contractor.

(2) Charging an individual who has been willfully misclassified as an independent contractor a fee, or making any deductions from compensation, for any purpose, including for goods, materials, space rental, services, government licenses, repairs, equipment maintenance, or fines arising from the individual's employment where any of the acts described in this paragraph would have violated the law if the individual had not been misclassified.

(b) If the Labor and Workforce Development Agency or a court issues a determination that a person or employer has engaged in any of the enumerated violations of subdivision (a), the person or employer shall be subject to a civil penalty of not less than five thousand dollars ($5,000) and not more than fifteen thousand dollars ($15,000) for each violation, in addition to any other penalties or fines permitted by law.

(c) If the Labor and Workforce Development Agency or a court issues a determination that a person or employer has engaged in any of the enumerated violations of subdivision (a) and the person or employer has engaged in or is engaging in a pattern or practice of these violations, the person or employer shall be subject to a civil penalty of not less than ten thousand dollars ($10,000) and not more than twenty-five thousand dollars ($25,000) for each violation, in addition to any other penalties or fines permitted by law.

(d) (1) If the Labor and Workforce Development Agency or a court issues a determination that a person or employer that is a licensed contractor pursuant to the Contractors' State License Law has violated subdivision (a), the agency, in addition to any other remedy that has been ordered, shall transmit a certified copy of the order to the Contractors' State License Board.

(2) The registrar of the Contractors' State License Board shall initiate disciplinary action against a licensee within 30 days of receiving a certified copy of an agency or court order that resulted in disbarment pursuant to paragraph (1).

(e) If the Labor and Workforce Development Agency or a court issues a determination that a person or employer has violated subdivision (a), the agency or court, in addition to any other remedy that has been ordered, shall order the person or employer to display prominently on its Internet Web site, in an area which is accessible to all employees and the general public, or, if the person or employer does not have an Internet Web site, to display prominently in an area that is accessible to all employees and the general public at each location where a violation of subdivision (a) occurred, a notice that sets forth all of the following:

(1) That the Labor and Workforce Development Agency or a court, as applicable, has found that the person or employer has committed a serious violation of the law by engaging in the willful misclassification of employees.

(2) That the person or employer has changed its business practices in order to avoid committing further violations of this section.

(3) That any employee who believes that he or she is being misclassified as an independent contractor may contact the Labor and Workforce Development Agency. The notice shall include the mailing address, e-mail address, and telephone number of the agency.

(4) That the notice is being posted pursuant to a state order.

(f) In addition to including the information specified in subdivision (e), a person or employer also shall satisfy the following requirements in preparing the notice:

(1) An officer shall sign the notice.

(2) It shall post the notice for one year commencing with the date of the final decision and order.

(g) (1) In accordance with the procedures specified in Sections 98 to 98.2, inclusive, the Labor Commissioner may issue a determination that a person or employer has violated subdivision (a).

(2) If, upon inspection or investigation, the Labor Commissioner determines that a person or employer has violated subdivision (a), the Labor Commissioner may issue a citation to assess damages set forth in subdivisions (b) and (c) in addition to any other penalties or damages that are otherwise available at law. The procedures for issuing, contesting, and enforcing judgments shall be the same as those set forth in Section 1197.1.

(3) The Labor Commissioner may enforce this section pursuant to Section 98 or in a civil suit.

(h) Any administrative or civil penalty pursuant to subdivision (b) or (c) or disciplinary action pursuant to subdivision (d) or (e) shall remain in effect against any successor corporation, owner, or business entity that satisfies both of the following:

(1) Has one or more of the same principals or officers as the person or employer subject to the penalty or action.

(2) Is engaged in the same or a similar business as the person or employer subject to the penalty or action.

(i) For purposes of this section, the following definitions apply:

(1) "Determination" means an order, decision, award, or citation issued by an agency or a court of competent jurisdiction for which the time to appeal has expired and for which no appeal is pending.

(2) "Labor and Workforce Development Agency" means the Labor and Workforce Development Agency or any of its departments, divisions, commissions, boards, or agencies.

(3) "Officer" means the chief executive officer, president, any vice president in charge of a principal business unit, division, or function, or any other officer of the corporation who performs a policymaking function. If the employer is a partnership, "officer" means a partner. If the employer is a sole proprietor, "officer" means the owner.

(4) "Willful misclassification" means avoiding employee status for an individual by voluntarily and knowingly misclassifying that individual as an independent contractor.

(j) Nothing in this section is intended to limit any rights or remedies otherwise available at law.

Added Stats 2011 ch 706 § 1 (SB 459), effective January 1, 2012.

PART 7

PUBLIC WORKS AND PUBLIC AGENCIES

Chapter 1

Public Works

Article 2

Wages

§ 1770. General prevailing wage rate; Determination; Payment of more than prevailing rate; Overtime work

The Director of the Department of Industrial Relations shall determine the general prevailing rate of per diem wages in accordance with the standards set forth in Section 1773, and the director's determination in the matter shall be final except as provided in Section 1773.4. Nothing in this article, however, shall prohibit the payment of more than the general prevailing rate of wages to any workman employed on public work. Nothing in this act shall permit any overtime work in violation of Article 3 of this chapter.

Enacted 1937. Amended Stats 1953 ch 1706 § 2; Stats 1976 ch 281 § 2.

§ 1771. Requirement of prevailing local rate for work under contract

Except for public works projects of one thousand dollars ($1,000) or less, not less than the general prevailing rate of per diem wages for work of a similar character in the locality in which the public work is performed, and not less than the general prevailing rate of per diem wages for holiday and overtime work fixed as provided in this chapter, shall be paid to all workers employed on public works.

This section is applicable only to work performed under contract, and is not applicable to work carried out by a public agency with its own forces. This section is applicable to contracts let for maintenance work.

Enacted 1937. Amended Stats 1953 ch 1706 § 3; Stats 1974 ch 1202 § 1; Stats 1976 ch 861 § 2; Stats 1981 ch 449 § 1.

§ 1771.2. Action against employer that fails to pay prevailing wage

A joint labor–management committee established pursuant to the federal Labor Management Cooperation Act of 1978 (Section 175a of Title 29 of the United States Code) may bring an action in any court of competent jurisdiction against an employer that fails to pay the prevailing wage to its employees, as required by this article. This action shall be commenced not later than 180 days after the filing of a valid notice of completion in the office of the county recorder in each county in which the public work or some part thereof was performed, or not later than 180 days after acceptance of the public work, whichever last occurs.

Added Stats 2001 ch 804 § 1 (SB 588).

§ 1771.3. Monitoring and enforcement of compliance; State Public Works enforcement Fund created; Loan; Regulations; Determination of rates; Costs; Applicability

(a) (1) The Department of Industrial Relations shall monitor and enforce compliance with applicable prevailing wage requirements for any public works project paid for in whole or part out of public funds, within the meaning of subdivision (b) of Section 1720, that are derived from bonds issued by the state, and shall charge each awarding body for the reasonable and directly related costs of monitoring and enforcing compliance with the prevailing wage requirements on each project.

(2) (A) The State Public Works Enforcement Fund is hereby created as a special fund in the State Treasury. All moneys received by the department pursuant to this section shall be deposited in the fund. Notwithstanding Section 13340 of the Government Code, all moneys in the fund shall be continuously appropriated to the Department of Industrial Relations, to monitor and enforce compliance with the applicable prevailing wage requirements on public works projects paid for in whole or part out of public funds, within the meaning of subdivision (b) of Section 1720, that are derived from bonds issued by the state and other projects for which the department provides prevailing wage monitoring and enforcement activities and for which it is to be reimbursed by the awarding body, and shall not be used or borrowed for any other purpose.

(B) Notwithstanding any other law, upon order of the Director of Finance, a loan in the amount of four million three hundred thousand dollars ($4,300,000) shall be provided from the Uninsured Employers Benefit Trust Fund to the State Public Works Enforcement Fund to meet the startup needs of the Labor Compliance Monitoring Unit.

(3) The Director of Industrial Relations shall adopt regulations implementing this section, specifying the activities, including, but not limited to, monthly review, and audit if appropriate, of payroll records, which the department will undertake to monitor and enforce compliance with applicable prevailing wage requirements on public works projects paid for in whole or part out of public funds, within the meaning of subdivision (b) of Section 1720, that are derived from

bonds issued by the state. The department, with the approval of the Director of Finance, shall determine the rate or rates, which the department may from time to time amend, that the department will charge to recover the reasonable and directly related costs of performing the monitoring and enforcement services for public works projects; provided, however, that the amount charged by the department shall not exceed one-fourth of 1 percent of the state bond proceeds used for the public works projects.

(4) The reasonable and directly related costs of monitoring and enforcing compliance with the prevailing wage requirements on a public works project incurred by the department in accordance with this section are payable by the awarding body of the public works project as a cost of construction. Notwithstanding any other provision of law, but subject to any limitations or restrictions of the bond act, the board, commission, department, agency, or official responsible for the allocation of bond proceeds from the bond funds shall consider and provide for amounts in support of the costs when allocating or approving expenditures of bond proceeds for the construction of the authorized project. The awarding body may elect not to receive or expend amounts from bond proceeds to pay the costs of the project; however, such election does not relieve the awarding body from reimbursing the Department of Industrial Relations for monitoring and enforcing prevailing wage requirements on the project pursuant to Section 1771.3 or any other applicable provision of law.

(b) Paragraph (1) of subdivision (a) shall not apply to any contract for a public works project paid for in whole or part out of public funds, within the meaning of subdivision (b) of Section 1720, that are derived from bonds issued by the state if the contract was awarded under any of the following conditions:

(1) The contract was awarded prior to the effective date of implementing regulations adopted by the department pursuant to paragraph (3) of subdivision (a).

(2) The contract was awarded on or after the effective date of the regulations described in paragraph (1), if the awarding body had previously initiated a labor compliance program approved by the department for some or all of its public works projects and had not contracted with a third party to conduct such program, and requests and receives approval from the department to continue to operate its existing labor compliance program for its public works projects paid for in whole or part out of public funds, within the meaning of subdivision (b) of Section 1720, that are derived from bonds issued by the state, in place of the department monitoring and enforcing compliance on projects pursuant to subdivision (a).

(3) The contract is awarded on or after the effective date of the regulations described in paragraph (1), if the awarding body has entered into a collective bargaining agreement that binds all of the contrac-

tors performing work on the project and that includes a mechanism for resolving disputes about the payment of wages.

(c) This section shall not apply to public works projects subject to Section 75075 of the Public Resources Code.

Added Stats 2011 ch 378 § 6 (AB 1023), effective January 1, 2012.

§ 1771.5. Labor compliance program as exception to Labor Code Section 1771; Reimbursement of costs; Requirements; Revocation; Regulations; Determination of rates; Costs; Deposit of amounts collected

(a) Notwithstanding Section 1771, an awarding body may choose not to require the payment of the general prevailing rate of per diem wages or the general prevailing rate of per diem wages for holiday and overtime work for any public works project of twenty-five thousand dollars ($25,000) or less when the project is for construction work, or for any public works project of fifteen thousand dollars ($15,000) or less when the project is for alteration, demolition, repair, or maintenance work, if the awarding body elects to either:

(1) Initiate and enforce a labor compliance program pursuant to subdivision (b) for every public works project under the authority of the awarding body as described in subdivision (e).

(2) Reimburse the Department of Industrial Relations for the cost of monitoring and enforcing compliance with prevailing wage requirements for every public works project of the awarding body as described in subdivision (f).

(b) For purposes of this section, a labor compliance program shall include, but not be limited to, the following requirements:

(1) All bid invitations and public works contracts shall contain appropriate language concerning the requirements of this chapter.

(2) A prejob conference shall be conducted with the contractor and subcontractors to discuss federal and state labor law requirements applicable to the contract.

(3) Project contractors and subcontractors shall maintain and furnish, at a designated time, a certified copy of each weekly payroll containing a statement of compliance signed under penalty of perjury.

(4) The awarding body shall review, and, if appropriate, audit payroll records to verify compliance with this chapter.

(5) The awarding body shall withhold contract payments when payroll records are delinquent or inadequate.

(6) The awarding body shall withhold contract payments equal to the amount of underpayment and applicable penalties when, after investigation, it is established that underpayment has occurred.

(7) The awarding body shall comply with any other prevailing wage monitoring and enforcement activities that are required to be con-

ducted by labor compliance programs by the Department of Industrial Relations.

(c) For purposes of this chapter, "labor compliance program" means a labor compliance program that is approved, as specified in state regulations, by the Director of Industrial Relations.

(d) For purposes of this chapter, the Director of Industrial Relations may revoke the approval of a labor compliance program in the manner specified in state regulations.

(e) An awarding body that elects to use a labor compliance program pursuant to subdivision (a) must use the labor compliance program for all contracts for public works projects awarded prior to the effective date of the regulations adopted by the department as specified in subdivision (g). For contracts for public works projects awarded on or after the effective date of regulations adopted by the department as specified in subdivision (g), the awarding body may also elect to continue operating an existing previously approved labor compliance program in lieu of reimbursing the Department of Industrial Relations for the cost of monitoring and enforcing compliance with prevailing wage requirements on the awarding body's public works projects if it has not contracted with a third party to conduct its labor compliance program and if it requests and receives approval from the department to continue its existing program.

(f) An awarding body that elects to reimburse the department for the cost of monitoring and enforcing compliance with prevailing wage requirements for public works projects of the awarding body, pursuant to subdivision (a), must, for all of its contracts for public works projects awarded on or after the effective date of the regulations adopted by the department as specified in subdivision (g):

(1) Ensure that all bid invitations and public works contracts contain appropriate language concerning the requirements of this chapter.

(2) Conduct a prejob conference with the contractor and subcontractor to discuss federal and state labor law requirements applicable to the contract.

(3) Enter into an agreement with the department to reimburse the department for its costs of performing the service of monitoring and enforcing compliance with applicable prevailing wage requirements on the awarding bodies' projects.

(g) The Department of Industrial Relations shall adopt regulations implementing this section specifying the activities which the department shall undertake to monitor and enforce compliance with the prevailing wage requirements on the public works projects, including, but not limited to, monthly review, and audit if appropriate, of payroll records.

(h) (1) The Department of Industrial Relations shall determine the rate or rates, which the department may from time to time amend, that the department will charge in obtaining reimbursement from awarding bodies for the reasonable and directly related costs of performing the specified monitoring and enforcement services, provided the amount charged by the department shall not exceed one-fourth of 1 percent of the total public works project costs.

(2) Notwithstanding paragraph (1), for public works projects paid for in whole or part out of public funds, within the meaning of subdivision (b) of Section 1720, that are derived from bonds issued by the state, the amount charged by the department shall not exceed one-fourth of 1 percent of the state bond proceeds used for the public works project.

(i) All amounts collected by the Department of Industrial Relations for its services pursuant to this section shall be deposited in the State Public Works Enforcement Fund.

Added Stats 2011 ch 378 § 8 (AB 436), effective January 1, 2012.

§ 1771.55. [Section repealed 2012.]

Added Stats 2009-2010 2d Ex Sess ch 7 § 7 (SB 9XX), effective May 21, 2009. Repealed Stats 2011 ch 378 § 9 (AB 436), effective January 1, 2012. The repealed section related to payment of the general prevailing rate of per diem wages or the general prevailing rate of per diem wages for holiday and overtime work for any public works project of twenty-five thousand dollars ($25,000) or less, or for any public works project of fifteen thousand dollars ($15,000) or less when the project is for alteration, demolition, repair, or maintenance work.

§ 1771.6. Notice of withholding

(a) Any awarding body that enforces this chapter in accordance with Section 1726 or 1771.5 shall provide notice of the withholding of contract payments to the contractor and subcontractor, if applicable. The notice shall be in writing and shall describe the nature of the violation and the amount of wages, penalties, and forfeitures withheld. Service of the notice shall be completed pursuant to Section 1013 of the Code of Civil Procedure by first–class and certified mail to the contractor and subcontractor, if applicable. The notice shall advise the contractor and subcontractor, if applicable, of the procedure for obtaining review of the withholding of contract payments.

The awarding body shall also serve a copy of the notice by certified mail to any bonding company issuing a bond that secures the payment of wages covered by the notice and to any surety on a bond, if their identities are known to the awarding body.

(b) The withholding of contract payments in accordance with Section 1726 or 1771.5 shall be reviewable under Section 1742 in the same manner as if the notice of the withholding was a civil penalty order of the Labor Commissioner under this chapter. If review is requested, the Labor Commissioner may intervene to represent the awarding body.

(c) Pending a final order, or the expiration of the time period for seeking review of the notice of the withholding, the awarding body shall not disburse any contract payments withheld.

(d) From the amount recovered, the wage claim shall be satisfied prior to the amount being applied to penalties. If insufficient money is recovered to pay each worker in full, the money shall be prorated among all workers.

(e) Wages for workers who cannot be located shall be placed in the Industrial Relations Unpaid Wage Fund and held in trust for the workers pursuant to Section 96.7. Penalties shall be paid into the General Fund of the awarding body that has enforced this chapter pursuant to Section 1771.5.

Added Stats 2000 ch 954 § 16 (AB 1646), operative July 1, 2001.

§ 1771.7. Labor compliance program where public works project uses funds derived from Kindergarten-University Public Education Facilities Bond Act of 2002 or Kindergarten-University Public Education Facilities Bond Act of 2004; Applicability; Requirements

(a) (1) For contracts specified in subdivision (f), an awarding body that chooses to use funds derived from either the Kindergarten-University Public Education Facilities Bond Act of 2002 or the Kindergarten-University Public Education Facilities Bond Act of 2004 for a public works project, shall initiate and enforce, or contract with a third party to initiate and enforce, a labor compliance program, as described in subdivision (b) of Section 1771.5, with respect to that public works project.

(2) If an awarding body described in paragraph (1) chooses to contract with a third party to initiate and enforce a labor compliance program for a project described in paragraph (1), that third party shall not review the payroll records of its own employees or the employees of its subcontractors, and the awarding body or an independent third party shall review these payroll records for purposes of the labor compliance program.

(b) This section applies to public works that commence on or after April 1, 2003. For purposes of this subdivision, work performed during the design and preconstruction phases of construction, including, but not limited to, inspection and land surveying work, does not constitute the commencement of a public work.

(c) (1) For purposes of this section, if any campus of the California State University chooses to use the funds described in subdivision (a), then the "awarding body" is the Chancellor of the California State

Appendix

University. For purposes of this subdivision, if the chancellor is required by subdivision (a) to initiate and enforce, or to contract with a third party to initiate and enforce, a labor compliance program, then in addition to the requirements described in subdivision (b) of Section 1771.5, the Chancellor of the California State University shall review the payroll records on at least a monthly basis to ensure the awarding body's compliance with the labor compliance program.

(2) For purposes of this subdivision, if an awarding body described in subdivision (a) is the University of California or any campus of that university, and that awarding body is required by subdivision (a) to initiate and enforce, or to contract with a third party to initiate and enforce, a labor compliance program, then in addition to the requirements described in subdivision (b) of Section 1771.5, the payroll records shall be reviewed on at least a monthly basis to ensure the awarding body's compliance with the labor compliance program.

(d) (1) An awarding body described in subdivision (a) shall make a written finding that the awarding body has initiated and enforced, or has contracted with a third party to initiate and enforce, the labor compliance program described in subdivision (a).

(2) (A) If an awarding body described in subdivision (a) is a school district, the governing body of that district shall transmit to the State Allocation Board, in the manner determined by that board, a copy of the finding described in paragraph (1).

(B) The State Allocation Board shall not release the funds described in subdivision (a) to an awarding body that is a school district until the State Allocation Board has received the written finding described in paragraph (1).

(C) If the State Allocation Board conducts a postaward audit procedure with respect to an award of the funds described in subdivision (a) to an awarding body that is a school district, the State Allocation Board shall verify, in the manner determined by that board, that the school district has complied with the requirements of this subdivision.

(3) If an awarding body described in subdivision (a) is a community college district, the Chancellor of the California State University, or the office of the President of the University of California or any campus of the University of California, that awarding body shall transmit, in the manner determined by the Director of Industrial Relations, a copy of the finding described in paragraph (1) to the director of that department, or the director of any successor agency that is responsible for the oversight of employee wage and employee work hours laws.

(e) Because the reasonable costs directly related to monitoring and enforcing compliance with the prevailing wage requirements are necessary oversight activities, integral to the cost of construction of the public works projects, notwithstanding Section 17070.63 of the Education Code, the grant amounts as described in Chapter 12.5 (commencing with Section 17070.10) of Part 10 of Division 1 of Title 1 of the Education Code for the costs of a new construction or modernization project shall include the state's share of the reasonable and directly related costs of the labor compliance program used to monitor and enforce compliance with prevailing wage requirements.

(f) This section shall only apply to contracts awarded prior to the effective date of regulations adopted by the Department of Industrial Relations pursuant to paragraph (3) of subdivision (a) of Section 1771.3.

Added Stats 2002 ch 868 § 2 (AB 1506). Amended Stats 2003 ch 834 § 2 (AB 324); Stats 2005 ch 606 § 1 (AB 414), effective January 1, 2006; Stats 2009-2010 2d Ex Sess ch 7 § 8 (SB 9XX), effective May 21, 2009; Stats 2010 ch 719 § 49 (SB 856), effective October 19, 2010; Stats 2011 ch 378 § 10 (AB 436), effective January 1, 2012.

§ 1771.75. [Section repealed 2012.]

Added Stats 2009-2010 2d Ex Sess ch 7 § 9 (SB 9XX), effective May 21, 2009. Amended Stats 2010 ch 719 § 50 (SB 856), effective October 19, 2010. Repealed Stats 2011 ch 378 § 11 (AB 436), effective January 1, 2012. The repealed section related to the labor compliance program where public works project uses funds derived from Kindergarten-University Public Education Facilities Bond Act of 2002 or Kindergarten-University Public Education Facilities Bond Act of 2004, applicability, and requirements.

§ 1771.8. [Section repealed 2012.]

Added Stats 2002 ch 892 § 2 (SB 278). Amended Stats 2009-2010 2d Ex Sess ch 7 § 10 (SB 9XX), effective May 21, 2009; Stats 2010 ch 719 § 51 (SB 856), effective October 19, 2010. Repealed Stats 2011 ch 378 § 12 (AB 436), effective January 1, 2012. The repealed section related to adoption and enforcement of a labor compliance program by the body awarding any contract for a public works project financed in any part with funds made available by the Water Security, Clean Drinking Water, Coastal and Beach Protection Act of 2002.

§ 1771.85. [Section repealed 2012.]

Added Stats 2009-2010 2d Ex Sess ch 7 § 11 (SB 9XX), effective May 21, 2009. Repealed Stats 2011 ch 378 § 13 (AB 436), effective January 1, 2012. The repealed section related to fees to support the department's costs in ensuring compliance with and enforcing prevailing wage requirements in contracts for public works project financed in any part with funds made available by the Water Security, Clean Drinking Water, Coastal and Beach Protection Act of 2002.

§ 1771.9. [Section repealed 2012.]

Added Stats 2009-2010 2d Ex Sess ch 7 § 13 (SB 9XX), effective May 21, 2009. Repealed Stats 2011 ch 378 § 14 (AB 436), effective January 1, 2012. The repealed section related to payment of fee and adoption of labor compliance program by body awarding contract for public works under the Safe, Reliable High-Speed Passenger Train Bond Act for the 21st Century.

§ 1772. Workers deemed employed upon public work

Workers employed by contractors or subcontractors in the execution of any contract for public work are deemed to be employed upon public work.

Enacted 1937. Amended Stats 1992 ch 1342 § 7 (SB 222).

§ 1773. Ascertainment of prevailing rate; Data considered

The body awarding any contract for public work, or otherwise undertaking any public work, shall obtain the general prevailing rate of per diem wages and the general prevailing rate for holiday and overtime work in the locality in which the public work is to be performed for each craft, classification, or type of worker needed to execute the contract from the Director of Industrial Relations. The holidays upon which those rates shall be paid need not be specified by the awarding body, but shall be all holidays recognized in the applicable collective bargaining agreement. If the prevailing rate is not based on a collectively bargained rate, the holidays upon which the prevailing rate shall be paid shall be as provided in Section 6700 of the Government Code.

In determining the rates, the Director of Industrial Relations shall ascertain and consider the applicable wage rates established by collective bargaining agreements and the rates that may have been predetermined for federal public works, within the locality and in the nearest labor market area. Where the rates do not constitute the rates actually prevailing in the locality, the director shall obtain and consider further data from the labor organizations and employers or employer associations concerned, including the recognized collective bargaining representatives for the particular craft, classification, or type of work involved. The rate fixed for each craft, classification, or type of work shall be not less than the prevailing rate paid in the craft, classification, or type of work.

If the director determines that the rate of prevailing wage for any craft, classification, or type of worker is the rate established by a collective bargaining agreement, the director may adopt that rate by reference as provided for in the collective bargaining agreement and that determination shall be effective for the life of the agreement or until the director determines that another rate should be adopted.

Enacted 1937. Amended Stats 1953 ch 1706 § 4; Stats 1968 ch 699 § 1, operative July 1, 1969; Stats 1971 ch 785 § 1; Stats 1976 ch 281 § 3. Amended Stats 1999 ch 30 § 1 (SB 16).

§ 1773.1. Per diem wages; What employer payments are included therein; Credits for employer payments; Computation of credits; Filing of collective bargaining agreements

(a) Per diem wages, when the term is used in this chapter or in any other statute applicable to public works, shall be deemed to include employer payments for the following:

(1) Health and welfare.

(2) Pension.

(3) Vacation.

(4) Travel.

(5) Subsistence.

(6) Apprenticeship or other training programs authorized by Section 3093, so long as the cost of training is reasonably related to the amount of the contributions.

(7) Worker protection and assistance programs or committees established under the federal Labor Management Cooperation Act of 1978 (Section 175a of Title 29 of the United States Code), to the extent that the activities of the programs or committees are directed to the monitoring and enforcement of laws related to public works.

(8) Industry advancement and collective bargaining agreements administrative fees, provided that these payments are required under a collective bargaining agreement pertaining to the particular craft, classification, or type of work within the locality or the nearest labor market area at issue.

(9) Other purposes similar to those specified in paragraphs (1) to (8), inclusive.

(b) Employer payments include all of the following:

(1) The rate of contribution irrevocably made by the employer to a trustee or third person pursuant to a plan, fund, or program.

(2) The rate of actual costs to the employer reasonably anticipated in providing benefits to workers pursuant to an enforceable commitment to carry out a financially responsible plan or program communicated in writing to the workers affected.

(3) Payments to the California Apprenticeship Council pursuant to Section 1777.5.

(c) Employer payments are a credit against the obligation to pay the general prevailing rate of per diem wages. However, no credit shall be granted for benefits required to be provided by other state or federal law. Credits for employer payments also shall not reduce the obligation to pay the hourly straight time or overtime wages found to be prevailing.

(d) The credit for employer payments shall be computed on an annualized basis where the employer seeks credit for employer payments that are higher for public works projects than for private construction performed by the same employer, except where one or more of the following occur:

(1) The employer has an enforceable obligation to make the higher rate of payments on future private construction performed by the employer.

(2) The higher rate of payments is required by a project labor agreement.

(3) The payments are made to the California Apprenticeship Council pursuant to Section 1777.5.

(4) The director determines that annualization would not serve the purposes of this chapter.

(e) (1) For the purpose of determining those per diem wages for contracts, the representative of any craft, classification, or type of worker needed to execute contracts shall file with the Department of Industrial Relations fully executed copies of the collective bargaining agreements for the particular craft, classification, or type of work involved. The collective bargaining agreements shall be filed after their execution and thereafter may be taken into consideration pursuant to Section 1773 whenever filed 30 days prior to the call for bids. If the collective bargaining agreement has not been formalized, a typescript of the final draft may be filed temporarily, accompanied by a statement under penalty of perjury as to its effective date.

(2) Where a copy of the collective bargaining agreement has previously been filed, fully executed copies of all modifications and extensions of the agreement that affect per diem wages or holidays shall be filed.

(3) The failure to comply with filing requirements of this subdivision shall not be grounds for setting aside a prevailing wage determination if the information taken into consideration is correct.

Added Stats 1959 ch 2173 § 1. Amended Stats 1969 ch 1502 § 1; Stats 1976 ch 281 § 4. Amended Stats 1999 ch 30 § 2 (SB 16); Stats 2000 ch 954 § 18 (AB 1646), operative July 1, 2001; Stats 2003 ch 839 § 1 (AB 807), ch 905 § 1 (SB 868).

§ 1773.2. Specification of prevailing wage rates in call for bids

The body awarding any contract for public work, or otherwise undertaking any public work, shall specify in the call for bids for the contract, and in the bid specifications and in the contract itself, what the general rate of per diem wages is for each craft, classification, or type of worker needed to execute the contract.

In lieu of specifying the rate of wages in the call for bids, and in the bid specifications and in the contract itself, the awarding body may, in the call for bids, bid specifications, and contract, include a statement that copies of the prevailing rate of per diem wages are on file at its principal office, which shall be made available to any interested party on request. The awarding body shall also cause a copy of the determination of the director of the prevailing rate of per diem wages to be posted at each job site.

Added Stats 1971 ch 785 § 2. Amended Stats 1974 ch 876 § 1; Stats 1977 ch 423 § 1. Amended Stats 1992 ch 1342 § 8 (SB 222).

§ 1773.3. Notifications of award of public works contract and of discrepancy in apprentices–journeymen ratio

An awarding agency whose public works contract falls within the jurisdiction of Section 1777.5 shall, within five days of the award, send a copy of the award to the Division of Apprenticeship Standards. When specifically requested by a local joint apprenticeship committee, the division shall notify the local joint apprenticeship committee regarding all such awards applicable to the joint apprenticeship committee making the request. Within five days of a finding of any discrepancy regarding the ratio of apprentices to journeymen, pursuant to the certificated fixed number of apprentices to journeymen, the awarding agency shall notify the Division of Apprenticeship Standards.

Added Stats 1972 ch 1399 § 2 as § 3098. Amended Stats 1974 ch 1095 § 1. Renumbered Stats 1978 ch 1249 § 6.

§ 1773.4. Procedure for review of rates

Any prospective bidder or his representative, any representative of any craft, classification or type of workman involved, or the awarding body may, within 20 days after commencement of advertising of the call for bids by the awarding body, file with the Director of Industrial Relations a verified petition to review the determination of any such rate or rates upon the ground that they have not been determined in accordance with the provision of Section 1773 of this code. Within two days thereafter, a copy of such petition shall be filed with the awarding body. The petition shall set forth the facts upon which it is based. The Director of Industrial Relations or his authorized representative shall, upon notice to the petitioner, the awarding body and such other persons as he deems proper, including the recognized collective bargaining representatives for the particular crafts, classifications or types of work involved, institute an investigation or hold a hearing. Within 20 days after the filing of such petition, or within such longer period as agreed upon by the director, the awarding body, and all the interested parties, he shall make a determination and transmit the same in writing to the awarding body and to the interested parties.

Such determination shall be final and shall be the determination of the awarding body. Upon receipt by it of the notice of the filing of such petition the body awarding the contract or authorizing the public work shall extend the closing date for the submission of bids or the starting of work until five days after the determination of the general prevailing rates of per diem wages pursuant to this section.

Upon the filing of any such petition, notice thereof shall be set forth in the next and all subsequent publications by the awarding body of the call for bids. No other notice need be given to bidders by the awarding body by publication or otherwise. The determination of the director shall be included in the contract.

Added Stats 1953 ch 1706 § 4.5. Amended Stats 1968 ch 699 § 2, operative July 1, 1969; Stats 1969 ch 301 § 1.

§ 1773.5. Rules and regulations

The Director of Industrial Relations may establish rules and regulations for the purpose of carrying out this chapter, including, but not limited to, the responsibilities and duties of awarding bodies under this chapter.

Added Stats 1953 ch 1706 § 5. Amended Stats 1989 ch 1224 § 5.

§ 1773.6. Change in prevailing per diem wage rate

If during any quarterly period the Director of Industrial Relations shall determine that there has been a change in any prevailing rate of per diem wages in any locality he shall make such change available to the awarding body and his determination shall be final. Such determination by the Director of Industrial Relations shall not be effective as to any contract for which the notice to bidders has been published.

Added Stats 1953 ch 1706 § 6. Amended Stats 1957 ch 1932 § 486; Stats 1963 ch 1786 § 68, operative October 1, 1963; Stats 1976 ch 281 § 6.

§ 1773.7. Charges for interagency services

The provisions of Section 11250 of the Government Code shall not be applicable to Sections 1773, 1773.4, and 1773.6.

Added Stats 1976 ch 281 § 8.

§ 1773.8. [Section repealed 1999.]

Added Stats 1968 ch 880 § 1. Repealed Stats 1999 ch 30 § 3 (SB 16). The repealed section related to specification requiring payment of travel and subsistence payment, and filing collective bargaining agreements to establish payment.

§ 1773.9. Determination of general prevailing rate of per diem wages

(a) The Director of Industrial Relations shall use the methodology set forth in subdivision (b) to determine the general prevailing rate of per diem wages in the locality in which the public work is to be performed.

(b) The general prevailing rate of per diem wages includes all of the following:

(1) The basic hourly wage rate being paid to a majority of workers engaged in the particular craft, classification, or type of work within the locality and in the nearest labor market area, if a majority of the workers is paid at a single rate. If no single rate is being paid to a majority of the workers, then the single rate being paid to the greatest number of workers, or modal rate, is prevailing. If a modal rate cannot be determined, then the director shall establish an alternative rate, consistent with the methodology for determining the modal rate, by considering the appropriate collective bargaining agreements, federal rates, rates in the nearest labor market area, or other data such as wage survey data.

(2) Other employer payments included in per diem wages pursuant to Section 1773.1 and as included as part of the total hourly wage rate from which the basic hourly wage rate was derived. In the event the total hourly wage rate does not include any employer payments, the director shall establish a prevailing employer payment rate by the same procedure set forth in paragraph (1).

(3) The rate for holiday and overtime work shall be those rates specified in the collective bargaining agreement when the basic hourly rate is based on a collective bargaining agreement rate. In the event the basic hourly rate is not based on a collective bargaining agreement, the rate for holidays and overtime work, if any, included with the prevailing basic hourly rate of pay shall be prevailing.

(c) (1) If the director determines that the general prevailing rate of per diem wages is the rate established by a collective bargaining agreement, and that the collective bargaining agreement contains definite and predetermined changes during its term that will affect the rate adopted, the director shall incorporate those changes into the determination. Predetermined changes that are rescinded prior to their effective date shall not be enforced.

(2) When the director determines that there is a definite and predetermined change in the general prevailing rate of per diem wages as described in paragraph (1), but has not published, at the time of the effective date of the predetermined change, the allocation of the predetermined change as between the basic hourly wage and other employer payments included in per diem wages pursuant to Section 1773.1, a contractor or subcontractor may allocate payments of not less than the amount of the definite and predetermined change to either the basic hourly wage or other employer payments included in per diem wages for up to 60 days following the director's publication of the specific allocation of the predetermined change.

(3) When the director determines that there is a definite and predetermined change in the general prevailing rate of per diem wages as described in paragraph (1), but the allocation of that predetermined change as between the basic hourly wage and other employer payments included in per diem wages pursuant to Section 1773.1 is subsequently altered by the parties to a collective bargaining agreement described in paragraph (1), a contractor or subcontractor may allocate payments of not less than the amount of the definite and predetermined change in accordance with either the originally published allocation or the allocation as altered in the collective bargaining agreement.

Added Stats 1999 ch 30 § 4 (SB 16). Amended Stats 2007 ch 482 § 2 (SB 929), effective January 1, 2008.

§ 1773.11. Contract with private entity for prevailing rate of per diem wages and prevailing rate for holiday and overtime work; Director to determine rates and respond to requests; Limited number of requests per calendar year

(a) Notwithstanding any other provision of law and except as otherwise provided by this section, if the state or a political subdivision thereof agrees by contract with a private entity that the private entity's employees receive, in performing that contract, the general prevailing rate of per diem wages and the general prevailing rate for holiday and overtime work, the director shall, upon a request by the state or the political subdivision, do both of the following:

(1) Determine, as otherwise provided by law, the wage rates for each craft, classification, or type of worker that are needed to execute the contract.

(2) Provide these wage rates to the state or political subdivision that requests them.

(b) This section does not apply to a contract for a public work, as defined in this chapter.

(c) The director shall determine and provide the wage rates described in this section in the order in which the requests for these wage rates were received and regardless of the calendar year in which they were received. If there are more than 20 pending requests in a calendar year, the director shall respond only to the first 20 requests in the order in which they were received. If the director determines that funding is available in any calendar year to determine and provide these wage rates in response to more than 20 requests, the director shall respond to these requests in a manner consistent with this subdivision.

Added Stats 2003 ch 343 § 1 (AB 852).

§ 1774. Payment of not less than specified prevailing rates to workmen

The contractor to whom the contract is awarded, and any subcontractor under him, shall pay not less than the specified prevailing rates of wages to all workmen employed in the execution of the contract.

Enacted 1937.

§ 1775. Forfeiture for paying less than prevailing wage rates; Amount of penalty; Payments to workers; Liability of prime contractor; Notification of complaint

(a) (1) The contractor and any subcontractor under the contractor shall, as a penalty to the state or political subdivision on whose behalf the contract is made or awarded, forfeit not more than two hundred dollars ($200) for each calendar day, or portion thereof, for each worker paid less than the prevailing wage rates as determined by the director for the work or craft in which the worker is employed for any public work done under the contract by the contractor or, except as provided in subdivision (b), by any subcontractor under the contractor.

(2) (A) The amount of the penalty shall be determined by the Labor Commissioner based on consideration of both of the following:

(i) Whether the failure of the contractor or subcontractor to pay the correct rate of per diem wages was a good faith mistake and, if so, the error was promptly and voluntarily corrected when brought to the attention of the contractor or subcontractor.

(ii) Whether the contractor or subcontractor has a prior record of failing to meet its prevailing wage obligations.

(B) (i) The penalty may not be less than forty dollars ($40) for each calendar day, or portion thereof, for each worker paid less than the prevailing wage rate, unless the failure of the contractor or subcontractor to pay the correct rate of per diem wages was a good faith mistake and, if so, the error was promptly and voluntarily corrected when brought to the attention of the contractor or subcontractor.

(ii) The penalty may not be less than eighty dollars ($80) for each calendar day, or portion thereof, for each worker paid less than the prevailing wage rate, if the contractor or subcontractor has been assessed penalties within the previous three years for failing to meet its prevailing wage obligations on a separate contract, unless those penalties were subsequently withdrawn or overturned.

(iii) The penalty may not be less than one hundred twenty dollars ($120) for each calendar day, or portion thereof, for each worker paid less than the prevailing wage rate, if the Labor Commissioner determines that the violation was willful, as defined in subdivision (c) of Section 1777.1.

(C) If the amount due under this section is collected from the contractor or subcontractor, any outstanding wage claim under Chapter 1 (commencing with Section 1720) of Part 7 of Division 2 against that contractor or subcontractor shall be satisfied before applying that amount to the penalty imposed on that contractor or subcontractor pursuant to this section.

(D) The determination of the Labor Commissioner as to the amount of the penalty shall be reviewable only for abuse of discretion.

(E) The difference between the prevailing wage rates and the amount paid to each worker for each calendar day or portion thereof for which each worker was paid less than the prevailing wage rate shall be paid to each worker by the contractor or subcontractor, and the body awarding the contract shall cause to be inserted in the contract a stipulation that this section will be complied with.

(b) If a worker employed by a subcontractor on a public works project is not paid the general prevailing rate of per diem wages by the subcontractor, the prime contractor of the project is not liable for any penalties under subdivision (a) unless the prime contractor had knowledge of that failure of the subcontractor to pay the specified prevailing rate of wages to those workers or unless the prime contractor fails to comply with all of the following requirements:

(1) The contract executed between the contractor and the subcontractor for the performance of work on the public works project shall include a copy of the provisions of this section and Sections 1771, 1776, 1777.5, 1813, and 1815.

(2) The contractor shall monitor the payment of the specified general prevailing rate of per diem wages by the subcontractor to the employees, by periodic review of the certified payroll records of the subcontractor.

(3) Upon becoming aware of the failure of the subcontractor to pay his or her workers the specified prevailing rate of wages, the contractor shall diligently take corrective action to halt or rectify the failure, including, but not limited to, retaining sufficient funds due the subcontractor for work performed on the public works project.

(4) Prior to making final payment to the subcontractor for work performed on the public works project, the contractor shall obtain an affidavit signed under penalty of perjury from the subcontractor that the subcontractor has paid the specified general prevailing rate of per diem wages to his or her employees on the public works project and any amounts due pursuant to Section 1813.

(c) The Division of Labor Standards Enforcement shall notify the contractor on a public works project within 15 days of the receipt by the Division of Labor Standards Enforcement of a complaint of the failure of a subcontractor on that public works project to pay workers the general prevailing rate of per diem wages.

Added Stats 1997 ch 757 § 2 (SB 1328). Amended Stats 2000 ch 954 § 20 (AB 1646); Stats 2003 ch 849 § 3 (AB 1418); Stats 2011 ch 677 § 1 (AB 551), effective January 1, 2012.

§ 1776. Payroll record of wages paid; Inspection; Forms; Effect of noncompliance; Penalties

(a) Each contractor and subcontractor shall keep accurate payroll records, showing the name, address, social security number, work classification, straight time and overtime hours worked each day and week, and the actual per diem wages paid to each journeyman, apprentice, worker, or other employee employed by him or her in connection with the public work. Each payroll record shall contain or be verified by a written declaration that it is made under penalty of perjury, stating both of the following:

(1) The information contained in the payroll record is true and correct.

(2) The employer has complied with the requirements of Sections 1771, 1811, and 1815 for any work performed by his or her employees on the public works project.

(b) The payroll records enumerated under subdivision (a) shall be certified and shall be available for inspection at all reasonable hours at the principal office of the contractor on the following basis:

(1) A certified copy of an employee's payroll record shall be made available for inspection or furnished to the employee or his or her authorized representative on request.

(2) A certified copy of all payroll records enumerated in subdivision (a) shall be made available for inspection or furnished upon request to a representative of the body awarding the contract, the Division of Labor Standards Enforcement, and the Division of Apprenticeship Standards of the Department of Industrial Relations.

(3) A certified copy of all payroll records enumerated in subdivision (a) shall be made available upon request by the public for inspection or for copies thereof. However, a request by the public shall be made through either the body awarding the contract, the Division of Apprenticeship Standards, or the Division of Labor Standards Enforcement. If the requested payroll records have not been provided pursuant to paragraph (2), the requesting party shall, prior to being provided the records, reimburse the costs of preparation by the contractor, subcontractors, and the entity through which the request was made. The public may not be given access to the records at the principal office of the contractor.

(c) The certified payroll records shall be on forms provided by the Division of Labor Standards Enforcement or shall contain the same information as the forms provided by the division. The payroll records may consist of printouts of payroll data that are maintained as computer records, if the printouts contain the same information as the forms provided by the division and the printouts are verified in the manner specified in subdivision (a).

(d) A contractor or subcontractor shall file a certified copy of the records enumerated in subdivision (a) with the entity that requested the records within 10 days after receipt of a written request.

(e) Except as provided in subdivision (f), any copy of records made available for inspection as copies and furnished upon request to the public or any public agency by the awarding body, the Division of Apprenticeship Standards, or the Division of Labor Standards Enforcement shall be marked or obliterated to prevent disclosure of an individual's name, address, and social security number. The name and address of the contractor awarded the contract or the subcontractor performing the contract shall not be marked or obliterated. Any copy of records made available for inspection by, or furnished to, a joint labor-management committee established pursuant to the federal Labor Management Cooperation Act of 1978 (29 U.S.C. Sec. 175a) shall be marked or obliterated only to prevent disclosure of an individual's name and social security number. A joint labor management committee may maintain an action in a court of competent jurisdiction against an employer who fails to comply with Section 1774. The court may award restitution to an employee for unpaid wages and may award the joint labor management committee reasonable attorney's fees and costs incurred in maintaining the action. An action under this subdivision may not be based on the employer's misclassification of the craft of a worker on its certified payroll records. Nothing in this subdivision limits any other available remedies for a violation of this chapter.

(f) (1) Notwithstanding any other provision of law, agencies that are included in the Joint Enforcement Strike Force on the Underground Economy established pursuant to Section 329 of the Unemployment Insurance Code and other law enforcement agencies investigating violations of law shall, upon request, be provided nonredacted copies of certified payroll records. Any copies of records or certified payroll made available for inspection and furnished upon request to the public by an agency included in the Joint Enforcement Strike Force on the Underground Economy or to a law enforcement agency investigating a violation of law shall be marked or redacted to prevent disclosure of an individual's name, address, and social security number.

(2) An employer shall not be liable for damages in a civil action for any reasonable act or omission taken in good faith in compliance with this subdivision.

(g) The contractor shall inform the body awarding the contract of the location of the records enumerated under subdivision (a), including the street address, city, and county, and shall, within five working days, provide a notice of a change of location and address.

(h) The contractor or subcontractor has 10 days in which to comply subsequent to receipt of a written notice requesting the records enumerated in subdivision (a). In the event that the contractor or subcontractor fails to comply within the 10-day period, he or she shall, as a penalty to the state or political subdivision on whose behalf the contract is made or awarded, forfeit one hundred dollars ($100) for each calendar day, or portion thereof, for each worker, until strict compliance is effectuated. Upon the request of the Division of Apprenticeship Standards or the Division of Labor Standards Enforcement, these penalties shall be withheld from progress payments then due. A contractor is not subject to a penalty assessment pursuant to this section due to the failure of a subcontractor to comply with this section.

(i) The body awarding the contract shall cause to be inserted in the contract stipulations to effectuate this section.

(j) The director shall adopt rules consistent with the California Public Records Act (Chapter 3.5 (commencing with Section 6250) of Division 7 of Title 1 of the Government Code) and the Information Practices Act of 1977 (Title 1.8 (commencing with Section 1798) of Part 4 of Division 3 of the Civil Code) governing the release of these records, including the establishment of reasonable fees to be charged for reproducing copies of records required by this section.

Added Stats 1997 ch 757 § 4 (SB 1328). Amended Stats 2001 ch 804 § 2 (SB 588); Stats 2002 ch 28 § 1 (AB 1448) (ch 28 prevails), ch 664 § 161 (AB 3034); Stats 2003 ch 62 § 205 (SB 600); Stats 2005 ch 500 § 1 (SB 759), effective January 1, 2006; Stats 2011 ch 481 § 1 (AB 766), effective January 1, 2012, ch 677 § 2.5 (AB 551), effective January 1, 2012.

§ 1777.1. Penalties for willful violations of chapter; Notice; Hearing

(a) Whenever a contractor or subcontractor performing a public works project pursuant to this chapter is found by the Labor Commissioner to be in violation of this chapter with intent to defraud, except Section 1777.5, the contractor or subcontractor or a firm, corporation, partnership, or association in which the contractor or subcontractor has any interest is ineligible for a period of not less than one year or more than three years to do either of the following:

(1) Bid on or be awarded a contract for a public works project.

(2) Perform work as a subcontractor on a public works project.

(b) Whenever a contractor or subcontractor performing a public works project pursuant to this chapter is found by the Labor Commissioner to have committed two or more separate willful violations of this chapter, except Section 1777.5, within a three-year period, the contractor or subcontractor or a firm, corporation, partnership, or association in which the contractor or subcontractor has any interest is ineligible for a period up to three years to do either of the following:

(1) Bid on or be awarded a contract for a public works project.

(2) Perform work as a subcontractor on a public works project.

(c) Whenever a contractor or subcontractor performing a public works project has failed to provide a timely response to a request by the Division of Labor Standards Enforcement, the Division of Apprenticeship Standards, or the awarding body to produce certified payroll records pursuant to Section 1776, the Labor Commissioner shall notify the contractor or subcontractor that, in addition to any other penalties provided by law, the contractor or subcontractor will be subject to debarment under this section if the certified payroll records are not produced within 30 days after receipt of the written notice. If the commissioner finds that the contractor or subcontractor has failed to comply with Section 1776 by that deadline, unless the commissioner finds that the failure to comply was due to circumstances outside the contractor's or subcontractor's control, the contractor or subcontractor or a firm, corporation, partnership, or association in which the contractor or subcontractor has any interest is ineligible for a period of not less than one year and not more than three years to do either of the following:

(1) Bid on or be awarded a contract for a public works project.

(2) Perform work as a subcontractor on a public works project.

(d) A willful violation occurs when the contractor or subcontractor knew or reasonably should have known of his or her obligations under the public works law and deliberately fails or refuses to comply with its provisions.

(e) The Labor Commissioner shall publish on the commissioner's Internet Web site a list of contractors who are ineligible to bid on or be awarded a public works contract, or to perform work as a subcontractor on a public works project pursuant to this chapter. The list shall contain the name of the contractor, the Contractors' State License Board license number of the contractor, and the effective period of debarment of the contractor. Contractors shall be added to the list upon issuance of a debarment order and the commissioner shall also notify the Contractors' State License Board when the list is updated. At least annually, the commissioner shall notify awarding bodies of the availability of the list of debarred contractors. The commissioner shall also place advertisements in construction industry publications targeted to the contractors and subcontractors, chosen by the commissioner, that state the effective period of the debarment and the reason for debarment. The advertisements shall appear one time for each debarment of a contractor in each publication chosen by the commissioner. The debarred contractor or subcontractor shall be liable to the commissioner for the reasonable cost of the advertisements, not to exceed five thousand dollars ($5,000). The amount paid to the commissioner for the advertisements shall be credited against the contractor's or subcontractor's obligation to pay civil fines or penalties for the same willful violation of this chapter.

(f) For purposes of this section, "contractor or subcontractor" means a firm, corporation, partnership, or association and its responsible managing officer, as well as any supervisors, managers, and officers found by the Labor Commissioner to be personally and substantially responsible for the willful violation of this chapter.

(g) For the purposes of this section, the term "any interest" means an interest in the entity bidding or performing work on the public works project, whether as an owner, partner, officer, manager, employee, agent, consultant, or representative. "Any interest" includes, but is not limited to, all instances where the debarred contractor or subcontractor receives payments, whether cash or any other form of compensation, from any entity bidding or performing work on the public works project, or enters into any contracts or agreements with the entity bidding or performing work on the public works project for services performed or to be performed for contracts that have been or will be assigned or sublet, or for vehicles, tools, equipment, or supplies that have been or will be sold, rented, or leased during the period from the initiation of the debarment proceedings until the end of the term of the debarment period. "Any interest" does not include shares held in a publicly traded corporation if the shares were not received as compensation after the initiation of debarment from an entity bidding or performing work on a public works project.

(h) For the purposes of this section, the term "entity" is defined as a company, limited liability company, association, partnership, sole proprietorship, limited liability partnership, corporation, business trust, or organization.

(i) The Labor Commissioner shall adopt rules and regulations for the administration and enforcement of this section.

Added Stats 1989 ch 1224 § 10. Amended Stats 1998 ch 443 § 1 (AB 1569); Stats 2000 ch 970 § 1 (AB 2513); Stats 2011 ch 677 § 3 (AB 551), effective January 1, 2012.

DIVISION 3

EMPLOYMENT RELATIONS

Chapter 2

Employer and Employee

Article 1

The Contract of Employment

§ 2753. Liability of person who advises employer to treat individual as independent contractor to avoid employee status

(a) A person who, for money or other valuable consideration, knowingly advises an employer to treat an individual as an independent contractor to avoid employee status for that individual shall be jointly and severally liable with the employer if the individual is found not to be an independent contractor.

(b) This section does not apply to the following persons:

(1) A person who provides advice to his or her employer.

(2) An attorney authorized to practice law in California or another United States jurisdiction who provides legal advice in the course of the practice of law.

Added Stats 2011 ch 706 § 2 (SB 459), effective January 1, 2012.

Chapter 4

Apprenticeship

§ 3099. Responsibilities of Division of Apprenticeship Standards

(a) The Division of Apprenticeship Standards shall do all of the following:

(1) On or before July 1, 2001, establish and validate minimum standards for the competency and training of electricians through a system of testing and certification.

(2) On or before March 1, 2000, establish an advisory committee and panels as necessary to carry out the functions under this section. There shall be contractor representation from both joint apprenticeship programs and unilateral nonunion programs in the electrical contracting industry.

(3) On or before July 1, 2001, establish fees necessary to implement this section.

(4) On or before July 1, 2001, establish and adopt regulations to enforce this section.

(5) Issue certification cards to electricians who have been certified pursuant to this section. Fees collected pursuant to paragraph (3) are continuously appropriated in an amount sufficient to pay the costs of issuing certification cards, and that amount may be expended for that purpose by the division.

(6) On or before July 1, 2003, establish an electrical certification curriculum committee comprised of representatives of the State Department of Education, the California Community Colleges, and the division. The following shall apply to the electrical certification curriculum committee:

(A) The committee shall establish written educational curriculum standards for enrollees in training programs established pursuant to Section 3099.4.

(B) If an educational provider's curriculum meets the written educational curriculum standards established in accordance with subparagraph (A), the committee shall designate that curriculum as an approved curriculum of classroom instruction.

(C) The committee may review the approved curriculum of classroom instruction of any designated educational provider. The committee may withdraw its approval of the curriculum if the educational provider does not continue to meet the established written educational curriculum standards.

(D) The committee shall require each designated educational provider to submit an annual notice to the committee stating whether the educational provider is continuing to offer the approved curriculum of classroom instruction and whether any material changes have been made to the curriculum since its approval.

(b) There shall be no discrimination for or against any person based on membership or nonmembership in a union.

(c) As used in this section, "electricians" includes all persons who engage in the connection of electrical devices for electrical contractors licensed pursuant to Section 7058 of the Business and Professions Code, specifically, contractors classified as electrical contractors in the Contractors' State License Board Rules and Regulations. This section does not apply to electrical connections under 100 volt-amperes. This section does not apply to persons performing work to which Section 7042.5 of the Business and Professions Code is applicable, or to electrical work ordinarily and customarily performed by stationary engineers. This section does not apply to electrical work in connection with the installation, operation, or maintenance of temporary or portable electrical equipment performed by technicians in the theatrical, motion picture production, television, hotel, exhibition, or trade show industries.

Added Stats 1999 ch 781 § 1 (AB 931). Amended Stats 2000 ch 875 § 3 (AB 2481); Stats 2002 ch 48 § 1 (AB 1087); Stats 2004 ch 183 § 262 (AB 3082); Stats 2006 ch 828 § 4 (AB 2907), effective January 1, 2007; Stats 2011 ch 693 § 1 (AB 1346), effective January 1, 2012.

§ 3099.2. Certification of electricians

(a) (1) Persons who perform work as electricians shall become certified pursuant to Section 3099 by the deadline specified in this subdivision. After the applicable deadline, uncertified persons shall not perform electrical work for which certification is required.

(2) The deadline for certification as a general electrician or fire/life safety technician is January 1, 2006, except that persons who applied for certification prior to January 1, 2006, have until January 1, 2007, to pass the certification examination. The deadline for certification as a residential electrician is January 1, 2007, and the deadline for certification as a voice data video technician or a nonresidential lighting technician is January 1, 2008. The California Apprenticeship Council may extend the certification date for any of these three categories of electricians up to January 1, 2009, if the council concludes that the existing deadline will not provide persons sufficient time to obtain certification, enroll in an apprenticeship or training program, or register pursuant to Section 3099.4.

(3) For purposes of any continuing education or recertification requirement, individuals who become certified prior to the deadline for certification shall be treated as having become certified on the first anniversary of their certification date that falls after the certification deadline.

(4) Individuals desiring to be certified shall submit an application for certification and examination that includes an employment history report from the Social Security Administration. The individual may redact his or her social security number from the employment history report before it is submitted.

(b) (1) Certification is required only for those persons who perform work as electricians for contractors licensed as class C-10 electrical contractors under the Contractors' State License Board Rules and Regulations.

(2) Certification is not required for persons performing work for contractors licensed as class C-7 low voltage systems or class C-45 sign contractors as long as the work performed is within the scope of the class C-7 or class C-45 license, including incidental and supplemental work as defined in Section 7059 of the Business and Professions Code, and regardless of whether the same contractor is also licensed as a class C-10 contractor.

(3) Certification is not required for work performed by a worker on a high-voltage electrical transmission or distribution system owned by a local publicly owned electric utility, as defined in Section 224.3 of

the Public Utilities Code; an electrical corporation, as defined in Section 218 of the Public Utilities Code; a person, as defined in Section 205 of the Public Utilities Code; or a corporation, as defined in Section 204 of the Public Utilities Code; when the worker is employed by the utility or a licensed contractor principally engaged in installing or maintaining transmission or distribution systems.

(c) The division shall establish separate certifications for general electrician, fire/life safety technician, residential electrician, voice data video technician, and nonresidential lighting technician.

(d) Notwithstanding subdivision (a), certification is not required for registered apprentices performing electrical work as part of an apprenticeship program approved under this chapter, a federal Office of Apprenticeship program, or a state apprenticeship program authorized by the federal Office of Apprenticeship. An apprentice who is within one year of completion of his or her term of apprenticeship shall be permitted to take the certification examination and, upon passing the examination, shall be certified immediately upon completion of the term of apprenticeship.

(e) Notwithstanding subdivision (a), certification is not required for any person employed pursuant to Section 3099.4.

(f) Notwithstanding subdivision (a), certification is not required for a nonresidential lighting trainee (1) who is enrolled in an on-the-job instructional training program approved by the Chief of the Division of Apprenticeship Standards pursuant to Section 3090, and (2) who is under the onsite supervision of a nonresidential lighting technician certified pursuant to Section 3099.

(g) Notwithstanding subdivision (a), the qualifying person for a class C-10 electrical contractor license issued by the Contractors' State License Board need not also be certified pursuant to Section 3099 to perform electrical work for that licensed contractor or to supervise an uncertified person employed by that licensed contractor pursuant to Section 3099.4.

(h) Commencing July 1, 2009, the following shall constitute additional grounds for disciplinary proceedings, including suspension or revocation of the license of a class C-10 electrical contractor pursuant to Article 7 (commencing with Section 7090) of Chapter 9 of Division 3 of the Business and Professions Code:

(1) The contractor willfully employs one or more uncertified persons to perform work as electricians in violation of this section.

(2) The contractor willfully fails to provide the adequate supervision of uncertified workers required by paragraph (3) of subdivision (a) of Section 3099.4.

(3) The contractor willfully fails to provide adequate supervision of apprentices performing work pursuant to subdivision (d).

(i) The Chief of the Division of Apprenticeship Standards shall develop a process for referring cases to the Contractors' State License

Appendix

Board when it has been determined that a violation of this section has likely occurred. On or before July 1, 2009, the chief shall prepare and execute a memorandum of understanding with the Registrar of Contractors in furtherance of this section.

(j) Upon receipt of a referral by the Chief of the Division of Apprenticeship Standards alleging a violation under this section, the Registrar of Contractors shall open an investigation. Any disciplinary action against the licensee shall be initiated within 60 days of the receipt of the referral. The Registrar of Contractors may initiate disciplinary action against any licensee upon his or her own investigation, the filing of any complaint, or any finding that results from a referral from the Chief of the Division of Apprenticeship Standards alleging a violation under this section. Failure of the employer or employee to provide evidence of certification or trainee status shall create a rebuttable presumption of violation of this provision.

(k) For the purposes of this section, "electricians" has the same meaning as the definition set forth in Section 3099.

Added Stats 2002 ch 48 § 2 (AB 1087). Amended Stats 2003 ch 884 § 2 (AB 1719); Stats 2006 ch 828 § 5 (AB 2907), effective January 1, 2007; Stats 2008 ch 558 § 1 (AB 3048), effective January 1, 2009, ch 716 § 2.5 (SB 1362), effective January 1, 2009; Stats 2011 ch 432 § 36 (SB 944), effective January 1, 2012, ch 693 § 2.5 (AB 1346), effective January 1, 2012.

DIVISION 4

WORKERS' COMPENSATION AND INSURANCE

PART 1

SCOPE AND OPERATION

Chapter 4

Compensation Insurance and Security

Article 4

Construction Permit

§ 3800. Certificate of consent to self–insure or of insurance

(a) Every county or city which requires the issuance of a permit as a condition precedent to the construction, alteration, improvement, demolition, or repair of any building or structure shall require that each applicant for the permit sign a declaration under penalty of perjury verifying workers' compensation coverage or exemption from coverage, as required by Section 19825 of the Health and Safety Code.

(b) At the time of permit issuance, contractors shall show their valid workers' compensation insurance certificate, or the city or county may verify the workers' compensation coverage by electronic means.

Added Stats 1941 ch 1010 § 1. Amended Stats 1945 ch 1431 § 69.5; Stats 1953 ch 552 § 1; Stats 1959 ch 361 § 1; Stats 1963 ch 1140 § 2; Stats 1988 ch 160 § 124. Amended Stats 1994 ch 178 § 2 (AB 443); Stats 1999 ch 982 § 9 (AB 1678).

DIVISION 5

SAFETY IN EMPLOYMENT

PART 1

OCCUPATIONAL SAFETY AND HEALTH

Chapter 6

Permit Requirements

§ 6501.5. Registration of persons doing asbestos–related work

Effective January 1, 1987, any employer or contractor who engages in asbestos–related work, as defined in Section 6501.8, and which involves 100 square feet or more of surface area of asbestos–containing material, shall register with the division.

The division may grant registration based on a determination that the employer has demonstrated evidence that the conditions, practices, means, methods, operations, or processes used, or proposed to be used, will provide a safe and healthful place of employment. This section is not intended to supersede existing laws and regulations under Title 8, California Administrative Code, Section 5208.

An application for registration shall contain such information and attachments, given under penalty of perjury, as the division may deem necessary to evaluate the safety and health of the proposed employment or place of employment. It shall include, but not be limited to, all of the following:

(a) Every employer shall meet each of the following criteria:

(1) If the employer is a contractor, the contractor shall be certified pursuant to Section 7058.5 of the Business and Professions Code.

(2) Provide health insurance coverage to cover the entire cost of medical examinations and monitoring required by law and be insured for workers' compensation, or provide a five hundred dollar ($500) trust account for each employee engaged in asbestos–related work. The health insurance coverage may be provided through a union, association, or employer.

(3) Train and certify all employees in accordance with all training required by law and Title 8 of the California Administrative Code.

(4) Be proficient and have the necessary equipment to safely do asbestos–related work.

(b) Provide written notice to the division of each separate job or phase of work, where the work process used is different or the work is performed at noncontiguous locations, noting all of the following:

(1) The address of the job.

(2) The exact physical location of the job at that address.

(3) The start and projected completion date.

(4) The name of a certified supervisor with sufficient experience and authority who shall be responsible for the asbestos–related work at that job.

(5) The name of a qualified person, who shall be responsible for scheduling any air sampling, laboratory calibration of air sampling equipment, evaluation of sampling results, and conducting respirator fit testing and evaluating the results of those tests.

(6) The type of work to be performed, the work practices that will be utilized, and the potential for exposure.

Should any change be necessary, the employer or contractor shall so inform the division at or before the time of the change. Any oral notification shall be confirmed in writing.

(c) Post the location where any asbestos–related work occurs so as to be readable at 20 feet stating, "Danger—Asbestos. Cancer and Lung Hazard. Keep Out."

(d) A copy of the registration shall be provided before the start of the job to the prime contractor or other employers on the site and shall be posted on the jobsite beside the Cal–OSHA poster.

(e) The division shall obtain the services of three industrial hygienists and one clerical employee to implement and to enforce the requirements of this section unless the director makes a finding that these services are not necessary or that the services are not obtainable due to a lack of qualified hygienists applying for available positions. Funding may, at the director's discretion, be appropriated from the Asbestos Abatement Fund.

(f) Not later than January 1, 1987, the Division of Occupational Safety and Health shall propose to the Occupational Safety and Health Standards Board for review and adoption a regulation concerning asbestos–related work, as defined in Section 6501.8, which involves 100 square feet or more of surface area of asbestos–containing material. The regulation shall protect most effectively the health and safety of employees and shall include specific requirements for certification of employees, supervisors with sufficient experience and authority to be responsible for asbestos–related work, and a qualified person who shall be responsible for scheduling any air sampling, for arranging for calibration of the air sampling equipment and for analysis of the air samples by a NIOSH approved method, for conducting respirator fit testing, and for evaluating the results of the air sampling.

The Division of Occupational Safety and Health shall also propose a regulation to the Occupational Safety and Health Standards Board for review and adoption specifying sampling methodology for use in taking air samples.

Added Stats 1985 ch 1587 § 9, effective October 2, 1985. Amended Stats 1986 ch 1451 § 10, effective September 30, 1986.

§ 6501.7. "Asbestos"

"Asbestos" means fibrous forms of various hydrated minerals, including chrysotile (fibrous serpentine), crocidolite (fibrous riebecktite), amosite (fibrous cummingtonite—grunerite), fibrous tremolite, fibrous actinolite, and fibrous anthophyllite.

Added Stats 1985 ch 1587 § 11, effective October 2, 1985.

§ 6501.8. "Asbestos–related work;" "Asbestos containing construction material"

(a) For purposes of this chapter, "asbestos–related work" means any activity which by disturbing asbestos–containing construction materials may release asbestos fibers into the air and which is not related to its manufacture, the mining or excavation of asbestos–bearing ore or materials, or the installation or repair of automotive materials containing asbestos.

(b) For purposes of this chapter, "asbestos containing construction material" means any manufactured construction material that contains more than one–tenth of 1 percent asbestos by weight.

(c) For purposes of this chapter, "asbestos–related work" does not include the installation, repair, maintenance, or nondestructive removal of asbestos cement pipe used outside of buildings, if the installation, repair, maintenance, or nondestructive removal of asbestos cement pipe does not result in asbestos exposures to employees in excess of the action level determined in accordance with Sections 1529 and 5208 of Title 8 of the California Code of Regulations, and if the employees and supervisors involved in the operation have received training through a task–specific training program, approved pursuant to Section 9021.9, with written certification of completion of that training by the training entity responsible for the training.

Added Stats 1985 ch 1587 § 12, effective October 2, 1985. Amended Stats 1986 ch 1451 § 11, effective September 30, 1986; Stats 1993 ch 1075 § 1 (SB 877).

Appendix

§ 6501.9. Duty to determine presence of asbestos before commencing work

The owner of a commercial or industrial building or structure, employer, or contractor who engages in, or contracts for, asbestos–related work shall make a good faith effort to determine if asbestos is present before the work is begun. The contractor or employer shall first inquire of the owner if asbestos is present in any building or structure built prior to 1978.

Added Stats 1985 ch 1587 § 12.5, effective October 2, 1985. Amended Stats 1986 ch 1451 § 12, effective September 30, 1986.

PENAL CODE

PRELIMINARY PROVISIONS

§ 23. Proceeding against person holding license to engage in business or profession; Appearance of state agency

In any criminal proceeding against a person who has been issued a license to engage in a business or profession by a state agency pursuant to provisions of the Business and Professions Code or the Education Code, or the Chiropractic Initiative Act, the state agency which issued the license may voluntarily appear to furnish pertinent information, make recommendations regarding specific conditions of probation, or provide any other assistance necessary to promote the interests of justice and protect the interests of the public, or may be ordered by the court to do so, if the crime charged is substantially related to the qualifications, functions, or duties of a licensee.

For purposes of this section, the term "license" shall include a permit or a certificate issued by a state agency.

For purposes of this section, the term "state agency" shall include any state board, commission, bureau, or division created pursuant to the provisions of the Business and Professions Code, the Education Code, or the Chiropractic Initiative Act to license and regulate individuals who engage in certain businesses and professions.

Added Stats 1979 ch 1013 § 34. Amended Stats 1989 ch 388 § 6; Stats 2002 ch 545 § 3 (SB 1852).

PART 1

CRIMES AND PUNISHMENTS

TITLE 10
Crimes Against the Public Health and Safety

§ 396. Overpricing of goods and services following state of emergency or major disaster; Penalty; Definitions

(a) The Legislature hereby finds that during emergencies and major disasters, including, but not limited to, earthquakes, fires, floods, or civil disturbances, some merchants have taken unfair advantage of consumers by greatly increasing prices for essential consumer goods and services. While the pricing of consumer goods and services is generally best left to the marketplace under ordinary conditions, when a declared state of emergency results in abnormal disruptions of the market, the public interest requires that excessive and unjustified increases in the prices of essential consumer goods and services be prohibited. It is the intent of the Legislature in enacting this act to protect citizens from excessive and unjustified increases in the prices charged during or shortly after a declared state of emergency for goods and services that are vital and necessary for the health, safety, and welfare of consumers. Further it is the intent of the Legislature that this section be liberally construed so that its beneficial purposes may be served.

(b) Upon the proclamation of a state of emergency resulting from an earthquake, flood, fire, riot, storm, or natural or manmade disaster declared by the President of the United States or the Governor, or upon the declaration of a local emergency resulting from an earthquake, flood, fire, riot, storm, or natural or manmade disaster by the executive officer of any county, city, or city and county, and for a period of 30 days following that declaration, it is unlawful for a person, contractor, business, or other entity to sell or offer to sell any consumer food items or goods, goods or services used for emergency cleanup, emergency supplies, medical supplies, home heating oil, building materials, housing, transportation, freight, and storage services, or gasoline or other motor fuels for a price of more than 10 percent above the price charged by that person for those goods or services immediately prior to the proclamation of emergency. However, a greater price increase is not unlawful if that person can prove that the increase in price was directly attributable to additional costs imposed on it by the supplier of the goods, or directly attributable to additional costs for labor or materials used to provide the services, provided that in those situations where the increase in price is attributable to additional costs imposed by the seller's supplier or additional costs of providing the good or service during the state of emergency, the price represents no more than 10 percent above the total of the cost to the seller plus the markup customarily applied by the seller for that good or service in the usual course of business immediately prior to the onset of the state of emergency.

(c) Upon the proclamation of a state of emergency resulting from an earthquake, flood, fire, riot, or storm declared by the President of the United States or the Governor, or upon the declaration of a local emergency resulting from an earthquake, flood, fire, riot, or storm by the executive officer of any county, city, or city and county, and for a period of 180 days following that declaration, it is unlawful for a contractor to sell or offer to sell any repair or reconstruction services or any services used in emergency cleanup for a price of more than 10 percent above the price charged by that person for those services immediately prior to the proclamation of emergency. However, a greater price increase is not unlawful if that person can prove that the increase in price was directly attributable to additional costs imposed on it by the supplier of the goods, or directly attributable to additional costs for labor or materials used to provide the services, provided that in those situations where the increase in price is attributable to the additional costs imposed by the contractor's supplier or additional costs of providing the service during the state of emergency, the price represents no more than 10 percent above the total of the cost to the contractor plus the markup customarily applied by the contractor for that good or service in the usual course of business immediately prior to the onset of the state of emergency.

(d) Upon the proclamation of a state of emergency resulting from an earthquake, flood, fire, riot, storm, or other natural disaster declared by the President of the United States or the Governor, or upon the declaration of a local emergency resulting from an earthquake, flood, fire, riot, storm, or other natural disaster by the executive officer of any county, city, or city and county, and for a period of 30 days following that proclamation or declaration, it is unlawful for an owner or operator of a hotel or motel to increase the hotel or motel's regular rates, as advertised immediately prior to the proclamation or declaration of emergency, by more than 10 percent. However, a greater price increase is not unlawful if the owner or operator can prove that the increase in price is directly attributable to additional costs imposed on it for goods or labor used in its business, to seasonal adjustments in rates that are regularly scheduled, or to previously contracted rates.

(e) The provisions of this section may be extended for additional 30–day periods by a local legislative body or the California Legislature, if deemed necessary to protect the lives, property, or welfare of the citizens.

(f) A violation of this section is a misdemeanor punishable by imprisonment in a county jail for a period not exceeding one year, or by a fine of not more than ten thousand dollars ($10,000), or by both that fine and imprisonment.

(g) A violation of this section shall constitute an unlawful business practice and an act of unfair competition within the meaning of Section 17200 of the Business and Professions Code. The remedies and penalties provided by this section are cumulative to each other, the remedies under Section 17200 of the Business and Professions Code, and the remedies or penalties available under all other laws of this state.

(h) For the purposes of this section, the following terms have the following meanings:

Appendix

(1) "State of emergency" means a natural or manmade disaster or emergency resulting from an earthquake, flood, fire, riot, or storm for which a state of emergency has been declared by the President of the United States or the Governor of California.

(2) "Local emergency" means a natural or manmade disaster or emergency resulting from an earthquake, flood, fire, riot, or storm for which a local emergency has been declared by the executive officer or governing body of any city or county in California.

(3) "Consumer food item" means any article that is used or intended for use for food, drink, confection, or condiment by a person or animal.

(4) "Repair or reconstruction services" means services performed by any person who is required to be licensed under the Contractors' State License Law (Chapter 9 (commencing with Section 7000) of Division 3 of the Business and Professions Code), for repairs to residential or commercial property of any type that is damaged as a result of a disaster.

(5) "Emergency supplies" includes, but is not limited to, water, flashlights, radios, batteries, candles, blankets, soaps, diapers, temporary shelters, tape, toiletries, plywood, nails, and hammers.

(6) "Medical supplies" includes, but is not limited to, prescription and nonprescription medications, bandages, gauze, isopropyl alcohol, and antibacterial products.

(7) "Building materials" means lumber, construction tools, windows, and anything else used in the building or rebuilding of property.

(8) "Gasoline" means any fuel used to power any motor vehicle or power tool.

(9) "Transportation, freight, and storage services" means any service that is performed by any company that contracts to move, store, or transport personal or business property or rents equipment for those purposes.

(10) "Housing" means any rental housing leased on a month–to–month term.

(11) "Goods" has the same meaning as defined in subdivision (c) of Section 1689.5 of the Civil Code.

(i) Nothing in this section shall preempt any local ordinance prohibiting the same or similar conduct or imposing a more severe penalty for the same conduct prohibited by this section.

(j) A business offering an item for sale at a reduced price immediately prior to the proclamation of the emergency may use the price at which it usually sells the item to calculate the price pursuant to subdivision (b) or (c).

Added Stats 1st Ex Sess 1993–94 ch 52 § 2 (AB 36 X), effective November 30, 1994.
Amended Stats 1995 ch 91 § 123 (SB 975); Stats 2004 ch 492 § 2 (SB 1363).

TITLE 13
Crimes Against Property

Chapter 5
Larceny

Penal Code § 490a, enacted in 1927, provides that whenever any statute refers to larceny, embezzlement, or stealing, it shall be read and interpreted as if the word "theft" were substituted therefor.

§ 484b. Diversion of money received for construction of improvements

Any person who receives money for the purpose of obtaining or paying for services, labor, materials or equipment and willfully fails to apply such money for such purpose by either willfully failing to complete the improvements for which funds were provided or willfully failing to pay for services, labor, materials or equipment provided incident to such construction, and wrongfully diverts the funds to a use other than that for which the funds were received, shall be guilty of a public offense and shall be punishable by a fine not exceeding ten thousand dollars ($10,000), or by imprisonment in a county jail not exceeding one year, or by imprisonment pursuant to subdivision (h) of Section 1170, or by both that fine and that imprisonment if the amount diverted is in excess of two thousand three hundred fifty dollars ($2,350). If the amount diverted is less than or equal to two thousand three hundred fifty dollars ($2,350), the person shall be guilty of a misdemeanor.

Added Stats 1965 ch 1145 § 1. Amended Stats 1974 ch 910 § 1; Stats 1975 ch 464 § 1; Stats 1976 ch 1139 § 219, operative July 1, 1977; Stats 1983 ch 1092 § 286, effective September 27, 1983, operative January 1, 1984; Stats 2009 ch 35 § 9 (SB 174), effective January 1, 2010; Stats 2009–2010 3d Ex Sess ch 28 § 14 (SB 18XXX), effective January 25, 2010; Stats 2011 ch 15 § 367 (AB 109), effective April 4, 2011, operative October 1, 2011.

§ 484c. Submission of false voucher to obtain construction loan

Any person who submits a false voucher to obtain construction loan funds and does not use the funds for the purpose for which the claim was submitted is guilty of embezzlement.

Added Stats 1965 ch 1145 § 2.

Appendix

Chapter 8

False Personation and Cheats

§ 532e. Rebating money furnished for constructing improvements

Any person who receives money for the purpose of obtaining or paying for services, labor, materials or equipment incident to constructing improvements on real property and willfully rebates any part of the money to or on behalf of anyone contracting with such person, for provision of the services, labor, materials or equipment for which the money was given, shall be guilty of a misdemeanor; provided, however, that normal trade discount for prompt payment shall not be considered a violation of this section.

Added Stats 1965 ch 1145 § 3.

Chapter 10

Crimes Against Insured Property and Insurers

§ 551. Referral to automotive repair dealer for consideration; Discounts intended to offset deductible

(a) It is unlawful for any automotive repair dealer, contractor, or employees or agents thereof to offer to any insurance agent, broker, or adjuster any fee, commission, profit sharing, or other form of direct or indirect consideration for referring an insured to an automotive repair dealer or its employees or agents for vehicle repairs covered under a policyholder's automobile physical damage or automobile collision coverage, or to a contractor or its employees or agents for repairs to or replacement of a structure covered by a residential or commercial insurance policy.

(b) Except in cases in which the amount of the repair or replacement claim has been determined by the insurer and the repair or replacement services are performed in accordance with that determination or in accordance with provided estimates that are accepted by the insurer, it is unlawful for any automotive repair dealer, contractor, or employees or agents thereof to knowingly offer or give any discount intended to offset a deductible required by a policy of insurance covering repairs to or replacement of a motor vehicle or residential or commercial structure. This subdivision does not prohibit an advertisement for repair or replacement services at a discount as long as the amount of the repair or replacement claim has been determined by the insurer and the repair or replacement services are performed in accordance with that determination or in accordance with provided estimates that are accepted by the insurer.

(c) A violation of this section is a public offense. Where the amount at issue exceeds nine hundred fifty dollars ($950), the offense is punishable by imprisonment in the state prison for 16 months, or 2 or 3 years, by a fine of not more than ten thousand dollars ($10,000), or by both that imprisonment and fine; or by imprisonment in a county jail not to exceed one year, by a fine of not more than one thousand dollars ($1,000), or by both that imprisonment and fine. In all other cases, the offense is punishable by imprisonment in a county jail not to exceed six months, by a fine of not more than one thousand dollars ($1,000), or by both that imprisonment and fine.

(d) Every person who, having been convicted of subdivision (a) or (b), or Section 7027.3 or former Section 9884.75 of the Business and Professions Code and having served a term therefor in any penal institution or having been imprisoned therein as a condition of probation for that offense, is subsequently convicted of subdivision (a) or (b), upon a subsequent conviction of one of those offenses, shall be punished by imprisonment in the state prison for 16 months, or 2 or 3 years, by a fine of not more than ten thousand dollars ($10,000), or by both that imprisonment and fine; or by imprisonment in a county jail not to exceed one year, by a fine of not more than one thousand dollars ($1,000), or by both that imprisonment and fine.

(e) For purposes of this section:

(1) "Automotive repair dealer" means a person who, for compensation, engages in the business of repairing or diagnosing malfunctions of motor vehicles.

(2) "Contractor" has the same meaning as set forth in Section 7026 of the Business and Professions Code.

Added Stats 1992 ch 675 § 9 (AB 3067). Amended Stats 1993 ch 462 § 1 (AB 438), effective September 25, 1993; Stats 1995 ch 373 § 1 (SB 639); Stats. 2009, Ch. 28 (SBX3 18).

TITLE 16
General Provisions

§ 667.16. Enhanced sentence for fraud in repairing natural disaster damage

(a) Any person convicted of a felony violation of Section 470, 487, or 532 as part of a plan or scheme to defraud an owner of a residential or nonresidential structure, including a mobilehome or manufactured home, in connection with the offer or performance of repairs to the structure for damage caused by a natural disaster, shall receive a one–year enhancement in addition and consecutive to the penalty prescribed. The additional term shall not be imposed unless the allegation is charged in the accusatory pleading and admitted by the defendant or found to be true by the trier of fact.

Appendix

(b) This enhancement applies to natural disasters for which a state of emergency is proclaimed by the Governor pursuant to Section 8625 of the Government Code or for which an emergency or major disaster is declared by the President of the United States.

(c) Notwithstanding any other law, the court may strike the additional term provided in subdivision (a) if the court determines that there are mitigating circumstances and states on the record the reasons for striking the additional punishment.

Added Stats 1994 ch 175 § 5 (SB 634), effective July 9, 1994.

§ 670. Scheme to defraud owner of structure regarding repairs for damage resulting from natural disaster for which state of emergency has been declared; Punishment

(a) Any person who violates Section 7158 or 7159 of, or subdivision (b), (c), (d), or (e) of Section 7161 of, the Business and Professions Code or Section 470, 484, 487, or 532 of this code as part of a plan or scheme to defraud an owner or lessee of a residential or nonresidential structure in connection with the offer or performance of repairs to the structure for damage caused by a natural disaster specified in subdivision (b), shall be subject to the penalties and enhancements specified in subdivisions (c) and (d). The existence of any fact which would bring a person under this section shall be alleged in the information or indictment and either admitted by the defendant in open court, or found to be true by the jury trying the issue of guilt or by the court where guilt is established by a plea of guilty or nolo contendere or by trial by the court sitting without a jury.

(b) This section applies to natural disasters for which a state of emergency is proclaimed by the Governor pursuant to Section 8625 of the Government Code or for which an emergency or major disaster is declared by the President of the United States.

(c) The maximum or prescribed amounts of fines for offenses subject to this section shall be doubled. If the person has been previously convicted of a felony offense specified in subdivision (a), the person shall receive a one–year enhancement in addition to, and to run consecutively to, the term of imprisonment for any felony otherwise prescribed by this subdivision.

(d) Additionally, the court shall order any person sentenced pursuant to this section to make full restitution to the victim or to make restitution to the victim based on the person's ability to pay, as defined in subdivision (b) of Section 1203.1b. The payment of the restitution ordered by the court pursuant to this subdivision shall be made a condition of any probation granted by the court for an offense punishable under this section. Notwithstanding any other provision of law, the period of probation shall be at least five years or until full restitution is made to the victim, whichever first occurs.

(e) Notwithstanding any other provision of law, the prosecuting agency shall be entitled to recover its costs of investigation and prosecution from any fines imposed for a conviction under this section.

Added Stats 1st Ex Sess 1989–90 ch 36 § 4 (AB 9), effective September 22, 1990. Amended Stats 2001 ch 854 § 38 (SB 205).

PART 2

CRIMINAL PROCEDURE

TITLE 3
Additional Provisions Regarding Criminal Procedure

Chapter 4.5

Peace Officers

§ 830.3. Investigators, inspectors, and other employees of specified agencies

The following persons are peace officers whose authority extends to any place in the state for the purpose of performing their primary duty or when making an arrest pursuant to Section 836 as to any public offense with respect to which there is immediate danger to person or property, or of the escape of the perpetrator of that offense, or pursuant to Section 8597 or 8598 of the Government Code. These peace officers may carry firearms only if authorized and under those terms and conditions as specified by their employing agencies:

(a) Persons employed by the Division of Investigation of the Department of Consumer Affairs and investigators of the Medical Board of California and the Board of Dental Examiners, who are designated by the Director of Consumer Affairs, provided that the primary duty of these peace officers shall be the enforcement of the law as that duty is set forth in Section 160 of the Business and Professions Code.

(b) Voluntary fire wardens designated by the Director of Forestry and Fire Protection pursuant to Section 4156 of the Public Resources Code, provided that the primary duty of these peace officers shall be the enforcement of the law as that duty is set forth in Section 4156 of that code.

(c) Employees of the Department of Motor Vehicles designated in Section 1655 of the Vehicle Code, provided that the primary duty of these peace officers shall be the enforcement of the law as that duty is set forth in Section 1655 of that code.

(d) Investigators of the California Horse Racing Board designated by the board, provided that the primary duty of these peace officers shall be the enforcement of Chapter 4 (commencing with Section 19400) of Division 8 of the Business and Professions Code and Chapter 10 (commencing with Section 330) of Title 9 of Part 1 of this code.

(e) The State Fire Marshal and assistant or deputy state fire marshals appointed pursuant to Section 13103 of the Health and Safety Code, provided that the primary duty of these peace officers shall be the enforcement of the law as that duty is set forth in Section 13104 of that code.

(f) Inspectors of the food and drug section designated by the chief pursuant to subdivision (a) of Section 106500 of the Health and Safety Code, provided that the primary duty of these peace officers shall be the enforcement of the law as that duty is set forth in Section 106500 of that code.

(g) All investigators of the Division of Labor Standards Enforcement designated by the Labor Commissioner, provided that the primary duty of these peace officers shall be the enforcement of the law as prescribed in Section 95 of the Labor Code.

(h) All investigators of the State Departments of Health Care Services, Public Health, Social Services, Mental Health, and Alcohol and Drug Programs, the Department of Toxic Substances Control, the Office of Statewide Health Planning and Development, and the Public Employees' Retirement System, provided that the primary duty of these peace officers shall be the enforcement of the law relating to the duties of his or her department or office. Notwithstanding any other provision of law, investigators of the Public Employees' Retirement System shall not carry firearms.

(i) The Chief of the Bureau of Fraudulent Claims of the Department of Insurance and those investigators designated by the chief, provided that the primary duty of those investigators shall be the enforcement of Section 550.

(j) Employees of the Department of Housing and Community Development designated under Section 18023 of the Health and Safety Code, provided that the primary duty of these peace officers shall be the enforcement of the law as that duty is set forth in Section 18023 of that code.

(k) Investigators of the office of the Controller, provided that the primary duty of these investigators shall be the enforcement of the law relating to the duties of that office. Notwithstanding any other law, except as authorized by the Controller, the peace officers designated pursuant to this subdivision shall not carry firearms.

(l) Investigators of the Department of Corporations designated by the Commissioner of Corporations, provided that the primary duty of these investigators shall be the enforcement of the provisions of law administered by the Department of Corporations. Notwithstanding any other provision of law, the peace officers designated pursuant to this subdivision shall not carry firearms.

(m) Persons employed by the Contractors State License Board designated by the Director of Consumer Affairs pursuant to Section 7011.5 of the Business and Professions Code, provided that the primary duty of these persons shall be the enforcement of the law as that duty is set forth in Section 7011.5, and in Chapter 9 (commencing with Section 7000) of Division 3, of that code. The Director of Consumer Affairs may designate as peace officers not more than 12 persons who shall at the time of their designation be assigned to the special investigations unit of the board. Notwithstanding any other provision of law, the persons designated pursuant to this subdivision shall not carry firearms.

(n) The Chief and coordinators of the Law Enforcement Branch of the California Emergency Management Agency.

(o) Investigators of the office of the Secretary of State designated by the Secretary of State, provided that the primary duty of these peace officers shall be the enforcement of the law as prescribed in Chapter 3 (commencing with Section 8200) of Division 1 of Title 2 of, and Section 12172.5 of, the Government Code. Notwithstanding any other provision of law, the peace officers designated pursuant to this subdivision shall not carry firearms.

(p) The Deputy Director for Security designated by Section 8880.38 of the Government Code, and all lottery security personnel assigned to the California State Lottery and designated by the director, provided that the primary duty of any of those peace officers shall be the enforcement of the laws related to assuring the integrity, honesty, and fairness of the operation and administration of the California State Lottery.

(q) Investigators employed by the Investigation Division of the Employment Development Department designated by the director of the department, provided that the primary duty of those peace officers shall be the enforcement of the law as that duty is set forth in Section 317 of the Unemployment Insurance Code.

Notwithstanding any other provision of law, the peace officers designated pursuant to this subdivision shall not carry firearms.

(r) The chief and assistant chief of museum security and safety of the California Science Center, as designated by the executive director pursuant to Section 4108 of the Food and Agricultural Code, provided that the primary duty of those peace officers shall be the enforcement of the law as that duty is set forth in Section 4108 of the Food and Agricultural Code.

(s) Employees of the Franchise Tax Board designated by the board, provided that the primary duty of these peace officers shall be the enforcement of the law as set forth in Chapter 9 (commencing with

Section 19701) of Part 10.2 of Division 2 of the Revenue and Taxation Code.

(t) Notwithstanding any other provision of this section, a peace officer authorized by this section shall not be authorized to carry firearms by his or her employing agency until that agency has adopted a policy on the use of deadly force by those peace officers, and until those peace officers have been instructed in the employing agency's policy on the use of deadly force.

Every peace officer authorized pursuant to this section to carry firearms by his or her employing agency shall qualify in the use of the firearms at least every six months.

(u) Investigators of the Department of Managed Health Care designated by the Director of the Department of Managed Health Care, provided that the primary duty of these investigators shall be the enforcement of the provisions of laws administered by the Director of the Department of Managed Health Care. Notwithstanding any other provision of law, the peace officers designated pursuant to this subdivision shall not carry firearms.

(v) The Chief, Deputy Chief, supervising investigators, and investigators of the Office of Protective Services of the State Department of Developmental Services, provided that the primary duty of each of those persons shall be the enforcement of the law relating to the duties of his or her department or office.

Added Stats 1968 ch 1222 § 1. Amended Stats 1969 ch 1511 § 1; Stats 1970 ch 468 § 2, ch 1454 § 4, ch 1589 § 1, ch 1591 § 1, ch 1592 § 3; Stats 1971 ch 631 § 3, ch 632 § 3, ch 701 § 2, ch 716 § 203, ch 1695 § 1; Stats 1972 ch 618 § 117; Stats 1974 ch 639 § 2, ch 1403 § 12; Stats 1975 2d Ex Sess ch 2 § 10.5, effective September 24, 1975, operative December 12, 1975; Stats 1976 ch 42 § 1, ch 1435 § 3; Stats 1977 ch 220 § 2; Stats 1978 ch 429 § 157.5, effective July 17, 1978, operative July 1, 1978, ch 1138 § 1; Stats 1979 ch 573 § 3; Stats 1980 ch 10 § 2, effective February 12, 1980, ch 1340 § 7, effective September 30, 1980; Stats 1981 ch 973 § 1, ch 975 § 22; Stats 1982 ch 548 § 2.5, effective August 24, 1982, ch 1277 § 4; Stats 1984 ch 57 § 1, effective March 28, 1984, ch 940 § 1; Stats 1985 ch 1241 § 1, effective September 30, 1985; Stats 1986 ch 898 § 2; Stats 1988 ch 685 § 1, ch 1552 § 2; Stats 1989 ch 886 § 101 (ch 1166 prevails), ch 1165 § 22 (ch 1166 prevails), ch 1166 § 3; Stats 1990 ch 82 § 8 (SB 655), effective May 2, 1990; Stats 1991 ch 877 § 2 (AB 1196), ch 910 § 5 (SB 249); Stats 1993 ch 409 § 2 (AB 2308), effective September 16, 1993; Stats 1996 ch 841 § 16 (AB 3220) (ch 841 prevails), ch 1023 § 390 (SB 1497), effective September 29, 1996; Stats 1997 ch 670 § 1.5 (SB 951), ch 704 § 7 (SB 826); Stats 1998 ch 485 § 132 (AB 2803); Stats 1999 ch 525 § 191 (AB 78), ch 840 § 2 (AB 900), effective October 10, 1999; Stats 2000 ch 857 § 78 (AB 2903); Stats 2003 ch 788 § 80 (SB 362); Stats 2006 ch 74 § 46 (AB 1807), effective July 12, 2006; Stats 2007 ch 483 § 41 (SB 1039), effective January 1, 2008; Stats 2010 ch 618 § 192 (AB 2791), effective January 1, 2011, ch 643 § 2 (SB 1254), effective January 1, 2011.

PUBLIC CONTRACT CODE

DIVISION 2
GENERAL PROVISIONS

PART 1
ADMINISTRATIVE PROVISIONS

Chapter 4
Subletting and Subcontracting

§ 4100. Citation of chapter

This chapter may be cited as the "Subletting and Subcontracting Fair Practices Act."

Added Stats 1986 ch 195 § 42.1.

§ 4101. Bid shopping and bid peddling

The Legislature finds that the practices of bid shopping and bid peddling in connection with the construction, alteration, and repair of public improvements often result in poor quality of material and workmanship to the detriment of the public, deprive the public of the full benefits of fair competition among prime contractors and subcontractors, and lead to insolvencies, loss of wages to employees, and other evils.

Added Stats 1986 ch 195 § 42.1.

§ 4103. Rights and remedies not diminished

Nothing in this chapter limits or diminishes any rights or remedies, either legal or equitable, which:

(a) An original or substituted subcontractor may have against the prime contractor, his or her successors or assigns.

(b) The state or any county, city, body politic, or public agency may have against the prime contractor, his or her successors or assigns, including the right to take over and complete the contract.

Added Stats 1986 ch 195 § 42.1.

Appendix

§ 4104. Listing of subcontractors in bid or offer

Any officer, department, board or commission taking bids for the construction of any public work or improvement shall provide in the specifications prepared for the work or improvement or in the general conditions under which bids will be received for the doing of the work incident to the public work or improvement that any person making a bid or offer to perform the work, shall, in his or her bid or offer, set forth:

(a)(1) The name and the location of the place of business of each subcontractor who will perform work or labor or render service to the prime contractor in or about the construction of the work or improvement, or a subcontractor licensed by the State of California who, under subcontract to the prime contractor, specially fabricates and installs a portion of the work or improvement according to detailed drawings contained in the plans and specifications, in an amount in excess of one–half of 1 percent of the prime contractor's total bid or, in the case of bids or offers for the construction of streets or highways, including bridges, in excess of one–half of 1 percent of the prime contractor's total bid or ten thousand dollars ($10,000), whichever is greater.

(2)(A) Subject to subparagraph (B), any information requested by the officer, department, board, or commission concerning any subcontractor who the prime contractor is required to list under this subdivision, other than the subcontractor's name and location of business, may be submitted by the prime contractor up to 24 hours after the deadline established by the officer, department, board, or commission for receipt of bids by prime contractors.

(B) A state or local agency may implement subparagraph (A) at its option.

(b) The portion of the work that will be done by each subcontractor under this act. The prime contractor shall list only one subcontractor for each portion as is defined by the prime contractor in his or her bid.

Added Stats 1986 ch 195 § 42.1. Amended Stats 1988 ch 1578 § 3. Amended Stats 1998 ch 1010 § 1 (AB 1092).

§ 4104.5. Date and time for closing of bids

(a) The officer, department, board, or commission taking bids for construction of any public work or improvement shall specify in the bid invitation and public notice the place the bids of the prime contractors are to be received and the time by which they shall be received. The date and time shall be extended by no less than 72 hours if the officer, department, board, or commission issues any material changes, additions, or deletions to the invitation later than 72 hours prior to the bid closing. Any bids received after the time specified in the notice or any extension due to material changes shall be returned unopened.

(b) As used in this section, the term "material change" means a change with a substantial cost impact on the total bid as determined by the awarding agency.

(c) As used in this section, the term "bid invitation" shall include any documents issued to prime contractors that contain descriptions of the work to be bid or the content, form, or manner of submission of bids by bidders.

Added Stats 1998 ch 1010 § 2 (AB 1092). Amended Stats 2002 ch 204 § 1 (SB 937).

§ 4105. Circumvention of subcontractor listing requirement

Circumvention by a general contractor who bids as a prime contractor of the requirement under Section 4104 for him or her to list his or her subcontractors, by the device of listing another contractor who will in turn sublet portions constituting the majority of the work covered by the prime contract, shall be considered a violation of this chapter and shall subject that prime contractor to the penalties set forth in Sections 4110 and 4111.

Added Stats 1986 ch 195 § 42.1.

§ 4106. Failure to specify subcontractor

If a prime contractor fails to specify a subcontractor or if a prime contractor specifies more than one subcontractor for the same portion of work to be performed under the contract in excess of one–half of 1 percent of the prime contractor's total bid, the prime contractor agrees that he or she is fully qualified to perform that portion himself or herself, and that the prime contractor shall perform that portion himself or herself.

If after award of contract, the prime contractor subcontracts, except as provided for in Sections 4107 or 4109, any such portion of the work, the prime contractor shall be subject to the penalties named in Section 4111.

Added Stats 1986 ch 195 § 42.1.

§ 4107. Substitution, assignment, and subletting; Notice and hearing

A prime contractor whose bid is accepted may not:

(a) Substitute a person as subcontractor in place of the subcontractor listed in the original bid, except that the awarding authority, or its duly authorized officer, may, except as otherwise provided in Section 4107.5, consent to the substitution of another person as a subcontractor in any of the following situations:

(1) When the subcontractor listed in the bid, after having had a reasonable opportunity to do so, fails or refuses to execute a written con-

tract for the scope of work specified in the subcontractor's bid and at the price specified in the subcontractor's bid, when that written contract, based upon the general terms, conditions, plans, and specifications for the project involved or the terms of that subcontractor's written bid, is presented to the subcontractor by the prime contractor.

(2) When the listed subcontractor becomes insolvent or the subject of an order for relief in bankruptcy.

(3) When the listed subcontractor fails or refuses to perform his or her subcontract.

(4) When the listed subcontractor fails or refuses to meet the bond requirements of the prime contractor as set forth in Section 4108.

(5) When the prime contractor demonstrates to the awarding authority, or its duly authorized officer, subject to the further provisions set forth in Section 4107.5, that the name of the subcontractor was listed as the result of an inadvertent clerical error.

(6) When the listed subcontractor is not licensed pursuant to the Contractors License Law.

(7) When the awarding authority, or its duly authorized officer, determines that the work performed by the listed subcontractor is substantially unsatisfactory and not in substantial accordance with the plans and specifications, or that the subcontractor is substantially delaying or disrupting the progress of the work.

(8) When the listed subcontractor is ineligible to work on a public works project pursuant to Section 1777.1 or 1777.7 of the Labor Code.

(9) When the awarding authority determines that a listed subcontractor is not a responsible contractor.

Prior to approval of the prime contractor's request for the substitution, the awarding authority, or its duly authorized officer, shall give notice in writing to the listed subcontractor of the prime contractor's request to substitute and of the reasons for the request. The notice shall be served by certified or registered mail to the last known address of the subcontractor. The listed subcontractor who has been so notified has five working days within which to submit written objections to the substitution to the awarding authority. Failure to file these written objections constitutes the listed subcontractor's consent to the substitution.

If written objections are filed, the awarding authority shall give notice in writing of at least five working days to the listed subcontractor of a hearing by the awarding authority on the prime contractor's request for substitution.

(b) Permit a subcontract to be voluntarily assigned or transferred or allow it to be performed by anyone other than the original subcontractor listed in the original bid, without the consent of the awarding authority, or its duly authorized officer.

(c) Other than in the performance of "change orders" causing changes or deviations from the original contract, sublet or subcontract any portion of the work in excess of one-half of 1 percent of the prime contractor's total bid as to which his or her original bid did not designate a subcontractor.

Added Stats 1986 ch 195 § 42.1. Amended Stats 1998 ch 443 § 2 (AB 1569); Stats 1999 ch 972 § 3 (AB 574); Stats 2003 ch 180 § 1 (AB 902); Stats 2009 Ch. 500 (AB 1059).

§ 4107.2. Subcontracting by carpeting subcontractor

No subcontractor listed by a prime contractor under Section 4104 as furnishing and installing carpeting, shall voluntarily sublet his or her subcontract with respect to any portion of the labor to be performed unless he or she specified the subcontractor in his or her bid for that subcontract to the prime contractor.

Added Stats 1986 ch 195 § 42.1.

§ 4107.5. Clerical errors in listing of subcontractors; Procedure for substitution

The prime contractor as a condition to assert a claim of inadvertent clerical error in the listing of a subcontractor shall within two working days after the time of the prime bid opening by the awarding authority give written notice to the awarding authority and copies of that notice to both the subcontractor he or she claims to have listed in error and the intended subcontractor who had bid to the prime contractor prior to bid opening.

Any listed subcontractor who has been notified by the prime contractor in accordance with this section as to an inadvertent clerical error shall be allowed six working days from the time of the prime bid opening within which to submit to the awarding authority and to the prime contractor written objection to the prime contractor's claim of inadvertent clerical error. Failure of the listed subcontractor to file the written notice within the six working days shall be primary evidence of his or her agreement that an inadvertent clerical error was made.

The awarding authority shall, after a public hearing as provided in Section 4107 and in the absence of compelling reasons to the contrary, consent to the substitution of the intended subcontractor:

(a) If (1) the prime contractor, (2) the subcontractor listed in error, and (3) the intended subcontractor each submit an affidavit to the awarding authority along with such additional evidence as the parties may wish to submit that an inadvertent clerical error was in fact made, provided that the affidavits from each of the three parties are filed within eight working days from the time of the prime bid opening, or

(b) If the affidavits are filed by both the prime contractor and the intended subcontractor within the specified time but the subcontractor whom the prime contractor claims to have listed in error does not submit within six working days, to the awarding authority and to the prime contractor, written objection to the prime contractor's claim of inadvertent clerical error as provided in this section.

If the affidavits are filed by both the prime contractor and the intended subcontractor but the listed subcontractor has, within six working days from the time of the prime bid opening, submitted to the awarding authority and to the prime contractor written objection to the prime contractor's claim of inadvertent clerical error, the awarding authority shall investigate the claims of the parties and shall hold a public hearing as provided in Section 4107 to determine the validity of those claims. Any determination made shall be based on the facts contained in the declarations submitted under penalty of perjury by all three parties and supported by testimony under oath and subject to cross–examination. The awarding authority may, on its own motion or that of any other party, admit testimony of other contractors, any bid registries or depositories, or any other party in possession of facts which may have a bearing on the decision of the awarding authority.

Added Stats 1986 ch 195 § 42.1.

§ 4107.7. Failure to pay hazardous waste hauler (First of two; Operative until July 1, 2012)

If a contractor who enters into a contract with a public entity for investigation, removal or remedial action, or disposal relative to the release or presence of a hazardous material or hazardous waste fails to pay a subcontractor registered as a hazardous waste hauler pursuant to Section 25163 of the Health and Safety Code within 10 days after the investigation, removal or remedial action, or disposal is completed, the subcontractor may serve a stop notice upon the public entity in accordance with Chapter 4 (commencing with Section 3179) of Title 15 of Part 4 of Division 3 of the Civil Code.

Added Stats 1987 ch 746 § 2.

§ 4107.7. Failure to pay hazardous waste hauler (Second of two; Operative July 1, 2012)

If a contractor who enters into a contract with a public entity for investigation, removal or remedial action, or disposal relative to the release or presence of a hazardous material or hazardous waste fails to pay a subcontractor registered as a hazardous waste hauler pursuant to Section 25163 of the Health and Safety Code within 10 days after the investigation, removal or remedial action, or disposal is completed, the subcontractor may serve a stop notice upon the public entity in accordance with Chapter 4 (commencing with Section 9350) of Title 3 of Part 6 of Division 4 of the Civil Code.

Added Stats 1987 ch 746 § 2. Amended Stats 2010 ch 697 § 43 (SB 189), effective January 1, 2011, operative July 1, 2012.

§ 4108. Bonds

(a) It shall be the responsibility of each subcontractor submitting bids to a prime contractor to be prepared to submit a faithful performance and payment bond or bonds if so requested by the prime contractor.

(b) In the event any subcontractor submitting a bid to a prime contractor does not, upon the request of the prime contractor and at the expense of the prime contractor at the established charge or premium therefor, furnish to the prime contractor a bond or bonds issued by an admitted surety wherein the prime contractor shall be named the obligee, guaranteeing prompt and faithful performance of the subcontract and the payment of all claims for labor and materials furnished or used in and about the work to be done and performed under the subcontract, the prime contractor may reject the bid and make a substitution of another subcontractor subject to Section 4107.

(c)(1) The bond or bonds may be required under this section only if the prime contractor in his or her written or published request for subbids clearly specifies the amount and requirements of the bond or bonds.

(2) If the expense of the bond or bonds required under this section is to be borne by the subcontractor, that requirement shall also be specified in the prime contractor's written or published request for subbids.

(3) The prime contractor's failure to specify bond requirements, in accordance with this subdivision, in the written or published request for subbids shall preclude the prime contractor from imposing bond requirements under this section.

Added Stats 1986 ch 195 § 42.1. Amended Stats 1991 ch 754 § 1 (SB 580).

§ 4109. Subletting or subcontracting in cases of public emergency or necessity

Subletting or subcontracting of any portion of the work in excess of one–half of 1 percent of the prime contractor's total bid as to which no subcontractor was designated in the original bid shall only be permitted in cases of public emergency or necessity, and then only after a finding reduced to writing as a public record of the awarding authority setting forth the facts constituting the emergency or necessity.

Added Stats 1986 ch 195 § 42.1.

§ 4110. Options of awarding authority upon violation of chapter

A prime contractor violating any of the provisions of this chapter violates his or her contract and the awarding authority may exercise the option, in its own discretion, of (1) canceling his or her contract or (2) assessing the prime contractor a penalty in an amount of not more than 10 percent of the amount of the subcontract involved, and this penalty shall be deposited in the fund out of which the prime contract is awarded. In any proceedings under this section the prime contractor shall be entitled to a public hearing and to five days' notice of the time and place thereof.

Added Stats 1986 ch 195 § 42.1.

§ 4111. Disciplinary action by Contractors State License Board

Violation of this chapter by a licensee under Chapter 9 (commencing with Section 7000) of Division 3 of the Business and Professions Code constitutes grounds for disciplinary action by the Contractors State License Board, in addition to the penalties prescribed in Section 4110.

Added Stats 1986 ch 195 § 42.1.

§ 4112. Noncompliance by contractor on defense in action by subcontractor

The failure on the part of a contractor to comply with any provision of this chapter does not constitute a defense to the contractor in any action brought against the contractor by a subcontractor.

Added Stats 1986 ch 195 § 42.1.

§ 4113. "Subcontractor"; "Prime contractor"

As used in this chapter, the word "subcontractor" shall mean a contractor, within the meaning of the provisions of Chapter 9 (commencing with Section 7000) of Division 3 of the Business and Professions Code, who contracts directly with the prime contractor.

"Prime contractor" shall mean the contractor who contracts directly with the awarding authority.

Added Stats 1986 ch 195 § 42.1.

§ 4114. Delegation of functions by board of supervisors

The county board of supervisors, when it is the awarding authority, may delegate its functions under Sections 4107 and 4110 to any officer designated by the board.

The authorized officer shall make a written recommendation to the board of supervisors. The board of supervisors may adopt the recommendation without further notice or hearing, or may set the matter for a de novo hearing before the board.

Added Stats 1986 ch 195 § 42.1. Amended Stats 1989 ch 43 § 1.

Chapter 6

Awarding of Contracts

§ 6100. Verification of contractor's license

(a) Any state agency or department, as defined in Section 10357, which is subject to this code, shall, prior to awarding a contract for work to be performed by a contractor, as defined by Section 7026 of the Business and Professions Code, verify with the Contractors' State License Board that the person seeking the contract is licensed in a classification appropriate to the work to be undertaken. Verification as required by this section need only be made once every two years with respect to the same contractor.

(b) In lieu of the verification, the state entity may require the person seeking the contract to present his or her pocket license or certificate of licensure and provide a signed statement which swears, under penalty of perjury, that the pocket license or certificate of licensure presented is his or hers, is current and valid, and is in a classification appropriate to the work to be undertaken.

Added Stats 1986 ch 1230 § 2.

Chapter 7

Contract Clauses

§ 7106. Form of required declaration

Every bid on every public works contract of a public entity shall include a declaration under penalty of perjury under the laws of the State of California, in the following form:
"NONCOLLUSION DECLARATION TO BE EXECUTED BY BIDDER AND SUBMITTED WITH BID

The undersigned declares:

I am the _____ of

_____ , the party making the foregoing bid.

The bid is not made in the interest of, or on behalf of, any undisclosed person, partnership, company, association, organization, or corporation. The bid is genuine and not collusive or sham. The bidder has not directly or indirectly induced or solicited any other bidder to put in a false or sham bid. The bidder has not directly or indirectly colluded, conspired, connived, or agreed with any bidder or anyone else to put in a sham bid, or to refrain from bidding. The bidder has not in any manner, directly or indirectly, sought by agreement, communication, or conference with anyone to fix the bid price of the bidder or any other bidder, or to fix any overhead, profit, or cost element of the bid price, or of that of any other bidder. All statements contained in the bid are true. The bidder has not, directly or indirectly, submitted his or her bid price or any breakdown thereof, or the contents thereof, or divulged information or data relative thereto, to any corporation, partnership, company association, organization, bid depository, or to any member or agent thereof to effectuate a collusive or sham bid, and has not paid, and will not pay, any person or entity for such purpose.

Any person executing this declaration on behalf of a bidder that is a corporation, partnership, joint venture, limited liability company, limited liability partnership, or any other entity, hereby represents that he or she has full power to execute, and does execute, this declaration on behalf of the bidder.

I declare under penalty of perjury under the laws of the State of California that the foregoing is true and correct and that this declaration is executed on _____ [date], at _____ [city], _____ [state]."

Added Stats 1988 ch 1548 § 1. Amended Stats 2011 ch 432 § 37 (SB 944), effective January 1, 2012.

PART 2

CONTRACTING BY STATE AGENCIES

Chapter 1

State Contract Act

Article 1

Scope of Chapter and General Provisions

§ 10111.2. Providing electronic copy of project's contract documents to contractor plan room

A department shall, upon request from a contractor plan room service, provide an electronic copy of a project's contract documents at no charge to the contractor plan room.

Added Stats 2010 ch 371 § 1 (AB 2036), effective January 1, 2011.

Article 4

Bids and Bidders

§ 10164. State licensing requirements where project involves federal funds

In all state projects where federal funds are involved, no bid submitted shall be invalidated by the failure of the bidder to be licensed in accordance with the laws of this state. However, at the time the contract is awarded, the contractor shall be properly licensed in accordance with the laws of this state. The contract shall not be awarded unless the state agency has verified that the contractor has a valid license in the appropriate classification for the work performed. Any bidder or contractor not so licensed shall be subject to all legal penalties imposed by law, including, but not limited to, any appropriate disciplinary action by the Contractors State License Board. The department shall include a statement to that effect in the standard form of prequalification questionnaire and financial statement. Failure of the bidder to obtain proper and adequate licensing for an award of a contract shall constitute a failure to execute the contract as provided in Section 10181 and shall result in the forfeiture of the security of the bidder.

Enacted Stats 1981 ch 306 § 2. Amended Stats 1983 ch 810 § 1; Stats 1994 ch 432 § 1 (AB 3365).

Article 8

Modifications; Performance; Payment

§ 10262. Payment to subcontractors

The contractor shall pay to his or her subcontractors, within seven days of receipt of each progress payment, the respective amounts allowed the contractor on account of the work performed by his or her subcontractors, to the extent of each subcontractor's interest therein. The payments to subcontractors shall be based on estimates made pursuant to Section 10261. Any diversion by the contractor of payments received for prosecution of a contract, or failure to reasonably account for the application or use of the payments constitutes ground for actions prescribed in Section 10253, in addition to disciplinary action by the Contractors' State License Board. The subcontractor shall notify, in writing, the Contractors' State License Board and the department of any payment less than the amount or percentage approved for the class or item of work as set forth in Section 10261.

Enacted Stats 1981 ch 306 § 2. Amended Stats 1998 ch 857 § 10 (AB 2084); Stats 2011 ch 700 § 8 (SB 293), effective January 1, 2012.

Chapter 2

State Acquisition of Goods and Services

Article 2

Approval of Contracts

§ 10295.4. State agency contracts with contractors appearing on tax delinquency list prohibited; Application

(a) Notwithstanding any other law, a state agency shall not enter into any contract for the acquisition of goods or services with a contractor whose name appears on either list of the 500 largest tax delinquencies pursuant to Section 7063 or 19195 of the Revenue and Taxation Code. Any contract entered into in violation of this subdivision is void and unenforceable.

(b) This section shall apply to any contract executed on or after July 1, 2012.

Added Stats 2011 ch 455 § 5 (AB 1424), effective January 1, 2012.

PART 3

CONTRACTING BY LOCAL AGENCIES

Chapter 1

Local Agency Public Construction Act

Article 1

Title

§ 20103.5. Effect of license requirement on bid

In all contracts subject to this part where federal funds are involved, no bid submitted shall be invalidated by the failure of the bidder to be licensed in accordance with the laws of this state. However, at the time the contract is awarded, the contractor shall be properly licensed in accordance with the laws of this state. The first payment for work or material under any contract shall not be made unless and until the Registrar of Contractors verifies to the agency that the records of the Contractors' State License Board indicate that the contractor was properly licensed at the time the contract was awarded. Any bidder or contractor not so licensed shall be subject to all legal penalties imposed by law, including, but not limited to, any appropriate disciplinary action by the Contractors' State License Board. The agency shall include a statement to that effect in the standard form of prequalification questionnaire and financial statement. Failure of the bidder to obtain proper and adequate licensing for an award of a contract shall constitute a failure to execute the contract and shall result in the forfeiture of the security of the bidder.

Added Stats 1990 ch 321 § 2 (SB 929) as § 20104, effective July 16, 1990. Renumbered § 20103.5 by Stats 1990 ch 1414 § 1 (AB 4165).

§ 20103.7. Providing electronic copy of project's contract documents to contractor plan room

A local agency subject to this chapter taking bids for the construction of a public work or improvement shall, upon request from a contractor plan room service, provide an electronic copy of a project's contract documents at no charge to the contractor plan room.

Added Stats 2010 ch 371 § 2 (AB 2036), effective January 1, 2011.

PUBLIC RESOURCES CODE

Division 15

Energy Conservation and Development

Chapter 5

Energy Resources Conservation

§ 25402.11. Establishment of administrative enforcement process for violation of a regulation and assessment of administrative civil penalty; Considerations; Orders; Cost; Exceptions

(a) (1) The commission may adopt regulations establishing an administrative enforcement process for a violation of a regulation adopted pursuant to subdivision (c) of Section 25402 and for the assessment of an administrative civil penalty not to exceed two thousand five hundred dollars ($2,500) for each violation. The process shall comply with the requirements of Chapter 4 (commencing with Section 11400) and Chapter 4.5 (commencing with Section 11500) of Part 1 of Division 3 of Title 2 of the Government Code.

(2) In assessing the amount of an administrative penalty, the commission shall consider all of the following factors:

(A) The nature and seriousness of the violation.

(B) The number of violations.

(C) The persistence of the violation.

(D) The length of time over which the violation occurred.

(E) The willfulness of the violation.

(F) The violator's assets, liabilities, and net worth.

(G) The harm to consumers and to the state that resulted from the amount of energy wasted due to the violation.

(b) If the commission finds that a violation of the regulations adopted pursuant to subdivision (c) of Section 25402 has occurred or is threatening to occur, the commission may refer the matter to the Attorney General to petition a court to enjoin the violation. The court may grant prohibitory or mandatory injunctive relief as warranted by issuing a temporary restraining order, preliminary injunction, or permanent injunction, and may assess a civil penalty not to exceed two thousand five hundred dollars ($2,500) for each violation, considering the factors specified in paragraph (2) of subdivision (a).

(c) Penalties collected pursuant to this section shall be deposited into the Appliance Efficiency Enforcement Subaccount, which is hereby established in the Energy Resources Program Account. The moneys in the Appliance Efficiency Enforcement Subaccount may be expended by the commission, upon appropriation by the Legislature, for the education of the public regarding appliance energy efficiency and for the enforcement of the regulations adopted pursuant to subdivision (c) of Section 25402.

(d) An order imposing an administrative civil penalty shall be subject to judicial review pursuant to subdivisions (a) and (b) of Section 25534.2.

(e) A person shall not be liable for a civil penalty pursuant to subdivision (b) if that person is subject to an administrative civil penalty pursuant to subdivision (a).

(f) In a civil action brought on behalf of the commission pursuant to this section, upon granting relief, the court shall award to the commission the reasonable costs incurred by the commission in investigating and prosecuting the action.

(g) The commission shall not initiate an administrative enforcement process pursuant to the regulations adopted pursuant to this section against an entity for the unlawful sale or the unlawful offer for sale of an appliance if both of the following apply:

(1) The appliance fully complies with all of the requirements of the regulations adopted pursuant to subdivision (c) of Section 25402.

(2) The only basis for the commission's potential enforcement action is that the appliance is not considered to be in compliance because of the commission's delay in reviewing and processing information submitted to it that demonstrates full compliance.

(h) In addition to the prohibitions specified in subdivision (g), the commission shall not initiate an administrative enforcement process pursuant to the regulations adopted pursuant to this section for a violation of a standard adopted pursuant to subdivision (c) of Section 25402 until both of the following occur:

(1) No fewer than 60 days have elapsed since the date when the standard was published in the California Register.

(2) No fewer than 30 days have elapsed since the date when the alleged violator received written notice of the alleged violation and date when the commission provided public notice of the standard.

Added Stats 2011 ch 591 § 3 (SB 454), effective January 1, 2012.

Appendix

Chapter 10

Enforcement and Judicial Review

§ 25900. Injunctive relief

Except as provided in Sections 25402.11 and 25531, if the commission finds that any provision of this division is violated, or a violation is threatening to take place that constitutes an emergency requiring immediate action to protect the public health, welfare, or safety, the Attorney General, upon request of the commission, shall petition a court to enjoin the violation. The court may grant prohibitory or mandatory injunctive relief as warranted by way of temporary restraining order, preliminary injunction, and permanent injunction.

Added Stats 1974 ch 276 § 2, operative January 7, 1975. Amended Stats 2011 ch 591 § 4 (SB 454), effective January 1, 2012.

PUBLIC UTILITIES CODE

Division 1

Regulation of Public Utilities

PART 1

PUBLIC UTILITIES ACT

Chapter 2.3

Electrical Restructuring

Article 16

California Renewables Portfolio Standard Program

§ 399.4. Policy and intent to administer cost-effective energy efficiency programs; Rebates or incentives for an energy efficiency improvement or installation; Evaluation of investments

(a) (1) In order to ensure that prudent investments in energy efficiency continue to be made that produce cost-effective energy savings, reduce customer demand, and contribute to the safe and reliable operation of the electric distribution grid, it is the policy of this state and the intent of the Legislature that the commission shall continue to administer cost-effective energy efficiency programs authorized pursuant to existing statutory authority.

(2) As used in this section, the term "energy efficiency" includes, but is not limited to, cost-effective activities to achieve peak load reduction that improve end-use efficiency, lower customers' bills, and reduce system needs.

(b) (1) Any rebates or incentives offered by a public utility for an energy efficiency improvement or installation of energy efficient components, equipment, or appliances in buildings shall be provided only if the recipient of the rebate or incentive certifies that the improvement or installation has complied with any applicable permitting requirements and, if a contractor performed the installation or improvement, that the contractor holds the appropriate license for the work performed.

(2) This subdivision does not imply or create authority or responsibility, or expand existing authority or responsibility, of a public utility for the enforcement of the building energy and water efficiency standards adopted pursuant to subdivision (a) or (b) of Section 25402 of the Public Resources Code, or appliance efficiency standards and certification requirements adopted pursuant to subdivision (c) of Section 25402 of the Public Resources Code.

(c) The commission, in evaluating energy efficiency investments under its existing statutory authority, shall also ensure that local and regional interests, multifamily dwellings, and energy service industry capabilities are incorporated into program portfolio design and that local governments, community-based organizations, and energy efficiency service providers are encouraged to participate in program implementation where appropriate.

Added Stats 2000 ch 1050 § 4 (SB 1194). Amended Stats 2006 ch 512 § 28 (SB 1250), effective September 27, 2006; Stats 2011 ch 591 § 5 (SB 454), effective January 1, 2012.

REVENUE AND TAXATION CODE

Division 2

Other Taxes

PART 1

SALES AND USE TAXES

Chapter 2

The Sales Tax

Article 2

Permits

§ 6070.5. Failure to resolve outstanding liabilities or to comply with terms of installment payment agreement as grounds for refusal to issue or revoke a seller's permit; Notice; Reconsideration

(a) The board may refuse to issue a permit to any person submitting an application for a permit as required in Section 6066 if the person desiring to engage in or conduct business as a seller within this state has an outstanding final liability with the board for any amount due under this part.

(b) In addition to the provisions of subdivision (a), the board may also refuse to issue a permit if the person desiring to engage in or conduct business as a seller within this state is not a natural person or individual and any person controlling the person desiring to engage in or conduct business as a seller within this state has an outstanding final liability with the board as provided in subdivision (a). For the purposes of this section, "controlling" has the same meaning as defined in Section 22971 of the Business and Professions Code.

(c) For purposes of this section, a liability will not be deemed to be outstanding if the person has entered into an installment payment agreement pursuant to Section 6832 for any liability and is in full compliance with the terms of the installment payment agreement.

(d) If the person submitting an application for a seller's permit has entered into an installment payment agreement as provided in subdivision (c) and fails to comply with the terms of the installment payment agreement, the board may seek revocation of the seller's permit obtained by the person pursuant to this section.

(e) (1) Whenever any person desiring to engage in or conduct business as a seller within this state is denied a permit pursuant to this section, the board shall give to the person written notice of the denial. The notice of the denial may be served personally, by mail, or by other means deemed appropriate by the board. If served by mail, the notice shall be placed in a sealed envelope, with postage paid, addressed to the person at the address as it appears in the records of the board. The giving of notice shall be deemed complete at the time of deposit of the notice at the United States Postal Service, or a mailbox, subpost office, substation or mail chute, or other facility regularly maintained or provided by the United States Postal Service, without extension of time for any reason. In lieu of mailing, a notice may be served personally by delivering to the person to be served and service shall be deemed complete at the time of the delivery. Delivery of notice by other means deemed appropriate by the board may include, but is not limited to, electronic transmission. Personal service or delivery by other means deemed appropriate by the board to a corporation may be made by delivery of a notice to any person listed on the application as an officer.

(2) Any person who is denied a seller's permit pursuant to this section may request reconsideration of the board's denial of the permit. This request shall be submitted in writing within 30 days of the date of the notice of denial. Timely submission of a written request for reconsideration shall afford the person a hearing in a manner that is consistent with a hearing provided for by Section 6070. If a request for reconsideration is not filed within the 30-day period, the denial becomes final at the end of the 30-day period.

(f) The board shall consider offers in compromise when determining whether to issue a seller's permit.

Added Stats 2011 ch 734 § 2 (AB 1307), effective January 1, 2012.

UNEMPLOYMENT INSURANCE CODE

DIVISION 1

UNEMPLOYMENT AND DISABILITY COMPENSATION

PART 1

UNEMPLOYMENT COMPENSATION

Chapter 2

Administration

Article 1

Employment Development Department

§ 329. Chairperson of Joint Enforcement Strike Force on Underground Economy; Duties of strike force; Membership of strike force; Reporting

(a) The director, or his or her designee, shall serve as Chairperson of the Joint Enforcement Strike Force on the Underground Economy provided for in Executive Order W–66–93. The strike force shall include, but not be limited to, representatives of the Employment Development Department, the Department of Consumer Affairs, the Department of Industrial Relations, the Department of Insurance, and the Office of Criminal Justice Planning. Other agencies that are not part of the administration, such as the Franchise Tax Board, the State Board of Equalization, and the Department of Justice, are encouraged to participate in the strike force.

(b) The strike force shall have the following duties:

(1) To facilitate and encourage the development and sharing of information by the participating agencies necessary to combat the underground economy.

(2) To improve the coordination of activities among the participating agencies.

(3) To develop methods to pool, focus, and target the enforcement resources of the participating agencies in order to deter tax evasion and maximize recoveries from blatant tax evaders and violators of cash–pay reporting laws.

Appendix

(4) To reduce enforcement costs wherever possible by eliminating duplicative audits and investigations.

(c) In addition, the strike force shall be empowered to:

(1) Form joint enforcement teams when appropriate to utilize the collective investigative and enforcement capabilities of the participating members.

(2) Establish committees and rules of procedure to carry out the activities of the strike force.

(3) To solicit the cooperation and participation of district attorneys and other state and local agencies in carrying out the objectives of the strike force.

(4) Establish procedures for soliciting referrals from the public, including, but not limited to, an advertised telephone hotline.

(5) Develop procedures for improved information sharing among the participating agencies, such as shared automated information database systems, the use of a common business identification number, and a centralized debt collection system.

(6) Develop procedures to permit the participating agencies to use more efficient and effective civil sanctions in lieu of criminal actions wherever possible.

(7) Evaluate, based on its activities, the need for any statutory change to do any of the following:

(A) Eliminate barriers to interagency information sharing.

(B) Improve the ability of the participating agencies to audit, investigate, and prosecute tax and cash–pay violations.

(C) Deter violations and improve voluntary compliance.

(D) Eliminate duplication and improve cooperation among the participating agencies.

(E) Establish shareable information databases.

(F) Establish a common business identification number for use by participating agencies.

(G) Establish centralized, automated debt collection services for the participating agencies.

(H) Strengthen civil penalty procedures to allow the strike force to emphasize civil rather than criminal penalties wherever possible.

(d) The strike force shall report to the Governor and the Legislature annually during the period of its existence, by June 30, of each year, regarding its activities.

The report shall include, but not be limited to, all of the following:

(1) The number of cases of blatant violations and noncompliance with tax and cash–pay laws identified, audited, investigated, or prosecuted through civil action or referred for criminal prosecution.

(2) Actions taken by the strike force to publicize its activities.

(3) Efforts made by the strike force to establish an advertised telephone hotline for receiving referrals from the public.

(4) Procedures for improving information sharing among the agencies represented on the strike force.

(5) Steps taken by the strike force to improve cooperation among participating agencies, reduce duplication of effort, and improve voluntary compliance.

(6) Recommendations for any statutory changes needed to accomplish the goals described in paragraph (7) of subdivision (c).

Added Stats 1994 ch 1117 § 5 (SB 1490), operative until January 1, 2000. Amended Stats 1999 ch 306 § 2 (SB 319), operative until January 1, 2006; Stats 2001 ch 180 § 1 (AB 202), repealed January 1, 2006; Stats 2002 ch 29 § 4 (AB 1729), repealed January 1, 2006. Amended Stats 2004 ch 685 § 6 (AB 3020).

Chapter 4

Contributions and Reports

Article 6

Records, Reports and Contribution Payments

§ 1088.5. Information to be reported relating to new employees

(a) In addition to information reported in accordance with Section 1088, effective July 1, 1998, each employer shall file, with the department, the information provided for in subdivision (b) on new employees.

(b) Each employer shall report the hiring of any employee who works in this state and to whom the employer anticipates paying wages.

(c) (1) This section shall not apply to any department, agency, or instrumentality of the United States.

(2) State agency employers shall not be required to report employees performing intelligence or counterintelligence functions, if the head of the agency has determined that reporting pursuant to this section would endanger the safety of the employee or compromise an ongoing investigation or intelligence mission.

(d) (1) Employers shall submit a report as described in paragraph (4) within 20 days of hiring any employee whom the employer is required to report pursuant to this section.

(2) Notwithstanding subdivision (a), employers transmitting reports magnetically or electronically shall submit the report by two monthly transmissions not less than 12 days and not more than 16 days apart.

(3) For purposes of this section, an employer that has employees in two or more states and that transmits reports magnetically or electronically may designate one state in which the employer has employees to which the employer will transmit the report described in paragraph (4). Any employer that transmits reports pursuant to this paragraph shall notify the Secretary of Health and Human Services

Appendix

in writing as to which state the employer designates for the purpose
of sending reports.

(4) The report shall contain the following:

(A) The name, address, and social security number of the employees.

(B) The employer's name, address, state employer identification
number (if one has been issued), and identifying number assigned to
the employer under Section 6109 of the Internal Revenue Code of
1986.

(C) The first date the employee worked.

(5) Employers may report pursuant to this section by submitting a
copy of the employee's W-4 form, a form provided by the department,
or any other hiring document transmitted by first-class mail, magnetically, or electronically.

(e) For each failure to report the hiring of an employee, as required
and within the time required by this section, unless the failure is due
to good cause, the department may assess a penalty of twenty-four
dollars ($24), or four hundred ninety dollars ($490) if the failure is the
result of conspiracy between the employer and employee not to supply
the required report or to supply a false or incomplete report.

(f) Information collected pursuant to this section may be used for
the following purposes:

(1) Administration of this code.

(2) Locating individuals for purposes of establishing paternity and
establishing, modifying, and enforcing child support obligations.

(3) Administration of employment security and workers' compensation programs.

(4) Providing employer or employee information to the Franchise
Tax Board and the State Board of Equalization for the purpose of tax
or fee enforcement.

(5) Verification of eligibility of applicants for, or recipients of, the
public assistance programs listed in Section 1320b-7(b) of Title 42 of
the United States Code.

(g) For purposes of this section, "employer" includes a labor union
hiring hall.

(h) This section shall become operative on July 1, 1998.

Added Stats 1997 ch 606 § 14 (AB 67), effective October 3, 1997, operative July 1, 1998.
Amended Stats 1998 ch 858 § 8 (AB 2169); Stats 2011 ch 296 § 293 (AB 1023), effective
January 1, 2012, ch 734 § 3, effective January 1, 2012 (ch 734 prevails).

§ 1095. Purposes for which director must permit use of information in his or her possession

The director shall permit the use of any information in his or her
possession to the extent necessary for any of the following purposes
and may require reimbursement for all direct costs incurred in pro-

viding any and all information specified in this section, except information specified in subdivisions (a) to (e), inclusive:

(a) To enable the director or his or her representative to carry out his or her responsibilities under this code.

(b) To properly present a claim for benefits.

(c) To acquaint a worker or his or her authorized agent with his or her existing or prospective right to benefits.

(d) To furnish an employer or his or her authorized agent with information to enable him or her to fully discharge his or her obligations or safeguard his or her rights under this division or Division 3 (commencing with Section 9000).

(e) To enable an employer to receive a reduction in contribution rate.

(f) To enable federal, state, or local government departments or agencies, subject to federal law, to verify or determine the eligibility or entitlement of an applicant for, or a recipient of, public social services provided pursuant to Division 9 (commencing with Section 10000) of the Welfare and Institutions Code, or Part A of Title IV of the Social Security Act, where the verification or determination is directly connected with, and limited to, the administration of public social services.

(g) To enable county administrators of general relief or assistance, or their representatives, to determine entitlement to locally provided general relief or assistance, where the determination is directly connected with, and limited to, the administration of general relief or assistance.

(h) To enable state or local governmental departments or agencies to seek criminal, civil, or administrative remedies in connection with the unlawful application for, or receipt of, relief provided under Division 9 (commencing with Section 10000) of the Welfare and Institutions Code or to enable the collection of expenditures for medical assistance services pursuant to Part 5 (commencing with Section 17000) of Division 9 of the Welfare and Institutions Code.

(i) To provide any law enforcement agency with the name, address, telephone number, birth date, social security number, physical description, and names and addresses of present and past employers, of any victim, suspect, missing person, potential witness, or person for whom a felony arrest warrant has been issued, when a request for this information is made by any investigator or peace officer as defined by Sections 830.1 and 830.2 of the Penal Code, or by any federal law enforcement officer to whom the Attorney General has delegated authority to enforce federal search warrants, as defined under Sections 60.2 and 60.3 of Title 28 of the Code of Federal Regulations, as amended, and when the requesting officer has been designated by the head of the law enforcement agency and requests this information in the course of and as a part of an investigation into the commission of

Appendix

a crime when there is a reasonable suspicion that the crime is a felony and that the information would lead to relevant evidence. The information provided pursuant to this subdivision shall be provided to the extent permitted by federal law and regulations, and to the extent the information is available and accessible within the constraints and configurations of existing department records. Any person who receives any information under this subdivision shall make a written report of the information to the law enforcement agency that employs him or her, for filing under the normal procedures of that agency.

(1) This subdivision shall not be construed to authorize the release to any law enforcement agency of a general list identifying individuals applying for or receiving benefits.

(2) The department shall maintain records pursuant to this subdivision only for periods required under regulations or statutes enacted for the administration of its programs.

(3) This subdivision shall not be construed as limiting the information provided to law enforcement agencies to that pertaining only to applicants for, or recipients of, benefits.

(4) The department shall notify all applicants for benefits that release of confidential information from their records will not be protected should there be a felony arrest warrant issued against the applicant or in the event of an investigation by a law enforcement agency into the commission of a felony.

(j) To provide public employee retirement systems in California with information relating to the earnings of any person who has applied for or is receiving a disability income, disability allowance, or disability retirement allowance, from a public employee retirement system. The earnings information shall be released only upon written request from the governing board specifying that the person has applied for or is receiving a disability allowance or disability retirement allowance from its retirement system. The request may be made by the chief executive officer of the system or by an employee of the system so authorized and identified by name and title by the chief executive officer in writing.

(k) To enable the Division of Labor Standards Enforcement in the Department of Industrial Relations to seek criminal, civil, or administrative remedies in connection with the failure to pay, or the unlawful payment of, wages pursuant to Chapter 1 (commencing with Section 200) of Part 1 of Division 2 of, and Chapter 1 (commencing with Section 1720) of Part 7 of Division 2 of, the Labor Code.

(*l*) To enable federal, state, or local governmental departments or agencies to administer child support enforcement programs under Title IV of the Social Security Act (42 U.S.C. Sec. 651 et seq.).

(m) To provide federal, state, or local governmental departments or agencies with wage and claim information in its possession that will assist those departments and agencies in the administration of the

Victims of Crime Program or in the location of victims of crime who, by state mandate or court order, are entitled to restitution that has been or can be recovered.

(n) To provide federal, state, or local governmental departments or agencies with information concerning any individuals who are or have been:

(1) Directed by state mandate or court order to pay restitution, fines, penalties, assessments, or fees as a result of a violation of law.

(2) Delinquent or in default on guaranteed student loans or who owe repayment of funds received through other financial assistance programs administered by those agencies. The information released by the director for the purposes of this paragraph shall not include unemployment insurance benefit information.

(o) To provide an authorized governmental agency with any or all relevant information that relates to any specific workers' compensation insurance fraud investigation. The information shall be provided to the extent permitted by federal law and regulations. For the purposes of this subdivision, "authorized governmental agency" means the district attorney of any county, the office of the Attorney General, the Department of Industrial Relations, and the Department of Insurance. An authorized governmental agency may disclose this information to the State Bar, the Medical Board of California, or any other licensing board or department whose licensee is the subject of a workers' compensation insurance fraud investigation. This subdivision shall not prevent any authorized governmental agency from reporting to any board or department the suspected misconduct of any licensee of that body.

(p) To enable the Director of the Bureau for Private Postsecondary and Vocational Education, or his or her representatives, to access unemployment insurance quarterly wage data on a case-by-case basis to verify information on school administrators, school staff, and students provided by those schools who are being investigated for possible violations of Chapter 7 (commencing with Section 94700) of Part 59 of the Education Code.

(q) To provide employment tax information to the tax officials of Mexico, if a reciprocal agreement exists. For purposes of this subdivision, "reciprocal agreement" means a formal agreement to exchange information between national taxing officials of Mexico and taxing authorities of the State Board of Equalization, the Franchise Tax Board, and the Employment Development Department. Furthermore, the reciprocal agreement shall be limited to the exchange of information that is essential for tax administration purposes only. Taxing authorities of the State of California shall be granted tax information only on California residents. Taxing authorities of Mexico shall be granted tax information only on Mexican nationals.

(r) To enable city and county planning agencies to develop economic forecasts for planning purposes. The information shall be limited to businesses within the jurisdiction of the city or county whose planning agency is requesting the information, and shall not include information regarding individual employees.

(s) To provide the State Department of Developmental Services with wage and employer information that will assist in the collection of moneys owed by the recipient, parent, or any other legally liable individual for services and supports provided pursuant to Chapter 9 (commencing with Section 4775) of Division 4.5 of, and Chapter 2 (commencing with Section 7200) and Chapter 3 (commencing with Section 7500) of Division 7 of, the Welfare and Institutions Code.

(t) To provide the State Board of Equalization with employment tax information that will assist in the administration of tax programs. The information shall be limited to the exchange of employment tax information essential for tax administration purposes to the extent permitted by federal law and regulations.

(u) Nothing in this section shall be construed to authorize or permit the use of information obtained in the administration of this code by any private collection agency.

(v) The disclosure of the name and address of an individual or business entity that was issued an assessment that included penalties under Section 1128 or 1128.1 shall not be in violation of Section 1094 if the assessment is final. The disclosure may also include any of the following:

(1) The total amount of the assessment.

(2) The amount of the penalty imposed under Section 1128 or 1128.1 that is included in the assessment.

(3) The facts that resulted in the charging of the penalty under Section 1128 or 1128.1.

(w) To enable the Contractors' State License Board to verify the employment history of an individual applying for licensure pursuant to Section 7068 of the Business and Professions Code.

(x) To provide any peace officer with the Division of Investigation in the Department of Consumer Affairs information pursuant to subdivision (i) when the requesting peace officer has been designated by the Chief of the Division of Investigation and requests this information in the course of and as part of an investigation into the commission of a crime or other unlawful act when there is reasonable suspicion to believe that the crime or act may be connected to the information requested and would lead to relevant information regarding the crime or unlawful act.

(y) To enable the Labor Commissioner of the Division of Labor Standards Enforcement in the Department of Industrial Relations to identify, pursuant to Section 90.3 of the Labor Code, unlawfully uninsured employers. The information shall be provided to the extent permitted by federal law and regulations.

(z) To enable the Chancellor of the California Community Colleges, in accordance with the requirements of Section 84754.5 of the Education Code, to obtain quarterly wage data, commencing January 1, 1993, on students who have attended one or more community colleges, to assess the impact of education on the employment and earnings of students, to conduct the annual evaluation of district-level and individual college performance in achieving priority educational outcomes, and to submit the required reports to the Legislature and the Governor. The information shall be provided to the extent permitted by federal statutes and regulations.

(aa) To enable the Public Employees' Retirement System to seek criminal, civil, or administrative remedies in connection with the unlawful application for, or receipt of, benefits provided under Part 3 (commencing with Section 20000) of Division 5 of Title 2 of the Government Code.

(ab) To enable the State Department of Education, the University of California, the California State University, and the Chancellor of the California Community Colleges, pursuant to the requirements prescribed by the federal American Recovery and Reinvestment Act of 2009 (Public Law 111-5), to obtain quarterly wage data, commencing July 1, 2010, on students who have attended their respective systems to assess the impact of education on the employment and earnings of those students, to conduct the annual analysis of district-level and individual district or postsecondary education system performance in achieving priority educational outcomes, and to submit the required reports to the Legislature and the Governor. The information shall be provided to the extent permitted by federal statutes and regulations.

Enacted Stats 1953 ch 308. Amended Stats 1971 ch 578 § 13, effective August 13, 1971, operative October 1, 1971; Stats 1973 ch 1206 § 57, ch 1207 § 57, ch 1212 § 157, operative July 1, 1974; Stats 1977 ch 1252 § 406, operative July 1, 1978; Stats 1979 ch 288 § 2; Stats 1982 ch 1080 § 2; Stats 1983 ch 175 § 1, effective July 11, 1983; Stats 1984 ch 1127 § 5; Stats 1985 ch 543 § 4; Stats 1986 ch 331 § 1; Stats 1987 ch 855 § 3; Stats 1990 ch 1024 § 1 (AB 3092), ch 1084 § 2 (SB 2053); Stats 1991 ch 659 § 6 (AB 1137); Stats 1992 ch 1352 § 9 (AB 3660), effective September 30, 1992; Stats 1993 ch 295 § 8 (SB 774), ch 891 § 3 (AB 1881), ch 1144 § 19 (SB 857); Stats 1994 ch 146 § 216 (AB 3601), ch 1049 § 4 (AB 3086) (ch 1049 prevails); Stats 1995 ch 313 § 16 (AB 817), effective August 3, 1995, ch 701 § 1 (SB 488); Stats 1996 ch 1124 § 1 (SB 1524), effective September 30, 1996; Stats 1997 ch 78 § 4 (AB 71), ch 810 § 1.4 (SB 132); Stats 1998 ch 217 § 2 (AB 2017); Stats 1999 ch 83 § 185 (SB 966); Stats 2002 ch 744 § 11 (SB 1953); Stats 2003 ch 789 § 26 (SB 364); Stats 2007 ch 272 § 1 (AB 798), effective January 1, 2008; ch 662 § 3.5 (SB 869), effective January 1, 2008; Stats 2008 ch 369 § 8 (AB 1844), effective January 1, 2009; Stats 2009–2010 5th Ex Sess ch 2 § 22 (SB 1XXXXX), effective April 13, 2010; Stats 2010 ch 139 § 1 (AB 2433), effective January 1, 2011.

DIVISION 3

EMPLOYMENT SERVICES PROGRAMS

PART 1

EMPLOYMENT AND EMPLOYABILITY SERVICES

Chapter 4

Programs

Article 1

Eligibility

§ 10501. Exemption of assistance recipient from examination or certification fees

Any public assistance recipient who successfully completes a job training program approved under this part shall be exempted from the payment of those fees normally associated with any examination or certification required by state law if the employment opportunity is for the job for which the recipient was trained.

Added Stats 1972 ch 1281 § 1.

VEHICLE CODE

DIVISION 12
EQUIPMENT OF VEHICLES

Chapter 2
Lighting Equipment

Article 3

Rear Lighting Equipment

§ 24615. Slow moving vehicle emblem

It is unlawful to operate upon a public highway any vehicle or combination of vehicles, which is designed to be and is operated at a speed of 25 miles per hour or less, unless the rearmost vehicle displays a "slow–moving vehicle emblem," except upon vehicles used by a utility, whether publicly or privately owned, for the construction, maintenance, or repair of its own facilities or upon vehicles used by highway authorities or bridge or highway districts in highway maintenance, inspection, survey, or construction work, while such vehicle is engaged in work at the jobsite upon a highway. Any other vehicle or combination of vehicles, when operated at a speed of 25 miles per hour or less, may display such emblem. The emblem shall be mounted on the rear of the vehicle, base down, and at a height of not less than three nor more than five feet from ground to base. Such emblem shall consist of a truncated equilateral triangle having a minimum height of 14 inches with a red reflective border not less than 1¾ inches in width and a fluorescent orange center.

This emblem shall not be displayed except as permitted or required by this section.

Added Stats 1969 ch 949 § 1. Amended Stats 1971 ch 287 § 1.

Article 7

Flashing and Colored Lights

§ 25260.1. Warning lights on vehicles engaged in construction, removal, or inspection of oil or gas pipeline

Vehicles actually engaged in the construction, removal, maintenance, or inspection of any oil or gas pipeline may display flashing amber warning lights to the front, sides, or rear when necessarily parked on a highway or when necessarily moving at a speed slower than the normal flow of traffic and only in accordance with Section 25268.

Added Stats 1978 ch 120 § 1.

Article 14

Vehicles Exempted

§ 25801. Special construction and maintenance equipment

The provisions of Sections 24012, 24250, 24251, 24254, 24400 to 24404, inclusive, 24600 to 24604, inclusive, 24606 to 24610, inclusive, Section 25950, and Articles 4 (commencing with Section 24800), 5 (commencing with Section 24950), 6 (commencing with Section 25100), 9 (commencing with Section 25350), 11 (commencing with Section 25450), 12 (commencing with Section 25500), and 13 (commencing with Section 25650) shall not apply to special construction or maintenance equipment, nor to motortrucks equipped with snow removal or sanding devices, but shall apply to motortrucks and automobiles used independently of such equipment.

The provisions of Section 25803 shall be applicable to such equipment.

Enacted 1959 ch 3. Amended Stats 1961 ch 1659 § 9; Stats 1972 ch 618 § 148.

Chapter 5

Other Equipment

Article 1

Horns, Sirens, and Amplification Devices

§ 27000. Horns; Backup device or alarm and video camera on garbage trucks

(a) A motor vehicle, when operated upon a highway, shall be equipped with a horn in good working order and capable of emitting sound audible under normal conditions from a distance of not less than 200 feet, but no horn shall emit an unreasonably loud or harsh sound. An authorized emergency vehicle may be equipped with, and use in conjunction with the siren on that vehicle, an air horn that emits sounds that do not comply with the requirements of this section.

(b) A refuse or garbage truck shall be equipped with an automatic backup audible alarm that sounds on backing and is capable of emitting sound audible under normal conditions from a distance of not less than 100 feet or shall be equipped with an automatic backup device that is in good working order, located at the rear of the vehicle and that immediately applies the service brake of the vehicle on contact by the vehicle with any obstruction to the rear. The backup device or alarm shall also be capable of operating automatically when the vehicle is in neutral or a forward gear but rolls backward.

(c) A refuse or garbage truck, except a vehicle, known as a rolloff vehicle, that is used for the express purpose of transporting waste containers such as open boxes or compactors, purchased after January 1, 2010, shall also be equipped with a functioning camera providing a video display for the driver that enhances or supplements the driver's view behind the truck for the purpose of safely maneuvering the truck.

(d) (1) A construction vehicle with a gross vehicle weight rating (GVWR) in excess of 14,000 pounds that operates at, or transports construction or industrial materials to and from, a mine or construction site, or both, shall be equipped with an automatic backup audible alarm that sounds on backing and is capable of emitting sound audible under normal conditions from a distance of not less than 200 feet.

(2) As used in this subdivision, "construction vehicle" includes, but is not limited to, all of the following:

(A) A vehicle designed to transport concrete, cement, clay, limestone, aggregate material as defined in subdivision (d) of Section 23114, or other similar construction or industrial material, including a transfer truck or a tractor trailer combination used exclusively to pull bottom dump, end dump, or side dump trailers.

(B) A vehicle that is a concrete mixer truck, a truck with a concrete placing boom, a water tank truck, a single engine crane with a load rating of 35 tons or more, or a tractor that exclusively pulls a low-boy trailer.

Enacted Stats 1959 ch 3. Amended Stats 1965 ch 1015 § 1; Stats 1982 ch 926 § 1, effective September 13, 1982; Stats 1983 ch 1144 § 8, effective September 28, 1983; Stats 1997 ch 945 § 27 (AB 1561); Stats 2005 ch 166 § 2 (AB 1637), effective January 1, 2006; Stats 2011 ch 235 § 1 (SB 341), effective January 1, 2012.

Article 3.5

Headsets and Earplugs

§ 27400. Wearing of headsets or earplugs

A person operating a motor vehicle or bicycle may not wear a headset covering, or earplugs in, both ears. This prohibition does not apply to any of the following:

(a) A person operating authorized emergency vehicles, as defined in Section 165.

(b) A person engaged in the operation of either special construction equipment or equipment for use in the maintenance of any highway.

(c) A person engaged in the operation of refuse collection equipment who is wearing a safety headset or safety earplugs.

(d) A person wearing personal hearing protectors in the form of earplugs or molds that are specifically designed to attenuate injurious noise levels. The plugs or molds shall be designed in a manner so as to not inhibit the wearer's ability to hear a siren or horn from an emergency vehicle or a horn from another motor vehicle.

(e) A person using a prosthetic device that aids the hard of hearing.

Added Stats 1973 ch 87 § 1. Amended Stats 1975 ch 495 § 1; Stats 1977 ch 348 § 1; Stats 1980 ch 107 § 1, effective May 20, 1980; Stats 1982 ch 542 § 1, effective August 18, 1982; Stats 1985 ch 736 § 2. Amended Stats 2003 ch 594 § 45 (SB 315).

WATER CODE

DIVISION 7
WATER QUALITY

Chapter 10
Water Wells and Cathodic Protection Wells

Article 3

Reports

§ 13750.5. Requirement of water well contractor's license

No person shall undertake to dig, bore, or drill a water well, cathodic protection well, groundwater monitoring well, or geothermal heat exchange well, to deepen or reperforate such a well, or to abandon or destroy such a well, unless the person responsible for that construction, alteration, destruction, or abandonment possesses a C–57 Water Well Contractor's License.

Added Stats 1986 ch 1373 § 2.5. Amended Stats 1996 ch 581 § 5 (AB 2334).

ADDITIONAL RESOURCES

All California codes listed below can be accessed through the
California State Legislature's Website, www.leginfo.ca.gov.

SUBJECT	RESOURCE
ACCESS FOR PERSONS WITH PHYSICAL DISABILITIES	
Disability Access Requirements	*California Code of Regulations,* Title 24 Part 2 (State Building Code) Part 3 (State Electrical Code) Part 5 (State Plumbing Code) (See also Parts 1, 8 and 12) Federal: The Americans with Disabilities Act (ADA) The ADA Accessibility Guidelines (ADAAG) California: 1988 Fair Housing Amendments Act
Publications	California:
California Accessibility Resource Manual	Copies are available through builders bookstores throughout California or the Division of the State Architect
California Code of Regulations, Title 24	Division of the State Architect or your local technical bookstore

SUBJECT	RESOURCE
Access Guide: Survey Checklist	ADA Technical Assistance Section, Department of Rehabilitation (916) 263-8674, Fax (916) 263-8671
A Guide to California Multi-Family Disability Access Regulations	California Building Officials 1225 8th Street, Suite 425 Sacramento, CA 95814 (916) 457-1103, Fax (916) 442-3616 www.calbo.org
Technical Assistance Manual on compliance	Federal: U.S. Department of Justice 950 Pennsylvania Avenue, NW Disability Rights Section – NYAV Washington, DC 20530 (800) 514-0301, (800) 514-0383 (TDD)
Americans with Disabilities Act Accessibility Guidelines (ADAAG)	U.S. Access Board 1331 F Street NW, Suite1000 Washington, DC 20004-1111 (800) 872-2253, Fax (202) 272-0081 (800) 993-2822 (TTY) www.access-board.gov
Telephone Assistance	
Begin by contacting	Local building department or jurisdiction

SUBJECT	RESOURCE
Code interpretations regarding all publicly funded buildings and privately funded buildings open to the general public	Division of the State Architect, Office of Universal Design Access Compliance 1102 Q Street, Suite 5100 Sacramento CA 95811 (916) 445-8100, Fax (916) 445-3521 *www.dsa.dgs.ca.gov*
Technical information or access policy, regulations and interpretations, or for information on plans approval processes for publicly funded schools, colleges, or universities	Division of the State Architect (916) 445-8100
General information regarding access requirements contained in Title 24 of the California Code of Regulations and the ADA requirements	Department of Rehabilitation, ADA Technical Assistance Section P.O. Box 944222 Sacramento, CA 94244-2220 (916) 263-8674, Fax (916) 263-8671 *www.dor.ca.gov*
Code interpretations relating to privately funded multifamily buildings	Department of Housing and Community Development/Codes and Standards Division 1800 3rd Street, Room 260 Sacramento CA 95814 (916) 445-9471, Fax (916) 327-4712 *www.hcd.ca.gov*
Federal accessibility requirements	Department of Justice or the Access Board, as listed above

Resources

SUBJECT	RESOURCE
ADVERTISING: ILLEGAL PRACTICES AND PENALTIES	
Advertising	Business & Professions Code Division 7, Part 3, Chapter 1
BONDS	
Bond and Undertaking Law	Code of Civil Procedure Title 14, Chapter 2
BUILDING STANDARDS	
State Housing Law, Building Standards Law	California Health and Safety Code Division 13
California Building Standards Code	California Code of Regulations Title 24
Publications	
California Building Standards Code with California Amendments (Title 24)	International Code Council 5360 Workman Mill Road Whittier, CA 90601-2298 (888) ICC-SAFE (422-7233), Fax (562) 692-3853 *www.iccsafe.org*

SUBJECT	RESOURCE
Other responsible agencies	Department of Industrial Relations
	Division of Occupational Safety and Health
	Division of the State Architect
	Department of Housing and Community Development
	Division of Housing Codes and Standards
	Department of Health Services
	California Energy Commission
	Office of State Health Planning and Development
	State Fire Marshal
EMPLOYMENT ELIGIBILITY VERIFICATION	U.S. Department of Justice, Immigration and Naturalization Service (INS), Office of Business
Responsible Agency	Liaison: Employer Information Line (800) 357-2099 National Customer Service Center (800) 375-5283, Fax (202) 305-2523 *http://uscis.gov*
EMPLOYMENT PRACTICES	
California Fair Employment and Housing Act	Government Code Title 2, Division 3, Part 2.8

Resources

SUBJECT	RESOURCE
EMPLOYMENT TAXES, FEDERAL	
Responsible Agencies	Internal Revenue Service (800) 829-1040 *www.irs.ustreas.gov* Social Security Administration (800) 772-1213 *www.socialsecurity.gov*
Publications	
Circular E Employer's Tax Guide	Internal Revenue Service
Employment Taxes and Information Returns	Internal Revenue Service
EMPLOYMENT TAXES, STATE	
Responsible Agencies	Employment Development Department (EDD) *www.edd.cahwnet.gov* or contact your local office Franchise Tax Board (FTB) *www.ftb.ca.gov* or contact your local office

SUBJECT	RESOURCE
Publications	
California Unemployment Insurance Code	Employment Development Department Business Operations Planning and Support Division, MIC 62 P.O. Box 826880 Sacramento, CA 94280-0001 Workforce Div.:(916) 654-6949
California Employer's Tax Guide	Employment Development Department
LABOR CODE	
Department of Industrial Relations	*Labor Code,* Division 1
Employment Regulation and Supervision	*Labor Code,* Division 2 Part 1. Compensation Part 2. Working Hours Part 3. Privileges and Immunities Part 4. Employees Part 7. Public Works and Public Agencies Part 9. Health
Federal Fair Labor Standards Act of 1938	*Code of Federal Regulations,* Title 29
Employment Relations	*Labor Code,* Division 3

Resources

SUBJECT	RESOURCE
Workers' Compensation	*Labor Code*, Division 4 Part 1. Scope and Operation Part 2. Computation of Compensation Part 3. Compensation Claims Part 4. Compensation Proceedings
Safety in Employment	*Labor Code,* Division 5 Part 1. Occupational Safety and Health Part 3. Safety on Building Part 7. Volatile Flammable Liquids Part 10. Use of Carcinogens
PUBLIC INFORMATION ACCESS	
Open Meeting Act	*Government Code:* Title 2, Division 3, Part 1
California Public Records Act	*Government Code:* Title 1, Division 7, Ch. 3.5.
Information Practices Act of 1977	*Civil Code:* Title 1.8, Division 3, Part 4, Ch. 1
Business Records	*Civil Code:* Title 1.82, Division 3, Part 4, Ch. 1-3
District Attorney	*Government Code:* Title 3, Div. 2, Part 3, Ch. 1

SUBJECT	RESOURCE
SAFETY AND HEALTH	
Publications	
California Occupational Safety and Health Standards— Title 8 California Code of Regulations *Cal/OSHA Guide for the Construction Industry* *Guide to Cal/OSHA*	Barclay's Official Code of Regulations P.O. Box 2006 San Francisco, CA 94126 (800) 888-3600, (415) 732-8800 Fax (415) 344-3906 barclaysccr@thomson.com or DOSH 1221 Farmers Lane, Suite 300 Santa Rosa, CA 95405 (800) 963-9424, (707) 576-2388 Fax (707) 576-2598 *www.dir.ca.gov*
Guide to Developing Your Workplace Injury and Illness Prevention Program	Department of Industrial Relations P.O. Box 420603 San Francisco, CA 94142-0603 (800) 963-9424, (916) 574-2339 *www.bni-books.com*
Information concerning Occupational Safety and Health requirements	Cal/OSHA Consultation Services (see list at the end of Chapter 7)
STATE SALES AND USE TAX	
Responsible Agency	California State Board of Equalization (800) 400-7115 *www.boe.ca.gov*

Resources

Index

Index

Index

Index

Index

CRIMINAL COMPLAINTS
Payment of penalties, B&P 7028.2 p. 285

CRIMINAL HISTORY
Applications
Corporations, requirements for, p. 23; B&P 7069 p. 321
Consumer Affairs, Department of Criminal background checks, required, B&P 144 p. 204

D

DEFECTS, STRUCTURAL, B&P 7091
p. 360; T16 CCR 861.5 p. 506
Actions for construction defects, requirements, CC 895-945.5 p. 589

DEMOLITION
Asbestos-containing materials suspected National Emission Standards for Hazardous Air Pollutants (NESHAP) requirements, p. 145

DENIAL OF LICENSE
Applicability, B&P 475 p. 238
Authorized actions by Board, B&P 488 p. 242
Conviction of a crime, substantial relationship required, B&P 480 p. 239; B&P 7069 p. 321
Exemptions, B&P 476 p. 238
Failure to comply with rules, grounds, T16 CCR 860 p. 506
False statement, B&P 475 p. 238
Grounds for denial, B&P 480 p. 239
Hearing, B&P 487 p. 242
Denial without hearing, B&P 489 p. 242
Procedure for board upon denial, B&P 485 p. 241
Reapplication after denial, B&P 486 p. 241
Rehabilitation, criteria for after, B&P 482 p. 240; T16 CCR 869 p. 510
Related crimes, criteria, B&P 481 p. 240; T16 CCR 868 p. 509

DEPUTIES
Authority of, B&P 10 p. 163

DESIGN PROFESSIONAL SERVICES
Contracts
Indemnify promisee against liability, invalidity of provisions to, CC 2782.8 p. 634

DIG ALERT. (*See* Regional Notification Centers)

DIRECTOR, DEFINED, B&P 23.5 p. 164

DIRECT SUPERVISION AND CONTROL, RESPONSIBILITY OF QUALIFYING INDIVIDUAL, B&P 7068.1 p. 318; T16 CCR 823 p. 472

DISASSOCIATION
Of responsible managing employee, B&P 7068.2 p. 319

DISASTERS
Cancellation of home improvement contract
Contract void under certain circumstances, CC 1689.14 p. 622
Crimes against public health and safety
Price gouging following state of emergency or major disaster, PC 396 p. 803
Fraud in repairing natural disaster damage
Enhanced sentence, PC 667.16 p. 809

DISCIPLINARY BOND. (*See* Bonds)

DISCIPLINARY GUIDELINES, T16 CCR 871 p. 515

DISCIPLINARY PROCEEDINGS
Action
Despite correction of condition, B&P 7090.5 p. 360
Jurisdiction, by another, B&P 141 p. 203; B&P 7103 p. 367

Index

Index

Index

Index

Index